As
Leaven
in the
World

As Leaven in the World

Catholic Perspectives on Faith, Vocation, and the Intellectual Life

Thomas M. Landy, Editor

SHEED & WARD

Franklin, Wisconsin

As an apostolate of the Priests of the Sacred Heart, a Catholic religious congregation, the mission of Sheed & Ward is to publish books of contemporary impact and enduring merit in Catholic Christian thought and action. The books published, however, reflect the opinions of their authors and are not meant to represent the official position of the Priests of the Sacred Heart.

2001

Sheed & Ward
7373 South Lovers Lane Road
Franklin, Wisconsin 53132
1800-266-5564

Cover and interior design by GrafixStudio, Inc.
Author photo by John Gillooly

Printed in the United States of America

Library of Congress Cataloging-in-Publication Data

As leaven in the world : Catholic perspectives on faith, vocation, and the
    intellectual life / Thomas M. Landy, editor.
        p. cm.
    Includes bibliographic references.
    ISBN 1-58051-089-2 (pbk.)
    1. Catholic—United States—Intellectual life.
    2. Spirituality—Catholic Church. I. Landy, Thomas M.

BX1407. I5 A8 2001
282'.73—dc21
        2001020547

1 2 3 4 5 / 04 03 02 01

Contents

Part I
Seven Opportunities

Part II
Marks of the Faith

Part III
Spiritualities: *Ora* Giving Life to *Labora*

Part IV
Discipleship and the Practices That Sustain Us

With special gratitude to four women
who played important roles in
bringing Collegium to life:

Mary Frances A. H. Malone
Alice Gallin, O.S.U.
Jeanne Knoerle, O.P.
Eva Hooker, C.S.C.

Acknowledgments

More people than I can count made this book possible. The essays arise out of many years of Collegium colloquies. Among many others, the four women acknowledged on the dedication page helped make Collegium possible. Friends at Fairfield University supported the idea through to its proposal, and the Lilly Endowment generously took the first steps to make it possible. Planners, speakers, mentors, and participants helped expand my thinking about faith and intellectual life and about the mission of Catholic higher education. Members of the Collegium board have helped steer it along, as have three Assistant Directors: Mary Beth Pinard, Caroline Lenox, and Jen Stojak. Paula Powell Sapienza, author of one of the essays in this volume, played a particularly valuable role strengthening and enabling Collegium's work for the last two years. I owe her a special debt of gratitude, as I do to my family, especially my mother, Janice, and to Felix, Christopher, and Mary Beth.

The authors in this volume took up the challenge to help broaden the way we think about Catholic intellectual life, and to share their own experiences. I feel especially grateful for what they accomplished.

A 1996 grant from the Lilly Endowment supported the publication of this book. Other donors deserve thanks including Amaturo Foundation, Inc., George and Marie Doty, the Mary J. Donnelly Foundation, the Koch Foundation, Inc., John McShain Charities, Inc., the William M. & Miriam F. Meehan Foundation, Inc., Our Sunday Visitor, Inc., the Raskob Foundation for Catholic Activities, Inc., Collegium alumni/ae, and a major donor who wishes to remain anonymous.

Introduction

Yeast and
Three Measures of Flour

Thomas M. Landy

Intellectuals, to put it mildly, have had a rather odd relationship with religion, including Catholicism, for quite a number of centuries. The old saws about the war between faith and reason, between science and superstition, between Galileo and the Church, are too many to chronicle. Yet the university itself, like most of America's private colleges and universities, was founded by religious people and religious institutions for religious purposes.

Sociologist Peter Berger is fond of saying that except among intellectuals, Americans are one of the most religious people on earth. Europeans visiting the United States are often shocked at the omnipresence of religion in a country that prides itself on "separation of church and state," However shallow Americans' beliefs may be at times, we hear fairly frequent reference to God in political rhetoric, over the airwaves, and in the culture at large. Although some facets and sectors of American life are clearly very secularized, religious institutions and ideas are very much a part of our culture, even though believers may not always agree with the ways religion is used. In academe, too, survey data suggest that more faculty are religious believers than one might expect, but the overall culture of the academy and of other American intellectual institutions has not been especially welcoming to religious belief.

I suspect that each of the authors in this book has experienced more than once the incredulity of another intellectual for being a believer, much less a Catholic. To many Americans, a "Catholic intellectual" is regarded at least as an enigma, if not a full-fledged oxymoron. Numerous critics have asserted that "real" Catholics are not able to think independently, and are thus not capable of being legitimate intellectuals. A much larger group of people, while not as hostile, would find the idea of religiously engaged intellectuals hard to grasp, because they regard religion as inherently private, or because they have scant understanding of why the Church would need intellectuals at all, other than theologians. John Henry Newman regretted this latter shortcoming among Catholic bishops and laypeople. Today, young Catholic scholars often tell me that they find themselves in a double bind: their academic colleagues have no interest in talking about religion except to caricature it; other Catholics seldom can relate to the academic work as potentially valuable from a religious point of view. When they ask people in ministry for help figuring out how to be disciples in the world, they are often sent away from intellectual pursuits, to volunteer in some sort of social service. Few of them are helped to explore deeply how the disciplinary work they are dedicating their talents to could also be a vocation.

Perhaps we fail to offer this kind of advice because we treat Catholicism as more static than adaptive, or because we have relegated religion to a number of limited spheres, which need not integrate with other aspects of life. In that light, we could grasp the idea that some intellectuals might "happen" to be Catholic, but usually fail to perceive any connection between intellectuals' work and faith. Colleges and churches do too little to help intellectuals deepen their understanding of the connections or to foster their vocations.

For nearly a decade, Collegium, a consortium of sixty Catholic colleges and universities headquartered at Fairfield University, has worked to foster Catholic intellectual life in America, and the mission of Catholic higher education.[1] Collegium's work has centered primarily on supporting faculty and mission enhancement at our sixty-member schools, but it has also expanded to emphasize the importance of Catholic intellectual life more generally. We began, and continue, to sponsor weeklong summer colloquies on faith and intellectual life for younger faculty at our member schools. We also offer fellowships to the colloquies to as many as twenty-five graduate students per year, in the hope that they will consider spending their careers in Catholic higher education and furthering its mission.

Collegium has never been primarily *for* Catholics, but has always sought out the participation of faculty who are not familiar with the Catholic intellectual tradition or the particular mission of their institution, and who the institutions believe will play an important role shaping the future of the colleges. I've been particularly proud of the work we've done to help faculty from other faith traditions to discern what important role—as Lutherans, Muslims, or Jews, with distinctive talents in particular disciplines—they have in shaping the mission of the Catholic institution where they teach. Collegium's starting point is Catholic higher education, but our focus has always been to provide an opportunity for *individuals* to shape their own vocations as intellectuals and to discern how they could best contribute to the mission of their institution, given their own particular faith, talents, and desires.

While our emphasis or niche has been in introducing young and non-Catholic faculty to conversations about Catholic mission and identity, our first year's work made it fairly clear that we had to do more to foster a more active, public Catholic intellectual life among Catholics who have already established reputations as scholars and intellectuals. We were conscious that there were more than a few great Catholic intellectuals, but that few of them were identified as such, and few (except for the theologians) knew one another well. The old "ghetto" Catholic institutions that provided networking opportunities for Catholic intellectuals had withered, but nothing vital had taken their place.

Recognizing the need for better networking and conversation, the Lilly Endowment, Inc. generously funded a special Collegium colloquy, Renewal '97, to help bring together prominent Catholic intellectuals and to invite them to help us think about the renewal of Catholic intellectual life. This book derives from that colloquy and seeks to expand on its work. The primary audience for this book is threefold. It aims in particular to reach Catholic and non-Catholic faculty at Catholic colleges and universities and, like Renewal '97, expands our reach to helping faculty at secular colleges and universities to think about their own vocations to the intellectual life.

In its structure, this book emulates the annual Collegium colloquies in a number of ways that participants have told us were particularly helpful to them. It offers new ways of thinking about the content and concerns of Catholic faith, and it tries to connect these to intellectual life in many disciplines; it explores prominent Catholic spiritualities as ways to help us discern and shape vocations; and it shares first-person accounts of how eight scholars have tried to shape vocations as intellectuals and faithful Christians. Collegium alumni/ae will find much that is familiar, as well as a great deal that is new here. My hope is that this book will help us to bring some of the best of Collegium to larger groups of people. In that light, in hopes of building some of the same depth of community that occurs at the colloquies, I especially hope that the book will be used by faculty groups—and by other groups of intellectuals—as a basis for shared discussion about mission and vocation. A number of faculty groups now gather regularly at secular and Catholic campuses for discussion on faith, vocation, and intellectual life. Conceived with those groups in mind, the chapters in this book should serve as a resource to help shape or launch their discussions.

While written primarily by Catholics, with reference to the Catholic intellectual tradition, this book is intended for Catholic college campuses to be a resource for *all* faculty who wish to discuss the mission of their institution. At one level, if colleges and universities describe themselves as Catholic, it seems important that all faculty are seriously encouraged and enabled to take time to understand what that means, although it certainly should not mean that all faculty will thus be expected to *be* Catholic. In light of *Gaudium et spes*, the crowning document of Vatican II,[2] I believe passionately that Catholic identity involves nothing short of full engagement with as many ideas and cultures as possible. That necessarily entails including faculty from other faith traditions to be part of the college, and makes these faculty anything *but* peripheral to the colleges' Catholic mission. Still, it is hard to carry out this engagement without some solid understanding of what "Catholic" stands for. Just as importantly, based on my experience at Collegium, the Catholic intellectual tradition and Catholic spiritualities provide a tremendous resource for faculty from any religious tradition to reflect on their own work, and to facilitate deeper vocational discernment.

For a number of reasons right now, many potential readers of this book undoubtedly are uncomfortable with emphasis on *Catholic* faith and intellectual life. Some of this may result from anti-Catholicism, which is hardly new to the academy, but many others feel particularly ill at ease with the present uses of authority in the Catholic Church and with actions that seem aimed at cutting off theological discourse. Many intellectuals who care about Catholicism feel that overt reference to Catholic identity on campus only invites problems for them today, and invites resistance to religious goals that might otherwise be more easily achieved to a similar, but less explicitly Catholic, good end.

For this and other reasons, a book focusing on *Catholic* faith and intellectual life may not seem too propitious today. A recent study of faculty at three Jesuit universities about the meaning of "Catholic" compared to "Jesuit" showed that Catholic was fairly often associated with "indoctrination," "rigidity," "hierarchy," "rules," "conservative," "hard on women and nonconformists of various kinds," "authority," "suppression," "anti-intellectual," and "exclusive." The perceptions revealed in that study were by no means all negative and, in fact, many suggested that Catholicism in their experience was just the opposite. By and large, though, the study showed that faculty tended to see Jesuit identity in quite opposite terms, as an *opportunity*, while seeing Catholic identity as a *liability* for a college.[3] My experience working with faculty at many colleges and universities suggests that this phenomenon is equally true of faculty at Benedictine or LaSallian or Franciscan colleges, or most any other colleges founded by religious communities of men and women. However highly the faculty rate the religious order's commitment to the intellectual life, it is always better regarded than is the larger Church's commitment.

Efforts to raise questions about *Catholic* identity, then, usually raise fears of exclusion. The great paradox is that that which is really a subset of Catholicism (e.g. "Franciscan") is taken to be more open and inclusive than Catholicism itself. Even faculty who have played central roles enlivening their institution for decades can suddenly fear that emphasis on what's "Catholic" will mean that they no longer belong there as first-class citizens. What the colleges might have done to prevent these perceptions years ago is one problem, but here the central difficulty raised is about why I would want to raise the issue of "Catholic" identity at all, instead of letting institutions stick to their identity as Mercy or Vincentian or Jesuit universities.

Because Catholicism includes all of these identities, it really cannot be taken as narrower than any one of them. I believe that it is important to keep remembering this—in order to keep a better sense of proportion, but also to keep insisting that Catholicism embrace its own catholicity. It is impossible to separate any of these particular identities from Catholic identity without doing them serious injustice. Rather, these identities are best seen as *ways* of being Catholic and Christian.

My aim in this book is to help readers imagine ways that Catholic identity might serve as an *opportunity* for colleges and universities and for the intellectual life. Although Catholicism might often be perceived primarily as a collection of "no's" or strictures—as if *not* giving out birth control on campus or *not* inviting certain speakers to campus is what makes a college Catholic—I would stress that Catholic Christianity is fundamentally about a series of affirmations, not negations. I am Catholic not because of what Catholicism tells me *not* to do (although there are instances when it does so) but because I believe that it fundamentally leads me to better understand the world and the purpose God intends for it, and it enhances my ability to know

God, however impossible that may sound. The Second Vatican Council (1962–1965) redefined and broadly expanded the Church's understanding of how it could learn from and contribute to contemporary culture, with the aim of reversing the defensive position the Church had fallen into previously. The Council positioned the Church to engage in richer dialogue with contemporary culture—both to learn more from it and to contribute more to it. In the wake of *Gaudium et spes*, we cannot justify or regard Catholic intellectual life or Catholic higher education in exclusionist terms. To be church at all, as we understand it, necessarily means going out to the world, to engage it—to bring the good news, but also to know that we are bringing it into a world where God is already active and engaged. Those who know the historical or present-day reality will readily call to mind justifiable examples of how the Church has failed at this openness and engagement. But this does not negate the need to keep reminding ourselves as church to work harder to be the people we believe we have been called to be.

In Matthew 13:33, Jesus claims, "the reign of God is like yeast which a woman took and kneaded into three measures of flour. Eventually the whole mass of dough began to rise." The title of this book draws from that parable, and from the insight of a great Jesuit scholar, Walter Ong, who used it to describe the mission of Catholic higher education. I would expand his use of the parable to describe the role of all Catholic intellectuals. For Ong, the parable's implications are embedded in the very choice of the word *Catholic*. He points out that the Latin western Church passed over the Latin term *universalis* to describe itself, and turned instead to a Greek term: *katholikos*. *Katholikos* conveyed a slightly different, but very important meaning: "through the whole," in the sense that the gospel metaphor of yeast uses it. If Catholic higher education wants to be Catholic, Ong asserts, it should keep the parable and image of yeast (or leaven) in mind. "Yeast not only grows quickly, but nourishes itself on the dough in which it grows."[4] It engages itself fully in the whole of the world, and does not retreat from it. I believe that this metaphor beautifully summarizes the function of Catholic intellectual life, to be as leaven in the world, both to help transform creation and to be transformed by it.

This book is a collection of essays by a variety of American Catholic intellectuals on their understanding of their work as Christian vocation. Its underlying thesis is that intellectual life is at least as vigorous and important to the Church as at any time in history, despite the inability of many people in our culture to grasp its existence or purpose. In the contemporary context, however, the work of Catholic intellectuals is often treated as secular, even where its impetus arises from deep moral convictions, and from a passion for knowing that seems inherently religious. For many reasons, we, as intellectuals, are not good at talking about the spiritual nature of our work, which is something I hope to help remedy.

In the last decade, Protestant and Catholic colleges have organized a number of conferences to discuss the future of religious identity at colleges and universities, the compatibility of faith and science, and other issues relating to faith and the intellectual life. A number of these events have featured talks roughly titled, "Athens and Jerusalem: Can They Meet?" Noting this historical title on the agenda of one meeting I attended not long ago, in one of my less patient moods, I said to myself, "Not again! We *know* that his answer is going to be yes, so let's get beyond this!" The talk, in fact, was given by an extremely talented scholar, and was better than my impatient self could have expected. Yet it did reflect the need I felt for taking a few steps forward in the conversation. At this point in history, despite too many low moments in the churches' encounter with the intellectual life, the fact that they can meet and coexist and even flourish together ought to be evident to all who have studied history over the last two millennia.

I have organized this book, then, with the hope of stepping a little bit beyond the "Athens and Jerusalem" question, or a generalized discussion on *theism* and the intellectual life. Many of the talks, articles, and presentations I have encountered make a fairly good case for the compatibility of a generalized—or generically Judeo-Christian—theism with the academic disciplines, but I have often been left to ponder what difference some of the most important specificities of Catholic, Christian faith might have. Does it matter a whit to the way we conceive the intellectual life that the God we worship is understood as Trinitarian? What real effect does the mission and preaching of Jesus have for my work as a sociologist?

My hope for this book has been to work to broaden and "flesh out" the conversations about Catholic higher education and Catholic intellectual life. Since I have not felt compelled to assemble the last or most comprehensive word on the Catholic intellectual tradition, I've had the luxury of being able to work with the authors to extend the conversation in ways that I hope will prove to be both novel and important, without having to be all-inclusive.

Almost all of the authors have participated in Collegium colloquies. They represent a mix of senior and junior scholars, providing insight from some of the most important voices in Catholic intellectual life today, as well as from a younger generation that brings with it slightly different perspectives and priorities. Given that the mission-and-identity conversation has found most of its more vocal proponents among men now late in their careers, I have made a strong effort to include younger—and female— authors. Unlike Collegium colloquies, the collection lacks voices of non- Catholic faculty, but this was a decision I made for the sake of including writers who could engage Catholic traditions particularly well. I do hope, as I indicated, that it will be read and discussed by many people who are not Catholic, and that their perspectives will be well-heard. Some readers will also be aware that while our subject is intellectual life, the context refers almost entirely to higher education. The professorate has surely worked hard to monopolize intellectual life in the United States, but here the constriction is simply practical, involving the need to at least try to speak to a specific audience. Nonetheless, on reading the essays, I feel confident that they can have a great deal to say to intellectuals who work outside of academe.

The essays are organized in four sections, each of which is aimed at developing and bringing to a larger audience some aspect of Collegium's explorations on faith and the intellectual life:

I. Seven Opportunities

Having often been struck by the extent to which identification with Catholicism is construed only or primarily in negative terms—as a series of constraints, whether against certain kinds of ideas or research topics or speakers—I wanted to begin this book by examining the *opportunities* that engagement with Catholic faith can provide. While undoubtedly there are things that I would not or should not do as a Catholic Christian, the essence of faith is opportunity, calling, and engagement—not constraint.

One of the most important things contemporary Catholicism can offer to public dialogue is its own long tradition of reflection on the good and on the conditions for human well-being. The Catholic intellectual tradition has made tremendous contributions in areas like the just war theory, social ethics, and bioethics. Richard Liddy's chapter helps us begin to examine how the Catholic intellectual tradition in arts, literature, and philosophy is an important resource for church and society, worth preserving and developing. Liddy's contribution reflects on how best to gain from such a tradition and take it seriously without being entombed in it.

Most of us think of the Catholic intellectual tradition as an opportunity for the Church to teach, but as church historians are inevitably aware, Catholic intellectual life has just as importantly been an opportunity for the Church to *learn*. Without such learning, it seems doubtful that the Church could have flourished or been able to preach the gospel in the many cultures it has encountered. Paula Sapienza's essay highlights the opportunity for learning that Catholic intellectual life provides for the Church, and identifies some surprising and important places where such engagement could be profitable.

Catholic intellectual life is all too often treated as if it were mostly about the rational and the philosophical. Yet visual symbols, images, metaphors, and the like have played an equally important role in Catholic Christianity and in the way we help the world to see and understand itself. Joanna Ziegler, an art historian, highlights the spiritual importance of helping students to really learn to see, and the opportunity that Christian reflective practices can play in that.

In all the talks and presentations I've heard in the last decade on Catholic identity in higher education, I've never heard the case made that to be Catholic means that we have an opportunity and an obligation to foster creativity. By failing to foster artistic and other forms of creativity, we sell our tradition short. I asked Eva Hooker, a poet, to reflect on the Church's obligation to foster creativity. Taking that creative challenge to heart more fully than I had conceived, she responded with an essay in prose strophes that engages the creative act as a fundamentally religious act.

Russ Butkus highlights another opportunity and responsibility of Catholic intellectual life, to foster individual and collective memory, especially memories we'd rather forget. This is a responsibility built into our theological understanding of the world and of how God works in it, and in a faith that we can come to know—however imperfectly—God's presence and desires by examining our own lives and history. To be faithful as Christians is to have an obligation to remember. Such impetus is also a tremendous opportunity for those of us who wish to preserve and engage history in a culture prone to devaluing it.

David Gitomer took on the task of discussing another core responsibility of Catholic intellectual life: serious, sustained engagement of other cultures and ideas. He acknowledges some of the difficulty of pluralistic engagement but, as a person who has worked to experience other religious traditions "from within," he points to the possibility for stronger understanding that engagement from "inside" can bring.

Finally, Jill Raitt explores the paradoxical ways in which many Catholic intellectuals' felt sense of marginality, both within the Church and the academy, also represents a special opportunity for them. Building on a conversation started at Collegium's Renewal '97, she opens up a number of ways of seeing "marginality" differently than we often tend to do.

II. Marks of the Faith

The second section of the book builds upon the opportunities presented in the first, but also raises questions about the potential relevance of particular, very central aspects of Catholic Christian faith. It aims to step beyond the "Athens and Jerusalem" or vaguely theistic examinations of faith and intellectual life, and asks the authors to identify how they think that some of the essentials of our faith have bearing on our vocation as intellectuals.

Our beliefs about creation and its value seem a good place to begin this questioning. Michael Himes does so by identifying a broad "sacramental" sense that derives from Catholicism's understanding of God's act of creation, and from the respect God showed creation by becoming one with the created world through his Son. Building on that core Catholic belief—that God is much more present and discernible in the world than he is absent from it— John Neary provides an example of how the sacramental vision has played itself out in contemporary American fiction.

In the first years of Collegium colloquies, we often asked a speaker to talk about the person of Jesus and his relation to the mission and ministry of Catholic higher education. I was surprised at how difficult this was for many people who care a great deal about being disciples of Jesus and about the future of Catholic colleges. Most found it easier, we realized, to consider "the Catholic university" as an ecclesial construct than to address the difference Jesus makes in the academic vocation. Diana Hayes helps us in this regard by looking at Jesus and the nature of discipleship in the intellectual life.

Dennis Doyle takes on the question of what difference Christian Trinitarian faith makes for the intellectual vocation. He applies a number of thinkers' reflections on the Trinity to lead us to new ways of thinking about the life of the mind. In the chapter that follows, I take on the task of reflecting on the vocational significance of the fact that Catholic practice is, at its very heart, eucharistic.

Three essays discuss aspects of Catholic ethical reflection. David Hollenbach turns to the signature document of the Second Vatican Council,

Gaudium et spes, and the social encyclicals of the Church to consider what difference it makes for Catholic intellectual life that the Church's own understanding of itself is as an institution oriented and obligated to the world. Therese Lysaught looks at our responsibilities as a people called to value life, the forms of bioethical reflection that have derived from this belief, and the challenges that lie ahead. Brian Linnane reflects on the notion of the person embedded in modern Catholic thought, and on how it serves as an alternative starting point to reductionistic understandings of the person, whether as consumer, rational actor, or the mere sum of chemical processes.

The effort to link faith and reason has been a hallmark of Catholic theology through much of the last two millennia. The last three essays of this section examine religious and rational knowledge. Dennis O'Brien visits the question of engagement between faith and reason from the vantage point of Jesus' claim that he came into the world to testify to the truth, and of Pilate's celebrated retort, "What is truth?" (cf. John 18:37–38). Michael Patella looks with skepticism at the truth claims of modernity, and suggests ways for Christianity to more fully engage at least some of the insights of postmodern thought. Alex Nava turns to the deep Judeo-Christian traditions of mysticism and prophecy to explore how they represent alternative ways at reaching truth. Whereas rationalists have often regarded the prophetic and mystical aspects of religion as antithetical to the pursuit of truth, Nava makes a case for how they can tremendously enrich Catholic intellectual life.

III. Spiritualities: *Ora* Giving life to *Labora*

Shortly before the first Collegium summer colloquy, two prominent Catholic intellectuals, both now friends, told me independently that they thought it was a mistake to try to integrate some form of retreat or spirituality into the colloquy. The week should be either a real academic conference or a retreat, but it was unwise to try to do both. By the end of the conference both decided, to their great surprise, that they had been wrong. They, and a great number of Collegium alumni/ae, have commented over the years that they think the greatest contribution Collegium has made is to weave together the spiritual and the intellectual in the same week's conference, as equally important elements of the Catholic intellectual vocation.

The desire to bound-off the "truly intellectual" aspects of Catholicism from the spiritual is not new, but it does strike me as a terrible mistake. Jean LeClercq's great study, *The Love of Learning and the Desire for God,* hints that it may be as old as the shift from monastic theology to "scientific," or more rationalist, theology.[5] Among contemporary scholars and would-be scholars who are members of religious communities, I have too often heard distinctions made between people who were "retreat types" (or "faith and justice types") and those who have genuine respect for the intellectual life. Such dichotomies, whether grounded in real experiences or misinterpretation, certainly undermine the work of the Church and the broader development of its members. When I first conceived of Collegium, I was especially concerned that Catholic colleges were not paying sufficient attention to the religious aspects of their central mission, which is intellectual formation. I lamented that while they tended to pay attention to their mission and identity in terms of service programs, retreats, and campus ministry, they downplayed the importance of a vital Catholic intellectual life on campus. Yet, as much as I wanted to shift the focus back to include the intellectual mission of the college, I did not believe that this should entail putting aside prayer and spirituality.

Still, it may seem strange to many readers to pick up a book on Catholic intellectual life that devotes a quarter of its attention to spirituality. In an age when the laity clearly constitutes the bulk of Catholic intellectual life, chapters on the spiritualities of various religious orders will also seem odd. Nonetheless, I regard these chapters as among the most important patrimonies of the Church to all persons seeking to find God and a sense of spirituality in their own life.

The word *spirituality* is not without its problems in terms of contemporary usage. Still, in an age when so many Americans seem absolutely *hungry* for a sense of spirituality, even as they are ambivalent about "religion," it seems to me that these spiritualities are among the best assets Catholicism has for inviting people to reflect deeply on faith and the intellectual life. For those unfamiliar with any of them, I would simply describe them as "ways to God"—practices of life and prayer developed in the context of lived communities as particular ways of being disciples.

Marie-Dominique Chenu, the great Dominican theologian, recognized the link between spiritual and intellectual life:

> The fact is that in the final analysis theological systems are
> simply the expression of spiritualities. It is this that gives them
> their interest and their greatness. . . . One does not enter into a
> system for the sake of the logical coherence of its structure or
> the plausibility of its conclusions; one finds oneself at home
> there because of the governing intuition which engages our
> spiritual life and the realm of intelligibility that it entails.[6]

Among the advantages over lay people that vowed religious have had in their formation was the opportunity to be formed in the context of a deep spiritual tradition while they were also being formed intellectually. These chapters aim to briefly introduce readers to the history, origin, and core insights of a particular spiritual tradition, but they also aim to focus on the *practice* of that spirituality. It seems to me that religious orders often do a reasonable job at introducing new faculty and staff to the "stories" of their founders ("shot in the leg by a cannonball," "bedside conversion," "started giving his Spiritual Exercises . . .") but are too slow to welcome faculty of all faiths into ways of praying with and living out that spirituality. These essays are meant to be a means of helping people not only learn the stories but also explore how the spiritualities are lived out, especially in the method of prayer. Each essayist had a large task at hand, to tell the story of the founders and followers (since the spirituality develops in real, lived history, not in ether), to talk about how it is practiced, and to indicate what the spirituality

might have to add specifically to the intellectual life. In spirituality in particular, understanding is seldom gained without practice.

These chapters highlight a number of Christian spiritual traditions that
have, among other things, provided numerous people with a motivation or
framework for pursuing the intellectual life. These spiritualities entail different practices and priorities, and have notably flourished in a number of
particular communal contexts, but have also proven to be flexible, adapt-
able, and helpful to people who have no intention of becoming members of
a religious order. I have been struck over the years at how deeply Collegium
participants—Catholic or not—have been attracted to spiritualities like Benedictine monastic prayer, despite the fact that they normally live lives far
removed from monasteries. In evaluations, a majority of the participants,
Catholic or not, tell us that the exposure to one or more spiritualities, and the
time to pray or reflect, was among the things they most valued about their
Collegium experience.

Three of the authors in this section—Katherine Kraft, Ingrid Petersen, and
Howard Gray—have very capably served as Collegium retreat directors. They
brought to light three of the great spiritual traditions of the Church, those
founded by Benedict and Scholastica, Ignatius Loyola, and Francis and Clare.
Since I also wanted this book to expand the present discourse on faith and intellectual life, I turned to several other writers for help exploring spiritualities that
had not been engaged on Collegium retreats. Joseph Kelley, an alumnus of the
first Collegium colloquy, has written on the spiritual tradition that aims to follow the example of one of the Church's greatest thinkers, Augustine.

Two other writers who had not participated in Collegium events have
helped to expand our thinking in new directions. Keith Egan delves into the
Carmelite tradition, known for its depth and its great mystics, although its
specific influence on university life has been more limited. Dennis
Holtschneider, a Vincentian priest, describes the deep concern for the poor
involved in the life of Saint Vincent de Paul, and gives some idea how that
could shape the vocations of persons and communities aimed at using education first and foremost to serve the poor.

IV. Discipleship and the Practices That Sustain Us

Perhaps because of my own formation in Ignatian spirituality, but also
because of my understanding of the Hebrew Scriptures as a "salvation history," I am thoroughly convinced that the stories of our lives are fundamentally the story of God's encounter with us. Because of this, they are
necessarily worth reflecting on prayerfully, and sharing with others. Collegium colloquies have always included this form of reflection as a core component of the week. Mentor faculty, and participants who wish to do so
reflect on their own past and share how it was that their vocation emerged in
both planned and unanticipated ways. A number of Collegium alumni/ae suggested that it would be important for this book to include autobiographical
reflections on faith and vocation, in order to stimulate the same kind of
reflection in readers.

Memoir is undoubtedly the literary form *de jour*, a form that can be narcissistic, uninspiring, or merely titillating. In the Christian tradition, it has a long and honorable tradition, beginning with no less a personage than Augustine. In the *Confessions*, Patricia Hampl has noted, Augustine show us that "memory [is] an instrument to seek God, to plumb the mystery of God's creation, not simply to seek out oneself."[7]

These first-person narratives have a special way of concretizing what Catholic intellectual life is in America. Indeed, the sociologist in me would say that if we were able to collect all the stories, we might have the best possible account of the meaning of Catholic intellectual life, perhaps more meaningful than any description of it as an ideal type. As these accounts begin to reveal, the lived experience of Catholics committed to the intellectual life is often messy and full of surprises and disappointments alongside moments of grace and insight.

Younger graduate students often find these stories helpful because they had been imagining that the sense of vocation that some of these more prominent faculty now have had always been clear to them, or developed in ways that were linear or were immediately apparent as they occurred. I don't expect that any readers will have to relate exactly to these accounts, but only that "mentor" stories will help readers begin to examine and interpret their own stories. In this last section, then, Elizabeth Johns, Cynthia Russett, Bruce Russett, John Thompson, Peter Dodson, William Gray, Ed Block, and Sidney Callahan all reflect on their own histories as Christians and intellectuals.

ALL THE ESSAYS in this book help to make the case that it is a genuine vocation—indeed, it is *holy work*—to teach others how to see or listen or remember. The possibility is no less real in the sciences, literature, or social sciences than in theology. Collectively, the essays help point to the existence of a vital Catholic intellectual life in disciplines and among persons often overlooked. I hope that they are seen as an invitation to many more people to take seriously their intellectual life as a vocation in service to others.

Notes

1. The best source of information about Collegium and its work is our website, www.fairfield.edu/collegiu. The site also contains bibliographies, resources, and links to books and articles on faith and the intellectual life, both from Catholic and ecumenical perspectives.

2. "Pastoral Constitution on the Church in the Modern World" (*Gaudium et spes*), in Walter M. Abbott, ed., *The Documents of Vatican II* (New York: America Press, 1966).

3. Judy Deshotels, "Report on AJCU Study 'Perspectives on Mission and Identity at Three Jesuit Universities." N.p. Jan 31, 2000.

4. Walter J. Ong, S.J., "Yeast, a Parable for Catholic Higher Education" *America* 162, April 1990, pp. 347–363.

5. Jean LeClercq, *The Love of Learning and the Desire for God; a Study of Monastic Culture*, trans. Catharine Misrahi (New York: Fordham University Press, 1961).

6. Marie-Dominique Chenu, *Une Ecole de Theologie: Le Saulchoir* (Paris: Editions du Cerf, 1985) p. 148. My gratitude goes to Alex Mikulich for drawing my attention to Chenu's words and to Joseph Komonchak for identifying their precise source.

7. Patricia Hampl, "First Person Singular: The Autobiographical Voice," address to Collegium's "Renewal '97," June 20, 1997, Fairfield University.

Part I

Seven Opportunities

The Catholic Intellectual Tradition: Achievement and Challenge

Richard M. Liddy

I fled Him down the nights and down the days;
I fled Him, down the arches of the years;
I fled Him, down the labyrinthine ways
Of my own mind; and in the mist of tears
I hid from Him, and under running laughter.
　　　　　　　　　—Francis Thompson,
　　　　　　　　　The Hound of Heaven

When I was a young student in the 1950s, I came across a book entitled *The Wisdom of Catholicism.* I liked it very much and bought a copy as a present for my parents. It was edited by Anton Pegis of the Medieval Institute in Toronto and contained selections from "the Catholic classics:" from Augustine's *Confessions* and the *City of God*, Thomas Aquinas's *Summae*, Dante's *Divine Comedy*, Thomas á Kempis's *Imitation of Christ*, Teresa of Ávila's *Interior Castle*, John of the Cross's *Ascent of Mount Carmel*, Blaise Pascal's *Pensées*, and John Henry Newman's *Apologia pro vita sua*. There were also more recent selections: papal encyclicals on Christian philosophy and on the reconstruction of the social order, as well as literary pieces such as Charles Péguy's *Vision of Prayer*, Paul Claudel's *The Satin Slipper*, and selections from Hilaire Belloc, G. K. Chesterton, Christopher Dawson, Sigrid Undset, Etienne Gilson, and Jacques Maritain. At the time it provided evidence for me of the superior wisdom of Catholicism. It was a wisdom achieved in the past and ours was the job of appropriating it and passing it on.

Recently there have again arisen references to "the Catholic intellectual tradition"—often in relation to Catholic studies programs—and I ask myself what difference there is between "the wisdom of Catholicism" as I conceived of it in the 1950s and as I look on it now.[1] In this article I would like to explore this question by first focusing on the problem of an inadequate, often classicist, conception of the Catholic intellectual tradition and by contrasting this with a more dynamic, historically conscious, understanding. Second, I would like to draw out the implications of this more adequate understanding of the Catholic intellectual tradition for the transformation of contemporary cultures. Throughout I will call attention to the role of "the Catholic classics," both artistic and theoretical, in this process of cultural transformation.

Classicism and Historical Consciousness

The historian Eric Voegelin wrote of "the hardening of the symbols," that is, the cultural process whereby an authentic tradition becomes disconnected from its roots in authentic living.[2] Bernard Lonergan has referred to one version of this as "classicism," that is, an a-historical mode of thinking in which "all the answers are in the book," that is, somewhere in Augustine or Aquinas or the Code of Canon Law or books and manuals that summarize all of the above. Somewhere you can find all the answers, a well-defined "block" of knowledge.[3]

Such a view can disguise a hidden agenda in which "the dead weight" of the tradition is used to attack others. In the name of the Catholic intellectual tradition we can attack "those conservatives" or "those liberals" and we can hold triumphalistic attitudes about the superiority of Catholicism. Just as there can be a fundamentalism that canonizes a particular nineteenth century form of American Protestantism, so there can be a Catholic fundamentalism of an ideal past that "had all the answers," leaving us with the sole responsibility of mindlessly passing on that tradition to the future.

Now I would submit that the Catholic intellectual tradition can be conceived merely as such an achievement completed in the past, or it can be conceived as a living tradition challenging persons to do in our day what that tradition accomplished in cultures gone by. For the Catholic intellectual tradition is not a pile of books or writings "out there"—it is not some "thing." Rather, it is a living meaning, very alive to some, less alive, perhaps even dead, to others.

For the authentic dynamism of the Catholic intellectual tradition has "power," the power reflected in the lives of the saints and great teachers of the Church, a power capable of shaping action in the present for the building of the future. In his *Essay on the Development of Christian Doctrine*, John Henry Newman wrote that the authenticity of a tradition—he called it "a living idea"—bore fruit in its "power of assimilation:" that is, its power to enter into various cultures and assimilate the best elements of those cultures into its own self-expression. Such "inculturation" is the ability of Christianity to be truly and authentically Christian while being at the same time truly and authentically Japanese, African, American, or whatever. The Catholic intellectual tradition is not a closed "canon" of Western works only. For many, Shusaku Endo's *Silence* has become a classic of the Catholic intellectual tradition from the world of Japanese Catholicism. And Vincent Donovan's *Christianity Rediscovered* appeals for respect for the native patterns of East

African cultural life—in terms of which alone the Gospel message can there be proclaimed.[4]

It is because of this transcultural dynamism that it is impossible to come up with a once-and-for-all definition of the "essence" of the Catholic intellectual tradition. For the tradition is always becoming incarnate in a particular historical context, either authentically or not. If it is becoming authentically incarnate in a culture, it will appeal to those who are seeking to be authentic and seeking expressions of authenticity. If they are not such seekers, they will either water down the tradition, or they won't care.

This is not to say that it is not a very good thing to read and reread the classics of the tradition. Although rooted in particular cultures, they transcend those cultures in their appeal to human authenticity, and we the readers must ask ourselves whether we in our context are listening to the appeal to authenticity and conversion that these classics constitute. For Christians, these classics would be, first of all, the Scriptures, "the Word of God," and also all the other Christian classics that help us listen to that Word in our lives. Among these sources of wisdom, Catholics also look to the authoritative teaching of the Church in their discernment of God's Word.

In our day there is a new context for the reception of the classics of the Catholic intellectual tradition. Unlike the culture of classicism, which saw itself as the one normative culture, today the context is one of historical consciousness. This emphasis on the ineluctably historical rootedness of our being has affected the reception of the classics, and even of the Scriptures. The result is not that the classics have ceased to be classics, but that the process of coming to appropriate them, especially in Western cultures, has become a far more rigorous process. Thus, Etienne Gilson, who for so long championed the scholarly historical retrieval of St. Thomas, used to maintain that Thomas was the last "Thomist"—so great had been the transformation of his thought in the hands of commentators.[5]

All of which highlights the importance of "method" as the Catholic intellectual tradition encounters modern and postmodern historical consciousness. That is why I would personally highlight the contribution of Bernard Lonergan to the contemporary situation of the Catholic intellectual tradition. If the Catholic intellectual tradition is truly to encounter contemporary consciousness, as Aquinas encountered the Aristotelianism of medieval culture, one needs a "map:" a map of modern scientific and philosophic consciousness, such as Lonergan laid out in his *Insight* (1956) and a map of historical consciousness and method, such as he set out in his *Method in Theology* (1972).

The problem with our ordinary thinking about the Catholic intellectual tradition, then, is that we tend to think of it, as we tend to think of all tradition, as just about the past. We tend to think that the Catholic intellectual tradition means merely reading Aquinas or Augustine or Dante. But if we truly understand the meaning of these writers, we will find ourselves invited to do in our culture what they did in theirs. The point of any authentic tradition is to change us in the present so that we can articulate the authentic meanings of the tradition into the future. If we read Augustine or Aquinas, and we are not changed so that we think and act differently, then we water down their meaning. We reduce them to our own narrow horizon. We inauthentically pass on the tradition—and as a result, the tradition becomes lifeless.

Again, Lonergan highlights this needed respect for the various cultures in which Christianity would take root. If the Christian message is to be communicated to "all nations," preachers and teachers need to enlarge their horizons to include an accurate and intimate understanding of the culture and the language of the people they address.

> They must grasp the virtual resources of that culture and that language, and they must use those virtual resources creatively so that the Christian message becomes, not disruptive of the culture, not an alien patch superimposed upon it, but a line of development within the culture. Here the basic distinction is between preaching the gospel and, on the other hand, preaching the gospel as it has been developed within one's own culture. In so far as one preaches the gospel as it has been developed within one's own culture, one is preaching not only the gospel but also one's own culture. In so far as one is preaching one's own culture, one is asking others not only to accept the gospel but also renounce their own culture and accept one's own. Now a classicist would feel it was perfectly legitimate for him to impose his culture on others. For he conceives culture normatively, and he conceives his own to be the norm. Accordingly, for him to preach both the gospel and his own culture is for him to confer the double benefit of both the true religion and the true culture. In contrast, the pluralist acknowledges a multiplicity of cultural traditions. In any tradition he envisages the possibility of diverse differentiations of consciousness. But he does not consider it his task either to promote the differentiation of consciousness or to ask people to renounce their own culture. Rather he would proceed from within their culture and he would seek ways and means for making it into a vehicle for communicating the Christian message.[6]

In our day the Catholic intellectual tradition must insert itself into a global culture. Dialogue with "the other" is essential, even to know who we ourselves are to be. This implies Catholic ecumenical dialogues with other Christians, inter-religious dialogues, and dialogues with the various cultures of the world, including Western secular culture. While challenging all forms of materialism and relativism, the Catholic tradition must interact with all that is good in contemporary cultures. If it is true that "God wants all to be saved," then a major challenge for the Catholic tradition is to articulate how it is indeed possible that God is truly at work in the lives and cultures of those who are not Catholic. A major challenge for Catholics—large "C"—is to be catholic—small "c."

At its best the Catholic intellectual tradition, the set of meanings and values rooted in Jesus of Nazareth, is a living tradition. It reflects and reflects *on* the Word of God which the Letter to the Hebrews called "living and active, sharper than any two-edged sword, piercing to the division of soul and spirit, of joints and marrow; and discerning thoughts and intentions of the heart" (Hebrews 4:12; RSV).

The Catholic Intellectual Tradition as Infrastructure

A curious aspect about the phrase "the Catholic intellectual tradition" is the possible implication that there could be any kind of genuine Catholic tradition other than an intellectual one. For if we agree with Thomas Aquinas that the human person is especially the human spirit or the human "mind"—*homo maxime est mens hominis* (the human person is especially the human mind)[7]—then any genuinely human tradition is an intellectual tradition. Of course, as we noted, a tradition may fade, become watered-down and lifeless; but it will only revive and come to life again to the extent that people begin to use their heads.

Such intellectual activity need not be limited to theorizing—to theology and philosophy—but it can also find expression in art and music, in symbol and dance, in architecture, in poetry and myth and, of course, in ritual. Dostoevsky caught this "ground level" intellectual activity in the songs of the Russian peasants as even during persecution they kept alive the image of Christ.

> The people acquired their knowledge in churches where, for centuries, they have been listening to prayers and hymns which are better than sermons. They have been repeating and singing these prayers in forests, fleeing from their enemies, as far back as the time of Batzi's invasion; they have been singing: *Almighty Lord*, be with us! It may have been then that they memorized this hymn, because at that time nothing but Christ was left to them; yet in this hymn alone is Christ's whole truth.[8]

In other words, in addition to the practical and social patterns of our human interaction, there is also the level of culture, that is, the meaning we find in our present way of life, the value we place upon it or, again, the things we find meaningless and stupid, wicked and disastrous. Dostoevsky's peasants illustrate culture in its immediacy. Their music expressed what they found to be meaningful and valuable and what they felt to be wicked and disastrous.

> In its immediacy the cultural is the meaning already present in the dream before it is interpreted, the meaning in a work of art before it is articulated by the critic, the endless shades of meaning in everyday speech, the intersubjective meanings of smile and frown, tone and gesture, evasion and silence, the passionate meanings of love and hatred, of high achievement and wrathful destruction.[9]

The Catholic intellectual tradition finds expression, then, not just in Augustine of Hippo and Thomas Aquinas—persons aware of the philosophical culture of their own day and expressing their faith in a theoretical way—but also in poetry (*The Divine Comedy*, the poems of Gerard Manley Hopkins) and art (frescoes, mosaics, icons, medieval, Renaissance and Baroque painting); architecture (Romanesque, Gothic, Baroque, "modern") and music (Gregorian chant and polyphony); as well as in the dramas of the medieval mystery plays. In addition, the Catholic intellectual tradition has found literary expression in works of practical spirituality that, at least for some communities within the Church, have attained the status of classics: for example, *The Rule of Saint Benedict, The Imitation of Christ, The Cloud of Unknowing, The Spiritual Exercises of Saint Ignatius*, Teresa of Ávila's *Interior Castle*, John of the Cross's *Ascent of Mount Carmel*, Francis de Sales' *Introduction to the Devout Life*, etc.

Now what all these works of art and literary expressions of Catholicism have in common is that they invite us to change; in fact, they aim at being mediators of conversion. They express in sensuous and imaginative form the religious, moral, and intellectual "vision" of their authors and creators—and they invite others to participate in that same transforming vision.

All such expressions of the Catholic intellectual tradition are expressions of a deeper, more primal intellectual experience, an experience inseparable from the reception in faith of the gospel message. That faith-reception of the gospel message involved decision and action—even to suffering and dying for the Lord—but it also involved acclamations acknowledging Jesus as Lord, confessions that God had raised him from the dead, as well as gradually developing and expanding formulas of belief. It was to provide a context for such acclamations, such confessions, such formulas, to clarify their meaning and preclude misinterpretation that memories of Jesus' earthly ministry were recalled and the classics that we call "the Gospels" were written.[10]

The Catholic Intellectual Tradition as Superstructure

But besides the meaning and value immediately intuited, felt, spoken, acted out, there is to any advanced culture a superstructure. Science is added to common sense; literary criticism to literature; philosophy to the proverbs of the wise. In every area of human living a superstructure of science, scholarship, and philosophy appears. "Besides the meanings and values immanent in everyday living there is an enormous process in which meanings are elaborated and values are discerned in a far more reflective, deliberative, critical fashion."[11]

Such is one function of the Catholic intellectual tradition. Rooted in the Word of God and celebrated in the eucharistic assembly, that Word was also preached not only to Jews but also to Gentiles and to all the communities of the civilized world. As is evident even in the pages of the New Testament, the Word faced new situations and new questions as it began to be preached throughout the Mediterranean world. Disputes arose: What is the exact meaning of the Word of God? What are its implications in this situation?—in Antioch? in

Corinth? in Rome? Early Jewish Christians wanted to hold Gentile converts to the whole Jewish law. Those influenced by Gnosticism wanted to reduce the Gospel to an esoteric sect. Innovators formed schools of theology that splintered off in various directions and, by their very separation and diversity, they emphasized a main, unchanging tradition.[12]

That main tradition itself was faced with ever deeper issues, including the issue raised by Arius: "In what sense can it be said that Jesus is the Son of God?" Is this just a metaphor in the sense that all humans are "children of God?" Or, as St. Athanasius held, is Jesus truly the Son of God in the sense that what is said of him is also said of the Father, except that he is the Son and not the Father? To express this truth Athanasius and those gathered at the Council of Nicea in 325 had to do a lot of prayer and reflection. That reflection resulted in adopting the nonscriptural technical term *homoousios* to express what they considered to be scriptural truth. This was a painful process. It was a process continued throughout the early centuries of the Church during which, in order to protect the Gospel, Christian teachers employed terms in senses unknown both to the Scriptures and to the earlier patristic tradition.[13] It is in reflecting on this whole process of development and in linking such development to ever new situations that theology developed as an academic subject at once intimately related to Christianity as a religion and at the same time as manifestly distinct from it.

In this sense we can say that the Catholic intellectual tradition emerged out of the bosom of the Church, out of its liturgical celebrations and its preaching. Eventually, however, it also found expression in a specifically theoretical way, preeminently in the great *Summae* of Thomas Aquinas, the *Summa Contra Gentiles*, and the *Summa Theologica*. This was a natural consequence of the movement of the Christian religion into the highly sophisticated culture of the medieval university. Lonergan describes this process:

> As we have seen, the principal part of human living is constituted by meaning, and so the principal part of human movements is concerned with meaning. It follows more or less inevitably that the further any movement spreads and the longer it lasts, the more it is forced to reflect on its own proper meaning, to distinguish itself from other meanings, to guard itself against aberration. Moreover, as rivals come and go, as circumstances and problems change, as issues are driven back to their presuppositions and decisions to their ultimate consequences, there emerges that shift towards system, which was named by Georg Simmel, *die Wendung zur Idee*. But what is true of movements generally, also is true of Christianity. The mirror in which it reflects itself is theology.[14]

This has been a long and difficult journey. John Henry Newman pays tribute to this journey as he surveyed the editions of the great teachers of the Church arrayed on his library walls:

Look along their shelves, and every name you read there is, in
one sense or other, a trophy set up in record of the victories of
Faith. How many long lives, what high aims, what single-
minded devotion, what intense contemplation, what fervent
prayer, what deep erudition, what untiring diligence, what toil-
some conflicts has it taken to establish its supremacy! This has
been the object which has given meaning to the life of Saints,
and which is the subject matter of their history. For this they
have given up the comforts of earth and the charities of home,
and surrendered themselves to an austere rule, nay, even to
confessorship and persecution, if so be they could make some
small offering, or do some casual service, or provide some
additional safeguard towards the great work which was in
progress.[15]

Recently, in his 1998 encyclical, *Fides et ratio*, John Paul II paid tribute to
this ancient process by which the meanings and values of the gospel are articulated philosophically in ever new cultural settings.[16]

The Catholic Classics

As we have seen, if a cultural movement is to last, if it is to enjoy any continuity in history, it must reflect on itself, on its encounter with other movements, and on its future direction. The beginnings of this process of
intellectualization can be discerned even within the pages of the New Testament where later formulations reflect the reframing and reconceptualization
of the gospel message in new circumstances. The Gospels themselves
remained normative for Christians, for they found themselves in these books
and the Scriptures helped them to orient their activities as they faced ever
new circumstances. Out of these Scriptures Christians have drawn different
emphases at different times, depending on the particular needs of the times.
"Every scribe who has been learned in the kingdom of heaven is like the head
of a household who brings from his storeroom both the new and the old"
(Matthew 13:52; NAB).

    Thus, the role of an intellectual tradition can be clarified if we just reflect
on the role of a *classic* within that tradition. The classic, through its impact
on those who receive it and reverence it, creates a "space" wherein it can be
interpreted and applied in ever new circumstances. Thus, David DeLaura, in
writing about John Henry Newman's *Apologia pro vita sua* could say:

The special distinction of the *Apologia* is that it does make its
way, as any prophetic book must in the modern world, on its
own and literarily; it creates its own authority and authenticity;
while it constitutes our whole experience for a time, its inherent thrust is to transform us in some more permanent way. In
this sense, the book's literary power, as the subtle revelation of

the religious progress of a highly gifted human being, makes
the *Apologia,* as it touches the deepest springs of the religious
impulse in man, an ever renewable force in the contemporary
world, in ways in which most of even the highest of modern art
does not.[17]

So a classic creates a "field" in which it is received, a field within which it is
interpreted and applied to new circumstances.[18] Of course, there are different
traditions, and different classics. *The Rule of Saint Benedict,* for example,
might not have the status of a classic for all Catholics, but it certainly does
for those who live within the Benedictine community. The universal Church
has officially deemed some of these classic Catholic writers as "doctors," an
official mark of approval enhancing the receptiveness for their writings
within the Church. Others, like Newman, await that official recognition while
the process of reception continues in various places and communities
throughout the world. People return to these classic writers again and again
to find ever new orientations for living their lives. As Friedrich Schlegel said,
"A classic is a writing that is never fully understood. But those that are educated and educate themselves must always want to learn more from it."[19]

Even within a particular tradition there arise questions about the authentic interpretation of the classic. There can be a deepening penetration of the
meaning of the tradition as when the disciples on the road to Emmaus
reflected, "Were not our hearts burning inside us as he talked to us on the
road and explained the scriptures to us?" (Luke 24:32; NAB). Or, on the other
hand, the interpreting tradition itself might be unauthentic, insensitive to the
authentic meaning of the classic and those that would interpret it authentically are ridiculed as was St. Paul when he quoted Isaiah to the Romans "Go
to this people and say: /you may listen carefully, yet you will never understand; /you may look intently, yet you will never see" (Acts 28:26, NAB).
Thus, the road from the New Testament to other Christian classics is a
process of discussion, disagreement, and spiritual discernment in ever new
circumstances of the meaning and values of the Christian tradition. Certainly,
ecclesial authority, the "magisterium," plays a major role in this process of
discernment. Newman graphically described this dialectic of reason and
authority:

> Catholic Christendom is no simple exhibition of religious
> absolutism, but presents a continuous picture of Authority and
> Private Judgment alternately advancing and retreating as the
> ebb and flow of the tide; it is a vast assemblage of human
> beings with willful intellects and wild passions, brought
> together into one by the beauty and the Majesty of a Supreme
> Power, into what may be called a large reformatory or training
> school, not as if into a hospital or prison, not in order to be sent
> to bed, not to be buried alive . . .[20]

The Transformation of Cultures

At this point we can simply ask, What is the Catholic intellectual tradition for? What is its purpose? What good is it? And we can answer these questions by pointing to its good for the individual and for the culture as a whole.

For one thing, for the born-Catholic who would come to an adult appreciation of his or her faith, the Catholic intellectual tradition aids in linking our faith with the rest of our lives. It aids us in articulating who we are as Christians as we live in the contemporary world: it serves as a mirror in which we can come to understand ourselves. Thus, Bernard Lonergan found Cardinal Newman's theory of knowledge in the *Grammar of Assent* a lifesaver as he struggled to articulate his own faith in the 1920s. As he put it years later:

> Newman's remark that ten thousand difficulties do not make one doubt has served me in good stead. It encouraged me to look difficulties squarely in the eye, while not letting them interfere with my vocation or my faith.[21]

For Christians need an articulation of the faith that is commensurate with their human intellectual development. If they tend to think theoretically in other areas of their lives, they will tend to need some theory to sustain their faith.

> . . . once consciousness is differentiated, a corresponding development in the expression and presentation of religion becomes necessary. So in an educated and alert consciousness a childish apprehension of religious truth either must be sublimated within an educated apprehension or else it will simply be dropped as outmoded and outworn.[22]

On the other hand, the Catholic intellectual tradition can be of help to those who are on their way to faith, or are interested in Christianity and in particular, in Catholicism. It can be a way of finding out how Catholicism relates to their own questions; that is, it has an *apologetic* function. Here the point of the Catholic intellectual tradition is not to create faith—only God does that—but it can help people integrate their faith with the rest of their lives.

> The apologist's task is neither to produce in others nor to justify for them God's gift of his love. Only God can give that gift, and the gift itself is self-justifying. People in love have not reasoned themselves into being in love. The apologist's task is to aid others in integrating God's gift with the rest of their living.[23]

At its best, the Catholic intellectual tradition provides the resources for the human spirit wherever it might be on its journey to authenticity.

> Religious conversion is an extremely significant event and the adjustments it calls for may be both large and numerous. For

some, one consults friends. For others, one seeks a spiritual director. For commonly needed information, interpretation, the formulation of new and the dropping of mistaken judgments of fact and of value, one reads the apologists. They cannot be efficacious, for they do not bestow God's grace. They must be accurate, illuminating, cogent. Otherwise they offer a stone to one asking for bread, and a serpent to one asking for fish.[24]

One can clearly see this process in the lives of converts to Catholicism: Ronald Knox picking up Chesterton's *Orthodoxy* on his way to Catholicism; Thomas Merton picking up Etienne Gilson's work, *The Spirit of Medieval Philosophy*; Avery Dulles picking up a work by Jacques Maritain. etc.[25] For these persons, the Catholic intellectual tradition served as a means of engendering sympathy and understanding for the meaning of Catholicism. Chesterton expressed his experience very graphically:

I had been blundering about since my birth with two huge and unmanageable machines of different shapes and without apparent connection—the world and the Christian tradition. I had found this hole in the world: the fact that one must somehow find a way of loving the world without trusting it. I found this projecting feature of Christian theology, like a sort of hard spike, the dogmatic insistence that God was personal, and had made a world separate from himself. The spike of dogma fitted exactly into the hole in the world—it had evidently been meant to go there—and then the strange things began to happen. When once these two parts of the two machines had come together, one after another, all the other parts fitted and fell in with an eerie exactitude. I could hear bolt after bolt over all the machinery falling into its place with a kind of click of relief. Instinct after instinct was answered by doctrine after doctrine.[26]

The Catholic intellectual tradition, then, functions in various ways. For born-Catholics it helps them deepen their understanding of the Catholic faith in the light of the problems and questions posed to them by their ever new cultural settings. It functions as *fides quaerens intellectum*, faith's ancient search for understanding, so that the faith can be lived and proclaimed "to the ends of the earth." On the other hand, for those in search of belief, the Catholic intellectual tradition functions in an apologetic way: it provides an articulation of how faith and belief relate to the rest of life.

To recall an emphasis we made at the beginning of this essay, because the Catholic intellectual tradition is a living tradition reflecting the gospel and calling for an ongoing conversion, the tradition concerns not just the past but also the future. It is a tradition that would penetrate every dimension of contemporary culture, not to control that culture, but to liberate it, to bring the best out of it. So, in today's world, when Christianity and Catholicism's

fortunes seem in many areas to have hit such a low ebb, it is extremely important to believe that the gospel contains seeds that would germinate in all areas
of contemporary culture: the arts and drama, literature and philosophy, the
sciences and scholarship, communications and public policy.

For faith not only helps us focus on God as our absolute value, but it also
helps us see what God would have us do in this world. Faith not only has an
absolute aspect that places all values in the shadow of the supreme value that
is God, but it also has a relative aspect by which that supreme value links
itself to all other values to transform, magnify, and glorify them. To quote
Lonergan: "Faith places human efforts in a friendly universe; it reveals an
ultimate significance in human achievement."[27]

Just as Aquinas provided the framework for Dante to write his *Divine
Comedy*, so insightful analyses of human consciousness can provide the
framework for the Catholic intellectual tradition to enter into the artistic,
poetic, literary, historical, and political worlds of our own times.

> In the medieval period theology became the queen of the sci-
> ences. But in the practice of Aquinas it was also the principle
> for the molding and transforming of a culture. He was not con-
> tent to write his systematic works, his commentaries on Scrip-
> ture and on such Christian writers as the Pseudo-Dionysius and
> Boethius. At a time when Arabic and Greek thought were pen-
> etrating the whole of Western culture, he wrote extensive com-
> mentaries on numerous works of Aristotle to fit a pagan's
> science within a Christian context and to construct a world
> view that underpinned Dante's *Divine Comedy*.[28]

Much remains to be done in our day. Catholic writers such as Walker
Percy, Flannery O'Connor, and Andre Dubus have done much to allow their
Catholic faith to find expression in contemporary cultural circles. But much
still remains to be done to allow gospel values and meanings to penetrate into
the various areas of contemporary life. As Lonergan addressed Jesuit scholastics in 1962: "Ours is a time for profound and far-reaching creativity. The
Lord be with us all—*ad maiorem Dei gloriam*—and, as I have said, God's
own glory, in part, is you."[29]

Notes

1. Cf. Francis W. Nichols, "Catholic Studies Are Here to Stay," and Andrew
   Greeley, "What Catholics Do Well," *Commonweal*, April 9, 1999, 26–32.
2. Cf. John Ranieri, *Eric Voegelin and the Good Society* (Columbia, MO: University of Missouri Press, 1995) 110–111.
3. Cf. Bernard Lonergan, *A Second Collection* (Philadelphia: Westminster
   Press, 1974) 92: "Classicist culture contrasted itself with barbarism. It was
   culture with a capital 'C.' Others might participate in it to a greater or less
   extent and, in the measure they did so, they ceased to be barbarians. In other
   words culture was conceived normatively. It was a matter of good manners

and good taste, of grace and style, of virtue and character, of models and ideals, of eternal verities and inviolable laws."

4. Vincent Donovan, *Christianity Rediscovered* (Maryknoll, NY: Orbis Books, 1982).

5. Cf. Bernard Lonergan, "The Scope of Renewal" (unpublished Larkin-Stuart Lecture at Trinity College in the University of Toronto, November 15, 1973) 2: "When the study of Aquinas was enjoined on all students of philosophy and theology, what was envisaged was the assimilation of the basic tenets of Thomistic thought. But the first concern of historical scholarship is not to set forth and convince readers or hearers of the profundity of an author's thought, the breadth of his vision, the universal relevance of his conclusions. That sort of thing may be allowed to pad a preface or to fill out a conclusion. But the heart of the matter is elsewhere. It is a long journey through variant readings, shifts in vocabulary, enriching perspectives—all duly documented—that establish as definitively as can be expected what the great man thought on some minor topic within the horizon of his time and place and with no great relevance to other times and places. Only from a long series of such dissertations can the full picture be constructed—a picture as accurate as it is intricate, broad indeed but with endless detail, rich in implications for other times if only one has the time to sort them out, discern the precise import of each, and infer exactly what does and does not follow."

6. Bernard Lonergan, *Method in Theology* (Toronto: University of Toronto Press, 1996) 362–363.

7. Thomas Aquinas, *Summa Theologiae*, 1–2, q. 29, a. 4 c.

8. Quoted in Denis Dirscherl, *Dostoevsky and the Catholic Church* (Chicago: Loyola University Press, 1986) 63.

9. *A Second Collection*, "Belief: Today's Issue," 91.

10. Bernard Lonergan, "Christology Today," *A Third Collection* (Mahwah, NJ: Paulist Press, 1985) 84. There Lonergan refers to the works of Heinrich Schlier and Franz Mussner.

11. *A Second Collection*, "Belief: Today's Issue," 91.

12. *Method in Theology*, 138.

13. Cf. Bernard Lonergan, "The Origins of Christian Realism," *A Second Collection*, 239–261.

14. *Method in Theology*, 139.

15. *Oxford University Sermons* (London: Longmans, 1896) 9.

16. John Paul II, *Fides et ratio*, September 14, 1998. The text is available on the worldwide web at http://www.vatican.va

17. David DeLaura, "Newman's *Apologia* as Prophecy," in David J. DeLaura, ed., *Apologia pro vita sua* (New York: Norton [critical edition], 1968) 496.

18. As Bernard Lonergan writes of the classic: "The classics ground a tradition. They create the milieu in which they are studied and interpreted. They produce in the reader through the cultural tradition the mentality, the *Vorverständnis* [the preunderstanding], from which they will be read, studied, interpreted." *Method in Theology*, 161–162.

19. *Method in Theology*, 161, quoting from Hans Georg Gadamer, *Varheit und Methode* (Tübingen: Mohr, 1960) 274.

20. John Henry Newman, *Apologia pro vita sua*, Martin J. Svaglic, ed. (Oxford: Clarendon Press, 1967) 226.

21. *"Insight* Revisited," *A Second Collection*, 263. Cf. "Reality, Myth, Symbol" in *Myth, Symbol and Reality*, ed. Alan M. Olson (Notre Dame, IN: University of Notre Dame Press, 1980) 32–33: "My fundamental mentor and guide has been John Henry Newman's *Grammar of Assent.* I read that in my third year philosophy (at least the analytic parts) about five times and found solutions for my problems. I was not at all satisfied with the philosophy that was being taught, and found Newman's presentation to be something that fitted in with the way I knew things. It was from that kernel that I went on to different authors."

22. *Method in Theology*, 139.

23. Ibid., 123.

24. Ibid.

25. For numerous examples of the apologetic role of the Catholic intellectual tradition, cf. Patrick Allitt, *Catholic Converts: British and American Intellectuals Turn to Rome* (Ithaca, NY: Cornell University Press, 1997).

26. G. K. Chesterton, *Orthodoxy* (Garden City, NY: Doubleday, 1959 [1908]) 79.

27. *Method in Theology*, 117. Cf. 116: "The power of God's love brings forth a new energy and efficacy in all goodness, and the limit of human expectation ceases to be the grave."

28. *A Second Collection*, 62.

29. Bernard Lonergan, *A Fourth Collection: Collected Works of Bernard Lonergan, Vol. 4* (Toronto: University of Toronto Press, 1988) 231.

2

Catholic Intellectual Life:
An Opportunity for the Church
to Continue to Learn

Paula Powell Sapienza

Our entire subject is humankind,
men and women:
whole and entire
with body and soul,
with heart and conscience,
with mind and will.
　　　　　　　　　—*Gaudium et spes* (Bill Huebsch, trans.)

This essay begins with the assumption that there is a desire among many if not most intellectuals for integration and wholeness in their lives. For those individuals who also profess faith in God, such a longing for unity of meaning and purpose may lead them to consider the relationship of their faith to their daily work, most specifically to their teaching and scholarship. Some of these same intellectuals may have had the occasion to share their ideas and experiences of integration achieved, thwarted, or desired with others in their academic institutions or faith communities. Many more may have never broached the topic at all, either publicly or privately. The discussion here seeks to break open and encourage consideration of the relationship between faith and the intellectual life, most specifically in the Catholic context. It begins with the idea of vocation, exploring what it might mean to view the intellectual life not as job or career, but as calling, and what such a theology of the intellectual life might entail. If we accept the intellectual life as vocation and, more importantly, claim it as our own, the question then becomes: How do we live our lives in faithfulness to God's call? And on a broader scale: What is the mission and ministry of Catholic intellectual life?

These questions can be answered in a number of different ways, some of which are the topics of other articles in this collection. The particular answer that we will explore here is that one function of Catholic intellectual life and the vocation of the intellectual is to help the church do its thinking. This answer is intentionally very broad in scope, catholic with a small "c," because in keeping with Catholic thought on the relationship between faith and reason, the two are understood to be inextricably and necessarily joined one to the other. There is no area of rational human inquiry that cannot potentially inform faith, just as there is no aspect of faith that is unable to impact our efforts to reason and make sense of our experiences. It is unreasonable, therefore, to define Catholic intellectual life in only narrow terms such as theology, philosophy, hermeneutics, and the like, although they all certainly constitute aspects of it. Instead, every field or discipline has a place within Catholic thought because every area of rational inquiry is a potential reflection upon and even mediator of God's presence in the world. This view is based upon what Catholics call *sacramentality*, the belief that God reveals God's self concretely in all of history and creation. Out of this worldview arises the call to observe God's self-disclosure, to behold and interpret reality, the sign of God's action in the world. This call is central to the vocation of the intellectual, the call to bear witness to God's self-revelation in the natural world and in human activity.

Intellectual Life as Vocation

The word *vocation* connotes something radically different from the meaning of career, occupation, job, or profession. The later are like restaurant advertisements, while the former could be compared to an invitation to share a meal in the home of a dear friend. There are of course certain similarities. For example all satisfy basic human needs; both the restaurant meal and the friend's meal will end one's physical hunger. Both vocations and careers answer the human need to act in the world, to work for the survival of one's self and one's loved ones.

Another similarity is that all promise some greater degree of gratification or fulfillment beyond the satisfaction of fundamental physical needs. Restaurant ads tempt potential patrons by offering nonessential pleasures such as a unique or luxurious atmosphere, "home-style" cooking or dishes that verge on art (gourmet food), an exceptionally attentive wait staff, convenience, etc. A meal at a friend's may share some of these attributes while also holding the promise of a meal chosen with you and your particular tastes in mind. Similarly, a career or vocation may offer individuals wealth beyond their needs, special challenges and opportunities such as international travel or continuing education, and certain degrees of status or respect, among other things.

It is the differences between the elements of the two groups that are of greater significance. The restaurant ad has as its primary purpose the generation of business. A dinner invitation from a dear and trusted friend is fundamentally a request for intimacy, for an opportunity to further deepen a shared relationship. Similarly, a career or job also has at its foundation the creation of a business relationship based on an exchange of goods and services in the marketplace. A vocation, however, is by its very definition an invitation to deeper relationship, relationship with God and God's people, by becoming a sign and witness of God's action in the world. Clearly, strong and meaningful relationships can be fostered in the course of business dealings. Greater love and intimacy, however, are not the necessary goals of such transactions as they are for a shared meal or one's vocation.

Vocation as an invitation or call (the word is derived from the Latin *vocare*, "to call") from God to a particular state of life leads to reflection upon how God calls people. Vocation is in no way one-dimensional. There are many vocations, and individuals may be called to any number over their lifetimes. There are, for example, personal vocations such as vowed religious, single, or married life, and there are uncountable social vocations that correspond by name to various jobs and professions but that, as discussed above, imply much more. No one vocation is superior to any other. All vocations ultimately serve one goal in the Christian context: to build up the Body of Christ and the kingdom of God.

Individuals may discern their vocation(s) in any number of ways, prayer certainly being an important part of any Christian's discernment process. Church tradition provides many spiritual avenues by which pray-ers might open themselves to God's Spirit through individual prayer, the guided process of spiritual direction, faith sharing within community, liturgy, and other means. It is not the purpose of this essay to outline or introduce ways of praying or specific spiritual traditions of the church. What is important to emphasize rather, is the need for daily prayer and discernment in the lives of believing intellectuals so that we might first cultivate an openness to the approach and call of God's Spirit and, second, foster the freedom and courage to respond to that call.

How then does a call to the intellectual life serve the goal of fostering the kingdom of God? The principle of sacramentality, "the notion that all reality, both animate and inanimate, is potentially or in fact the bearer of God's presence and the instrument of God's saving activity on humanity's behalf" (McBrien 1989: 1148) logically demands that God's presence and action in the world have witnesses. A Catholic theology of the intellectual life as vocation certainly places this task before the intellectual. It is fundamentally linked with the search for knowledge and truth to which scholars and teachers dedicate themselves, and for Catholic (and all believing) intellectuals, the search for disciplinary knowledge and truth potentially and explicitly leads to knowledge of the truth that is God (which is not to say that only believers can come to know God's truth in their work, but that they consciously and expressly link the two together).

A Catholic Theology of the Intellectual Life

The continuity of reason and faith is a central pillar in Catholic thought. The most recent example of this profession is John Paul II's 1998 encyclical letter *Fides et ratio*. There the pope affirms the Catholic teaching that the human quest for truth, most particularly the truth that transcends us and is God, is a quest to grow in our humanity, a quest to know who we are as humans and to know our place in the natural world. What is more, the human desire to know is given to us by God, a gift that comes from God's own desire to be known. In other words, human striving toward knowledge and truth can result in the fulfillment of God's will, an assent to God's dream that we might come to know God as God is. Intellectuals clearly have a role to play in this search, a search that is not for the benefit of themselves alone but for the benefit of all people.

Before considering this role in more specific terms, it may be useful to outline briefly some additional principles that, together with the ideas above, begin to constitute a Catholic theology of the intellectual life. It is by no means complete or exhaustive. Rather, its purpose is to present certain assumptions that Catholic thinkers might be said to generally share and to encourage discussions of other premises that might undergird a Catholic vision of the intellectual life. At the very least, this discussion further reveals some of this writer's own beliefs, commitments, and assumptions, something that all intellectuals must do if they are to honestly enter into dialogue with one another, whether or not they profess faith in God.

To believe that God gives us the means by which we might truly know God logically dictates that rational knowledge and faith's knowledge, because they both have their source in God, cannot contradict each other. To proclaim God's unity is not, however, to ascribe perfection to our human interpretations of the knowledge God gives. Catholics' assent to God as the source of all truth clearly does not accord humanity knowledge of that truth in its fullness. Indeed, the profound humility that this knowledge engenders needs to be at the very heart of the stance of the Catholic intellectual in the world. We are, as *Lumen gentium* ("The Dogmatic Constitution of the Church" from the Vatican II Council) proclaims, a "pilgrim people," imperfect in our striving toward God.

It is, therefore, not confidence in our own intellectual abilities that is to sustain Catholic intellectuals' search for truth, but our faith, hope, and trust in God. Jesus is the human embodiment of such a humble faith. As someone who knew himself to be God's beloved Son *and* servant, Jesus never fell victim to the vice of human arrogance that "deems equality with God." As Catholic thinkers and teachers, we must constantly ask ourselves where it is we place our own faith as we carry out our scholarship and communicate our knowledge with our students, colleagues, and the larger communities of which we are members. In other words, what assumptions do we bring to our work as Catholics, and are we willing to not only publicly acknowledge these assumptions but also reflect on how they might impact and even enrich our fields of study?

An honest and thorough exploration of our assumptions demands dialogue. It is through honest, faithful, and open discourse with others, especially those who do not share our worldview, that we are best able to identify and critically assess the premises upon which we base our thinking. This fact points to another essential feature of the intellectual life, that it engage the world. This task and challenge is of special urgency for Catholic intellectuals in the post-Vatican II church. Vatican II was the first worldwide council of the church to produce a document (*Gaudium et spes*, "The Pastoral Constitution on the Church in the Modern World") that addressed itself to the whole of humanity and stressed the two-way relationship or interdependence that must exist between the church and the world. The following passage is of particular significance for intellectuals:

> [The Church] profits from the experience of past ages, from the progress of the sciences, and from the riches hidden in various cultures, through which greater light is thrown on the nature of man [*sic*] and new avenues to truth are opened up. In this way it is possible to create in every country the possibility of expressing the message of Christ in suitable terms and to foster vital contact and exchange between the Church and different cultures. Nowadays when things change so rapidly and thought patterns differ so widely, the Church needs to step up this exchange by calling upon the help of people who are living in the world, who are expert in its organizations and its forms of training, and who understand its mentality, in the case of believers and nonbelievers alike. With the help of the Holy Spirit, it is the task of the whole people of God to listen to and distinguish the many voices of our times and to interpret them in the light of the divine Word, in order that the revealed truth may be more deeply penetrated, better understood, and more suitably presented ("Pastoral Constitution on the Church in the Modern World," 1975: n. 44).

This passage points directly to three actions that are critical to the work of the intellectual: listening, distinguishing, and interpreting. To be both an intellectual and a Catholic, then, is to be in a particularly advantageous position from which to facilitate and produce the types of exchanges necessary for proclaiming the gospel. There is an additional province of the intellectual that also translates directly into the work of the church: the responsibility of criticism, which is also the call of the prophet.

These intellectual projects serve not only to better connect the church with the larger world but also to keep the church honest with itself. Certainly dialogue between intellectuals and the institutional church has undergone a wide range of successes and failures. There are not just bitter intellectual disputes in the church's history, but also personal tragedies suffered by individuals within and outside of the church at the hands of members of the Body of Christ, both religious and lay. Because of the suffering that has taken place on all sides, some groups and individuals have chosen to reject any degree of interaction, intellectual or otherwise, with the institutional church. Regrettably, the church's hierarchy has at times arrogantly stifled dialogue by either seeming to or in fact labeling certain issues as not open to discussion. Certainly individuals and institutions alike must be prepared to argue strongly and with conviction for the principles and beliefs they hold most dear. And yet, if we do not allow our beliefs, our assumptions, our principles, our faith, to be subjected to scrutiny and even shaken by doubt, then how is it that we can ultimately say that we chose them in freedom? If we as humans are truly free to either reject or accept God, then the possibility of rejection must exist and be open to exploration. The same must be true for all ideas and beliefs. For the church to disallow any such questioning is perilous and shortsighted, for it flies in the face of the church's teachings that God's fidelity is without end, and that God's mercy is forever. For the church, therefore, to forsake dialogue with any human being, let alone individuals laboring for intimacy with God, is to reject the example of right relationship that God gives to us.

The type of genuine dialogue that allows for thoughtful and thorough consideration of disparate beliefs is something wholly different from mere tolerance of differing viewpoints. Agreeing to disagree may be the most expedient or even comfortable route to take in the course of a difficult exchange, but it certainly will not bring the two parties any closer together. Critical to any dialogue that springs from Christian principles is certainly the virtue of faithfulness, faithfulness first of all to the other as a human being. Such faithfulness requires a loving and respectful approach that engenders trust and goodwill even in the absence of agreement. Second, there must be faithfulness to the process of dialogue itself, which should naturally flow from one's faithfulness to the other. If I truly respect and love you as the person you are, then it stands to reason that I will take seriously your ideas and beliefs and give them a careful and deliberative hearing.

Clearly, for such a dialogue to take place, *both* parties must be committed to these principles. For Catholic intellectuals interacting with peoples and institutions that do not subscribe to such ideals, there will certainly be times when dialogue is not possible, or at least when it must be suspended with the hope of renewal. For Catholic intellectuals who wish to engage one another and the institutional church, however, these results should not be the outcome. The responsibility for keeping the channels of communication open lies equally with all parties.

The choice Catholic scholars and the church must make about whether they will faithfully engage one another is that of any two people called to dialogue. This choice is based on answers to important questions such as: Do I want this relationship to grow in greater intimacy? What injuries need to be reconciled or forgiven? What joys need to be celebrated? What meaning do I find in this relationship? How does it help me to become more fully human? How does it do the same for the other in the relationship? There are other questions that could be raised in this context. For Catholics who have discerned the intellectual life to be their vocation, engagement with the church seems a necessary part of their call. The question for them then becomes how to faithfully place their work in the service of others in the spirit of Jesus Christ.

How Do We Do What We Do?

The first half of this paper has attempted to lay down a very basic set of assumptions about the intellectual life in the Catholic context: that it is a vocation discerned in prayer, rooted in humility, and based in dialogue that answers God's call to behold and interpret (come to know or understand) God's action in the world. Catholic intellectual life, therefore, is an opportunity for the church (in the broadest sense of the word) to learn, and the second half of this paper will focus on the question of how Catholic intellectuals might approach their work so as to answer the church's (and, indeed, humanity's) need to grow in knowledge of the truth that God reveals.

One premise of this discussion is that every discipline has the potential to inform and challenge our understanding of who God is and what relationship with God means and requires, in other words, the questions that are central to religious thought and moral praxis. Similarly, just as our research can and must impact our faith, faith in God can offer an important and potentially enlightening point of departure in academic research. A fundamental question to ask, therefore, as we formulate our research strategies is: How do we frame the subject matter at hand and what assumptions do we bring to the projects we undertake?

It is today a truism that our ability to rationalize about human culture and the natural world is shaped by our environment and culture. Even the natural sciences cannot claim true objectivity. Positivistic illusions have been shattered. The challenge for intellectuals, then, becomes to unveil the sources of our epistemological commitments as scholars. What are our ways of knowing? For Catholic intellectuals, this question raises the issue of faith as a way of knowing, as a potential starting place for research. There are two seemingly polar concepts within Catholic thought and faith that can serve as springboards to thinking about the nature and limits of human knowledge. The first, which we have already begun to explore, is *sacrament*. The second is *mystery*.

Mystery refers to the infinite incomprehensibility of God. Because our human senses are unable to determine the existence of God, we never experience God directly, only indirectly. Our encounters with God are always mediated by people, events, things, and states of mind that our senses perceive firsthand. For Catholic scholars, mystery is at once a reminder that our knowledge will never be complete, will never embrace the totality of God— and yet it also points to the importance, once again, of the *sacramental nature of all that is*. God, although incomprehensible, nevertheless constantly reveals God's self in all of history and creation. God's self-revelation or self-communication is what Catholics call grace, and when we perceive God's grace in our midst, we call the object, person, event, etc., that we have come to recognize as a sign of God's grace sacrament. Anything can be a sacrament because God is always present, always revealing God's self. As Christians, Catholics profess that the greatest or "first" sacrament is Jesus Christ. It is the mystery of the Incarnation—of God's becoming a human being in Jesus Christ—that challenges us most profoundly to see the sacred in the secular, to find God in all things.

And yet, there is a paradox. God, the ultimate mystery, of which we can never conceive, is nevertheless immanent. God is always everywhere. God is "pure presence." Such a faith perspective has tremendous potential as an entrée into the discourse on the "postmodern condition." One of postmodernism's foundational philosophers, Jacques Derrida, bases his critique of Western philosophy's quest for an ultimate source of meaning on an analysis of communication that argues that signs (e.g., gestures, hieroglyphs, words, etc.), because they can be cited, because they are iterable, break with their given context. Therefore, he maintains, contexts are "without any center of absolute anchoring" (Derrida 1982: 320). In other words, meaning cannot be pinned down. Conscious intention is untranslatable through the use of signs.

Derrida does *not* argue that meaning itself does not exist (although such conclusions have been drawn from his argument by others), but rather that the Western faith that words embody truth is fallacious because the signifier (e.g., the word) does not equal the signified (that to which the word refers). Instead, all words are metaphors, approximations, comparisons, and "literal meaning" turns out to be an oxymoron. Put differently, all signs defer rather than confer meaning because they symbolize or re-present that which is present.

The notion of mystery can be understood as a qualified confirmation of this idea. Derrida's argument can be understood at a certain level as a critique of fundamentalism, which insists on the absolute inerrancy and literal truth of the Scriptures. For Derrida, such an idea is clearly anathema. For Catholics, divine inspiration and inerrancy are attributed to the Scriptures. However, the authority Catholics ascribe to Scripture exists only in the context of the church's living tradition and its teaching authority. In other words, the interpretation of Scripture is not literally fixed. The truth (authority) of Scripture is found not in the words alone, but rather as the word of God is revealed in human community and interpreted through human discourse. This idea is not new to Christianity, but rather flows out of the Jewish tradition of midrash, exegesis of the Jewish Scriptures that presumes a standard of truth yet allows for an infinite array of interpretations by the rabbinical community.[1]

To Derrida's belief that language leads not to clearer, more focused, sharper meaning, but to an ever greater multiplication of meanings, a Catholic could say "Yes, the word of God is boundless; the mysteries it reveals are not finite, but infinite, and ultimately unknowable. God is mystery." However, the word of God, perhaps not surprisingly, carries an additional and no less important meaning for Catholics.

Christian faith proclaims that Jesus Christ is the Word (Gk., *Logos*) of God *made flesh* (see John 1:1–14). In other words, the Word of God is "pure presence," an idea to which we will return shortly. The understanding of Jesus as Logos developed in the second century as Christians found it necessary to translate Christ's significance to the Hellenistic world. Logos, which for the Greeks was the divine reason (intention) governing the universe, in John's Gospel is God's preexisting Word who formed creation and was incarnated in Jesus Christ. In other words, the early Christians proclaimed that in Jesus Christ the barrier between God and humanity had been broken. Jesus Christ, by his very being, was the embodiment of God's Word, the fulfillment of the Hebrew Scriptures, the *full revelation of the conscious intention of God*, what Derrida seems to mean when he writes of "pure presence."

Derrida's argument presupposes that there is no experience of pure presence, however, and based upon this assumption, he asserts his analysis as valid for all experience, not just signs alone (p. 318). For Catholics, however, pure presence did and does exist in Jesus Christ as well as through God's grace, God's self-communication which, when it takes on a form recognizable by our senses, becomes sacrament. Such communication, because it is of God, is perfect, "pure." The mystery of Christ's Incarnation is, therefore, for Catholics a disputation of any absolutist view that would reject the sacramental nature of all that is, signs included. The Catholic presumption is that God is fully present everywhere and always. God is not iterable because God simply is ("I am")—which is why modern science is unable to prove God's existence—God cannot be subjected to repeatable experiment. Pure presence is thus foundational to all that is. The problem, then, is not that we have no experience of pure presence, of God, but rather that because God's presence is immanent, we are unaware of it, desensitized to it as always being present. It therefore becomes the task of Catholic scholars to sensitize themselves to the presence of God in their disciplines, to become aware of the sacramental nature of what they study.

There is one point that needs to be clarified before continuing. Namely, I do not mean to suggest that Catholic intellectuals would be right to dismiss Derrida's argument in a scholarly forum on the basis of their faith in God's immanent presence. George Marsden (1997) argues quite clearly that Christian scholars must maintain standards in their work that, regardless of any Christian underpinnings, make their work accessible to others operating out of different sets of assumptions. In other words, scholars' argumentation cannot introduce or depend upon "special or private revelations" that others cannot verify (p. 48). This requirement does not preclude allowing revelation to inform our work, however. And so in this particular instance for a Catholic scholar to assume, based on faith, that pure presence can be experienced, that God is pure presence and communicates God's self perfectly, is no less reasonable than Derrida assuming that pure presence is impossible.

The difficulty for the Catholic intellectual then becomes how to respond to the paradox. If God communicates God's self perfectly *and* God is infinitely incomprehensible, then where does this conundrum leave us? The question is by no means new, as it is central to the human quest for meaning and purpose in life, and of course numerous people have offered numerous responses to it. The answer I wish to present and explore here comes from the twentieth-century Russian philosopher Mikhail Bakhtin. In his book on Dostoevsky, Bakhtin argues, in the words of Caryl Emerson (1990), that:

> Dostoevsky's dialogic mode of thinking gave new meaning to the idea of an "ideological quest": it ceased to signify the search for impersonal disembodied truth and became instead an exchange, an act of personal address. But can such a dialogically interdependent world acknowledge any genuine authority? Bakhtin says yes, and submits as his (and Dostoevsky's) ideal the image of Christ. Christ's truth is real, but its authority cannot be known as dogma or as proposition. Genuine truth always involves more work and more risk than dogma or propositions require of us. Because the task of life is always posited

and created rather than merely given, any truth we might
achieve in life is available only as a relationship (p. 113).

Emerson goes on to cite Bakhtin directly: "Quests for my own word are in
fact quests for a word that is not my own, a word that is more than myself;
this is a striving to depart from one's own words, with which nothing essential can be said" (p. 113).[2] The central task of Emerson's essay is to assess
the ways in which Bakhtin can be said to be a thinker in the Russian Orthodox tradition. This topic is not of concern to us here. However, it is necessary
to consider how Bakhtin's ideas can be understood as allied with Catholic
thought.

The critical point to take from Bakhtin is that to follow Christ means to
reject dogma and discover God in communion, in relationship, where dogma
is understood to be any human teaching deemed immutable and therefore
closed to critical evaluation and development. The Gospels tell of many
instances when Jesus questions the Jewish authorities' interpretations of
God's law. Jesus exposes many of their readings of the law as human distortions of God's intent:

> He said to them, "Isaiah prophesied rightly about you hyp-
> ocrites, as it is written, 'This people honors me with their lips,
> but their hearts are far from me; in vain do they worship me,
> teaching human precepts as doctrines.' You abandon the com-
> mandment of God and hold to human tradition" (Mark 7:6-8).

At issue here is not whether there is a law given by God. Clearly Jesus affirms
that there is, and, moreover, that he has come to fulfill it (see Matthew 5:17).
Instead, Jesus challenges us to always measure our interpretations of God's
law and our actions that flow from it against the standard of love, love of God
and love of neighbor. In other words, Jesus calls us first and foremost into
loving relationship. It is upon such communion that any understanding and
fulfillment of God's law depends.

It is also worthwhile to note that Bakhtin's idea is clearly consonant with
the Christian teaching of the Trinity, which proclaims one God in three Persons. This diversity of persons assumes a relationship between the three, a
relationship that Augustine describes in *On the Trinity* (see esp. Book 15,
chapter 17 ff.) as lover, beloved, and the love between them. If these images
are true, therefore, if God is relationship, if God is love, and, to return to an
earlier image, if God is truth, then it is reasonable to conclude with Bakhtin
that truth is found only in relationship, which presupposes dialogue.

The citation above from Bakhtin then holds a particular significance for
intellectuals. He says that our search for the "right" words, our (inadequate)
striving to communicate knowledge and truth, is not about the struggle to
understand our own words, but to understand the words of others. In terms of
our relationship with God, this idea challenges us to constantly open ourselves to and behold God's ever-present grace. In terms of our relationships
with other people, it demands a genuine, even radical form of empathy. In

intellectual terms, then, the true and ultimate object of the work of Catholic scholars is not intellectual "progress" (i.e., greater knowledge), no matter how foundational knowledge is to our enterprise, but instead the central mark of the intellectual vocation is greater love.

Ralph Williams, a gifted teacher and professor of English at the University of Michigan, was honored with a prestigious teaching award by the student body in 1992. The highlight of the award is an opportunity for the recipient to give (and for students and faculty to hear and enjoy) his/her "lecture of a lifetime." The talk can be on anything, any topic the award-winner wishes to explore. Ralph Williams chose to speak on the relationship of knowledge and action. He spoke first of the tragedy of imperfect knowledge that leads to wrong action, and then went on to contrast it with inaction that results from the desire for perfect knowledge. Using the holocaust as his primary example, he focused most specifically on the failure of human beings to cry "violence" and act against violence when the "other" cries out in pain and sorrow. The only option we have as human beings, he concluded, is to strive for a unity of knowledge and love as our response in all situations, with the emphasis being, when our knowledge is imperfect, as it always proves to be, to act out of love, and to take this ideal as our guiding principle in life.

The marriage of word and deed is clearly central to what Jesus taught: "Not everyone who says to me, 'Lord, Lord,' will enter the kingdom of heaven, but only the one who does the will of my Father in heaven" (Matthew 7:21). And the greatest commandment, of course, is to love. To love God and our neighbor as we love ourselves must clearly remain the core moral teaching for any Catholic intellectual. That such love is always based in relationship places a particular emphasis on the ways in which our work as scholars draws us into relationship with God and others, and the necessity for honest and open dialogue to be at the heart of our research.

In a recent article on the legacy of Vatican II, Scott Appleby (1999) assesses among other things the current state of Catholic theology. He writes:

> Theologically, John Paul has attempted to lead the church away from the promise (or peril, depending on one's perspective) of pluralism—the acceptance and further deepening of the plurality of the theological methods and sources recovered, developed, celebrated, and anticipated by the (mostly) white male European theologians who shaped Vatican II. Catholic theologians teaching in American colleges and universities are more diverse than ever, however, in terms of their intellectual training, social background, race and gender. This tension forms the backdrop to the brouhaha brewing between some bishops and some Catholic theologians and university administrators over the implementation of *Ex corde ecclesiae*, the pope's encyclical on higher education (p. 27).

I raise this issue at the peril of seeming to imply that in the final analysis Catholic intellectual life boils down to theology. Nothing could be further from the truth. Rather, the point of including Appleby's assessment here is to remind us that there is always a danger in every academic discipline for one methodology, one epistemology, one set of normative questions, to take root and potentially choke off or at least hinder the growth of others. It is important to keep in mind that the intellectual life does not produce pluralism but, instead, is a response to it (see Landy [n.d.]: 37). Intellectual life is a translation between natures, a translation between cultures, a translation between worlds that to us seem fragmented.

Faith, however, tells the Catholic intellectual that all are in fact one. Such faith in a universal truth has throughout history, unfortunately, been a source of oppression and suffering. Therefore, in the post-Enlightenment, to affirm one's faith in God and hence the existence of perfect truth has often been to encounter ridicule and censure. The fault, however, lies not in our faith in God, our faith in absolute truth, but in our faith in ourselves to understand God in truth absolutely. John Paul II (1998) has written in *Fides et ratio* that "to believe it possible to know a universally valid truth is in no way to encourage intolerance; on the contrary, it is the essential condition for sincere and authentic dialogue between peoples" (VII: n. 92). Such loving communion is the necessary foundation for intellectual questioning, for academic research, and for Catholic intellectual life as a whole. The better Catholic intellectuals model such behavior, the more genuine, rewarding, and beneficial will our research be, for it will open us to God's grace made visible in the sacraments that are our disciplines and the people whose lives our work touches.

Mission and Ministry in the Catholic Intellectual Life

If these reflections can be said to be a reasonable starting place for thinking about Catholic spirituality and its implications for our intellectual work, most specifically our research, then the final question to which this essay must turn is: How are Catholic intellectuals to make their specific research choices? In other words, how do we quantify and qualify the mission and ministry of Catholic intellectual life in our academic research?

John Haughey, S.J. (1996) has laid out a two-pronged approach to the question, challenging faculty to embrace what he calls a "metaethics or spirituality of research," and calling Catholic institutions to reward faculty research that embodies such principles. Haughey outlines six essential attributes of the spirituality of research: 1) *call*—the intellectual's sense of vocation; 2) *self-appropriation or interiority*—taken from Bernard Lonergan, it is the idea that we must take our deepest desires seriously and be true to them; 3) *the sovereignties of disciplines*—the need for a "transcendent horizon" in our research that extends beyond the smaller worlds of our fields of study; 4) *the common good*—the need to address explicitly the question of who benefits from our research; 5) *stewards of the goods of information*—the need to reflect upon how we choose to share the fruits of our research, what media do we use to disseminate our research results and who benefits as a result;

and 6) *discernment*—the need for Ignatian indifference in and toward our research (i.e., to value and prefer things only insofar as they help us to attain the end for which God created us, an idea that comes from the "First Principle and Foundation" of *The Spiritual Exercises of St. Ignatius*) (pp. 26–29). In terms of discernment, Haughey sees "intellectual consolation and a growth in being related to others, including those who will benefit most from the research" as two important signs that one's research choices are consistent with God's call (p. 29). Clearly, the need for dialogue discussed earlier is essential to and implicit in all six elements.

If scholars develop their research projects while operating out of such a spirituality, research agendas quite different from what is currently the norm will certainly result. Haughey describes five characteristics of such scholarship that he believes would ensue, and argues that it is the Catholic institutions of higher education that must encourage and support such research in clear and tangible ways if faculty research is to support the mission and ministry of the institution. The five "fruits" of spiritually based research that he outlines are projects that: 1) lend themselves to unity and integration; 2) facilitate inquiry into and dialogue with faith; 3) serve the causes of humanity and consider the ethical implications of the research; 4) dialogue with the church's tradition; and 5) struggle against injustice (pp. 30–31). To this list I would explicitly add research that is ecumenical in nature and seeks discourse not only with other theological traditions, but with nonbelievers as well.

What is critical for these and any similar suggestions to come about is for faculty and administrators to act courageously. Do we allow our faith to transform the university system in which we work, or do we back down from our beliefs in the face of a system that perhaps has yet to fulfill its promise of serving God in all things? It is clearly one thing to draft a mission statement, but quite another to live it out. And yet the identity crisis that Catholic schools began to experience in the 1960s need not describe the current state of Catholic higher education today. There are clear and present signs that in many Catholic colleges and universities faculty and administrators have been asking important questions and searching for the answers that will facilitate the type of work that is essential for the church to do its thinking. Surely the resources we need for this work God will provide. We need only to be faithful to the relationships that will sustain our vocations.

Notes

1. On the implications of *midrash* for literary studies, see *Midrash and Literature*. 1986. Geoffrey H. Hartman and Sanford Budick, eds. New Haven and London: Yale University Press.
2. Emerson takes the citation from Bakhtin, Mikhail, 1986. "From Notes Made in 1970–71." *Speech Genres and Other Late Essays*. Vern W. McGee, trans. Austin: University of Texas Press. 148–149.

Sources

Appleby, Scott. 1999. "The Contested Legacy of Vatican II." *Notre Dame Magazine* 28(2): 23–27.

Derrida, Jacques. 1982. "Signature Event Context." In: *Margins of Philosophy.* Alan Bass, trans. Chicago: University of Chicago Press, 1982. 307–330.

Emerson, Caryl. 1990. "Russian Orthodoxy and the Early Bakhtin." *Religion and Literature* 22(2–3): 109–131.

The HarperCollins Encyclopedia of Catholicism. 1995. Richard P. McBrien, gen. ed. First edition. San Francisco: HarperCollins Publishers, Inc.

Haughey, S.J., John C. 1996. "Catholic Higher Education: A Strategy for Its Identity." *Current Issues in Catholic Higher Education* 16(2): 25–32.

Ignatius of Loyola. *The Spiritual Exercises of Saint Ignatius: A Literal Translation and a Contemporary Reading.* Ed. and trans., David L. Fleming. St. Louis, MO: Institute of Jesuit Sources, 1978.

John Paul II. 1998. *Fides et ratio.*
http://www.vatican.va/holy_father/john_paul_ii/encyclicals/
documents/hf_jp-ii_enc_15101998_fides-et-ratio_en.html

Landy, S.J., Thomas M. [N.d.]. *Fostering Catholic Intellectual Life in a Post-Vatican II Context: A Theological Framework and Pastoral Strategy.* Unpublished thesis. Cambridge: Weston School of Theology.

Marsden, George. 1997. *The Outrageous Idea of Christian Scholarship.* New York and Oxford: Oxford University Press.

"Pastoral Constitution on the Church in the Modern World (Vatican II, *Gaudium et spes*, 7 December, 1965." 1975). In: *Vatican II, The Conciliar and Post Conciliar Documents.* Austin Flannery, O.P., ed. Newly revised edition, 903–1001. New York: Costello Publishing Co.

The Pastoral Constitution on the Church in the Modern World: Study Edition. Trans. Bill Huebsch. Thomas More Press, 1997.

3

Practice Makes Reception: The Role of Contemplative Ritual in Approaching Art

Joanna E. Ziegler

In the midst of a demanding and often exhausting personal and professional life, I have one hope for my work: that teaching the practice of looking at art should have a central place in the creation of a meaningful spiritual life in the Catholic academy. It trains the beholder—indeed the emphasis is on the beholder—by its discipline and daily routine and by its continual and repetitive confrontation with a work of art, to be ready to "see" in the fullest way. It teaches humility by training students to be open to the work of art on its own terms, rather than approaching it as a mirror of their own will and desires; it teaches them to pay attention, not just as a cerebral activity but one that involves the entire body and senses. It teaches an approach to what Esther de Waal calls "mindfulness, an awareness," which turns the process "from a cerebral activity into a living response."[1]

The practice of looking, as I propose to teach it, comes very close to introducing students to a form of contemplative practice, such as those identified with the great spiritual and mystical traditions of Christianity and Eastern religions, such as Zen Buddhism.[2]

It is fitting to begin with a quotation from de Waal's splendid book on Benedictine spirituality, *Seeking God: The Way of Saint Benedict.*[3] She shows us how to find the Benedictine spirit in the contemporary world of housewives, academics, and office workers—people like ourselves—by teaching us how to live that spirit in our daily lives. The theory of Benedictine spirituality does not, indeed cannot, as de Waal insists, exist apart from how one is actually to live a Christian life: "I have one hope in writing this book and that is that it may serve as a first step to an encounter with the Benedictine way, for reading about it is no substitute for living it."[4] Although this is not an essay about Benedictine spirituality, it urges the reader to consider precisely this point: that the pursuit of a meaningful spiritual life is not the result of amassing erudition and theory but of learning how one is to lead that life in a routine daily way. Art gives us one way to learn to do this. In Chapter III, de Waal has a good place from which to begin our own exploration. Although she talks about "listening," let us include—in our mind and for our purposes—the word seeing:

> The very first word of the Rule is "listen." From the start the disciple's goal is to hear keenly and sensitively that Word of God which is not only message but event and encounter . . . To listen closely, with every fibre of our being, at every moment of the day, is one of the most difficult things in the world, and yet it is essential if we mean to find the God whom we are seeking. If we stop listening to what we find hard to take then, as the Abbot of St. Benoit-sur-Loire puts it in a striking phrase, "We're likely to pass God by without even noticing Him."[5]

This essay explores the ways in which viewing art—the practice, the very act itself, of viewing works of art—can be profoundly spiritual. I would call us away from thinking about art in the usual ways, as something to do for mere recreation or entertainment, in our leisure or spare time. Of course looking at art is entertaining. We like to visit museums during vacations and attend concerts and plays in order to relax, to escape from the demands of our overly pressured lives. On the other hand, when the religious purpose of art is raised, immediately we think of art with a religious subject matter. The history of art, especially from the medieval, Renaissance, and Baroque periods, is rich with paintings and sculptures of biblical narratives of Mary and Jesus, saints, martyrs, popes, and sinners—the redeemers and the redeemed.

Catholics, therefore, presume that for their art to be spiritually enriching, it must be religious art about the figures, symbols, and stories of Christianity. This essay proposes, however, that there is another role for art, one that is neither entertaining nor didactic in the ways we have come to presume: beholding art is a practiced discipline and, as such, teaches us to see closely, "with every fibre of our being," as de Waal would have it. This goal—to see "keenly and sensitively"—is essential if we are to be ready for an encounter *with things as they are* rather than as we would have them. With daily practice, what really looking at art gives us—openness to whatever and however one defines "the transcendent," either as God or "the other"—becomes something more than a scholarly exercise in rhetoric; it becomes attainable in actuality.

The discipline of art history, at least at this moment, has little to offer the person intent upon probing the deeper truths that art might have to offer, for it is more interested in social and political issues than philosophical or spiritual ones. This is not to say that there are no resources in the history of the discipline, but they are fragmentary, isolated cases of scholars here and there trying to introduce a personally meaningful element into writing about art.[6] Since the nineteenth century, art history has been concerned with developing a "scientific" approach, in the early modern academic sense of the word, which would ensure a place within the established hierarchy of disciplines in the academy. The earliest practitioners of art history were dedicated, therefore, to developing methods with a claim to objectivity through fact gathering and dependable documentary study. My goal is to promote an enlightened experience of art, too, but by using less objectifying means than current academic practice sanctions. My emphasis first is on *today's* viewers, who can find themselves on deeply intimate terms with works of art, without becoming scholars or academics. If prepared through practice, viewers can experience works of art as immediate experiences, things to be penetrated with their entire being rather than objects of intellectual stimulation that are preserved in theories and reclaimed through books with very specialized access, at best. To approach art with a desire to grasp it fully is to approach it with reverence for what is divine in human creation and with the conviction that it has the power to lift us above the mundane and make us aware of the mystery and wonder of the human spirit. To do so is demanding; it requires discipline, practice, and preparedness.

It might be appropriate to examine some of the religious uses of art in the past: Why have people *really looked* at art? This is an interesting and complex topic in its own right, very well studied and documented, and of interest to us primarily insofar as it helps us understand how it differs from the present project. Most curious is the Church's position on images, its anxiety and recurrent attempts to prevent the laity from engaging in what it perceived as idol worship. This was especially problematic in the later Middle Ages, when religious images were readily available in churches, on street corners, in graveyards, in the home—even to the person of humblest means.[7] It was a time of intense piety, and images shaped the religious imagination as much as preaching did. In fact, preachers adopted many of their narrative anecdotes for sermons from available statuary and painting.[8] In many ways, the Church's attitude toward religious imagery confirms the power not only of imagery itself but repetitious looking, which, after all, is integral to idol worship as an activity. However, the spiritual value of looking at art ought not be limited to religious imagery.

Other periods and styles of art can be profoundly transforming, too. Things today, for example, are vastly different from the way they were in the Middle Ages. Art has been secularized, to use a favorite art historical term, which means the subject matter seldom is concerned with religious themes. Also, there are many new formats and techniques that were not available to artists of earlier times: photography, lithographic printing, installation, silkscreen, video, and so on. Yet, art without religious subject matter can be as much about creation and offers as many opportunities for spiritual transformation as can strictly religious works of art. I should make it clear that for the time being, I use the word *art* to mean the art of museums: the paintings, sculpture, and drawings of the past. We will—and should—extend that meaning to include other art forms, such as music, dance, singing, and acting. When we learn to open our eyes, minds, and hearts to the life of the human spirit in art—indeed, when that is our fundamental reason for viewing art— the categories and terminology that specialists use to distinguish one art form from another, or the implications about importance or value which they draw from such distinctions, quickly become immaterial. As de Waal shows her readers the way "from the monastery to the kitchen," I similarly encourage the present reader to make the practice of looking at art as lived experience—as much for the housewife as for the scholar.

Some Moments in the History of Looking at Images

Although it is beyond the scope of this essay to provide more than a brief look at the role of religious images in Western civilization, history offers crucial evidence of the power of looking, as a religious activity, as well as insight into our own views—dare I say prejudices—on the value of art as a religious experience today.

In the history of Christianity, there have been two periods when the response to the worship of religious images was violent in the extreme: in Byzantium between 726 and 842, and in Western Europe during the sixteenth century.[9] In both periods, the conflict over religious images was tantamount to civil warfare. On the one side, the *iconoclasts* attacked the veneration of images as "idolatry" and, on the other, the *iconophiles* literally wept with anguish over the desecration of sacred sites and imagery. In the latter period, the Reformation, churches were sacked and burned; sculptures were beheaded, urinated on, and thrown into rivers; altars were overturned; and consecrated hosts were fed to animals. The accounts from both periods of the destruction reveal the sadness and horror of watching as nearly everything considered materially holy was literally cast down, trodden upon, and otherwise desecrated. The consequences of the Reformation are still with us, much more tangibly than those of the earlier Byzantine Iconoclasm. After all, Protestant attitudes toward imagery, which draw the line between material and spiritual worship, have defined one of the central differences between Protestants and Catholics.[10]

Although the Catholic Church, since Vatican II in the 1960s, has downplayed the external objects of devotion—the material imagery and church ornaments—the newer Catholic churches nonetheless reflect a tradition of imagery, in banners and stained glass, which Protestantism has scorned since the sixteenth century. What these periods of violent destruction of images reveal is how deeply affective images could be, positively as well as negatively. One is not moved to destroy sculptures and paintings without having witnessed their effect on people.[11] As art historian David Freedberg describes in his monumental study, *The Power of Images*, "People have smashed images for political reasons and for theological ones; they have destroyed works which have roused their ire or their shame; they have done so spontaneously or because they have been directed to do so. The motives for such acts have been and continues to be endlessly discussed, naturally enough; but in every case we must assume that it is the image—whether to a greater or lesser degree—that arouses the iconoclast to such ire."[12] Freedberg insists that "the power of images is much greater than is generally admitted."[13] This is important. On some basic level, religious images have been deemed dangerous because they appear to steer the believer away from a cerebral, fully spiritual, and immaterial knowledge of God and toward a sense that the material thing itself, that is, the painting or sculpture, is somehow interchangeable—if not identical—with what is represented. We have a powerful reminder of this in the mighty wrath of Moses, incurred when he saw his people worshiping a graven image as though the image itself was divine. Even in our own time, religious images such as Michelangelo's Pieta in St. Peter's Basilica in Rome still arouse anger and violence as well as— perhaps even because of—displays of intense piety and affection. Ironically, Michelangelo himself found excessive devotion to religious images to be extremely distasteful.[14]

Current attitudes toward religious art bear some imprint of this past ambivalence and conflict. There is a view, perhaps a fear, that religious imagery can occupy the believer with an artificial presence rather than with a genuinely spiritual response. Church furnishings and decoration became noticeably spare since Vatican II, after which there evolved two, almost mutually exclusive, generations of believers: the older, clinging to their statuary, calendars, and household pictures of Jesus, Mary, and the saints; the younger, finding such images anachronistic, unnecessary, even somewhat ludicrous. Most of my current students at the College of the Holy Cross, for instance, claim that they have never prayed to a statue.

The academic disciplines, on the other hand, are fascinated by the isolated continuation of traditional devotion to images. Anthropology has produced numerous studies, for example, on Italian feast days such as those centered on effigies of St. Anthony, or practices of ritual, image devotion among the native Americans in the Southwest. The academic study and individual enclaves of active image devotion, particularly in Hispanic cultures, stand apart from the attitude of most practicing Catholics in America and Europe (albeit not the oldest generation), who generally find any form of devotion to imagery excessive and even ridiculous.

Yet, the irony is that people still generally believe that for art to be spiritually efficacious, it must portray or reflect religious subject matter. There is a clear separation of religious from secular art, in the minds of most people fostering spiritual purposes. Liturgical art guilds today, for example, are dedicated to promoting artists but the art produced must be religious in nature, either in function (liturgical vestments, for example) or subject matter (portrayals of Christ and the holy family, and so on). Even folk music, introduced as part of the Catholic liturgy in the 1960s, makes reference in its lyrics to the sacred nature of things and experience. Study groups at local churches sponsor talks and workshops on the history of religious art and music. Although the changes in forms and attitudes in the second half of this century from devotional art of the past have been radical, to say the least, what has not changed is the belief that for art to be useful in a spiritual way, it does so by communicating and narrating Christian themes, motifs, and persons. In other words, religious art has undergone significant changes in the twentieth century, with one fundamental exception: for art to serve a religious purpose it still must be concerned with religious subject matter.

Contemplation and Looking

In the history of Christian art there have been times when the activity of art—making it and looking at it—has been viewed as a serious and worthy spiritual activity in its own right. In the fourteenth and fifteenth centuries, nuns and beguines were involved in art-making practices that constituted a form of prayer: making was praying. The beguines, lay holy women who lived a communal religious life, provide a fascinating example of the identification of detailed manual work with prayer.[15]

As a way of grasping what we are about to explore, it is not at all inappropriate, I believe, to call to mind the modern image of the beguines as thoroughly rapt in the activity of making lace, for which they were renowned. Early twentieth-century beguines often were photographed bent over their little lace looms, heads hung as hands carried out the exquisitely detailed work of creating the ornamental patterns of the lace. Modern tourism, in fact, equates the religious life of the beguines with the manual life of their manufactured product, lace. Day in and day out, the beguines' world looks inward on the combined activities of work and prayer, often merging as though they are one. These modern icons of lace-making beguines are signposts, guides into the past. They reveal a tradition in the beguines' life of a merging, an identity, of close, repetitious manual labor and the prayer life.

Since earliest times, beguines were engaged in the cloth-making industry: spinning, carding, dying, and weaving wool. They also cleaned, scrubbing floors and washing laundry, and gardened. They baked and counted hosts for the liturgy. Their days were dedicated mostly to this sort of repetitious manual labor. It seems appropriate, then, that when beguines began to make art, it was the art of handicraft. The first creations for which they become known were so-called enclosed gardens, which were little worlds populated by religious figurines, in lavish artificial settings, and framed with glass.[16] The beguines made all parts themselves. For them, the discipline and concentration required for making the gardens was a form of religious activity, a form of prayer, if you will. Like the chanting of the holy Hours of the day (*prime, terce, sext,* and so on), the making of these highly detailed shrines was itself a daily ritual realized, however, in manual rather than vocal form.

Art historian Jeffrey Hamburger raises a similar issue in his book, *Nuns as Artists.*[17] Hamburger studies twelve drawings produced around 1500 at the convent of St. Walburg—near Eichstatt in Franconia, which now is part of Bavaria, Germany—seeking to understand them within the devotional practices of the nuns who made and used them. He believes the drawings—with their unusual iconography and childlike drawing style—to be the work of a single, anonymous nun. Although engaging in its own right, Hamburger's study offers some points that directly relate to the concerns of this essay. In the first place, he contends that the nuns' devotions were enacted through their eyes: "As defined by the drawings, to look is to love, and to love is to look;"[18] "Sight itself becomes the subject of the image."[19] The drawings have unusual images, such as those titled *The Heart on the Cross* or *The Heart as a House,* whereby the nuns were drawn through the wound of Christ's heart to the soul "nesting" there, "like a bird . . . in the clefts of the rock, in the hollow places of the wall."[20] This devotion to Christ's heart is what Hamburger calls the "wounding look of love."[21]

Looking, then, is praying, according to Hamburger. For these nuns, the goal of mystical devotion was to unite with Christ and to feel his love. As we learn, some incredibly imaginative nun fashioned that love into images of Christ's own heart which literally could be penetrated, entered, and felt sensuously *just by looking*. This goes far beyond our customary understanding of devotional practices that involve contemplating images or symbols of Christ. In Hamburger's view, passionate looking is a devotional end in itself. Looking is praying. Hamburger argues that, "In the handiwork of nuns, the two meanings [of *operor,* "to keep busy" and "to be engaged in worship"] converged: work itself was a form of worship."[22] In keeping with the Benedictine ideal of *ora et labora* (prayer and work), religious women throughout the Middle Ages were instructed to lead a life of pious work and prayer—"laboring like the Virgin with her spindle and thread."[23] Although Hamburger only hints at the true nature of this activity, he understands that repetitive work like weaving, calligraphy, and drawing—what we moderns now call "art"—is grounded in the body, encoded as eye-hand skills. Making is therefore intimately intertwined with seeing and feeling: hand, eyes, and heart as the vehicles and the ends of prayer.

There is a lesson to be drawn from these medieval examples: that there is a link between spirituality and the physical body; that perhaps the way to reach the divine is achieved by not only moving beyond the body but also by deepening the experience of the body through daily, concentrated, disciplined physical activity. Might there not be intrinsic value in work, defined this way then, not as a reference to ourselves (as self-promotion or self-gratification) but as a way to create a time for contemplation and a body that is ready for the physical demands of contemplation? Nuns and beguines were motivated by their superiors and conditioned by the religious culture of the time to pursue work as a form of prayer. How, then, can we achieve, within the nature of our largely secular reality, some of the same integration? Let us consider some thoughts on accomplishing this goal.

Ora et labora: **Practice and Contemplation Today**

Should we wish to deepen our spiritual lives, we must find dependable, workable forms of such practice, as well as times when we can prepare the body to work with the eyes and the heart—as did the nuns and beguines in earlier times. Our means will differ from theirs, of course. Our culture differs; our daily routines and habits differ; and our expectations and reasons for pursuing spiritual matters differ. Even if religion is important to us, the context in which we live is a largely secular one. I contend, however, that learning to make art and look at art are wholly appropriate to our present culture. This is achieved by heightening the skills of looking and listening, which can only be gained through discipline, rigor, and daily routine. Beholders eventually assume some identity with the art and ultimately the artist.

Although young people like to believe creativity is a possession—either you have it or you don't—creativity actually is a product, built on a foundation of practice. The very essence of practice is habit and daily routine. The dancer, for instance, must exercise daily and in a dependable, repeatable pattern. Ballet class always begins with the dancers doing simple arm and leg movements at the barre, then movements on the floor, and finally rehearsing strenuous choreography involving the entire studio space. Every ballet dancer knows this sequence by heart—in body as well as mind. Certain movements become entirely inscribed in the body—for example, specific arm positions—so that they no longer need to be consciously recalled when learning choreography or when actually giving a performance. Routine practice gives rise to creative expression: it is not identical with it but is its prerequisite. Artistry is when technique is so encoded in the body that pure freedom from technique can be achieved. For artist and audience—which is the point I wish to emphasize—the fullest experience of an art form comes with practice. Like the pianist practicing her scales, so too must beholders practice, if they are to penetrate the deeper meaning of creative expression.

Where contemplation enters this picture is that the discipline of daily, habitualized repetitive activity, encoded in the body, is a form of contemplative practice. Asian practices of yogic meditation and the martial arts have long been recognized as demanding daily repetition of prescribed physical activity. Western art also affords this possibility of providing the practical discipline that underlies the contemplative act—for artist as well as audience.

To introduce students to the theory and practice of these ideas, I require them to visit the local museum, the Worcester Art Museum, on a weekly basis. (Ideally, daily visits would be preferable but are not possible for college students.) It has been an effective and wonderful assignment, which students often have resisted at first but embraced by the end—one of the best signs that practice works. Students were asked to choose a painting by one of three artists: Thomas Gainsborough (English, eighteenth-century portraitist and landscape painter), Claude Monet (the French Impressionist), or Robert Motherwell (American Abstract Expressionist). None of these pictures, by the way, has a religious subject matter. The students were required to write one paper a week on the same painting for the entire semester—thirteen weeks, thirteen papers in all—each essentially the same, but reworked, refined, and rewritten. Students were asked not to consult any outside reading, even including the wall text provided by the museum. Instead, I asked them to describe, as simply and directly as they could, what they see, what is on the canvas, in a maximum of five typed pages. Notes and paper had to be turned in every week, and the students—in addition to other classroom work—returned to the museum to repeat the assignment the following week.

The students were resistant at first, anxious over whether they would be able to find anything to write about, especially thirteen times in succession. Also, the notion of a repetitive activity other than sport or bodybuilding (examples of great value in this context, by the way, for their nature as daily routine leading to "performance") was downright unattractive. The results, however, have been remarkable. The essays transformed tangibly from personalized, almost narcissistic, responses to descriptions firmly grounded in the picture. Descriptions evolved from being fraught with willful interpretation, indeed selfishness (students actually expressed hostility at being made to go the museum once a week), to revealing some truth about the painting on its own terms. Most importantly, students developed a personal relationship with what became known as "my" work of art. It was a work they knew by heart, could describe from memory—brushstroke, color change, and subtlety of surface texture. Through repeated, habitual, and direct experience (not working from slides or photographs but confronting the real work of art), students were transformed from superficial spectators, dependent on written texts for their knowledge, into skilled, disciplined beholders with a genuine claim to a deep and intimate knowledge of a single work of art—and they knew it. Moreover, they learned that with practice, any work of art could be accessible to them on its own terms.

This assignment bears the essential ingredients for becoming a practiced beholder of any art form—be it music, dance, acting, or the visual arts. In the first place, the activity is a part of daily life. Students came to depend on the time in the museum as the one routine in their harried lives they could count on. Many of them described it as "my time in the week when I get to be alone: just me and my painting." Looking at "their" work of art became a habit. It was a habit not only because it occurred weekly, but because there was a repeated pattern to the activity, which I prescribed: taking a cab at the same time each week, entering the same door of the museum, sitting in the same place, looking at the same object, indeed returning time and again to one place. Interestingly, this resonates with at least one form of instruction in prayer: Ignatius of Loyola, founder of the Jesuits, instructed his followers to return to the same place at the same time every day as an aid to prayer and preparation to hear the word of God.[24] At the heart of the contemplative activity lies repetition, for that is what frees the mind. With daily practice, the whole being and the whole person become ready to look and to listen. As my students experienced, full awareness of the object of their attention was possible only when looking had become habitual routine rather than demanding drudgery. Similar to other forms of genuine contemplative activity, looking also demands concentration, the result of routine physical discipline. To be ready—to be open—arises first from practice.

Although an assignment given to college students, this practice has a message for teaching us a range of ways to strengthen our inner lives. Becoming a practiced beholder of art is actually a wide-ranging exercise that can become a vital part of spiritual experience because, above all else, it teaches us how to cultivate concentrated awareness by repetition and physical ritual. Although, as I indicated, I focused on looking at paintings in museums, the pattern of activity is applicable to other art forms. Learn one work well, and experience it routinely. Pick a Beethoven piano sonata, for example, and learn it by heart. Play the same compact disc again and again, until every line and every nuance is second nature. Then begin to listen to other performances, learning those equally well by heart. Do this every day, at the same time and in the same place. You will come to know, in the deepest sense, a work of incomparable creativity—as well as at least one of the performances that has brought this work into being. This is nothing short of a contemplative activity, which has opened you to the full expressive power of a work of art.

Learning one work of art well is demanding. It requires discipline and practice, as well as a commitment to developing a long-term routine. Every art form makes essentially the same demands upon its practitioners. Audiences should approach art with the same spirit, if they wish to enter fully into the creative wonder.

The same fundamental principle holds true in the performing arts. Performance is the result of rigorously encoded physical and mental habits. Singers and musicians begin their study, as well as their practice sessions, with the most repetitive activity imaginable: scales. Individual works are committed to memory by hours of daily repetition; they become inscribed in the mind and body of the performer.

Many actors do the same, although audiences are less prepared to understand the nature of creativity in theater than in almost any other art form. Acting is so much a product of the marketplace, with its celebration of superficial values of stardom, that the power and beauty of the art form are all but completely obscured. Yet, acting is an art form, too, whose artistry is the result of practice and discipline. That genius of the theater, Konstatin Stanislavski, developed a system for teaching acting that was grounded in the principles of physical repetition and routine activity. Actors are taught to come into contact their emotions through repeated physical actions. By disciplining one's body the emotions could be channeled. Audiences have little knowledge of such practices. Yet, returning to the same performance over and over will reveal the effectiveness of such practices. It is essential to understand that this is not as simple as recognizing that "practice makes perfect." We enter the full artistry of the actor's art only by repeated viewing and greater awareness of the foundation in repeated, encoded, physical action. This entails, as well, a transformation in our own practices and habits.

Conclusion

Habitualized practice is a foundation for what we earlier called "mindfulness." It gives beholders access to works of art as genuine embodiments of the human spirit. I emphasize, however, that what I mean by this is that daily practice can teach us to enter into a work of art as a thing in its own right. It teaches us to leave our will behind and approach objects on their own terms. There are two wonderful lessons in this that unite in a single idea: the search for truth requires discipline *and* habit and it is attainable in things outside ourselves. This is a contemplative practice. The development of concentrated awareness—"mindfulness"—is essential if we mean to find the spiritual life we are seeking. It involves the whole person—mind, heart, and body—which for centuries has been the vital sign of meaningful spiritual experiences.

Concentrated awareness must be learned, however. My goal is to teach students that art offers the unique opportunity for experiencing the great paradox of creativity: it is a function of extreme rigor and practice and, at the same time, the manifestation of true freedom. There is something genuinely spiritual in this paradox, for contemplative ritual teaches artist and beholder alike about stability, fidelity to one thing. Perseverance and steadfastness promise readiness—and only with readiness can the freedom to transcend the activity and journey to the utterly spectacular realm of creativity become reality.[25] "Let your heart take courage, yea, wait for the Lord" (cf. Psalm 27:14). "Love the art in yourself, not yourself in the art" (Stanislaviski).

Notes

1. Esther de Waal, *Seeking God: The Way of Saint Benedict* (Collegeville, MN: The Liturgical Press, 1984), p. 43. Hereafter referred to as *Seeking God*.
2. Two institutions have helped to encourage these ideas: Collegium and The Center for Contemplative Mind in Society. The visits with the participating fellows changed my thinking about contemplation and its importance to education. I cannot thank sufficiently Tom Landy for getting me "on my way" by accepting me to attend Collegium in 1996 and The Center, along with the Nathan Cummings Foundation, for supporting the development with Joe Lawrence (Department of Philosophy, College of the Holy Cross) of a course on this material in 1998.
3. *Seeking God.*
4. *Seeking God*, p. 12–13.
5. *Seeking God*, p. 42–43.
6. I am relying in this paragraph on the work of Kathryn Brush, who has been researching the formative years of art history. In her first book, she was especially interested in the splitting apart of personal versus objective writing styles. In addition to her many articles, see *The Shaping of Art History: Wilhelm Voege, Adolph Goldschmidt, and the Study of Medieval Art* (Cambridge: Cambridge University Press, 1996).
7. Joanna E. Ziegler, *Sculpture of Compassion: The Pieta and the Beguines in the Southern Low Countries, c.1300–c.1600* (Brussels and Rome: 1992).
8. The classic history of the migration from image to word is in Franciscan preaching, particularly the recipes they used called *exempla*. One may consult various works by Caroline Walker Bynum, Walter Simons, and Jean-Claude Schmitt on this topic.
9. There were other iconoclastic movements during the French and Russian Revolutions. Western Europe lost for the second time many of its religious artifacts during the Napoleanic Occupations.
10. Carlos M. N. Eire, *War Against the Idols: The Reformation of Worship from Erasmus to Calvin* (Cambridge: Cambridge University Press, 1986).
11. Consult the brilliant though much-neglected short essay by David Freedberg, *Iconoclasts and Their Motives* (Maarssen: 1985).

12. David Freedberg, *The Power of Images: Studies in the History and Theory of Response* (Chicago: University of Chicago Press, 1989), p. 10–11.

13. Freedberg, p. 429.

14. Joanna Ziegler, "Michelangelo and the Medieval Pieta: Sculpture of Devotion or the Art of Sculpture?" *Gesta* XXXIV/1 (1995): 28–36.

15. I first introduced the spiritual nature of the relationship between the beguines and their manual labor in *Sculpture of Compassion* (c.f. footnote 7).

16. Joanna Ziegler, "Beguines," *Dictionary of Art*, vol. 3 (New York: Grove's Dictionaries, 1996), 502–505.

17. Jeffrey F. Hamburger, *Nuns as Artists: The Visual Culture of a Medieval Convent* (Berkeley, Los Angeles, London: University of California Press, 1997).

18. Hamburger, 129.

19. Hamburger, 130.

20. Hamburger, 116, 166, 219.

21. Hamburger, 128.

22. Ziegler (1992), 95–113; Hamburger, 184.

23. Hamburger, 186.

24. I wish to thank Brian Linnane, S.J., and Jim Hayes, S.J., for this insight. Father Linnane led a mini-retreat at Collegium in 1996, where he outlined the idea of repetition as a preparation for prayer, that it offers something dependable and reliable when we often are not in our moods and emotions. Father Hayes taught a class in *The Art of Contemplation* seminar in 1998, covering many of the issues of prayer and practice.

25. As always, I thank Joe Vecchione for his unwavering interest in my work and his willingness to discuss it on what must seem endless occasions. I thank him for his editing, as well, which is always the paragon of sensitivity.

The Clothier's Yard:
Church and the Imagination

An Essay in Prose Strophes

Eva Hooker, C.S.C.

Until a thing is made, it is an unstruck bell. It lacks figuration. It lacks domestic detail. It has no resting place. It is no-thing.

∼

The un-made is like a possum which hides under a house waiting for the green apples to fall. It is keen yearning.

∼

Church is a wind-lull in which spirit collects itself. Church weighs lightly on imagination. Church weighs heavy, like an iron fist. In the tension between these opposing modes of being acted upon, the imagination sifts, gains the cankered limbs it needs to work itself to the edge, to crawl to the sharp. Imagination, then, can seek and fall to the place where the hard light of transfiguration burns.

∼

Church is a shape-shifting rock. She who imagines, she who chisels within her, upon her is both deaf mute and blind seer. Her task is to fetch light and sound and color.

∼

Church stalks the imagination. Church provides for certain kinds of interiority by means of a lush sacramental ordering, even office. Think of the phrase: "to sing the office." Think "office": a room, a place, a work or duty, a chore, "little domestic offices," something done for another, the ordering of the psalms, my work. Imagination is office.

∼

Imagination is my office, my work, my ordering, my something done for another. I keep office hours, post them outside my door.

∾

If you attempt this, offer praise.

∾

What if when we look at ourselves, we fail, unlike Hamlet, to see a noble piece of work? What if, what if, we fail to see? What if we only see a map, lines of dim cartography? Lines of desire, unclear directions for folding a tent, careless use of detail, poor perspective? What if we see nothing at all?

∾

In the desert, light can peel your eyes.

Our wit's diseased.

∾

Church offers quintessence of dust.
Church offers silence that cracks a wall.
Church offers us God in our hands.

∾

Church offers what our hands cannot hold. In making, our hands try. Church offers us dumb shows and melody, shape and shape-shifters. Water, wine, oil, body, blood. A fire walking. The green mountain.

∾

Imagination wants to press down and make into the verb TO BE.
Church offers the bare tree.

∾

Did I tell you Moses pruned the burning bush?
God burned his feet.

Making is a thrashing.

∾

A word is a leading.

Stile & gate, a foot-path.
Let me mow the grass. Turn its surge,
make yet again press-money for the crow-keeper,
or a clothier's yard.

～

Church clusters people together. Shadow is inside. That is its office. Augustine asks, "Where, then, did I find you so that I could learn of you? For you were not in my memory before I learned of you." Shadow is inside. That is its office. That is my office.

To remember is an office.

～

Scrutiny of shadow. Witness to collaboration.
The shaping of memory. That is our office.

～

Church offers us the gift of cell, the room of solitude where we can see acquittal. Sing shadow song. There I find knowledge. There I find obsession.

～

Tsvetaeva tells us creation is a state of possession: "obeying an unknown need, you burn the house down, you push a friend off the top of a mountain." Possession is written down or painted or sculpted; the permission of violence is in the art. Only there. You imagine what you do not do, should not do, cannot do if you are to be fully human. You imagine no limit. You mediate.

～

Church reminds us through the cell's shattering solitude that in art we give permission to mediated violence. To create is to dream of breaking things. Thus it is that painting is permitted; we shape the icon that we must not worship. Thus it is that writing is permitted; we write the icon that we must not worship.

～

To make is to dream of breaking the self. To make is to break down. Church gives us cell for place of breakage.

~

I know now that plain song is fragile, a privacy
trained to fold like an envelope.

Bottom said that, after. His dream broke him. He had no cell.

~

I heard of a thing called Redemption which rested men and women.

~

Church gives cell as a place of mourning.

Ovadiah writes: "an individual who has acquired knowledge should lead the afternoon and evening and morning services, for the more he prays and the more he multiples the saying of kaddish, the better for the souls of the dead; and an individual who does not possess the strength or the knowledge to say all the prayers will say kaddish, so that nothing is lacking." He says further that through this office, the son attributes merit to the father.

~

Who has such strength? Such knowledge? Such power to attribute merit?

They who are housed in cell.

~

In making, we break so that we may mourn.
You might weep at this courtesy.
She writes, *Wonder stings me.*
Rude mouth music.

~

If you attempt this, offer praise.

~

Making is lying.

When your child opens her dark mouth, hungry, would you give her a stone? You give her bread. She watches you with large eyes.

Making is truth-telling.

~

Poor old Polonious made the mistake of asking Hamlet what it was that he was reading. Hamlet answered without courtesy, without patience: *Words, words, words.*

Make it plain, make it plain.

~

Real edge, the kind found in the high mountain, just breaks off. It does not announce itself. We'd better be ready.

The art of our necessities is strange.

~

Church nurtures readiness. It has seven words:

       water   oil   fire

  tree   bread   wine   eat.

~

Church does not ask, like Rilke, what is your most suffering experience. She provides for sundering.

~

In the sundering-place, we find what we need.
Words for preying ellipsis.

~

Making is out of our hands.

Making is laying on of hands.

~

Suddenly you are full, candid.
No longer fugitive.

∿

The art of our necessities is strange.
If you attempt this, offer praise.

∿

Notes

Reference is made either by adaptation or direct quotation to the following
sources:

Page 44: "Our wit's diseased," William Shakespeare, *Hamlet* 3.2.294.
Page 45: ". . . make yet again press-money for the crow-keeper," William
Shakespeare, *King Lear* 4.6.105–107.
Page 45: Tsvetaeva tells us . . . " from Marina Tsvetaeva, *Art in the Light of
Conscience* (Cambridge, Harvard University Press, 1992), 68–69.
Page 46: "I heard of a thing . . . " adapted from Letter 3, *The Master Letters of
Emily Dickinson*, edited by R. W. Franklin (Amherst, Amherst College Press,
1986).
Page 46: "Ovadiah writes: . . . " found in Leon Wisseltier, *Kaddish* (New York,
Knopf, 1998), 418–419.
Page 46: "Wonder stings me," adapted from Letter 2, *The Master Letters of Emily
Dickinson.*
Page 47: "Words, words, words," *Hamlet* 2.2.192.
Page 47: "The art of our necessities is strange," William Shakespeare, *King Lear*
3.2.73.

5

Dangerous Memory: The Transformative Catholic Intellectual

Russell A. Butkus

Introduction:
Commodity Culture and the Role for Catholic Intellectual Life

There is a cartoon on my office door that, through its amusing caricature, communicates a disturbing truth about North American culture. In the center of the picture is an oversized upright one-hundred-dollar bill in the grasp of a large hand resting upon an altar. Half a dozen people in various postures of oblation surround the sacred object. One particular obeisant character—obviously the high priest—is standing with arms raised (holding wand with a dollar sign on it) stating, "The thing I like most about this religion is the total lack of hypocrisy." It serves as a humorous reminder to me of the real religion of the dominant culture in the U.S., where "power and money talks" and where the "thingification" of life, human and nonhuman, is paramount. It also serves to introduce this essay by raising an essential question: What ought to be the role of Catholic intellectual activity in a culture that worships at the altar of the commodity?

According to John Francis Kavanaugh, North American culture is aptly defined by what he calls the "commodity form," the hallmarks of which are producing, marketing and consuming."[1] He argues that ultimately the commodity form:

> . . . is a revelation of ourselves as replaceable objects whose goal and value is dependent upon how much we market, produce, and consume. With our worth and purpose dependent upon the commodity, we ourselves are reduced to the qualities of commodity: quantifiably measurable, non-unique, price-valued, replaceable objects.[2]

The ideological and idolatrous praxis of the commodity form is pervasive. Legitimated and promoted by the powerful economic dogma of late industrial capitalism—which would appear to reign supreme in our contemporary world—the commodification of life is relentlessly communicated through the ubiquitous network of media advertising. The ultimate result of this destructive pattern of thinking and acting is the de-valuation of creation. According to Kavanaugh, the commodity form:

> . . . means . . . that there is no intrinsic human uniqueness or irreplaceable value. The person is only insofar as he or she is marketable or productive. Human products, which should be valued only insofar as they enhance and express human worth, become the very standards against which human worth itself is measured.[3]

This aspect of the commodity form is, from a Catholic theological view, a direct contradiction to the foundation of the modern Catholic rights tradition. Known as the doctrine of the *imago Dei*, it is the assertion that human beings, created in the image and likeness of God, are endowed with intrinsic worth, dignity, and value. This linchpin of the tradition forms the very basis of the entire concept of human rights, which seeks to protect and promote the dignity of persons in society. Furthermore, the doctrine of the *imago Dei* implies, at least in Catholic social teaching, that systemic-institutional transformation is necessary—a notion inherent to the concept of social and ecological justice.[4] The commodity form, on the other hand, systematically erodes human worth, reducing persons to instrumental value. Moreover this pervasive characteristic is socio-economically reinforced by a class structure that relegates many to the margins of society.

Under closer scrutiny it is not difficult to ascertain how, through its praxis of domination and violence, the commodity culture systematically destroys the dignity of persons. In the U.S. we have heard, for some time now, that we are in the longest uninterrupted period of economic growth since the end of the Second World War. Yet, what is discovered when the thin veneer of this ideological claim is unmasked? In other words, are these the real signs of the times? According to the U.S. Census Bureau there were approximately 35.6 million poor people (or 13.3 percent of the population) in the U.S. in 1997. Interestingly the bureau's 1997 "Poverty Highlights" reads: "The 1997 poverty rate was not statistically different from the rate in 1989, when a low point of 13.1 percent was achieved during the economic expansion of the 1980s."[5] Consider the fact that, of the 35.6 million poor, 40 percent are children, although children compose only 26 percent of the total population. The poverty rate of children is higher than any other age group. Moreover almost half (49 percent) of the children living in poverty were from female-headed families. According to a U.S. Census Bureau working paper, "trends in child poverty, according to official statistics, are not encouraging. After a period of improvement in the 1960s, child poverty worsened over the last three decades."[6] These statistics are revealing and are strongly suggestive that a relatively permanent underclass of poor exists in our midst, composed largely of women and children who have not benefited from the protracted period of economic expansion.

Factors like hunger and health care also shed light on the inner workings of the commodity form. According to the Food Research and Action Center (FRAC), 34 million persons in the U.S. are affected by food insecurity— defined by the USDA as "limited or uncertain affordability of nutritionally adequate foods."[7] FRAC estimates that 13.6 million children under twelve years of age "live in families that must cope with hunger or the risk of hunger during some part of one or more months of the year."[8] Lack of health care coverage is also an important issue to consider. The U. S. Census Bureau estimates that in 1997 close to 44 million people in the U.S. lacked health insurance coverage. In their May 1998 policy statement, the American Academy of Pediatrics stated that "the number and proportion of American children lacking health insurance increased in 1996 to the highest levels ever recorded by the Census Bureau's Current Population Survey. In 1996, 15.1% (11.3 million) of children younger than 19 were uninsured, up from 14% (10.3 million) who were uninsured in 1993 . . ."[9]

Add to the poverty, hunger, and lack of health insurance coverage, the stark fact that the commodity form is driven by voracious consumption and, consequently, ecological devastation—and the scenario of the commodity form grows even bleaker. According to the U. S. Catholic bishops, "Consumption in developed nations remains the single greatest source of global environmental destruction."[10] The bishops go on to state:

> A child born in the United States, for example, puts a far heavier burden on the world's resources than one born in a poor developing country. By one estimate, each American uses 28 times the energy of a person living in a developing country. Advanced societies, and our own in particular, have barely begun to make efforts at reducing their consumption of resources and the enormous waste and pollution which result from it.[11]

Much more could be said about the commodity form but the above snapshot clearly indicates that our commodity culture is by no means benign and is perpetuated at great cost particularly to the poorest and most vulnerable in our midst. It was into this cultural milieu, albeit during a much earlier historical time, that the majority of Euro-ethnic Catholics were assimilated, and it is within this commodity culture that most have prospered. Given this cultural scenario, in juxtaposition with the historical uniqueness of the Catholic tradition, such as the doctrine or the *imago Dei*, what ought to be the role of Catholic intellectual activity? The answer, and this essay's primary thesis, is that the function and goal of Catholic intellectual life ought to be the transformation of North America's commodity culture. Furthermore, given the unique history of North America's immigrant Catholics, past and present, this essay will propose a unique strategy for promoting cultural transformation—the strategy of evoking "dangerous memory," defined as the remembrance and suffering of freedom. But first, the notion of the transformative intellectual must be considered.

The Transformative Intellectual

The sociology of knowledge has taught us to recognize that knowledge and the activity that produces it cannot be socially or politically neutral. Knowledge is power and always stands in a particular relationship—to legitimate or de-legitimate—the sphere of social, economic, and political institutional activity of any given society. Also, the knowledge and the intellectual who produces it are always contextualized to some degree and shaped by, but not limited to, such factors as socio-economic class, gender, race, etc. According to Stanley Aronowitz and Henry Giroux, "There is a correspondence between the social function of one's intellectual work and the particular relationship it has to modifying, challenging, or reproducing the dominant society."[12]

Aronowitz and Giroux offer a helpful typology that categorizes the social function of intellectual activity and the knowledge produced. The categories or types of intellectuals are hegemonic, accommodating, critical, and transformative. The hegemonic intellectual is one who knowingly and intentionally aligns himself or herself with the dominant culture and class in an uncritical manner. Aronowitz and Giroux state that hegemonic intellectuals "self-consciously define themselves through the forms of moral and intellectual leadership they provide for dominant groups and classes; the interests that define the conditions as well as the nature of their work are tied to the preservation of the existing order."[13] The hegemonic intellectual is a legitimating ideologue for existing socio-economic structures.

The next type is the accommodating intellectual. He or she has usually embraced a specific ideological position and intellectual praxis that tends to validate the dominant culture and its ruling elite but, unlike the hegemonic type, accommodating intellectuals do not—according to Aronowitz and Giroux—"define themselves as self-conscious agents of the status quo . . ."[14] They often claim, for intellectual or professional reasons, to be "above" direct political engagement or affiliation. Nevertheless the intellectual activity of the accommodating intellectual tends to function in a legitimating capacity by uncritically mediating the institutionally based knowledge and practice that reproduce the existing dominant culture.

The activity of critical intellectuals is clearly geared toward protest. Their intellectual activity is defined, in part, as ideological critique of existing social, political, and economic arrangements. Aronowitz and Giroux claim that critical intellectuals "are ideologically alternative to existing institutions and modes of thought, but they do not see themselves as connected either to a specific social formation or as performing a general social function that is expressively political in nature."[15] They often, with great passion, identify and critique social forms of inequality and injustice but, for whatever reason, are unable or unwilling to engage in forms of genuine solidarity with those who suffer injustice or who are marginalized.

The final type is the transformative intellectual who, like the critical intellectual, passionately exposes and critiques prevailing ideologies and social practices that destroy creation and produce injustice and who, unlike the critical type, commits to forms of political solidarity with those groups engaged in the struggle for freedom. The underlying interest of this form of intellectual activity is emancipatory and seeks to transform culture into one that is more just and humane for all—human and nonhuman. Within an educational context, the transformative intellectual is prepared to engage students in critical reflection and dialogue over those aspects of culture that have been identified as the commodity form. Here critical reflection and action become, according to Aronowitz and Giroux, "part of a fundamental social project to help students develop a deep and abiding faith in the struggle to overcome injustices and to change themselves."[16] Moreover, the transformative intellectual labors, in the midst of struggle, "to make despair unconvincing and hope practical."[17]

These are, of course, ideal types, and most intellectuals, except for the most ideologically committed, are not usually typified by a single position but, most likely, assume a variety of intellectual postures depending on concrete institutional circumstances. Perhaps this is as it should be. There are elements of any society, our own North American commodity culture included, that should be endorsed and affirmed. An example might be John Courtney Murray's eloquent Vatican II validation of the concept of religious liberty, a defining characteristic of U.S. culture. Nevertheless, the typology of Aronowitz and Giroux does highlight the various social functions of intellectual activity and reminds us that intellectual work always carries significant ramifications for one's culture. It challenges the intellectual to engage in critical self-reflection and ponder the ultimate horizon and purpose of one's work.

At its roots, the Roman Catholic tradition is, as a particular historical embodiment of the gospel, a potential countercultural force. In contradistinction to the commodity form, the gospel is, according to Kavanaugh, "the most countercultural and the most significantly revolutionary document one could ever hope to find. It reveals the meaning and purpose of human life in terms which are closer to being absolutely contradictory to the form of perceiving and valuing human persons in our culture."[18] Grounded in the faith of the gospel and open to its eschatological hope, the task of the Catholic intellectual in the midst of a commodity culture is to unmask and critique the prevailing patterns of domination and violence that are deeply embedded in the commodity form. In solidarity with all oppressed creation and through the utilization of the unique characteristics of the Catholic tradition, the meta-purpose of Catholic intellectual activity is to promote cultural transformation in hopeful anticipation of the eschatological coming of God.

Theologically, the relationship between the transformative Catholic intellectual and the commodity culture is best described in H. Richard Niebuhr's long-standing Christ-culture paradigm as "Christ the transformer of culture."[19] In his effort to describe the multifaceted relationship between Christianity and human culture, Niebuhr attempts to typify five possible responses ranging from one extreme, Christ *against* culture, to the other, Christ of culture. While any typology is limited, the posture that best describes the thesis of the present essay is Christ the *transformer* of culture. Exemplified in Christian history by Augustine, the transformist "seeks to hold together in one movement the various themes of creation and redemption, of incarnation and atonement."[20] On one hand, the transformist takes seriously the "corruption" of human culture and yet, on the other hand, this view is mediated by a profound hope in redemption. According to Niebuhr, "The conversionist, with his view of history as the present encounter with God in Christ, does not live so much in expectation of a final ending of the world of creation and culture as in awareness of the Lord to transform all things by lifting them up to himself."[21] In this view the reign of God is human culture transformed and redeemed, and the historical praxis of the Catholic transformative intellectual is to labor toward that hoped-for future.

However, how should one proceed to provoke cultural transformation given the commodity form and the unique historical experience of North American Catholics?

Perhaps the historical factors of immigration and assimilation, hallmarks of the Catholic experience in this culture, may suggest some clues.

The American Catholic Experience: Immigration, Assimilation, and the Problem of Social Amnesia

The history of North America's Catholics is punctuated by the experience of immigration and assimilation. In other words, the Roman Catholic community of North America is largely comprised of immigrants, past and present, who have struggled and continue to struggle for acceptance into the dominant culture. A cursory review of American Catholic history reveals definite patterns of ethnic Catholic immigration. Prior to the Civil War, when the massive influx of immigration began, the predominant flow of Catholic immigrants arrived from Ireland and Germany. Later, the patterns of Catholic immigration began to shift to include more eastern and southern European immigrants, especially Poles and Italians. Catholic immigration from eastern and southern Europe continued unabated until the end of the First World War, when federal legislation severely curtailed and controlled all immigration into the U.S. More recently, particularly during the latter part of the twentieth century, Latin American peoples have come to compose a significant and growing proportion of North American Catholics. These newer Catholic immigrants continue to endure the socio-economic struggles of assimilation into the dominant Anglo culture.

This historical scenario clearly indicates that the roots of most American Catholics extend back to the massive waves of foreign immigration during the mid-nineteenth and early twentieth centuries. By and large, these ethnic-immigrants were poor with little or nothing in the way of economically useable resources. Philip Gleason correctly asserts, "From the onset of mass immigration before the Civil War until the middle of the present century, Catholics were predominantly a low-status, working class population."[22] Historian David O'Brien writes, "From the flood of Irish immigration in the 1840s until World War II American Catholicism was a Church of immigrants and workers."[23] The story of Catholic immigration is a rich and varied one, often fraught with the experience of discrimination and injustice and the pursuit for social justice. More recent Catholic immigrants continue to struggle against cultural marginalization and oppression, an experience typical of the historical dialectic between immigration and assimilation. This body of historical experience forms the basis of what will be referred to later in this essay as "dangerous memory," the past memory of suffering and freedom.

However, despite the ethnic-immigrant roots of American Catholics, a dramatic change has occurred in the North American Catholic community in the last 150 years, particularly for those of European origin. O'Brien succinctly describes this dramatic and oftentimes painful transformation: "American Catholics, traditionally associated with immigrant working class minorities, are now firmly integrated into the main currents of American life."[24] The process of integration, or what is commonly called assimilation, began as soon as American Catholics landed upon these shores. In other words, the American Catholic journey is in some respects a story of their Americanization and, according to O'Brien, "the concept of Americanization provides an indispensable key to the past, for upward mobility and acceptance into American culture were indeed objectives of immigrant Catholics and their leaders."[25] While O'Brien's assessment does not reveal the whole story and is, therefore, somewhat overstated, it points to the truth that the objectives of which he speaks have been attained. The majority of North American Catholics, particularly those of European ethnic extraction, are now Americanized and middle class.[26]

The consequences of cultural assimilation, particularly for those Catholic immigrants who arrived during the nineteenth and early twentieth century, have been significant. First, as a result of Americanization, these Euro-ethnic Catholics are no longer considered a foreign Church. Closely associated with the loss of foreignness has been the waning of ethnic loyalties among American Catholics. By the late 1960s, Gleason could readily declare:

> The generation now entering society as young adults hardly even remembers the period of "Protestant-Catholic tensions" in the early 1950s to say nothing of the Ku Klux Klan of the Al Smith days—but it does remember that John F. Kennedy was a Catholic who became President of the United States. Hence these young people have little to think of themselves as a minority threatened by the society around them, but good reason to believe that they are pretty much the same kind of American as everyone else.[27]

A second major consequence of assimilation is the fact that Americanization among immigrant Catholics has resulted in the attainment of social and economic success and parity with the dominant American culture. As Catholic immigrants became assimilated, that is, as they shed their foreignness and ethnic customs and appeared more American, they began to make significant socio-economic progress, eventually attaining middle-class status. However, it was only after World War II that this upward mobility became truly phenomenal. Gleason writes that "the post-World War II era of prosperity coincided with the maturation of American-born generations even among the more recent Italian and Slavic immigrant groups, and the last quarter-century has witnessed a remarkable improvement in the socio-economic status of American Catholics."[28] In short, the last fifty years have been an American success story for most Catholics who are now, and have been for some time, full participants in the American, middle-class way of life.

A third consequence, and perhaps the most important for our analysis, is the fact that the assimilation process resulted in the adoption of prevailing attitudes and values by American Catholics. Gleason asserts that "assimilation on the individual level has not only brought Catholics abreast of their fellow citizens in respect to social and economic status, it has also resulted in a new self-conception for those who have increasingly adopted the attitudes and beliefs prevailing in secular society."[29] The implication here is that the process of Americanization, which accelerated the internalization of dominant values and attitudes, has brought European ethnic Catholics to a point of accepting and adopting *status quo* arrangements. In other words, the majority of American Catholics, through the process of assimilation, have embraced the commodity form defined by the values of producing, marketing, and consuming.

One of the more dangerous and insidious side effects of cultural assimilation yet to be addressed is the problem of social amnesia. Social amnesia can be defined as the phenomenon whereby segments of one's collective story or tradition are lost to consciousness and forgotten. When applied to the American Catholic community, it refers to the refusal or inability of Catholics to remember their collective formative history in North America, especially the tradition of suffering and the attempts to alleviate injustice that lie embedded in that collective past. This development holds potential serious consequences. According to Vigilio Elizondo, "When one forgets the experience of suffering, as has happened to many immigrant groups in the U.S.A.—such as the Irish in Boston—then they simply inflict the same insults and worse upon others that had previously been inflicted upon them."[30] This form of social amnesia among contemporary American Catholics is directly related to their attainment of socio-economic success. In other words, social amnesia is constitutive of assimilation, middle-class consciousness and the commodity form.

To some degree, successful cultural assimilation cannot occur without some loss of memory. It is, in other words, constitutive of the process whereby new forms of social engagement are internalized, that is, retrojected into consciousness, thereby altering it. For the ethnic-immigrant, the experience of assimilation involved two poles of tension united by the process of integration into the host society. One pole was the old—that is, the old ways, customs, language and worldview of the foreign born immigrant. The other pole was the new—the new American ways of living, thinking, and acting into which foreign-born immigrants and their children were socialized. Social amnesia began as soon as the old ways were abandoned in practice. The pressure to forget the past and the old ways was directly related to the pressure to adopt new ways. As the assimilation process continued, greater distance was experienced between immigrants and their old ethnic ways.

Consequently, social amnesia resulted as greater geographical, cognitive, generational, and social distance occurred.

Key historical factors in the immigrant Catholic experience of assimilation that produced social amnesia were the arrival of American-born generations and the relatively rapid upward shift in socio-economic class. As the assimilation process unfolded, the American-born ethnic-immigrant generations ascended the socio-economic ladder into higher and more prestigious social classes. The result of this generational and social class movement was a change in consciousness and the production of knowledge leading gradually to social amnesia—the forgetting of the collective past.

In addition to assimilation, the cultural milieu into which immigrant Catholics were socialized—the commodity form—also perpetuates social amnesia. Kavanaugh reminds us that "the Commodity form dulls us into forgetting our truest identity and so separates us into isolated competing units . . ."[31] Russell Jacoby, in his book *Social Amnesia*, makes a similar claim. He argues that social amnesia is caused by the economic life of North American society. For Jacoby, memory is driven out of mind "by the social and economic dynamic of this society."[32] Social amnesia is the effect of reification, which for Jacoby is rooted in capitalist economic activity. He states:

> To pursue this for a moment: this form of reification is rooted in the necessities of economic life. The intensification of the drive for surplus value and profit accelerates the rate at which past goods are liquidated to make way for new goods; planned obsolescence is everywhere from consumer goods to thinking to sexuality. Built-in obsolescence exempts neither thought nor humans . . . Social amnesia is society's repression of remembrance—society's own past. It is a psychic commodity of the commodity society.[33]

An important aspect of economically produced social amnesia to which Jacoby alluded is the notion that planned obsolescence refers also to human beings. In other words, social amnesia encompasses the human cost of economic activity and success. It also incorporates the natural world whereby creation is forgotten in its instrumental reduction to "natural resources." Clearly, this is revealed in the capitalist commodification of creation and the objectification of human labor as commodities to be bought and sold, hired and fired, and employed and unemployed (or under-employed) according to the whim of market conditions. This is precisely what Kavanaugh refers to as the commodity form. The commodity form defines the reified matrix of our capitalist existence, and it serves as a potent legitimation for the devaluation of creation and the objectification of human beings.

Furthermore, economic reification means that the exploitation, domination, and poverty—which is constitutive of capitalist economic activity, and upon which it is built and maintained—is also lost to memory. In human terms, we are speaking of suffering, injustice, and death caused by an economic praxis rooted in the domination of creation, human and nonhuman.

Social amnesia, therefore, is not merely forgetting the past, for the past is an empty abstraction capable of being filled with whatever contents we choose. No, social amnesia is forgetting people, that is, the traditions of human suffering, oppression, and injustice that are embedded in our history of economic activity. Given this pernicious scenario, one strategy for the transformative Catholic intellectual to pursue, in the hope of promoting cultural transformation, is the evocation of dangerous memory.

Dangerous Memory and the Project of Cultural Transformation

The notion of dangerous memory, as a theological category within the Catholic tradition, can be traced to Johann Baptist Metz. In his book, *Faith in History and Society*, Metz expands the concept of political theology into a fundamental theology grounded in three practical philosophical categories: praxis, memory, and narrative. To begin, Metz understands memory in two ways. First, it is a basic category of practical reason and, second, memory is essentially the remembrance of suffering and freedom. Narrative is inextricably linked to memory because the articulation of the memory of suffering is always practical. According to Metz, memory "is never purely argumentative but always narrative in form, in other words, it takes the form of dangerous and liberating stories."[34]

Ultimately, Metz considers his use of memory as dangerous because it has the capacity to subvert existing ideologies and oppressive social structures. The subversive and dangerous potential exists because dangerous memories are:

> ... memories which make demands on us. There are memories in which earlier experiences break through to the centre point of our lives and reveal new and dangerous insights for the present. They illuminate for a few moments and with a harsh and steady light the questionable nature of things we have apparently come to terms with, and show up the banality of our supposed "realism." They break through the canon of the prevailing structures of plausibility and have certain subversive features. Such memories are like dangerous and incalculable visitations from the past. They are memories that we have to take into account, memories, as it were, with a future content.[35]

For Metz, this concept of dangerous memory also embodies the notion of solidarity and it becomes, therefore, a form of anamnetic solidarity with the victims of suffering and oppression. Furthermore, dangerous memory is understood historically "as a remembered history of suffering."[36] As the historical remembrance of suffering, dangerous memory incorporates a subversive and "dangerous tradition." In this capacity, dangerous memory functions as a socio-historical category that reflects a collective remembrance of suffering and freedom. Finally, dangerous memory has a future content that must be taken into account. This means that dangerous memory contains the possibility of promoting an emancipatory praxis aimed at a liberated future. Metz claims that "every rebellion against suffering is fed by the subversive power of remembered suffering."[37]

Theologically, memory and narrative are, for Metz, practical categories of salvation. As such, memory and narrative are seen as promoting historical and religious identity and protecting it from disintegration. According to Metz, memory and narrative are "fundamental categories used in ascertaining and saving identity in the historical struggles and dangers in which men experience themselves and are constituted as subjects."[38] Here memory is a "definite memory" of the human salvific process of becoming subjects in the presence of God. Metz writes:

> In this memory of suffering, the history of men as subjects in the presence of God is evoked and Christians are compelled to respond to the practical challenge of this history. In its praxis what will emerge . . . is [the recognition] that all men are called to be subjects in the presence of God.[39]

As a category of salvation, memory encompasses two significant dimensions. First, salvific memory refers to the "dangerous memory of the freedom of Jesus Christ" and, second, it refers to the "future in the memory of suffering."[40] The dangerous memory of the freedom of Jesus Christ focuses on the centrality of Jesus' life, death, and resurrection for Christian faith. In this context, Metz interprets memory as "the fundamental form of expression of Christian faith" and "the central and special importance of freedom in that faith."[41] The memory of freedom in Jesus is rooted in Jesus' own life and praxis: his proclamation of the kingdom, his solidarity with victims, his suffering and death, and his liberation from death through the Resurrection. A constitutive dimension of Jesus' life and our faith response is freedom—liberation—salvation.

In this context the Church, as the sacrament of Jesus Christ, becomes the public expression of the dangerous memory of Jesus. As a public witness, the Church must constantly remind the world of God's freedom eschatologically won in Jesus' death and resurrection. Moreover, the Church must criticize and oppose all ideologies, economic systems, and totalitarian regimes that deny human dignity and freedom. Metz declares that "the Church is an emancipative memory liberating us from all attempts to idolize cosmic and political power and make them absolute."[42]

The memory of the freedom of Jesus also contains a future, eschatological dimension, and it is what Metz calls "the future in the memory of suffering." In this capacity, the remembrance of Jesus' suffering, death, and resurrection is an anticipatory memory which, according to Metz, "intends the anticipation of a particular future of man as a future for the suffering, the hopeless, the oppressed, the injured and the useless of this earth."[43] This eschatological vision of God's reign holds two significant claims upon the Church and Christian praxis. First, it requires that the Church can never simply accept and take for granted social, political, and economic power and domination. As a sign of the anticipated future in the memory of suffering, the Church must demand justification of existing social arrangements in terms of actual suffering. Second, the future vision of the kingdom demands a praxis of solidarity and political engagement for justice. Metz states that "the memory of suffering . . . brings a new moral imagination into political life, a new vision of others' suffering which should mature into a generous, uncalculating partisanship on behalf of the weak and unrepresented."[44]

When applied to the North American Catholic experience, dangerous memory means several things. First, dangerous memory refers to the disturbing socio-economic conditions of the "Old World" and the experience of displacement that brought many Catholic immigrants, past and present, to these shores. It refers to the historical reasons, such as social upheaval, war, and famine, that drove Catholics to search for a better life in America.

Second, dangerous memory refers to the actual immigrant experience in North America: the struggle, poverty, injustice, and marginalization that many Catholics encountered. While the experience of immigration should not be overestimated or blown out of proportion, it does, nevertheless, indicate a very real dimension of the past history of American Catholics, which is a submerged or forgotten past of that history.

Third, dangerous memory refers to the Church's response to the immigrant experience: the search for freedom and social justice. In this context, dangerous memory is understood as the Church's historical praxis for freedom and justice, and it embodies a subversive tradition of Catholic voices, activists, and movements that supported and worked for justice in the early decades of the twentieth century. From mainline reformers like Orestes Brownson and John A. Ryan to more radical activists like Dorothy Day and Daniel Berrigan, the Catholic tradition embodies a subversive tradition that has repeatedly challenged the commodity form of North American culture.

Finally, dangerous memory refers to the theological tradition of the Church. It includes the gospel, "the dangerous memory of the freedom of Jesus Christ," and the entire biblical demand to do justice. It also includes the social teachings of the Church, which, while unique in the world's traditions of human rights, is a component of the Church's tradition that is often either overlooked, or worse, simply forgotten. The elements of the modern Catholic rights tradition, with its emphasis on the dignity of the human person and the need to care for all creation, are potentially dangerous because they stand in direct contrast to our commodity culture.

Dangerous memory, however, can never refer exclusively to the sufferings of a particular group such as ethnic-immigrant Catholics. Because of its privileged status, the American Catholic community—in order to maintain itself as a "community of memory," to use Robert Bellah's language—must attend to the suffering of all who have been subjected to oppression on this continent and beyond. Bellah writes, "If the community is completely honest, it will remember the stories not only of sufferings received but of suffering inflicted—dangerous memories, for they call the community to alter ancient evils."[45] Bellah's interpretation of dangerous memory to mean the remembrance of suffering received and inflicted challenges North American Catholics to critically examine their own participation in the construction and maintenance of the commodity form and to remember all, human and nonhuman, who have suffered in its wake. In the remembrance of suffering and freedom, a genuine community of memory can challenge the sacred canons of the commodity form and, consequently, create a hopeful vision for cultural transformation in the interest of the common good of all creation. Bellah states:

> The communities of memory that tie us to the past also turn us toward the future as communities of hope. They carry a context of meaning that can allow us to connect our aspirations for ourselves to those closet to us with the aspirations of a larger whole and see our own efforts as being, in part, contributions to a common good.[46]

There is no guarantee, of course, that the evocation of dangerous memory will produce the desired outcome of transforming our commodity culture. But as a strategy for the transformative Catholic intellectual, the remembrance of suffering and freedom holds the potential of becoming a critical epistemological force that directly challenges the commodity form. The communication of dangerous memories can critique and negate the prevailing social arrangements that perpetuate suffering and injustice. In other words, dangerous memory can de-legitimate the plausibility structures that maintain and validate the commodity form through the creation of critical consciousness and the promotion of transformative action. It is the unique and essential responsibility of the transformative intellectual to assist the members of the Catholic community in North America to remember its past, the memories of suffering received and inflicted, for the purpose of creating a hoped-for future that anticipates our shared horizon of faith in the reign of God. In this endeavor, perhaps the newer Catholic immigrants, like the Hispanic community, will play a crucial role. Referring to the Mexican-American experience of rejection and marginalization, Elizondo maintains:

> . . . it is precisely out of the condition of suffering that the poor are chosen to initiate a new way of life where others will not have to suffer what the poor suffered in the past. . . . The greater the suffering and the more vivid the memory of it, the greater the challenge will be to initiate changes so as to eliminate the root causes of the evils that cause suffering. It is the wounded healer who has not forgotten the pain of the wounds who can be the greatest healer of the illnesses of society.[47]

Conclusion

No historical community can exist for long without a shared identity and a collective memory. In order to preserve itself against disintegration, any historical community must repeatedly recall its stories and share in the remembrance of things past; otherwise, in time, it will cease to exist. Included in the retelling of the past must be the stories of shared suffering, those dangerous memories that have a unique and subversive quality that, according to Metz, "break through the canon of the prevailing structures of plausibility." This task is never easy and it is made particularly difficult when the historical community, like Catholics in America, has become prosperous in a commodity culture where the propensity for social amnesia is a constant threat against communities of memory. Perhaps the North American Catholic community has reached an important historical nexus between its past and its possible future, where the tension between remembering and forgetting is real and immediate. John Coleman points in the direction of Catholic social amnesia when he declares that "most American Catholics are near illiterates in their own history. American Catholic history is conspicuously absent from parochial schools, church colleges and even seminaries."[48] Echoing a similar sentiment, the U.S. Catholic bishops state in their economic pastoral letter that "today, as many Catholics achieve greater economic prosperity, we are tempted like the people of Exodus to forget the powerless and the stranger in our midst."[49] If these observations are correct then the specter of social amnesia is upon us. Consequently, the urgency is greater than ever for America Catholic intellectuals to provoke the memory of suffering and freedom for the sake of preserving our collective memory and identity and, in doing so, to seek to negate the power of the commodity form in favor of the way of Christian discipleship.

Notes

1. John Francis Kavanaugh, *Following Christ in a Consumer Society* (Maryknoll, NY: Orbis, 1981), 41. Kavanaugh's idea of the commodity form is based, in large measure, on Karl Marx's notion of the fetishization of commodities that is defined in *Das Kapital*, wherein Marx draws an analogy between the curious phenomenon of the commodity with the "mist-enveloped regions of the religious world." Commenting on the commodity fetish on pp. 5–6, Kavanaugh states that Marx "compares our relationship to commodities with his notion of religion, wherein humans subject themselves to the imagined products of their thoughts. Thus he sees the commodity functioning as a god or, more specifically, a 'fetish': relating to a mere part of the beloved as if it were the entire beloved. The commodity, like a god, achieves an independent existence over and against men and women. We begin to worship things, to relate to them as if they were persons; and we relate to other persons as if they were things." The cartoon that introduces this section is a humorous depiction of the commodity fetish and is used here not as a critique of genuine, authentic religion but as a lampoon of our North American commodity culture, which worships the almighty dollar.

2. Ibid.

3. Ibid., 22.

4. In the Roman Catholic rights tradition human dignity indicates that human persons possess transcendental worth. This foundation and fundamental

norm of the tradition is based on the theological doctrine known as the *imago Dei*. From this perspective rights are the minimal conditions necessary to protect and promote human dignity. According to David Hollenbach, S.J., "The central theological affirmation at the foundation of the Roman Catholic rights theory is that the human person is a living image of God." He goes on to state that "respect for the dignity and worth of persons is the foundation of all the specific human rights and more general social ethical framework adopted by the encyclicals and other Church documents." For a complete treatment of this concept see David Hollenbach, *Claims in Conflict* (New York: Paulist Press, 1979), pp. 41–50; 108–118.

5. U.S. Census Bureau website, "Poverty: 1997 Highlights," http://www.census.gov/hhes/poverty/poverty97.

6. U.S. Census Bureau website, "Poverty Measurement Working Papers," http://www.census.gov/hhes/poverty/povmeas/papers/iceland/john.html. Readers should be aware of two recent reports issued by the U.S. Census Bureau that have a direct bearing on the information in this section. The first report on Household Income and Poverty, dated September 30, 1999, indicates, in a very positive fashion, that rising income levels have lifted about 1.1 million Americans out of poverty in 1998. However the report also indicates that the income inequality gap between poor and rich in the U.S. remained unchanged. For an interesting news summary of the report see the *New York Times*, October 1, 1999. For an online summary of the report itself see http://www.census.gov/Press-Release/www/1999/cb99-188.html. The second report, dated October 4, 1999, is less upbeat. It indicated that approximately 44.3 million people in the U.S., about 16.3 percent of the population, had no health insurance coverage in 1998. This represents an increase in about 1 million people over 1997 data. For an online summary of this report see http://www.census.gov/Press-Release/www/1999/cb99-189.html.

7. Food Research and Action Center (FRAC) website, "Hunger in the U.S.," http://www.frac.org/html/hunger_in_the_us/hunger_index.html.

8. Ibid.

9. American Academy of Pediatrics website, "Policy Statement," http://www.aap.org/policy/re9745.html.

10. "Renewing the Earth," *Origins* (December 1991), 430.

11. Ibid.

12. I would agree with Aronowitz and Giroux who, drawing on Antonio Gramsci, argue that "all people are intellectuals in that they think, mediate, and adhere to a specific view of the world." Stanley Aronowitz and Henry Giroux, *Education Under Siege* (South Hadley, MA: Bergin and Garvey Publishers, 1985), 34–35.

13. Ibid., 39.

14. Ibid.

15. Ibid., 37.

16. Ibid., 36.

17. Ibid., 37.

18. Kavanaugh, 69.

19. H. Richard Niebuhr, *Christ and Culture* (New York: Harper and Row, 1956), 190–229.

20. Ibid., 193.

21. Ibid., 195.

22. Philip Gleason, ed. "The Crisis of Americanization," *Contemporary Catholicism in the United States* (Notre Dame: University of Notre Dame Press, 1969), 9.

23. David O'Brien, *The Renewal of American Catholicism* (New York: Oxford University Press, 1972), 6.

24. Ibid., 208–209.

25. Ibid., 61.

26. By and large, the more recent Catholic immigrants from South and Latin American countries do not share in the benefits of middle class status that most other Catholic immigrant groups have attained. Consequently they still struggle against serious marginalization and poverty. For excellent historical-theological analyses of the Hispanic community in the U.S., especially the Mexican-American experience, see Virgilio Elizondo, *Galilean Journey* (Maryknoll, NY: Orbis Press, 1983).

27. Ibid., 11.

28. Ibid., 9–10.

29. Ibid., 27.

30. Elizondo, 101.

31. Kavanaugh, 125.

32. Russell Jacoby, *Social Amnesia* (Boston: Beacon Press, 1975), 4.

33. Ibid., 4–5.

34. Johann Baptist Metz, *Faith in History and Society* (New York: Seabury Press, 1980), 110.

35. Ibid., 109–110.

36. Ibid.

37. Ibid.

38. Ibid., 66.

39. Ibid., 68.

40. Ibid., 90.

41. Ibid.

42. Ibid., 91.

43. Ibid., 117.

44. Ibid., 117–118.

45. Robert Bellah, et. al. *Habits of the Heart* (New York: Harper and Row, 1986),153.

46. Ibid.

47. Elizondo, 101.

48. John Coleman, S.J., *An American Strategic Theology* (New York: Paulist Press, 1982), 159.

49. "Catholic Social Teaching and the U.S. Economy," *Origins* (November 1984), 348.

6

"Tell me One Thing, Krishna . . ."
A Personal Reflection on Catholic Faith and Religious Pluralism

David L. Gitomer[1]

"You bewilder my mind
with these contradictory statements.
Determine that one thing by which
I may attain the highest good.
Then speak to me."
—Arjuna to Lord Krishna(*Bhagavad Gita*, 3.2)

This is a reflection on a kind of theological praxis by a nontheologian, what I would like to call a "dynamic Catholic pluralism." It is an argument by way of ideas, by way of images, by way of experience and, sometimes, by way of rhapsody. I am a Sanskritist by training, a scholar of ancient Indian epic and drama by inclination, and a teacher of South Asian culture and religion by vocation. I teach in the Religious Studies Department of a large, urban Catholic university, but was trained in language and literature rather than religion or theology. I was a lover of the Indian everyday experience and the civilizational achievements of South Asia before I became a Catholic.

Conversion for me brought a passionate interest in the insides of the religious worlds which animated the cultural forms that so long appealed to me. Because I had discovered the *inside* of the cultural forms and theological formulations of Christianity—the life-altering, world-altering love of Jesus Christ—I became alive to Spirit in traditions I had already known for years. Later, even religions that had never engaged me before began to lay hold of me. Although many of my colleagues would sharply disagree, I now feel strongly that without trying to convey the *absolutely compelling* qualities of these religious traditions—their *truths*, if you will—the study of religion simply becomes another way of doing the history of culture. And this willingness, which becomes a hunger, to discover and experience these absolutely compelling qualities in a variety of traditions means that I am a pluralist.

This claim may seem puzzling to readers who try to fit this kind of pluralism into a conventional tripartite taxonomy of exclusivism ("we have the only truth"), inclusivism ("our truth is so rich it includes your truth"), and pluralism ("truth is plural, so truth abides in my tradition and in your traditions"). Am I not, then, actually speaking of a kind of inclusivism? After all, if it is because of an immersion in Catholicism that I discover other religions, is there not at least the implication that Catholicism includes them? Granted, this is a subtler or softer kind of inclusivism than the missionizing variety that wants to see monastic contemplative modes in Buddhist meditation, God the Father in the monistic Hindu Brahman, or saints and angels in polytheism.

Any comparison, of course, begins with imaginative assimilation, but my hope is that what I am doing stops short of the appropriation involved in inclusivism. Pluralism, as a number of theologians have pointed out, is a position with problems. What does it mean to say that truth is plural? Can truth be "anything"? Even if we avoid the slide into philosophical or cultural relativism, does pluralism simply give up on truth as a meaningful notion? Then how can truth have any meaning? If truth is plural (many) rather than everything (all), then are there some religions that embody it and some that do not?

In this essay, I want to talk about truth in a perhaps messy way—as an experiential quality rather than a proposition. Thus, for me, while Catholic experience as reflected in its theology becomes the impetus for a profound appreciation of other faiths, there is the realization that this experience cannot engulf the other and so cannot be "inclusive" in the conventional sense. Rather, it takes its cues from the pluralism already present within Catholicism, as we shall see, a pluralism in which the experience of the center and the experience of the margins are in dynamic dialogue.

Attempting to explain the connections between belief, spirituality, and teaching practice involves me in using certain words in ways that may seem unconventional, joined together to form an unfamiliar discourse—although I hope to show that it is nonetheless profoundly Catholic. For example, in my department, a true religious studies department in which Christianity is not privileged but taught along with other faiths and traditions (although we also have in our university a program in Catholic Studies), some of my colleagues, both believers and nonbelievers, would be uncomfortable with the notion of "religious truth" as a category in the study of religion, at least as it operates in the economy of Abrahamic revelation—as a discursive proposition stemming from a divine historical event, say, God's revelation of himself to Abraham, Moses, and Muhammad, or God's revelation of his nature as providential, or God's revelation in the form of Law. Many of us who belong to these traditions are accustomed to thinking about truth as the claims that our religions make in the form of statements based on a history that is recorded in our holy books. Since we know that arguments based on these books do not persuade in the commonly allowed arguments of the academy, we avoid making them the center of our study and teaching. Certainly, in the multireligious environment of the classroom, it is neither appropriate nor effective to bring a religious tradition to life by asserting the truth (in this doctrinal sense) of its teachings.

Outside the Abrahamic traditions, truth has different kinds of meanings. For example, in certain traditions where ritual is central, the notion of truth might have reference to the efficacy of a ritual. In other religions, such as Buddhism, the truth might be an ontology, a theory of the way things are. The Buddha-dharma, for example, is a new way of seeing the world as the Buddha described it, as impermanent and contingent. When I use the word *truth* as a kind of shorthand for the apprehensions of the absolutely compelling qualities of a tradition, I am evoking a sense that is aesthetic, existential, and performative, as when we speak of the "truth" of a piece of art or music, of an actor's work, of a conversation or wordless encounter between friends. In a religious tradition, truth is a quality of experience that excites, invites, and challenges, which makes overwhelmingly clear why a person would find a faith impossible to ignore in its totality. It is a quality that makes a person say, "Yes, this changes me, this changes everything."

This is a conversion perspective (certainly the perspective of a convert) and it could be argued that it does not address the experience of the majority of religionists who are born into a tradition. But, like the mystic, the convert (and, of course, a convert could be converted into her own religion) does something other than find the teachings of the tradition attractive; she, in some sense, has the experience of the founding genius, the compelling experience of being called, being consecrated, being initiated, or being awakened. For Catholics, this truth of seeing, of experiencing, is incarnational and sacramental: it is embodied in the Person, in a concrete symbolic act that virtually *is* the Person. In my own experience, shaped by grace and an openness to the sacred in other traditions, the discursive, catechetical propositions—the "truth statements" of Catholic Christianity—are "only" true in a derivative or secondary way insofar as they attempt to describe the mystery of Person and Sacrament. They have no truth apart from the reality of that mystery, nor can they substitute for it. However helpful, teaching formulations are guides or signposts, articulated formulas which attempt to express a reality that cannot be reduced. Christians believe that language of another order—the scriptural Word—does have the potential for conveying the symbolic mystery; and so we are called on to cultivate an encounter with this Word. Yet, too often the yearning for language to be a transparent window to the divine, found in many cultures, hijacks this cultivation. Thus, the sacramental, symbolic Word is flattened into a sign, becoming just so much more catechism.

This a why a distinction between the "outside" and the "inside" of a religion can be helpful, at least provisionally. When I speak of the "outside" and the "inside," I do not exactly mean the popular distinction between "religion" as a formal social institution with structure, rules, and hierarchy, as opposed to "spirituality" as private religious feeling. In a Catholic version of this distinction, for example, the organizational structure of the Church, the body of church doctrine, and the "laws" of the Church would be set against an individual's emotions about God, feelings in prayer, etc. This distinction is a product of a nonreligious modernity, and especially of an American, adolescent way of viewing the world—"(the real) me against (the false) them." It makes romantic, psychologistic assumptions about the autonomy of the individual and naively ignores the given reality of community, especially the Catholic Christian notion of the people of God as the Body of Christ.

Rather, I mean this distinction in the following way: the "outside" of a tradition is the way the tradition articulates itself in teaching formulas both for its members and for outsiders. The "inside" of the tradition is the collective experience of the reality expressed in those formulas, a reality which, as the Catholic and other traditions teach, cannot be fully expressed in ordinary human language. In Catholicism we have, of course, the theological formulations about transubstantiation and the "laws" about the eucharistic fast, but what holds Catholics together as community is the distinctly Catholic experience of the Eucharist, an experience cooked by tradition, liturgical style, social history and, yes, theological inquiry. Folks in the pews say that through all their disagreements with the teachings of Rome on church governance and sexual ethics, it is the truth of the Eucharist that keeps them coming to Mass. And it is the same compelling quality of the living incarnate God that guides Catholics in an apprehension of the meaning of sexuality, an apprehension that begins with the same vision of the holiness of the body that the magisterium teaches, but often arrives at different conclusions about what to do with our bodies. Whether we are celibate or not, all of us who meet Jesus Christ in the Eucharist experience his humanity: Jesus must have known the divine gift of sexuality in his incarnate life. And so this truth of incarnation infuses and transforms even the way we experience our appetites.

As we begin to apprehend the inside of a religious tradition, we begin to understand its power to lay hold of imagination and forge a comprehensive vision of the world and its meaning. Without necessarily accepting the truth claims formulated by other faiths, we can nevertheless understand the capacity of another tradition to make a total meaning for its followers. Then the specific religious insights of other traditions may contribute to our own. In other words, grasping the *experiential* truth in one's own religious place enables an openness to the quality of compelling meaning in religious places that are not one's own. For example, I harbored suspicions about Islam for more than four decades from my Jewish childhood, my Hindu acculturation, and specters created by the media. Then, a few years back, I was recruited to co-direct a foreign study program in Morocco and, for the first time, experienced a "truth" in Islam. In all my years of going to India, of teaching—superficially—about Islam, I had never understood the brilliance of the revelation to Muhammad and the beauty of Islamic culture.

Of course, this discovery might never have taken place in a country where Islam was more "compulsory," yet Morocco is profoundly Islamic in its own way. Hearing the call to prayer, my cultivated, highly intellectual Muslim host colleagues modestly excuse themselves to slip into a mosque for twenty minutes or join a cook and a dishwasher in the back of a cafe, and I am shaken by an awed sense that Muhammad has gotten monotheism exactly right: God is everything; God knows us intimately; God made us absolutely free, not disposed to sin, but placed us in a world with his moral design to reach our fullness in discovery and conformity to that moral design; God has no likeness to a person, nor does God need any persons to proxy for him. It was the combination of a thoroughgoing rejection of anthropomorphism with the assertion of God's omniscient Providence that struck me as the perfection of the Abrahamic experience. A new dialogue had sprung up within me, in which I acknowledged that we as Christians have much to learn about God from Muslims. The radical monotheism of Islam *should* make us continually ponder how we conceive of God in Christ. Do we let the awe of Abraham and Muhammad seep away in a false familiarity with Jesus? These unsettling questions came because I allowed myself to be invited into the *inside* of the Islamic experience, trusting that the God who made all must be in this experience, and so going deeper into my own Christian experience. Subsequently this "insideness" opened aspects of the "outside" of Islam that I had been blocked from seeing: *Qur'anic* admonitions about the fire tell us that the business of living is serious because Allah's world is given to us already infused with moral meaning. Do we too often forget this in our own daily experience of the created world? After this opening, I began to look for opportunities to present Islam to students, and to engage Muslim students on other religions.

I am gratified that young Pakistani American Muslim women, their heads in scarves out of newly born Islamic pride, will take my Hindu Thought and Culture course. They know that I not only will help them make sense of this aggressively pluralistic and *pictorial* religion that is the very antithesis of Islamic monotheism but also that I respect Islam and Islamic culture. They, like me, discover in the Brahman of the Upanishads a notion of the Absolute which, although impersonal and abstract, takes me further into the experience of God's transcendence (and immanence, in a metaphysical way) than most of the scriptural resources of my own tradition. On the other hand, the florid incarnations of the gods and goddesses challenge all of us to ponder our claims of Christ's uniqueness or, at the least, to ponder what exactly we mean when we speak of incarnation. Further, in both Hinduism and Buddhism, the "technology" of spirituality in meditation and self-purification through a spiritual path has been developed to a degree not found in other traditions.

God, of course, is the only God, the God who made Muslims and Hindus and Buddhists. Thus "our" God does not belong to us, but belongs to all and made all. God made Muhammad and God made the sages of the Upanishads. God made yoga and God made the Buddha's Four Noble Truths about the nature of suffering and its resolution. This is the starting point of my pluralism as it was for Gandhi and the nineteenth-century Hindu saint Ramakrishna. Alas, the more recent rise of Hindu nationalism and Hindu fundamentalism has disclosed a hateful poison in human nature (and in the legacy of colonialism) that mocks the optimistic tolerance of Gandhi and the mystical experiments of Ramakrishna. But it still could be said that Hindus have a head start on pluralistic thinking, since they grow up with Hindu neighbors who worship different gods, or because they learn theistic monism almost as early as they learn theistic pluralism. It is an experience that feels very different than the ideas expressed in the generous but still limited inclusivism of the Vatican II declaration on non-Christian faiths.

To return to the notion of truth discussed above, this sort of inclusivism assumes that the Christian God has revealed "himself" to non-Christian peoples; that the Christian truth *includes* the truths of other faiths. This is not what I intend: it does not go far enough. If that were sufficient, we would not be called to encounter the "Real" in other cultural places when that real does not look like "God." And if that were the case, the torchlight that the study of non-Christian faiths provides would illumine only what we already know about the gospel from our own tradition. What I see happening, in fact, is that the study of non-Christian religions opens up ways of thinking about the gospel implicit but not yet emerged within Christian communities. From the margins of "theology," this study challenges the center—or that which has become so comfortable with itself that it imagines itself to be the center—just as Catholic communities at the margins, thrilling to the call of Christ to the outcastes, will transform the established power at the center simply by being faithful to the gospel.

It is in teaching that I experience, even discover, this dynamic Catholic pluralism. A student once told me that in the first course he took with me he was convinced I was a Buddhist until I told him otherwise. By the time he took the introductory Hinduism course, he knew that I was Catholic but told me that several of his classmates thought I must be Hindu.

The "witness" of teaching the tradition from the inside is a witness not to relativism, but to what I feel comfortably, if unconventionally, calling the power of the gospel. For contrary to what some might think, to teach a non-Christian tradition at arm's length is to say that God's love does not have the power to come to us, to illumine us, and to ignite us. And if Christianity is about nothing else, it is about that. When the student asked how I could be a Christian and be so passionate about Hinduism and Buddhism, I had to reply that it was *because* of Christianity that I could be astonished by other religions. If this is a kind of "inclusivism," it is not the kind that allows you to see only what you came to find, but the kind that changes you.

In the classroom, I usually do not directly reveal that I am Catholic, although I do make it clear that I am not a Hindu or a Buddhist. It sometimes seems appropriate to make this point because students not uncommonly believe that my commitment to presenting the inside of these traditions must mean that I am a partisan. And so they learn that it is acceptable, even necessary, that one who studies the religion of another has an obligation to explain what there is about that religion that makes it so compelling that someone would choose it. This validates those traditions as integral in themselves as well as the possibility of conversion.

But students do inevitably discover that I am Catholic and that I have *chosen* Catholicism, and they are left to puzzle two opposite yet identical questions: Why is he who is so immersed in the study of South Asian religions, who so well understands their beauty and power, a Roman Catholic by choice? Why is he who was so transformed by the eucharistic reality of the Holy Spirit and the eucharistic community of the Church so immersed in the study of Hinduism and Buddhism?

The answers are in one sense historical (I began studying South Asian culture about ten years before I became a Catholic), but more profoundly theological. For if my baptismal vocation and my professional vocation did not have some profound interrelationship, one would have had to go. In the initial white heat of my Christian awakening, the study of India seemed like an artifact that would eventually wither, especially when I began to pursue work that seemed to me to be more directly ministerial. But a mentor, a scholar of China about thirty years my senior and a convert to Catholicism as well, suggested what seemed like a preposterous idea at the time—that the academic life could be a Christian vocation as well. I decided to remain in academia not in direct consequence to the magnificent idea suggested by Professor De Bary, but because of a more practical point he had raised when I said I thought I might be more cut out for a "religious" rather than an academic vocation. He simply pointed out that as a graduate instructor, part-time adjunct, and even a full-time replacement, I had never really given a full commitment to an academic vocation. Vocations, he said, require full-time commitment.

In a somewhat mysterious although entirely predictable fashion, my interest in the culture of India turned toward the religious in the next few years. For those outside the field of South Asian studies who see traditional India and perhaps even modern India as saturated in spirituality, this statement may seem peculiar in its obviousness. However, in my professional formation as a Sanskritist, I have learned to view the relationship between religion and civilization in ways that have helped me understand the contemporary reality of religion in our own culture, but which nevertheless enabled my turning away from religion *per se* in thinking about ancient India. In all premodern cultures, even in the West before the Enlightenment, the spheres of religion and the rest of life were inseparable. This does not necessarily mean that people were more fixed on transcendent values, but the discourse of all endeavors from scientific inquiry to statecraft was woven into the discourse of what we would call religious structures. So I learned that in order to see this civilization more fully and clearly, I would need to see intellectual activity, aesthetics, and socio-political and economic forces as independent variables in the civilization. In other words, I ought to see the civilization with a different, perhaps even marvelous, content, but not functioning by a different set of principles than any other civilization. In my own work on epic and drama, I struggled to discern the human experience within devotional gestures and theological conflicts. It was not that I didn't appreciate the unique beauty that the theology, metaphysics, and "god-style" of Hinduism imparted to the artifacts its civilization produced; rather, it was that I was keenly aware of the dangers of minimizing the human and material dimensions of that civilization in favor of a "spiritual" view, a colonial distancing view that both romanticizes and demonizes India as the opposite "other" of the rational West.

While all this is true, I have in the years since my conversion come to see more complexity in the situation. I first realized that my views of Indian civilization were shaped not only by an aspiration in my profession to see the culture more fully but also by a learned professional prejudice against students and more senior scholars who had "allowed themselves" to become personally involved in various forms of Hindu spirituality, whether through the advanced study of yoga, meditating under the guidance of a guru, or personal conversion to a devotional love of Krishna. Of course, it was necessary as a scholar to participate in Hindu life, but one should guard against allowing it to have too strong a claim on one's consciousness. This can be broadly linked to the "deal" Descartes cut with the Church to divide the mind (and the world) into reason and religion, and the subsequent impoverished notion of academic objectivity that for centuries was its legacy, not to mention the impoverished, otherworldly notion of religion that has remained. Even more, I began to see that under the guise of objectivity, there was being fostered a late colonial remnant of European racism against the conquered peoples and the attendant shame of "going native" hurled against missionaries, administrators, and military personnel whose original work of control had been "undermined" by a genuine appreciation for the people among whom they found themselves. I realized this disdain was still alive among certain colleagues who, although having spent their lives studying India, maintained a more or less constant bemusement (sometimes veering into vicious contempt) for the culture. Since I was not solidly in the field of religious studies at the time, I did not know that other than places like seminaries or departments of theology, this cool distancing from the *power* contained in the "object of study" was all too often the order of the day. Even now, I hear colleagues amused at students who assume that their professors are religious because they teach in a religious studies department.

But what I see in many of our students is that the turning point is not (or not only) when they decide they "like" a particular religious tradition, find its images, ideas, and practices engaging, but when they awaken to religion as a phenomenon. They may become fascinated first with Hinduism but it's not, I think, because they have decided Hinduism or Native American religion or Islam is interesting. Rather, it's because those traditions are the means by which the light goes on about the importance of the inner life, of the quest, the spirit, the transformation—because they know it's "real." And this pluralistic "real" may be discovered within the walls of our churches, especially in our urban churches, or wherever the cultural diversity of Catholicism is seen.

In fact, I first began to think about this theme—"dynamic Catholic pluralism"—during a Good Friday liturgy at one such church that for me embodies our diversity and reminds me of the incredibly different cultural and religious settings in which the gospel has been received. The homilist brilliantly brought to life the powerful, even repugnant, act we were about to do. He spoke of the many kinds of processions that occur during Holy Week, reviewing the Palm Sunday triumphal procession, continuing with the procession from the church to the sanctuary to venerate the Eucharist, the procession in the city streets to reenact, and re-imagine the Stations of the Cross;

and the processions to come, including the illumination of the paschal candle in the chill darkness. But the Good Friday procession, in the words of the homilist, was to be the strangest of all, the procession to kiss the Cross, the procession to kneel and clasp and kiss two wooden beams upon which the Lord was tortured and killed. In our church, the Latino community and the Anglo community—which is really an English liturgy community that includes the usual Chicago Catholic ethnic spread of German, Polish, Italian, Nigerian, Filipino, South Asian, Haitian, and African Americans, not to mention a healthy attendance of physically and mentally disabled people—begin the Good Friday liturgy in separate spaces and remain separate through the reading of the Passion and the great intercessions. Then the main doors at the front of the church are thrown open and reveal a large cross supported by a Mexican American man and woman, along with the priest (our pastor) who has been celebrating the liturgy in Spanish in the chapel. The English liturgy priest and the young men and women who serve on the altar process down the center aisle to the doors to solemnly welcome the cross and the part of the community who brings it. As the servers go to greet the cross, their censers fill the church with the pungent, otherworldly odor and smoke, transporting the faithful beyond the everyday experience of suffering, which is part of the cross but which does not explain the cross. What is outside? What is inside?

The English liturgy leaders turn to face the altar and the entire procession—cross, cross bearers, priests, and lectors from both liturgies, altar servers censing the faithful with by-now almost suffocating smoke (at least for those of us eager enough to be sitting on the aisle)—begins to move slowly toward the altar. Hispanic men, women, teenagers, and young children fill in the alternating rows that have been reserved for them up to the front of the church, and the community becomes, at least for this holy time, nearly one. What is outside? What is inside?

The Veneration of the Cross and the Communion Rite that follows is, indeed, a strange pair of processions. Moving toward the cross takes much longer than the usual stand, turn, and walk toward the Eucharist on an ordinary Sunday, and the brief, preconsecrated Communion Rite takes much, much less time than the usual Sunday walk. But it is in these two oddly disjunct processions that I feel myself to be most Catholic, profoundly Christian, but least generically "Christian." In part, this is because of the thoughtfully planned and humanely realized liturgy, solemn but not stiff, that this church, St. Nicholas in Evanston, Illinois, does so well. But in part, paradoxically, my experience of this liturgy comes from decades-long study and teaching of non-Western religious traditions.

How appropriate that it should be the Spanish-speaking community that brought in the cross, for in several neighborhoods in Chicago and its near suburbs, Latino congregations enact the Passion on Good Friday in the streets, as does ours. If we look beyond the American, somewhat Protestant-influenced, "churchy" way of being Catholic, toward European Catholicism, especially the parts of Europe with remnants of peasant culture, toward the Catholicism of Latin America, the Catholicisms of Africa and of Asia, we see a Catholicism of ritual, of relics, of pilgrimage, and of healings. We see a Catholicism that invokes sacred power to strengthen the vulnerable, to ward off demons of illness and despair, to make whole the incomplete and broken.

We see a Catholicism in which saints—those who had the genius while living to show the way to power, wholeness, and balance—remain accessible after death to those who live and struggle. They are the part of our community that, although unseen, or even because unseen, has access to the sacred power that comes from the unseen world but manifests itself through irruptions into the mundane world in holy places and at holy times. We see a Catholicism in which priests and other practitioners, both men and women, are acknowledged to have undergone powerful journeys through sickness and despair to wholeness and vision, who now have the wisdom and skill to heal individuals by calling down sacred power, and by readjusting a social order that fragments and wounds. They do as Jesus did. We see a Catholicism in which believers may feel reverence and awe in the presence of physical things—holy water, golden crucifixes, pearl rosaries, body parts that survive death like bones and teeth and hair, garments that must retain the sacred power of the godly people who wore them. Or a fragment of the True Cross that might burn, might heal, might speak, or might contain a silent mystery.

Perhaps most important, we see a Catholicism in which men, women, and children are inspired, comforted, and challenged by visions of a divine woman who appeared in the air as true female paradox beyond reason—Mother and Virgin—a divine woman who was nearer than the distant, mysterious, and sometimes cruel sky father. If we value Catholicism as the tradition that, during the masculinist retrenchment of the Reformation, held on to the autochthonous feminine in the cult of Mary, Mary's virginity must be more than a magic trick; it must be the hyper-female generativity, the hyper-generativity of God himself underscored by god-to-woman "virgin" birth. It is because peoples in both preindustrial peasant Europe and the contemporary vibrant Catholicism of the non-West envisioned goddess Mary differently from her spectrally virginal official persona, that Catholic Christianity has always provided a source for the rediscovery and revalorization of the feminine.

If we are truly Catholic, "that" Catholicism is ours. For centuries, that which has been outside—that which has seemed exotic, overly vivid—to those on the inside, *has* been coming inside, *has* been us, *is* us. True, we see a Catholicism riddled with abstruse, even absurd theological formulations of this primal power of the sacred, a Catholicism led by men who governed by fear and guilt, a hierarchical Catholicism so out of touch with the sacred power Jesus called on and identified with that it would not recognize him within its fortress walls or outside among the people it purports to serve and lead. After the Reformation and the Enlightenment, the primal mysteries of Catholic Christianity became a kind of hermetic, hieratic magic encased in triumphalism, although for European Catholic peasants, "benighted with superstition," a vital connection to the rhythms of earth, with its old gods and goddesses, remained a conduit to a subversive pluralism, with local rites and celebrations that varied from Romania to Ireland, from Sicily to Germany.

Then the Church triumphant, through its Catholic proxy states, turned its efforts toward people who were often seen as subhumans in the new worlds. But the great irony of the monolithic imperialist missionizing efforts to Africa, Asia, and the Americas was that it has yielded a harvest of internal pluralism that frightens those most responsible for the effort to "win souls" for Christ. This is a pluralism that brings through the doors of the Church the "unholy" religions of the missionized continents transformed by the gospel, transformed by the Cross. This has been the dynamic process of Christianity since Jesus, since Paul.

At the door to our Church stand the heirs of a great civilization which understood that the work of maintaining the cosmos will require blood and sacrifice, that there are mysteries of regeneration more primal than can be expressed in encyclicals. The conquest was by the sign of the Cross, but the conquered understood that Cross better than the conquerors. The Cross, instrument of torture and death; the Cross, emblem of the suffering nature of the world, the shape of our lives as the Buddha taught, as Jesus lived; the Cross, instrument of transformation beyond good and evil, the uniquely Christian version of a manifestation of the sacred power that wells up in all cultures and all times. A primal "fetish," it must be revered for its power to heal and transform. It must be touched. We must kneel before it, clasp it, kiss it.

To kiss the wood on which our dying and rising God was tortured, the Cross which, in some sense, *is* our God. This unavoidable, disturbing confrontation with our misery, our cruelty, and our salvation, the image of bloody Mother Kali in sexual union with the corpse of Shiva, cannot be explained, it can only be fiercely kissed as the truth. "For Jews demand signs and Greeks seek wisdom, *but we preach Christ crucified, a stumbling block to Jews and folly to Gentiles*, but to those who are called, both Jews and Greeks, *Christ the power of God* and the wisdom of God" (1 Corinthians 1:22–23).

In Paul's accounts of his missions and in the Acts of the Apostles, we read of the gospel taking root among peoples who had no experience with the cultural statutes of the law of Moses, including those concerning food and circumcision. But we must also look to our history to see how the Corinthians, the Romans, the Celts, the Incas, and others brought new light and life to the gospel. If we want to reflect on the centrality of pluralism to the mission of the Church, we have to think differently, for the ideas of "centrality" and "pluralism" seem to be almost contradictory, as if some Zen master had set us to work on a koan: that which is central ought to be one thing, and pluralism by its very nature is neither one (because it admits that the truth is plural) nor a thing (because pluralism is a practice). Perhaps anticipating that two thousand years later some readers would call the text contradictory and inconsistent, traced through with influences from Buddhism and marginal Yogic gnosticism, the author of the *Bhagavad Gita* (Did you think I have some other text in mind?) has Arjuna beg Lord Krishna to tell him "one thing" by which he might know the truth. But Krishna leads him through a labyrinth of monistic transcendence, ritual duty, theological reasoning, ascetic withdrawal, and the yoga of detached action, until finally he reveals his cosmic form as the lord of creation and destruction, the very "meaning" of history. Arjuna now knows that all the paths are Krishna's paths; they lead to him and proceed from him. But they are very confusing to hear about, and for us to read about, because they all lead to one another as well. Still, Arjuna is transformed—"saved"—by listening to Lord Krishna, by seeing Lord Krishna.

Notes

1. I wish to express my thanks to members of St. Nicholas parish in Evanston, Illinois, which is referred to later in this essay. Fr. Robert Oldershaw is pastor, and Fr. James Halsted also celebrated the liturgy discussed. Christine Neff is the director of liturgy, and Tim Estberg the director of music. The essay could not have reached its present form without the wise comments of my friend and colleague, Dr. Jeffrey Carlson.

7

Speaking of Margins . . .

Jill Raitt

T his essay has its origin in a grand Collegium gathering called Renewal '97. The primary speaker was Patricia Hampl, author of *Virgin Time*[1] and other works and collections of poetry and stories. During one of her two lectures, Hampl described herself as a marginal Catholic, that is, one who adheres to the Catholic Church but who is not in complete agreement with the demands of its Roman hierarchy. I have heard others say something similar by claiming to be Catholic but not Roman. That is not Hampl's position. She is Roman Catholic, but she keeps distance between herself and the Roman Catholic Church's "center," making it clear that notions of marginalization, whether challenged or accepted, are of some significance to these mostly Catholic intellectuals. The meaning of *margins*, then, became the subject of part of the discussion following each of Hampl's two lectures. During the discussion, themes emerged which helped to provide the framework for this essay.

Before taking up the themes concerning marginality, it may be helpful to remember that Jesus of Nazareth began a movement that was doubly marginal.[2] The first Christians were marginal members of the Jewish religion, itself marginal, although exempt from religious persecution, in the Roman Empire. Before the end of the first century, the Christian Jews were expelled from the synagogues and Christianity became subject to Roman demands of conformity to Roman religious practice and therefore subject to persecution when they refused to conform. Antwaun Smith comments:

> Being aware of Jesus' marginal state and that of the movement he began, should cause Christians to reflect on how they treat their own margins and to remember how their Church has marginalized, even persecuted, members of other religions such as the Jews and indigenous peoples. Theologically speaking, I think a profound appreciation of Jesus as marginal, in all the complexity of meanings discussed in this essay, would be an effective antidote to triumphalist notions of Christ and Christianity.[3]

Appropriately reminded of Christianity's origins on the margins, we turn to a thematic discussion of margins under four themes: Marginalia, Finding the Center, Margin as Borderland, and Beyond the Margins.

Marginalia

Bernard J. Lee, co-author of a recent book on small faith communities,[4] called my attention to a fascinating book on medieval marginalia, *Image on the Edge: The Margins of Medieval Art* by Michael Camille.[5] Camille's study provides insight into the interplay of marginalia and central texts. Medieval illustrators' work flourished not only in the margins but also reached into the central text playing a game of text vs. anti-text before the reader's eye. In fact, the marginalia may so impinge upon the text that it is difficult to distinguish one from the other.[6]

Medieval illuminators illustrated and at the same time laughed at the dangerous edges of the world as represented by the pages on their desks. Nor did they keep the strange humanoids, flora, and fauna only at the edges, but linked them to the body of the texts, nearly always pious texts, that they were "illuminating." The beasts and monsters were referred to as *babuini* (baboons) because of the multiplicity of simian figures frolicking among the vines and leaves that often half-hid them. All the oddities imagination could conjure abandon themselves to forbidden behaviors and visual conundra. For example, a running wooden-legged man wielding scissors tries to cut the fur from a large hare scampering ahead of him into the text.[7] Monkeys climb into the text or dangle from its letters while farting and nibbling another simian's turds. A typical one is a page from a Book of Hours in the Pierpont Morgan Library. The central illustration is of the flagellation of Christ. The text is *Deus in adiutorium meum intende; Domine ad adiuvandum me festina* (God come to my help; Lord hurry to help me.), a prayer that opens each of the hours. Above the margin, immediately under the first line of the psalm, a naked man bowls. From the same Book of Hours, at the bottom of the prayer to the Holy Spirit, *Accende lumen sensibus, infunde amorem cordibus* (Light your light in our senses, pour love into our hearts), a naked figure's bottom protrudes from an oven. Art historians have interpreted these irreverent figures in various ways, most often by separating them from the text as mere fancies and fun that would not impede pious prayer. But such interpretations artificially isolate the marginalia that, in fact, extend tendrils and tails into the center of some of the texts. Indeed, some of the tails of letters such as "p" become the tails of monkeys or chimerae. While putting aside interpretations that separate the sacred and the profane, Camille takes care not to fall into another critical trap and simply "postmodernize" his view of medieval marginalia. Nevertheless, in the Middle Ages as in this:

> Things written or drawn in the margins add an extra dimension, a supplement, that is able to gloss, parody, modernize and problematize the text's authority while never totally undermining it. The center is, I shall argue, dependent upon the margins for its continued existence.[8]

What sort of a culture plays with such counter-texts in and surrounding a text intended for prayer and meditation? One could ask as well what sort of a world gives rise to cathedral architecture whose borders and boundaries also abound in gargoyles, fanciful figures, and animals and birds with humanoid faces carrying a book in a procession that mock the processions occurring with the Church?[9] The mixing of animal and human forms, Camille tells us, violates "the taboo that separates the human and the animal. Christianity held it essential that man and nature were 'discontinuous,' but marginal art constantly mixes them up."[10] One could argue, as Camille does in this place, that in order to keep the center smooth, orderly, and holy, the bizarre, the irrational, and the vicious had to be kept to the margins. Thus, maps depicted the known area of Europe as ordered while the unknown territories beyond the ocean were inhabited by monsters: "blemyae and cynocephali (men with eyes in their chests and dog-headed persons), giants, pygmies . . . a sciapod. . . ."[11] God and the holy were at the center and cosmic models hurled, with centrifugal force, all that was deformed, disordered, dangerous, to the perimeter. How account then for the intrusion of disordered forms into the center of the page,[12] the top of the interior pillars of a cathedral,[13] even into the illustration of Christ who is represented as a man with a long bird's beak?[14] Camille remarks:

> We should not see medieval culture exclusively in terms of binary oppositions—sacred/profane, for example, or spiritual/worldly—for the Ormesby Psalter suggests to us that people then enjoyed ambiguity. Travesty, profanation and sacrilege are essential to the continuity of the sacred in society.[15]

Marginalia are then intentional counterpoints to the text, to the building, to the city, to the country. These marginalia represent the ambiguity and disorderliness of life as we experience it and refuse to allow a neat separation of the holy from the profane, of virtue from vice. One might conjecture further that the experience of the spiritual life is not dissimilar. At one stage, one sees certain actions as wholly God-inspired, as virtuous. At another stage, one recognizes the self-seeking that was present at the same time, and one realizes the ambiguity at the core of all one's actions, prayer, participation in liturgy. Perhaps it was this sense of ambiguity that those using the illuminated psalters immediately understood.

Marginalia can also protest that the center itself is ambiguous. How could it be otherwise when the subject is the Church? As understood by Christians, the Church has always been a mix of the worst and the best, of Peter's denial and his martyrdom, of corruption and heroic charity, of rigidity and principled flexibility, of saints in rags and sinners in vestments and vice versa. Marginal Christians as individuals and marginal Christian small communities are not different in this respect. They have their personal and their social ambiguities. But their very existence is also a critical protest against a center that demands unambiguous affirmation of its self-proclaimed unambiguous righteousness. It is intriguing to note that nightmarish marginalia disappeared when the Church as center began to be challenged and replaced by the Renaissance turn *ad fontes* (to the sources), and the Reformations of the sixteenth century that proliferated their own certainties about reasonable centers and unambiguous texts. The clarity of the printed page and the less versatile printing presses also ended marginal illuminations but made possible the equally irreverent broadsides. Broadsides, however, no longer illustrated a text; they were independent texts themselves. Plurality replaced ambiguity in a developing modern world.[16]

In a postmodern world of bewildering multimedia, we entertain both plurality and ambiguity, a more frightening and challenging condition than ambiguity within one view of God and creation or of plurality within which one theological view claims certainty against the others. But where pluralism gives rise to tolerance and is accepted as appropriate, and where ambiguity is no less present, finding a center becomes more difficult and, for that reason, for some people, more urgent.

Finding the Center

When marginal people and groups reach into the center of the text, the center of the institution itself, they challenge prevailing notions of what is central and what is peripheral. In fact, in the handing on of a text, sometimes the marginal remarks become incorporated into the main text. Is this not what happened when theologians who were banished and silenced in the 1950s became the *periti*, the experts, invited in the 1960s to assist the bishops at Vatican II?[17]

A similar concern was voiced by one of Terry Veling's respondents in his exploration of life in the margins:[18]

> I think the terminology of "marginalized" communities underscores a definition that directly implies "the institution is center." For me, the question is more accurately: *why* have Christian communities emerged in such numbers? In the U.S. there are thousands and this is just the beginning. Why do these communities illustrate a *new center* to the church? What are the errors that the institutional church is making on such a widespread scale that people are searching out and forming their own bases of church?[19]

A new center? Or a broader understanding of what "church" is? For example, challenges to the hierarchical and patriarchal dominance of the Vatican are also challenges to "tradition" as it is represented by the center. Scholars understand that the "tradition" has never been static. For example, interpretations of liturgy, of the Bible, of who is and who is not a "Christian," have been developed as theologies and handed on, "traditioned." Cultural influences over time have altered, enriched, challenged, or traduced traditions.[20]

Is it possible, then, to talk about "margins" without also talking about how margins and centers have shifted over two thousand years? Veling summarizes ways in which sociologists (Robert Bellah, et al.), anthropologists

(Victor Turner), ecclesiologists, and theologians (Rosemary Radford Ruether, Leonardo Boff) have seen institutions and communities, centers and margins. All of these theologians find life in a creative tension between the margin and the center, and death when they come into absolute opposition. Ideally, the center, or the larger Church, and the margin, or intentional communities,[21] provide stability and identity on the one hand and creative exploration on the other. When the larger Church sets individuals and communities outside its self-defined perimeters, using its power to "marginalize" communities in tension with it, it cuts itself off from the dynamic life expressed in those communities, a life that could prevent the sterile ossification of the institution itself. When small intentional communities break from the institution, when the *ecclesiolae in ecclesia* renounce their citizenship in the larger Church, they renounce the living relationship that feeds their dynamic continuation. Rosemary Ruether advises, rather, that:

> One must learn to make creative use of existing institutions without being stifled or controlled by them. In the process these institutions become more flexible and become vehicles for further creativity. This is precisely what is meant by the positive working of the dialectic of spiritual community and historical institution.[22]

Veling also expresses the relationship as a positive dialectic. He sums up the margins and the intentional communities dwelling there as "critical space, decentering space, transgressing, de-institutionalizing, impulsive and spontaneous, unsettled and unsettling, loyal yet opposing, rending yet renewing, disruptive yet transforming."[23]

A recent study by Bernard Lee based on extensive research on small faith communities reveals a different reality. Contrary to Lee's own expectations, he found that the majority of intentional communities consists of people who do not consider themselves marginal, people who are among the most active in their parishes.

> About three-fourths [of small Christian Communities] have parish connections of one kind or another, from having a specific place in parish structure to being in communities in which most individual members are active in their parish. In the interviews with members, many stated that the small community deepened their connection with the parish.[24]

On the other hand, Lee comments that most of these communities (Hispanic communities excepted) consist of a population better educated than the average Catholic population "which in turn is better educated that the general U.S. population."[25] It is no surprise, therefore, that members of these communities are critically reflective and seek a truly adult faith. This marriage of faith and reason, Lee argues, is what Pope John Paul II's *Fides et ratio* is about. There is good reason, therefore, for the institutional Church to reach out to these small communities, to include them in dialogue, rather than to "marginalize" them. True enough, but it seems that the members of most of these communities, if indeed they are "on the margins," reach to the center through their participation and leadership in their parishes and dioceses.

In fact, for some time now, many bishops and parish priests have fostered small faith communities through Renew, Disciples-in-Mission, and other diocesan and parish-based movements. So it would seem that there is also movement from the institutional center toward the margins and recognition, on the part of some "central" figures in the Church, of the healthy nature of well-developed small lay communities spread throughout the Church, from its center to its periphery. One may hope that recognition of lay-led small groups is leading to a shift of the center itself toward a degree of decentralization.

So what does it mean that the marginalia stretch into the center and that the center itself shifts? It means minimally that the life and development of an institution require lively growth at its margins. Those margins feed the center and protect it from ideas and movements that the center is not yet ready to encounter. The margins provide a place to experiment and to adapt to cultural changes so that the whole Church will be able to sustain and even profit by such encounters when they do occur. Margins can be seen, then, as borderlands, as places that mediate between what is inside and what is outside.

Margin as Borderland

Margin can also mean a boundary between two geographical territories.[26] It is therefore not "at the edge" but "between" countries or cultures. In this sense, the ethnic minorities in the United States are people who share in two cultures. They are people who combine these cultures in themselves and in their communities. Thus Asian Americans, Hispanic Americans, and African Americans are marginal to the Anglo American culture that dominates in the United States; they are called *minority groups*. But these minorities are also writing not only in the margins of the dominant culture, they are writing across the text, in between the lines and, in so many ways, altering the page on which they live with Anglo Americans. They do more; they mediate between their homeland culture and American culture. For example, European Americans living in Miami experience what is common to many Europeans: to step outside the area where everyone speaks the same language, enjoys the same sort of food, hears the same kinds of music. Miamians, whatever their ethnic background, must learn to speak, eat, see, hear, experience, different cultures. Miami is a border rather than a margin. It provides a critical point of view of the U.S. as well as a multicultural place on the margin of the geographical United States.

Another instance of cultural mediation is the way in which creative thinkers combine cultural traditions in ways that affect not only their own times, but reach through the centuries to our own day. Cultural boundaries can be merged and yield extraordinary results in the minds of individuals.

Thus Augustine of Hippo was on the boundary between two cultures: the hellenized Roman Empire and the Catholic Church.[27] Augustine's blend of Christianity and Neoplatonism has had a deep and continuing influence on the culture and the theologies of Western Christendom. Another example is the use by Thomas Aquinas of Aristotle's works as received through Islamic scholars living on Europe's borders in Sicily and Spain. Indeed, the eclecticism of every age, it may be argued, is precisely that which gives that age new life and a more vibrant legacy to hand on to succeeding ages.

The pages of the Church, then, are made up almost entirely of marginalia that subsequently become central to its self-perception, some positively, some negatively. An example is the doctrine of transubstantiation, an interpretation drawn entirely from philosophy and applied to Jesus words: "Take and eat this all of you, this is my body which is given up for you" (cf. 1 Corinthians 11:24, Luke 22:19). In the twelfth and thirteenth centuries, transubstantiation proved to be a useful explanation of a long tradition of the presence of the eucharistic Christ and of the words, "This is my body." But when challenged by protesting reformers in the sixteenth century, Trent moved the philosophically based theologoumenon called "transubstantiation" to the center of its eucharistic understanding. The doctrine of transubstantiation, then, became an embattled theological distraction from the purpose of Jesus' gift of the Eucharist. *Embattled,* because armies clashed over it in the sixteenth century. *Distraction,* because the purpose of the Eucharist is the continuing sanctification of the faithful community for whom it is the central liturgical action and the source of sacramental grace for the members of the community, the Body of Christ, the Church. Jesus said the Eucharist is his body "given *for you*" (Luke 22:19, emphasis added). This is just one example in which a marginal idea, Aristotle's doctrine of substance and accidents, entered the center of the Church's teaching, was itself altered by that application, and then dominated the doctrinal life of the Church from the Council of Trent until the present. For some Catholics, it remains a test of orthodoxy long after its terminology has ceased to be current. One may indeed ask, concerning this doctrine: What is central, what is marginal, and what is beyond the margins?

Beyond Margins

In the consideration of margins thus far, it is apparent that margins are ambiguous, that they are places where nothing can be pronounced simply positive or simply negative, whether we look at margins as borderlands or as the space beyond the print on a page.

If other religions are "other books," are they merely discrete volumes in the library called "Religions," or do their contents occasionally speak to each other?[28] The answer becomes obvious if one acknowledges both the previous argument about cultural influences on the one hand and the movements of peoples and their interactions throughout history on the other. For example, the Holocaust is "on the pages" of the Catholic Church. While some Catholics died in the concentration camps, others watched millions of Jews being rounded up and taken away. The debate continues about the concordat between the Church as represented by Eugenio Pacelli, the future Pius XII, and Hitler. Recently, the beatification of Edith Stein raised more questions about the relation of the Catholic Church, the Jews, and the Holocaust. The suggestion that Pius XII be beatified raises the volume of voices engaged in this debate. As institution and through its members, the Catholic Church was engaged in Nazi Germany. How can Jews be "off the page" or outside the book? Here again, a religion—Judaism, that is a volume in itself and therefore outside the volume called "Catholicism"—reaches into the center of Catholicism's pages, challenging its contents and demanding its reinterpretation.

Another challenge comes from indigenous peoples who were the objects of missionary activities of the Catholic Church. Surely they are "marginal" and remain at the edges of the Church and even of this discussion. While enculturation occurred in the sixteenth and seventeenth centuries in China and Japan until it was officially ended by Rome,[29] there were only rare efforts to accommodate Catholicism to the cultures of the peoples of the Americas, of Polynesia, of Africa.[30] These peoples could become part of the book only by giving up the culture they had valued and that had given them their identity. Even then, as slaves, as servants, as confined to reservations, they remained marginal. To them, too, apologies and reparations are overdue.

Enculturation is now at least being discussed and, in some areas, a beginning has been made. Where that occurs, the way the Catholic Church thinks of itself, describes itself, has also to change. Enculturation is dialogical or it is not enculturation but remains the continuing imposition of a foreign (Western European) culture. The Catholic Church has become newly apologetic, in the modern sense of the term, as it acknowledges its past errors and sinful policies with regard to Jews and now also to other religions and groups of peoples. Because of those who at first glance seemed to be outside the book, the contents of the book are being reviewed and the inclusion acknowledged, with apologies, of the history and influence of these peoples.

Conclusion

We have looked at margins as the space around the text in a book that becomes filled with illuminations that reach into the text and offer an artist's commentary, sometimes ribald, sometimes a counter-thesis to the text. We have considered margins as the place where the jottings or highlighting of previous readers direct the reader's eye and mind in ways that the text by itself would not have done. Sometimes the marginalia challenge the text, sometimes they are commentary on it. In any case, marginalia are on the page, in the book, and so they alter the reading of the text by their very presence. To speak of margins is also to speak of centers. But, we noted, when margins reach into the center, they become part of the text even though their presence there may be regarded as intrusive. Given time, however, the intruding marginalia are accepted and become part of the new modified page; the text acquires new meanings. Margin as border becomes a place of mediation between two cultures either temporally or geographically. As those margins expand, not only the nature of the page changes, but the nature of the book itself changes, and its text becomes more inclusive.

Our conversation about margins was inspired by Patricia Hampl's remarks about being a marginal Catholic. Often that means that one sees the structures of the Catholic Church as too rigid. In reaction, spontaneous movements arise; among them, the move to small, intentional communities, or small faith groups. While many of these groups are in tension with the hierarchical Church and exhibit the characteristics of the *liminal communitas* described by Victor Turner,[31] most of these small groups do not consider themselves as oppositional or as cut off, but as connected vitally with the hierarchical Church. Increasingly, too, it seems, the Church is fostering groups of this kind, recognizing that parishioners crave the more intimate relations that such small faith groups provide and that the faith of the members is thereby strengthened. The groups in tension with the Church, who want an alternative community and no longer attend a parish church, may consider themselves as truly marginal with little or no contact with the structured center. But their presence is a challenge that nevertheless requires attention to the matters such groups protest. They may hope that one day the page will read quite differently because of their persistence on the margin. Lastly, those who have written their own texts and exist principally in other books, in other religions, even those have been in the book, on the pages of the history of the Church and in the Church's present dialogues with other religions. These groups, too, have reached sometimes to the center and caused it to change, to reread itself in relation to them, and so to become more flexible.

The author of this essay hopes that these pages offer wide margins for others to illuminate and in which commentary may develop so that this text is itself changed. It is the hope of both editor and author that others comment, highlight, scratch out, or add new phrases to the ones that previous readers have already entered into the text.

Notes

1. New York: Farrar Straus Giroux, 1992.
2. I was reminded to include the "marginality" of Jesus and the first Christians by Antwaun Smith, a graduate of the Department of Religious Studies at the University of Missouri, 1998, a Harvard University graduate student (1998) and Rhodes Scholar (1999–2001).
3. Antwaun Smith, conversation with Jill Raitt after reading "Speaking of Margins . . . ", August 11, 1999.
4. Michael A. Cowan and Bernard J. Lee, *Conversation, Risk, and Conversion: The Inner and Public Life of Small Christian Communities*. Maryknoll, NY: Orbis Books, 1997.
5. Cambridge: Harvard University Press, 1992.
6. My contribution to the Renewal discussion was inspired by a tape of Bernard Lee speaking about small faith communities. I noted, among other things, that whether one picks up a used and "highlighted" book or one in which the reader has put only stars and exclamation marks in the margin, one's eye

cannot help but pay particular attention to the highlighted portions or argue with the appropriateness of the exclamation point. To be in the margin is still to be on the page and in some way, part of the text.

7. Ibid., p. 50.
8. Ibid., p. 10.
9. Ibid., p. 76–77.
10. Ibid., p. 72.
11. Ibid., p. 14.
12. Ibid., p. 51.
13. Ibid., p. 82ff.
14. Ibid., p. 29.
15. Ibid.
16. On rereading Umberto Eco's *The Name of the Rose*, it occurred to me that ambiguity was as distasteful to medievals as it is to moderns or to most people in most places in most times. Humans like definition and try hard to define this group against that from children's peer groups to hate groups. Given the philosophical situation in the fourteenth century, these marginalia might also represent William of Ockham's nominalist world *de potentia absoluta*, according to which God could indeed make water run uphill or even effect redemption through an ass. The central text, on the other hand, represents the world *de potentia ordinata*, the world as, in fact, God has created and established it.
17. For example, Ives Congar, Henri de Lubac.
18. Terry A. Veling, *Living in the Margins: Intentional Communities and the Art of Interpretation*. NY: The Crossroad Publishing. Co., 1996.
19. Ibid., p. 10.
20. Five detailed examples of developing (changed) traditions were given by John T. Noonan at the Catholic Theological Society of America's annual meeting in Miami, Florida, in June 1999—changes in attitudes toward the death penalty, for example, and toward usury.
21. Veling says he uses the word "*intentional* to distinguish the life of small communities in the relatively affluent, middle-class cultures of Western societies . . . from the life of those communities situated in Third World contexts and generally referred to as *basic* or *base* communities. *Intentional* means 'deliberate,' 'attentive,' or 'actively pursued.' Small-community life does not come naturally for members of Western, individualistic cultures. It is something we must consciously choose and consistently work at." p. 3.
22. Rosemary Radford Ruether, *Women-Church: Theology and Practice*. San Francisco: Harper& Row, 1986, p. 39 as cited in Veling, p. 14.
23. Veling, p. 15.
24. *National Catholic Reporter*, July 16, 1999, p. 10.
25. Ibid.
26. Philip Gleason raised this idea of "margin" during the discussion following Hampl's first lecture.
27. After Hampl's second lecture, Peggy Steinfels, editor of *Commonweal*, returned the discussion to "margins" and contributed the example of St. Augustine.

28. Cynthia Russet raised this issue and used the example of the Holocaust.
29. Matteo Ricci, S.J., *The True Meaning of the Lord of Heaven*. Translated by Douglas Lancashire and Peter Hu Kuo-chen. A Chinese-English translation edited by Edward J. Malatesta, S.J. St. Louis: Institute of Jesuit Sources, 1985; Josef Franz Schütte, S.J. *Valignano's Mission Principles for Japan*. two vols. Translated by John J. Coyne, S.J. St. Louis: Institute for Jesuit Sources, 1980,85. See also Jonathan D. Spence, *The Memory Palace of Matteo Ricci*. New York: Viking Penguin, 1984, and George Minamiki, *The Chinese Rites Controversy : From Its Beginning to Modern Times*. Chicago: Loyola University Press, 1985.
30. Father De Smet, the indefatigable Jesuit missionary to many of the midwestern and western Native Americans, went some distance to accommodate the liturgy by the use of familiar symbols and dress. See Robert C. Carriker, *Father Peter John de Smet: Jesuit in the West*. Norman, OK: University of Oklahoma Press, 1995; and Hiram Martin Chittenden and Alfred Talbot Richardson, editors. *Life, Letters, and Travels of Father de Smet*. New York: Arno Press, 1969.
31. Victor W. Turner, *The Ritual Process: Structure and Anti-Structure*. Chicago: Aldine Publishing Co., 1969, pp. 106–107.

Part II

Marks of the Faith

8

"Finding God in All Things": A Sacramental Worldview and Its Effects

Michael J. Himes

What is it that makes Catholicism Catholic? There are, after all, many ways of being Christian: the rich Orthodox traditions, the Anglican tradition, the Lutheran tradition, the Reformed traditions, and the Evangelical traditions, to name the most obvious. All of these traditions have wonderfully wise, insightful, powerful, things to tell us about Christianity. And there is the Catholic tradition.

What has Catholicism to tell about Christianity? What makes Catholicism Catholic? I suggest that the most important answer to these questions is the *sacramental principle*. I must offer a provisional statement of the sacramental principle, one which will, I hope, become clearer as we go on. The *sacramental principle* means that what is always and everywhere the case must be noticed, accepted, and celebrated somewhere sometime. What is always and everywhere true must be brought to our attention and be embraced (or rejected) in some concrete experience at some particular time and place.

Talking about God

To explain why I think that this sacramental principle is so important, I must ask your indulgence while I lay some deep foundations. Consider the word *God*. "God" is the theological shorthand that we use to designate the Mystery which grounds and undergirds all that exists. One could call it something else, perhaps, but "God" is handy. It is short, three letters, one syllable, it has been around for a good while, and it has the advantage of familiarity, so let us use it. If we are talking about God, the ultimate Mystery, that which grounds all that exists, then we are speaking about that which is itself not grounded on or in anything else. The ultimate Mystery is ultimate, not itself dependent on another. Everything that exists and is not that ultimate Mystery is the universe. Thus, we cannot account for the universe's existence in such a way that it is understood as giving something necessary to God.

I teach at Boston College, a Jesuit university. Perhaps for that reason, I think in this context of the familiar Jesuit motto, *Ad majorem Dei gloriam*: "For the greater glory of God." As a description of the motive of our actions, that motto is very powerful and very challenging, indeed. But it ought not be taken as a theological statement, i.e., a statement that tells us something about God. God does not need greater glory; God has tons of glory. God is never going to use up all the glory God has. God has closets full of it. God does not require creatures to tell God that God is great. Presumably, God has noticed. God does not need us to glorify God. Why does anything other than God, i.e., the universe, exist? Not so that it can give something to God but so that God can give something to it. The universe (or, as we more often call it in religious language, *creation*) exists as the recipient of a gift.

What is it that God, the ultimate Mystery, gives to creation, the universe whose being is grounded in that Mystery? There are only two possibilities: either God gives something other than God, which would simply be more of the universe, another creature; or God gives God. Here is the great Christian claim about the universe's origin in Mystery: creation exists so that God can give God's self to it. Creation exists so that God can communicate God's self to creation. That gift of self is what is meant by *agape*, love. Creation exists because it is the object of love. Love, *agape*, is the only ground for its existence. So deep is this claim in the Christian tradition that Christianity actually insists that it is the least wrong way to understand what we mean by the Mystery that grounds and surrounds all that exists.

I tell beginning students in theology that theology, certainly Christian theology, is always done between two poles. One pole is probably best summed up by Ludwig Wittgenstein. The final proposition in the only book published by Wittgenstein during his lifetime, the *Tractatus Logico-Philosophicus* (you may have seen the film), is arguably the most famous single sentence in twentieth-century philosophy: "Of that about which we can say nothing, let us be silent." If I may paraphrase less elegantly, "If you don't know what you're talking about, shut up." That is an enormously important religious counsel. If God is Mystery, then let us not natter on about God like we know what we're talking about.

A great problem of religious language and imagery is that we use it too confidently. We speak as if what we are talking about—God—is perfectly clear and fully intelligible. Any language about God that is perfectly clear is certainly wrong. We are, after all, daring to speak about ultimate Mystery, and whatever we say, we must not, under pain of blasphemy, lose a profound sense of awe before the Mystery which undergirds all that exists. The first commandment of the Decalogue in both Exodus and Deuteronomy is not to fabricate any image of God: "I am the Lord, your God, who brought you out of the land of Egypt, out of the house of bondage. You shall have no other gods before me; you shall not make for yourself a graven image . . . you shall not bow down to them or serve them (Deuteronomy 5:6–8; Exodus 20:2–4; RSV) of me." That is a commandment to be taken to heart by all religiously interested people, because it counsels against the too easy idolatry of religious language. For we all make images of God.

For two pages now I have been referring to *God*, yet I suspect that no one reading this has stopped to ask, "Who is he talking about?" We automatically begin with some idea of what the word means or might mean. When I say the word *God*, something goes on in your mind. Now, however wonderful, however deep, rich, powerful, consoling, however philosophically informed, however metaphysically precise, however traditionally grounded, however scripturally sound, however magisterially orthodox, whatever that idea in your mind is, it is not God. And that is the most important thing to know about God: that what you have in your mind when you hear or speak the word *God* is an image of God, and the First Commandment is against the making of images of God. So we must be very cautious not to confuse what we think when we hear or speak the word *God* with God.

The Second Commandment of the Decalogue, of course, flows directly from the first. The Second Commandment, as you recall, is, "You shall not take the name of the Lord your God in vain" (Exodus 20:7; Deuteronomy 5:11; RSV). We have done terrible things to this. We have diminished it into a commandment against profanity: "Don't use bad language." (Should you be asked what Himes's position is on profanity, you can answer that he is against it. But I strongly suspect that Moses had more on his mind at Sinai than how colorfully the Israelites were swearing at the foot of the mountain.) The Second Commandment is not about profanity. Rather, it states the obvious consequence of the First Commandment: do not take the name of God in vain. Do not talk about God like you know what you're talking about. Far from a commandment against profanity, it is a warning against overconfident theology and too-simple preaching. We must be very, very, cautious about how we use the word God because, more often than not, we use it in vain. If we speak of Mystery, we must acknowledge that ultimately we do not know what we are talking about. Wittgenstein's caution is immensely important.

However, this insight must be balanced by another pole—and the statement of that other pole I borrow from T. S. Eliot. (Eliot was talking about poetry, but I think I can borrow the statement and apply it to religious language without distorting it too much.) Eliot wrote that there are some things about which we can say nothing and before which we dare not keep silent. There are some subjects about which we know in advance that anything we say will be inadequate. But these issues that are so important, so crucial, that we dare not say nothing.

Let me offer an image taken from a Woody Allen film. (I am a New Yorker, indeed, a Brooklynite, by origin. All New Yorkers have an immediate affinity with Woody Allen films. Elsewhere, people think Woody Allen makes comedies; New Yorkers know Woody Allen makes documentaries. He sets up a camera on the Upper West Side and films what is going on. The rest of the world thinks it is funny; New Yorkers know it is life.) In one of his films, *Manhattan*, he plays a man who is deeply in love with a younger woman who has no idea that he is romantically attracted to her. She thinks of him as merely a good friend and is utterly unaware that he is pining for her. Throughout the film, Allen tries to work up the nerve to tell the woman how he feels, and finally two-thirds or three-quarters of the way through the film, in the middle of a conversation about something else entirely, he simply can stand it no longer and blurts out, "I love you." Immediately he catches himself and says, "No, no, no, I don't. I llllove you. No, no. I looooove you." He continues to go through a dozen different ways of saying precisely the same three words. Why? The point of the scene is, I think, that the moment he says those three words, "I love you," he knows how hopelessly inadequate they are. They are such a cliché, so banal. They've been so used and misused and overused in the English language that to say "I love you" does not begin to convey what this man wants to say to that woman.

Were Wittgenstein looking over Allen's script, he would have advised him to end the film at that point. If it cannot be said, be silent. If you do not know how something can be said correctly, do not say it. But Eliot wisely knows that there are some things that are so important you dare not keep silent. You know that you cannot say "I love you" in any way that is adequate, but you also know that you cannot simply be silent, that you have to try to say something, however badly. There are those things so important that one simply cannot be silent about them. This is preeminently true when we speak of God.

At this point, I should add a caution. When the Christian tradition speaks of God, it does not mean a great big person out there somewhere, older, wiser, stronger, than you and I. That is Zeus, not God. One can baptize Zeus, but Zeus always remains Zeus. A baptized Zeus is not what Christians mean when we talk about God. I often tell students that the Christian statements about God are ways of answering the question, "Do you think that there are meaning, purpose, and direction to your life, and do you think that you are not the one who decides that meaning, purpose, and direction?" That question, however it is answered, is the question of God. Does my life have meaning and, if so, do I create and impose that meaning or do I discover it? How we answer that question is how we answer the God question. It is an unavoidable question. We cannot dismiss it as too difficult or impossible of final and sufficient resolution and so decline to ask it. We cannot *not* ask that question, implicitly or explicitly. It cannot be answered finally, but it is too impossible not to answer it in some way. That is where we find ourselves in religious language, language about Mystery. Theology, like all religious language, is caught between Wittgenstein's caution and Eliot's insight.

How, then, do we talk about God, recognizing that we cannot speak of God adequately but must say something? We do what the great users of language—poets—do when trying to say the unsayable: we pile up metaphors. Let me use my favorite example of this from Shakespeare, certainly by anyone's standard a great user of language. I call to your recollection act 5, scene 5 of *Macbeth.* Macbeth's world is falling apart. The English and the Scottish rebels are drawing closer to Dunsinane. As Macbeth gives his frantic orders for defending the castle, there comes a scream from offstage. To learn the cause of the cry he sends his servant who shortly returns and announces, "The queen, my lord, is dead." Then Shakespeare does what he often does at such moments in the plays: he has a character say that he cannot speak about the crisis. Hamlet dies saying that "the rest is silence." Othello kills himself while talking about an irrelevant action long ago in Aleppo. King Lear's last words dissolve into sound and rhythm. And Macbeth says, more to himself than to his servant, "She should have died hereafter;/ There would have been a time for such a word."

There are no words for Lady Macbeth's death, at least not at that moment. Macbeth cannot talk about it—but, of course, he does. He launches into his great soliloquy: "Tomorrow, and tomorrow, and tomorrow/ Creeps in this petty pace from day to day . . . " And we come to the extraordinary moment when Macbeth says, "Life is . . . " Realize what the death of this woman means to this man. She was not only his wife; she was the only other human being who shares the guilt, the only other person who knows all the horror—and she is gone. Macbeth is now utterly alone, alone as few, if any, are ever alone. So the loneliest human being in the world is about to tell us what life is like for him.

And how does he do it? He gives us three metaphors. "Life's but a walking shadow." A shadow, nothing, merely the absence of light. But a walking shadow—animated nothingness. Now hold that image in mind, but shift your angle of vision, as it were. Life is also "a poor player / That struts and frets his hour upon the stage / And then is heard no more." A bad actor—Shakespeare had probably known many. An actor who gets on stage and flubs his lines and muffs his gestures and bumps into props. The audience wants him to get off so that the play can go on; when he does exits, the audience immediately forgets him. Now, hold that image in mind, too, and shift your perspective to still another angle. Life is "a tale / Told by an idiot, full of sound and fury, / Signifying nothing." I suspect that most of us, if not all, have had the experience of being harangued by someone who was overwrought and out of control, who spluttered on about—what? Something, nothing; whatever it was, we did not understand it. A moment of pure frustration. A tale full of sound and fury told by an idiot. (Teachers have probably had such experiences. Believe me, anyone who has spent any time in ministry knows what it is like to be buttonholed by someone who carries on at length about something that apparently means a great deal to him or her and that remains thoroughly impenetrable to the captive listener.) Three images. Draw out the lines of those three perspectives and, where they intersect, that is how life looks to the loneliest human being on earth. When trying to say the unsayable, we pile metaphor on metaphor on metaphor. Shakespeare, of course, does it better than the rest of us.

That is precisely what we do in religious language when we try to speak about God. And so we say that God is creator, judge, parent, spouse, shepherd, king, lawgiver, rock, leader in battle, savior, and on and on. We pile image on image on image on image, metaphor after metaphor after metaphor. But there must be some control on these metaphors. After all, some ways of describing God are simply abhorrent to the Christian tradition, e.g., God is evil or God is hatred. So we ask: Is there some fundamental metaphor for God according to the Christian tradition which can provide a guideline for talking about God, a metaphor with which all other metaphors must be in accord in order to be deemed acceptable? Granted that no way of talking about God is the right and fully adequate way, is there some way of talking about God that is less hopelessly inadequate than other ways?

The Christian tradition says yes. There is a fundamental metaphor for talking about God with which all the other metaphors we use for God must

fit. (I suspect, by the way, that this idea of a fundamental metaphor for ultimate Mystery is applicable to all great religious traditions, but at this moment
we are interested in Christianity, especially in its Catholic form.) The fundamental metaphor for God in the Christian tradition is suggested over and over
again in the New Testament but finds its clearest, sharpest, most succinct
statement in one of the last documents of the New Testament collection written, what we call the First Letter of John, at 4:8 and again at 16: "God is love"
(NRSV).

A Fundamental Metaphor for God

But this love which is offered as the fundamental metaphor for God is a peculiar kind of love: *agape*. This is not the usual Greek word for "love" in the
New Testament era. That would be *eros*, a perfectly fine word and a marvelous concept, but not the one early Christians chose as the metaphor for the
ultimate Mystery. *Eros* is a love that seeks satisfaction from the person or
thing loved. Thus, it clearly includes what most of us think of first when we
hear of erotic love, i.e., sexual love. But it also means what we refer to in
English when we say, "I love that movie" or "I love playing tennis." These
are instances of what the Greek-speaking world called "erotic" love, because
the lover finds satisfaction and pleasure in that which is loved. There is certainly nothing wrong with *eros*; it is simply something other than *agape*.
Agape is love to which satisfaction is irrelevant. The lover seeks nothing from
the beloved, not even gratitude. The lover simply gives the lover's self to the
beloved. Rather than "love," which has become a word with so many (probably too many) uses in English, I prefer to translate *agape* as "self-gift," the
gift of the self to the other asking nothing in response. *Agape* is pure gift of
self to the other. This is what the Christian tradition claims is the least wrong
metaphor for God.

The whole Christian doctrinal tradition is an expansion of this fundamental claim, that God, the Ultimate Mystery which undergirds the existence
of all that is, is least wrongly thought of as pure and perfect self-gift. I might
exemplify this at great length, but you will be thrilled to know I shall not. But
we should note that, while the fundamental Christian metaphor for God is
agape, pure other-directed love, "love" is not the name of a person but rather
of a relationship among persons. So we are saying that the least wrong way
to think about God, the foundational Mystery that grounds and surrounds all
that exists, is not first and foremost as a person but as a relationship. You may
well think that this is a bizarre claim, and in many ways it is. But I am sure
that it is scarcely a claim that you have not heard before, although perhaps
not in quite these words. In fact among Christians, certainly Catholic Christians, we make this claim all the time. We often affirm that we do or say
something "in the name of the Father and of the Son and of the Holy Spirit."
When we do so, we assert that God is to be thought of first not as "the One,"
but as the relatedness of "the Three." The central point of the doctrine of the
Trinity is that God is least wrongly understood as a relationship, as an eternal explosion of love.

When he wrote *De Trinitate*, St. Augustine acknowledged that the Church had language for the Trinity from the New Testament itself. At the end of the Gospel of St. Matthew (28:19), we find the command to go out and baptize all nations "in the name of the Father and of the Son and of the Holy Spirit" (NRSV). But, Augustine suggested, however biblically rooted such language may be, it is not especially helpful in trying to show the meaning of the Trinity for people's lives. After all, he reasoned, if we are created in the image and likeness of God and God is Triune, then ought we not be able to see traces of the Trinity in our own experience? So he set out to find alternate terminology that might better convey the meaning of the Trinity, coming up with two sets of terms that he seems to have particularly liked—and I must confess that I like them, too. Augustine suggested that perhaps "Giver, Recipient, and Gift given" might be more useful for teaching and preaching, rather than "Father, Son, Spirit"; or as yet another alternative, "Lover, Beloved, and the Love between them." This is what Christians mean when they talk about God: from all eternity the Mystery at the root of all that exists is endless self-gift, endless outpouring of self; for all eternity the Mystery is endless acceptance of the gift of that outpouring and rejoicing in it; and for all eternity the Mystery is the outpouring. God is the Lover, the Beloved, and the Love between them; the Giver, the Recipient, and the Gift given. When we use the word *God*, the Mystery that grounds and surrounds all that exists, we speak of the infinite and eternal explosion of self-gift.

That allows me to pose another question: Why does God create? Think with me for a moment about the question that Martin Heidegger maintained was the beginning of all metaphysics, i.e., of all accounts of how things finally fit together: Why is there being rather than nothing? There are many ways in which that question has been answered, many metaphysics. The Christian tradition's answer, as I understand it, is, "Because it is loved." The reason that anything exists is that it is the object of love. All things that are, are loved into being. The fundamental ground for anything is that it is called into being because God loves it. As I noted earlier, the universe gives nothing to God; rather, God gives something to it, namely God's self. Why? Because God gets a kick out of it. Because that's what God's like: overflowing love. Please notice: I am speaking about the reason *anything* exists, not only *anyone*. This overflowing love is the reason for not only your existence and mine, but for the existence of the chair on which you are sitting and the pen you are holding, the existence of the leaves on the trees and your pet cat and your favorite rhododendron and the furthest supernova. It is the ground of the existence of the universe, everything that ever has, ever will, or ever can exist. Why does anything exist rather than nothing, in Heidegger's question? The Christian tradition's answer is because it is loved.

What makes us unique as human beings (at least, as far as we know) is that we are the point in creation that can acknowledge that we are infinitely loved and either accept or reject it. We can embrace being loved or deny and turn away from it. The desk at which I am writing cannot know that it is loved; it cannot accept or refuse being loved. It is, however, as truly and perfectly loved as I am. Please notice: everything is loved perfectly because

God, being God, does nothing imperfectly. God is God and therefore always acts in a God-like way, which is to say, God does everything perfectly. God does not love a little today and a bit more tomorrow and perhaps a bit less the day after. God loved you on Tuesday, but then Wednesday you sinned, so God loved you less; then on Thursday you repented, so God loves you again: that is pure mythology in which God is reduced to Zeus or Odin. Rather, God loves everything in a God-like way, perfectly, completely, one hundred percent. Not every creature can know and accept this love, of course. The desk is loved perfectly, and so is Himes. The difference is that Himes knows it and the desk does not. Sometimes Himes accepts it, and sometimes, tragically, he refuses it. But God remains God.

Nothing you can do can make God not love you. If there were, then you would be more powerful than God, in that you could cause God to change. I sometimes use this image when I preach, and it ruffles some feathers, but feather-ruffling is by no means a bad thing to do in the pulpit. Let me dare to make a claim about how things look from God's perspective: from God's point of view, there is no difference between Mary and Satan; God loves them both perfectly. The difference is on the side of the two creatures: Mary is thrilled and Satan hates it. In the *Summa Contra Gentiles*, St. Thomas Aquinas raises a question: If God is everywhere, is God in hell? His answer is that, indeed, God is in hell. Of course, his next question is: And what is God doing there? And Thomas's answer is that God is in hell loving the damned. The damned may not love God, but the damned cannot make God not love them. Since the perfect love which is the least wrong metaphor for God is the reason for our being, the opposite of being loved by God is not damnation, but non-being. Not to be loved by God is not to exist. Everything that is, to the extent that it is, is loved.

The Sacramental Principle

Let me introduce another piece of theological shorthand: grace. *Grace* is the word by which we traditionally designate the *agape* of God outside the Trinity, the *agape* of God calling all things into being. In Christian theology, grace is the self-giving of God outside the Trinity bringing all things into being.

With the introduction of the word *grace*, I want to turn our attention to a difficulty. Consideration of the difficulty for a moment will lead us back to the sacramental principle. If the agapic love of God or grace is omnipresent, if everything is loved or engraced, if everything we are and everything we encounter is rooted in grace, grace may go unnoticed. What is omnipresent is more often than not unnoticed. For example, the whole time you have been reading this, you have been blinking. Now, unless this paper has been preternaturally boring, you have not been counting your blinks. After all, who thinks about blinking? This example struck me a few years ago because I was hit with a bout of Bell's palsy. The left side of my face froze, and one of the consequences was that my left eye could not blink. Throughout the day I periodically had to hold my left eyelid down, and at night I taped the eye shut. One becomes very conscious of blinking when one cannot do it, yet I never thought about it until Bell's palsy called my attention to it.

What we do all the time we seldom, if ever, think about. What is always there gets little or no attention. For example, we never think about the oxygen in a room until the air starts to become stale. We do not think about our heart beating, although if it stopped, we would notice as we slumped to the floor. So if grace is omnipresent, grace is likely to go unnoticed. We require occasions when grace is called to our attention, when it is made concrete for us, when that which is always the case is made present in such a way that we cannot help but notice it and may either accept or reject it and, if we accept it, celebrate it. I remind you of my preliminary description of what I called the *sacramental principle*: that which is always and everywhere the case must be noticed, accepted, and celebrated somewhere sometime.

In the Catholic tradition, we call the occasions when grace is made effectively present for us *sacraments*. I am not referring here primarily to the seven great public rituals that Catholics celebrate (although I am by no means excluding them). By *sacrament* I mean any person, place, thing, or event, any sight, sound, taste, touch, or smell, that causes us to notice the love which supports all that exists, that undergirds your being and mine and the being of everything about us. How many such sacraments are there? The number is virtually infinite, as many as there are things in the universe. There is nothing that cannot be a sacrament, absolutely nothing—even, as St. Augustine observed, sin. Within the context of repentance, sin can become an occasion when we discovers how deeply loved we are. This is what he meant when he called the sin of Adam and Eve *felix culpa,* a happy fault, a phrase the Church still sings in the Easter Proclamation every Holy Saturday. There is nothing that cannot become a sacrament for someone, absolutely nothing.

We all have our personal sacraments. For all of you who are married, I hope that one of the deepest, richest, most profound experiences of the fundamental love that undergirds being is your spouse. For those who are parents, I hope your children are such experiences. To your neighbors, they may be the little pests who live next door, but to you they are sacraments. We all have our own array of sacraments that are absolutely necessary for us.

This, by the way, is an important element in Catholic liturgy. The fundamental principle of Catholic liturgy is that everything and the kitchen sink have a place within it. Why? Because everything is potentially sacred. Everything is engraced. So everything is fair game for liturgy. So we sing, dance, parade, wave banners, ring bells, play organs, blow horns, sound trumpets—and sometimes we are still and silent. We eat, drink, bathe one another in water, pour oil on one another, put one another to bed when we get married and into the earth when we die. We waft incense, hang paintings, put up mosaics, erect statues, construct extraordinary buildings and illumine them through stained glass. We appeal to sight, sound, taste, touch, and smell. Historically, the principle on which the liturgy operated was, "If it works, throw it in." The reason for such inclusiveness is the deep Catholic conviction that nothing is by definition profane. Everything is potentially sacramental.

The great nineteenth-century English Jesuit poet Gerard Manley Hopkins has an especially beautiful phrase for this. It is a line in one of his best-known and most frequently anthologized poems, "Hurrahing in Harvest." At the time he wrote the poem, Hopkins was teaching at a Jesuit boys' school in Wales. At the opening of the poem it is the fall and Hopkins is disheartened by the disappearance of the summer's beauty and the coming onset of winter. But he begins to consider the clouds scudding across the sky, the way the wind blows off the Irish Sea at that time of year in Wales, the joy of people bringing in the harvest, and the changing color of the leaves. How beautiful it all is, yet he does not notice it while he worries about what is gone and dreads what has not come. All the while, he fails to notice what is here at the moment. In what is, in my opinion, the single most beautiful statement in English of the Catholic sacramental principle—and Hopkins was Catholic to the tips of his fingers—the poet wrote, "These things, these things were here and but the beholder / Wanting." The leaves have not suddenly changed their colors at that moment, nor has the sky been transformed. All that beauty was already there. What changed? Hopkins. The splendor was there, but he did not notice it. Then he becomes a beholder and sees what is there to be seen. The whole Catholic sacramental life is a training to be beholders. Catholic liturgy is a lifelong pedagogy to bring us to see what is there, to behold what is always present, in the conviction that if we truly see and fully appreciate what is there, whether we use the language or not, we will be encountering grace. We will see the love which undergirds all that exists.

Those who have been fortunate to have seen the film *Babette's Feast* might recall how the little band of Lutheran sectarians learn to appreciate what has been placed there before them by the French chef, Babette. They learn to savor the taste, the aroma, the color of the food and drink and, in discovering the goodness of the physical world, are led to reconciliation with one another. At the end of the extraordinary meal, they go outside into the little square of the village where they have stood countless times, look up at the stars, join hands, and begin to sing. At one marvelous, closing moment, one of the two elderly sisters says to the other, "The stars look very close tonight," and the other replies, "Maybe they are every night." That night they could see what was there every night because Babette's feast had made them beholders. That is what sacramentality does.

But what has all this to do with education and the intellectual's vocation? As a Catholic and an educator, I think that it may suggest a very important perspective on education. If we accept what I have said about the sacramental principle, then anything that awakens, enlivens, and expands the imagination, opens the vision, and enriches the sensitivity of any human being is a religious act. Although we may not use this language, education is or can be training in sacramental beholding.

At the very beginning of the twentieth century, Baron Friedrich von Hügel, one of the most profoundly Catholic people of that century, was invited to give a talk to a Christian students' association at Oxford. (Despite the Austrian name, he was, in fact, an Englishman. His father had been an Austrian and a baron of the Holy Roman Empire, but his mother was a Scot.

He was brought up in England and English was his first language.) In his lecture to this group of presumably earnest Christian students, von Hügel spoke of asceticism, self-discipline, as a traditionally important part of the Christian life. He asked a rhetorical question: Who is the most striking example of asceticism in the nineteenth century that had just ended? I suspect that his answer must have shocked those sober young Christian gentlemen in Oxford, for he said that he thought, beyond doubt, that the great example of asceticism in the nineteenth century had been Charles Darwin. Darwin, according to von Hügel, had, with immense discipline and over a long period of time, subordinated his extraordinarily keen, powerful intellect and astonishing energy to the painstaking observation of the varieties of barnacles and the shapes of pigeons' bills. With astonishing clarity and intensity, Darwin had forced himself to observe what was there. And that, claimed von Hügel, is what asceticism is all about.

Asceticism is not self-denial in order to please a mildly sadistic deity. Rather, its goal is to discipline oneself sufficiently so that one can move beyond one's hopes, dreams, fears, wants, and expectations to see what is, in fact, there. Asceticism is a training to see reality, not what one expects, hopes, or fears to see. I have often told students that the point of asceticism is to stop looking in the mirror long enough to look out the window, to stop gazing at oneself long enough to see something else. The Catholic conviction is that if one sees what is there to be seen, one will discover grace, the love that undergirds all that exists. The ascetic beholds the omnipresence of grace.

Where do people today learn that kind of self-discipline? There are, I think, many ways in which life teaches us asceticism. Marriage is a splendid school of self-discipline for those who live it well and wisely, as is parenthood. Paying off the mortgage and managing our credit cards can be excellent paths of ascetical training. They are all ways of coming to grips with what is there, not what we would like to be there.

And certainly, one of the most rigorous and effective ways of self-discipline is science. Following von Hügel's claim about Darwin, I suggest that there is a profoundly sacramental dimension to all the sciences because they are all training in intellectual self-discipline. After all, we often call our fields of study *disciplines*. When we study anything, we "discipline" ourselves.

Anything that expands the imagination, enriches the vision, liberates the will, frees the vision, and disciplines the attention is a profoundly religious act. Indeed, so convinced am I of this that I could have come at this same point from an entirely different angle from the way I have done thus far. I could have developed this same conclusion starting from a consideration of what Christians mean by the *Incarnation*. Catholics try to hold this belief radically and so insist that in Christ God does not merely seem to be human or act in a human way, but has become human. In the words of an ancient hymn quoted in Philippians 2:6–11, he has become human as all human beings are human, that he is like us in all things except sin. The Catholic tradition has recognized that, if this radical claim of the Incarnation is true, then you and I and God share humanity in common and so, to become like God, we should be as fully human as we can. Thus, whatever enriches and deepens our humanity, whatever makes us braver, wiser, more intelligent, more responsible, freer, more loving, makes us holy, i.e., like God. Thus, education, which certainly should aim at making human beings braver, wiser, more intelligent, more responsible, freer, and more loving, is a work of sanctification. This is why the Christian community has always been involved in education and not only in catechetics. A good Catholic university or college is not a place where we allow people to study mathematics or history or literature so that we can get them to sit through a religion course. We do not admit people to the business school so that we can require them to take a minimum number of credits in theology. Rather, any and every field of study is ultimately religious in nature if everything rests on grace and humanity is shared with God in Christ.

This sacramental conviction shapes Catholicism at its best. Of course, Catholicism is not always at its best, and so does not always act in accord with its sacramental vision. But were we all to require ourselves to live up to our best vision all the time, which of us would have gotten out of bed this morning? Still, at its best and wisest, Catholicism is shaped by the conviction that grace lies at the root of all reality. And if that conviction is true, all the humanities as well as all the sciences become religious enterprises.

Let me offer a closing image. In the *Divine Comedy*, you will recall that Dante allots hell, purgatory, and heaven each thirty-three cantos. The whole of the great poem is completed with a hundredth canto in which Dante attempts to do what Wittgenstein would have told him he should not even try: to describe to the reader the vision of God. In the ninety-ninth canto of the poem, the thirty-third of the *Paradiso*, Beatrice has conducted Dante to the highest circle of heaven. She points him toward Bernard of Clairvaux, a symbol of all that was richest and best in the spiritual tradition of the Middle Ages. Looking in awe at Bernard, Dante realizes that Bernard is gazing steadily across at someone else, and he follows Bernard's gaze to Mary. And he is overwhelmed with ·the sight of Mary until he sees that she has her look fixed steadily upward. Dante follows Mary's glance and beholds at the end of canto ninety-nine the vision of God. In canto one hundred, he tries to do the undoable. Needless to say he fails, but Dante's failures are more interesting than almost anyone else's successes. He says that he was dazzled by a light that initially blinded him. But as the intense light burned his eyes, it healed them so that he began to discern that the light was actually the interaction of three concentric globes of three colors, his image for the Trinity. As his eyes were simultaneously seared and strengthened, he could look into the very depth of the light, and there he saw one exactly like himself. In one of the greatest statements of the Catholic humanist tradition, Dante saw that, as a result of the Incarnation, at the heart of God is one like him and you and me.

And so, in the great final line of the great poem, the line to which the whole *Divine Comedy* has been leading, his recognition of *"l'amor che move il sole e l'altre stelle,"* "the love that moves the sun and other stars." This is Dante's statement of the sacramental principle: the universe, the sun and all the stars, is grounded and governed by love. It exists because of infinite self-gift. That is what enlivens the Catholic tradition at its best.

Sources

Scripture quotations from the Revised Standard Version (RSV), copyright 1946, 1952, and 1971 by the Division of Christian Education of the National Council of the Churches of Christ in the USA. Used by permission, all rights reserved.

Scripture quotations from the New Revised Standard Version of the Bible (NRSV), copyright 1989 by the Division of Christian Education of the National Council of the Churches of Christ in the USA. Used by permission, all rights reserved.

9

Twin Peaks and *Columbo*: Two Ways to Imagine God

John Neary

Some years ago I was hooked on film director David Lynch's television series *Twin Peaks*. I was fascinated by the show's twisting, twisted story, eccentric characters, and overall weirdness. But when I mentioned *Twin Peaks* to a good friend who is a Catholic theologian, he told me with some embarrassment that he found the show off-putting; it was "too Protestant," he said.

When I asked my friend what he meant, he handed me an article by Fr. Andrew Greeley from a 1991 issue of *America*. In this article Greeley, invoking theologian David Tracy's "magisterial *The Analogical Imagination*" (285), describes two religious imaginations, two ways of using images to suggest a transcendent reality: the "dialectical" and the "analogical" imaginations. Borrowing from David Tracy's ideas, Greeley claims that within modern Christianity, Protestantism tends to nurture a dialectical imagination and Catholicism an analogical or sacramental imagination:

> The analogical or Catholic imagination, to summarize and simplify David Tracy, emphasizes the presence of God in the world. It perceives the world and its creatures and relationships and social structures as metaphors, sacraments of God, hints of what God is like. I often illustrate the theory by noting that Catholics have angels and saints and souls in purgatory and statues and stained glass windows and holy water, and an institutional church that itself is thought to be a sacrament. Protestant denominations, on the other hand, either do not have this imagery or do not put so much emphasis on it. "One side, the Catholic analogical imagination, leans in the direction of immanence; the other, the Protestant dialectical imagination, leans in the direction of transcendence. Which is better? Neither. Which is necessary? Both" ("Catholic Imagination," p. 286).

My Catholic theologian friend noted that David Lynch's dark, depraved town of Twin Peaks is a place that is dialectically divorced from the good. The hero, FBI agent Dale Cooper, comes from somewhere else, and until late in the series, he stays pure, untouched by the depravity around him; impeccably well-groomed and wholesome, his worst vice being a passion for coffee and cherry pie. Cooper's access to truth is less through his interaction with the people of Twin Peaks than through insights and visions that transcend the mundane mess around him. My friend said that he preferred *Columbo*, a detective show in which everybody is partly good and partly bad. This show's grumpy, rumpled hero bumbles his way to the truth because truth is there, available within the imperfect but not hopelessly depraved world around him.

When it occurred to me that these two imaginative relationships with ultimate reality have shaped much modern fiction, I decided that an examination of the two imaginations could be a valuable way to reflect on the different views of the Ultimate that inhere in various modern fictional works. I quickly discovered that Greeley's assertion that the dialectical imagination is "Protestant" and the analogical is "Catholic" is too facile; Greeley himself acknowledges that "the analogical and the dialectical imaginations are not mutually exclusive. No individual is completely possessed by one or the other, nor does any denomination or group have a monopoly on one or the other" ("Catholic Imagination," p. 286). But after reading much theology and literary criticism and reflecting on some of the most compelling English-language fiction of the last one hundred years, I am convinced that the overall insight is very fruitful. So I propose that David Tracy's description of two kinds of religious imagination, the "dialectical" and the "analogical," provides a good model for talking about modern fiction and its vision of what Tracy calls the "whole" of reality. For the dialectical imagination, ultimate reality is radically other, unlike earthly reality, while the analogical, sacramental imagination finds metaphors and images that suggest similarities between human reality and the Ultimate.

The concept of the analogical and the dialectical imaginations strikes me as particularly useful in the current "postmodern" academic climate because both imaginations are able to take seriously the "linguistic turn," the turn toward metaphor and narrative. In *Postmodernity*, a book-length anatomy of postmodernism, Paul Lakeland describes the "linguistic turn" (a term coined by Richard Rorty) that virtually all contemporary thinkers have taken: "It is not Being or God or *nous* or reason that is the foundation of thinking, and hence of the subject, but language. What can be said lays down the boundaries of what can be thought, and this insight has profound historicizing and contextualizing implications" (p. 19). After the postmodern linguistic turn, Lakeland says, "knowledge cannot be pure, may not even aspire to the condition of purity. Language is not, as Heidegger would have it, the 'house of Being,' but simultaneously its creator and destroyer" (p. 19).

Of course, this "linguistic turn" has led some thinkers—including Rorty himself—to a relentless atheism. "Death of God" theologian Carl A. Raschke, for instance, asserts that postmodern deconstruction, which he calls "the interior drive of twentieth-century theology rather than an alien agenda," is "*the death of God put into writing*" (p. 3). But literary theorist Kevin Hart claims that what is at issue in postmodern skepticism is not the reality of God but only the limitations of human knowledge and the radical incompleteness of all human systems (including Raschke's). Hart argues that postmodern deconstruction is "not a collection of first-order propositions about knowledge or being but a second-order discourse on epistemology and ontology, one that traces the effects of their will to totalise" (p. 173). Postmodernism's claim that experience is mediated through representation or sign, that humans experience a deferred or contextualized rather than absolute presence, is similar, Hart suggests, to traditional "negative theology," which emphasizes the fact that any God concept is always already a representation, a sign, not a presence (p. 186). For negative theology, says Hart, "one gains 'knowledge' of God by successively abstracting God from images of Him" (p. 190), hence guaranteeing "that human speech about God is in fact about *God* and not a *concept* of God" (p. 192). Such a mystical form of theism, however "negative," is hardly a proclamation of the "death of God."

So I suggest that the current awareness of the thickly particularized contexts within which humans experience reality (contexts governed by historical placement, social position, gender, etc.), and of the fact that these experiences are always linguistically—metaphorically—mediated, does not render religious approaches to literature obsolete. Rather, it justifies a close examination of the various ways people have imagined the holy, the specific textures of human representations and signs of God. If answers seem more than ever to be beyond definitive reach, the big questions, what Tracy calls the "limit" questions, remain as real and pressing as ever. The question of how and to what extent, if at all, language and metaphor can mediate some transcendent reality is a key modern-day religious question—and one that ought to bring theologians together with literary critics, who study texts explicitly founded on metaphors and fictions. This is a question about religious *imaginations*, about the ways people have imagined ultimate reality—an essentially unnameable reality that is of ultimate concern, that at the limit, seems to reveal itself even through the web of intertextuality in which postmodern theory has shown the imagining human self to be enmeshed. And I wish to propose that in Christian theological history, two religious imaginations have dominated; borrowing David Tracy's terminology and conceptual framework, I will call them the "dialectical" and the "analogical" imaginations.

These two kinds of imagination approach ultimate reality differently. Again I turn to Andrew Greeley for a succinct description of these two imaginations; although Greeley's definitions are lacking in nuance, they provide a useful starting point:

> The central symbol is God. One's "picture" of God is in fact a metaphorical narrative of God's relationship with the world and the self as part of the world. It was precisely at this point that Tracy's work made its major contribution to my own thinking. . . . On the basis of his study, he suggested that the Catholic imagination is "analogical" and the Protestant imagination is "dialectical." The Catholic "classics" assume a God who is present in the world, disclosing Himself in and through creation. The world and all its events, objects, and people tend to be somewhat like God. The Protestant classics, on the other

hand, assume a God who is radically absent from the world
and who discloses Herself only on rare occasions (especially in
Jesus Christ and Him crucified). The world and all its events,
objects, and people tend to be radically different from God.

. . . Tracy argues that the two approaches to human society
of the respective traditions are shaped by these imaginative
pictures. The Catholic tends to see society as a "sacrament" of
God, a set of ordered relationships, governed by both justice
and love, that reveal, however imperfectly, the presence of
God. Society is "natural" and "good," therefore, for humans,
and their "natural" response to God is social. The Protestant,
on the other hand, tends to see human society as "God-
forsaken" and therefore unnatural and oppressive. The individual stands over against society and is not integrated into it.
The human becomes fully human only when he is able to
break away from social oppression and relate to the absent
God as a completely free individual (*Catholic Myth*, 45).

In these definitions, Greeley effectively captures the essential characteristics
of each of the two religious imaginations: the dialectical emphasizes the gaps
and dissimilarities between things (sacred and secular, human and world,
human and transcendence) while the analogical emphasizes the connections,
the similarities.

As I have noted, both kinds of imagination are grounded on the insight
that the transcendent "limit-dimension" is an absent presence that can be
mediated only metaphorically. Where these imaginative visions differ is in
their attitudes toward this insight—their willingness or unwillingness to go
ahead and use positive metaphors to suggest that which is beyond literal naming. The dialectical imagination, hyper-aware of the metaphoricity of religious language and image, constantly and explicitly drives a wedge between
human images and the limit-dimension; for this imagination, ultimate reality
is what we do *not* possess, what our metaphors and images cannot express.
But the analogical imagination celebrates the metaphors, weaves them,
asserting the proportionate (*ana-logos*) relationship between things, the
carrying-between (*meta-pherein*) of meaning. This imagination affirms
analogies and metaphors, although it is always at least implicitly aware of
their partiality, their hypothetical and playful nature, the fact that ultimate
reality can be present not directly but only analogically. At their most sophisticated, both forms of imagination possess an awareness that, in Tracy's
words, "theological interpretation, like all such interpretations, must always
be a highly precarious mode of inquiry," because theological interpretation
reflects "on Ultimate Reality, and thereby on the limit questions of our existence. . . . Theologians can never claim certainty but, at best, highly tentative
relative adequacy" (*Plurality and Ambiguity*, p. 84–85).

Certainly Greeley's linkage of the dialectical imagination with Protestantism and the analogical with Catholicism is too facile; Catholicism has its

stern dialectical strains, and much Protestantism is very open to God's gracious self-manifestations. Nonetheless, the great theologians of the Reformed tradition have often emphasized God's radical transcendence, God's wholly—and holy—otherness. And Catholicism's distinctive sacramental focus does lead it to imagine the immanent presence of the divine within ordinary human reality, and a lot of modern Catholic fiction embodies a kind of imagination that David Tracy calls "analogical."

In David Tracy's analysis, then, the dialectical imagination emphasizes the gaps and dissimilarities between things (sacred versus secular, world versus self, transcendent versus human) while the analogical emphasizes the connections, the similarities. At the risk of seeming to be operating dialectically myself, I must first describe the dialectical imagination in order to more clearly differentiate the analogical imagination from it. The roots of the dialectical imagination are very deep within the Jewish-Christian tradition, perhaps as deep as the book of Genesis and the story of the Fall. The second Mosaic commandment (deleted, interestingly, from the Catholic list of Ten Commandments) is one source of this imagination: "You shall not make for yourself an idol, whether in the form of anything that is in heaven above, or that is on the earth beneath, or that is in the water under the earth" (Exodus 20:4). Yahweh's command reflects the Hebrew principle—embraced by the Christian dialectical imagination—that the absolute cannot be mediated through any human/worldly image.

One obvious biblical "classic" expression of dialectical imagining is Paul, especially in a text that has been of particular importance to the Protestant neo-orthodox tradition: the Letter to the Romans. This is the letter in which Paul proclaimed the principle adopted by the Protestant Reformers— that human beings are justified by faith rather than by works—and he founds this principle on a conviction that humans, in their sinfulness, are radically separated from the good, and that hence there can be no bridge between the human world and the divine:

> For we know that the law is spiritual; but I am of the flesh, sold into slavery under sin. I do not understand my own actions. For I do not do what I want, but I do the very thing I hate. Now if I do what I do not want, I agree that the law is good. But in fact it is no longer I that do it, but sin that dwells within me. For I know that nothing good dwells within me, that is, in my flesh (Romans 7:14–18).

In analyzing this passage, the Protestant theologian Karl Barth argues that by "flesh" Paul does not just mean the physical body; Paul is not dichotomizing physical and mental, body and soul. Rather, says Barth, "flesh" is for Paul the entire human self: "We must, of course, bear in mind the meaning of the word *flesh*: unqualified, and finally unqualifiable, worldliness; a worldliness perceived by men, and especially by religious men; relativity, nothingness, non-sense. That is what I am!" (p. 263). Paul, then, establishes the dialectical vision of *nature* as profoundly unsound, cut off from the good. And the emphases on human fallenness and on the not-yet of religious reality are the primary marks of the dialectical imagination.

Following Paul, Martin Luther carries out a key dialectical strategy: he claims that humans are immersed in the profane, non-transcendent world, which reveals the sacred only by dialectical negation. For the dialectical imagination there is no way for humans to approach the divine, so the only available avenue is a descent into the profane world itself, where God is revealed as a radical antithesis, an absence: "Thus, you say, 'How do we fulfill the law of God?' I answer, Because you do not fulfill it, therefore we are sinners and disobedient to God" (p. 62). It is this intense awareness of sin that crushes Christians down—impotent, despairing, in need of grace (which is radically other, unmediated by any human act, ritual, or analogy).

The great dialectical reformer John Calvin discusses images of God, but they are not sacramental images, outward signs of inward grace. Rather, for Calvin, divine images—such as Christ crucified—are anti-images, images that reveal God's absence rather than presence:

> God, indeed, from time to time showed the presence of his divine majesty by signs, so that he might be said to be looked upon face to face. But all the signs that he ever gave forth aptly conformed to his plan of teaching and at the same time clearly told men of his incomprehensible essence. For clouds and smoke and flame [Deut. 4:11], although they were symbols of heavenly glory, restrained the minds of all, like a bridle on them, from attempting to penetrate too deeply" (p. 102).

The dialectical imagination, powerfully exemplified by the quintessentially dialectical Kierkegaard, proclaims a radical either/or: a rift between the religious and the secular, the sacred and the profane, the *agapic* and the erotic, God and fallen nature. The analogical imagination's *ana-logos*, however, is founded on a both/and.

Mapping out his analogical theology, David Tracy defines as "religious" those experiences, situations, and questions that make humans confront a *limit*. This concept allows Tracy to imagine a wafer-thin line between the human and the divine; experiences of a limit to worldly reality and existence are fully human, but they also disclose at their very borders a "limit-of whose graciousness bears a religious character" (*Rage*, p. 106). For Tracy, the limit-*to* is the wall of helplessness and impotence that all humans ultimately confront (most clearly in the fact of mortality itself). But the limit-*of* is a kind of graciousness beyond the limit-to, a discovery that the apparent wall is, in a sense, the surface of a hand that lovingly holds and supports humanity. Tracy suggests:

> . . . that reflection upon limit-questions and limit-situations does disclose the reality of a dimension to our lives other than the more usual dimensions: a dimension whose first key is its

> reality as limit-to our other everyday, moral, cultural, and polit-
> ical activities; a dimension which, in my own brief and hazy
> glimpses, discloses a reality, however named and in whatever
> manner experienced, which functions as a final, now gracious,
> now frightening, now trustworthy, now absurd, always uncon-
> trollable limit-of the very meaning of existence itself. I find
> that, although religiously rather "unmusical" myself, I cannot
> deny this reality. . . . A neologism does not really seem needed
> here: that reality is religious (*Rage,* p. 108–109).

Since for Tracy, limit-to experiences also mediate an experience of a grounding reality, a limit-of, there may at least be bridges (metaphors, "carryings-
between") linking the ordinary and the transcendent.

The metaphorical picture of God that Tracy paints contains just such a
bridge. If "God" is a metaphorical image of the gracious limit-of disclosed
through a confrontation with the limit-to, then such a reality could not be
utterly removed, distant, sublimely disinterested, and unchangeable. Tracy
suggests that the God imaged by analogical Christianity is "dipolar"—both
the "wholly other" God of the Barthians and the immanent, relational God of
natural religion.

While a dialectical imagination drives a wedge between the secular/
historical on the one hand and the sacred on the other, the analogical, sacramental imagination is a yes to both. "Indeed a sacrament," says Tracy, "is
nothing other than a decisive re-presentation of both the events of proclaimed
history and the manifestation of the sacred cosmos." Sacrament yokes
together, declares analogous, what dialectics wrenches apart. The dialectical
way of describing the human relationship with the whole is a *not-yet,*
"charged with the prophetic, apocalyptic, eschatological sense of a 'great
refusal' to the present order of things" (*Analogical Imagination,* p. 312); the
analogical way, however, is an *always-already*—"the exaltation of a fundamental trust, a wonder at the giftedness of life itself, a radical, universal and
finally incomprehensible grace, a pervasive sense of a God of love who is
never an 'inference' but an always-present reality to each and to all" (*Analogical Imagination,* p. 311). The analogical imagination entertains a most
stunning analogy or simile: "If Jewish, Christian or Islamic, the texts will
witness to a faith that the whole is like a who, involved in self-manifestation
in the event or events to which these texts bear witness" (*Analogical Imagination,* p. 255).

If the prophetic and the Pauline traditions are biblical sources of the
dialectical imagination, the Wisdom and Johannine traditions are sources of
the analogical. The female personification of God in the Wisdom literature is
much more immanent, more connected with humanity and nature, than the
starkly transcendent God who warns Moses not to image the divine in any
way. And John's gospel story of the Logos made flesh is a good imaginative
presentation of divine reality as always-already, especially for those who eat
the flesh and drink the blood of the Christ.

The most obvious blossoming of the analogical imagination in Christian history is in Thomism, and then in Thomism's encounter with mysticism and phenomenology in such modern theologians as Baron Friedrich von Hügel and Karl Rahner. For example, Rahner's notion of the divine self-communication as inherent in human consciousness—its intentionality, its transcendence of itself—sharply distinguishes Rahner from those who claim that the secular and the sacred are separated by an absolute abyss. Rahner describes grace not as something radically other but as (to use Tracy's term for the analogical) *always-already*. And God, Rahner says, is "present for us in an absolute self-communication, . . . present in the mode of closeness, and not only in the mode of distant presence as the term of transcendence" (p. 119). The connection of humanity to God is not a dialectical negation of the natural order, but rather "a modality of [humanity's] original and unthematic subjectivity" (p. 129). And such feminist theologians as Sallie McFague have gone on to use this Rahnerian analogical insight that humans are connected, however imperfectly, to the divine to weave new images and metaphors of God—not as a distant king but as mother, lover, and friend (see *Models of God*).

Clearly, then, the analogical imagination, like the dialectical, is relevant to literature. It is concerned with metaphoricity itself and with the most important challenge of metaphoricity: the use of images to mediate ultimate reality. I will end this presentation of the two imaginations by showing examples of each occurring in two works of contemporary fiction that explicitly deal with religious issues: John Updike's *Roger's Version* and Andre Dubus's *Voices from the Moon*. Updike's novel exemplifies a dialectical metaphorical mediation—or non-mediation—of ultimate reality, while Dubus uses an analogical imagination to accomplish a kind of sacramental mediation between the human and the transcendent.

Updike is a writer whose Protestant heritage and Christian faith are deeply important to him, and his sense of his vocation as a writer of Christian fiction represents a very nuanced and thoughtful articulation of the dialectical imagination: "Is not Christian fiction, insofar as it exists, a description of the bewilderment and panic, the sense of hollowness and futility, which afflicts those whose search for God is not successful? And are we not all, within the churches and temples or not, more searcher than finder in this regard?" ("Disconcerting Thing," p. 9). Many of Updike's other novels are arguably as analogical as they are dialectical, but *Roger's Version*—with a protagonist/narrator, Roger Lambert, who is a Barthian theologian, and a particularly severe one at that—seems to me a sharp modern literary embodiment of the dialectical way of imagining humans' relationship with what David Tracy calls the "limit-dimension." Although the novel as a whole may to a degree ironize Roger's fierce negativity, it is Roger's imagination that dominates the book—and a more dialectical imagination would be difficult to find.

The novel itself is designed dialectically. Virtually every section is organized around a conflictual or at least tense situation between some pair from among the major characters: Roger himself, a sternly skeptical Barthian theology professor at what appears to be Harvard Divinity School, who thinks that God, if there is one, is radically absent from the human world; Dale Kohler, a young Christian computer scientist, who believes in an immanent God and is determined to prove God's existence scientifically; Esther Lambert, Roger's wife; and Verna, daughter of Roger's half-sister, Edna. There are a variety of dialectical pairings throughout the book, but the book's main plot deals with Roger's theological opposition to Dale Kohler; Roger pits his radically transcendent God against Dale's immanent God. For Roger, unlike Dale, God is not a graceful presence experienced within nature, but is precisely that which we humans feel painfully cut off from. Religion for this deeply dialectical theologian is an experience of depravity and deprivation rather than of fullness.

Dale's God is one who shows a face within nature, a God who is not separated from the human world by an abyss. "The physicists are getting down to the nitty-gritty," Dale proclaims; "they've really just about pared things down to the ultimate details, and the last thing they ever expected is happening. God is showing through" (p. 9). This God, Dale says, is not some safe object for academic study; it is a real, living God—"God as a *fact*, a fact about to burst upon us, right up out of Nature" (p. 19). And, since Dale imagines God analogically, he believes that the parts of the universe are microcosmic mirrors of God; thus, he proposes to analyze parts of the natural world with a computer to show that God, or God's ordering principle, is contained within these parts. Dale describes God as having a "face" which is "breaking through": "They've been scraping away at physical reality all these centuries, and now the layer of the little left we don't understand is so fine, God's face is staring right out at us" (p. 20).

But Roger sneeringly dismantles this inappropriate metaphor: "Sounds rather grisly, frankly. Like a face through a frosted bathroom door. Or like . . . that poor young sailor from the Franklin expedition they found this past summer up in Canada, nicely preserved by the ice. He was staring right out at us, too" (p. 20). Dale, in other words, employs his metaphors to affirm their at least partial adequacy to reality, but Roger employs his to dialectically expose and explode metaphoricity itself. Reflecting on the need to keep God utterly disentangled from nature and the human, Roger plays with, and imaginatively explodes, a metaphor for transcendent imagining: "Barth had been right: *totaliter aliter.* Only by placing God totally on the other side of the humanly understandable can any final safety for Him be secured. . . . All else is mere philosophy, churning the void in the hope of making butter, as it was put by the junior Oliver Wendell Holmes" (p. 32). Holmes's comical metaphor is what the analogical imagination can look like to one who imagines in a sternly dialectical way: soft, buttery, futile.

In place of Dale's analogies, Roger offers Tertullian's dialectical affirmation via negation: "'*Certum est*,' I murmured, '*quia impossible est*'" (p. 180). Instead of trying to imagine a reconciliation between seeming incompatibles, Roger yanks them apart and proclaims the dialectical paradox: it is certain because it is impossible. Flesh cannot be reconciled with spirit, nor can God's incarnation in Christ be made understandable through human metaphor. Roger neatly sums up his attitude about analogical models that attempt to mediate the truth about the absolute: "If it's a faithful model," he says, "it'll plead the Fifth Amendment, just like the real thing" (p. 109).

Appropriately, then, Roger's most intensely religious experience in the novel is dark, morally disturbing—an act of sex with his niece, Verna. The situation could hardly be seamier. Not only will sex with Verna be adulterous (Roger is married); not only will it be incest. Roger and Verna finally have an occasion to have sex because of an act of child abuse: Verna's illegitimate baby has to be hospitalized because Verna has badly struck her, and Roger and Verna will conveniently have Verna's apartment to themselves.

Roger is aware of the sordidness of the situation, but for him this very sordidness gives the experience a religious edge, and his description of the sexual act sums up the dialectical imagination. He makes it clear that this is a religious experience—an experience of the sacred, but only through its absence, through a dialectical immersion in the profane. Roger describes it this way:

> When I was spent and my niece released, we lay together on a hard floor of the spirit, partners in incest, adultery, and child abuse. We wanted to be rid of each other, to destroy the evidence, yet perversely clung, lovers, miles below the ceiling, our comfort being that we had no further to fall. Lying there with Verna, gazing upward, I saw how much majesty resides in our continuing to love and honor God even as He inflicts blows upon us—as much as resides in the silence He maintains so that we may enjoy and explore our human freedom. That was my proof of His existence, I saw—the distance to the impalpable ceiling, the immense distance measuring our abasement. So great a fall proves great heights. Sweet certainty invaded me. "Bless you" was all I could say (p. 302).

This key passage is not without metaphors and analogies: Roger describes relationship with God in terms of a fall, the distance from a ceiling, and so forth. But these are images and metaphors that dialectically unmake themselves, the kind described by John Calvin as dark, veiled, shadowy images that convey God's "incomprehensible essence" by restraining "the minds of all, like a bridle, from attempting to penetrate too deeply" (p. 102). Roger's images, like Calvin's, restrain rather than enlighten. The sacred, for Roger, is revealed only in its absence, only through a radical descent into the profane. The final "Bless you" is a shock, an absurd and unexplainable grace.

Andre Dubus's prose exemplifies the linguistic spareness of much American writing, and as such it has a severe, New England Puritan texture. But the devoutly Catholic Dubus embeds a sacramental spirituality in his fiction that makes it a fine model of the analogical imagination, a use of worldly images as epiphanies of an immanent spiritual presence. Catholic sacramentality is deeply embedded in Andre Dubus's religious imagination. If Protestant Christianity is one of Updike's most important personal and artistic formative influences, Roman Catholicism is equally important in Dubus's development as person and storyteller. Dubus's description of his own reception of the Eucharist is a good reflection on the way, in a sacrament, the transcendent is manifested through the fleshly and mundane:

> This morning I received the sacrament I still believe in: at seven-fifteen the priest elevated the host, then the chalice, and spoke the words of the ritual, and the bread became flesh, the wine became blood, and minutes later I placed on my tongue the taste of forgiveness and love that affirmed, perhaps celebrated, my being alive, my being mortal. This has nothing to do with immortality, with eternity; I love the earth too much to contemplate a life apart from it, although I believe in that life. No, this has to do with mortality and the touch of flesh. . . . (*Broken Vessels*, p. 77).

Dubus here precisely captures the sacramental, analogical imagination as I have been describing it in these pages: a graciousness (forgiveness and love) is experienced through concrete details (host, chalice, words, bread, flesh, wine, blood, tongue, the earth) in a specific, worldly time and place (this morning at 7:15). Dubus's best-known work is perhaps his novella *Voices from the Moon*, which ends with a scene that effectively embodies such an analogical, sacramental imagination.

Dubus's novella is, in many ways, similar to rather than different from John Updike's *Roger's Version*. Both works have a realistic narrative texture and are set in middle-class, suburban New England; both deal with troubled families who engage in seedy (even incestuous) sexual activities; both explicitly grapple with religious issues. But where *Roger's Version* tends to wrench apart the sordid human from the transcendent divine, the movement of *Voices from the Moon* is toward an integration of these realities: the novel depicts a young protagonist, Richie Stowe, who is learning to join together God, self, and world. It is this ultimate *joining together* that makes the book's vision essentially analogical. What Richie learns is how God and God's love are *like* worldly realities and human love.

Richie is a twelve-year-old Catholic boy who intends to become a priest. He feels that this will be difficult, though, because his family is hardly supportive. They are entangled in all sorts of familial and sexual problems, and Richie fears that he himself has inherited the twisted family *eros*—a "feeling that usually he associated with temptation, with sin, with turning away from Christ" (p. 8). Trying to guard his own chastity, Richie attempts to stay away from Melissa, a rather tough, slightly older, cigarette-smoking girl whom he finds very attractive. He thinks, rather prudishly, that he should love others only coolly, from a distance, "and he could do that only with Christ, and to receive Christ he could not love Melissa. He knew that from her scents this morning, and her voice, and her kiss" (p. 92).

The book ends, however, with a gently erotic scene between Richie and Melissa. Through this innocent encounter with Melissa, Richie experiences

God—not as a fierce, distant judge (as Roger does with Verna) but as something close, analogous to Melissa herself.

The scene is tender, with a touch of comically melodramatic eroticism:
"He was watching her mouth, and he swallowed, and knew he was lost. If
only he could be lost without fear" (p. 357). Richie, very aware of the way
his feelings are tugging him, looks to the transcendent stars, hoping they will
dialectically negate this fleshly experience—although he already suspects
that the stars may *side with* this experience: "If only he could look to the
stars—and he did: abruptly lifted his face to the sky—and find in them
release from what he felt now, or release to feel it" (p. 357).

All that actually happens between Richie and Melissa is that they hold
hands and have a conversation: "He watched the stars, and talked" (358). But
there is now no gap between the mundane and the cosmic—talking and
watching the stars are not in opposition. The entire ambience is one in which
everything is linked: Richie, Melissa, the night air, the grass, the stars, God;
eros, agape. This may mark the beginning of the end of Richie's journey
toward the seminary, but it is not an unreligious moment:

> What he felt was the night air starting to cool, and the dew on
> the grass under his hand holding Melissa's, and under his arms
> and head and shirt, and only its coolness touching his thick
> jeans, and the heels of his shoes. He felt Melissa's hand in his,
> and the beating of his heart she both quickened and soothed,
> and he smelled the length of her beside him, and heard in the
> trees the song of cicadas like the distant ringing of a thousand
> tambourines. He saw in the stars the eyes of God too, and was
> grateful for them, as he was for the night and the girl he loved.
> He lay on the grass and the soft summer earth, holding
> Melissa's hand, and talking to the stars (p. 358).

Dubus does not achieve this analogical connectedness in an easy, senti-
mental way. The Stowe family *eros,* of which Richie is awakening to traces,
is very dark indeed; Richie's brother, Larry, in reflecting on sordid sexual
games that he and his ex-wife, Brenda, used to play, remembers them as a
kind of addiction, a proof that humans cannot avoid willing the bad: "[I]t
was . . . [Brenda] who said finally: *There's something dark in us, something
evil, and it has to be removed, and he told her, We can just stop then; we
won't even talk about it again, not ever, it'll be something we did one year*"
(p. 320). There is, in other words, a dark side to the human (and erotic)
nature that Richie is being initiated into, one that is profoundly separate
from—and self-consciously aware of its absence from—the ordered and the
decent. Human nature is hardly ideal in this novel; the closest thing to a
"moral" the book has is Larry and Richie's mother's quiet oracular statement to Larry: "We don't have to live great lives, we just have to understand
and survive the ones we've got" (p. 355). But despite this revelation of the
limit to human greatness, an underlying graciousness also reveals itself. As
John Updike puts it in his review of *Voices from the Moon,* appropriately

entitled "Ungreat Lives": "The family and those intimate connections that make families are felt by this author as sharing the importance of our souls, and our homely, awkward movements of familial adjustment and forgiveness as being natural extensions of what Pascal called 'the motions of Grace'" (97). This is the analogical imagination: a vision of the homely and awkward as sacrament, a natural extension of grace. Over the course of *Voices from the Moon,* Richie finds—and the book as a whole affirms—that *eros* is more like *agape* than it sometimes seems to be, and that talking to a girlfriend is like talking to the stars.

I hope I haven't sided too heavy-handedly with the analogical imagination and against the dialectical. The fact is, I find *Twin Peaks* more stimulating than *Columbo*; the two imaginations need each other to create a vision that is sharp, rich, and whole. Tracy himself claims that the analogical imagination needs to be supplemented by the dialectical lest it become vacuous: "Where analogical theologies lose that sense for the negative, that dialectical sense within analogy itself, they produce not a believable harmony among various likenesses in all reality but the theological equivalent of 'cheap grace': boredom, sterility and an atheological vision of a deadening univocity" (*Analogical Imagination*, p. 413). Hence, it is good that the *Twin Peaks* imagination is still very much alive in modern fiction. The avant-garde Thomas Pynchon, who strips away image and metaphor to expose underlying absence, is in the American dialectical tradition, as are such fine writers as Joseph Heller, Don DeLillo, and John Updike, as well as such young chroniclers of urban and suburban *angst* as Douglas Coupland (*Generation X*).

But surprisingly, just when contemporary literary theory seems to have embraced absence, a postmodernist rejection of any real presence or center or ground, many modern and contemporary fiction writers seem to be discovering sacramental spiritual presence. The quintessential modern analogical novelist is, I think, James Joyce, who is able to make the most secular of moments (what could be more seemingly profane than Stephen Dedalus and Leopold Bloom's outdoor pee at the end of *Ulysses*?) epiphanic revelations of the gracious limit-of grounding all reality. Such Catholic writers as Graham Greene, Muriel Spark, and Mary Gordon—but also writers from other traditions (notably Toni Morrison, Alice Walker, Anne Tyler, and plenty of others)—crack open the material surface of things to reveal a kind of sacramental radiance that bubbles up, in Gerard Manley Hopkins' words, "like the ooze of oil / Crushed" ("God's Grandeur"). Maybe it is not really surprising that such a literary imagination keeps reemerging; as my theologian friend might point out, *Columbo* may lack the fierce intensity of *Twin Peaks,* but it has lasted on television a lot longer.

Works Cited

Barth, Karl. *The Epistle to the Romans.* Edwyn C. Hoskins, trans. London: Oxford University Press, 1933.

Calvin, John. *Institutes of the Christian Religion,* Volume 1. Ford Lewis Battles, trans. Philadelphia: Westminster Press, 1960.

Dubus, Andre. *Broken Vessels*. Boston: Godine, 1991.

_____.*Voices from the Moon*. In *Selected Stories*. Andre Dubus. New York: Vintage, 1989.

Greeley, Andrew M. "The Catholic Imagination and the Catholic University." *America,* 16 March 1991: 285–288.

_____.*The Catholic Myth: The Behavior and Beliefs of American Catholics*. New York: Macmillan, 1990.

Hart, Kevin. *The Trespass of the Sign: Deconstruction, Theology, and Philosophy.* Cambridge, New York, Cambridge, 1989.

Lakeland, Paul. *Postmodernity: Christian Identity in a Fragmented Age*. Minneapolis, MN: Fortress, 1997.

Luther, Martin. "Heidelberg Disputation." Harold J. Grimm, trans. In *Career of the Reformer*, Volume 1. Harold J. Grimm, ed. Philadelphia: Huhlenberg Press, 1957.

McFague, Sallie. *Models of God: Theology for an Ecological, Nuclear Age.* Philadelphia: Fortress Press, 1987.

New Revised Standard Version of the Bible, copyright 1989 by the Division of Christian Education of the National Council of the Churches of Christ in the USA. Used by permission. All rights reserved.

Rahner, Karl. *Foundations of Christian Faith: An Introduction to the Idea of Christianity*. William V. Dych, trans. New York: Seabury, 1978.

Raschke, Carl A. "The Deconstruction of God." In *Deconstruction and Theology.* Thomas J. J. Altizer et al. New York: Crossroad, 1983.

Tracy, David. *The Analogical Imagination: Christian Theology and the Culture of Pluralism*. New York: Crossroad, 1981.

_____.*Blessed Rage for Order: The New Pluralism in Theology*. New York: Seabury Press, 1975.

Tracy, David. *Plurality and Ambiguity: Hermeneutics Religion, Hope*. San Francisco, Harper & Row, 1987.

Updike, John. "A Disconcerting Thing." *America.* 4 October 1997: 8–9.

_____.*Roger's Version*. 1986; New York: Fawcett Crest, 1987.

_____."Ungreat Lives." *New Yorker,* 4 February 1985: 94–101.

A fuller treatment of the material discussed in this essay can be found in John Neary, *Like and Unlike God: Religious Imaginations in Modern and Contemporary Fiction* (Scholars Press, 1999).

10

Walking with Jesus in Our Everyday Lives: The Role of Christian Faith in Teaching

Diana Hayes

Introduction

I have deliberately grounded this paper in the reality of the U.S. as it is today, an increasingly secularized nation which has enabled, in Stephen Carter's words, a "culture of disbelief" to come into existence, a culture where religious debate, discourse, and even faith—except in its most radical or regimented forms—is too often relegated to the sidelines of everyday life. Carter asserts that the U.S. has become a nation where:

> On the one hand, American ideology cherishes religions, as it
> does all matters of private conscience . . . At the same time,
> many political leaders, commentators, scholars, and others are
> coming to view any religious element in public moral discourse
> as a tool of the radical right for reshaping American society.[1]

Carter calls us to acknowledge that in many ways, as intellectuals, we have failed to engage all of the publics, whether academic, political, legal, or social, with which we, as scholars, should have an ongoing dialogue. The most critical of these, he asserts, is the dialogue between the world of academia and that of politics, a dialogue that should emerge from and be affected by moral values arising from the faith of those engaged in the dialogue. In our sensible zeal to keep religion from dominating our politics, we have created a political and legal culture that presses the religiously faithful to be other than themselves, to act publicly, and sometimes privately as well, as though their faith does not matter to them.[2]

As a lawyer who is also a man of faith comfortable with discussing and writing about those values integral to our way of life, Carter is concerned about the wall that has been erected between church and state in the United States to such an extent that any efforts to bring a religious perspective into political discourse are seen as constitutionally invalid. This is a misreading of the antiestablishment clause of the Bill of Rights which forbids the establishment of any particular religion as the official religion of the nation but says nothing about precluding dialogue between the two or among its citizens who are both politically and religiously minded.

The result, increasingly, is a religious vacuum in political offices in which the voices of religious intellectuals—or, put another way, of scholars who are also people of faith—are infrequently heard and too often dismissed as forms of irrational or illogical speech. Their credibility is questioned, and sometimes their sanity, because of what is publicly seen as their belief in the irrational, namely in God and the Son of God, Jesus Christ, and their willingness to act on that belief. In secular universities, especially those under state funding, a similar vacuum exists, as fear of overstepping the boundaries requires that the study of religion(s) takes place only from an objective, detached stance and that same detachment governs the discussion of moral virtues and values that may have a religious undertone. Thus, ethical discourse on issues such as abortion, euthanasia, human sexuality, genetic experimentation, drug use and abuse, war, etc. are robbed of a particular and significant context when all arguments, for or against, can be used except those that are religiously grounded.

Catholic intellectuals especially often have their credentials and credibility questioned because of the prevalent movement to the "right" of the institutional Church and the still persistent belief by many that Roman Catholics lack the right or the ability to think for themselves. To many, the return to what is seen as a "legalistic, authoritative" form of pronouncing edicts and condemnations, which has emerged in the past twenty years, is stifling in many ways what had been a growing openness to dialogue, both ecumenical and internal. Whereas the U.S. Catholic bishops' pastoral letters on peace and on the economy were models of consultation, reason, maturity, and moderation, raising political discourse to a higher moral place, today we are left with politicians' sound bites.

It is both tragic and paradoxical that now, just as the nation is beginning to invite people into the public square for the different points of view that they have to offer, people whose contributions to the nation's diversity come from their religious traditions are not valued unless their voices are somehow esoteric.[3] As a consequence, the vacuum is increasingly being filled by those with a more rigidly doctrinal religious perspective that often *does* violate the constitutionally mandated separation of church and state. In their religious fervor, they seek to coerce the entire nation, regardless of individual creeds, political views, or cultural differences, into an acknowledgment that their way is the only legitimate one, their truth the only truth, thereby stifling dialogue at all levels. David Tracy has also treated this issue of public and private spheres of accountability for intellectual life. He raises the following question: "In a culture of pluralism must each religious tradition finally either dissolve into some lowest common denominator or accept a marginal existence as one interesting but purely private option?"[4] Tracy's response is that neither role is satisfactory, especially for anyone "seriously committed to the truth of any major religious tradition. The need [he concludes] is to form a new and inevitably complex theological strategy that will avoid privatism by articulating the genuine claims of religion to truth."[5]

Carter's work, written more than a decade later, implies that this strategy, as yet, has not been completely successful. The question we must therefore address is: Why has it not been successful? What has occurred in our nation and the world that has led to the relegation of religion and its values to the sidelines of public discourse at almost every level in society today?

We are one of the most religious nations on the earth, in the sense that we have a deeply religious citizenry; but we are also perhaps the most zealous in guarding our public institutions against explicit religious influences. One result is that we often ask our citizens to split their public and private selves, telling them in effect that it is fine to be religious in private, but there is something askew when their private beliefs become the basis for public action.[6]

Again, why is this so? My response is that, as Christians and especially as Catholic Christians, we no longer feel comfortable in articulating our faith in a public way. In other words, we no longer have a sacramental, incarnational worldview in which God, especially in the person of Jesus Christ, is seen as active in all things, in, by, and through us all, and bringing all to Him. Thus, our praxis—that is, our reflection on and our action emerging from that reflection in the world—has become absented in many ways from the world. We have become dualistic—perhaps schizophrenic would be a better term—dividing and separating our life of the intellect, especially when it engages in questions of moral values, from our participation in the pluralistic society which is the U.S. We have also become an increasingly individualistic and materialistic society in which decisions are made based solely on their impact on or benefit to us as individuals and those with whom we most closely identify. The needs and/or concerns of others are of little or no importance.

In order to participate in such a society, arguments and critiques that are religiously based are required to be "restated in other terms," thereby forcing one to bracket one's "religious convictions from the rest of [one's] personality, essentially demanding that [one] split off a part of [one's very] self."[7] As legal theorist Walter Perry notes: "to bracket them [one's religiously based assertions, that is] would be to bracket—indeed, to annihilate—herself. And doing that would preclude *her*—the particular person she is—from engaging in moral discourse with other members of society."[8]

Once again we are caught in paradox. As intellectuals, whether social, political, or religious, it is incumbent upon us to recognize that we *do* have public responsibilities to engage in genuinely public discourse for the society as a whole. This, above all else, should be the mandate for our life and work in guiding our students to develop critical minds capable of reflecting upon, analyzing, and questioning the world around them. That analysis, reflection, and questioning should have a moral grounding which, for Catholic professionals, can be found in the mission and ministry of Jesus the Christ. Our failure or hesitance to do so has consequences, as I've already shown. If humanists, Tracy notes, "including theologians in the realm of culture, continue to accept their marginalized status, then the alternatives are the short-run enhancement of self-fulfillment and the long-term despair of societal value bankruptcy."[9]

Today we must ask ourselves as Catholic scholars, whether on religious or secular campuses, what is the place of our faith as Catholic Christians in our everyday lives and in our lives of teaching and scholarship? Who is Jesus the Christ for us? What is his significance and why? How can we incorporate our understanding of Jesus' mission and ministry into our teaching in a way that does not threaten those who are non-Christian or nonreligious but does allow us to speak of the "hope that lies within us?" (cf. 1 Peter 3:15).

This article is an effort to show that we can do this because, as Catholic teachers and scholars whose faith, hopefully, is inseparable from our identity, we must participate in the public debates regarding value and moral systems that are taking place throughout the U.S. today. To fail to do so would be to fail ourselves, our students, and most of all, the very faith we claim to have. These debates are taking place at different levels of our society, in government and business circles, in religious circles and in academia. In a sense, our participation will simply live up to our nation's historical understanding of what a university or college should be: a place where new ideas are discussed and old ones challenged; where issues that will have an impact, both inside and outside of the university, are debated on as if they matter, which they do; and where the minds and hearts of our students and ourselves become fully engaged. To do this also means bringing our students, in whatever field of study they are, to the awareness that with higher education comes privilege, yes, but also responsibility: to be available for and to others unlike themselves and to become comfortable in dialoguing with them.

For just as the face of the Catholic Church in the United States and, in actuality, throughout the world, is changing, reflecting the growing presence of the formerly colonized and enslaved, so are our nation's institutions of higher learning, Catholic as well as secular, changing as young persons of color seek to take advantage of the doors and opportunities open to them to gain a higher education and therefore the hope of greater success in the world outside our gates. Therefore, in discussing the meaning of Jesus' mission and ministry in our lives today, we must be aware of the changing contexts in which and with which we find ourselves in dialogue. What does Jesus have to say, not only to us as academicians but to our students, many of whom are relatively new to the halls of academe but have rich, ancient, and diverse roots in the Catholic faith?[10] What role does our understanding of Jesus, as man and incarnate God, have in enabling us to be more assured in our faith and its moral values without falling into a form of proselytization and narrow parochialism?

The Jesus of History

What do we know of the man Jesus? Actually, very little. It is said that he was born during the time of Caesar Augustus when Israel was under the control of the Roman Empire. He was raised in a small, insignificant village by a young woman with an older husband, as was often the case then. He grew up, learned the trade of his father, carpentry, until suddenly around the age of thirty, he left his village, Nazareth of Galilee, and began the life of an itinerant preacher and teacher, gathering followers, both male and female, and, it was claimed, performing miraculous acts of healing while teaching a new message of love, love of God and neighbor. As his following grew, those in positions of authority, both Roman and Jewish, as often happens, felt threatened, and sought to put a stop to his preaching. He was therefore arrested and executed by crucifixion, a death usually reserved to common criminals. His ministry lasted only three short years, yet the result was a global religion that, almost two thousand years later, reveres this humble preacher/teacher as the Son of God, God made flesh.

What was so significant about the life of this man that his memory is revered to this day even though his death, at the time, was little noted? What was the message that he taught that so transformed the world? Jesus' first sermon, given in his small village, was brief and simple. As we read in the Gospel of Luke, he first read the words of the prophet Isaiah from the Torah scroll:

> The Spirit of the Lord is upon me,
>> because he has anointed me
>>> to bring good news to the poor.
> He has sent me to proclaim release to the captives
>> and recovery of sight to the blind,
> to let the oppressed go free,
>> to proclaim the year of the Lord's favor (4:18).

He then returned to his seat in the synagogue and quietly stated: "Today this scripture has been fulfilled in your hearing" (4:21). Most were amazed at the apparent wisdom of the carpenter's son but were soon angered by his ensuing words that questioned their acceptance of him as a rabbi (teacher) and predicted their inability to accept him as a prophetic teacher. Confirming his prediction, they attempted to kill him but were unsuccessful.

What was significant about these words, both then and now? Jesus, in their presence, proclaimed himself a prophet of God, one who would not be welcomed in his own village and whose words of wisdom would be rejected, as they were. But more importantly, he called their attention to a renewed understanding of God's law. Throughout the Old Testament (the Hebrew Scriptures), we read of God's constant reminder to God's people that their God is a God of justice and righteousness. God rejects the burnt offerings of the people and requires only that they "do justice, and . . . love kindness, and . . . walk humbly with your God" (Micah 6:8).

The people of Israel, although they were under the thumb of Rome, had yet grown complacent and comfortable. They no longer paid full attention to the demands God had placed upon them as part of their covenant agreement, but were seen to have acquiesced—especially those in positions of power and authority, the scribes and Pharisees and the members of the Sanhedrin (the Council)—to the demands of Rome. Those who were poor were neglected; their needs ignored. Many had lost their lands and property but could look to no one for redress. The Temple Courts were filled with moneylenders, places of greed and profit rather than veneration of the one God.

Jesus was, like the prophets of old, bringing God's message warning God's people that they were straying from the path they, in covenant with God, had agreed to walk. The times were difficult, yes; false prophets and messiahs could be found preaching everywhere, but this man was Jesus. He asked nothing for himself; he sought no payment for his healing touch and challenging words. He simply sought a renewal of faith, a conversion of the hearts and minds of those who listened to him. As he affirmed, he did not come to change the laws by which the Jews had lived for so long but to give them new and vigorous life. This man Jesus appealed to the common folk rather than the learned or wealthy. He was born poor like them and lived the life of an itinerant, never knowing where he would lay his head at night or what food there would be for his table.

As Christians, we are called to imitate the life of Christ; we are called to follow his path of perfection. Yet, at the same time, it is recognized that we will never be fully able to become perfect because, unlike Jesus who was the Son of God, we are very much human, weighted with the frailties of finite life. The command, however, is still the same: "to be perfect as your heavenly father is perfect" (Matthew 5:48). And Jesus tells us how this is possible by giving us the Great Commandment, the one that shapes and affects the whole of our lives: "Love God and your neighbor as yourself" (see Mark 12:28–31).

Such a command may seem, on the one hand, quite simple, but this commandment overrides all others. To love God, we must find ourselves in union with God, in harmony with God's laws, in love, with all our heart, mind, and soul, with God. Many of us feel we have that stance perfected. We speak of a one-on-one relationship with God; a personal relationship with God that guides and nurtures us. But is that really true? As affirmed in the First Letter of John, how can we claim to love God while we hate one another (see 21–22)? We do not know God. God is mystery in its deepest sense. Yet, we know our neighbors, or should. But we find it so much easier to speak of our love for this God, whom we can't see, while failing to love those who live around us everyday. We hate them because of their skin color, their religion or faith, their gender or sexual orientation, and/or their economic status, because it is greater or less than ours. We argue with our colleagues, disagree with our administrators, are envious of those who win fellowships or publish books that we feel we should have won or published. We are frustrated, angry, and confused and, too often, we look to God, not for guidance or assistance, but for affirmation of our exalted or injured sense of self.

There is a popular saying today that can be found on clothing, bracelets, and necklaces: "WWJD"—What would Jesus do? What would Jesus do when confronted with disrespectful students who don't want to learn but want to graduate with high-paying jobs awaiting them, who want to know only the minimum necessary for them to get a good grade without too much effort on their parts? What would Jesus do about colleagues who have grown complacent in their tenured positions and teach the same material year after year to the boredom and frustration of their students? What would Jesus do about administrators who are more concerned about the bottom line in their budgets than the need for the expansion of the library, the technological advances that are taking place, or simply the need of their faculty for a decent living in order to pay back their own educational loans and adequately support a family? What would Jesus do about the state legislators and members of Congress who seem less concerned about the quality of education provided at a particular institution than they are about who is teaching what and which students are being provided financial opportunities withheld for decades. What would Jesus do?

We don't really know. The times in which Jesus lived are vastly different from contemporary times. But we have been given his words in sacred Scripture and the teachings handed down through our Catholic tradition to guide us on our journey. Jesus spoke of the coming Kingdom of God where all would be at peace, but the Church had to develop an ongoing understanding of that kingdom so that in the years until it came people could prepare themselves.

We are the Church, the People of God in its fullest understanding. Through our baptism in Christ, we have been commissioned to serve as God's ministers in whatever walk of life we find ourselves. That ministry and its corresponding mission also involve a responsibility to discern the signs of the times for our generation and to act in accordance with those signs for the benefit of ourselves and our students. It also requires us to be open to being ministered to by others, including our students, because we do not know when or from whom we will see the face of Jesus shining forth.

As teachers, we have the privilege, although it may not always seem so, of preparing for our nation's future by preparing the leaders of that future. We do this through the young people with whom we come into contact and whom we seek to influence in ways that will be beneficial not just for them as individuals but for all of us. We have the responsibility of passing on knowledge to our students in ways that will enable them to develop and lead moral and responsible lives. That knowledge should not and cannot be limited simply to facts, statistics, dates, and formulas, but must also provide our students with a foundation upon which they can build and develop moral lives that will be of value to the nation as a whole. We are following directly in the footsteps of Jesus when we do so, guiding and providing our students with what they need in order to live lives of justice, kindness, and righteousness, as Micah stated. This is our responsibility, whether we teach in the field of science, the humanities, business, law, medicine, or any other field.

But how do we do this? This is the more difficult question to answer.

The Christ of Faith

In order to live out our faith in the various publics in which we find ourselves engaged, whether as professors, parents, spouses, and/or friends and neighbors, we need an understanding of that faith that goes beyond the religious instruction we received while in elementary or high school. An eighth grade education is adequate for eighth graders but not for assumedly mature adults who are responsible for making decisions that can impact, positively or negatively, on the lives of those around us, whether we acknowledge their presence and humanity or not.

An adult understanding of Jesus Christ and the significance of his life, death, and resurrection provides a fuller foundation in our faith; one that challenges us to live out our lives in *imitatio Christ*, in imitation of Christ as personified particularly in the mission and ministry of Jesus. The history of the developing understanding of the role that sacraments play in the Catholic Church is one way in which to explore the significance of how we are called to participate in Jesus' life on earth.

Saint Thomas Aquinas was instrumental in making the critical link between Jesus and the Church as instruments of salvation for all. For Aquinas, the "sacraments incorporate the Christian into the body of Christ and confer the Spirit promised by the risen Christ . . . (They) are the sign of the Incarnate Word, his passion and resurrection which sanctifies the participant. God accomplishes this through the humanity of Jesus manifest in the sacramental sign itself."[11] With the shifts in understanding that took place with the Second Vatican Council and the accompanying liturgical renewal of that time period, a reconciliation of the Christian, especially his or her inner attitude, with the mystery of Christ as experienced in liturgy and sacraments took place. Christ is seen as the original sacrament, while the Church becomes the foundational sacrament of the seven ecclesial acts we recognize as sacraments: baptism, confirmation, Eucharist, reconciliation (or penance), anointing of the sick, marriage, and holy orders. The result is a shift in our understanding of Jesus as the Christ, the Savior, and of ourselves as participants in Jesus' ministry. Rather than an emphasis on the sacraments in and of themselves, this understanding emphasizes God's encounter with humanity as God's self-communication of self to finite humanity. Our response to that communication "signals a shift from emphasizing Christ's presence in the sacraments to the community's transformation through sacraments."[12] As a result, sacraments are no longer seen simply as things that act upon us, but as events that place a responsibility on the participant in the sacrament to a certain type of lifestyle afterwards. Thus, just as Jesus' new life of ministry was signaled by his baptism in the Jordan, our own baptism calls us into being as sharers in that same ministry.

This more holistic and communitarian understanding is in keeping with liberation theology's emphasis on humankind's engagement in sacraments as a challenge "to live the justice and peace of God's kingdom which is experienced in sacraments. The liberative power of sacraments is thus to be channeled into a way of living life that reveals the liberative power of the gospel of justice and peace."[13]

The Eucharist: Forming a Community that Acts

The sacrament of the Eucharist is itself an excellent way to explore more fully the significance of sacrament and how it enables us to have a sacramental worldview in which Jesus as both God and man enables and encourages our participation in the world around us.

In the Eucharist, we commemorate the life, death, and resurrection of Jesus the Christ; by our own participation in its celebration we are ourselves transformed through the grace of God, and in our coming together as a community, reflective of all the peoples of the world, we foretell the future not only of the world but of the end-time.

In the Constitution on the Liturgy of Vatican II, we read that "the sacramental worship of the Church is given a certain primacy over all the forms of Christian life."

> The Liturgy is the summit toward which the activity of the Church is directed; it is also the fountain from which all her power flows. For the goal of the apostolic works is that all who are made [children] of God by faith and baptism should come together to praise God in the midst of His Church, to take part in her sacrifice and to eat the Lord's supper (*Sacrosanctum concilium* n.10).

As Church, the People of God, we *are* a eucharistic community, one that gathers to live out again and again the sacrifice of Jesus Christ. It is most particularly in the celebration of the Eucharist that we become one—a people united by faith. This formation of community has accompanying responsibilities, however, for it is only in giving ourselves that we are able to receive the grace of the sacraments. It is only in modeling that future glory, not just during the celebration but when we go out from the church, back to our own life's duties, that we are truly Church, truly sacrament.

Theologian Avery Dulles speaks of the significance of viewing the Church and thereby the world as sacrament. He states:

> [Humanity] comes to [it]self by going out of [it]self. [It] becomes active only in reception, and receives only through encounter with the world . . . The body mediates that encounter. Without contact with the world through the body, the spirit simply would not actuate itself . . . The structure of human life is therefore symbolic. The body with all of its movements and gestures becomes the expression of the human spirit. The spirit comes to be what is in and through the body . . . the expression and the realization accompany and support each other . . . [14]

The celebration of the Eucharist goes beyond our own immediate experience to celebrate mystery by means of signs and symbols. While signs have conventional meanings that have been established by a particular community, symbols can be ambiguous, capable of multiple meanings and associations that emerge from a "given historical, cultural, ethnic, and social community. They can [then] assume levels of meaning that make sense of birth, life, and death—by means of tradition, community and grace." The greatest mystery of all is Jesus, God become human, human like us in all things but sin yet also God, the Savior of the world.

God's incarnation as Jesus reveals to us the significance of the changes taking place in the Church today, especially in terms of liturgical inculturation but also in how we see ourselves as Church and welcome those "others," historically marginalized, as neighbor in its fullest understanding. We are called to become familiar with the cultures and languages of those once marginalized, made voiceless and invisible in our Church and society. We must engage them in dialogue not only on the future of the Church but the future of our society as a morally grounded society for they are often the ones raising the most challenging questions today. They bring a communitarian understanding of life and faith which is sacramental in its fullest meaning as the entire world is seen as being impacted by God's guidance. In other words, without faith, there is no life. [Sacraments, therefore, can never be seen as] individual transactions. Nobody baptizes, absolves, anoints himself, and it is anomalous for the Eucharist to be celebrated in solitude. [We] come into the world as a member of a family, a race, a people. [We] come to maturity through encounter with our fellow men [and women]. Sacraments have a dialogic structure. They take place in a mutual interaction that permits the people together to achieve a spiritual breakthrough that they could not achieve in isolation. A sacrament is therefore a socially constructed or communal symbol of the presence of grace coming to fulfillment.[15]

And it is in that coming together as human beings "bound together in grace by a visible expression" that the Church, *as sacrament* becomes itself an actual act of grace. But "sacramentality by its very nature calls for active participation."[16] Thus:

> . . . only those who belong . . . and actively help to constitute (the Church) as a sign share fully in its reality as a sacrament. The actions by which they help the Church achieve itself as a visible, social embodiment of God's grace in Christ are the means by which their own spiritual life is sustained, intensified, and channeled in constructive ways.[17]

It is in the going out of ourselves, the giving of ourselves, to and for others, that we, in turn, truly become sacramental beings—vehicles of grace. It is in teaching, guiding, mentoring, nurturing, consoling, healing, and shaping the hearts and minds of those with whom we come in contact—whether on a daily basis or just once in our lives, whether with our colleagues, students, or the greater society around us—that we become most fully human. And it is only then that we truly participate fully in the mission and ministry of Jesus, individually and as a body that makes up the Church. Karl Rahner notes that "the sacraments must not merely be considered as actions of the Church in view of individual members. They must also be considered as means by which the Church *in* its members (and its members through the Church) lives and acts in . . . response toward God."[18]

Participation in the sacraments thus calls for a response by those participating, both as individuals and in community, as the people of God who make up the Body of Christ, the Church. We are called and commissioned through our baptism to proclaim the Good News to all with whom we come in contact, to attempt in our daily lives, whether at home, in the classroom, or other places of work, to witness to our faith in Jesus Christ and to so live out our lives that we model Christ's life as best we can. Otherwise, by participating in the sacraments—especially the Eucharist, the sign of our union with God and each other which erases all humanly conceived obstacles and boundaries in our lives—without living our lives in accord with that union, we are living a lie.

An Incarnational, Sacramental Worldview

This incarnational, sacramental way of being in the world is one that requires the Church, in its members today, to live in recognition of the newly emerging world.

The Church must experience and express itself through the cultural riches not only of Western peoples. For these are the "tribes and tongues and peoples and nations" mentioned frequently in the Bible, to whom the Church is divinely sent, for whom the Church exists, and from whom the Church is called into historically tangible existence.[19] The Church, therefore, must incarnate itself in every culture in the same way that Jesus was himself incarnated in the Jewish culture. This will necessitate a shift in our societal, ecclesial, and academic discourse to make it more reflective of the catholicity of our faith. Yet, we must also be aware that such a shift is out of sync with the current political and religious temperament of our nation today which rejects intellectuals as well as intellectual discourse, especially if it is religiously based, and which denies, for the most part, intellectual capabilities to women, blacks, Latinos/as, and any and all others who do not fit their narrow self-definition. We cannot allow the discourse to be sidetracked, however. As David Tracy affirms:

> . . . any major religious tradition does disclose in its symbols
> and in its reflections upon those symbols (i.e., its theologies)
> some fundamental vision of the meaning of individual and
> communal existence providing disclosive and transformative
> possibilities for the whole society. Both ethos and worldview
> are disclosed in any religion. One need not minimize the need
> for reasoned public discourse upon all claims to truth in order
> to recognize the indispensable role that cultural symbols,
> including the religious, can play in the wider society.

This remains especially true of a society like our own, characterized in fact by cultural pluralism and committed in principle to a democratic polity. Where art is marginalized, religion is privatized. Indeed, religion suffers even greater losses than art by being the single subject about which more intellectuals can feel free to be against. Often abetted by the churches, they need not study religion, for everybody already knows what religion is: it is a private consumer product that some people seem to need.[20]

What is lacking, I believe, is a dialogue, not necessarily along the lines of specific religious faith but one in keeping with the realization that "human beings have a deep need to have their lives make sense, to transcend the dynamics of individualism and selfishness that predominate in a competitive market society and to find a way to place their lives in a context of meaning and purpose."[21] Our God-talk today, however, is too often confused with the "bully" pulpits of those who, without any clear-cut counterresponse from other people of faith act and speak as if the have a monopoly on both God and God's concerns in the world. Yet, a sacramental, incarnational worldview that focuses on the significance of Jesus' mission and ministry to bring all to God denies this. A dualistic worldview that divides the sacred and the secular, denying the significance of the world's reality for a spiritual understanding that uplifts some while condemning the great majority, is inherently invalid for it divides the Body of Christ itself. Salvation history reveals a God active in history on the side of the "least among us" while offering redemption to all irrespective of race, class, ethnicity, gender, or political persuasion. For Rahner, God communicates God's self to humanity through Jesus Christ, God Incarnate: "by virtue of the Holy Spirit as the divine personal bond who dwells in Jesus Christ in divine fullness . . . The Spirit . . . is present . . . efficaciously, perpetually poured out by God on mankind and the world.[22]

All Christians have a responsibility, in keeping with their creation and redemption by God and their participation in the building up of the Body of Christ, the Church, to be open to the working of the Spirit in and through them for the transformation of the world. We are thus challenged by our participation in the sacraments not just to celebrate our individual union with God. We celebrate God's actions that make disparate individuals into a community that gathers to celebrate, give thanks, and live out the mandate of their calling.

If we continue to assume the value of reasoned public discourse in a critical and argued fashion, if we continue to affirm the related values for a democratic polity, then the discussion of these conflicts cannot be left to either a technological and bureaucratic elite nor to the happenstance of special-interest groups.[23] The Rev. Dr. Martin Luther King, Jr., recognized this mandate and attempted to live it out in his day in an effort to follow Christ. For King, the early church of the first century was the type of church needed today. The early Christians modeled a sacramental worldview in their lives and martyrdoms. King notes that the early church was:

> . . . not merely a thermometer that recorded the ideas and principles of popular opinion, it was a thermostat that transformed the mores of society. . . . Whenever the early Christians entered

> a town the power structure got disturbed and immediately sought to convict them for being "disturbers of the peace" and "outside agitators." But they went on with the conviction that they were a "colony of heaven" and had to obey God rather than man. They were small in number but big in commitment. They were too God-intoxicated to be astronomically intimidated.[24]

What must it feel like to be so drunk with the love of God that you care not for the consequences of your actions: arrest, jail, perhaps loss of position, of tenure, or even silencing by the very Church on whose behalf you believed you were speaking? This was Jesus' own experience and it led to his death.

Indeed, the penalties for stepping out on faith can be severe but perhaps not as final as in his time. Yet, if we understand "religion as (an) independent moral force" that acts, correctly, to subvert a society that dehumanizes, impoverishes, and alienates a great many of its citizens, then we are left with few alternatives but to act as if our lives and the lives of others truly mattered to us.

What Would Jesus Do?

A sacramental, incarnational worldview, one in which the subversive memory of Jesus is actively present, guiding us in all that we do, does not permit us to turn our backs on the needs and concerns of others, nor to live our lives as if our faith does not matter. If we as Christians are to resurrect the positive aspects of such a worldview while avoiding the narcissistic aestheticism it can fall captive to, we must seek to connect all things and all peoples with God, for only then can we cease to participate in activities that make our fellow human beings things to be ignored, silenced, manipulated, used up, and destroyed. For it must be acknowledged that:

> We, as a nation, are now more than ever possessed by our own possessions. Wisdom leads the list of casualties in a conflict of values where greed, promoted by the popular culture, is on the rise, and sacrifice, proclaimed as a value by the Catholic tradition, is on the decline.[25]

There is little or no time today for students or their teachers to cultivate the values of the mind, to spend time in reflection, to work toward gaining insight, or to journey after wisdom. Rather, we find ourselves on a daily round of often meaningless tasks and errands that take us further from our ties to a sacramental life, reducing us to cogs in a manic ever-spinning wheel of production.

We have to fight against these dehumanizing trends prevalent in modern society and, instead, call for the sacramental tradition of our faith, bringing that understanding to bear at every level of daily life—and most especially in the halls of academe. Our students must be empowered to learn for the pure joy of learning, as well as for their own benefit and the good of others, rather than only for grades and better options for graduate school.

Recognizing our co-createdness by a God who loved us into life and wishes only our good, we can't afford the illogical ideologies that set us against each other on issues of race, gender, and class. We cannot continue refusing to acknowledge those unlike us perhaps in skin color, culture, or language but who share our Catholic and Christian faith. We cannot look away from the abuse and maltreatment of women, children, and the elderly, especially those who are poor, in a society in which poverty is once again being seen as a judgment by God rather than the result of a cynical and selfish callousness found in all areas of public and private life. Nor can we continue to allow our students to grow to supposed maturity ignorant of the peoples and nations who make up this nation and contributed to its success.

As Christian intellectuals, we cannot act in this way. It is a denial of the very ground of our faith and a failure to live out our mission in Christ. We must recognize that we who engage in reflection (which should resolve itself in action) on issues pertaining to the meaning of human events and the interpretation of human experience cannot afford the luxury of objectivity. It is neither a value nor is it truly viable. We all participate in discussion, dialogue, and debate from particular cultural stances developed over a lifetime. Those who claim objectivity when talking about the powerful realities of today's world should be immediately suspect, because it is impossible for us as finite human beings to live apart from this world, untouched and uninfluenced by it. Books, journals, and newspapers that we've read, conversations we've overheard or engaged in, films and/or television programs we've watched, family and social events, and our faith itself have all had a hand in shaping us into the persons we are today.

For myself, as a lay black female Catholic theologian in the early years of this new century, I find that I cannot be dispassionate and impartial. I cannot because what is happening in this world affects me, either positively or negatively. I am not free to deny my identity—my skin color and texture of my hair will not allow me to. However, this does not mean I wallow in despair or am uncritically biased. Being subjective—being aware, that is, of one's subjectivity, rather than forcing an impossible objectivity—is, in many ways, freeing. Having acknowledged my context, I can then critically analyze it and that of others, recognizing that there are overlaps but also disparities. My subjectivity challenges me to be open to and respectful of the perspectives of others, even though I may disagree with them and intend to bring all of my intellectual capabilities to bear to help them see my reason, while respecting their right to do the same. It forces me to participate in the public discussions taking place which affect the very nature of who we are as a Church and a nation today.

Because this is what Jesus did. He did not stand aside and watch passively as life went by him. Rather, he urged his fellow Jews to respond to the presence of the kingdom within their midst if they could but believe and act on that belief. Jesus is, for us, the sign that points to that sacred presence in the world, both then and now. He is the sacrament of God, freely given, whose death saved us all and transformed our world and whose mission and ministry to all of God's people now becomes our responsibility.

A Faith of Praxis

Let me be more specific. Certainly, if you are a professor or administrator at a Catholic college or university or at an institution of higher learning that is religiously based, your situation is quite different from that of someone at a secular or state-funded institution. In the latter two, especially, the wall of separation can be almost impenetrable for someone seeking to work within their faith-context. Departments of religion or religious studies exist and, often, the objective is to study religions of all kinds in the way one would study any other academic subject: objectively examining the attributes, teachings, and practices without placing any type of value judgment on any of them.

There are difficulties in all of these situations, however. For example, a Catholic theologian on a Catholic campus should, realistically, have few problems with expressing his or her own religious perspective in or out of class. The reality, of course, is that that is not always the case as Catholic schools become more pluralistically as well as racially and ethnically diverse and "touchy" issues therefore arise. How does one discuss the current situation in the Middle East in a classroom of not only Christians from every church but Muslims, Jews, and others—as well as atheists and agnostics? How does one discuss the recent and ongoing events in the Balkans where not only Christians and Muslims have been at war with each other but so, too, have Roman Catholics and Orthodox Christians? How do you walk the tightrope of presenting issues clearly and allowing your students the freedom to discuss and debate from their perspective, while allowing yourself the same freedom? It can be done but it must be done honestly, openly, and with a painstaking regard for the concerns of others who disagree or agree with you and one another. Whether a theologian or a professor of history, biology, languages, or sociology, one can bring one's own faith into the dialogue and encourage one's students to do likewise by critically exploring the subjective aspects of a particular field that enables the sharing of experiences, cultural perspectives, and attitudes and their impact, both positive and/or negative, conscious and/or unconscious on the discussion.

An equally difficult situation arises when a professor has a more progressive or conservative stance than those with whom or to whom he or she teaches. The responsibility still remains, however, to engage in dialogue from the stance of one's faith and understanding of that faith as it correlates to the topic under discussion. Not to do so is self-alienating and helps neither the student nor the professor.

Another question challenging Catholic institutions today is how to maintain both catholicity and Catholicity without treading painfully on the beliefs of others. Too often, by default, discussions of faith stances, as in the public arena, are shoved aside in order to maintain what is seen as an "open" mind but which, in reality, forfeits the opportunity for a truly rigorous exploration, discussion, and dialogue. Edward Malloy, C.S.C., President of Notre Dame notes:

> A Catholic university must be a hospitable environment where the life of the mind and the urgings of the heart are taken seriously . . . A truly Catholic university, which is simultaneously faithful to its distinctive legacy and promotes an open forum for contrary points of view, will require continuous attention to the kind of atmosphere that pervades among faculty and students.[26]

What would Jesus do? We cannot forget that Jesus, born of the poor, lived, to a degree unusual for his time, a life without boundaries. He challenged the prevailing thought and praxis of those around him, especially those in positions of power, speaking to any and all, consorting and eating with outcastes such as prostitutes and tax collectors, treating women as his equal, listening to and accepting criticism from those his fellow Jews would never have listened to, let alone spoken to. Jesus challenged his own culture and religion, reminding not only his fellow Jews but all with whom he came into contact that we are all God's children, created in God's image and likeness, and therefore deserving of treatment worthy of our human dignity. He was a constant witness to his belief in a God of love who required that same love of us all for our fellow human beings. Unafraid to step beyond the limits set by society, Jesus expressed views contrary to those in all positions of power and authority in secular and religious society, whether Jewish or Roman.

We, too, are called to do likewise as best we can. We are called to speak of our faith as the treasure that it is in order to witness to the love within us. Many of our students have no experience of an altruistic love of others in our "me-first" society. They have been brought up thinking that it is better to receive than to give, taking what they want if necessary; to demand rather than share, to fight their way through life in competition against their neighbors, and to blame others when they fail rather than accept responsibility for their own actions. Life is a bitter struggle to succeed regardless of the costs, whether personal, emotional, or physical, to themselves or to others. It is our responsibility to show them other ways to live.

> [W]e must seek simultaneously to build a new human being and a new earth, although the newness of the new human being will not attain fulfillment realistically and collectively except through *active participation* in striving to build a new earth . . . The formal standpoint from which Christianity projects its liberating work is not that of power or domination but service . . . The university of Christian inspiration is not a place of security, selfish interests, honor or profit, and worldly splendor, but a place of sacrifice, personal commitment, and renunciation.[27]

But what if you teach in a secular institution? How do you speak of the "hope that lies within you" (cf. 1 Peter 3:15) without crossing that boundary or barrier that serves to separate a lived (orthopraxic) faith from one which is merely taught (orthodox)? Certainly, there are greater difficulties but it must also be recognized that, regardless of what we think, we are each a composite of the disparate factors and experiences that have impacted our lives, shaping and forming us into the unique individuals that we are. One of these factors is religion, and our religious experience has helped form us, consciously and unconsciously. We can no more shed that experience and foundation than we can shed our very skins. So what can we do and how can we do it?

The role of various religions in shaping and forming the world in which we live today is both obvious and yet often obscured. In the United States and Western society, the role of Christianity, especially its Western European expression, has been critical to our understanding of ourselves as a nation. That faith can be discussed objectively, as a set of teachings and understandings that inspired the founding of a democratic republic based on the equality of all and justice for all. At the same time, as an adherent of that faith, I can speak subjectively of my own experience of the Christian religion and how it has impacted on my life and that of others, both positively and negatively. In classes such as Western civilization, religion/religious studies, and similar humanities courses, this is not difficult to do. But such an approach is also viable in the sciences, as biologists, anthropologists, geneticists, and others discuss the origins of humanity, the significance of genetic evolution, the emerging possibility of cloning, thereby creating, human beings. Physicists discuss the formation of atoms and order and chaos in the universe—are they evidence for or against the existence of God? Mathematicians extrapolate formulas that raise similar questions. The Catholic Church, at one time, played a critical role in the development of scientific study, one that enabled creative leaps forward and also restricted scientific progress. Scientists themselves are today dialoguing with theologians about God, faith, and religion in ways that enable persons of faith, whether scientist or theologian, to speak from a truth stance that is religiously grounded.

Again, what would Jesus do? He was a simple man; his miracles might, in various ways, be explained as psychological or physical phenomena. But that does not take away from the significance of his life and mission of making us whole in all ways. He accepted the limitations of those with whom he lived and worked, including his own followers, and spoke to them, using stories and examples that came from their everyday lives and experiences, speaking of a shepherd losing and searching for one lost sheep, and faith as small as a mustard seed. He was teaching them about the unteachable, the infinite, unknowable mystery that was God, but the means he used were those of his time and situation. As he taught by example and faith, enabling people he encountered to free themselves of their fears and prejudices, so can we teach our students to be open to new ideas and understandings that challenge their assumptions about persons unlike themselves whose cultures and social and economic backgrounds may differ but who also desire to learn and improve their lives and that of others.

Jesus' mission was to spread the good news of the coming Kingdom of God, a kingdom based on love and community, a "kin-dom" in which all would be welcomed regardless of race, gender, or class. It was left to those of us who, believing in his message, called ourselves Christians, to prepare ourselves and our world for that coming. We cannot do so by hiding our light of faith and knowledge for fear of negative responses. We cannot hold fast to it nor deny it to others, for we will then lose it ourselves.

Our faith can grow only if it is brought out into the light of day, watered by the challenging exchange of ideas and experiences, and nurtured and sustained by being an active and engaged part of our lives.

Walking with Jesus

As Ignacio Ellacuria, one of the Jesuit martyrs of El Salvador, affirmed:

> Correctly understood, Christianity defends and promotes a sense of fundamental values which are essential to our current process in history and therefore very useful to a universal endeavor committed to that process in history . . . Christianity regards the poorest as both the redeemers of history and the privileged of this world. Christianity struggles vis à vis those things that dehumanize, such as the yearning for wealth, honors, power, and the high regard of the powerful in this world; it strives to replace selfishness with love as the driving force in human life and in history and it is centered on the other and on commitment to others rather than in demands made on others for one's own benefit. Christianity seeks to serve rather than to be served; it seeks to do away with unjust inequalities; it asserts the transcendent value of human life, and the value of the person from the standpoint of God's son, and hence, it upholds solidarity and kinship of all human beings; it makes us aware of the need for an ever greater future and this underlies the active hope of those who work to make a more just world in which God can thereby become more fully manifested. Christianity regards the rejection of human beings and of human kinship as the radical rejection of God and, in that sense, as the rejection of the source of all reality and of all human realization.[28]

Jesus died so that we all might have life in abundance but not at the expense of our fellow human beings. His ministry was to the lowliest in his community, the illiterate fishermen, the sick and the lame, the outcasts, those for and about whom no one cared. We, as professors, are privileged to be the molders of the future by teaching our students—modeling for them a life that makes a difference—to become other than what they thought themselves capable of becoming.

Jesus is the sacrament of God, God incarnate. Through his ministry of love, he gave all of us who dare to call ourselves Christian a mission: to go therefore and do likewise, teaching all nations and striving for the perfection in life that only he was truly capable of achieving. Jesus did not hold back from offering himself fully, risking his life for the sake of others. Today, perhaps we are not called to such a harsh sacrifice, but we are all called to witness to our faith in him in all that we say and do.

We do this by placing God, not humanity, at the center of our lives. This calls for a corresponding praxis. With God at the center, modeling myself on the Jesus of history, I cannot engage in individualistic, selfish actions that may better my life but will damage the lives of others. If God is at the center, then the great commandments set by Jesus, to "love the Lord your God with all your heart, and with all your soul, and with all your mind" and to "love your neighbor as yourself" (Matthew 22:38–39) must be lived out in the world not apart from it. My neighbor, then, becomes everyone with whom I come into contact, not just those with whom I have a particular relationship. It means that I cannot slip and slide into a relationship with God that allegedly nurtures me but does not, at the same time, prod me into taking a stand for others, for righteousness sake. In order to attain to God's grace, I must be open to it through and by means of how I live out my life *in* the world.

As a liberation theologian, I see myself as an "organic intellectual," one who has emerged, as many of us have, from within a particular community, and recognized, affirmed, and sent forth by that community to garner knowledge and skills and then return to the people to work with and for them, to bring about their and my own empowerment. An "organic intellectual" is grounded in a community and works on behalf of that community, serving as teacher but also listener, as mediator and conduit, as source of strength and hope, as gentle guide and guided. In many ways, he or she must be, like Jesus, the servant of the servants.

To be an "organic intellectual" is to see yourself as Jesus did, as one in solidarity with others, especially the least among us, working to bring about a better world for all people. It is to recognize that we are called by our baptism, anointed through confirmation, and commissioned daily through our celebration of the Eucharist to live out the message of God's salvific plan *in* the world.

Thus, for me to be an intellectual is to be called forth and commissioned. It is a vocation not just a job I happen to like; it is a mandate from God to use the intellect and talents given so generously to me by God, not for self-aggrandizement but for the betterment of all humankind. I do not have the luxurious option of sitting in an ivory tower expounding on ideas that have no connection with the reality around me.

It means taking risks, stepping out on faith, leaving the ivory tower, and mixing and mingling with ordinary people. It means raising questions that annoy and anger the powers that be about *their* complicity in a *status quo* that relegates hundreds of thousands to the lowest rungs of life in this and other nations. It means, as the poet Audre Lorde noted, "standing alone and at times rejected" because you refuse to act as if your faith was meaningless and your love for God "foolishness." It means that the university or college setting in which you work becomes, in the words of Leo O'Donovan, President of Georgetown University, a "community of wisdom" where discerning the signs of the times and learning to make wise choices are constant concerns for all of its faculty and students, administrators and staff.

Jesus *is* in all things. Jesus *is* all around us—looking out of the eyes of a homeless man, an abandoned child, a battered mother, but also shining in the face of a businesswoman, a teacher, a student who has suddenly realized the incredible joy of learning simply for learning's sake.

We are a people called to be Church, gathered by the Holy Spirit to celebrate daily in joyful remembering the life, death, and resurrection of Jesus the Christ through the Eucharist—the sacrament of unity for us all. How we choose to celebrate—the style of music, the prayers and language used, the forms of expression—may and do often differ, but we are united as one Church catholic because our celebration of the sacrament of Christ that makes of us a sacrament, an event of grace for others. We must express that unity in all that we say and do, thereby enabling others to become truly empowered in themselves.

As Catholic Christian intellectuals, we must bring that gift of catholicity to a wounded and weary world, sharing with them not simply our faith but the ground of that faith, that in Christ Jesus we are all one in ways that unite and welcome rather than intimidate and coerce.

The world is the sacrament of God because as principal cause, all grace comes from God whose incarnation in Jesus Christ and by means of the Holy Spirit offers grace to us all. If we are open to God as revealed in *all* people, we, too, will serve as vehicles of grace, helping to bring about that time when, in the words of Dame Julian of Norwich, all shall be *well,* and all *shall* be well, and *all* shall be very well.

I close with a question that I hope will be a challenge for us all:

Can we, as we look around and see the present state of affairs in our nation, our churches, and in our world, afford to demand professional competency in all of the major areas of our lives except those areas that relate to issues of value?

Notes

1. Stephen Carter, *The Culture of Disbelief: How American Law and Politics Trivialize Religious Devotion* (New York: Basic Books, 1993), p.3.
2. Ibid.
3. Ibid., p. 57.
4. David Tracy, *Analogical Imagination: Christian Theology and the Culture of Pluralism* (New York: Crossroad Publishing, 1983), p. xi.
5. Ibid.

6. Carter, p. 8.
7. Ibid., p. 56.
8. Cited in Carter, p. 56, fn. 22.
9. Tracy, p. 75.
10. See for example Cyprian Davis, O.S.B., *The History of Black Catholics in the United States* (New York: Crossroad Publishing, 1990), chapters 1–2.
11. Joseph Komonchak, ed., *The New Dictionary of Theology* (Collegeville, MN: The Liturgical Press, 1993), pp. 915–916.
12. Ibid., p. 920.
13. Ibid., p. 921.
14. Dulles, *The Craft of Theology: From Symbol to System* (NY: Crossroad, 1995) p. 60.
15. Ibid., pp. 61–62.
16. Ibid., p. 67.
17. Ibid.
18. Karl Rahner, ed., *Sacramentum Mundi: Encyclopedia of Theology* (New York: Herder and Herder, 1968), p. 1481.
19. Komonchak, p. 512.
20. Tracy, pp. 12–13.
21. Carter, p. 19.
22. Rahner, p. 1484.
23. Tracy, p. 9.
24. Joseph M. Washington, ed., *A Testament of Hope: The Essential Writings of Martin Luther King, Jr.* (New York: Harper and Row, 1986).
25. William Byron, S.J., "The Widening World of Primary, Secondary, and 'Tertiary' Education." In *Reading the Signs of the Times: Resources for Social and Cultural Analysis.* ed. T. Howland Sanks and John A. Coleman (Mahwah, NJ: Paulist, 1993).
26. Edward A. Malloy, C.S.C., *Culture and Commitment: The Challenge of Today's University* (Notre Dame, IN: University of Notre Dame Press, 1992).
27. John Hasselt and Hugh Lacey, eds, *Towards a Society That Serves Its People: The Intellectual Contributions of the El Salvador Murdered Jesuits* (Washington, DC: Georgetown University Press, 1991), p. 206.
28. Ibid.

Scripture quotations are from the New Revised Standard Version of the Bible, copyright 1989 by the Division of Christian Education of the National Council of the Churches of Christ in the USA. Used by permission. All rights reserved.

Quotations from the documents of the Second Vatican Council are from *Vatican Council II; The Conciliar and Post Conciliar Documents*, Gen. ed. Austin Flannery, O.P. (Collegeville, MN: Liturgical Press, 1975).

11

The Trinity and Catholic Intellectual Life

Dennis M. Doyle

The Catholic intellectual life could never be simply a dry, mundane affair. Being Catholic and being intellectual make vital demands upon each other. In this essay, I use the doctrine of the Trinity as a point of reflection to explore how the Catholic intellectual life is rooted in mystery, tradition, spirituality, a personalist ontology, and a concern for justice.

The Trinity is at once the most central yet most incomprehensible of Christian teachings. Christian authors throughout the ages have contemplated its impenetrable majesty. In the final canto of *The Divine Comedy*, Dante encounters the Trinity:

> Within its depthless clarity of substance
> I saw the Great Light shine into three circles
> in three clear colors bound in one same space;
>
> the first seemed to reflect the rest like rainbow
> on rainbow, and the third was like a flame
> equally breathed forth by the other two.
>
> How my weak words fall short of my conception,
> which is itself so far from what I saw
> that "weak" is much too weak a word to use![1]

The Trinity leaves even Dante short on words. His climactic vision is of the Christian mystery that is at once the most important yet the least comprehensible.

Intellectual Life Rooted in Mystery

One who accepts the doctrine of the Trinity embraces a mystery. A sense of mystery at the heart of the intellectual life creates a tension with some modern assumptions about epistemology. Most Catholics are not rejecters of the modern world, but most of us manage a critical distance from it as we participate either whole or three-quarters-heartedly. In the modern world, what you know, you understand, and what you don't understand, you don't know.

A similar thing is true of belief: what you believe you don't know, and vice-versa.

In the encyclical *Fides et ratio*, John Paul II draws upon an alternative philosophical tradition familiar to Catholics. Belief is a way of knowing. Some things you know because you found out for yourself. Other things you know because you accept them from someone you trust. Believing even has some advantages over immanently generated knowledge, because it is relational and based on trusting another. It is quite common, in this approach, to know something to be true even though you do not understand it.

This is how it is with the doctrine of the Trinity. We believe its truth as revelation through our acceptance of the Christian faith, but it remains ever beyond our comprehension. Now we see as through a glass, darkly. The sense of mystery permeates our intellectual life.

Modern Challenges

The doctrine of the Trinity has posed a particular intellectual challenge for Christians of the last two centuries. Immanuel Kant (1724–1804) taught that nothing could be known about God through theoretical reason; human beings "know" God only through practical reason, with moral practice as the ground for judgment. Kant draws out the implications: "From the doctrine of the Trinity, taken literally, nothing whatsoever can be gained for practical purposes, even if one believed that one comprehended it—and less still if one is conscious that it surpasses all our concepts."[2]

The German Protestant theologian Friedrich Schleiermacher (1768–1834) followed Kant in holding that the Trinity, while it expresses the Christian experience of God, reveals nothing knowable about God in God's own self. Schleiermacher compared the trinitarian doctrine of Athanasius (c. 296–373) that influenced the early councils with the modalism of the heretic Sabellius (excommunicated c. 220). *Modalism* is the belief that there is only one person in God who has acted or appeared to act in three different modes. Schleiermacher argued that one really cannot know whether Athanasius or Sabellius were correct. And, although he maintained formal neutrality, Schleiermacher seemed, in the end, to prefer the position of Sabellius.[3] In an age when even traditional religious believers often buy into a kind of functional agnosticism in the public sphere, the grounds for belief in the Trinity become difficult to articulate.[4]

Another difficulty arises in the particularity of the doctrine. The Trinity is a belief that distinguishes Christian teaching from Jewish and Islamic teaching. It distinguishes it from virtually all other religious teaching as well, although a great number of archetypal parallels can be found.[5] Many modern thinkers have shown a bias for principles that are sufficiently universal as to provide connections among the religions. "Love your neighbor" is relatively easy to generalize; the Trinity is not. Among Catholics of the immediate post-Vatican II period, the tendency can be traced to highlight what is common with others and to put all else to the side. It is hard to justify a belief that seems, at least on the surface, to divide rather than connect Christians with other human beings.

Intellectual Life Rooted in Tradition

Much twentieth-century reflection on the Trinity has been in response to these modern challenges. Belief in the Trinity gives evidence of an intellectual life rooted in tradition. At the first moment of my first day in my Catholic grade school in Philadelphia in 1958, Sr. Bernard Patrick, S.S.J., drew three circles on the blackboard. She then formed the word *God* by altering only slightly the outer two of the three circles. She changed the first circle into a "G," and the third circle into a "D." That there were three circles out of which my teacher made the one word for God was highly significant. I would learn much about this topic over the next eight years.

Images and concepts of the Trinity surrounded us. Lesson three of my *Baltimore Catechism* was on "The Unity and Trinity of God." We often made the sign of the cross. At the end of each decade of the rosary, we would declare: "Glory be to the Father, and to the Son, and to the Holy Spirit: as it was in the beginning, is now, and ever shall be, world without end." The Creed that we recited at Mass each Sunday was trinitarian in structure. On selected Sundays, for the concluding hymn at Mass we would belt out:

> O, Most Holy Trinity, undivided unity
> Holy God, mighty God,
> God immortal, be adored.

The three persons were encountered on a daily basis. We frequently prayed the Our Father; a crucifix loomed on the wall of each classroom to remind us of what Christ had done for us; we received the Holy Spirit (in those days, the "Holy Ghost") in confirmation; and we learned that our bodies were temples of the Holy Spirit.

In class, we were told the story of how St. Patrick had used a clover to teach this doctrine to the Irish. One sister told us the story of how St. Augustine, contemplating the Trinity as he walked along the beach, came upon a boy trying to pour the ocean into a small hole he had dug, pail by pail. Augustine told the boy that his task was impossible. "So too," said the boy to Augustine, "is it impossible for you to understand the mystery you are contemplating." Then the boy disappeared.[6]

Belief in the Trinity goes hand in hand with an intellectual life that is more inclined to treasure than to suspect a religious tradition. This does not mean that we are uncritical. We are not devotees waiting to be liberated from mindless traditions. But we tend to see tradition as offering a help rather than a hindrance in providing a context within which an intellectual life can be pursued.

The act of belief in the Trinity requires a hermeneutic of appreciation toward the Christian tradition. Christian teaching employing philosophical terms and concepts to express that there are three Persons in one God developed gradually over a period of several centuries. A three-fold experience of God, however, finds expression in New Testament witness that represents the faith of the earliest Christian communities. Some modern scholars stress discontinuity between the diversity of New Testament witness and the trinitarian doctrines that were formulated later. These scholars tend to construe the doctrine of the Trinity as a construct super-added to the original Christian faith experience. Such an approach, however, runs counter to the overwhelming bulk of Catholic, Orthodox, and Reformational teaching, which affirms a fundamental connection between New Testament witness and the trinitarian formulations that develop over the centuries.

The Dominican theologian William J. Hill is perhaps the best representative of the many scholars who use contemporary methods of study to support traditional claims about Christ and the Trinity. Hill maintains that trinitarian beliefs and formulas developed of necessity in the New Testament as supporting cast accompanying claims about Jesus. While surveying the diversity of the New Testament witness, Hill places a stress on continuity between early christologies and the later doctrine of the Trinity.

Hill focuses on a range of titles given to Jesus, such as Son of God, Son of Man, Logos, and Lord, as well as on various references to the Holy Spirit. Hill finds these terms and concepts to be expressive of a deeply shared Christian experience of God's loving presence in Jesus and, after Jesus' death, in the community. That is, Hill shows how the New Testament bears witness to their experience of God in Jesus, in the Father to whom Jesus prayed, and in the ongoing guidance of the Holy Spirit. The movement from the faith-experience of Jesus as Son of God and Lord to an identification of Jesus as a preexistent divine person is gradual and not uniform. Still, argues Hill:

> The New Testament itself does not make the explicit transfer from "son of God" to "God the Son." But it does provide the matrix for the later Church's doing so—in the sense that an implicit trinitarianism is gradually coming to light in the New Testament itself in function of some of its developing christologies.[7]

In other words, Christians make the claim that God has become incarnate in the person of Jesus Christ. Without the reality of the Trinity, Jesus is just a great teacher or a prophet, not God incarnate. Claiming that Jesus is one in being with the Father has implications not only for who Jesus is, but also for what God is like. Hill makes the case that later Church Fathers and councils, in elaborating the doctrine of the Trinity, are not engaging in mere speculation, but are expressing what lies at the very core of the earliest Christian faith-experience.

Accepting this process of doctrinal development as valid requires an intellectual orientation toward affirming a tradition. Those predisposed to make skepticism their deepest guiding principle, or those inclined to see original manifestations of a phenomenon as authentic and later developments as corruptions, would not be inclined to follow William Hill in affirming the indispensability of the doctrine of the Trinity.

Intellectual Life Rooted in Spirituality

Contemporary reflection on the Trinity has been linked with a communitarian personalism that challenges Enlightenment-style assumptions about individual, rational subjects living in a mechanical world. It might seem strange that I would begin this part of the discussion on the doctrine of the Trinity by referring to the Jewish philosopher Martin Buber (1878–1965). It is Martin Buber, however, who perhaps best typifies the theological personalism that has accompanied so much of the current trinitarian emphasis among Christians.

Buber, in fact, is frequently quoted by contemporary Christian theologians for his distinction between "I-It" relationships on the one hand and "I-You" relationships on the other.[8] The first phrase indicates the world of separated egos in relation to which the rest of reality is reduced to manipulated objects. The second phrase indicates a world of relationality in which subject connects with subject. In this world of relationality, the very mystery of God is encountered as a "You" rather than as a thing. This relational world is also a world of community, in which subjects are aware of a basic interconnectedness that precedes and sustains the distinctions among individual persons. This communal world is furthermore a world of social commitment, which calls subjects forth to action.

The late feminist theologian Catherine Mowry LaCugna (1952–1997) is the best-known Catholic proponent of a personalist rendering of the doctrine of the Trinity.[9] She argues that the Trinity is the most practical and relevant of Christian doctrines. Finding fault with traditional thinkers who have emphasized the doctrine's direct application to God in godself, LaCugna chooses applied spirituality over ontology as her focus. She minimizes any emphasis on intra-divine relations. The Trinity is for her above all a doctrine about how God and human beings are interrelated with one another. It is a doctrine that tells Christians that they must live their lives not individualistically but relationally.

LaCugna's constant focus is soteriological; that is, how is the Trinity expressive of the types of relationships that save and liberate? Christians have encountered the personal reality of God in the face of Jesus and in the activity of the Holy Spirit. LaCugna depicts the Trinity as a communion of Persons in mutuality, equality, freedom, inclusivity, and reciprocity. She draws upon the Greek term, *perichoresis*, to envision trinitarian reality ultimately as a cosmic divine dance that includes God and human beings in interpenetration. This vision of the Trinity expresses the reality that:

> . . . *living as persons in communion, in right relationship, is the meaning of salvation and the ideal of Christian faith.* God is interactive, neither solitary nor isolated. Human beings are created in the image of the relational God and gradually are being perfected in that image (*theosis*), making more and more real the communion of all creatures with one another. The doctrine of the Trinity stresses the relational character of personhood

over and against the reduction of personhood to a product of
social relations. Thus it can serve as a critique of cultural
norms of personhood, whether that of "rugged individualism"
or "me first" morality, as well as patterns of inequality based
on gender, race, ability, and so forth.[10]

LaCugna interprets the Trinity finally as a call for Christians to live their
lives in praise of God's glory and in loving relationship with one another. She
does little to challenge modern skepticism about the doctrine's ability to tell
us anything about God in godself; some scholars see this point as a weakness
in her otherwise beneficial approach. Still, LaCugna argues forcefully that the
Trinity remains a most relevant and practical teaching for Christian living. The
Catholic intellectual life is rooted in praise and right relationships. There is to
be no divorce between intellectuality and spirituality.

The Vatican II document *Lumen gentium* also connects the Trinity with
spirituality; spirituality is spoken of in terms of Christian discipleship, and
the mark of the true disciple is love. To love is to follow Jesus in seeking and
doing the will of the Father. The will of the Father is known through listening to the promptings of the Holy Spirit.

Vatican II thus presented Christian spirituality as most properly a trinitarian spirituality. This is true even though many Christians in practice seem
to relate primarily to one Person of the Trinity more than another. Catholics
of my generation, for example, tended to equate "God" with "Father." I have
noticed, however, that many of my Catholic students of post-Vatican II education tend to equate "God" with "Jesus." I have known Catholics involved
with the charismatic renewal who think of "God" primarily as "Holy Spirit."
I do not think of such selective emphasis as a problem. It is important,
though, that the spirituality of the Church as a whole be trinitarian, and that
ultimately each Person of the Trinity be understood in relation to the other
Persons.

The Catholic intellectual life is grounded in a trinitarian spirituality.
Such an intellectual life can be distinguished, but not entirely separated, from
a life rooted in love and Christian discipleship. Knowledge can be pursued
for its own sake insofar as one's motivating force can be a sense of wonder
and appreciation of the marvels of creation. But knowledge cannot be pursued simply for its own sake if that means that intellectual pursuits are
entirely cut off from the service of human beings and God. Spirituality and
intellectual pursuits go hand in hand.

Intellectual Life Rooted in a Personalist Ontology

In contrast with LaCugna's focus, some recent attention to the doctrine of the
Trinity has been linked with a personalist metaphysics or ontology, understood here as philosophical and theological approaches that place subjectivity, freedom, human experience, and solidarity at the heart of reality. Greek
Orthodox theologian and bishop John Zizioulas expresses the belief that at
the core of being itself—at the very heart of all that exists—there lies a

community of Persons.[11] This community of Persons is formed by the three Persons in one God.

Zizioulas contrasts his Christian personalist worldview with a Greek metaphysics, that apprehends God as monistic and deterministic, as well as with certain modern, scientific worldviews that are fundamentally materialistic. For Zizioulas, personhood, freedom, and relationality are not optional extras added over and above a prior and more basic objective, material universe. Rather, the universe itself is basically personal. Christians are aware of this because of the way in which they have encountered and experienced God as a communion of Persons.

According to Zizioulas, the eucharistic assembly best expresses the personalism of ultimate reality as experienced by Christians. He emphasizes the presence there through memory and invocation of the communion of saints and of the three Persons in God. The eucharistic assembly anticipates the Kingdom of God to such a degree that it offers a foretaste of heavenly and divine reality.

The Church, in this Eastern view, functions like a school in which Christians learn to be in the way that God is. Christians learn to overcome their individualistic, biologically determined, ego-centered life stances to learn that community precedes individuality. Individuals remain real and important but only within the context of a prior human interconnectedness and solidarity. Rather than isolated and determined, Christians experience their personhood as relational and free. They learn to exist as persons in the way that the three Persons in God exist. The Persons in God take on their distinctiveness and freedom not as isolated individuals but in relation to each other. Being in relationship does not impose limitations on them, but frees them to be who they are. Relationality provides the context within which they take on their personhood.

Zizioulas describes how the formal doctrine of the Trinity was developed by fourth-century Greek fathers such as Athanasius, whose work influenced the Council of Nicea (325), and the three Cappadocian fathers, Basil of Caesarea (c. 329–379), Gregory of Nazianzus (c. 325–389), and Gregory of Nyssa (d. after 385), whose work influenced the Council of Chalcedon (451). These thinkers used technical Greek terms, such as *hypostasis* (individual as encountered) and *ousia* (being), to explain the divinity/humanity of Christ as well as the reality of three Persons in one God. The key point, for Zizioulas, is that in this merging of the Christian experience of God with Greek metaphysics, Christian experience emerged as the dominant partner. The Greek terms became tools for expressing what the universe must be like for the Christian experience of God and reality to be possible. At the basis of all reality is the Trinity. At its most ultimate, being is communion.

Jesuit theologian Joseph Bracken performs a marriage between the doctrine of the Trinity and the process metaphysics of Alfred North Whitehead (1861–1947).[12] Bracken finds the Western metaphysical tradition with its focus on substance to be too limited for expressing the reality of God when compared with a process approach that focuses on dynamic interrelationships. He proposes that the three "Persons" of the Trinity be understood along the lines of "societies" (in Whitehead's language, personally ordered societies of actual occasions) who together constitute the communitarian reality of God. The Trinity thus becomes the ground of creativity in an ever-evolving universe. At the core of reality lies not "substance," but "subsistent relations." Bracken writes:

> . . . Creativity may be termed the power of divine intersubjec-
> tivity. For, in virtue of Creativity, each of the divine persons is
> constituted at every moment both as an individual entity and
> as a member of a structured society, namely, the divine com-
> munity. The reality of the one is inseparable from the reality
> of the other. The divine community only exists in virtue of the
> self-constituting activity of the persons at every moment, and
> the persons in their self-constitution are shaped by the com-
> mon element of form proper to their existence as a divine
> community.[13]

Bracken is in line with LaCugna in his insistence that the three Persons in God are radically equal and provide the grounds for an equality among human persons. Bracken, however, explicitly extends this equality to various nonhuman environments within the cosmos. Also, Bracken insists, contrary to LaCugna, that the doctrine of the Trinity is not only about how Christians have encountered God but also as importantly about the very reality of God in godself. Bracken urges Christians to live relationally because that is the way that God truly is.

In fact, Bracken's main purpose in offering his trinitarian reflections is to provide the ground for a social ontology. He holds that a radically intersub-jective reality cannot have as its ground a oneness. Society or community must be the first category of being. Bracken believes that if Christians are to make a significant contribution to the emerging global dialogue concerning cosmology, the Trinity must be put forward as "archetype or model for the world of creation."[14] The Catholic intellectual life cannot be divorced from a personalist and relational view of the cosmos.

Intellectual Life Rooted in a Concern for Justice

Where Zizioulas and Bracken have concentrated on the ontological dimen-sions of the Trinity, the German Protestant political theologian Jürgen Molt-mann has emphasized implications of trinitarian relationality for political and social concerns. Following the work of Erik Peterson[15] (1890–1960), Molt-mann links monotheism with monarchical and even dictatorial forms of gov-ernment.[16] He charges that Christianity, unfortunately, has often functioned as a monotheism supporting such power arrangements. When Christianity is true to its trinitarian heritage, however, it challenges structures that promote dominating and abusive forms of power. The God of love, the self-emptying God, the God who is willing to suffer for the sake of humankind, "is not the archetype of the mighty ones of this world." As Jesus became the brother of the oppressed, so the glory of God is reflected in the fellowship of believers and of the poor.

Moltmann promotes a political and social personalism that is not unlike the metaphysical personalism of Zizioulas:

> We have said that it is not the monarchy of a ruler that corresponds to the triune God; it is the community of men and women, without privileges and without subjugation. The three divine persons have everything in common, except for their personal characteristics. So the Trinity corresponds to a community in which people are defined through their relations with one another and in their significance for one another, not in opposition to one another, in terms of power and possession.[17]

Moltmann does not lay out a specific political or economic program. He rejects totalitarian government on the one hand and bourgeois liberal economies on the other. His key categories are freedom, responsibility, and the Kingdom of God. The freedom associated with the Trinity, he says, is creative, oriented toward the future, and linked with the building of community.

Liberation theologian Leonardo Boff, a former Franciscan priest who left the order after several clashes with the Congregation for the Doctrine of the Faith, espouses ideas similar to those of Moltmann from within his Brazilian context. Boff is known for his radical critiques of Church and society; he depicts the Trinity as a community that provides a model for how Church and society should be conceived:

> We are not condemned to live alone, cut off from one another; we are called to live together and to enter into the communion of the Trinity. Society is not ultimately set in its unjust and unequal relationships, but summoned to transform itself in the light of the open and egalitarian relationships that obtain in the communion of the Trinity, the goal of social and historical progress. If the Trinity is good news, then it is so particularly for the oppressed and those condemned to solitude.[18]

Boff also applies these relational categories to the Church while still making clear the link between the Trinity and social justice. The Church is the "sacrament of trinitarian communion," called to uproot injustices within itself and within the world. For Boff, "the universe exists in order to manifest the abundance of divine communion."

The best known of all liberation theologians, Peruvian priest Gustavo Gutiérrez, makes a similar connection between the Trinity and social liberation. Gutiérrez argues that God, love, and justice need always to go together. A person who tries to embrace God and love without embracing justice is missing a key ingredient in the divine recipe. Gutiérrez's approach to the Trinity at first sounds fairly traditional:

> The Father, communicator of life, is the God "who is love."
> The Holy Spirit is the bond of love between Father and Son,
> between God and us, and between human beings. The presence
> of the Spirit in our hearts enables us, like Jesus, to call God
> *Abba* (see Gal 4:6). The mystery of the Trinity shows the full-
> ness of life that is in God.[19]

Gutiérrez then contextualizes this traditional view, however, within a vision
of liberation:

> The God of life manifests love by forming a family of equals
> through an act of liberation in which God does, and demands,
> justice amid the people and enters into an irrevocable
> covenant with them in history. Liberation, justice, and
> covenant imply one another; each is necessary for the full
> meaning of the others.[20]

For Gutiérrez, then, as for Boff, it requires but a short series of deductions to
move from the belief that there are three Persons in one God to the demand
to work for justice in this life. The doctrine of the Trinity expresses the Christian experience of the God who liberates through Christ and the Spirit. This
liberation always has both interpersonal and social dimensions.

Catholic feminist theologian Elizabeth Johnson, C.S.J., draws upon classical Christian sources to construct a theological approach that is both trinitarian and inclusive.[21] For Johnson, the Catholic intellectual life must
manifest a concern for the flourishing of women, which in turn calls for an
understanding of God and religious tradition that is gender-sensitive. She
wants to get beyond the "isolated patriarchal God of the Enlightenment," the
God who is not only male but a loner. Johnson finds a relatedness at the heart
of all reality, "a mystery of personal connectedness." The Triune God
emerges in the conclusion of her book *SHE WHO IS* as the indicator that
relatedness, mutuality and equality, and the outpouring of compassionate,
liberating love lie at the core of all. The patriarchal God is overcome by a
community in diversity whose mutual interaction can be imaged as a joyous,
revolving dance: "Casting the metaphor in yet another direction, we can say
that the eternal flow of life is stepped to the contagious rhythm of spicy sal-
sas, merengues, calypsos, or reggaes where dancers in free motion are yet
bonded in the music."[22] Understood in this way, the Trinity can function "as
a model of mutual love stressing the equality of all persons." Johnson detects
not a detached, above-it-all God, but a God who is related, a compassionate
God who suffers.

Johnson emphasizes that the Triune God of Christianity is beyond being
male or female. She connects the Holy Spirit with the wisdom, or *Sophia*, of
the Old Testament. Wisdom is often spoken of in feminine terms and images.
It is this wisdom that fills the spirit of Jesus, especially in the Gospel of Luke.
Jesus is filled with the spirit of *Sophia*. Jesus himself calls God "Father," but
he also uses a feminine metaphor to speak of how God cares in a way that a

mother hen cares for her chicks. Johnson believes that the exclusive use of male metaphors to speak of God is unscriptural and has contributed to the marginalization of women. She proposes that for a time, Christians should use only feminine images of God in order to redress the balance. The title of her book, *SHE WHO IS*, is itself a feminine rendering of "I AM WHO AM."

Intellectual Life Rooted in Humility

The doctrine of the Trinity goes to the very heart of the Christian experience of God and proves quite relevant for the contemporary world. The intellectual life that accompanies belief in the Triune God is rooted in tradition, spirituality, a relational ontology, a concern for justice, and a sense of mystery. The Catholic intellectual is not likely to be the solitary inquirer seeking knowledge solely for its own sake, but rather a member of a community of learners who blend mind and heart. After all, the one God is a community of Persons who love one another.

Despite the many challenges posed by the modern age, the Trinity remains the greatest and most incomprehensible of Christian mysteries. There is a story of a medieval monk who had a dream in which the mystery of the Trinity was fully revealed to him. When he awoke, he remembered that the mystery had been revealed, but he could not remember any of the specific content. This monk thanked God for this, for how could he live the humble life to which he was called in the monastery if he carried within him so great a knowledge?

Notes

1. *The Portable Dante*, trans. and ed. Mark Musa (New York: Penguin Books, 1995), 584.
2. *Der Streit der Fakultäten*, PhB 252, p. 33. This translation taken from Jürgen Moltmann, *The Trinity and the Kingdom: The Doctrine of God*, trans. Margaret Kohl (San Francisco: Harper and Row, 1981 [German original, 1980]), 6.
3. "On the Discrepancy between the Sabellian and Athanasian Method of Representing the Doctrine of the Trinity in the Godhead," trans. M. Stuart, in *Schleiermacher and Stuart on the Doctrine of the Trinity*, reprinted in book form with no publication data from *Biblical Repository and Quarterly Observer*, April and July 1835.
4. The main theme of Karl Rahner's *The Trinity*, trans. Joseph Donceel (New York: Herder and Herder, 1970 [German original, 1967]) is that the Trinity as experienced by Christians in history (the economic Trinity) and the Trinity as expressive of God in godself (the immanent Trinity) are identical.
5. For comparative discussions that link the Christian Trinity with other world religions, see William Hill, *The Three-Personed God*, 307–314; Raimundo Panikkar, *The Trinity and the Religious Experience of Man* (New York: Orbis Books; London: Darton, Longman, and Todd, 1973); Ewert Cousins, "The Trinity and World Religions," *Journal of Ecumenical Studies* 7 (1970):

476–498; Roger Corless and Paul F. Knitter, eds., *Buddhist Emptiness and Christian Trinity: Essays and Explorations* (New York: Paulist, 1990); and Joseph A. Bracken, *The Divine Matrix: Creativity as Link between East and West* (Maryknoll, NY: Orbis Books, 1995).

6. In different versions of this medieval legend, the boy turns out to be an angel or the baby Jesus. The tale is immortalized in a Botticelli painting in the Uffizi in Florence. See *Bibliotheca Sanctorum* (Rome: Instituto Giovanni XXIII, 1961), 502; 599. Augustine authored *The Trinity*, trans. Edmund Hill, O.P. (Brooklyn, NY: New City Press, 1991 [Latin original, 419]).

7. William Hill, *The Three-Personed God: The Trinitarian Mystery of Salvation* (Washington, D.C.: The Catholic University of America Press, 1982), 26.

8. *I and Thou*, trans. Walter Kaufmann (New York: Charles Scribner's Sons, 1970 [German original, 1923]).

9. *God for Us: The Trinity and Christian Life* (San Francisco: HarperCollins, 1991).

10. Ibid., 292.

11. *Being as Communion: Studies in Personhood and the Church* (Crestwood, NY: St. Vladimir's Seminary Press, 1985).

12. Joseph A. Bracken, *Society and Spirit: A Trinitarian Cosmology* (Cranbury, NJ: Associated University Presses, 1991).

13. Ibid., 128.

14. Joseph A. Bracken, "Trinity: Economic and Immanent," *Horizons* 25 (Spring 1998) 7–22, at 22.

15. Moltmann refers to Peterson's famous 1935 essay, "Monotheismus als politisches Problem," in *Theologische Traktate* (Munich, 1951), 48–147.

16. Jürgen Moltmann, *The Trinity and the Kingdom: The Doctrine of God*, trans. Margaret Kohl (San Francisco: Harper and Row, 1981 [German original, 1980]. See also a book by Miroslav Volf, who studied under Moltmann: *After Our Likeness: The Church as the Image of the Trinity* (Grand Rapids: Eerdmans, 1998). Volf develops a trinitarian ecclesiology from a Free Church perspective.

17. Moltmann, *The Trinity and the Kingdom*, 198.

18. Leonardo Boff, *Trinity and Society*, trans. Paul Burns (Maryknoll, NY: Orbis Books, 1988 [Portuguese original, 1986]), 158.

19. Gustavo Gutiérrez, *The God of Life*, trans. Matthew J. O'Connell (Maryknoll, NY: Orbis Books, 1991 [Spanish original, 1989]), 2.

20. Ibid.

21. Elizabeth A. Johnson, *SHE WHO IS: The Mystery of God in Feminist Theological Discourse* (New York: Crossroad, 1996).

22. Ibid., 221

12

The Eucharist:
Faculty, Community, and the
Priority of Paying Attention

Thomas M. Landy

The question posed in this essay is a seemingly simple one. What difference does it make to our work as scholars, teachers, and intellectuals that the Christian community to which Catholics are committed is, at its very heart, a eucharistic community? Many Christian communities model themselves on other, noneucharistic aspects of Jesus' ministry. With some great measure of grace, but without the Eucharist, their members commit themselves to follow Christ—to be "disciples"—in some instances through intellectual work. Yet, Catholicism is, to its core, a eucharistic community. Catholics are marked perhaps most of all by a faith in Jesus' commitment of self in and through gifts of bread, wine, and his own body. Surely, in the eyes of faith, at least for the Catholic, this commitment is relevant to the individual, and has enormous transformative and salvific power. But how is this relevant to the life of the college or university community, to the broader intellectual community, or to the life of the mind?

While framed empirically, the question might well be framed ideally, *Could* commitment to a eucharistic community make a difference to our work as scholars, teachers, and intellectuals? As a sociologist, my first and deepest instinct in response to a question like this is to want to find an empirical answer. What I propose here is to try to steer a middle path: to ground this reflection not in the generalized correlations found in a huge population sample, or in theological and philosophical speculation, but rather to rely primarily on the empirical but largely anecdotal experience of a number of persons, including myself. Perhaps the experience of the persons cited here will revive dormant connections in readers' minds, or the possibilities are still yet to be realized. In any case, I invite readers to hold up these assertions to the light of their own experience, and thereby to consider how real the possibilities are raised in what follows.

I should note that I am not trained as an expert on liturgy or ritual. Still, I have given myself over to participation at Eucharist for countless hours. I have sometimes been lost to myself in those hours, which is variously a good or bad thing, but like to think that I have paid attention a good deal—perhaps even been taught how to pay attention—in the course of the communal rituals of the Eucharist. Some theological training along the way has undoubtedly supplemented and shaped the way I see the Eucharist, but always, as indicated, to the extent that it has genuinely helped to make sense of experience.

Having indicated that the primary question of this essay concerns the difference the Eucharist makes or might make for us, I also want to pose in the latter part of this essay a second, equally important question: In the context of a pluralistic culture, can the Eucharist serve as our foundation and source of mission for any but individuals or exclusive communities? At Catholic universities or colleges, which are necessarily engaged in a pluralistic context and conversation, is it really possible to use the liturgy—Masses of the Holy Spirit and other eucharistic celebrations—to unite and guide the institution in its mission, or does that simply draw or highlight the lines of division? I have had many occasions to see that the Eucharist has served both as the most important source of unity, and also as a deep source of division. Protestants and those who are not Christian often experience it as an exclusionary moment. Persons deeply troubled over women's exclusion from the priesthood have told me that they go away more spiritually hungry than nourished from attendance at the Eucharist. I raise this problem at the beginning of the essay so that even as we move along through examination of what has been most deeply moving and inspiring about the Eucharist, we do not lose sight of the profound paradox that the Eucharist presents to the Church today.

Learning to Pay Attention

In *The Sociology of Religion*, Max Weber took a dim view of the influence of the Mass on everyday life and action.[1] Weber compared the experience of "attending" Mass to viewing a play, albeit a beautifully staged or even interesting play at that. He asserted that both events, no matter how beautiful and inspiring at the moment, have little influence on the ethical character of persons after they walk out the door. Each has its own "moment" and a logic that dominates that moment. Thus, there can be little interaction in between. The play would seem to be an escape, not an influence on daily life.

Weber had in mind the "passive" quality of the Tridentine Latin Mass, as my use of the word *attend* suggests. In the Tridentine context, Weber believed, what counted most was attendance. There, grace was produced, *ex opere operato*, independently of any requirement of religious conversion. Such ritualism, Weber asserted, served most of all to divert us from everyday life, rather than to exert any direct influence on life. Indeed, for Weber, even the devotion that it might induce outside of the liturgy was regarded as a distraction from this-worldly realities.

Weber's critique is probably shared by a great number of people, even in an era when liturgy is celebrated in the hundreds of native tongues and can sometimes be overwhelmed by "participation." I have at times had to confront my own failure—sometimes even a few minutes after Mass—to live out what I had just witnessed at the altar. In research on American Catholics, I have spoken to more than a few people who were troubled at having observed persons who attended Mass and then behaved in less than charitable ways. Even the late theologian Henri Nouwen has felt compelled to ask whether what happens to him and his friends daily at the table of the Eucharist really does enough to shape their lives, or whether it is used only as a soothing, comforting ritual.[2]

Contrary to Weber's assertion, however, I have also seen evidence that the Eucharist is actually very much a way of *learning to pay attention.* Jonathan Z. Smith has argued that conclusions like Weber's are the outcome of a Reformation polemic that equated all ritual with "blind and thoughtless habit." Smith has gone so far as to suggest, as I believe, that ritual "first and foremost" directs attention. "It is a process for marking interest."[3] Certainly, as the Eucharist is described in New Testament accounts, it was used by Jesus to focus people's attention on what was happening or about to happen in their midst. The more one considers the claims made at the Eucharist, particularly the claim "This is my body," the more one *has* to pay close attention, because so much is riding on such an outrageous claim. Our culture may go to great lengths to sanitize that claim, like many other aspects of bodily death and suffering, but the claim of the Eucharist is strikingly blunt in demanding our attention.

Michael Himes's chapter in this collection already makes a compelling case for the power of Catholicism's sacramental vision to reveal God to us. The Eucharist, following from the Incarnation itself, is the font of this vision. Arguably, it is Eucharist that has most kept alive that sacramental sense and made it real to us. The willingness of a transcendent God to manifest himself fully through physical reality is extraordinary. As Himes points out, that gift ought to impel us to recognize all reality as sacred, created to communicate something about God's love. This sacramental perspective, taken seriously, impels us to pay attention to all material things, out of a sense that they mediate God's presence to us by their very existence. That claim that God is really present in the world is made real in the most profound way by the Eucharist, by Jesus' claim to be fully present to us through bread and wine in the midst of the community.

The two major eucharistic accounts in the Gospel—Jesus' initial offering of self at the Passover Last Supper, and the encounter with two disciples on the road to Emmaus—point out exactly how much the institution of the Eucharist calls us to pay attention. At the Last Supper, Jesus draws the disciples' attention to what is being fulfilled in their midst and why. By speaking to them in this way, and sharing a meal, he points out to them how to understand and interpret what they are about to see.

On the road to Emmaus, the two disciples who meet up with Jesus are unable to recognize fully what was happening in their midst, until Jesus blesses and breaks bread with them. The story takes place after the crucifixion, the same day that Mary and the other women had returned from the tomb with confusing news about the whereabouts of Jesus. On the road from Jerusalem, two disciples encounter Jesus, although they do not recognize him. They explain to him all that has happened in the past days, and in doing so make clear their pain and confusion, their dashed hopes and uncertainty about what to make of the women's news that Jesus had risen. "Beginning with Moses and all the prophets," Jesus "interpreted to them the things about himself in all the Scriptures" (Luke 24:27; NRSV). Still, as the encounter is recorded, the disciples were not aware of who this was among them. On arriving at Emmaus near the close of the day, the two disciples invited the man to stay with them.

> When he was at table with them, he took the bread, blessed and broke it, and gave it to them. Then their eyes were opened and they recognized him, and he vanished from their sight. They said to each other, "Were not our hearts burning within us while he was talking to us on the road, while he was opening the scriptures to us?" (Luke 24:30–32; NRSV).

Jesus' use of the breaking of bread to help his disciples see suggests to me that it is holy work—a form of discipleship of a kind of minor Eucharist—to teach someone else how to pay attention. That includes teaching them to recognize some facet of the created world or to recognize injustice or to appreciate a creative act.

The late writer Andre Dubus apparently had a deep faith in this possibility, which seemed to shape his vocation as a father and writer. In his last collection of short essays, he bears witness in story after story to the power of the Eucharist in his life.[4] A daily communicant for most of his life, Dubus quite clearly found God all around him, and did not hesitate to let others know. He also wrote of having found God driving to his daughters' school to meet them, exercising his crippled body, making love. Dubus recounted how, making sandwiches to bring to his daughters, he began "to focus on this: That sandwiches are sacraments. Not the miracle of transubstantiation, but certainly parallel with it, moving in the same direction."[5] Like all of us, Dubus does not always recognize the grace of God that is present in his daily life, but the sacrament that is the Eucharist makes all these other sacraments come to life. Sacraments, he said, make love tactile. It is not enough for him to try to remember or desire it in his head,

> ... for I cannot feel joy with my brain alone. I need sacraments I can receive through my senses. I need God manifested as Christ, who ate and drank and shat and suffered, and laughed. So I can dance with Him as the leaf dances in the breeze under the sun. Not remembering that we are always receiving sacraments is an isolation the leaves do not have to endure: they receive and they give, and they are green. Not remembering this is an isolation only the human soul has to endure.[6]

Coming to Know Ourselves

In a memoir of his experience of coming to grips as an adolescent with his own homosexuality, author/editor Andrew Sullivan called attention to one way that the Eucharist worked powerfully and concretely in his own life and helped him to face a truth he did not want to face. In an essay published in the *South Atlantic Quarterly*, and revised as the prologue to his first book,[7] Sullivan recalled the awkwardness of coming to terms with his attraction to men. Recognizing the too-painful threat of rejection from friends and others, Sullivan felt as a young teenager that he had to work to cover up a quality in himself that could never be shared with others. He imagined personae and roles for himself that would obviate even needing to face up to what he feared. While he "knew" about his sexual identity, Sullivan says he couldn't allow himself to give a name to what he felt, to acknowledge to himself that he was what he was taught he should never want to be, a homosexual. But eventually Sullivan did admit it and even talk about it:

> Eventually, I succumbed to panic and mentioned it before God. I was in the communion line at my local parish church, Our Lady and Saint Peter's, the church that was linked to my elementary school. Please, I remember asking of the Almighty almost offhandedly as I walked up the aisle to receive communion from the mild-mannered Father Simmons for the umpteenth time, please, help me with that.[8]

He had apparently previously been able to articulate or admit to himself only who he wasn't—a person who would be at home in the world of dating girls. At the Eucharist, before God, he found the freedom to face who he is, not just who he is not. "Looking back, I realize that that moment at the communion rail was the first time that I had actually addressed the subject of homosexuality explicitly in front of anyone."[9] Rather than finding certain destruction in the presence of God, as the ancients feared, Sullivan found a God before whom he could face up to a most fearful truth, and find love.

Sullivan has described elsewhere, quite eloquently, times in his adult life when he turned to the Eucharist for sustenance. Many other people, no doubt, have been led to a different experience at the thought of bringing truths we fear into the presence of God. And the Church has too often fostered the notion that one must first be purified to approach God in the Eucharist. But such purification comes first through God's grace, not our actions. In the several years immediately following college, as questions about who I was and what I wanted in life proved difficult, it often seemed to me that the only thing that kept me attached to the Church, in ways that felt both powerful and tenuous, was the Eucharist. Repeatedly I felt called back, despite confusion and resistance, to the table of the Eucharist. Like Sullivan, those visits did bring me to face squarely truths that others had been calling me to recognize. Ultimately, it was that repeated presence at the table that helped me recognize concretely and piercingly who I am as a human being—a sinner loved by God. Coming in contact with Christ present in the Eucharist has helped me, when I have needed it most, to face up to both the reality of my own limitation and sinfulness and the sheer miracle of being unequivocally loved. It has helped me to accept at the same time (a) that I am not God, and (b) that I am absolutely loved by God, a God who would suffer and cross time, space, and physical reality to make sure that I know that. The latter recognition, communicated to me in the Eucharist, makes it much easier to face up to the former.

Any parallel to Sullivan's recognition of his own sexual identity at the Eucharist may seem shocking to some readers, but I am struck by the possibility that the encounter at the Eucharist can provide a chance to face up to truths we might otherwise want to avoid. Drawing from J. B. Metz, Russ Butkus's essay in this collection refers to these truths as "dangerous memories." One could draw a very long list indeed of the harms that can come of avoiding some frightening truth when we teach or write or research. The Eucharist, I have seen, can help us to build up the courage to face these things in true freedom. While I can make no claim to having lived up fully to it, such freedom, I must believe, is a true mark of the gospel.

Covenant, Communion, and Memory

When the term *ritual* is used pejoratively, it is often to signal that repetition dulls the mind. In another essay in this collection, Jody Ziegler talks about the discipline of returning to a work of art and contemplating it repeatedly to learn how to see. Doing this, she makes clear, requires some measure of discipline, patience, and guidance from another person—some reinforcement to help us recognize what's before us to behold. Our need for help to learn to see never ends. Neither does our need to remember how we got where we are.

Eucharist means "act of thanksgiving." Thanksgiving derives from remembrance, because being thankful requires calling to mind what it is that we are thankful for. Like most forms of liturgy, Eucharist aims to make the past very real and present to us. It seeks to remind us who we are and how we came to be.

For Jews, memory is particularly important. In Hebrew Scripture, one of the worst things a Jew could do was to forget the great things that Yahweh had done for Israel. The Passover celebration is a liturgy to commemorate, by reenacting it in part, the events of the saving act of God, which freed a band of slaves from Egyptian bondage and made them into a Chosen People. The command to remember "I am Yahweh who brought you out of the desert" is even referred to by theologians as the "Yahwist liturgy." Psalm 137 uses vibrant imagery to caution the people in exile to cling to their memory of the Temple and thus to God's promise to be with them and watch over them:

> If I forget you, O Jerusalem,
>   let my right hand wither!
> Let my tongue cleave to the roof of my mouth,
>   if I do not remember you,
>   if I do not set Jerusalem
>   above my highest joy (5–6; RSV).

The law, the gift of God, should never be forgotten either:

> [T]hese words which I command you this day shall be upon
> your heart; and you shall teach them diligently to your chil-
> dren, and shall talk of them when you sit in your house, and
> when you walk by the way, and when you lie down, and when
> you rise. And you shall bind them as a sign upon your hand,
> and they shall be as frontlets between your eyes. And you shall
> write them on the doorposts of your house and on your gates.
> And when the Lord your God brings you into the land which
> he swore to your fathers . . . and when you eat and are full, then
> take heed lest you forget the Lord, who brought you out of the
> land of Egypt, out of the house of bondage (Deuteronomy
> 6:6–12; RSV).

The fact that the Eucharist has so long served as the central act of
Catholic and Orthodox worship suggests how fundamental memory is to
Catholic and Orthodox faith. Scripture also serves as a means to communicate memories of God's actions through prophets, disciples, and Jesus himself. But Eucharist, I would suggest, is an added effort to make the past fully
present today. Daniel Donovan has made clear how radical the sense of memory is meant to be in Catholic liturgy. The name theologians give to this is
anamnesis, a Greek term that means "memorial" or "memory," but which
evokes it in an extremely powerful way:

> In the Eucharist we make memory of the death and resurrec-
> tion of Jesus and of his future coming. What is intended here
> is more than mere remembrance. In the biblical sense of the
> word, memorial suggests a rendering present of a past event so
> that new generations can encounter its power for life and sal-
> vation. That such a thing was possible was the conviction that
> gave the Jewish celebration of the Passover its unique value.
> The same conviction lies at the heart of the Christian liturgy.[10]

The Eucharist does make a powerful claim, that what happened long ago
is fully present and meant to be equally transformative today. For good or ill,
memory can shape us as a community. Eucharist shapes our memory around
a saving, redemptive act as the basis for our shared identity. Enda McDonagh
asserts, "Remembering in Christian liturgical terms is sharing. Persons and
events are not merely recalled but participated in."[11]

The power of Eucharist to bring a prior event to life can be extraordinarily unsettling, but it also can be an extraordinarily centering experience.
Through remembrance, the Jewish people knew, we come to recognize who
we are, individually and collectively. As Jane Redmont has put it, "All
remembering, especially ritual prayer, is re-membering: bringing together,
making whole. To bind together, to re-connect, *re-ligere* in Latin: that is the
root meaning of the word 'religion.'"[12]

Unity and Diversity

The binding potential of liturgy is extraordinary. Faculty often remark about this on occasions of great loss, such as when the campus needs to mourn the death of a student or other important person from the college.

One story stuck with me a long time, told by a friend whose graduate student had participated in Collegium one summer. The week at Collegium was the first in-depth opportunity that the student, a Lutheran woman, really had to encounter so many Catholics together at work, play, and prayer. As my friend recounted it, on her return home she asked the student many questions about how the week went, how the speakers were, etc. Somewhere in the course of this, however, she noted a bit of hesitation about something, and asked the student what that meant. After even further hesitation, the student replied, "Well, it's hard to understand. The Catholics there seemed to disagree on so many things—about the Church, politics, academics. They'd have it out over these topics in conversation, and then later they'd go to Mass and come together as if their disagreement meant nothing. Then they might go to dinner and enjoy themselves but have it all out again, and the next day do the same, then go to church . . ." "Yes! That's it!" my friend responded. "You've got it. That's exactly how we are."

Certainly the Lutheran liturgies that the graduate student had attended all her life were marked with the presence of God. Yet, I have seen within the Eucharist a powerful ability of the Eucharist to reconcile and hold together disparate groups of people. That certainly seems to be true in terms of the diversity of views among Catholics. Despite deeply felt differences on a number of important "issues" relating to the Church and morality, people manage to gather together as one around the table. One might be tempted, on observing this, to think that this simply signals that the Eucharist is about not paying attention to matters of real importance, but I would suggest that it is a time when we somehow recognize that these differences are not the only factor of importance.

In an era when the social distance along class lines is deepening, I have noticed how often this seems to be significantly overcome at the Eucharist. I know well that the people I pray with at church on Sundays are by no means a random cross-section of Boston society, or even of Boston Catholics. Despite the very urban location of the church, there are relatively small numbers of Hispanic and African American and Asian people in church. Nearby there are predominantly Black, Hispanic, and Chinese Catholic churches.

Still, I'm often even more struck to see who *is* there, especially when I find people worshiping together who are otherwise at different ends of the spectrum of class, status, education, and income hierarchy that exists in America. A mentally and physically handicapped man puts his wheelchair in the front row and manages to sing loudly and far off-key to half the songs. I pray there with another man who is troubled by alcoholism and other demons, who spends much of his time in transient homes and shelters, and who comes to church holding on for dear life. There are many other people like them, mixed in with the middle class and the very well off. There are many people who, left to my own devices, I would probably never bother to know at all.

Colleges and universities, it should almost go without saying, are extremely hierarchical institutions. Faculty and staff often have little interaction; students and others can readily treat housekeeping or food service staff like hired help rather than fellow workers. Among faculty alone, hierarchies emerge and are sometimes guarded ruthlessly. Some of this emerges for reasons that hardly seem functional for running any organization effectively. The scholar's particular and persistent responsibility for critiquing and assessing creates hierarchies and divisions as well.

For this very reason, the idea of the university as community faces a troubling paradox. The university is fundamentally and ideally a critical institution where ideas are made public so that they might be critiqued and evaluated. When faculty are doing their job well, they will be willing to engage and critique the ideas of others.[13] This critique need not be rancorous, of course, but it certainly makes community ties more difficult to foster and even potentially counterproductive. Some degree of confrontation and hierarchy are built into academic life, but as our own experience and the pages of the Chronicle of Higher Education too regularly reveal, they can also become unrelenting and dehumanizing. Too often, our professorial roles can simply take over better human instincts, and we can forget how to step out of them.

Not long ago, I visited a Catholic university where I joined a large lunch table that included the president, a vice-president, several faculty, support staff, and ground crew; all were seated together, kibitzing. I was startled and pleased to learn that this was the norm at the university. The setting was the one-time refectory of the priests' community, now open to all staff, including the priests. While I would not want to reduce Eucharist to lunch, my time at these tables struck me as marvelously eucharistic. I like to hope that the Eucharist is what keeps making the lunch possible.

I'm told that historian Jakob Burckhardt once likened academic gatherings to "dogs sniffing at one another." Unless we simply conflate our faculty or scholarly roles with our own self, it ought to be a marvelous and freeing opportunity to step out of those roles a bit at times to find some breathing room and freedom. On campus, as elsewhere, Eucharist offers us a chance to step out of our roles in some very important ways, and to mitigate some of the various hierarchies we live in. At the eucharistic table we have an opportunity to see one another not simply as "Jews or Greeks, slaves or free" (1 Corinthians 12:13; RSV). When we move away from the table and back to work, we may not be able or want to eliminate all of the academic equivalents of "Jew or Greek," but we might be better able to keep from becoming trapped in those roles and distinctions alone. Those same persons I prayed with may still have to decide whether to grant or deny me tenure or a promotion, but our presence together at the table, taken seriously, can allow that any of those decisions comes from the responsibility of a single role, and does not reflect our whole selves.

Liturgist Kathleen Hughes, R.S.C.J., has used Victor Turner's insights to illuminate the opportunity that the Eucharist represents for us. Liturgical ritual can create a kind of "liminality . . . placing men and women temporarily outside of everyday structural positions and demands." Such liminality provides a genuine opportunity for a "state of freedom and creativity realized by people set apart for awhile from what Turner calls inhibiting 'status incumbencies.'" This freedom, as I see it, is a freedom to step away from the roles that define us long enough, or sufficiently, in order to be able to redefine our relation to one another. It is an opportunity to strip away what is burdensome and unhealthy and possibly overly inhibiting about our roles.[14] I would not want to seem naive about the possibility or ease of shedding our roles. At the same time, I can vouch for having experienced this at Eucharist, and having been grateful for it.

I have no doubt that it is healthy to step out of role sometimes, to keep from confusing oneself with one's role(s). At the same time, I would hope that participation in the Eucharist would help transform the role of the intellectual. Eva Hooker's words resonate when I think of this transformation: "If you do this, offer praise." The habit of praise is not often much at home in higher education or in other realms of intellectual life. We try in many areas of endeavor to outdo or critique others so as to make a name for ourselves, which makes it hard to offer such praise. A good critique is more widely respected than is equally open praise. Yet, really good pedagogy, I believe, does require habits of praise. Good teachers know the power that appropriate and generous praise can have. How we praise God can help us improve our openness to praising the good in others, just as how we act in other contexts can decrease our ability to praise God with full power and force.

More Still to Be Mended

Unfortunately, as I indicated earlier, the Eucharist has also proved to be fractious in many ways. Because of the Church's claim that it has no authority to ordain women, the Eucharist has been a painful experience for many women, and some men as well—a symbol not of inclusion in the kingdom, but of exclusion. Many traditionalist Catholics have separated themselves from other Catholics over the post-Vatican II replacement of the Tridentine (Latin) Mass with the Pauline (vernacular) Mass. Catholics who are less extreme about the near-demise of the Tridentine Mass still often disagree a great deal over the way the liturgy is celebrated. And when Protestants and Catholics come together to pray, the Eucharist (or its absence) often serves as the most significant reminder of division.

That recognition has sometimes caused faculty and administrators on Catholic campuses to want to shy away from campus-wide eucharistic events like the Mass of the Holy Spirit or the Baccalaureate Mass. Although in one sense that motivation is laudable, it also has the tendency to deprive the Catholic institution of its core communal experience and inspiration. Some years ago I was consulting to a university in an effort to develop some extended faculty workshops on faith and intellectual life. In the schedule, I had suggested that each day there be a more ecumenical morning or evening prayer, as well as a celebration of the Eucharist. Others were implementing and making final decisions about the program, but when the time for the workshops rolled around, I discovered that almost all of the Masses had been replaced with paraliturgical events, out of a fear of being exclusionary. The result, I observed, was that despite creative efforts to make them interesting and relevant, the number of participants who attended the paraliturgies declined each day. I don't think that eucharistic celebrations at mixed-faith Collegium events have ever drawn one-hundred-percent attendance, but I have never seen attendance decline so much as when we tried to develop liturgies suitable for all.

Sociologist Andrew Greeley has asserted repeatedly that the Eucharist is the most important thing that keeps Catholics attached to the Church. My own experience has suggested the same. When in my early twenties my faith felt as if it were hanging by a thread, that single thread was the Eucharist itself. It proved to be a more remarkably strong thread than I could have imagined.

The great paradox, as I see it, is that no words that I can offer can undo the difficulties of exclusion, although we can always communicate to others that we desire deeply that they gather with us around the table of the Lord. I do know Protestants who gain sustenance from our practice of Eucharist, and would rather that Catholics celebrate in a way that is truest to their identity and traditions, rather than have to turn their back on these traditions. Countless women draw great sustenance from the Eucharist, although they long very much to see feminine presiders at the table. And the Eucharist has benefited women even in apparently oppressive situations. Feminist historian Carolyn Walker Bynum has brilliantly helped us appreciate the extent to which the Eucharist helped women appreciate and value the sacredness of physicality and of their own bodies in past epochs when society devalued women for being more "physical" and thus less "spiritual."[15] Yet, I have also had to watch women I love leave the Church for other churches because they were unable to pray any longer at Catholic Eucharist.

While I cannot undo the difficulties of exclusion, I have to add that I cannot imagine the Catholic Christian community without the Eucharist. Perhaps more than any pragmatic argument for what Eucharist "does" for us or our scholarship, I can't imagine supporting the "Catholic" in Catholic intellectual life very long without it.

Conclusion

Communities of any sort exist only as communities of memory and shared commitment. We define ourselves as a group in large part according to a commitment to shared stories that define us. In the life of a college, rituals can be central to the college's sense of self. Commencements, presidential installations, inaugurations for holders of endowed chairs, regular lecture series, the rituals of scholarly academies, football games—even the rituals of obtaining tenure—can all have a profound effect on the unity of a college. Communal rites of mourning have often helped campuses recover from deaths and other tragedies, and rituals have been used to unite students against issues of injustice. In the long run, I would suggest that the memories and rituals we gather around shape and define who we are. It is important that we commit ourselves to these rituals, out of all the rituals that otherwise compete for our attention. As Catholic Christians, that presence of the body of Christ makes and affirms who we are. Augustine's famous words at Communion, "Receive what you are, the Body of Christ," eloquently makes that case.

On a more mundane or practical level, how does this relate to our work as teachers, writers, or researchers? I would suggest that at the very least it gives those of us who work in these areas a high standard to aspire to. Much of our work is aimed at helping to preserve memory, to see what has not been adequately perceived before, to discover anew, to share what we know and can achieve. It doesn't in any way reduce or trivialize the Emmaus account to compare the disciples' joy at their sudden recognition of Jesus' presence among them to the joy of finding deep insight into a problem or text that has confused us for a long time. The two disciples felt an obligation to share their discovery with others in all its fullness. Knowing, from our own grasp of the Emmaus experience, what it's like to have our hearts burn within us, we can aspire to help students to recognize some truth or insight at the deepest level possible, to see all that is present, and not simply to be content with surface-level understanding.

Historians could also be comforted and challenged by the reminder the Eucharist poses: that remembrance is crucial to human existence, not an extracurricular or merely specialist concern. Christian faith in the Eucharist is a theological reminder that ours is a God who really wants us to see and remember, and thus to know how we are obligated to one another.

Notes

1. Max Weber, *The Sociology of Religion* (Boston: Beacon Press, 1963), p. 152–153, originally published as part of his grand theoretical summary, *Wirtzschaft und Gesellschaft*.
2. Henri J. M. Nouwen, *With Burning Hearts: A Meditation on the Eucharistic Life* (Maryknoll, NY: Orbis, 1994).
3. Jonathan Z. Smith, *To Take Place: Toward Theory in Ritual* (Chicago: University of Chicago Press, 1987), p. 96–103.
4. Andre Dubus, *Meditations from a Movable Chair* (New York: Alfred A. Knopf, 1998).
5. Ibid., p. 89.
6. Ibid., p. 87.
7. Andrew Sullivan, "Virtually Normal," *South Atlantic Quarterly*, Volume 93, Number 3 (1994). The essay was revised for the prologue of Sullivan's book by the same title, *Virtually Normal: An Argument About Homosexuality* (New York: Alfred A. Knopf, 1995). The *SAQ* volume was subsequently published as *Catholic Lives, Contemporary America* (Durham, NC: Duke, 1997).
8. Sullivan, 1995, p. 7.
9. Sullivan, 1997, p. 172.

10. Daniel Donovan, *Distinctively Catholic: An Exploration in Catholic Identity* (Mahwah, NJ: Paulist, 1997), p. 110.
11. Enda McDonagh, *The Making of Disciples* (Wilmington, MA: Michael Glazier, 1982), p. 39.
12. Jane Redmont, *When in Doubt, Sing: Prayer in Daily Life* (San Francisco: HarperCollins, 1999), p. 105.
13. Alan Wolfe, "Higher Learning," *Lingua Franca*, 6 (March/April 1996), p. 70–77.
14. H. Kathleen Hughes, R.S.C.J. "Liturgy and Justice: An Intrinsic Relationship," in Kathleen Hughes, R.S.C.J., and Mark R. Francis, C.S.V., editors, *Living No Longer for Ourselves: Liturgy and Justice in the Nineties* (Collegeville, MN: Liturgical Press, 1991), p. 46–47. Victor Turner, "Passages, Margins and Poverty: Religious Symbols of Communitas," *Worship* 46 (1972) p. 399.
15. Caroline Walker Bynum, *Fragmentation and Redemption: Essays on Gender and the Human Body in Medieval Religion* (New York: Zone Books, 1991.

13

Catholicism's Communitarian Vision: The Church in the Modern World

David Hollenbach, S.J.

The beginning of the twenty-first century confronts all religious communities with a fundamental challenge: how to relate their distinctive visions of the good human life with growing awareness that all persons are linked together in a web of global interdependence. The diverse communities of the world today are increasingly bound together in the world market, by their mutual dependence on the biophysical environment that knows no boundaries, by cultural interactions made possible by communications technology, by migration and forced refugee movements, and by the transnational transmission of threats to human life and health such as the AIDS virus, drugs, and weapons of war. In this interdependent world, the need for a clear vision of the common good of the whole human race is evident.

This interdependent world, however, is increasingly aware of its religious and cultural pluralism. *Pluralism*, by definition, means that there is no agreement about the meaning of the good life. In addition, the complexity of emerging world realities is leading many communities to seek reaffirmation of the distinctive traditions that set them apart from others. Thus, we face an apparent paradox: attaining a vision of the global common good is increasingly problematic precisely at a historical moment when the need for such a vision is growing.

Catholic social thought has sought to address this paradox by remaining deeply rooted in biblical and theological sources, while also seeking to make its ethical vision intelligible to those of other communities through reasonable discourse, ecumenical understanding, and interreligious dialogue. The Catholic community, of course, is still learning how to be faithful to its own beliefs while making a contribution to the global common good. But I want to try to shed some light on the pathway Catholicism is seeking to travel.

In the century before the Second Vatican Council, the main lines of Catholic social teaching were based on the conviction that human reason is capable of discovering the basic outlines of the human good. From Pope

Leo XIII's encyclical *Rerum novarum* in 1891 to Pope John XXIII's *Pacem in terris* in 1963 during the Council, Catholic contributions to social morality regularly appealed to human reason to discern the moral demands of human nature. Since human nature was created by God, and since human reason is one of the Creator's greatest gifts to human beings, this natural law approach to social morality was seen as fully compatible with Christian biblical faith. Indeed, a reason-based social ethic was understood as a direct implication of Roman Catholic faith.

This natural law approach in official Roman Catholic social teaching reached its clearest expression in John XXIII's affirmation of a charter of human rights in *Pacem in terris*.[1] This encyclical declared human rights are founded on human dignity, whose clearest manifestation is rationality and freedom. The encyclical added that human rights will be esteemed more highly when considered in the light of revelation and grace, for Christian faith reinforces a sense of human worth through its belief in God's redemptive love for all people in Christ.[2] But it is clear that the pope proposes an ethical standard that can be known by those who are not Christian and to which all people can be held accountable independent of their religious or cultural traditions. Thus, John XXIII went on to present a list of human rights very similar to the United Nations Universal Declaration of Human Rights. In this natural law ethic, human rights were seen as universal, transcultural, and suited to the promotion of the common good of a religiously pluralistic world.

This sort of natural law-based, universalist ethic has deep roots in the Roman Catholic tradition. Saint Paul, in the letter to the Romans, and Thomas Aquinas, for example, maintained that the most basic requirements of human morality can be known by Christian believers and unbelievers alike. Christian morality is not sectarian in the sense Ernst Troeltsch used this term, i.e., it is not a morality for Christians only. The desire to find common moral ground between Christians and non-Christians is a deep impulse in the Catholic tradition because of its belief that one God has created the whole of humanity and that all human beings share a common origin, destiny, and nature. This universalism has continued to be a strong emphasis in Catholic social teaching in the decades since Vatican II.

However, the Council introduced some complexities into the Catholic affirmation of universalist natural law. The Second Vatican Council was an assembly of Roman Catholic bishops drawn from most of the diverse cultures around the world and from societies where all of the great world religions play significant roles. As Karl Rahner pointed out, Vatican II was a unique event in the history of the Catholic community in that it was "in a rudimentary form still groping for identity, the Church's first official self-actualization as a world Church" rather than as a European religion to be exported to the rest of the world along with European culture.[3] This historical and sociological fact had considerable influence on the teaching of the Council, including its social teaching. It led to heightened awareness that the cultural and religious pluralism of the world has an effect on what people see as reasonable interpretations of the human good, and thus as the reasonable demands of social morality. Despite the growing sense of the unity of the human family and the heightened exchange of ideas across cultural and religious boundaries, "the very words by which key concepts are expressed take on quite different meanings."4 This broadening of the Church's self-consciousness at Vatican II called into question the robust confidence that universal norms of social morality are readily evident to all reasonable people.

Thus, one can legitimately discern in some of the texts of Vatican II an incipient emergence of what has since come to be called the postmodern suspicion of universalism. In fact, this postmodern critique in the West has been aimed at the eighteenth-century Enlightenment's belief that pure reason could discover the human good on its own, without reliance on the inherited presuppositions of cultural or religious traditions. It is clear that Catholicism had never accepted the presuppositions of Enlightenment rationalism. But some eighteenth- and nineteenth-century Catholic thinkers, including moral theologians and social ethicists, were subtly affected by this rationalism in their apologetic efforts to defend Catholic thought in the face of the challenges raised to it by West European modernity. They adopted the methods of their rationalist adversaries to counteract the substance of rationalist arguments.5

The Council, however, affirmed an important role for distinctive biblical faith and Christian theological convictions in the formation of Roman Catholic social thought, although it did not abandon its commitment to universality. In fact, it saw a need to revitalize the distinctively Christian basis of the Church's response to pressing moral problems. The Council's Decree on Priestly Formation called for a renewal of Catholic moral thought through livelier contact with the mystery of Christ and the history of salvation.6 This renewal of biblical and theological roots is evident in the entire first part of the Council's Pastoral Constitution on the Church in the Modern World, which provides the overarching vision of recent Catholic social teaching. The document's treatment of three fundamental topics—the dignity of the human person, the importance of the vocation to community in solidarity, and the religious significance of this-worldly activity—is supported both by distinctively Christian theological warrants as well as by natural law warrants based on reason.

For example, in line with the natural law approach of John XXIII, the Council continued to affirm that the dignity of the human person is discernible in the transcendent power of the human mind, in the sacredness of conscience, and in the excellence of liberty. Thus, this dignity can be recognized by all human beings and makes claims upon all, both Christian and non-Christian. Nevertheless, human dignity is known in its full depth only from Christian revelation. The Bible uncovers this depth in its affirmation that human beings are created in the image and likeness of God and therefore possess a sacredness that is properly religious. Further, redemption and recreation in Christ means that human dignity has a theological dimension that only Christian faith can see. In a highly significant passage, the Council argued that an understanding of and response to the person of Jesus Christ is necessary for the attainment of an adequate grasp of the human: "The truth is that only in the mystery of the incarnate Word does the mystery of the human person take on light."7

Such an affirmation challenges the rationalist idea that Christian ethical reflection can rely exclusively on philosophical reason and natural law. It shows that the Church's social mission is a religious one that flows from the heart of Christian faith. This emphasis has been developed and refined in the post-conciliar official social teachings and in movements such as liberation and political theologies, both of which have strong biblical roots. It shows that the Church seeks to bring a distinctively Christian orientation to debates about social existence in a world increasingly conscious of itself as divided and pluralistic.

Thus, the Council seems to want to have it both ways. It reaffirmed a universal ethic or common morality that is normative in all cultures and for all religious communities; it also affirmed a distinctively Christian foundation for this ethic and an epistemology based on revelation through which this foundation can be known. The same dual approach is present in the recent writings of Pope John Paul II.[8] Is such a position coherent?

There are several interpretations of the relationship between universalist and particularist sources that could explain this two-fold approach. First, one could affirm that universal moral standards are in principle knowable by all persons but that in practice revelation is needed because of the weakness of the human mind and its further distortions by sin. In the concreteness of the actual existence of most people, revelation and grace are needed to know and live by the natural law. This position can be found in Augustine and Thomas Aquinas in the Catholic tradition and especially in the work of John Calvin in the Protestant tradition. The disadvantage of this approach is that it sometimes fails to attend sufficiently to the presence of sin in the Christian community itself.

Second, one could argue, as has Pope John Paul II, that the authoritative teaching office of the Roman Catholic Church guarantees that the magisterium is capable or discerning and teaching the universally normative natural law in ways that are preserved by the Holy Spirit from sinful distortions. This stance, however, risks undermining its own claims to provide a common morality for a pluralistic world by suggesting that only the magisterium of the Roman Church can in practice know what that morality is.

A third approach, which can be called dialogic universalism, offers a more promising possibility. The Council's approach combined the emphasis on the distinctively religious basis of Catholic social teaching with its recognition of pluralism through a new stress on dialogue. Dialogue means starting the pursuit of a common morality from the vantage point of the Church's own theological convictions. But it also means bringing these convictions into active encounter with other religious communities and with other traditions with different, non-Western histories. This method of dialogue does not imply relativism. In fact, the commitment to dialogue and mutual inquiry suggests just the opposite—that there is a truth about the human good that must be pursued and that makes a claim of the minds and hearts of all persons.[9] Only the pursuit of such truth makes dialogue worth pursuing. Relativists have no reason to engage in it; if no understanding of the human is any better than another, why bother?

Thus, when the Council stressed the particularity of its theological understanding of human dignity, this did not lead it to deny the universality of the morality rooted in this theology. Indeed, the affirmation of the universal dignity of the person is itself the reason dialogue is so important.[10] It opens the Church to learn more of the truth wherever it is found—in the sciences, the arts, and philosophy.[11] Other documents of the Council stress inter-Christian ecumenical dialogue and dialogue with the other great world religions as sources of such growth in understanding.[12]

This commitment to dialogue is both a demand of Christian faith and a requirement of reasonableness. Christian faith entails care and respect for all persons, and respect for their dignity means listening to their interpretations of the human good. Further, Christian love calls for the building up of the bonds of solidarity among all persons, and such solidarity requires efforts to understand those who are different, to learn from them, and to contribute to their understanding of the good life as well. Similarly, a reasonableness that avoids the rationalist dismissal of historical traditions and communal particularities will take the diverse traditions and cultures of the world seriously enough to both listen carefully to them and to respond with respect. It is a reasonableness that expects both to learn and to teach through the give-and-take of dialogue. For Christians, such dialogue, therefore, embodies a dynamic interaction between the biblical faith handed on to them through the centuries of Christian tradition and the reason that is a preeminent manifestation of the *imago Dei* in all human beings.

This dialogic and dynamic linkage of faith and reason has implications for a number of the substantive questions of social morality today. The most obvious is in the broad area of an ethic of human rights. Freedom of speech, association, assembly, and political participation are among the concrete expressions of any ethic committed to genuine dialogue. Where these freedoms are denied, dialogue is impossible. Where the rights to these freedoms are not respected, persons are treated neither as the gospel requires nor as reasonableness demands. Thus, Vatican II could state that "the right to religious freedom has its foundation in the very dignity of the human person, as this dignity is known through the revealed word of God and by reason itself."[13] Indeed, Vatican II linked its support for the full range of human rights with both the very core of Christian faith and with the continuing commitment to a kind of natural law morality understood by reason. For it declared both that "by virtue of the gospel committed to it, the Church proclaims the rights of the human person"[14] and that the social nature of human beings and their intrinsic dignity means that "the goal of all social institutions is and must be the human person."[15]

The location of this commitment to human rights in the context of an ethic of dialogue has important implications for the way these rights are understood. Religious freedom, for example, is sometimes understood in the more secularized sectors of Western societies in a way that would marginalize religion from active presence in the public life of society. In this view, religion will be tolerated as long is it remains a private matter within the individual's conscience or the walls of the sanctuary or sacristy. Vatican II's vision of religious freedom is quite different from this privatized account. For the Council stated that "It comes within the meaning of religious freedom that religious bodies should not be prohibited from freely undertaking to show the special value of their doctrine in what concerns the organization of society and the inspiration of the whole of human activity."[16] The free exercise of religion is a social freedom and the right to freedom of religion includes the right to seek to influence the policies and laws by which a free people will be governed and the public culture they share. The dialogic ethic underlying this claim means that protection of active engagement of religious believers in public life, not privatization of religion, is part of the substantive meaning of the right to religious freedom. It also means that such engagement must be conducted with deep respect for those who hold differing beliefs. Thus, believers should "at all times . . . refrain from any manner of action which might seem to carry a hint of coercion."[17] Persuasion through reasonable discourse is the proper mode of public participation by religious believers, especially when they seek to influence law or public policy.

More broadly, such a dialogic understanding has implications for how to address the meaning of the full range of human rights. In the days of the recently ended Cold War, for example, the West was largely inclined to conceive human rights in individualistic terms and to give priority to the civil and political rights to free speech, due process of law, and political participation. In contrast to this emphasis, Eastern bloc nations and some in the Southern hemisphere that adopted Marxist-inspired ideologies stressed social and economic rights such as those to adequate food, work, and housing. A dialogic ethic suggests not only that these two traditions ought to learn from the strengths of the other but also that the opposition between individual freedoms on the one hand and mutual solidarity in society on the other is a false dichotomy. Persons can live in dignity only when they live in a community of freedom, that is a community in which both personal initiative and social solidarity are valued and embodied. The give-and-take of dialogue is the intellectual manifestation of such a linkage of personal initiative and social solidarity. But this linkage has material dimensions as well and will be manifest only when persons have both economic and political space for action (civil and political rights) and the material and institutional prerequisites of communal life that make such action possible (social and economic rights). Thus, both civil-political and social-economic rights are genuine human rights that should be respected in all societies. This sets a large agenda before the nations of our interdependent world. But despite the challenging nature of this agenda, it can give substantive guidance for social, political, and economic institutions that a one-sided emphasis on the pluralism of interpretations of human rights in our world fails to provide.[18]

This vision of social interdependence has important implications for the intellectual life and for the life of the university. It calls for education in *social solidarity*, a form of education that opens the minds of the students and faculty of the university to the reality of human suffering in a world marred by the grinding poverty of so many in the world, by lack of health insurance for large numbers of Americans, by the attempts at genocide in Bosnia and

Rwanda, by the fate of refugees in throughout the world—to name only a few of the most obvious manifestations of the long history of human beings' sinful propensity to treat one another in inhuman ways. As Michael Buckley has noted, the origins of the Catholic university in the Middle Ages and its development by the Jesuits and other religious communities at the dawn of the modern period were manifestations of the conviction that a Christian humanism is both possible and required by the dynamic of Christian faith itself. The challenge of Christian humanism remains central to the identity of universities today. But today that humanism must be a social humanism, a humanism with a deep appreciation for not only the heights to which human culture can rise but also the depths of suffering to which societies can descend.[19] There are strong currents in American life today that insulate both professors and students from experience of and academic reflection on these sufferings. An intellectual life that aspires both to be Catholic and to serve the common good must do more than include nods to the importance of social solidarity. We must translate this into teaching and research priorities, and actualize these priorities in day-to-day activities in classroom and library. This will take both the courage and the humility that the privileged learn only when they encounter the reality of poverty and other forms of suffering.

The same need for a dialogical or solidarity approach to the interpretation of human rights is evident in the way we address the issue of religious diversity in the world today. It raises particularly pointed questions about the relation between the particularity of different religious traditions and the universality claimed for human rights norms. Human rights, of course, are moral norms proposed as protections for the sacredness of persons as such, independent of their religious or cultural traditions. They apply universally to all persons. Western Enlightenment thought interpreted this claim to universality to mean that human rights are moral standards that stand independent of all traditions, cultures, and religions. Indeed, in some interpretations, a human rights ethic challenges all traditions as forms of benighted narrowness. On the other hand, the contemporary awareness of the historical embeddedness of rationality has caused others to reject the very notion of human rights as an Enlightenment illusion. Catholic social thought, however, continues to affirm the reality of human rights as compatible with the importance of religious tradition. Such a continuing defense of human rights is crucial in today's interdependent world, for threats to human dignity continue today on a massive scale. But any such defense must take account of the ways the justification of human rights norms and the interpretation of their concrete implications vary in notable ways from one philosophical, ideological, or religious tradition to another.[20]

The history of Catholic tradition provides some noteworthy evidence that discourse across the boundaries of diverse communities is both possible and potentially fruitful. The Catholic tradition, in its better moments, has experienced considerable success in efforts to bridge the divisions that have separated it from other communities with other understandings of the good life. In the first and second centuries, the early Christian community moved from being a small Palestinian sect to active encounter with the Hellenistic and

Roman worlds. In the fourth century, Augustine brought biblical faith into dialogue with Stoic and Neoplatonic thought. His efforts profoundly transformed both Christian and Graeco-Roman thought and practice. In the thirteenth century, Thomas Aquinas once again transformed Western Christianity by appropriating ideas of Aristotle he had learned from Arab Muslims and from Jews. And although the Church resisted the liberal discovery of modern freedoms through much of the modern period, affirmation of these freedoms has been transforming Catholicism once again through the last half of our own century. The memory of these events in social and intellectual history as well as the experience of the Catholic Church since the Second Vatican Council leads me to the hope that communities holding different visions of the good life can get somewhere if they are willing to risk serious conversation and sustained argument about these visions. Injecting such hope back into the public life of the United States would be a signal achievement.

What might such public discourse look like? Broadly speaking, it will be conversation and argument about the shape of the culture the participants either share through their common traditions or could share in the future through the understanding of each other they seek to achieve. The forum for such discussion is not, in the first instance, the legislative chamber or the court of law. It is the university and all the other venues where thoughtful men and women undertake the tasks of retrieving, criticizing, and reconstructing understandings of the human good from the historical past and transmitting them to the future through education. It occurs, as well, wherever people bring their received historical traditions on the meaning of the good life into intelligent and critical encounter with understandings of this good held by other peoples with other traditions. It occurs, in short, wherever education about and serious inquiry into the meaning of the good life takes place.

Further, the achievement of such a truly free dialogue about the meaning of the good life has direct implications for the role of religion in the university. Our culture needs much more conversation about the visions of the human good held by diverse religious communities and real intellectual engagement with these religious visions. The Catholic tradition and many Protestant traditions as well reject the notion that religious faith must be irrational and, therefore, out of bounds within the intellectual forum of the university. In both the Catholic and Calvinist views of the matter, faith and understanding are not adversarial but reciprocally illuminating. This invites those outside the Church to place their self-understanding at risk by serious conversation with religious traditions. At the same time, the believer's self-understanding will be challenged to development or even fundamental change by dialogue with the other—whether this other be a secular agnostic, a Christian from another tradition, a Jew, a Muslim, or a Buddhist.

Although serious dialogue is risky business, at least some religious believers have been willing to take it. The future of the common good in our interdependent world could be considerably enhanced by the willingness of a larger number of people to take this risk of religious and cultural dialogue, whether they begin as fundamentalists convinced of their certitudes or agnostics convinced of their doubts. Our society needs more imagination about how to deal creatively with its problems than it appears to possess today. Religious traditions and communities are among the principal bearers of such imaginative sources for our understanding of the human, and the Catholic tradition is perhaps uniquely positioned to make important intellectual contributions of this sort today. Catholicism can evoke not only private self-understanding but public vision as well. Both believers and unbelievers alike have reason to risk considering what contribution religious traditions might make to our understanding of the public good. The principal place where this can happen is the university, as the Catholic tradition has long known. Today, the university needs to be much more open to such dialogue than it is inclined to be. Collegium is embarked on the task of helping you envision your role as intellectuals in the university and the larger society in ways that will help remedy this limitation in our culture.

In conclusion, the challenge of today's pluralistic and interdependent world leads to a new way of conceiving the ancient question of the relationship between faith and reason in the development of an ethic that can guide the Church's action in society. This new relationship is a dynamic process of interaction between fidelity to the distinctive religious beliefs and distinctive traditions of Christianity on the one hand, and the pursuit of an inclusive, universal community on the other. Dialogue—the active engagement of listening and speaking with others whose beliefs and traditions are different—is the key to such dynamism. Where such dialogue is absent, the chances of obtaining a vision of the common good of the world we are entering will be small to the point of vanishing. The Second Vatican Council launched the Roman Catholic community on this path of dialogue. Since the Council, there has been both progress and retreat. Addressing the future requires renewed commitment to the agenda set by Vatican II.

Notes

1. John XXIII, *Pacem in terris*, no. 9. Trans. in David J. O'Brien and Thomas A. Shannon, eds., *Catholic Social Thought: The Documentary Heritage* (Maryknoll, NY: Orbis Books, 1992).
2. *Pacem in terris*, no. 10.
3. Karl Rahner, "Toward a Fundamental Theological Interpretation of Vatican II," *Theological Studies* 40 (December 1979): 716–727, at 717.
4. Vatican Council II, *Gaudium et spes* (The Pastoral Constitution on the Church in the Modern World), no. 4. All references to Vatican II documents are from Walter Abbott and Joseph Gallagher, eds., *The Documents of Vatican II* (New York: America Press, 1966).
5. For a discussion of the effect of such apologetic efforts on theological responses to modern atheism, see Michael J. Buckley, *At the Origins of Modern Atheism* (New Haven: Yale University Press, 1987).
6. Vatican Council II, *Optatam totius* (Decree on Priestly Formation), no. 16.
7. *Gaudium et spes,* no. 22.
8. See, for example, John Paul II's encyclicals *Veritatis splendor* and *Evangelium vitae*.

9. See Alasdair MacIntyre, *Whose Justice? Which Rationality* (Notre Dame, IN: University of Notre Dame Press, 1988) chapter XVIII. See also MacIntyre, *Three Rival Versions of Moral Enquiry: Encyclopedia, Genealogy and Tradition* (Notre Dame, IN: University of Notre Dame Press, 1990) chapter X, which relates this treatment of how traditions develop to the task of the university.

10. *Gaudium et spes*, no. 40.

11. *Gaudium et spes*, no. 44.

12. See Vatican Council II, *Unitatis redintegratio* (Decree on Ecumenism) and *Nostra aetate* (Declaration on the Relationship of the Church to Non-Christian Religions).

13. Vatican Council II, *Dignitatis humanae* (Declaration on Religious Freedom), no. 2.

14. *Gaudium et spes*, no. 41.

15. *Gaudium et spes*, no. 25.

16. *Dignitatis humanae*, no. 4.

17. *Dignitatis humanae*, no. 4.

18. For a fuller discussion of this point see my "A Communitarian Reconstruction of Human Rights" and "Afterword: A Community of Freedom," in *Catholicism and Liberalism: Contributions to American Public Philosophy*, ed. R. Bruce Douglass and David Hollenbach (Cambridge and New York: Cambridge University Press, 1994), 127–150 and 323–343.

19. See Michael Buckley, "The University and the Concern for Justice: The Search for a New Humanism," *Thought* 57 (1982): 219–233, and "Christian Humanism and Human Misery: A Challenge to the Jesuit University," in Michael J. Buckley, et al., eds., *Faith, Discovery, Service: Perspectives on Jesuit Education* (Milwaukee: Marquette University Press, 1992), 77–105.

20. For one effort along these lines see the *Declaration Toward a Global Ethic* issued by the 1993 Parliament of the World's Religions held in Chicago, in Hans Küng and Karl-Josef Kuschel, eds. *A Global Ethic: The Declaration of the Parliament of the World's Religions,* trans. John Bowden (New York: Continuum, 1993), and commentaries on this Declaration from representatives of many traditions in Hans Küng, ed. *Yes to a Global Ethic*, trans. John Bowden (New York: Continuum, 1996).

14

The Seamless Garment of the Intellectual Life: Reflections from Bioethics and the Consistent Ethic of Life

M. Therese Lysaught

Most readers of this volume find themselves, by virtue of their social location, participants in what is often referred to as the "Catholic Intellectual Life." Whether we are Catholics teaching at secular institutions, skeptics teaching at Catholic institutions, or somewhere in between, our vocations as academics—professors, researchers, colleagues, citizens—are ineluctably shaped by Catholic traditions.

What difference might this social location make? In what ways might a Catholic ethos positively shape the academic life? To answer these questions, I would like to begin with a brief vignette.

A cold morning in January 1998 found eight of us gathered, bleary-eyed in the wan winter 8-a.m. light: two philosophers, two theologians, two professors (one of education and one of psychology), the director of campus ministry, an engineer, and a biologist. The year's first meeting of the university's Ethical Decisions Committee was convened, and we were charged to reflect on a question brought forward by the biologist: Should the University of Dayton develop a policy regarding the use of human embryonic stem cells in biological research on campus?

This question launched a yearlong process of research, reflection, writing, study, and conversation. In the process, we found ourselves turning to more fundamental questions:

- What might be the scientific elegance and clinical merit of such research?
- How might incipient developments in public policy create new possibilities or new pressures for biological research programs?
- What were the relevant federal policies or state or federal laws?
- What does it mean to be a Catholic and Marianist[1] institution with a doctoral program in biology?

- Which church teachings might shed light on the issue?
- For a biologist, ought the Catholic context of one's teaching and research make a difference?
- How do we balance the interests of the individual against those of the institution?
- What are our responsibilities to our students? What are the standards of our discipline?
- How might a biologist's faith commitments play into the negotiation of these relationships with students, science, discipline, institution, and society?
- Is there a call for individuals or the institution to witness an alternative to society?
- What difference might the commercial dimensions of biotechnology make in our assessment of it?

Science, policy, faith commitments, church teaching, professional identity discipleship, and economic considerations flowed seamlessly together. No one question, we found, could be considered in isolation from the others.

Clearly, this process was a challenge. We were on new and unfamiliar ground. Few of us even knew what a stem cell was. Thus, our necessary first step was to educate ourselves on the science. From there, our self-education broadened to encompass state and federal law, NIH policy, the policies of our university, the policies of other similarly situated secular and Catholic universities, church teaching, Catholic and Christian theology, philosophical reflection, and the realm of business.

In doing so, we found ourselves in the middle of a lively interdisciplinary exchange. As one can imagine, members of the committee did not always agree with each other. We found our own disciplinary perspectives both challenged and enhanced by the presentations of others; as we learned more from each of the other disciplines, we learned more about our own work.

And as if being pushed beyond our disciplinary comfort zones and having to learn serious science, policy, and theology were not enough, we were then charged with a task foreign to most of us: the task of creating a policy. This policy was clearly a "public" policy, insofar as it would affect the lives of some thirteen thousand people at the university (however tangentially) and become part of the wider public conversation about the propriety of human embryonic stem cell research. Thus, suddenly immersed in the middle of an ongoing public debate, we found ourselves pushed beyond theory to application.

That this conversation occurred at all reflected our location in shared Catholic context. The committee's dynamic embodied the best of what a Catholic university can be: a place for sustained intellectual analysis, debate, and dialogue; for reflection on the relationship between faith and intellectual/professional vocations; and for moving toward practical implementation of change in the world. For those readers who hail from disciplines not represented in the committee's make-up, had you been part of the work of such a committee, what questions would you have asked and issues would you have raised? What resources would you have been able to bring from your own disciplinary perspective? In what ways would this process have challenged your own perspective, both personally and professionally?

While the committee process embodied a Catholic university at its best, it also modeled—unbeknownst to the participants—the essence of the Catholic tradition of reflection on human life issues. I would like to suggest that this strand of the Catholic tradition—from the discipline of bioethics to the metaphor of the "consistent ethic of life"—provides a model that challenges academics across disciplines to think differently about our academic vocations. Roman Catholic bioethics stands before us as an exemplar of how the vocation of the academic is to forge new intellectual paths. Moreover, by bringing key theological concepts and convictions into the realm of practice, Catholic bioethical reflection provides a springboard from which to develop and deepen the vision of the academic life. Catholic bioethics helps us think about the academic life as, on the one hand, a form of discipleship, and on the other, as one of seamless integration and public witness rather than narrow professional reductivism. Keeping the opening vignette in mind as we move forward, consider now how Roman Catholic bioethics and the consistent ethic of life model possibilities for the integration of faith and vocation across disciplines.

Catholic Intellectual Life: Forging New Intellectual Paths

To locate oneself as an intellectual within the Catholic tradition is to find oneself immersed in a motley communion of forebears. For, contrary to the stereotype of Catholicism as an institution that stifles creative exploration by dogmatically requiring obedient adherence, its history is peopled with those who—trained within a Catholic way of thinking and raised within a Catholic ethos—creatively push disciplinary boundaries, becoming architects of new ways of understanding and negotiating the world. The very existence and character of contemporary bioethics is a case in point.

A mere four decades ago, "bioethics" as a distinct discipline of professional inquiry and practice did not exist. Today, however, it is a field in its own right, complete with professional associations, a plethora of academic journals, and career positions as hospital-based clinical ethicists, policy wonks, and academic experts. Unlike other academic specialties, it has become part of the fabric of everyday life, omnipresent to public consciousness through print and news media as well as through concrete encounters with the reality of medicine.

The establishment of bioethics has recently led a number of prominent figures to begin to write the history of the discipline's genesis and development. As with the writing of any such history, the perspectives and agendas of the storytellers inevitably shape the way that the story is told, but there is consensus on two points. First, bioethics as a contemporary phenomenon emerged in the mid to late 1960s. During this period, moral reflection on medicine underwent a "metamorphosis" or "renaissance."[2] Although moral reflection on medicine began well before the 1960s (most trace its beginnings back to the Hippocratic tradition in fourth century B.C.E. Greek culture), clearly the tenor, method, and content of such reflection underwent a radical and qualitative shift during this time. Second, analysts who study the 60s in detail lay responsibility for this renaissance at the feet of one group: theologians. As Albert R. Jonsen, author of the magisterial *The Birth of Bioethics* notes, at the dawn of bioethics, "theologians were the first to appear on the scene."[3] Protestant, Jewish, and Catholic alike, theologians brought to the burgeoning conversations amongst scientists and physicians two key advantages. They were equipped with a language and intellectual practice that enabled them to locate techniques and technologies within a broader vision of human life and its individual, social, and ultimate ends. And Catholics, especially, could avail themselves of lengthy traditions of moral reflection, particularly upon the moral dimensions of medical practice.

However, Catholics were more than simply present at this rebirth. It is clear that Catholic laity—by virtue of their position of engagement with both the Church and the world—were principle architects of the new field, both institutionally and substantively.[4] A pivotal event in this nativity, glossed over in many secular histories of the field, proved to be Pope Paul VI's 1968 papal encyclical *Humanae vitae*. The story begins in 1963/1964 with the encyclical's precursor, the Pontifical Study Commission on Family, Population, and Birth; the study group convened to examine the question of contraception. Two aspects of the commission itself were significant. First, it was interdisciplinary, comprised of moral theologians, reproductive biologists, physicians, demographers, economists, sociologists, and pastoral chaplains. Natural and social scientists, policy analysts, and theologians came together to deliberate on a new technology and an important human question. In addition, of the fifty-eight members of the commission, the majority were lay professionals and intellectuals, an important innovation in church processes. As such, the commission modeled the face of bioethics to come, serving as "a precursor to the national and presidential commissions established in the United States in the 1970s," secular commissions that determined the substance and course of bioethics in the 1980s and 1990s.[5]

Not only did the commission model the future development of this nascent discipline. The commission itself captured the hearts and attention of key Catholic lay people. Two of these are of signal significance. The first was the young Dutch-born but United States-based obstetrician-gynecologist, André E. Hellegers. A member of the commission, Hellegers was particularly impressed with the commission's interdisciplinary interactions and sought in his subsequent work to replicate its conversations between medicine and theology. In addition, the ongoing work of the commission captured the attention of leading lay Catholic leaders in the U.S., including moral philosopher Daniel Callahan, then editor of the leading American Catholic intellectual journal, *Commonweal*. As is clear from his writings between 1964 and 1969, his engagement with medical ethics began with the related questions of contraception and abortion and the work of the commission. In 1968, the encyclical itself was released, rejecting the majority recommendations of the Pontifical Commission. Both Hellegers and Callahan were dismayed; the encyclical seemed to both disregard the findings of science relative to moral evaluation and to dishonor the process of study and effort mounted by commission members.

These experiences could not help but have shaped their subsequent moves. Undeterred, in 1969, Daniel Callahan founded, with colleague Willard Gaylin, the Institute of Society, Ethics, and the Life Sciences, a center for bioethics research and education that would eventually be renamed the Hastings Center. In 1971, Hellegers followed suit, convincing the Joseph P. Kennedy Foundation to provide initial funding for what would become the Kennedy Institute for Ethics at Georgetown University (and would later sponsor the first graduate programs in bioethics). In so doing, Callahan and Hellegers, two leading lay Catholic intellectuals, established what have become the two premiere centers for research and education in bioethics and the two most significant influences on the development of the field, equaled only by the National and Presidential Commissions for Bioethics.

The story of Catholic involvement in the renaissance of bioethics could go on. In so doing, it would need to recount the significant contributions of moral theologians, such Bernard Häring, Charles Curran, Richard McCormick, Germaine Grisez, Albert Jonsen, Margaret Farley, and Lisa Cahill; jurists such as Ninth Circuit Court justice John Noonan; physician-philosophers like Edmund Pellegrino; and attorneys like Paul Armstrong, who argued and won the case of Karen Ann Quinlan laying the groundwork for current consensus on the right to refuse treatment.[6] These compatriots, trained within a Catholic way of thinking and raised within a Catholic ethos, have again and again creatively pressed beyond traditional disciplinary boundaries to shape one of the most socially influential disciplines in late twentieth-century Western culture.

Is this a phenomenon limited to theology and philosophy? I would like to suggest that it is not, but rather reflects a dynamic internal to the Catholic tradition. What might one find if one were to turn to the history of one's own discipline, looking for the contributions and innovations of Catholic practitioners? Would one find these practitioners raising questions of the deeper meaning of technical innovations, of the impact of such innovations on both the dignity of individuals and on the broader good of society, and seeking the answers to such questions at interdisciplinary boundaries? Bioethics as a discipline peopled and shaped by Catholics challenges us to historicize our own professional disciplines in order to foster a truer and more nuanced understanding of our own intellectual heritage.

While bioethics challenges us to reconsider our histories, it likewise points us toward the future. How are we, as participants within the Catholic intellectual tradition, negotiating the current boundaries of our disciplines? In our research and professional life, do we find ourselves safely treading water within the confines of well-established parameters? Or do we see ourselves as likewise called to forge new intellectual paths, risky and uncharted though they may be? I would argue that such creativity-in-community—whether manifest as globally as the development of a new discipline or as locally as the work of the University of Dayton Ethical Decisions Committee—is the hallmark of the Catholic intellectual. The Catholic intellectual life, like the life of faith, calls us beyond our comfort zones.

Catholic Intellectual Life: Following the Call to Discipleship

While the mere existence of the discipline of bioethics illuminates important characteristics of an intellectual life rooted in a Catholic ethos, the content of Catholic reflection on human life issues provides more substantive guidance. For consideration of moral issues in medicine from a Catholic perspective is rooted in a theological vision of the world in which the actions of physician, patient, and community are ideally construed under the rubric of discipleship. Thus, Catholic intellectuals who turn to the legacy of Catholic medical ethics for insight into their own vocation will find themselves called beyond narrowly defined professional identities to a broader construal of the academic life as a life of discipleship.[7]

The starting point of Roman Catholic medical ethics and, indeed, much of Roman Catholic moral reflection in general is the human person. But behind the human person stands a vision of God. To understand the life to which humans are called requires first an understanding of God.

Who is this God? First and foremost, God is the Creator, the one out of whose gracious love all being has come into existence and who sustains all of creation in divine grace. Faith in this creative God leads to an affirmation of the goodness of life and all created things, as Genesis notes again and again, "God saw that it was good" (cf. Genesis 1:1–13). While good, however, all creation remains just that—a creation; none of God's creation (nor any of our own creations, for that matter) is God.

But while none of God's creation is God, as God's handiwork creation (or nature) is understood to be revelatory of God's intention for the world and human persons. As such, nature points toward how God intends each creature to flourish. One can look to nature, and by the use of reason through study, observation, and reflection (i.e., science) one can ascertain two important elements that direct human persons toward their proper goals. On the one hand, one can discern regularities and patterns in nature that point toward the purposes, ends or goods which are necessary for human growth and fulfillment. (Given their necessary character, these are also sometimes referred to as "needs" or "laws.") The ultimate end of all of creation, including humanity, is union with God. In the tradition of Augustine and Aquinas, as all of creation proceeds from God's gracious love, so likewise it is on a return course: God has created all things so that their truest fulfillment is to return to God. But more proximate ends built into human nature by God can likewise be discerned; these can be categorized as biological (e.g., life, food, shelter, health), psychological (e.g., love, belonging), social (e.g., friendship, family, autonomy), and spiritual and creative (e.g., knowledge, prayer).

This creative God is not a distant, deist god. This God who "so loved the world" (John 3:16) sings the goodness of the creation by becoming radically present to it in the Incarnation. An incarnational faith affirms that the character of the divine is displayed best in the person of Jesus Christ. The

Incarnation points to the ongoing care, presence, and providence of this creative God, a care and presence that seeks and desires wholeness, well-being, and the fullest flourishing of all of creation. Jesus' life attests to the divine healing imperative; God's ongoing creativity seeks to recreate fallen materiality.

Faith in the Incarnation disallows any separation of the material from the spiritual—the wholeness sought is physical, social, and spiritual at once. Human bodies are equally objects of God's care as is the soul. Jesus' healings not only liberated sin-burdened souls and mended broken bodies; through his special attention to the poor and outcast, the marginalized were re-engrafted into the community from which their sickness or disability had separated them. In keeping the material, the social, and the spiritual together, the Incarnation argues against a solely "spiritual" approach to the healing of the body and suggests that, as a creative God, God works and heals "mediately through secondary causes and not immediately without the help of human causes. . . . In the area of healing, human means of curing illness have been encouraged, for in this way the doctor is cooperating in God's work . . . To relieve suffering and strive for healing is viewed as working with God."[8]

Not only does Jesus heal; Jesus suffers. Inextricable from the Incarnation is the passion. Jesus' passion critiques pollyanna visions of the Christian life and disallows faith to serve as a panacea. Instead, it displays in a graphic way the continuing presence of evil and how, most often, the body becomes the site upon which evil works its power, with death as its aim. The gospel witness affirms the reality and power of suffering and death, that not even God was spared. Yet, it also affirms that God's response in the face of evil is one of presence and creative love, a love that loves both the besieged and besetter toward the eschatological end of redemption and wholeness.

For the passion and death of Jesus are not the end of the story. The Resurrection attests to the fact that God's ultimate intention is for the world to be renewed, made whole again, for its brokenness to be healed, for it—in its very embodied materiality—to be redeemed. The Risen Christ sends to his followers the Paraclete, the Advocate, the Holy Spirit, which empowers the nascent Church to follow in his path and be "images" of God in the world. With this third "Person," we close with the mysterious affirmation that the God that is known through Jesus Christ in the Christian tradition is a trinitarian God.

If this account at least begins to display the Person who God is, then we, who are created in the image of God find ourselves called to likewise be certain kinds of persons, to embody certain virtues, and to image God in the world. This is the task of discipleship into which we are baptized. For it is God's peculiar logic that it is through human beings that God is present in the world. As Benedict M. Ashley and Kevin D. O'Rourke note in their definitive work in Catholic bioethics, *Healthcare Ethics: A Theological Analysis*, "the ultimate ethical norm is not a set of ethical rules but Jesus Christ—God become truly human. Therefore, he is our model of what it is to be human."[9] Who God is and how God acts becomes the primary norm, model, or standard for human actions.

What might the academic life look like when shaped by such a vision? Mirroring the trinitarian God, we find that the fullest exercise of the intellectual life is essentially social, relational, and communal. While reason and rational capacity remain distinctively human, such rationality must be embedded in a thickly interpersonal network—colleagues, students, disciplinary ancestors, those beyond the academy.

Furthermore, as images of a creative God, we find ourselves called to faithfully embody creativity in the world by utilizing our skills and talents to celebrate, nurture, and steward God's creation. That it is God's creation, however, cautions us not to allow celebration to slip into idolatry as those goods we pursue—whether the goods of technology, life, health, or the body, pursued by science and medicine or the goods of knowledge, publication, art, or social effectiveness pursued by other disciplines—threaten to become ends in themselves. Normed by God's vision for creation, the intellectual life should seek to promote human flourishing by responding to the complex needs, ends, and purposes of human life.

As disciples of an Incarnate God, moreover, a Catholic intellectual seeks and finds God in all things, not the least of which is the search for truth and the process of discovery. Knowing God's sustaining presence reminds us (as many an academic may need to be reminded) that we are not gods unto ourselves. It reminds us, as well, that in our vocations we are continually called to be present to others—to nurture, preserve, care for, heal, forgive, and not abandon. An incarnational approach to the intellectual life will also challenge the reductionisms characteristic of so much of society and our professions— whether it be the reductionistic tendencies of technology and medicine or the specialized reductionism of academic analysis.

Finally, imaging God calls us to direct our work in tangible service of the poor, vulnerable, disabled, and marginalized, and to work against those elements of our culture that conspire to render people isolated and invisible.[10] In short, we are called to be vehicles of the in-breaking of the kingdom, agents of God's grace in the world. Such a fight—for a fight it is—may certainly entail suffering. As a fight against the powers of evil, however, it may become a mysterious sharing in the suffering, death, and resurrection of Jesus. But such a vocation is possible for those confident that God's grace is stronger than the powers of evil.

Do we, then, understand the academic life as a "vocation," as a way of life in service to God? How might our relationships with students and colleagues look different if we sought to embody these sorts of convictions in our daily interactions? How might the focus of our research differ if we took seriously a vision of the world normed by Jesus, God Incarnate? How are we present—daily and in our research—to the outcast, the poor, the marginalized, and the handicapped? Do we work for full human flourishing in our communities and in our world? Or is our work isolated, detached from persons and creation?

Clearly, professional norms and academic culture at many institutions often work against the living out of these sorts of convictions. But as Catholic bioethics seeks to incarnate them in the realm of bioethics, so those in other disciplines are called to reflect on how such norms might practically be enfleshed, both in their lives as professors and colleagues and in their intellectual work.

Catholic Intellectual Life: Witnessing in the Public Realm

The vision of the intellectual life as a vocation of discipleship presents a compelling challenge. But for those interested in plumbing the depths of the Catholic medico-moral tradition for insight into our professional identities, one challenge remains. And this challenge comes from a relatively new addition to the Catholic lexicon: Cardinal Joseph Bernardin's consistent ethic of life. Here the cardinal challenges the Catholic community to be not only consistent in its moral positions, seeing heretofore unrelated issues as but a piece of "a seamless garment," but to "share our vision with the wider society."[11] In short, Bernardin renews the New Testament call for Christians see the connections between diverse issues in their communities and to witness to these connections and their commitments in the public realm.

The phrase "the consistent ethic of life" entered Catholic moral vocabulary on December 6, 1983, as the centerpoint of Cardinal Bernardin's Gannon Lecture at Fordham University.[12] He had been invited to speak on the pastoral letter recently issued by the National Conference of Catholic Bishops, *The Challenge of Peace: God's Promise and Our Response.*[13] A leader in the NCCB, Bernardin had chaired the committee whose multi-year study of the issue of nuclear arms led to the 1983 publication of the pastoral letter. In that letter, the bishops articulated a vision of a consistent ethic:

> When we accept violence in any form as commonplace, our sensitivities become dulled. When we accept violence, war itself can be taken for granted. Violence has many faces: oppression of the poor, deprivation of basic human rights, economic exploitation, sexual exploitation and pornography, neglect or abuse of the aged and the helpless, and innumerable other acts of inhumanity. Abortion in particular blunts a sense of the sacredness of human life. In a society where the innocent unborn are killed wantonly, how can we expect people to feel righteous revulsion at the act or threat of killing noncombatants in war?[14]

In 1983, with the ink on the pastoral letter barely dry, Bernardin was appointed chairman of the Catholic Bishops' Committee for Pro-Life Activities. He now confronted the linkage of the issues above not from the perspective of war but from the perspective of abortion.

In taking the helm of the committee, Bernardin faced a number of challenges. First, even a casual observer of U.S. politics would note that by 1983 the term "pro-life" had become reductively equated with the issue of abortion.

He saw a need to reclaim and redefine the term. Second, the efficacy and credibility of the Church's abortion stance was radically undermined by its inconsistency between social positions related to life:

> Consistency means we cannot have it both ways: We cannot urge a compassionate society and vigorous public policy to protect the rights of the unborn and then argue that compassion and significant public programs on behalf of the needy undermine the moral fiber of the society or are beyond the proper scope of governmental responsibility.[15]

Third, although *The Challenge of Peace* contained a vision of a consistent ethic, Bernardin believed that the pastoral neither sufficiently argued the case for linking the spectrum of issues nor provided a fully articulated theological or ethical framework. Both tasks lay before him.

His Gannon Lecture became the first step in forging a theologically grounded, broader moral vision. Echoing the theological vision outlined above, he notes:

> We believe that life is a gift from God and therefore must be protected and nourished at every stage of development. Furthermore, we believe not only that life is a sacred reality but also that it has a social dimension . . . therefore, it is the obligation of society to protect life and to provide things needed to enhance that life. That is the theological basis and starting point for the consistent ethic.[16]

His creative vision lies in applying this principle to an amazing range of issues, where the direct linkage to "life" may not be as clear:

> . . . genetics, including genetic counseling and genetic engineering; abortion; war; capital punishment; euthanasia and care of the terminally ill; pornography; hunger; homelessness; unemployment; education of the illiterate; undocumented migrants; sexism; racism; welfare reform; working mothers and single parents; birth technologies; health care reform; care of the disabled; care of the elderly; inhumane living conditions; inhumane working conditions; violence; exploitation; tolerance of poverty; international justice and peace.

In Bernardin's vision, these and any issue in which life or human dignity is threatened or diminished constitute a "seamless garment," a metaphor he later employed.[17] These issues weave a theologically informed tapestry: a desire for the full flourishing of human persons in terms of all the ends of human life, not simply the biological; an incarnated vision of the goodness of creation, holding together the bodily, spiritual, and communal; a recognition the reality of suffering, the power of evil, and our call to fight against it.

Succinctly encapsulating the Catholic tradition, he notes that "everything that protects, enhances, and nourishes life is good, is necessary. Those things, though, that in some way either destroy or diminish life are not good."[18] The purpose of articulating such a vision was both intellectual and strategic. This new synthesis, he argued, would facilitate the intellectual analyses of compelling moral and social issues, highlighting general moral principles as well as important distinctions between cases. On the strategic level, action might be pursued in a number of different ways. Individuals serving their local communities, for example, clearly give witness to their convictions, to their students and colleagues, as well as to those they work with and serve. Beyond local service, such witness might entail a more "heroic" social ethic; in what remains a controversial position, the consistent ethic of life, he suggested, "can and should be used to test party platforms, public policies, and political candidates."[19] Beyond electoral politics, such witness will find itself manifest in the development of public policy, one of the primary foci of the discipline of bioethics.

While not absolving individuals of responsibility to be involved in action beyond the confines of the academy, the consistent ethic moves the locus of responsibility for enacting social change from the individual to the community. As he notes: ". . . [N]o one can do everything. There are limits to both competency and energy. . . . [But] in this way, the Church will sustain a variety of individual commitments."[20] As importantly, the consistent ethic urges a move from theory to praxis, from thought to action.[21]

It is here, of course, that many academics and intellectuals will cringe. For again, the academic culture of many disciplines and institutions works against the transgressing of boundaries between the academy and "society." Work in the local communities which surround many of our institutions is not academically valued, at least when tallying one's accomplishments for tenure and promotion. Insofar as these sorts of activities take time away from central activities of teaching and research, young academics are in fact often discouraged from pursuing them. What ought to be considered a central component of our vocations as "holy work" becomes marginalized by the standards of the secular academy.

Yet, the consistent ethic provides a number of challenges to all intellectuals who locate themselves within a Catholic ethos. At minimum, it calls us to see our work as part of a larger whole. Simply within the academy, the consistent ethic models a more holistic, inclusive, perhaps "catholic" vision of the university. Premised on the value of knowledge as an important human good, the "seamless garment" of the intellectual life will posit relationships heretofore unseen—between art, science, business, sociology, and theology. Premised upon the overall good of human flourishing and the unity of the human person, such a "seamless garment" will likewise counter the artificial separation between the academic or intellectual life and the personal life— on the part of both students and faculty. In short, re-envisioning the university under the model of the "seamless garment" counters the traditional hostility or ignorance that separates the disciplines and fosters a broader view of the pursuit of knowledge and personal formation.

Beyond this, however, the consistent ethic clearly calls academics and institutions beyond their normal activities. It challenges Catholics and those within a Catholic environment to translate their convictions into action, to witness to their beliefs in the public realm, through both concrete service and their academic research. The tradition maintains that the issues named above—genetics; abortion; war; capital punishment; euthanasia and care of the terminally ill; pornography; hunger; homelessness; unemployment; education of the illiterate; undocumented migrants; sexism; racism; welfare reform; working mothers and single parents; birth technologies; health care reform; care of the disabled; care of the elderly; inhumane living conditions; inhumane working conditions; violence; exploitation; tolerance of poverty; international justice and peace—are interconnected and are important responsibilities for Catholic institutions and for those who work within such institutions. How does our work—in the classroom and in publication—attend to these issues? How do we think about our own disciplines in relation to these issues?

In giving a name to this vision, Cardinal Bernardin clearly forged a new intellectual path—pushing Catholic moral theology and social ethics beyond their traditional boundaries, linking Catholic attention to biomedical "life" issues with the Church's positions on war and social justice. In doing so, he did not claim to be creating something new but instead suggested that he was simply retrieving a vision rooted in and widely dispersed throughout the Catholic tradition.[22] His platform presented a theologically rich vision of a social life shaped by the canons of discipleship wedded to a notion of public witness that engaged the formation of public policy.

And it was the question of policy that faced our committee that cold January morning in 1998. We embarked on an intellectual journey together, seeking as a community of scholars to forge something new, to engage the broader public debate over an issue germane to the protection of human life, to publicly witness to our identity as a Catholic institution. Our journey returned us to the traditions that shaped us, to appreciatively listen for wisdom that would both challenge contemporary presuppositions and assist us in creatively constructing new alternatives. In the end, we agreed: a policy was necessary. Now we face the task of writing one. Can we give it a voice with resounding theological vision such that it incarnates our vocation as disciples? This remains our next challenge.

Notes

1. The Marianists, or more properly, the Society of Mary, is a religious order of brothers and priests founded in 1817 by the French cleric Fr. William Joseph Chaminade. The Marianists sponsor the University of Dayton, as well as two other institutions of higher education in the U.S., St. Mary's University in San Antonio, Texas, and Chaminade University in Hawaii. As with most institutions of Catholic higher education, the University of Dayton strives to live and work in accordance with not only its Catholic identity but

also with its Marianist identity and heritage. The Marianists should not be confused or associated with those contemporary movements that display a more apocalyptic devotion to Mary.

2. Edmund Pellegrino, "The Metamorphosis of Medical Ethics," in *Journal of the American Medical Association* 269, no. 9 (3 March 1993): p. 1158–1162; and LeRoy Walters, "Religion and the Renaissance of Medical Ethics in the U.S.: 1965–1975," in *Theology and Bioethics*, ed. by Earl Shelp (Boston: D. Reidel, 1985), p. 3–16.

3. Albert R. Jonsen, *The Birth of Bioethics* (New York: Oxford, 1998), p. 34. See also Walters, p. 3.

4. This account draws largely on Leroy Walters' persuasive piece, "Religion and the Renaissance of Medical Ethics in the U.S.: 1965–1975." Although Walters examines the role of religion generally, his narrative highlights the key role played by Catholics in giving birth to this new discipline.

5. Walters, p. 6.

6. Paul Armstrong is, the author must add, a graduate of the University of Dayton.

7. The following section relies heavily on the National Conference of Catholic Bishop's concise and practical *Ethical and Religious Directives for Catholic Health Care Services* (Washington, D.C.: United States Catholic Conference, 1995).

8. Charles E. Curran, "Roman Catholic Medical Ethics," in *Transition and Tradition in Moral Theology* (Notre Dame, IN: University of Notre Dame Press, 1979), p. 174–175.

9. Benedict M. Ashley and Kevin D. O'Rourke, *Healthcare Ethics: A Theological Analysis*, third edition (St. Louis: Catholic Health Association of the United States, 1989), pp. 9–10.

10. As Häring notes, "A person cannot know and love the invisible God unless he knows and loves the visible man. This is a theology springing from the dogma of the Incarnation," in *Medical Ethics* (Notre Dame, IN: Fides Publishers, 1973), p. 6.

11. Joseph Cardinal Bernardin, "A Consistent Ethic of Life: An American-Catholic Dialogue" (Gannon Lecture: Fordham University, 1983), *Origins* 13 (1983): 494.

12. The texts for the ten addresses in which Cardinal Bernardin applied or elaborated on the consistent ethic of life concept can be found on at http://www.catholic.org/pfl/magisterium. They are also collected in Thomas G. Fuechtmann, ed., *Consistent Ethic of Life* (Kansas City: Sheed & Ward, 1988). In the first two addresses, the Gannon Lecture at Fordham in December 1983 and the Wade Lecture at St. Louis University in March 1984, Bernardin explores and develops the principle itself. In his next six addresses, he applies it to specific issues: abortion (Kansas City, 1985), pornography (Cincinnati, 1984), poverty (Catholic University, 1985), health care (Loyola University, 1985 and Jamaica, New York, 1986), and the death penalty (Criminal Court of Cook County, Illinois, 1985). In the last two addresses, at Seattle University in 1986 and Portland in 1986,

Bernardin further develops the concept, now in light of three years of critique and response, and applies it more explicitly than in his other addresses to the relationship of religion and politics. It is important to note that his initial articulation of the consistent ethic of life took place in public addresses at Catholic universities.

13. National Conference of Catholic Bishops, *The Challenge of Peace: God's Promise and Our Response* (Washington, D.C.: U.S. Catholic Conference, 1983).

14. Ibid., paragraph 285.

15. Bernardin, 493.

16. "The Consistent Ethic of Life: An Interview with Joseph Cardinal Bernardin," in *Second Opinion* 8 (1988): 104.

17. Joseph Cardinal Bernardin, "A Consistent Ethic of Life: Continuing the Dialogue," the Wade Lecture (St. Louis University in March 1984), in Thomas G. Fuechtmann, ed., *Consistent Ethic of Life* (Kansas City: Sheed & Ward, 1988).

18. *Second Opinion*, p. 104.

19. Bernardin, Wade Lecture, p. 20.

20. Ibid.

21. I would like to thank my colleague Margaret M. Strain for articulating these last two points, as well as for her close reading of drafts of this text and her helpful editorial comments.

22. Thomas G. Fuechtmann, ed., *Consistent Ethic of Life* (Kansas City: Sheed & Ward, 1988), v. Bernardin himself maintains that in naming the principle he was simply articulating the moral vision underlying the work of the National Conference of Catholic Bishop's Respect Life Program. As he notes, when the bishops inaugurated this program in 1972, "they invited the Catholic community to focus on the 'sanctity of human life and the many threats to human life in the modern world, including war, violence, hunger, and poverty.'" *Address at Consistent Ethic of Life Conference*, Portland, OR, October 4, 1986.

15

The Dignity of Persons and the Catholic Intellectual Vision

Brian F. Linnane, S.J.

An account of the human person is of central importance to Roman Catholic theological reflection and pastoral teaching. While the concept of the person has always had a vital role in Christian thought generally, the Catholic emphasis on the person has become more pronounced, even dominant, in the last fifty years. Within the theological disciplines there has been a pervasive methodological commitment to human experience as the appropriate starting point for theological reflection. Theology, it is argued, must be consistent with our experience of ourselves and our world if it is to be credible to contemporary persons. Further, the graced encounter with God which makes theology and theologizing possible can only occur within the context of lived human experience.[1]

Following this commitment to the priority of human experience, recent Catholic moral and pastoral teaching has had its foundations in an appeal to the fundamental dignity of all persons simply as persons. This dignity, grounded in the potential for a God-human relationship, generates an obligation to respect certain fundamental human rights. This new emphasis on the person—its capacity for self-transcendence and its inviolable dignity—has provided an important and rich antidote to reductionist anthropologies that view the person simply as the product of its environment or as a mere consumer subject to the manipulations of the marketplace. Further, this tradition has generated a strong and consistent defense of human integrity in an era characterized by rapid cultural, political, and scientific change that, at times, has had the potential to undermine the essential dignity of individuals and communities.

This essay proposes to examine the theological sources and moral implications of recent Roman Catholic thinking on the notion of personhood and to defend its ongoing relevance in light of significant challenges. These challenges are both practical and theoretical in nature. On the level of practice, some persons question the Catholic Church's commitment to the dignity of all persons as persons in light of its perceived patriarchal nature. Thus, some critics argue that the Church does not live up to its own commitment to the essential human dignity of all persons insofar as it devalues the talents and experience of women. On the theoretical level, postmodern perspectives raise important questions about the intellectual coherence of any theory that is foundational in nature (the person as normative starting point) and universal in scope (applicable at all times and in all places). In this essay, I will argue that the Catholic tradition has the resources to address the more theoretical challenges to its account of the person and its dignity. Such resources can be found in the writings of Catholic feminist thinkers who, while rescuing the theological anthropology, issue a challenge that all Catholics recognize the full humanity of women.

The Scope of the Problem

For persons who are attentive to recent Roman Catholic teaching as well as to contemporary social and political discourse, it might seem difficult to believe that the notion of the person as the possessor of a fundamental dignity and as a bearer of inalienable rights is under intense, critical scrutiny. Official Catholic responses to questions ranging from human salvation to economic justice, from the meaning of suffering to sexual morality, are grounded in an appeal to the essential and fundamental worth of all persons *simply as persons*. In the United States, the foundational political documents are based upon an appeal to value of persons and seek to safeguard certain basic rights that are not merely granted to its citizens by the Republic, but are bestowed by Nature on all persons. Discussions of governmental policy—both foreign and domestic—frequently draw attention to concerns for "basic human rights." And in popular discourse, appeals to autonomy, to a perceived right to chart one's own destiny, to be free from uninvited interference, find regular expression. Further, the tendency to view tolerance of diversity and respect for the individual as a hallmark of the just society suggests that an appreciation for the obligating features of persons endures. The person and its due respect are taken for granted it seems, at least in practice.

Within the academy, however, appeals to any objective, universal foundations—epistemological, metaphysical, or ethical—are increasingly suspect. As we will see, persons in a variety of disciplines not only raise questions about the possibility of such an objective account of the person as a starting point for moral reflection but also suggest that attempts to generate rights based upon perceived obligating features of persons can be ultimately oppressive. Such perspectives are often referred to as postmodern, antifoundational, or constructivist. Many intellectuals, working from what might be referred to as a liberationist perspective, have used these insights fruitfully to expose the ways in which power relationships within particular cultures—often understood as merely reflecting the exigencies of human nature—actually serve to undermine human dignity. As helpful as these intellectual perspectives have been in exposing the structural oppression of persons of color, women, and sexual minorities, significant questions remain. First, it remains to be determined whether or not an authentic, cross-cultural ethic of liberation can be developed without some appeal to the fundamental and universal dignity of persons. Second, it must be determined whether one must necessarily reject the possibility of an objective account of the person and its obligating features as abstract, individualistic, and ahistorical. In other words, is the postmodern rejection of the subject ultimately adequate to human experience?

An evaluation of these concerns and their intellectual implications in light of the distinctively Catholic commitment to the person is the focus of this essay. Attention to the contemporary Catholic understanding of the person will, I believe, have two important effects on Catholic intellectual and ecclesial life. First, Catholic concern for the person, rooted in the documents of the Second Vatican Council and the theology they have generated, can make an important contribution to postmodern discussions on the status of the person and the possibility of objectively obligating features of personhood. Far from being limited to philosophical and theological discourse, Catholic understandings of the human person are relevant to scientific inquiry, the economic realm, public policy, cultural analysis, and beyond. Second, attention within the academy to the implications of Catholic thought on the person and its essential dignity can help the Church itself appropriate the insights of modern conciliar documents like *Gaudium et spes* (The Pastoral Constitution on the Church in the Modern World) and *Dignitatis humanae* (The Declaration on Religious Freedom) more completely.

The Person in Modern Catholic Thought

Concern for the dignity of the human person and for the promotion of basic human rights is for the Roman Catholic Church, as well as for the international community, a relatively recent development. While this is not to suggest that the Catholic tradition was necessarily or overtly hostile to concerns for human dignity prior to the Second Vatican Council, it was the case that the Church resisted many of modern reforms that protected the rights of individuals until the advent of modern Catholic social teaching. Although Leo XIII's encyclical, *Rerum novarum* (1891), which is at the foundation of this tradition of social teaching, does affirm the dignity of persons and champion the rights of workers, the Vatican resisted some dimensions of what are often taken to be basic human rights—including freedom of conscience— until the council which concluded in 1965.[2] The Church's commitment to primacy of human dignity is not, however, without strong theological roots. While a full account of the history and development of these theological resources is beyond the scope of this essay, it will be important to note some of them briefly before turning to a discussion of modern theological developments and their implications for the intellectual vocation.

Christian concern for the dignity and inviolability of all human persons is frequently linked to basic theological doctrines such as creation, Christology, soteriology, and eschatology. These doctrines, while not generating a full theological anthropology in themselves, do highlight the uniqueness of the personal God-human relationship and so serve to provide a theological foundation for an account of the obligating features of human persons. The Christian understanding of creation, dependent as it is on the Genesis accounts of God's creative activity, understands the human person as "the image of

God" (cf. Genesis 1:26). To understand the person as the *imago Dei* indicates both God's unique relationship with humankind as well as the potential for individual, personal union with God. With regard to christology, the doctrine of the Incarnation invests the human person with a particular dignity and status insofar as it holds that God became human in the person of Jesus of Nazareth. The soteriological implications of the Incarnation—that is, the understanding that God became human in order to heal the breach between humankind and God as well as to enable personal salvation—similarly reflects the high status of persons in the Christian theological tradition. Catholic eschatology, following the *exitus/reditus* theme developed by Thomas Aquinas (1224/5–1274), suggests that the person is created by God for ultimate union with God, although prospects for the divine-human relationship are compromised by the reality of sin. These fundamental Christian doctrines support the view that God is deeply concerned for not only humankind in general but for the well being of individuals.

The dignity of the person is also supported by the Catholic natural law tradition. This tradition, which claims to be accessible by human reason alone and so is not dependent upon special revelation, finds its classical statement in the thought of Thomas Aquinas.[3] For Aquinas, natural law suggests that human reason is capable of determining—by reflection upon human experience—those actions and behaviors that are conducive of individual and communal flourishing. Insofar as Aquinas understands that human reason can grasp the conditions necessary to promote human well-being, actions that serve the human good become obligatory and those that thwart the human good are proscribed. In this regard, he writes:

> There is in man an inclination to good, according to the nature of his reason, which is proper to him: thus man has a natural inclination to know the truth about God, and to live in society: and in this respect, whatever pertains to this inclination belongs to the natural law; for instance, to shun ignorance, to avoid offending those among whom one has to live, and other such things regarding the above inclination.[4]

In this way, an absolute requirement to respect and promote the conditions of human flourishing can be effectively linked to a concern for human dignity. The role of natural law remained the central one in the modern Catholic defense of human dignity and rights until the time of Vatican II. One sees in John XXIII's *Pacem in terris*, for example, the way in which the Catholic natural law theory is used to bolster claims for human rights. In that encyclical, John XXIII gives an exhaustive list of rights including respect for persons, rights of conscience, education, and "a share in the benefits of culture" which are derived from natural law.[5]

This brief survey helps us to see the ways in which the concept "person" has been significant in traditional Catholic thought. What is missing, however, is a full account of the person in light of modernity's "turn to the subject." This shift in the intellectual history of the modern period involves a move away from metaphysical approaches to understanding reality, as in the schools of thought that claim to follow Aquinas, and a new commitment to the experience of the human person as free and knowing and so capable of self-transcendence. The integration of modernity's turn to the subject into Roman Catholic theology enables a "sea-change" in the Catholic understanding of human person. For an articulation of this important theological development and its implications for a Catholic understanding of human dignity, we can find no better source than the theological anthropology of Karl Rahner.

The Contribution of Karl Rahner

The work of the great Jesuit theologian Karl Rahner (1904–1984) and its historical context can helpfully illumine the centrality of the human person in Roman Catholic theological reflection and pastoral practice. This is the case because Rahner's theology provided the intellectual resources that served to generate a distinctively theological account of the dignity of the person in the postwar period and because, as a German beginning his academic career in the 1930s, he experienced the threats of both the Nazi and the Communist totalitarianism which the Church perceived to undermine both human dignity and Christian identity.[6]

His theology, with its integration of modernity's "turn to the subject," has its starting point in the experience of the human subject. The human person and its experience is of vital importance for Rahner because of his understanding of the person's potential to both apprehend and respond to God's free self-communication in history.[7] This potential for encountering God's free word and so for relationship with God is, for Rahner, the source of human dignity; or, to use a term favored by Rahner's student Herbert Vorgrimler, "human greatness."[8] This understanding of the human person as "great" not only serves to exalt the human subject but also reflects the awesome responsibility that the free subject has to both God and neighbor. The responsibility that adheres to the human subject of divine self-revelation is awesome because its prospects for self-realization are at stake. Insofar as the divine self-revelation is addressed to human freedom, there exists the possibility that human agents can reject the invitation to relationship with God and its implications for our relations with other persons. Commenting on Rahner's thought on this point, Vorgrimler writes:

> Rahner [claims], someone who does not recognize the innermost nearness of the incomprehensible mystery or at least have intimations of it does not know himself. He does not grasp his own greatness and significance, the call of infinite mystery, and therefore is threatened by the danger of failing to recognize the true magnitude and significance of his fellow human beings—in whom alone this infinite mystery dwells. Not to have such self-knowledge is to go against the innermost tendency of every human being. Moreover it would go against the ultimate determination of humanity.[9]

The danger, then, that individuals face in failing to recognize that as persons they are potential vehicles of divine self-communication is that they would fail to recognize this same capacity—which grounds human dignity and establishes an absolute requirement of respect—in other persons.

Failing to recognize and respect the dignity of others is, for Rahner, a failure of neighbor love that is also always a rejection of God. In Rahner's account, love of neighbor is understood to be the central human act because it is the only means by which the subject decides about itself and so simultaneously decides about God. As such, this love is *caritas*, "a love of neighbor whose movement is directed to the God of eternal life."[10] One must be clear on this point: in Rahner's transcendental method this unity of love of neighbor and love of God is not simply causal—in loving one's neighbor one is really loving God—or motivational. He asserts:

> [E]ven the explicit love of God is still borne by that opening in trusting love to the whole of reality which takes place in the love of neighbour. It is radically true, i.e., by an ontological and not merely "moral" or psychological necessity, that whoever does not love the brother whom he "sees," also cannot love God whom he does not see, and that one can love God whom one does not see only *by* loving one's visible brother lovingly.[11]

Insofar as respecting the dignity of the other who is a potential bearer of God's self-revelation is the *sine qua non* of neighbor love, one can see that the theological stakes involved in promoting the dignity of persons are very high in Rahner's account.

Having established the centrality of the human subject and its experience in Rahner's thought, we must now briefly consider his understanding of the basic dimensions and features of the person and their moral implications. As we will see, Rahner's theological account of the person is consistent with the essential dimensions of the account of human dignity defended by many liberal democracies as well as that of the Vatican II's *Gaudium et spes*.

In an address given to the Austrian Catholic Congress in 1952, Rahner outlined the "specifically created and human characteristic(s)" of the person.[12] He isolates five distinct characteristics of persons that underscore its uniqueness: the person as Spirit, as free, as an individual, as social or community-building, and as embodied.[13] The person's spiritual nature indicates its complete dependence upon God; that the person alone is capable of self-transcendence and so of union with God. The notion of the person as free necessarily flows from the spiritual constitution of the human subject and reflects its capacity for radical self-definition vis-à-vis God by means of self-emptying neighbor love.[14] To speak of the human subject as an individual is to suggest that each person is unique and equal in value. As unique the person is "not merely an instance of the universal" that can be understood as interchangeable or disposable.[15] As unique and equally valuable, no person may be sacrificed for the good of another person or community. This emphasis on the uniqueness of the person does not generate an exaggerated individualism; rather, Rahner asserts the essential social and communal nature of the human subject.[16] Given the centrality of neighbor love in his understanding of the self-realization of the person before God, it follows that relationality and community are basic dimensions of human flourishing. Finally, Rahner emphasizes that bodies are essential to human personhood and not mere accessories in the process of self-realization.[17] Human relationality and the subjective demands of neighbor love can only be accomplished by an *embodied* spirit.

In addition to these five characteristics, it is important to emphasize that for Rahner, the person is also always a historical being.[18] In his account of the person and its destiny, human self-realization takes place "precisely in and through his being in the world, in time, in history."[19] This characteristic is certainly implied by the social and embodied nature of the human subject; nonetheless, it is worth emphasizing in light of those critics who might claim that Rahner's subject is overly abstract and ahistorical.[20]

For Rahner, these characteristics are not merely descriptive, but they also function as obligating in that it is these features of the person that generate a fundamental requirement of respect. In this regard he writes:

> In so far as man is a person, who possesses himself knowingly and in freedom—in other words, is always objectively referred to *himself* and hence does not ontologically have the character of a means but of an end, an end by reference away from himself indeed, to persons but not to things, he has an absolute value and hence an absolute dignity. . . . The human person by its nature and dignity demands an unconditional respect which is independent of any freely exercised determination of an end and value—i.e., is absolute.[21]

The person considered in its fullness, which for Rahner includes an account of the subject's spiritual destiny, generates an obligation to treat the person as an inviolable "end" in itself. All of these features—capacity for transcendence, relationality, freedom, and embodiment—are oriented toward and necessary for the subject's self-realization before God, which necessarily occurs in the midst of a particular personal and communal history.

As we have seen, human dignity for Rahner is both a preestablished reality and a task that confronts persons. That is, it demands "both respect and protection *as well as realization* both in its relations to others and in itself."[22] As a preestablished reality, the essential dignity of the person can never be lost. It adheres to the very nature of the person by virtue of the obligating features outlined above. However, by means of the exercise of freedom at the deepest level of the person, the task of self-realization can go unfilled, and so it can be said that human dignity can be degraded and lost. Because Rahner understands that human self-realization can only be achieved in history by means of neighbor love, this task includes a moral dimension. While self-realization is always a personal and unique task, it is not achieved in a random, idiosyncratic manner.

Thus, Christian self-realization is distinct from the sort of self-love or radical autonomy so valued in the contemporary West, which manifests itself by "doing its own thing."[23] Rather, Christian self-realization has a distinctive telos or goal: radical obedience to the command encountered in God's gracious self-communication—an obedience that always entails the "commandment" to love.[24] While respect for persons and their dignity does not exhaust Rahner's understanding of neighbor love, it is an absolute minimum requirement. Indeed, it might be argued that respect for persons reflects Rahner's understanding of the mysticism of daily life. That is to say that love of neighbor need not be construed as heroic, but can come about in ordinary human interaction that is respectful, charitable, or reconciling.[25]

Rahner's theological concern for persons and their dignity has implications for both political and ecclesial life. With regard to political life, he asserts that "[t]he state exists for man and not vice versa. It must serve the personal dignity and freedom of man."[26] The state, then, is the protector and not the source of basic human rights and liberties. Thus, insofar as the human person is defined as relational, for example, the rights of those fundamental human relationships which exist prior to the state (marriage, family, clan, and the like) are understood to be immune from political manipulation or coercion. Liberty of the conscience is another value that, for Rahner, is of paramount importance in both civil society and in the Church.[27] The dictates of personal conscience are, for Rahner, "the voice of God" and the decision to act in conscience is always a fundamental decision for God.[28] Because of this reality, Rahner argues that the Church must take the lead in defending freedom of conscience by means of example. Insofar as this liberty of conscience is essential to a free and loving response to divine self-revelation, the Church cannot deny such liberty within the Church and must also be an agent promoting it within civil society.[29]

Rahner's insights into the theological centrality of the human person reflected important political developments in the West and foreshadowed the theological blueprint for the Church's engagement with the modern world, *Gaudium et spes*. The Universal Declaration of Human Rights adopted by the General Assembly of the United Nations in 1948, for example, affirms its "faith in fundamental human rights," and "in the dignity and worth of the human person."[30] This faith, while generating an account of the obligating features of persons and their attending rights that is remarkably similar to Rahner's, is necessarily quite distinct from the faith which grounds Rahner's theological account of human dignity. The United Nations Declaration is based upon a political faith; that is, a confidence shared—to greater and lesser degrees—by member states that respect for the person and the protection of basic human rights would serve to both prevent atrocities, like those experienced in the early and middle decades of the twentieth century, and provide the strongest foundation for personal and social development.

Despite the evident similarities, however, there are important differences between Rahner's account of the implications of human dignity and the program advanced by the UN Declaration. Consider, for example, the commitment of the Declaration to participatory government and universal suffrage as a fundamental human right (Article 21). This reflects the understandable influence of the victorious liberal democracies in the aftermath of World War II. As such, it commits itself to a particular form of government as constitutive of human dignity and so fails to respect historico-cultural distinctiveness. Rahner, on the other hand, makes no such commitment. While acknowledging that "universal and equal suffrage may *in a certain historical situation be* . . . indispensable,"[31] he is unwilling to claim that any particular form of government or social arrangement necessarily is essential to the protection of human dignity. While in no way lessening his commitment to human dignity, Rahner acknowledges that it can be fostered in a variety of socio-cultural contexts.

With regard to other postwar developments in the Catholic Church, the final conciliar document of Vatican II, *Gaudium et spes*, gives protecting and promoting the dignity of persons pride of place in the Church's pastoral program. In the discussion that follows, we will see a sensitivity to the "incultured" nature of human dignity that we observed in the thought of Karl Rahner.

The Achievement of Vatican II

A reading of the documents of the Second Vatican Council clearly demonstrates the council Fathers' concern for human personhood and the conditions necessary for its flourishing. This concern finds it clearest expression in *Gaudium et spes*, the conciliar document that outlines and addresses the basic problems facing humankind. It is in this context that the Fathers assert and defend the essential dignity of all persons most explicitly. In this regard, they write that, "this Council lays stress on reverence for man; everyone must consider his every neighbor without exception as another self, taking into account first of all his life and the means necessary to living it with dignity," (n. 27). One finds many similarities between the council's account of the foundations and implications of human dignity and Rahner's theological anthropology. This is not surprising, as Rahner, who participated as a theological expert in the council, is thought to have been influential in an early draft of the constitution.[32] It will not be necessary, then, to fully rehearse the dimensions of the document's theological anthropology. Rather, this discussion will focus on the Pastoral Constitution's understanding of the requirement of respect for human dignity as both essential to persons and as conditioned by history and culture.

The understanding of human dignity as essential to persons is characteristic of the natural law tradition that characterizes modern Catholic social thought prior to *Gaudium et spes.* The natural law rights and dignities that one sees affirmed in *Pacem in terris*, for example, are understood to be universal rights applicable to all persons without reference to historical period or cultural exigencies. *Gaudium et spes*, on the other hand, while not denying the essential nature of human dignity, acknowledges the ways in which the rights that this dignity generates are shaped by historical and cultural forces. Indeed, the Constitution demonstrates the council Fathers' awareness of the dramatic historical developments of the twentieth century and the implications of these developments for a future characterized by ongoing social and cultural change. Their account of this change alternates between caution and hope.

> Today, the human race is passing through a new stage of its history. Profound and rapid changes are spreading by degrees around the whole world. Triggered by the intelligence and creative energies of man, these changes recoil upon him, upon his decisions and desires, both individual and collective, and upon his manner of thinking and acting with respect to things and to people (n. 4).

This new historical situation which threatens and promises calls for a new response; a response that affirms human dignity while recognizing that there can be no single, definitive account of the way in which that dignity is realized.

This understanding of the historically conditioned character of human dignity and the rights that attend it is, David Hollenbach argues, the Second Vatican Council's "most important contribution to the human rights tradition."[33] Thus, we see the *Gaudium et spes* forcefully defending basic human rights like "the right to choose a state of life freely and to found a family, . . . [the right] to respect, . . . [and the right] to activity in accord with the upright norm of one's own conscience" (n. 26), while acknowledging that the human person can only achieve self-realization within particular cultures and historical periods (see n. 53).

Human dignity, in this account, while based on essential features of the person and generating universal requirements of respect, does not suggest that the manner in which human dignity is respected must always and everywhere be the same. *Gaudium et spes* recognizes that different cultures can and will instantiate respect for human dignity in diverse ways, all of which are acceptable insofar as they are consistent with essential obligating features of persons. These obligating features flow from the Constitution's understanding of person as created in the image of God, as divinely endowed with the capacity for both free action in accord with the dictates of moral conscience and interpersonal relationships. So that while these obligating features do not require particular political and social relations, such as a democratic republic, they do serve to critique those political and social arrangements that undermine the conditions for human dignity. Furthermore, by acknowledging the historical nature of human dignity and its attending rights, the Constitution does not naively assert that the human autonomy that is at the heart of human dignity is unlimited or unconditioned. Human dignity is not then an abstract and ahistorical value for Catholic thought after the Second Vatican Council; rather, it is necessarily shaped and conditioned by unique cultures and historical epochs. This appeal to historical and cultural particularity can, as we will see, provide a counterbalance to postmodern critiques of objective obligating features of persons which ground human dignity and rights.

This new emphasis on the person as the starting point for theological reflection and as the bearer of a profound dignity signals not only an acceptance of some of the most rich insights of modernity by the Catholic Church but also an integration of these insights into the Church's pastoral and social mission. It is on the basis of this development that the Catholic Church has become outspoken on behalf of human rights and a defender of the poor, the oppressed, and the marginalized. Within a few decades of this new emphasis, however, the very idea that one could isolate an account of the essential features of persons which would serve as the basis for a universal obligation of respect was under scrutiny within the academy and beyond. We turn now to a discussion of this critical perspective that is broadly construed as "postmodern," before developing a Catholic, feminist response to it.

Postmodern Critiques of the Concept of the Person and Its Obligating Features

Significant intellectual trends, influential during the last two decades of the twentieth century, have raised doubts about the ability of the concept of person to ground universal claims obligating respect for human dignity. These developments, often referred to as *postmodern, constructivist,* or *anti-foundational,* challenge the existence of an objective, pre-cultural account of the human subject or of human nature. Accounts of human nature and, indeed, of the human self are not, from these perspectives, based upon some unbiased view of the basic structures of reality but are, rather, "constructed" by particular cultures and societies in ways that reflect and maintain prevailing power arrangements. Not only are such accounts of the person literally without foundation, it is argued, but they are constructed in such a way as to be harmful and repressive.[34]

Feminist thinkers, for example, have been especially critical of appeals to human nature or other abstract qualities like autonomy or rationality as a basis for generating obligating features of persons. While feminists affirm the support for personal self-direction implied in concepts like autonomy, they worry about the tendency of theories based on such concepts to be overly individualistic and inattentive to the particularities of real, historical persons. Seyla Benhabib writes of this as the problem of the "generalized other."[35] She contrasts this "generalized other" drawn from abstract universal human features with what she refers to as the "concrete other," an account of the person that "requires us to view each and every rational being as an individual with a concrete history, identity, and affective-emotional constitution."[36] To understand the human person as a generalized other in the manner of the Kantian autonomous subject, Benhabib argues, is to understand the person as "an empty mask that is everyone and no one."[37] Indeed, the mask is not so much empty as a reflection of the interests and concerns of those who are most powerful in particular societies. Thus, some feminists claim that to argue that persons are ends in themselves and ought never be treated as means only may reflect the moral interactions and experience of white men with certain levels of education and wealth, but it has not been the universal moral experience of women, the poor, and persons of color. Such persons, in their concrete, historical existence, have at times been deprived of meaningful autonomy and have experienced themselves as valued not in themselves but for their usefulness.

Attempts to base moral obligations on an account of a "generalized other" are problematic for some feminist thinkers not only because they tend to be inattentive to concrete lived experience of women and other marginalized persons but also because they imply a standard of moral accountability inconsistent with the actual freedom available to such persons. An example might help to make these difficulties clear. During my seminary studies, I spent a summer working as an intern in pastoral services department of an urban medical center affiliated with a mainline Protestant church. During my internship, the housekeepers and kitchen staff went out on strike to obtain better wages and working conditions. The interns were urged to cross the picket line and take up the duties of the striking workers. The director of my program, a clergyman, faulted the striking workers for failing to live up to their vocations as healthcare workers. He argued that when he entered the clergy he turned away from a lucrative career in the law. In addition to a financial sacrifice, he knew that the conditions of his ministry would often be inconvenient but that it would be his responsibility to fulfill his duties despite such inconveniences, and so it should be with these workers. He argued that since these persons chose to work in healthcare, they must accept the financial and personal hardships that accompany this "vocation."

This man's argument does a double disservice to the persons—principally recent immigrants and women of color—he criticized. First, he assumed that all persons have an equal ability to determine their life course regardless of their concrete circumstances. Second, he used this "presumed autonomy" to generate a responsibility of accepting passively the full implications of these "free" choices. Not only does freedom of choice fail to adequately reflect the actual experience of these persons, it is used to coerce acquiescence to a set of arrangements harmful to them but beneficial to the more powerful.

This example also demonstrates the ways in which the more powerful, usually affluent men, understand their experience as normative and so fail to attend to the experience of women and the poor. The Roman Catholic Church, with its male-based authority structure, is often cited as an example of a powerful institution that is not immune from difficulties of this sort. Many feminists fault Roman Catholic ethical teaching on gender relations and the family precisely because they are written by men and does not, in their view, attend to the lived realities of women.[38] As Susan Secker has noted, "[w]omen's experience . . . has critical implications for official Catholic ethical teachings. It brings into sharp relief the partiality of its universalist assumptions and calls into question the normative standards built on these presuppositions."[39] If Catholic claims about the fundamental dignity of all persons are to be credible, feminists argue, the account of the person such claims are based upon must do justice to the fullness of human experience.[40]

This perceived lack of attention to the particularities of concrete individual lives that has the effect of serving the interests of the more powerful brings many feminist thinkers to affirm a social constructivist understanding of the human person and the obligating features that are said to adhere to persons. Social constructivism, as has been noted, denies that there are any essential features of persons or natural structures of reality that obligate respect for the dignity of persons universally. Rights, and indeed all normative claims, ultimately reflect and support the prevailing power arrangements within particular cultures and societies. Such power arrangements and the practices they generate are so subtle and pervasive that they are construed as "natural" or as simply given in the order of things. From this perspective, it is argued, feminist and other liberationist thinkers can "de-construct" those arrangements and so expose the ways in which such arrangements are oppressive of persons.

As persuasive as the deconstructivist critique can be in demonstrating the constructed nature of norms and social arrangements, there are important reasons to question the wisdom of completely abandoning the concept of person as bearer of certain universal obligating features. For, as Lisa Sowle Cahill has pointed out, while a deconstructivist approach can expose oppression and lead to a greater appreciation for difference, it is unable to generate an account of authentic human liberation.[41] In other words, social contructionist approaches can delineate the ways in which power relationships can be oppressive within particular cultures; they do not, however, provide a basis or rationale for protecting persons or promoting a vision of human flourishing. This is the case because constructivist approaches are necessarily relativistic. They suggest that we cannot object to the practices of another society that we perceive as demeaning or oppressive because there is—in constructive approaches—no objective standard to judge the practices of other cultures.[42] Nor is there an objective account, wholly unaffected by particular cultures, of what constitutes human flourishing or well-being. To abandon an account of the person that generates universally valid obligating features seems, in fact, dangerous to those persons it seeks to liberate from oppressive circumstances.

It appears that the Roman Catholic account of the person and its relevance to political, social, and ecclesial life is threatened precisely at a time when its contributions are most urgently needed. Thus, it is of vital importance to determine whether the Catholic commitment to the person as deserving respect in every context can be sustained in light of postmodern critiques. In order to explore the continued prospects of this tradition, we will turn to Catholic feminist theology. It is somewhat ironic to turn to feminist sources for a rearticulation of Catholic account of the person and its fundamental dignity given the mutual suspicion between some members of the Roman Catholic hierarchy and the feminist community. Many Catholic feminists are critical of the hierarchical and male-based power structure of the Church, while many holding positions of authority within the Church view most feminists as "radical" and see their critiques as contrary to the notion of church established by Christ.[43] Nonetheless, a number of Roman Catholic feminist theologians have been attentive to the problem of nonfoundationalism and have attempted to articulate a foundational account of the person that is sensitive to historical and cultural particularity. Their work in this regard has given a new voice to the concerns about the person found in the thought of Rahner and the Vatican Council. The final section of this paper will consider the contributions of these theologians.

Roman Catholic Feminist Responses to Postmodern Critiques of the Person

As we have noted, feminist theorists have generally shared a postmodern skepticism about the possibility of an objective account of the nature of the human person and its universally binding obligating features. Their skepticism on this point is well grounded. Historical and anthropological study gives evidence to the ways in which patterns of human interaction, such as gender roles, that are thought to be natural or simply given in the order of things are, in fact, discrete manifestations of particular cultures. Such investigations have also demonstrated that modern understandings of the person (as rational and autonomous, for example) that claim to generate requirements of respect for all persons as *persons* (always treat persons as ends in themselves and never as only a means) are not necessarily able to extend this respect to everyone. Thus, feminists are legitimately skeptical of those essentialist perspectives that support the "natural" inferiority of women or that claim a universal and inviolable right of autonomy that is inconsistent with actual lived experience of many women, persons of color, and other marginalized persons. Many Catholic feminist thinkers, while agreeing with the perceived dangers of an overly abstract and ahistorical account of the human person, are reluctant to abandon an account of the person that serves to generate requirements of respect for human dignity. They look to generate a normative account of personhood that is sensitive to values that include the embodied, relational, and historical dimensions of the human subject. Thus, Catholic feminist theologians like Margaret Farley[44] and Lisa Sowle Cahill,[45] to name only two, attempt to mediate between a strict constructivism and an abstract essentialism and in doing so they affirm—at least implicitly—the theological anthropology evident in Karl Rahner's thought and in the documents of the Second Vatican Council. In addition, insofar as Catholic feminist accounts of the human person are especially attentive to human historicity and the concrete lived experience of all persons, they serve to challenge earlier Roman Catholic accounts of the person to a greater inclusivity. In the discussion that follows, I will focus principally on Margaret Farley's account of persons and their dignity.

As a feminist theologian and ethicist, Farley is acutely aware of the dangers to women that would result from a rejection of an understanding of the person as the bearer of universally binding obligating features. She sees, for example, that the moral and political commitments of most feminists can be sustained only by some foundational understanding of the dignity of persons.[46] Her point is that if feminism is committed to safeguarding and promoting the physical integrity and moral agency of all persons, it can only do so based on some type of universal morality that recognizes basic human dignity. If one concedes, then, that human rights and moral norms merely reflect the interests of the more powerful, societies, in particular, rather than some human features inherently worthy of respect, those persons with less power—usually including most women—are always at a disadvantage, if not at risk.[47] Cahill makes a similar point in her discussion of the tendency of many feminist thinkers to advance a politics of difference at the expense of ethically normative accounts of the human persons. She writes:

> It cannot be emphasized too strongly that, despite the immediate practical importance of recovering the differences (whether racial, ethnic, economic, or religious) of women who have too quickly been assimilated to a white, middle-class paradigm of "women's experience," the eradication of all unity worldwide among women or, for that matter among men and women, would have monstrous moral consequences. As an Asian feminist has written, "the very theme of difference, whatever the differences are represented to be, is useful to the oppressing group . . . To demand the right to Difference without analyzing its social character is to give back the enemy an effective weapon."[48]

Further, Cahill shares Farley's concern about feminism's ability to advance the cause of women without some appeal to moral foundations that support the dignity of persons. In Cahill's view, an antifoundationalist feminism is intellectually inconsistent in that it supports liberal values like respect for autonomy and equality that it cannot defend theoretically.[49] In light of these concerns, some Catholic feminist theologians seek to generate accounts of human dignity that incorporate feminist concerns about avoiding descriptions of the person that are overly abstract, unduly individualistic, and insensitive to historical particularity.

Careful to avoid any totalizing or overly exalted claims for the shared dimensions of human experience, Farley nonetheless argues that "persons can and ought to experience moral claims in relation to one another and that some of these claims can and ought to cross (through not ignore) the boundaries of history and culture."[50] Indeed, Farley's appeal to these shared dimensions of the human experience seems to echo the opening lines of *Gaudium et spes*:

> The joys and hopes, the griefs and the anxieties of the men of this age, especially those who are poor or in any way afflicted, these too are the joys and hopes, the griefs and anxieties of the followers of Christ. Indeed nothing genuinely human fails to raise an echo in their hearts . . . [t]hat is why this community realizes that it is truly and immediately linked with mankind *and its history* (n. 1, author's emphasis).

Farley develops her conviction about the moral implications of these shared experiences in the following terms:

> . . . in the experience of what it means as a human person to
> rejoice and to be sorrowful, to be protected or violated, nur-
> tured or stifled, understood or misjudged, respected or used.
> Whatever the differences in human lives, however minimal the
> actuality of world community, however unique the social
> arrangements of diverse peoples, it is nonetheless possible for
> human persons to weep over commonly felt tragedies, laugh
> over commonly perceived incongruities, yearn for common
> hopes. And across time and place, it is possible to condemn
> commonly recognized injustices and act for commonly desired
> goals.[51]

Farley, then, like Rahner and the Fathers of the Second Vatican Council, recognizes morally relevant common dimensions of human personhood that also
allows for the historical and cultural uniqueness of individuals and communities.

Chief among the attributes of persons that, in Farley's view, generate
moral demands are autonomy and relationality. Human capacity for relationship, she argues, is a characteristic as significant as the capacity for self-
direction.[52] In asserting the moral significance of personal autonomy, Farley
is not simply reiterating traditional, modern views of autonomy. Rather, in her
account, autonomy is always understood within the context of relationality. In
Farley's view, then, relationality both enables human freedom *and* is a source
of the particularity that conditions individual autonomy. So then, while the
histories of real persons can and often do give witness to harsh limitations on
personal self-governance, the possibility of relationship and affective commitment always remains an arena of self-determination. This is the case, Farley argues, because persons as relational beings are self-transcending; that is,
they are "expansive beyond what they are at any given moment—and self-
possessing—capable of knowing and loving themselves not in spite of knowing and loving others, but through it and in it."[53]

In her understanding of autonomy and relationality as obligating features of persons that mutually condition each other, Farley is able to address
a number of criticisms directed against feminist concerns about autonomy
and relationality as isolated concepts and so safeguard a commitment to
respect for persons. Against modern conceptions of the self that tend to be
abstract and individualistic, she shows that autonomy is ultimately for the
sake of relationship. Against conservative forms of communitarianism that
often favor traditional gender roles and relationships, Farley argues that patterns of relationship that do not respect individual autonomy are destructive
of persons and so ultimately of community. Finally, against postmodern
conceptions of the self as a construction of "a network of systems and the
womb of language," she claims that the autonomous self is made possible by
means of enduring relationships.[54] It is in the possibility of loving and com-
mitting oneself to the other (or to others) that we encounter our essential
freedom, according to Farley. Autonomy in this sense is not a freedom to
become or do whatever one might want or desire, but to commit oneself to

human flourishing—one's own and that of others—by means of love.[55] In this it is possible to detect a basic affinity with the thought of Karl Rahner and insights of Vatican II.

Rahner has referred to freedom as "a dialogic capacity of love."[56] In a way that might seem paradoxical to many contemporary readers, he argues that freedom increases insofar as one commits it (and so apparently limits it) in love.[57] As we have seen, such a commitment in Rahner's theology is a fundamental "yes" to God by means of a concrete commitment to the human other. Human autonomy is the freedom to affirm or deny God's gracious call to ultimate human fulfillment by means of love. In discerning and answering God's call to neighbor love, the human person does not surrender its autonomy but, instead, finds the highest and fullest expression of human freedom. As is the case with Farley, Rahner understands that freedom is not an end in itself; rather, it serves a definite, objective purpose that is the flourishing of individuals and communities.

Farley's own commitment to the possibility of autonomy in and through concrete, historical human relationships helps us to see a similar theological commitment in the anthropology of Karl Rahner and the documents of Vatican II, especially *Gaudium et spes*. The historical and cultural sensitivity of these two intellectual and spiritual sources is often overlooked and so they can be dismissed with other modern accounts of human persons and their rights and dignity. Farley's contribution shows that there is a way to approach human personhood that integrates universally obligating features of persons with attention to historical and cultural particularity. In doing so as a Catholic, feminist scholar, her work reflects and calls to mind of important resources within the Catholic community for generating a requirement to protect and respect all persons in a postmodern intellectual context. Her goal in this regard is not simply to advance the Catholic conception of the person and its dignity but also to challenge the Church to appropriate for itself the full implications of this teaching. The theological anthropology of the modern Catholic Church, with its commitment to the historical and particular nature of human personhood, is capable of accommodating an inclusive and diverse range of human experience. Insofar as Catholic teaching and theology continues to demonstrate a partiality to the experience of clerics and males generally, Farley argues, it will fail to advance the pastoral mission of the Church in a credible way.[58]

Conclusion

By all accounts, the human rights tradition that is predicated upon the dignity and inviolable worth of all persons is one of the most significant intellectual and political achievements of the twentieth century. This essay has surveyed the Roman Catholic contribution to this important tradition and argued for its continued relevance despite serious challenges. Following David Hollenbach's claim that the understanding of the person and its dignity as historically and culturally conditioned is Catholicism's greatest contribution to human rights discourse,[59] I have argued that an attempt to reject this understanding of human dignity as unduly abstract and inattentive to particularity cannot be sustained. Indeed, considerable support for the basic insights articulated in the theology of Karl Rahner and in the documents of Vatican II can be found in the work of feminist theologians.

The works of Margaret Farley and others challenge Catholics to a renewed commitment to the respect both the unique experience and the basic moral capacity of all persons, particularly those persons whose dignity has been traditionally discounted or undermined. Such a commitment is of particular urgency for Catholics committed to scholarship and teaching. For it must inform the treatment of human subjects in scholarly research—scientific, social scientific, literary, and beyond—as well as our treatment of students and colleagues. To behave in such ways, as we have seen, is consistent with some of the richest insights of the contemporary Church as well as the basic evangelical commitment of all baptized Christians.

Notes

1. On this point see John R. Sachs, "Transcendental Method in Theology and the Normativity of Human Experience" in *Philosophy and Theology* 7: 213–255 (1993).
2. For an account of the centrality of concern for human dignity in Leo XIII's thought, see David Hollenbach, *Claims in Conflict: Retrieving and Renewing the Catholic Human Rights Tradition* (New York: Paulist Press, 1979), 43–50.
3. Thomas Aquinas, *Summa Theologiae* I–II, 94.2.
4. *ST* I–II, 94, 2c.
5. John XXIII, *Pacem in terris* (*Peace on Earth*), n. 14.
6. For an account of Rahner's life and its implications for understanding his work, see Herbert Vorgrimler, *Understanding Karl Rahner: An Introduction to His Life and Thought*, trans. J. Bowden (New York: Crossroad, 1986).
7. ". . . the spiritual creature is constituted to begin with as the possible addressee of such a divine self-communication. The spiritual essence of man is established by God in creation from the outset because God wants to communicate himself: God's creation through efficient causality takes place because God wants to give himself in love." Karl Rahner, *Foundations of Christian Faith: An Introduction to the Idea of Christianity*, trans. W. Dych (New York: Seabury, 1978), 123. Also see Rahner, *Hearer of the Word*, trans. J. Donceel (New York: Continuum, 1994), 76.
8. Vorgrimler, 14.
9. Ibid., 14–15.
10. Karl Rahner, "Reflections on the Unity of Love of Neighbour and the Love of God" in *Theological Investigations* 6 (New York: Crossroad, 1982), 241.
11. Ibid., 247, author's emphasis.
12. Karl Rahner, "The Dignity and Freedom of Man" in *TI* 2 (New York: Crossroad, 1990), 239.
13. Ibid.

14. See Karl Rahner, "Theology of Freedom" in *TI* 6, 178–196. "Freedom, if it is to be able to effect salvation or damnation and hence the determination of the whole man, of itself brings into play the whole man with his mutually interactive relations to his origin and future. Freedom is always self-realisation of the objectively choosing man seen in view of his total realisation before God. In this way, considered as a capacity of the 'heart,' it is the capacity of love." 187.

15. "The Dignity and Freedom of Man," 239.

16. See Kevin Hogan's discussion of this point, "Entering into Otherness: The Postmodern Critique of the Subject and Karl Rahner's Theological Anthropology" in *Horizons* 25:2 (Fall 1998), 181–202, especially 192–193.

17. See Rahner's discussion of the body as the *Realsymbol* of the soul, "The Theology of the Symbol" in *TI* 4 (New York: Crossroad, 1982), especially 224–227, 246–247.

18. Rahner, *Hearer of the Word*, 94.

19. Rahner, *Foundations of Christian Faith*, 40.

20. Johannes Baptist Metz is most often associated with such criticisms. See chapter 9 in *Faith in History and Society* (New York: Seabury Press, 1980) for a concise statement of his influential critique of Rahner on this point. A full discussion of this criticism is beyond the scope of this essay, but an effective response to it has been advanced by Mary V. Maher; see her essay, "Rahner on Human Experience of God: Idealist Tautology or Christian Theology?" in *Philosophy and Theology* 7: 127–164 (1993). Also on this point, see Herbert Vorgrimler's essay, *"Der Begriff der Selbsttranzendenz in der Theologie Karl Rahners"* in *Wagnis Theologie: Erfahrungen mit der Theologie Karl Rahners*, H. Vorgrimler, ed. (Freiburg: Herder, 1979), 242–258, especially 258. Critiques like Metz's resonate with postmodern perspective which find attempts to articulate an account of the person insufficiently attentive to the concrete circumstances of actual persons.

21. Rahner, "The Dignity and Freedom of Man," 245, author's emphasis.

22. Ibid., 236, author's emphasis.

23. For Rahner, genuine freedom is both the goal and a presupposition of the moral law. Ibid., 246.

24. See my discussion of a positive fundamental option as neighbor love manifested as a "dying with Christ," "Categorical and Transcendental Experience in Rahner's Theology: Implications for Ethics" in *Philosophy & Theology* 10:1 (1997), 199–226, especially 219–224. "With regard to transcendental experience, Rahner understands dying with Christ to refer to radical self-disposal of the subject to God which necessarily occurs when the subject affirms both self and God in any genuine act of freedom. With regard to categorical experience, he situates the experience of dying with Christ in the concrete manifestation of love . . . " 220.

25. See Rahner's account of this in "Reflections on the Experience of Grace" in *TI* 3, especially 87.

26. Rahner, "The Dignity and Freedom of Man," 255.

27. Rahner, "Conscience" in *TI* 22, 6.

28. Ibid., 10.

29. Rahner, "The Dignity and Freedom of Man," 258–259.
30. The Universal Declaration of Human Rights, Preamble.
31. Ibid., 257, author's emphasis.
32. Lois Ann Lorentzen, *"Gaudium et spes,"* The New Dictionary of Catholic Social Thought, J. Dwyer, ed. (Collegeville, MN: Liturgical Press, 1994), 406.
33. Hollenbach, 70–71.
34. While not unique to his work, such ideas are often linked to Michel Foucault. See especially, *The History of Sexuality*, Robert Hurley, trans., 3 volumes (New York: Random House, 1978, 1985, 1986); and *Discipline and Punish: The Birth of the Prison*, Alan Sheridan, trans. (New York: Pantheon Books, 1977).
35. Seyla Benhabib, "The Generalized and the Concrete Other" in *Ethics: A Feminist Reader*, E. Frazer, J. Hornsby, S. Lovibond, eds. (Oxford: Blackwell, 1992), especially 280–286.
36. Ibid., 281.
37. Ibid., 283.
38. See Susan L. Secker, "Human Experience and Women's Experience: Sources for Catholic Ethics" in *Dialogue About Catholic Sexual Teaching*, C. E. Curran and R. A. McCormick, eds. (New York: Paulist Press, 1993), 577–599.
39. Ibid., 588.
40. Margaret A. Farley, *Personal Commitments* (San Francisco: Harper and Row, 1986), 81–82.
41. Lisa Sowle Cahill, *Sex, Gender, and Christian Ethics* (Cambridge: Cambridge University Press, 1996), 28.
42. See Martha Nussbaum on this point, *Sex and Social Justice* (Oxford: Oxford University Press, 1999), especially 35ff.
43. Margaret Farley discusses some of these tensions in her paper, "The Church in the Public Forum: Scandal or Prophetic Witness?" Unpublished Presidential Address, Catholic Theological Society of America, 12 June 2000. Forthcoming in *Proceedings*.
44. Farley, "Feminism and Universal Morality" in *Prospects for a Common Morality*, G. Outka and J. P. Reeder, Jr. eds. (Princeton: Princeton University Press, 1993), 170–190; and "A Feminist Version of Respect for Persons" in *Journal of Feminist Studies in Religion* (Spring 1993), 183–198.
45. Cahill, *Sex, Gender, and Christian Ethics*, especially chapter 2; "Feminism and Foundations," and chapter 3, "Particular Experiences, Shared Goods." Limitations of space prevent a full consideration of Cahill's account of the person. She does develop an interesting "critical realist" approach to a theory of human flourishing. As she develops this approach for a contemporary Catholic sexual ethic, she develops a fruitful dialogue with modern Catholic natural law theory.
46. Farley, "A Feminist Version of Respect for Persons," 185.
47. Farley, "Feminism and Universal Morality," 178.

48. Cahill, 28–29. The passage she quotes is from T. Minh-ha Trinh, "Difference: A Special Third World Women Issue" in *Feminist Review* 25 (1987), 18.

49. Ibid., 29.

50. Farley, "Feminism and Universal Morality," 178.

51. Ibid.

52. Ibid., 182.

53. Ibid.

54. Ibid.

55. Farley herself does not often use the term "love" in this context, preferring "relationality" or "commitment." Love can be a problematic concept in feminist analysis because it is frequently related to romantic bonding or, in Christian contexts, to self-sacrifice. For some feminists, romantic love in its traditional forms can be a means of "seducing" women into subordinate roles; while Christian self-sacrificing love or *agape* is criticized when it is construed as a particularly feminine virtue which is ultimately oppressing rather than liberating. I take it that love is a legitimate expression of Farley's relationality insofar as one understands that it is a love requiring mutuality and equality; that is a relationship that involves both giving and receiving.

56. Rahner, "Theology of Freedom," 186ff.

57. Rahner, "On the Theology of the Incarnation" in *TI* 4, 117.

58. Farley, "The Church in the Public Forum," 4–5. Also see her essay, "New Patterns of Relationship: Beginnings of a Moral Revolution" in *Theological Studies* 36/4: 627–646 (1975).

59. Hollenbach, 70–71.

Citations from the Second Vatican Council: *The Documents of Vatican II*, W. Abbott, S.J., ed.

16

Truth and Presence

Dennis O'Brien

R oman Catholic Christianity has had a special concern for Truth, revealed *and* rational. In his 1998 papal encyclical, *Fides et ratio,* John Paul II singles out denial of rational truth by philosophical relativism and pluralism as the besetting sins of the age. Yet, this Catholic defense of reason and philosophy is not without puzzles. Richard Collins in *Collegium News* more or less unwittingly states the problem. "The document [*Fides et ratio*] is optimistic about the ability of philosophy to discover the truth about the meaning of life, although, of course, without faith the meaning of existence is utterly beyond our grasp."[1] Just how reason (philosophy) can discover the truth about a mystery utterly beyond our grasp would seem at best a *prima facie* paradox.

While it is heartening to have the pope defend reason as an ally of faith, reason has not always repaid the compliment. Convinced rationalists often look on Christian faith as antithetical to the truths of reason. In the words of the great apostate emperor, Julian: "Reason enables us to attain a knowledge of the divine essence quite independently of any disclosures on the part of Moses, Jesus, or Paul. [The God of the Bible] is short sighted, resentful, capricious, sectional and particularist . . ."[2] Modern rationalists use the same epithets—maybe absent "resentful." Believers do not stand in the universal posture of reason; they are "particularist." Belief itself is "capricious" and "sectional" (sectarian)—the assertion of mere subjectivity against the common, universal truths which only reason can affirm.

The relation of *fides* and *ratio* is more than a conundrum for transcendent theologians; it is an ever present issue for Catholic academics and their universities and colleges. When the AAUP promulgated its statement about academic freedom in 1940, it made a grudging exception for religious colleges, allowing that they might put some restrictions on inquiry because of prior faith commitments. If, in a recent reflection on academic freedom, the general secretary of the AAUP declared that the exception was no longer necessary for Catholic colleges since they had become so open, one would not know whether to rejoice with the AAUP or fret with the pope, e.g., in *Ex Corde Ecclesiae.*[3]

Recently, the academic commitment to universal reason has come under question, not from some faith without but from "sectarian" demands within. Contemporary movements like feminism, deconstruction, ethnic studies, and queer theory have all, in their different ways, challenged the pretensions of or to "universal" reason. That supposed voice of reason is said to be mere male patriarchy or heterosexual hegemony in disguise. Multiculturalism (a generic term for the various individual ethnic claimants) demands that the *particularist* voices of women, blacks, and gays be heard in the icy mansions of academia. It is not surprising that these clamors raise the very issues of relativism and pluralism that so perturb John Paul in his encyclical. If it is every man, woman, black, white, gay, and bisexual for him/herself, what hope is there for Truth?

The challenge of multiculturalism is serious and the apparent threat of relativism disturbing but, before defending Truth, it is important to understand that this grand notion operates quite differently in a variety of contexts. As *Fides et ratio* itself affirms, "a single term conceals a variety of meanings. Hence the need for a preliminary clarification."[4] No less true of "Truth." In this essay I want to sketch out three important but significantly different contexts in which the word *truth* functions: scientific, artistic, and religious— specifically the Jewish-Christian context. While there is legitimacy to the use of "truth" in these differing contexts, the varied meanings of truth can be quite incompatible. My ultimate concern is with the "truth of faith" which, I believe, is fundamentally distorted if placed in either the scientific or artistic context. By understanding the radical difference between contexts of truth, I hope to illuminate what is the *Truth* in the truth of faith.

Truth and Science: The Truth of Doctrine

Any useful analysis of "Truth" should start with a commonsense model: the truth of propositions. The dominant model for verifying the truth of propositions is "science" broadly conceived. It is certainly the modern university's model for truth. What is crucial to science is the stance of the "scientist." The scientific observer is "neutral" extracted from "particularist" characteristics: sex, nationality, religious belief, time, place. There is no female or Chinese or Buddhist physics and results are time and space neutral. If the observer is neutral so are the data. A neutrino is the same wherever, whenever, and no matter what one's sexual orientation.[5] The scientific model is qualified when one turns to other parts of the standard curriculum. The great nineteenth-century historian Leopold von Ranke was naive to claim that his histories described "How things really were." Historians write from their own times and interests, which inevitably color their accounts. Nevertheless, Ranke rightly stated a necessity for historical study: no matter how colored a history, it must not be fiction. The historian must refer to data which would be open to any other investigator. Open data for open minds is a dictum even for "humanistic" studies. The literary critic who claims that Shakespeare was the Earl of Oxford, misogynous, and misandrous, or that Lear is a flawed play, points to data which he expects others to accept as proof. It is not his/her *personal* opinion or feeling that counts as scholarship. (I have to tell my students who give me their personal opinions about Plato that I am not interested in their autobiographies.)

In the ideal of science, *any* observer should be able to access *available* data—thus the insistence of natural science that experimental results be duplicable by other experimenters. Such stringent conditions cannot, however, apply in all circumstances. The contemporary historian cannot observe the past about which he writes. Even in natural science, we must sometimes rely on nonrepeatable observation. If the first astronaut to land on Mars is also the last, then his/her observations will have special authority. The astronaut would be a *privileged witness*. Reliance on the privileged witness as an *authority* does not, however, fundamentally deviate from the "scientific" model. Perhaps only one astronaut made it to Mars, but the assumption is that any other astronaut could confirm or disconfirm the initial report. In the case of history, if we happened to have H. G. Wells's time machine, we could travel in time as the astronaut travels in space. The time machine would allow later observers to confirm past historical facts. The privileged witness assumption is a conditional: *if* one were to be in the same situation as the privileged witness, then one would be in a position to validate the report. Unhappily the conditions for reconfirmation are technically impossible (no time machine, no appropriations for further Mars exploration).

I have explicated the authority-of-privileged-witness scenario since it is often taken to be the model for access to Christian Truth. "Only the Son knows the Father" (Cf. John 5:20). Jesus is the source of a truth about the will of the Father that he and he alone knows. Jesus is the authority, a privileged witness, and we come to believe the Truth that He reveals. The function of the Church is to pass on the truths revealed by the privileged witness.

The problem with truth-by-privileged-witness as the model for Christian truth is that it denies the central tenet of Christianity: the unique status of Jesus of Nazareth. Jesus does *not* say, "I am revealing a truth" he says "I *am* the Truth" (Cf. John 14:6). If Jesus were only a "privileged witness," he would be a prophet, not a Savior. Islam is very clear that Mohamed is "the seal of the prophets" who *reports* the word of God. The prophet is privileged but is in no way "divine." Muslims regard Christian claims about the divine nature of Jesus as blasphemous, an offense to the One God. Blasphemy was the accusation of the Sanhedrin in the trial of Jesus. Any privileged witness— even a prophet—is theoretically dispensable. Mohammed is so "dispensable" that some pious Muslims believe that the prophet was illiterate. He did not write the revelation; rather, he was only a writing instrument of Allah.

If there is a problem for Christianity with the status of the witness, there is a parallel problem in terms of *what* is revealed. In the normal case of a privileged witness, that which the witness reveals is something that others might well have known or come to know when they are brought face to face with what the original witness revealed. But in the Christian case, God is and remains an eternal mystery. Only the Son *does* know the Father.

In the Christian tradition, Jesus is more than a "privileged witness"; Jesus is the "unsurpassable Word of God" (Karl Rahner's phrase). As Savior, he is the indispensable Word: "*I* am the Truth." If Jesus is the Truth—and the Way and the Life—then his relation to God is more than witness; Christians say he is the Son of God and all the Trinitarian complexities begin to unfold. But the problems are not only with the metaphysics of divinity; they are also with the nature of the following of Jesus, which we call the "Church." What is the revelation taught, the *teaching* passed on by the Church?

If one considers the normal *teaching* situation, the role of the teacher is to reveal and display the *truths of the subject*. The aim of the teacher is to create students of the subject, *not* disciples of the teacher. It is utterly subversive for the teacher to say, "I am the Truth," as if the only avenue to revelation were through his/her personal powers. Contrast Jesus and the Buddha. The Buddha is a teacher; he preaches the Four Noble Truths; Buddhism stems from acceptance of the Truths, not of Siddhartha Gautama. Buddhism is not the worship of Gautama. Christianity, on the other hand, *is* the worship of Jesus of Nazareth. Christians *are* disciples of the Teacher.

To put the problem most paradoxically, at a first approximation there is no Christian "truth" to be passed along, no "teaching" in the sense that a university professor would recognize. If there is a Truth to be passed along, it is not a teaching; it is the *Teacher:* Jesus is the Truth. What is handed down from generation to generation is Jesus as Risen Lord. One could say that, for Catholics, the Church is centered in the Eucharist, not in the encyclicals. (For Protestants, it is the living word of preaching that makes God present to the faithful.) The Eucharist—like the Church as the body of Christ—is what is offered as the meaning of life, the ark of salvation. Christians are disciples of the Teacher as he is present in the Church. In the older Catholic ecclesiology: the Church is the Mystical Body of the Lord.

I once supervised an undergraduate philosophy thesis for a young woman who wanted to write on the "meaning of life." Her assumption was that there was some sort of answer like "power corrupts" or "the unexamined life is not worth living." She wanted a "doctrine" (a true statement) that settled the question. But I think Wittgenstein gets it right about questions on "the meaning of life":

> For an answer which cannot be expressed the question too cannot be expressed.
>
> ~
>
> If a question can be put at all, then it *can* also be answered.
>
> The solution to the problem of life is seen in the vanishing of the problem.
> (Is not this the reason why men to whom after long doubting the sense of life became clear, could not say wherein this sense consisted?)[6]

Reverting to Richard Collins's notion that philosophy raises a question about meaning that faith answers, I would say, following Wittgenstein, that the answer to a *philosophical* question (What is the meaning of life?) would have to be a *philosophical* answer. And if philosophy is an exercise of *ratio,* then the answer would have to be an exercise in like *ratio*—something like the verifiable "doctrine" my earnest student was seeking.[7] One may, adopting Wittgenstein's language, find the meaning of life as a disciple of Jesus Christ but be unable to "say wherein this sense consisted."

Truth and Art: Re-Presenting the Spirit

I am convinced that Christianity is committed to the strange logic I have outlined: what is "taught" is the Teacher, what is True is this Jesus, what is handed over is Christ's presence. The essence of Christianity is the presence of the Teacher, the presence of Jesus in the Church. The notion that "truth" is somehow essentially bound up in a specific named, historical person is fundamentally antithetic to the assumptions of universal reason and scientific truth. This was precisely the basis of Julian the Apostate's rejection of the need for revelation attached to any historical person, whether it be Moses, Jesus, or Paul.

Given the biblical notion of revelation to specific individuals and the even more uncanny notion that this Jesus *is* the Truth, it is worth looking at the particularist claims of contemporary multiculturalism for possible support and comparison. As explicated previously, the "scientific" notion of "truth" is essentially *un*historical. For true knowledge, all the characteristics that define an individual as an actual historical existent are negated and transcended. The one who knows is neither male or female, ancient or modern. This is precisely what multiculturalists deny; they say it is sheer illusion to think that one can or ought to transcend one's particular history; there is no truth-as-*universal*; rather, there is only my, his, and her "truth."

Let me call the multicultural claim a demand for *signatured truth*: John Doe's truth, Jane Roe's truth. From the perspective of universal, i.e., scientific-rational, knowledge, signatured truth is utterly subversive. However, if one turns to the arts, *signatured* "truth" is fundamental. (The sense in which signatured "truth" is truth in any sense will be integral to the exposition that follows.) Signatured truth attaches to a specific person, and so it seems to resemble the Jesus-truth that the Church proclaims. In the long run, the artistic model, like the scientific, fails to capture the peculiarity of religious proclamation, but an explication of artistic signature will introduce concepts and methods that recur within the religious dimension.

I have said that the Church does not teach a universal truth; rather, it makes present this Jesus. There seems to be a clear analogy in the arts. In music, one *re*-presents a Beethoven symphony—the very reality of Beethoven's work is present to the hearer. The re-presentation offers the unique "voice" of the composer; the work is signatured to the unique artist. Even when we do not know the names of the artists, we give them unique descriptions—the Master of Three Angels, the Rhine Painter, and so on—because we believe that there is something uniquely personal to the artist's work. Artworks as *signatured* are *essentially historical* in so far as they are connected to and express unique, particular visions. The work is Rembrandt not Lievens, Beethoven not Rossini. In contrast, *Newton's* theory is Newton's only *honoris causa*; there is nothing finally English, male, donnish or seventeenth century about the inverse square law.

One may readily admit that there is something personal, signatured, about works of art, but doesn't the variability of differing artistic styles preclude the sort of objectivity and universality that are taken to be essential marks of "truth"? In what sense, if any, does the notion of "truth" arise in the realm of the arts? Certainly not as propositional depiction of a reality. We may assess which portrait of George Washington is the most accurate and truest depiction, but then none of the paintings may be "true" art. There are two clear uses of "true" in regard to art. First is it "true" art and, if it is truly art, is there something *about which* it is true? Does this portrait of Washington, although not the most accurate depiction, capture the true nobility of the person?

If one asks, Is it true/truly art? the *manner* in which that question is answered is significant. In so far as we are concerned with the value of some work *as art,* we operate in a manner radically different than when we ask whether a putative scientific theory is true. The difference will be significant in the religious case as well. The morning paper carried photos of a hotel room in New York dripped with 1000 pounds of cheese. Is it art or a practical joke on art, the public, or the hotel? How would we judge? We make the decision in a manner analogous to how we judge an authentic Rembrandt. We fit the present object into the already present history of what is clearly "authentic": the *already* attested works of Rembrandt, the *already* attested exemplars of art. The cheese room is ranged alongside something—Gaudi's *Sagrada Familia* Church?—and a decision is made to enter it into the history of *art*, rather than the history of jokes or psychopathology.

True art is what is "valuable/valued" *artistically*—not every drip of concrete or cheese may be valuable (real, true) art.[8] The crucial point is that in the area of what is signatured, the criteria for value is an accepted *tradition*. The only standard for authentic/valuable art is the existence of actual valued exemplars. Comparison of present work to past exemplars affects past and present. It can happen that the newer work casts older work into the shadow. We see that previous examples are less valuable because the newer work reveals with clarity what was awkward and muddled in the earlier vision. On the other hand, in a developed and deeply historical tradition such as the history of visual representation, we would be prepared to reject out of hand any new development that claimed to undermine the value of Rembrandt.

The validation of art by an extant tradition clearly distinguishes art from the universal (nonsignatured) truth of science, a truth that is validated by observation or experiment, not great exemplars. The notion of true (truly valuable) art and its validation within *tradition* also constitutes a fundamental rejection of the "relativist" assumptions of multiculturalism. In the peculiar way that opposites are similar, the multicultural critique of "scientific," unhistorical, universalist knowledge turns out to be thoroughly *un*historical on its own grounds. If every reader has his or her own text, his or her own here-and-now interpretation, then historical placement is unnecessary or impossible, and canonic (traditional) works are political artifacts (thus the present-day canonic wars in American colleges). Shakespeare is whatever I make of him—and if I prefer Mickey Spillane or Jacqueline Suzanne, why not? It is that sort of evaluative free-for-all that concerns John Paul II in *Fides et ratio*. The danger is that in rejecting the outcome of the multiculturalist critique, one will fall back on some version of universal truth based on the logic of science, verifiable propositions, and true doctrine.

It is clear enough that we value works of art, and that works of art are uniquely *signatured,* but in what sense are works of art "true"? It may be *truly art,* but is it true *of* anything. Can one claim some "truth" for the world-as-seen-by-Rembrandt? To the extent that there is a "truth" in Rembrandt's vision, it necessarily moves beyond (or below) the scientific model of truth. The "self" of the rational, scientific mind is sexless, above culture, transcendent, without birth or death: a timeless, passionless observer. Unhappily, however, actual human beings are *not* timeless passionless observers. The world that living human beings "know" is precisely the world of historical position, passion, and emotion that the transcendent observer abandons. Art depicts the deep textures, the deep truths of all-too-human experiences. One brings humanity to the arts, and the arts, in turn, become the schools of humanity.

One might well admit, as multiculturalists are like to do, that humanity comes in only signatured, historically particular works, but then use that very fact to point up the difference between the *universality* of science and the variability of human sensibilities, moral, and aesthetic values. The relativists whom John Paul II opposes hold that truth is unattainable because cultures differ too widely; there are no human universals. It may be that Shakespeare is authentic art in the Western tradition but would not be so recognized in other cultures. For years, the artifacts of African tribes were placed in ethnographic museums because they were not regarded as "art" in the European *beaux arts* tradition.

I consider the notion of radical separation of cultures false in fact—a failure of nerve and thus an easy method of affirming one's own prejudices. That radical separation is false in fact seems clear enough from the fact of universal artists: Shakespeare has had a rich history in Japan. Of course, there is something *different* about the fact that the plays are translated into Japanese, but then the contemporary Royal Shakespeare Company does not perform in the manner of the English seventeenth century or the nineteenth century or even the 1920s. Push the argument far enough, and there is not enough commonality from year to year to talk about *culture* at all, not to mention *multicultures.* The very fact that we have now transferred African masks from the natural history museums to art museums suggests that the art of varied cultures can be appropriated. As to failure of nerve: posting a multicultural signpost at the beginning of crosscultural dialogue signals the basic futility of the enterprise. In proclaiming my broad tolerance of the other culture, I am also making sure that my own views are sealed from comparison and critique.

The paradox of *great* art is that it is, on the one hand, signatured, deeply historical, a unique personal voice and vision, while on the other hand, it transcends its mere periodicity and personal quirks. Shakespeare is certainly a unique voice; he is also very much a writer of his age. We can dissolve him into a specimen of sensibilities, style, and vision, which he shared with his contemporaries like Beaumont and Fletcher. Scholars do that. But it is the mark of great art that, while speaking from the person and of the age, it contains a core that can be constantly revived in radically different societies. If there is a *tradition* of art, it is not simply because there are historical precursors; rather, it is because some of those historical precursors are more than historical curiosities. Tradition bears upon the present as the standard of value because great art of the past moves beyond its historical placement to comment on present practice.[9] Great art is universal and true to the *human* condition.

Christian Truth: Real Presence

I have offered a sketch of the "logic of the arts" in order to suggest that neutral rationality does not command the entire territory of "truth." There is signatured truth, truth attached essentially to the vision and insight of individuals. As humans not angels, as living persons not transcendent observers, artists (broadly defined) reveal to us the truth of the human world of life and desire, passion and pride, good and evil. Art is always personal and thus signatured, which means that it must also be appropriated by the viewer-as-person. A great *universal* artist is not universal because he/she transcends person, history, sex, self—but because the sense of self expressed is so enriched that it can speak to other histories, other selves. Art is appropriated as a dialogue of historical selves.

The logic of the arts is structured in ways that parallel the logic of Jewish-Christian religious sensibility. Art depends on *exemplars* that are *canonic*. It is not too much of a stretch to regard these exemplars as *revelations*. There is no inner natural necessity that leads to say, landscape painting. Many cultures—even highly developed painting cultures—just don't do it. But if a Poussin or Turner or Cézanne comes along and paints landscapes, these are novel revelations, exemplars for the tradition of landscape painting. In art, we depend on the genius, the inspiration, of the artist to create and initiate the form. So inspired is the artist, that the ancients literally thought the godlike muses were prompting the artist's work. In that sense, then, art is deeply historical, dependent on what happens to be created.

The parallel to the role of revelation in the biblical sense is striking. Quite contrary to the universal rationalism of Julian, who held that Reason could discover the divine essence, the Bible affirms that we can know God only through specific revelation of, to, and in Abraham, Moses and, latterly, Jesus. These great revelations initiate a tradition that becomes canonic and is used to validate later revelations. The gospel writers did not refer to the Hebrew Bible for nothing! Biblical revelation is, then, canonic for true religion as Rembrandt is for true art. (That is the biblical claim. I am not going to defend it here; I only wish to state the logic of canonic valuation as essential to this tradition.)

Because art and religion depend on actual individual exemplars or revelation, the critical language that grows up around these initiating realities must be regarded as "parasitic." Artistic criticism and theological commentary are secondary discourses that receive validation only in the face of the exemplar or the revelation. We have extensive descriptions of ancient Athenian wall paintings but none of them have survived. Lacking the actual example, we really do not know what they were as art. I may tell you that Van Gogh uses a thick brush and vivid colors, but until you actually see a Van Gogh painting, you don't really know what I am talking about. Whatever the revelation in Jesus—which I will discuss more extensively—theology and doctrinal statements are finally interpreted to that actuality. We don't start with theological doctrine and then deduce the reality; rather, we start with the reality and try to understand what the theologian may be pointing to. "Jesus is the Son of God" can only be interpreted into the life of Jesus of the Gospels.

Just as Shakespeare's signatured genius is a universal claimant upon poets and our sense of humanity, so with Jesus. If we re-present Shakespeare from age to age, so does the Church re-present Jesus. As art is a dialogue of persons in their historical rootedness, so there is a dialogue with the revelation in Jesus. That there is a two-way dialogue clearly implies that re-presentation is not necessarily replication. It is interesting to see Shakespeare done on the stage of the reconstructed Globe, but too much fuss over periodicity may block the universal import of the work. Similarly, return to New Testament practices in the Church may revive externals but miss the living power of the original. Later ages may have their own Shakespeare—still the Bard— while later ages of Christianity may find new depths and directions in their Lord.

Comparing art and religion in this fashion has apologetic value for religion. Organized religion has been having a hard time of late, but the museums are crowded and drama festivals abound. If religion is like an artistic "vision," one could soften or perhaps eliminate the dogma and doctrinal controversies (the scientific model of truth) that have marred its history and make it "unbelievable" to the modern, rational mind. Freud thought that art was an "illusion" that allowed us to fantasize a more livable world, but because we recognize that art is an illusion it is a benign illusion. Religion, on the other hand, Freud judged as an illusion that people take "for real" and it thereby distorts their lives. Robert Frost said that poetry does not effect the real, it does not eliminate suffering; rather it "lifts suffering to a plane of higher regard."

Reducing religion to art—or making art a new religion—has its attractions, but it hardly conforms to the actuality of religious history and practice. The Bible is really not a very satisfactory "work of art" for all the power of the psalms, the denunciations of the prophets, or Jesus' parables. Religions have not offered themselves as artistic visions for contemplation, but as disciplines, life commandments, and commitments—and that is certainly how believers have reacted to religious teachings. To access the religious, one must in some sense move beyond art to life itself—what is "for real!"

A perceptive differentiation of art and life occurs in Henry James's preface to *The Spoils of Poynton*. James tells how the novel emerged: he was attending a fashionable London affair and overheard a story of a messy inheritance. He saw in that story what he called a "germ," a set of complications that could become the narrative of his novel. As the conversation proceeded, the actual history turned out quite different from the course of the novel. James reflected on the difference between life and art:

> Life being all inclusion and confusion, and art being all dis-
> crimination and selection, the latter in search of the hard latent
> *value* with which it is concerned . . . the artist finds in his tiny
> nugget washed clean of awkward accretions and hammered
> into sacred hardness the very stuff for a clear affirmation . . .
> for the indestructible. At the same time, it amuses him again
> and again to note how, beyond the first step in the actual case
> . . . life persistently blunders and deviates, losing herself in the
> sand. The reason, of course, is that life has no direct sense of
> the subject and is capable, luckily for us, of nothing but splen-
> did waste.[10]

If one contrasts religion and art, the Bible and poetry, one could say, echoing James, that the Bible is the "germ" from which *actual* lives, not novels, are "written." Art is the luminous, clear, Platonic form: hard, golden, indestructible. Life, on the other hand, is all "inclusion and confusion," capable only of "waste." In the gospel, what we have is not a work of art but depiction of a life full of loss, betrayal, confusion, death—waste. Christians, of course, affirm Jesus' life as *splendid* waste. In Jean-Paul Sartre's novel *Nausea*, the protagonist contrasts the "too much" of actual existence to the gem-like purity of art. What Sartre's atheism perceives as absurd and nauseous (waste), the saint perceives as the overflowing glory of God (splendid waste).

Powerful and important as art certainly is, it is in its own way an "abstraction" from life as lived. Art is symbolic, something shaped into a "clear affirmation" that reflects everywhere the controlling sensibility of the signatured artist. From the standpoint of Christianity, that is where art is finally abandoned as *only* an illusion. A vivid example of the *failure* of art is Elie Wiesel's comment that only the art of children produced in the concentration camps is adequate to the experience of the Holocaust. Once the cultivated sensibility of the adult artist starts to reshape the events as James extracted his germ from a messy history, the horror is placed at a distance and thus far falsified. Let me label the art of children in this instance as "iconic." An icon, unlike a symbol, *participates in the reality that it depicts.* (Thus the various controversies about icons in the Eastern Church. Are the icons mere *depictions* of the holy, or do they actually *participate* in the holy?) The art of children from the camps is immediate, unfiltered by Art, a direct reaction to the events, and thus it participates in the very event that is depicted.[11]

Wiesel chooses the work of children because he wants to make the experience of the Holocaust *present*—there is to be no aesthetic *distance* between the viewer and the event to be remembered, no artistic intermediary. In Catholic Christianity the central ceremony of remembrance of the Lord's passion is said to constitute *real presence.* In life's great loves and losses, what we want, what we need, is *presence.* Job's comforters are too full of moral injunction to be present to his distress. In the long run we don't need moralisms, teachings—even great poetry; we want the presence of the other, the one who loves. Real presence, then, goes beyond re-presenting a (the artist's) vision. Catholics claim a "real" presence of Jesus in the Eucharist and they reject the notion of "symbolic" presence. Clearly the Eucharist is not the literal body of the Nazarene who lived two thousand years ago, but the Catholics are right to reject the notion that it is merely a symbol or remembrance. Sacramental presence iconic: it is a symbol that participates in the reality which it depicts, just as the children's art is a symbol that is infected with the very *presence* of the event depicted.

In this essay, I have sketched out three contexts in which "truth" may function. There is the propositional truth exemplified by the sciences, artistic truth, and Jesus as Truth. Scientific truth, despite its power and scope, requires an ascetic transcendence of all-too-human experience. Artistic truth engages with human life as lived shaping and molding it, giving to suffering Robert Frost's attitude of "higher regard." But finally, art may fail before the enormity of suffering, the sheer "blunder" and "waste" of life. This is a final, ultimate truth. Is there a saving "word" for this final truth? What "utterance" could encompass, comprehend, the density, confusion, "waste" of actual life? It would be a "word" that is itself a *life*. Only word which is a life or a life which is itself a "word" could "depict" life. Thus the word is not a scientific proposition or doctrine, not even a great tragic poem; rather, it is a very life to very life. And if it is claimed as the life alongside *all* lives, surely it reaches toward God's life.

At the conclusion of a short story by John L'Heureux, *An Expert on God*, a disbelieving priest chances on a deadly auto crash on a lonely road. Reverting to his official role, he manages to rip open the car and anoint the driver, a young boy.

> He began to pray, aloud, which struck him as foolish: to be holding a dying boy in his arms and reciting rote prayers about our Father in heaven . . . What could he do? What could he say at such a moment? What would God do at such a moment, if there was a God? . . .
>
> His doubts became a certainty and he said, "It doesn't matter," but it did matter and he knew it. What could anyone say to this crushed, dying thing, he wondered. What would God say if he cared as much as I?
>
> . . . [A]t once the priest, faithless, unrepentant, gave up his prayers and bent to him and whispered, fierce and burning, "I love you," and continued until there was no breath, "I love you, I love you, I love you."[12]

Life's final truth is chanciness, the blundering accident, the awesome density of life and suffering. If there is any salvation, any "word," it is to be held, to have the presence of the other who says, "I love you."

L'Heureux ironically titles his story *An Expert on God*. The expert, it seems is "faithless, unrepentant." Is he? Does it matter, make any sense, to hold a "crushed, dying thing" and say, "I love you" until no breath remains? Being present to another, present to one unconscious and dying, saying "I love you" may really be nonsense—it doesn't matter. But the priest knows that it does matter, although he cannot say a prayer or articulate a belief. It is in holding and loving that he is "the expert on God." An "expert on God" who pronounced true doctrine could only articulate the sense of the senseless action of the priest in this story. Theology, belief, or doctrine only sketches out a world in which holding and loving make some final sense in the great cosmic order of things.

Notes

1. Richard Collins, "Toward a Counter-Cultural Dialogue," *Collegium News*, Volume 1, issue 8, p. 5. (*Collegium*: Fairfield University, 1999).
2. C. N. Cochrane, *Christianity and Classical Culture* (New York: Oxford University Press, 1957), p. 266, Cochrane is summarizing from Julian's *In Galileos*.
3. Mary Burgan, "Scholarly Ideals and Changing Reality," in *Academic Questions*, Volume 10, #4, pp. 22–24.
4. John Paul II, *Fides et ratio*, 4.
5. One might qualify this statement in two ways, neither of which is fundamental to the essential contrast. There is the fascination with certain quantum phenomenon in which it is postulated that some interaction with the observer qualifies what is observed. However one wants to understand this claim, it seems to do nothing to the basic "neutrality" of scientific observation. Quantum physicists do not publish their results like poets manifesting and seeking the personal voice. The second qualification is that science is itself a human artifact. To be sure—and many cultures have been as uninterested in science as Byzantine artists were in landscape painting—but the *culture* of science when it is practiced aims at the personal neutrality of the observer which is commensurate to the sheer givenness of empirical fact. Not all scientists may be up to the asceticism of the neutral observer, but that is the psychic ideal.
6. Ludwig Wittgenstein, *Tractatus Logico-Philosophicus*, 6.5, 6.521.
7. I am using "philosophy" in its technical sense as developed reason and argument. Of course, in some large and vague sense, one could talk about the "philosophy" of Rembrandt as displayed in his paintings. It seems better to speak of Rembrandt's "vision" or some such, however, since presumably he offered no arguments for his deeply humane presentations. Wittgenstein's own statements are "philosophical" but, as readers of the *Tractatus* recognize, Wittgenstein characterizes the claims of the *Tractatus* as "nonsense"— not rational arguments but "elucidations."
8. Of course, there is a merely descriptive sense of art which is used to distinguish works of nature from works of human hands. Barring an explosion in a cheese factory, dripped cheese is likely to be a work of human hands. For all that, not all art-done is art-valuable.

9. Shakespeare may or may not be the best example for a universal artist of humanity. Wittgenstein did not much like Shakespeare. "People stare at him in wonderment, almost as at a spectacular natural phenomenon. They do not feel that this brings them into contact with a great *human being*." (quoted by Iris Murdoch, *Metaphysics as a Guide to Morals*, New York, Viking, 1993. p. 112.) On the other hand, Harold Bloom, *Shakespeare: the Invention of the Human* (New York: Riverhead, 1998), thinks that Shakespeare *defines* what it is to be human. The *universality* of Shakespeare, it seems, can be taken as if he lacked a *personal* core (like a natural phenomenon) or as if he defined *all* that is human. The problematics of this difference are not unlike what one might apply to Jesus of the Gospels.

10. Henry James, *The Spoils of Poynton* (New York: Scribner, 1908) pp. v–vi.

11. It is worth noting that much of contemporary art, sensitive to the Holocaust and the other terrors of the century, seeks to deny the "arty," seeking in apparently "primitive" scrawls, quasi-random configurations, the sort of direct involvement that would move beyond art. In a sort of ironic similarity to Christian practice, the artist may even perform him/herself as the work of art.

12. John L'Heureux, *The Expert on God*, in *Celestial Omnibus: Short Fiction on Faith,* eds. J. P. Maney and Tom Hazuka (Boston: Beacon Press, 1997).

The Church in the (Post)Modern World

Michael Patella, O.S.B.

Christianity is closing its second millennium and opening its third. In approaching such a milestone we can look back as well as forward. Perhaps more than others, scholars are more likely to assume this Janus-like pose. As the ones responsible for upholding and furthering two thousand years of thought and discovery, we could be quite attuned to the new directions civilization might now take. This situation may be particularly true for Catholic intellectuals, since Catholicism has played such a large role in so much of Western civilization. We might wonder how our intellectual and cultural history can continue to be involved in the world. The question gains special importance as postmodern thought deconstructs, or at least strongly challenges, previously held assumptions, assumptions built on a perception of reality that has defined Western, and thus, in a large way, Christian civilization for two millennia. This Christian perception of reality has been defined by Erich Auerbach as an "antagonism between sensory appearance and meaning,"[1] an exercise of observing empirical data and interpreting it.

What follows is an exploration of this very issue of observation and interpretation. I would like to investigate some of the foundations of Christian thought, formed in that "antagonism between sensory appearance and meaning," and observe how they became the building blocks of our civilization. I would also like to continue the exploration into the realm of postmodernism. To further this end, I have divided Western civilization into three major phases of development: the premodern, the modern, and the postmodern periods. This essay ends with several thoughts about future directions.

J. Bottum states, "[I]t is premodern to seek beyond rational knowledge for God; it is modern to desire to hold knowledge in the structures of human rationality (with or without God); it is postmodern to see the impossibility of such knowledge."[2] This aphorism sums up the broad lines of Western, intellectual history, and in it, modernism appears as the anomaly. Bottum continues, "Though they disagree on whether God exists, premoderns and postmoderns share the major premise that knowing requires His existence. Only for a brief period in the history of the West—the period of modern times—did anyone seriously suppose that human beings could hold knowledge without God."[3]

In monastic thought, all learning and study have as their goal union with God; any new insights reflect his greater glory. Medieval thought could not conceive of knowledge divorced from God. The modern period pulled truth away from God and set it on rationality, and now postmodernism has removed truth from rationality. Thus, although postmodernism does not see God as the repository of truth, the medieval and postmodern minds at least agree that rationality alone is not the depository of truth either. So begins the discourse of monastic theology with the contemporary world. Indeed, the ethos inherent in monastic theology may very well provide the means for dealing with the postmodern mindset.[4]

By proposing such a dialogue, I am not advocating a return to a period in Western civilization that existed before the Enlightenment. Rather, in acknowledging that the postmodern critique of modernism has much to recommend it, Catholic discourse can, in Bottum's words, "[R]establish our communion" with the premodern community of faith,[5] a community of faith that existed in time, but a community of faith that transcends time. It is to our misfortune that stresses within Western history have caused these bonds of communion to break in the first place. Several factors have joined together in causing the ropes to snap.

The Enlightenment and Modernism

The Age of Reason, or the Enlightenment, was a logical development from the humanist tradition of the Renaissance. The Renaissance itself saw intellectuals building the foundation of the modern scientific enterprise by their interest in the workings of the world around them.[6] The Reformation and the resulting wars of religion—the Thirty Years' War in particular, ended by the Treaty of Westphalia in 1648—catalyzed the Enlightenment's arrival on the scene, a period that can be dated roughly as 1650–1781.The publication of Kant's *Critique of Pure Reason,* an "effective challenge to many of the presuppositions"[7] of the Enlightenment, can be considered of the period. Noteworthy, too, and somewhat of an epistemological declaration of independence, is Kant's essay, "Was ist Aufklärung?" in which he calls for autonomous reason not beholden to anyone or anything. Thus, the thought born in the Age of Reason grew to dominate the modern[8] era which itself is now passing.

Before the Reformation, the foundational anthropological outlook was the Great Chain of Being. God was at the top, with all life, knowledge, and salvation coming from him. Angels, in their differing ranks, followed, and right behind them stood human beings, after which, in the succession, came the rest of creation. This chain was not static, however. God acted in human history through the creation of Adam and Eve, revelations to Abraham and Moses, and most effectively, through the incarnation of his Son, Jesus Christ. This revelation was seen as a constant movement toward the salvation of humanity now mediated through the Church and its graces. The Renaissance, with its interest in humanism, gave rise to reason as a guiding principle for human interaction with creation. The Great Chain, including the mediation of the Church, however, still held together.

The pressures of the Protestant Reformation began to divide the interrelationship between revelation and reason. Since Protestants saw grace as already having been mediated through the death of Christ, the Church, as an authority structure, no longer had value for the Protestants, and the Bible, their sole source of revelation and authority, quickly filled this gap. This resulted in a widening divide between reason and revelation. Nonetheless, for both Catholics and Protestants, God still held the premier position in the chain.

This chain is broken with the Enlightenment. Rather than the human story finding its value in God, God found his value in the human story.[9] Human beings now became the rulers. Ironically, the end result was both an exaltation and a debasement. Where, in an earlier period, humans may have served God, in the Enlightenment, despite their self-exaltation, they lose their the position of being stewards of the created order and end up being ordinary players in an impartial universe.

It is not by accident that this great shift occurred after a time of great societal upheaval. The Thirty Years' War, with all its attendant atrocities, among other things, destabilized the faith in Christian doctrine. That armies unfurled the banner of one or another tenet of faith as they savaged Europe caused thinkers and others to look for new, less divisive ways around which to organize thought. In addition, the philosophical revolution initiated by René Descartes, which preferred knowledge based on the reasoned truth of mathematics over the knowledge gleaned from empirical observation, placed the rational human mind in the central position. Sir Isaac Newton's scientific discoveries functioned as the second revolution. Newton's aim was to lay out the laws by which the universe operates.

The Enlightenment worked on the basis of applying the rigor and necessity of mathematics to empirical observation and reason. Eventually, mathematics provided the model of proof and, ultimately, of reason itself, while observation provided the content. This they contrasted to the subservience of reason and observation to authority (be it Bible, Church, Aristotle, prejudice, superstition, etc.) in ages past. The Enlightenment emphasized the autonomy of reason and, with that, gave reason an objectivity and neutrality.

Although both Descartes and Newton did not want to disparage theology—rather, they aimed to complement it with reason—some have concluded that the momentum of these two revolutions forced theology to give way to the natural sciences.[10] Whereas revelation previously functioned as the highest court of appeal in decisions concerning truth, that position was ceded to reason in the Enlightenment. The social and political ramifications of this sea change are best reflected in the American Declaration of Independence, the United States Constitution, and the French Revolution. In addition, technological inventions such as the steam engine, medical developments such as small pox vaccination, and discoveries in such natural phenomena as the Atlantic Gulf Stream, all fed into the belief of the inevitability of human progress. In each case, the principles of mathematics and the scientific method, either separately or together, were responsible for this progress in alleviating human servitude and suffering. Humanity could improve its lot without the interference of the religion.

The Enlightenment and modernism maintain the optimistic view in the goodness, certainty, and objectivity of human knowledge. In the American Experiment, the Enlightenment's great laboratory, this optimism is reflected in the country's many movements and policies: democracy, temperance, abolition, women's suffrage, populism, progressivism, the New Deal, the Marshall Plan, the Great Society. It now appears to many, however, that this modern optimism and faith in the inevitability of human progress is gasping for breath, and, indeed, may have already breathed its last. As a case in point, the cyber and computer revolution, although hailed for the accessibility to information it affords, also raises more serious questions about privacy and use of information, and community. For many, the microchip is greeted begrudgingly as a necessary evil rather than enthusiastically as the great liberator of humankind. Why the change in attitude?

Some consider that the first volley against modernism occurs in the last half of the nineteenth century with Friedrich Nietzsche's *Also Sprach Zarathustra*.[11] In the prologue, Zarathustra, along with the townspeople, is watching a rope dancer. A man comes out of door right where one end of the rope is fastened, walks toward the rope dancer, jumps over him, and throws the dancer off balance; the dancer falls. As the dancer lies on the pavement, Zarathustra kneels beside him. "I knew long ago that the devil would trip me up," the rope dancer says. "Now he draggeth me to hell: wilt thou prevent him?"[12] When Zarathustra assures him that there is neither a devil or hell ("Thy soul will be dead before thy body; fear, therefore, nothing any more!") the rope dancer replies, "If thou speakest the truth . . . I lose nothing when I lose my life. I am not much more than an animal which hath been taught to dance by blows and scanty fare."

One speaking from a premodern perspective would be concerned about a last confession and the sacraments, for saving the dancer's soul is the only important thing. One speaking from modernism might try to see the dancer's fall as a failure to regard the laws of nature and to take proper precautions. Zarathustra, in his words of consolation, appeals neither to revelation nor to reason. There is no meaning to the rope dancer's life and no salvation in death; there is only nihilism.

Perhaps nihilism lurked in modernism's background all along, like Hamlet prowling the shadows of Elsinore. Gertrude and Claudius suspect something is amiss, but do not know quite how to handle the situation. For example, a little over a century before Nietzsche, Goethe has Faust, in his opening soliloquy, lamenting his education and training. As he catalogues his degrees, he takes a special stab at theology, the worst of all the subjects he studied, "Und leider auch Theologie."[13] Nonetheless, Faust feels equally as empty with philosophy, law, and medicine. Certainly, Goethe does not have his characters end up in the same meaningless web as Nietzsche's, but we feel that Goethe has a sense that something is lacking in the Enlightenment's claims.

Just as the premodern, medieval worldview fell apart after the ravages of the Thirty Years' War, the modern worldview collapsed with the catastrophes of the twentieth century, particularly the Second World War and the birth of the atomic age. Descartes' reason and Newton's science, practically unfettered for nearly three hundred years, brought the world to near annihilation. On the European continent, the literary and artistic worlds looked to Dadaism and Existentialism; in the United States, these movements found their expression with the "beat generation." Although these schools of thought were examples of and precursors to the postmodern world, they were, at that time, the intellectual and cultural property of the academic and artistic communities. Only now, at the close of the millennium, does it appear that postmodernism is the stock in trade of the greater society.

Postmodernism

Lyotard asks whether modernism is, "the constitution of sociocultural unity within which all the elements of daily life and of thought would take their places as in an organic whole?" or whether, "the passage that has to be charted between heterogeneous language games—those of cognition, of ethics, of politics—belong to a different order from that?[14] Lyotard holds that postmodernity must examine the Enlightenment's basic idea that there is a "unitary end of history and of a subject."[15]

Since modern discourse between various components of society necessitates a "consensus between partners over a certain knowledge and certain commitments," modernism cannot exist without a "shattering of belief."[16] This is because modernism relies on the premise that everything in the cosmos and every human experience can be presented and explained. If something cannot be presented or explained, we have to assume that, nonetheless, a rational explanation exists. Attempts to provide the depiction or explanation of the nonpresentable, no matter how much they fall short in their objective, must rely on the consensus of all parties to assume that explanation is true. This process is the "shattering of belief"; to wit, it is the atheism demanded by modernism. In other words, to return to the metaphor from literature, Queen Gertrude and King Claudius of modernism must agree (a consensus) to pretend ("shatter" their belief) that a knowing Hamlet, whose nihilistic personality defies presentation, is not lurking in the wings.[17] It is this intellectual subterfuge which Lyotard speaks against. Lyotard sees postmodernism as having a "stronger sense of the unpresentable" which we can observe in the medium itself.[18]

With this said, the term *postmodernism* is most difficult to describe. Stephen D. Moore, for example, offers nine different definitions of the word, but a characteristic common to all is that postmodernism refuses belief in absolute truths.[19] It can be said that in the Enlightenment, humans put themselves in the place of God; in postmodernism, that place is gone.

The Non-Presentable in Postmodernism

Moore, in his *Poststructuralism and the New Testament,* has a chapter entitled "Poststructuralist Historiography: Foucault at the Foot of the Cross."[20] In this section, Moore demonstrates that, unlike Bultmann and other modern exegetes following the historical-critical method, Foucault understands perfectly well what death on the cross actually means. The moderns, generally embarrassed by the concept of divine atonement, try to gloss over it, something which is difficult to do, especially when reading St. Paul. Therefore, reading Foucault with St. Paul in the background, Moore arrives at a poststructuralist interpretation of the death of God's Son. As any political ruler might sentence, torture, and dispatch a transgressor as a way of enforcing obedience from members in the society, God sentences, tortures, and dispatches his Son in order to impose disciplined docility on any who would follow.[21]

Moore interprets Foucault as seeing this docility as the end result of Christianity's ethical teaching, a teaching based on the cross.[22] The crucifixion was an instrument of torture for Christ. Over time, the torture mutated into something more insidious than the physical suffering undergone by Christ; the new torture touched the fiber of our being. In a premodern mindset, this torture was having our innermost soul controlled by an all-seeing God through the power structure of the Church best exercised by the sacrament of penance. In modernism, the instruments of torture were transferred to the psychiatrist and social scientists.

We could, perhaps, make a case supporting part of Moore and Foucault's respective positions. Many people have been terrorized by divine anger preached from a pulpit, and confidences spoken in both the confessional and on the couch have been used to manipulate. Nevertheless, there is the same major shortcoming in both their arguments, and here I am limiting my comments to matters of faith.

The greatest human pain is caused by the power of suffering and death as suffering and death. Is the pain of those mourning the death of a loved one or of those undergoing the ravages of cancer to be put on the same plane as the pain of those managing under the onus of Church teaching or practice, if indeed they even think of it as an onus? Is there any postmodern critique on the terror of death or the purpose of life? In addition, we must take issue with the Pauline interpretations Foucault and Moore are using to build their argument.

True, Paul calls Christians to submit to the power of the cross, but that is in order to rise with Christ. Moore relies on Romans 8:27 but ignores Romans 8:30. He refers to Romans 6:6 but does not read on to Romans 6:7–11.The heart of the Christian message is that human suffering, shame, guilt, and death, through the death and resurrection of Christ, are transformed into joy, honor, righteousness, and eternal life. If Moore, along with Foucault, would like to see a better life and promise for a Christian, what would that be?

Whether or not we may agree with Foucault or Moore, we can at least credit them with seeing that which modernism would prefer to overlook: Christ's crucifixion is ugly and full of suffering, and the blood spilled affects all believers, at least, if not all humanity. In this sense, Foucault and Moore give full value to patristic and Anselmian interpretations of the death of Christ, a point that disciples of modernism ignore.

Monastic Theology

For Christian discourse, a major preoccupation has been attempting to explain the meaning of the "nonpresentable" and "inexplicable" appearance of the passion, death, and resurrection of the Son of God. This is certainly the objective of monasticism. To return to Auerbach, the Christian perception stands as an "antagonism between sensory appearance and meaning."[23] Auerbach sees this antagonism as the Christian view of reality. I would venture, however, that it is also the stimulus for reality, if not the view of it, for both modernism and postmodernism.

Monastic Interpretation

Monasticism started in the desert regions of the Empire shortly after the Edict of Milan.[24] From that point, monasticism in the East, first, but particularly in the West, became the home to scholarship for the next one thousand years. Monastic schools themselves lacked formal instruction in theology. The science of theology was not included in monastic training because, for the monk and nun, religious study was tied to religious formation, and this occurred under the direction of an abbot or abbess through the reading of biblical and patristic literature.[25] Jean Leclerq describes this endeavor, and the writings flowing from it, as having a "mystical orientation . . . directed to personal union with the Lord here below and later in beatitude; it is marked by intense desire and by a longing for ultimate consummation."[26] In the monastic school, then, all learning was for the sake of contemplation and union with God. In time, the scholasticism of the universities not only acquired the dominant role in development of theology but also was responsible for turning theology into a scientific discipline in its own right. Since reading lies at the core of monastic culture, instruction in grammar assumed a high priority and was the foundation of all study.

Scripture

With a background in grammar, there arose an analysis of Scripture that naturally resulted in great importance being given to the texts and words.[27] In a monastic context, the reading of Scripture, or *lectio divina,* because it has wisdom and appreciation as its object, "begins with grammar, terminates in compunction, in desire of heaven."[28] A whole system for *lectio divina* developed toward this end.

Lectio divina is a threefold process. One begins by reading the text aloud. This procedure, still used by many language teachers today, functions as something more than an aid in mental memorization; it serves to involve one's whole being in the exercise. In order to make this reading profitable for life, the reader engages in *meditatio.* Arising from the *lectio, meditatio* frees itself from the discipline and rules of study and draws together various associated ideas that the mind may stumble upon, ideas stimulated by the reading.[29] *Meditatio* is then a process of "memory training, storage, and retrieval" in which the reading is completely internalized.[30]

The next step for the medieval scholar lay in digesting the read material. This process employs a term, *ruminatio*, which has analogous overtones to eating. As a bee makes honey or a cow chews a cud, so is a reading to be ruminated and digested. *Ruminatio* depends on having the material memorized, and reading aloud (*murmur*) is not only a valuable aid in the process, but it also maintains the metaphor between eating and reading.[31] Moreover, the metaphor becomes more graphic, for ruminatio carries the intended idea of regurgitation, with memory being the stomach and the texts therein being the cud.[32] The concept of *ruminatio*, then as now, is a pillar of monastic prayer. As a consequence, as we meditate on the sacred word, we memorize it, or better, inscribe it on our hearts.

By filling our every thought with God's holy Word, this act of meditative memorization aims to sanctify a person, guiding every deed toward strengthening the bond we have with Christ. Among the saints and mystics, and not necessarily only the Benedictine ones, this process became so successful that nearly every utterance, either immediately or remotely, was connected to Christ.[33] The aim of all this endeavor was to understand Scripture better. In the words of Columba Stewart, "Scripture helped to create the world . . . and [Scripture] was the key to interpreting it."[34] In this manner, the scriptural metaphors, supplemented by study of the classics and patristic literature, helped the early monks and nuns to understand humankind's place within creation.

Present Relevance

It goes without saying that the world has vastly changed over the past twenty-five hundred years. Very little of the Greco-Roman or early Christian society remains. Yet, Catholics in particular, also other Christians and, allowing for confessional differences, Jews as well, still proclaim the message of a premodern community. Is it not time for the world to give up the Judeo-Christian ghost?

On the heels of the age of discovery came the development of speedy communication and transportation. New cultures and lands were not only increasingly accessible to a greater number of people, but communication within the world now has become instantaneous on an almost universal level. This development has tested the validity of other premodern communities,[35] including Christianity's. In the West, on the intellectual level at least, this test has come from postmodern thought. With so many peoples, nations, and cultures, can we be so bold as to say that the one worldview, so much a part of the post-Constantinian Mediterranean and European civilization, is still an idea worth maintaining or achieving? Reality would necessitate that we answer the question in the negative. To assume that Christianity is or should be the only show in town is a romantic pipe dream—and a dangerous one at that.

Such an answer begs another question. If the one worldview of Christianity is no longer the ideal, does it mean that Christian thought has no place in the world? I maintain that the answer to this question is also negative. Christian thought has a viable, important, and legitimate claim on the world; in fact, Christianity sees the world as Christ's mystical body and for Christianity to silence itself would be to shrug off the redemption. It is at this point that the Christian community meets the postmodern critique.

Postmodern thought maintains that no philosophical, political, or faith system is better than any other, and any attempt on our part to argue or assume otherwise results in force or oppression. Hence, the Christian vocation to lead humanity to Christ might very well be interpreted by those within and without as religious, if not political, fascism. The monastic interpretation of the Christian experience, however, may very well offer a way for Catholic intellectuals and Christian believers to engage the contemporary discourse.

Monastic View

Auerbach's assessment that Christianity exhibits an "antagonism between sensory appearance and meaning" is seen in the passion, death, and resurrection of Christ. The monastic life was in the past and is now a continuous meditation on this antagonism using the privileged texts of the Christian community for its central metaphors. Throughout history, the aim of monastic meditation has not been to seek a rational answer or resolution to the antagonism, for surely there can be none. Rather, it has been to lead to mystical union with God. The mental and physical activity involved in *lectio divina* create an environment in which this mystical union can take place; it is an act of sanctification.

The premodern period saw the sensory appearance as being under divine control, as for instance, sunrises and sunsets were the result of a fine working, *primum mobile*. In addition, the premodern found the meaning of this appearance in the divine revelation; the daily rhythm was all for God's greater glory. With modernism, although the sun appears to rise and set, in actuality, the earth is spinning on its axis as it revolves around the sun. Any meaning is found in the laws of nature and reason. In postmodernism, the laws of nature are considered to be appearances and fictions and, of course, there is no meaning to any of them. If both modernism and postmodernism cannot acknowledge God, a trait they share in common, can it be that this has led them both to ask the wrong question?

In critiquing the Judeo-Christian narrative, modernism prefers to see it as a superstitious, or at least unscientific, explanation of phenomena. This is very much evident in the recent debates over teaching evolution in public schools. A postmodern approach, as demonstrated by Foucault and Moore, views the Judeo-Christian story as but another example of one group of people suppressing and undercutting another. In either case, modernism and postmodernism share the same anthropological stand: the human being is at the center of the universe. In the premodern understanding of the cosmos, however, God is at the center. This difference in the anthropology determines the questions we ask.

Monastic theology is based on Plato and Augustine, while scholastic theology relies on Aristotle and Aquinas. Nonetheless, both were able to see God at center of the universe, each with its own respective philosophy.[36] Modernism, for the reasons discussed, rejects those concepts and prefers a scientifically verified positivism. Postmodernism may be an *enfant terrible*,[37] but it is the child of modernism and, despite its valid critique of modernism, it has inherited its parents' myopia. Both modernism and postmodernism look at the Judeo-Christian narrative and ask how? The premodern monk or scholastic, perceiving the same story, asks why?

Monastic scholarship was built on *lectio divina*, the slow, deliberate, prayerful reading of scriptural and early Christian texts. That much of the monastic, biblical interpretation was so highly allegorical is proof that nuns and monks never saw the text as something to be taken literally. Their subsequent study of patristic literature and the classics along with the bestiaries and lapidaries demonstrates that they sought to broaden and complete their understanding of the universe. Nuns, monks, and their students searched for the truth beyond the fact. They did not suffer illusions concerning the meaning of life: life on earth ended in death, but it was a death from which they were redeemed.

The Rule of Benedict reflects the anthropological position of the age in which it was written. When examining the Rule, we observe that every prayer, thought, and deed is performed for one purpose: union with God. This purpose is particularly evident in chapter four, the "Tools for Good Works," and chapter seven, with its "Steps of Humility." Among the tools for good works, one of the most telling is to keep death daily before our eyes.[38] This advice is not to scare or intimidate disciples; rather, it is to remind them of their place in the universe, a point substantiated by the last tool for good works, "[n]ever lose hope in God's mercy."[39]

The Steps of Humility have a similar focus. The first step is to keep the fear (*timor*) of the God before our eyes,[40] an echo of the tools for good works. Here, too, we are reminded of our place in the universe, but this place has both a present and a future orientation, "Through this love, all that he [the monk] once performed with dread, he will now begin to observe without effort, as though naturally, from habit, no longer out of fear of hell, but out of love for Christ, good habit and delight in virtue. All this the Lord will by the Holy Spirit graciously manifest in his workman now cleansed of vices and sins."[41] Further on, we read, "Let them prefer nothing whatever to Christ, and may he bring us together to everlasting life."[42] The Christian life, as expressed in Benedictine monasticism, sees both a realized and future eschatology. True perfection occurs in union with God, but those who work at achieving that union can have a foretaste of it here on earth. In this sense, monasticism sees, pace postmodernism, the "unitary end of history and subject" but in manner quite different from the Enlightenment's.[43]

We can arrive at such a life of beatitude by asking of the Christian narrative not the modern or postmodern question "how," but the premodern question, "why." Hence, in encountering the creation story in Genesis 1–3, if we ask, "how," we will remain stuck in the ceaseless debate between evolutionary theorists and creationists. If, however, we ask "why," the discussion can open up to possibilities of divine love, disfavor, grace, and restitution, and can do so without compromising the integrity of evolutionary science. In fact, the two, science and theology, can walk quite well with each other in Chardinian fashion.[44] When we ask, "Why the cross?" subsequent questions and answers take on a geometric progression.

Foucault and Moore Revisit the Cross

Foucault and Moore, despite their postmodern and poststructuralist stance, view the cross as modern, impartial observers. If they wish to critique Christianity, they should at least embrace the cross as one living the Christian life embraces it. If they were to do so, they would see the world as the Son of God saw the world while hanging on the gibbet in absolute powerlessness, and dare it be said, despair. They would hear the crowds of the world jeering at him, and they could say, as Christ said, "Father forgive them; for they do not know what they are doing" (Luke 23:34).

If Foucault and Moore would be able to move beyond the antiseptic clinic of their "postmodern modernism," they could form a relationship with the God who chooses to manifest himself in weakness, and they would experience the power of that weakness just as the poor and oppressed have always experienced it, even if the oppression came *from the Church which professes Christ.* They would open their intellectual life to a sapiential component, one that seeks the truth beyond the fact. They would then be able to know why people like Sojourner Truth, Dietrich Bonhoeffer, Bishop Romero, four Jesuits and their housekeeper, Cesar Chavez, Dorothy Day, Cassie Bernall,[45] and countless others lived and died the way they did.

Christian Postmodernism

Postmodern nihilism is not so much a negation of truth inasmuch as it is an appeal for truth. With all modernism's formulae and explanations, the universe is still dark, cold, and foreboding. This would come as no surprise to early and medieval Christian minds; God was at the center of the universe, and the meaning of their lives were tied with his.

We may laugh or chafe at some of the allegorical interpretations given to Scripture before the Enlightenment. The countless allegories demonstrate, however, that God is a mystery, a mystery that is *fascinans et tremendans* and yet one to which persons have access. Saints and the not so saintly somehow made their way there. The divine mystery is never exhausted, but it is known through a deep and abiding relationship. There is Truth, but we will always have an incomplete view of it even as we draw closer to it.

Lyotard sees postmodernism as calling into question the Enlightenment's view that there is a unitary end of history and subject. If the postmodern is asking the world this question, maybe the best answer comes from the Benedictine motto, a motto that makes both the claims of modernism and postmodernism suspect: *ut in omnibus glorificetur Deus,* "that in all things, God may be glorified."[46]

I suggest that the time is right for Christianity to stand with postmodernism and declare that modernism is spiritually dead; indeed, that it ever could offer anything salvific to the human race has been a seductive fallacy all along. Simultaneously, Christianity should challenge postmodernism's nihilism. In so doing, Christianity can witness for this postmodern world an intellectual community that has within its tradition the means to think, search, and probe the universe in a manner that acknowledges the truth beyond the fact.

Notes

1. *Mimesis, The Representation of Reality in Western Literature*, trans., Willard R. Trask (Princeton: Princeton University Press, 1953), 49.
2. "Christians and Postmoderns," in *First Things*; 40 (February 1994), 29.
3. Bottum. "Christians," 29.
4. Jean Francois Lyotard defines "postmodern" as "the state of our culture following the transformations which, since the end of the nineteenth century, have altered the game rules for science, literature, and the arts. *The Postmodern Condition: A Report on Knowledge,* trans., Geoff Bennington and Brian Massumi; *Theory and History of Literature*, 10 (Minneapolis: University of Minnesota Press, 1997), xxiii. See also Madan Sarup, *Post-structuralism and Postmodernism, second edition* (Athens, GA: The University of Georgia Press, 1993).
5. Bottum. "Christian," 32.
6. Stanley J. Grenz. *A Primer on Postmodernism* (Grand Rapids, MI: William B. Eerdmans Publishing, 1996), 58.
7. Grenz. *Primer,* 60.
8. Lyotard defines "modern" as "any science that legitimates itself with reference to a metadiscourse of this kind [legitimation with respect to its own status] making an explicit appeal to some grand narrative, such as the dialectics of Spirit, the hermeneutics of meaning, the emancipation of the rational or working subject, or the creation of wealth. *Postmodern,* xxiii (parenthetical added by author).
9. Grenz. *Primer,* 61.
10. Grenz. *Primer* 67. Ironically, however, Newton wrote more on Scripture than on science.
11. Grenz. *Primer,* 83.
12. Friedrich Nietzsche. *Thus Spake Zarathustra*, trans., Thomas Common (New York: Heritage Press, 1967), 12.
13. *Goethes Faust, Der Tragodie erster und zweiter Teil Urfaust*, line 356. (Hamburg: Christian Wegner Verlag, 1963), 20.
14. Lyotard. *Postmodern,* 72.
15. Lyotard. *Postmodern,* 73.
16. Lyotard. *Postmodern,* 77.
17. Of course, this begs the question concerning modernism and atheism. When does pretending become a belief? To believe in atheism is still a belief.

18. For example, in Joyce's *Ulysses* the writing style describes what can only be partially grasped. Lyotard, *Postmodern*, 80–81.
19. *Poststructuralism and the New Testament* (Minneapolis: Fortress Press, 1994), 131.
20. *Poststructuralism*, 95–112.
21. Moore. *Poststructuralism*, 108–109.
22. Moore. *Poststructuralism*, 108–112.
23. Auerbach. *Mimesis*, 49.
24. Scholars are unsure whether monasticism arose first in Egypt or in Palestine. Timothy Fry, OSB, *et al.*, eds. *RB 1980* (Collegeville, MN: The Liturgical Press, 1981), 17–19.
25. Jean Leclerq. *The Love of Learning and the Desire for God*, trans., Catherine Misrahi (New York: Fordham University Press, 1982), 2.
26. Leclerq. *Love*, 6.
27. Leclerq. *Love*, 72.
28. Leclerq compares this process to the scholastic one which takes on the *quaestio* and *disputatio* in which the reader questions the text and then questions himself or herself on the subject matter. Here, the objective is science and knowledge, not wisdom and appreciation. *Love*, 72.
29. Mary Carruthers. *The Book of Memory; A Study of Memory in Medieval Culture* (Cambridge [England]; New York: Cambridge University Press, 1990).
30. Carruthers. *Book*, 163.
31. Carruthers. *Book*, 164.
32. Carruthers. *Book*, 165.
33. One finds this phenomenon, for example, in Hildegard von Bingen's poetry. It is so replete with chains of biblical images that she often invented her own terms to express the connections between them all.
34. *Prayer and Community, the Benedictine Tradition* (London: Darton, Longman, and Todd, 1998), 41.
35. N.b. the Chinese Cultural Revolution of thirty years ago.
36. Monastic or patristic theology saw this life as a reflection or shadow of the Godhead; scholastic theology saw God behind this life as being the First Act.
37. Moore describes poststructuralism as historical criticism's id. *Poststructuralism*, 117.
38. Rule of Benedict 4:47 in *RB 1980*, 183–184.
39. Rule of Benedict 4:74, *RB 1980*, 185.
40. Rule of Benedict 7:10, *RB 1980*, 193.
41. Rule of Benedict 7:68–70, *RB 1980*, 201–203.
42. Rule of Benedict 72:11–12, *RB 1980*, 295.
43. See Lyotard. *Postmodern*, 73.
44. Teilhard de Chardin's *The Divine Milieu*, despite some of its limitations, makes a very good beginning in melding the discussion between science and divine initiative.
45. Cassie Bernall, a student at Columbine High School, was found praying when her killers arrived in the library. They asked her if she believed in God. She said she did, and they asked her why. Not waiting for an answer, they

shot her. John Garvey, "Kids Killing Kids," in *Commonweal;* CXXVI, 11 (4 June 1999), 10.

46. Rule of Benedict 57:9, *RB 1980,* 267.

18

Mystics, Prophets, and the Status of Religion in Contemporary Intellectual Life

Alex Nava

The study of religion in the modern university is faced with many obstacles, ranging from total suspicion to an enlightened indifference and neglect of the question. To be sure, there are important differences among the various American universities and such negative attitudes toward the study of religion do not prevail everywhere. Catholic universities specifically engage the question of religion and require that students be exposed to the question of God. Such a requirement is unique to denominationally affiliated universities and is clearly not the case at secular universities, private or public. In these secular settings, the study of religion is a barely discernible presence, if it is a presence at all.

This attitude toward religion in secular universities is not surprising if one reflects on the fate of religion since the birth of modernity. In the modern world religion has become an Other: it is that Other that does not conform or cohere with post-Enlightenment methods of rationality and empirical investigation. Religion has suffered the fate similar to colonized peoples in modern times: it is deemed irrational, primitive, superstitious and, thus, an obstacle to historical progress, critical reasoning, and individual autonomy. Religion has been marginalized by the modern West. Religion continues to play a significant role in the lives of individuals. But while religion remains largely relegated to the private sphere, it is generally distrusted or altogether silent in the public sectors of our society.

If it is at all true that the location of religion in the modern West is in the margins, then it is not all that surprising to witness some major theologians engaging in postmodern discussions and speaking of a return of the question of God in contemporary academic circles.[1] While debates concerning the meaning and character of postmodernity are certainly beyond the scope of this work, I believe that it is fair (and not too contentious) to state that many postmodern thinkers seek to redirect the critical reasoning of the modern West against itself. The ambiguity of modernity is exposed and the illusion of Western innocence, of any self-congratulatory and triumphalistic narrative, is excoriated. While few postmodern thinkers wish to reject all the achievements of modern times, attention to the underside of modern progress and modern scientific-technological-rationality is underscored. Even Jurgen Habermas, the great defender of modernity, warns of the danger of the colonization of the lifeworld by technological rationality. Postcolonial critics clearly and powerfully demonstrate, moreover, how the colonization of whole peoples, traditions, and communities has been a legacy of the modern West and is inextricably linked with the celebration of Western scientific and cultural achievements.

With some of these postmodern perspectives in mind, I will consider the work of David Tracy as an example of a theologian involved in some postmodern debates. I will also reflect on two particular religious types, mystics and prophets, and the possible contribution of these figures to the diverse vocations of Catholics and others in the university today.

While David Tracy's work on the nature and meaning of postmodernity is rich and complex, in his most recent work he has highlighted three major separations that, he contends, were fostered by modernity: the separation of theory and practice; the separation of rationality and sensibility/feeling; the separation of form and content.[2] Each of these separations have had a profound effect on the substance and form of academic reflection in the modern West. In Tracy's current work on the naming of God, he explores the implications for the modern intellectual world of such separations and engages many classic premodern and some contemporary postmodern thinkers on how they interrupt and transgress such separations. As an instance of such a challenge, this work will analyze the form and content of mystics and prophets.

Mystical Discourse

While the term *mysticism* and *mystic* are common and widely employed terms (not only in theological circles but also in contemporary U.S. culture), the actual meaning of such terms is far from clear. The New Age movement has seemed to appropriate this term with an unparalleled eagerness. Besides an association with idiosyncratic practices and experiences (use of crystals, prediction of the future, levitation, the power of certain geographical locations), the New Age movement makes a clear and unequivocal distinction between mysticism and religion. This suggests that mysticism or spirituality is separate from and independent of concrete religious traditions; one can be mystical without belonging to a religion. By contrast, the meaning of mysticism in Western civilization has almost always been linked with, and an element of, a particular religious community and tradition. Even in the case of revolutionary mystics who call into question traditional theological conceptions or who challenge religious authority, such figures were products of a tradition and were unavoidably shaped by the images, symbols, ideas, practices, institutions, and myths of a specific religion. Insofar as they learned to speak a certain language, and subsequently seek to communicate their ideas and experiences through language, they are part of a tradition. In the words of one contemporary scholar of mysticism, Bernard McGinn: "No mystics (at least before the present century) believed in or practiced 'mysticism.' They believed in or practiced Christianity (or Judaism, or Islam, or Hinduism), that is, religions that contained mystical elements as parts of a wider historical whole."[3]

The fact that mysticism has been traditionally tied to religious communities does not imply that there is a clear and univocal meaning of such a term even within the same religious community. In the Christian tradition, mysticism has been associated with many of the following ideas: union with God, deification, ecstasy and rapture, locutions, birth of the Word in the soul, contemplation, visions. Often it was employed in the adjectival form, specifically in relation to the interpretation of Scripture or to the Church (e.g., mystical meaning of Scripture, mystical body of Christ). Bernard McGinn has provided a very helpful definition of mysticism that tries to accommodate the diversity of mystical expressions. In his view, mysticism is "preparation for, consciousness of, and reaction to, the immediate or direct presence of God."[4]

There are many advantages of such a definition. For one, it suggests that mysticism is related to an entire way of life. The tendency today is to reduce mysticism to a special, extraordinary experience without attention to the forms of training and practices that are at the heart of a mystical way of life. The use of terms such as *preparation for* and *reaction to* (an immediate sense of divine presence) imply the importance of the total life of the mystic, including participation in liturgy, forms of meditation, reading of Scripture, works of charity, etc. The choice of the term *consciousness of* (rather than *experience*, for instance) seeks to highlight the birth of a new awareness and consciousness of God, self, and cosmos. A new theological vision arises from such an encounter. It is for this reason that McGinn is insistent upon the study of mysticism as inextricably linked to the study of theology. Great mystics are great theologians.

Finally, the choice of the term *immediate* or *direct* is intended to underscore the claim of many mystics to a special union with God, a union that is not mediated exclusively by the Church. Certainly, it is this aspect that often leads mystical figures into conflict with religious authorities and traditional doctrines.

One major characteristic of mysticism in the West is also the apophatic dimension of mysticism. At the heart of most major mystical figures is the bold claim that the truths (or Divine Truth) about which they speak cannot be captured by language. No idea, metaphor, image, or experience can fully capture the Divine Other. God's transcendent nature eludes any attempt to systematize or delimit the identity of God. For Meister Eckhart, even the term God is not fully sufficient, as when he invokes the "God beyond God." Silence, many mystics suggest, is perhaps the most appropriate form of communication with God. Silence, no doubt, is still a form of speaking; it is still tied to the possibilities and limits of language. And certainly a mystic, in order to share her or his message, must communicate through oral and written form. One cannot teach via silence. In emphasizing the limits of language, however, mystical language performs a function that is self-nullifying; that is, it functions to relativize concepts and, in effect, deny what has just been stated. At the same moment that a mystic seeks to communicate a new consciousness, he or she reminds us of the metaphorical and symbolic nature of their writing and, hence, of the limits of literal communication.

This leads me to a key point concerning the mode of understanding in mystical thought: rather than being primarily *informational,* mystical knowledge is *transformational.* Without undergoing a transformation of one's consciousness and one's entire way of life, knowledge of the Wholly Other is impossible. Because of the failure of abstract ideas and concepts in speaking about God, mystical thought seeks not merely to inform, but more precisely to provoke and ignite in the reader or hearer a form of understanding that is deeply affective and passionate. A sense of awe and wonder; a feeling of joy and ecstasy; the experience of love: all such experiences in the life of the individual are conditions for the possibility of knowledge of God. As the great Catholic theologian Bernard Lonergan insisted, faith is a knowledge born of love.[5]

The requisite transformation at the heart of mystical discourse, then, serves to emphasize the limitation of any academic discourse (or at least in the humanities) that is purely abstract, objective, detached. It is no wonder that mystical texts have been often compared with poetic texts or seen in relation to art or music. In this regard, David Tracy is illuminating when he highlights the connection between mysticism and aesthetics.[6] In the aesthetical dimension, truth is indeed inaccessible via detached rational inquiry; one must be willing to let go of the controlling mind and remain attentive, receptive to the manifestation of truth. Truth is more of a happening or an event than a conceptual correspondence to an objective reality. For example, having accurate information about T. S. Eliot's *The Four Quartets* may provide a college student with adequate information necessary for an exam, but such preparation will finally prove inadequate if not accompanied by participation with the poem. As Tracy explains about any classic text, comprehension is more than a matter of objective knowledge: understanding happens when the vision of reality of that text resonates with the reader, or more radically, when that text elicits a shock of recognition in the attentive person. The demand for transformation, for a new way of thinking, feeling, and acting cannot be evaded without the price of misunderstanding.

The great Latin American writer Jorge Luis Borges (himself fascinated by both mysticism, especially the Jewish Kabbalah, and poetry) contends that an "aesthetic event" is central to poetry. For him such an event is fundamentally indescribable. "The aesthetic event," writes Borges, "is something as evident, as immediate, as indefinable as love, the taste of fruit, of water. We feel poetry as we feel the closeness of a woman, or as we feel a mountain or a bay. If we feel it immediately, why dilute it with other words . . ."[7] The ineffable nature of the aesthetic event makes indispensable a personal engagement with the subject-matter of a poem or a mystical text. What cannot be put into words calls for experience. For those that lack that experience, St. Bernard of Clairvaux insists, let them burn to have it.

The aesthetic dimension of mysticism also involves appreciation for the manifestation of God through all forms of beauty. The disclosure that occurs through the beauty of nature, or that of an icon or a cathedral or through a particular human form, is an expression of divine communication or revelation. What is intangible becomes tangible, concrete and incarnate—whether through a painting, a sculpture, a mountain, or one's beloved. In his *Journey of the Soul to God*, St. Bonaventure, clearly influenced by his teacher St. Francis, spoke of nature as a ladder by which we ascend to God. For the mystical poet Dante, the meaning of grace is both a gift of divine love and that passionate force (*eros*) that instills the human heart with a yearning for God. Indeed, for Dante, the manifestation of grace is mediated to the pilgrim poet (in his journey to paradise) through the awe-inspiring and wondrous beauty of his beloved Beatrice. The grace manifested by her beauty is nothing less than a divine magnet attracting him to the supreme Beauty of God.

There is another key that makes evident the connection between mysticism and aesthetics: the actual form of mystical texts. A study of the content of mystical texts is insufficient if one disregards the form of the writing. Again, similar to poetry, mystical texts seek to highlight both the possibilities and limits of language. The function of the texts is to inspire, provoke, and heighten the consciousness of the reader in a way that depends upon an attraction to the form of the text beyond the mere ideas. The metaphorical, symbolical character of mystical texts serves to arouse desire in the reader or hearer. This is especially true in the poetry of John of the Cross, in the music of Hildegard of Bingen, in the prayers of Augustine in *The Confessions*, or through the daring use of metaphors in the texts of Pseudo-Dionysius, but is also obvious when one recalls that in the Middle Ages many spiritual writings were read out loud.[8] The involvement of one's senses was to make clear the summons of the whole person in the experience of mystical exercises.

To be sure, in the thought of mystics, the separations of theory and practice or reason and sensibility (in addition to form and content) would equally be unimaginable. As mentioned before, mysticism was never a pure experience detached from a life of spiritual training and religious commitment. One could never come to knowledge of God by pure theory. The creation of arguments for or against God's existence in the modern period, for instance, seem to imply the sufficiency and cogency of pure, rational argument. It is assumed that the decision for or against God can be established and justified by reason alone. As the great critic of modernity, Søren Kierkegaard, and the twentieth-century theologian Paul Tillich understood, belief in God is a matter of passion. Mystical theology makes evident both the necessity of passion and the necessity of action (especially *caritas*) as the basis for belief in God. While the sophisticated and exact use of reason is never absent from mystical discourse, knowledge of the heart (in Pascal's sense) is the privileged path to theological wisdom. Forms of thought that employ theory without practice and that address the faculty of reason without moving the sensibility of the person are foreign to mystical discourse. Saint Augustine corroborates such a vision when he insists, in *De Doctrina Christiana*, that the object of theology is to teach, delight, and move. For Augustine, the study of rhetoric is particularly helpful in delighting readers or hearers and in moving them to conversion. Surely, he was aware of the unity of theory and practice, reason and sensibility, form and content.

Prophetic Discourse

If mysticism is deeply tied with aesthetics, then the prophetic tradition is grounded in ethics. If the message of the mystics is elusive, metaphorical, and intentionally indeterminate, then the message of the prophets is striking by its clarity, precision, and comprehensibility. The classic Hebrew prophet is one who announces or proclaims the Word of God in the form of rebuke, exhortation, or warning against the sins and injustices of the people in a particular historical circumstance.

It should be granted that such a rough definition of a prophet is most germane to what is considered the classic stage of prophecy (roughly 800–500 B.C.E.). Clearly, there are different characteristics associated with the prophetic vocation that complicate a monolithic understanding of the prophet. What has been considered "early prophecy" shows affinities with techniques of Near Eastern divination, with experiences of ecstasy and frenzy, with the interpretation of dreams, and with the prediction of future events. The Book of Numbers distinguishes between Moses and other prophets:

> When there are prophets among you,
>   I the LORD make myself known to them in visions;
>   I speak to them in dreams.
> Not so with my servant Moses;
>   he is entrusted with all my house.
> With him I speak face to face—
>   clearly, not in riddles . . ." (Numbers 12:6–8).

Such a passage accepts the validity (even if imperfect) of a more archaic revelation of God through dreams and visions. Some of the early prophets are also portrayed as ecstatics, as with Samuel, Elijah, and Elisha. In 1 Samuel, Samuel is told that he will come upon a band of prophets playing music, in a state of prophetic frenzy. "Then the spirit of the LORD will possess you, and you will be in a prophetic frenzy along with them and be turned into a different person" (10:6). With Moses and his followers, the classic prophets, however, proclamation of the divine Word (the Law) to the people plays the crucial role. Allegiance to the covenant and ethical responsibility come to govern the prophetic message in a more prominent manner than in early prophecy. The classic prophets do not seem to exhibit significant ecstatic behavior.

Thus, the classic prophet speaks, at times seemingly against his will, the Word of God. The context of the prophet is also a key component of prophetic discourse. Less connected to nature as with the mystics, the prophetic vocation is implicated in history, a history that is often the site of conflict and suffering. Indeed, the classic prophet is all too suspicious of any religious sensibility that locates God in the forces of nature; such a temptation is named *idolatry*. If the mystics give expression to almost a kind of pantheism, or more precisely a panentheism, the prophets give voice to a theology of history. God is revealed through the events of history, from Exodus through the Babylonian exile to the period of the Second Temple. Their message hopes to stimulate an attentiveness to the barely audible Word of God, obscured and hidden by the more obvious signs of suffering and oppression. If the hearers of their word (or rather of the Divine Word speaking through the prophet) do not respond, then the prophet's message serves only as a warning for an imminent judgment or doom.

While it is certainly a caricature, and an unfair one, to state that mystics are only concerned with timeless, eternal truths, one cannot help noticing a fundamental absence in much mystical thought; namely, the lack of sensitivity to wide-scale injustice and oppression of whole groups and nations. If prophets give off the impression of pessimism (Jeremiah for instance), it is because they witness with such lucidity and honesty the terror of history around them. The horror of war, the cries of the poor and the destitute, the condition of servitude of the Israelite people, communicate loudly to the prophet the suspect nature of happy-go-lucky and naively optimistic portrayals of history and the human condition. In general, the prophets remind us that much of history (especially that of Israel) is a history of suffering. The mystics do not announce the same message with such force.

The history of interpretation of the prophets is as diverse and rich as the history of mysticism. Since a historical overview of such a phenomenon is beyond the limits of this work, I would like to focus on one major trend that represents well the passion and vision of the prophets. Liberation theology is one form of contemporary thought that creatively articulates the concerns of the biblical prophets. By excoriating the apathy and complacency of the more privileged, wealthy nations, liberation theology heightens our awareness of the affliction of the poor and oppressed, especially in the Third World. Far from soothing and consoling the modern conscience (a conscience so wary of guilt), liberationists seek to disturb and rouse the conscience of the modern person. Uneasiness is the legitimate response of us all, whether the part we play in the face of suffering is direct cause or complicity and neutrality. The contribution of liberation theology is, in part, the single-minded attention to the ethical demands and responsibilities of the Christian life, especially in relation to the weakest and most forgotten of history and society. Cultic worship, in this understanding, is misguided when it displaces aid to the poor and the widow, the hungry, and the naked (see Isaiah 1:10–17; Hosea 6:4–6).

While liberation theologians have had little or nothing to say about debates concerning modernity or postmodernity (often seen as First World academic reflections), there is perhaps one point of contact between liberation theology and postmodernity: attention to the ambiguity of modern progress, especially in light of the exercise of power and violence (through colonialism and imperialism) in the formation of modern history. Liberation theology demands that the voices and stories of the victims of history be heard to prevent the subjugation and destruction of their traditions and histories. Modern civilization is more than a story of triumph and enlightenment; it includes the enslavement and exploitation of whole peoples based on Eurocentric claims of superiority. Such claims to superiority are often justified at the level of intellectual, ethical, and even aesthetical standards. Not only are non-European peoples (of Africa, India, the Americas, Asia) less rational, but they are indolent, mendacious, and given to theft; in a word, primitive. Even their physical characteristics indicate inferiority: the color of skin, the shape of noses and ears, the shape of skulls. The history of racism, classism, and sexism stains modern history and liberation theology is all too aware of the effects of such a stain on the lives of Third World peoples and on the disenfranchised and immigrants of First World countries.[9]

In relation to the three separations that we have been discussing, liberation theology, not unlike the Frankfort school of critical theory, has focused much attention on challenging the separation of theory and practice. The widely appropriated term *praxis* is meant to signify the interaction between theory and practice. Following Marx's famous dictum, "Philosophers have interpreted the world in various ways; the point however is to change it," liberationists demand that theology exercise its influence for the purpose of social change. The temptations of any academic discourse, temptations that isolate intellectuals of the "ivory tower" from issues affecting the masses in society, are the targets of criticism by liberation theologians insistent upon a more pragmatic role for theology. While most liberation theologians seek to persuade us of the intellectual credibility of their ideas, their primary intent is to work to incarnate the ideas of theology (the Kingdom of God, for instance) in history and society. Part of such a concern is evident in materialistic critiques. Eschewing a fearful rejection of the social and human sciences, they argue that theology should be willing to dialogue with the such disciplines in order to effect change at the level of economics, politics, and culture. In this understanding, a theology that is narrowly spiritual unjustly employs the title "Christian" insofar as it neglects the bodily dimension of human life. Certainly, as is clear in so many parables of Jesus, providing food for the hungry, clothing for the naked, healing for the sick, shelter for the homeless, etc., are spiritual obligations of the Christian life. When reflection on justice or the good becomes separate from an embodiment and realization of justice and goodness, the decadence of theology becomes most apparent. Not only is an academic form of theology in danger of becoming irrelevant, therefore, but a purely theoretical theologizing fails in its task of adequately interpreting and promoting the gospel of Jesus Christ. In the words of the liberation theologian Gustavo Gutierrez: "Reflection on the mystery of God (for that is what a theology is) is possible only in the context of the following of Jesus."[10]

While reflection on the separation of form and content is not a discernible presence in liberation theology, criticism of the separation of reason and sensibility does play a role in some liberationists. Gutierrez, along with many others post-Vatican II theologians, finds great fault with modern European scholasticism, not only insofar as it exacerbates the separation of theory and practice but also in its dry and lifeless reasoning. Gutierrez's theology is intent on challenging forms of theology that are not infused with love and spirituality. Insofar as Gutierrez claims that spirituality is at the heart of liberation theology (a claim contrary to many caricatures of liberation theology to be simply political), he argues that the effect of theologizing ought to be conversion to a new way of life. The pursuit of knowledge, then, is incomplete without the participation of the emotional depths of the human person. The understanding of knowledge in the Scriptures, Gutierrez contends, "is a very rich concept that is not limited to the intellectual realm but also connotes taste, fellow feeling, and love. Knowledge here is a direct and profound kind of knowledge that embraces all dimension of the person who is known and loved."[11] Part of Gutierrez's interest in challenging the ossification of scholastic theology is not only to highlight the centrality of love in the Christian tradition but also to undermine an intellectual elitism that devalues the lives and experiences of the masses, especially of the poor majority of the world. In this light, liberation theology is a representation of the potential wisdom among the illiterate and destitute of the world today.

Catholics and Contemporary Intellectual Life

My contention in this work is that study of the mystics and prophets can enrich the life of any intellectual, especially one who has been nurtured by the Catholic tradition or who embraces the richness and diversity of Catholicism. In many ways the vision of the mystics and the voice of the prophets can illuminate and guide those committed to both a Catholic vocation and a life of scholarship and learning in the university of today. As we have seen, the surprising interest in the mystics among contemporary academic circles has many facets, but one key theme seems to be mystical languages of unsaying: that is, the way in which mystical discourse undoes or negates the tendency to literalize concepts, metaphors, images, etc. The mystics witness to a God beyond Being and beyond all human attempts to circumscribe the Wholly Other. This interest in the mystics is evident beyond circles of theology and includes such a thinker as Jacques Derrida, who has engaged many themes of apophatic or negative theology and has spoken of the return of religion in contemporary times.[12] As suggested earlier, it is not inconceivable that some postmodern thinkers are rethinking the meaning and status of religion in contemporary times, given the fate that religion has suffered in modern times. The critique of modernity, even when fundamental themes of modernity are defended, has made possible more careful and thoughtful reflections on religion that challenge totalizing repudiations of the phenomena "religion."

This work also suggests that what accompanies the apophatic dimension of mystical discourse is an appreciation of mysticism as an entire way of life located within particular religious traditions. In contrast to many New Age renditions of mysticism (which often reduce this phenomena to idiosyncratic and fantastic experiences), mysticism has traditionally been linked to methods of spiritual training, liturgical and ascetical practices, and theological reflection. In light of this emphasis on the entire way of life of the mystic, the goal of mysticism is the transformation of the student/disciple, not merely the transmission of information.

Certainly, this theme has rich consequences for the academic world in general, but the implications are especially significant for Catholics in intellectual life. As Jesuit education has always understood, the formation of more critical, thoughtful, attentive, and responsible students should be the *telos* of all Catholic education. When this mission is surrendered in the interest of intellectual credibility (a credibility based on secular norms), not only will the spiritual mission of Catholic education be lost, but the intellectual distinctiveness and creativity will suffer. The mystics can only enrich and deepen this vision of Catholic education by insisting on the spiritual dimension of learning and on the cultivation of the mind, heart, and spirit of every student. By forging the integration of theory and practice, feeling and rationality, and form and content in intellectual life, this holistic understanding of higher learning, especially in relation to the vocation of Catholics in academia, will be furthered.

No less than this mystical dimension to learning, the prophetic voice signals to us the importance of justice in higher education. A spirituality without attention to instances of violence, poverty, racism, and sexism in history and society does not merit the name Christian. The prophetic traditions demand that reflection on justice inform and transform the form and content of academia, not only in the humanities and social sciences, but surely among the hard sciences and engineering as well. The temptation of academic life to become self-absorbed, elitist, and purely theoretical is a real threat to the integrity of Catholic education and to the vocation of Catholics in the university today. Defending the unity of theory and practice on the issue of justice, for instance, was central to the lives of the martyred Jesuits of San Salvador. In their understanding, the task of the university is to witness to Christ by defending the interests of the least of society, by being voices for the voiceless, and by confronting the powers that abuse and dehumanize the poor.[13] Perhaps such a vision is more difficult to pinpoint and realize in the context of the North America (although it is also a mission less dangerous, less prone to death), but it is certainly not rendered irrelevant by this First World context.

Certainly one other theme among prophetic trajectories has profound implications for intellectual life today; namely, the broadening of intellectual horizons beyond that of Europe. The inclusion of voices traditionally subjugated and ignored by academia and the ruling classes is a task that goes deeper (for a Christian) than the aims of multiculturalism. From a Catholic perspective, such an inclusion of non-European, colonized, and immigrant peoples is nothing less than fidelity to a universal God who is disclosed in the faces of all peoples, especially in the faces of those afflicted and oppressed Others. Witness to Christ Crucified is not a task for the biblical scholar of the passion narratives, but, instead, is an obligation incumbent upon all Christians to attend to the ways in which Christ continues to be crucified. I believe that the sixteenth-century Dominican priest, Las Casas, said it best when he exclaimed, "In the face of the afflicted Indians of the Americas, Jesus Christ is beaten, scourged and crucified not once, but thousands of times."[14] And the great philosopher and scientist Pascal spoke in a like manner in his summons to vigilance in the face of suffering: "Jesus will be in agony until the end of the world. There must be no sleeping until that time."[15] Surely the aim of higher education should be to promote and give birth to such a vigilance and prophetic responsibility and, concomitantly, to shatter the forces of apathy and weariness that turn a blind eye to injustice in history and society. A Catholic intellectual serious about a commitment to both the Catholic tradition and the intellectual life should aspire to provoke a mystical-prophetic sensitivity in the person of the student and to embody such a vision in one's own life and calling.

Notes

1. See David Tracy, "Literary Theory and Return of the Forms for Naming and Thinking God in Theology," *Journal of Religion*, volume 74, number 3 (July 1994); Jean-Luc Marion, *God Without Being*, trans., Thomas Carlson (Chicago: University of Chicago Press, 1991); John Milbank, *The Word Made Strange: Language, Theology, Culture* (London: Blackwell, 1997).

2. For his reflections on these matters, see his forthcoming book *On Naming and Thinking God.*

3. See Bernard McGinn, *The Foundations of Mysticism* (Crossroad: New York, 1991), p. xvi.

4. Ibid.

5. See Bernard Lonergan, *Method in Theology* (New York: Seabury Press, 1979).

6. See David Tracy, *The Analogical Imagination: Christian Theology and the Culture of Pluralism* (New York: Crossroad, 1991), pp. 205–208 and elsewhere.

7. See his chapter titled "Poetry" in *Seven Nights* (New York: W. W. Norton and Company, 1984), p. 81.

8. See Jean Leclercq's classic text *The Love of Learning and the Desire for God: A Study of Monastic Culture* (New York: Fordham University Press, 1982).

9. For a great example of a liberationist interpretation of the effects of colonialism in the modern world, see Gustavo Gutierrez, *Las Casas: In Search of the Poor of Jesus Christ* (New York: Orbis Books, 1993). For a postcolonial critic, see Edward Said, *Culture and Imperialism* (New York: A. A. Knopf, 1993).

10. Gustavo Gutierrez, *We Drink From Our Own Wells* (New York: Orbis Books, 1984), p. 136.

11. Gustavo Gutierrez, *The God of Life* (New York: Orbis Books, 1991), p. xiv.

12. See *Derrida and Negative Theology*, eds. Harold Coward and Toby Foshay (Albany: State University of New York Press, 1991); *Religion*, eds. J Derrida and G. Vattimo (Stanford: Stanford University Press, 1998).

13. See *Companions of Jesus*, ed. Jon Sobrino (New York: Orbis Books, 1990).

14. Quoted by Gustavo Gutierrez in *Las Casas: In Search of the Poor of Jesus Christ* (Maryknoll, NY: Orbis Books, 1993), p. 62.

15. Blaise Pascal, *Pensees* (New York: Penguin Books, 1966), fragment 919, p. 313.

Part III

Spiritualities: *Ora* Giving Life to *Labora*

19

Benedictine Spirituality:
A Way of Living for God,
Others, and the World

Katherine Kraft, O.S.B.

Robert Benson, in his book entitled *Between The Dreaming and the Coming True*, records the following words of Hazel McComas, whom he describes as "a kind and gentle woman, a teacher, a woman of prayer . . . whose spirit bears witness to her having spent a life seeking for glimpses of and listening for whispers of God particularly in the ancient prayers of the Chosen People."[1] Hazel says:

> This is what I believe. We were with God in the beginning. I do not understand that exactly—what we looked like, what we did all day, how we got along, any of it. Then we were sent here. And I am not sure that I understand that very well either. And I believe that we are going to God someday, and what that will be like is as much a mystery to me as any of the rest of it. But I believe those things are true and that what we have here on earth in between is a *longing—for the God that we have known and for the God that we are going home to. God has always known us, it seems*[2] (emphasis added).

Longing for the God we have known, the God who has always known us, and spending a lifetime looking for glimpses of God seems a particularly apt description of Benedictine spirituality, or of any spirituality for that matter, if one accepts the definition that spirituality is a way of understanding and living one's life in relation to a Transcendent/Spiritual Reality or God. While we might not express our desire for God in the straightforward and homey way of Hazel McComas, if we resonate with her longing to know God in a deeply personal way, Benedictine spirituality may have something to offer. Desire for God is the central aspiration that moves the Benedictine to spend a lifetime seeking God in specific and concrete ways. In fact, Benedict, the founder of the monastic order of Benedictines and author of the *Rule of Benedict*, identifies as the single determining quality for entrance into the monastery whether "the novice truly seeks God" (*RB* 58, 7).[3]

Hazel's desire is, I believe, the desire of many human beings, perhaps even constitutive of what it means to be human. Karl Rahner describes human beings as ontological capacities for God.[4] Mircea Eliade, the scholar of the holy, believes that the sacred is an innate quality of human existence and that we are always living out of some spiritual will-to-meaning, whether or not that impulse is recognized as spiritual.[5] Philip Sheldrake puts it this way:

> Despite frequent comments about secularization in Western society and a decrease in church membership, there is widespread evidence of a hunger for the spiritual. . . . The interest in spirituality is certainly not confined to church-goers or those commonly identified as religious people.[6]

Not long ago, a local newspaper included the following item:

> In a recent survey when a sample of Americans were asked what they considered necessities: 58% stated that a home computer was necessary. 41% felt that two or more phone lines were needed. However, the largest percentage, 82%, said that a quiet place for meditation was most essential.[7]

If we accept the claim that all of us are God-Seekers, hungry for the Transcendent, however we understand it, if we hear ourselves saying interiorly, "I can't live on bread and work alone; there has to be some way to nourish the soul, to attend to God, and to integrate my life around what really matters," we may want to find specific ways of tending the spirit that are possible, given the actual circumstances of our lives. What follows is a description of Benedictine spirituality (how Benedictines understand and live their lives in relation to God) together with practical suggestions intended for persons looking for ways of deepening their relationship with God. Dictates of space and audience led me to select those central elements and spiritual practices most relevant for non-Benedictines: a sacramental view of reality, the search for God, biblical liturgical prayer, *lectio divina,* work, and community. More suggestions will be made than can be adopted; all are offered for your consideration.

It might be helpful to read the description of Benedictine spirituality and the practices that incarnate that spirituality with these two questions in mind: 1) Am I drawn to Benedictine spirituality and practice? 2) What, if anything, could I adopt/adapt, given the actual circumstances of my life? Ultimately, each of us decides whether anything about a particular spirituality or practice resonates with our own spiritual quest and needs.

Benedict and the *Rule of Benedict*

Benedict of Nursia, Italy (480–547 c.e.), is called the Father of Western Monasticism because of the singular influence of the *Rule* he authored more than 1500 years ago. This rather brief document, adapted to the contemporary situation, remains the guide and norm of life for Benedictines today. World-wide, there are approximately 25,000 Benedictines: 17,000 women and 8,000 men. In the United States alone there are sixty Benedictine monasteries of women and fifty-one monasteries of men.[8] However, interest in Benedictine spirituality is not limited to members of monasteries. Kathleen Norris's recent best-seller, *The Cloister Walk*, written during an extended stay in a Midwestern Benedictine monastery, describes the relevance of Benedictine spirituality for lay persons like herself. A similar purpose shapes what follows.

Benedictine Spirituality: A Sacramental Way of Life

Benedict would probably have been uncomfortable with the word "spirituality" because it suggests the *interior* or *spiritual* as opposed to and separate from the rest of life.[9] Work, relationships, social obligations, leisure activities, and public responsibilities pull us outside ourselves. Often enough, we experience being torn between the inner self and the outer world, and we yearn for wholeness, some unifying thread or integrator to hold our lives together.

For Benedict, there is no real separation or dichotomy between inner and outer, sacred and secular, material and spiritual. It is not the case that prayer is sacred and work secular, that God is found in silence but not in others, that material things are worldly and spiritual things holy. His worldview is thoroughly *sacramental*, meaning everything and everyone can reveal God, because all is God's creation and God is present in the midst of life. ". . . God's gaze is upon you wherever you go" (*RB* 4, 49). ". . . we believe that God is always present to us" (*RB* 7, 2). Surprisingly, it is God who actively seeks us: "Seeking his [worker] in a multitude of people, *the Lord calls out to him [her]. . .*" (Prologue to *RB* 1, 14; emphasis added).

Seeking the God Who Seeks Us First

The central passion of Benedictine life is not an abstract ideal of goodness, not an ethical system, not even some dream of what life in this world might be like, but Someone, namely, the God we have come to know, believe in and love in Jesus Christ. Benedict's God is clearly not the remote God of Deists or philosophers, but the God of the Bible: near, relational, holy, challenging, the God whose saving intention for creation is unrelenting and certain. This God is the God of Israel, at one and the same time accessible and ineffable. The *Rule* is replete with biblical texts that express both God's immanence and transcendence. For Benedict, God is above all else the One who has become incarnate in Jesus Christ and who in Christ speaks the Word of life. We are to "prefer nothing whatever to Christ" (*RB* 72, 11). The *Rule* itself takes second place to the gospel, which is the primary rule of life to which all are called. ". . . let us set out on this way, with the Gospel for our guide . . . " (Prologue to *RB* 1, 21).

Benedict gives prayer and sacred reading priority as ways of seeking God, but this is not because God is less present in other activities, or in the rest of life. Everything—nature, work, study, silence, speech, rest, preparing a meal, interacting with community members and guests—is a way of encountering God. Life is *all of a piece*; there is nowhere God is not. Could such a way of viewing our life, whether harried and fragmented, dull and routine, exhilarating and satisfying, free us to accept it anew? While we may find it necessary to reorder priorities and make changes, believing God is present in the daily, in ordinary events and persons, could open us to finding God where we least expect. What difference might it make to view a typical day, task, or person through the sacramental lens of an everywhere-present God? Committee meetings, preparing lectures, research, teaching, office hours with students, budgeting: all are God-filled. A sacramental perspective could help alleviate the agitated "kicking against the goad" of our lives, an exercise bound to yield mostly frustration and discontent.

Biblical Liturgical Spirituality: Listening with the "Ear of the Heart"

Toward the end of his life, Abraham Heschel spoke of wonder as the most appropriate response to the mystery of life and God. "I did not ask for success; I asked for wonder. And You gave it to me."[10] For Heschel, wonder and prayer are related; wonder evokes a sense of God, which in turn, leads to prayer. About prayer he said, "The issue of prayer is not prayer; the issue of prayer is God."[11] Similarly, Benedict understood that prayer and worship begin with *attentiveness and listening*, qualities that are effective ways of lowering the threshold to God's entrance into our lives.

"Listen carefully, my [child], . . . and attend with the ear of your heart" are the opening words of the *Rule*. This striking image, *a heart with "ears," a heart that hears,* connotes keen listening from the center of one's being, sensitively tuning oneself to catch God's voice. Immediately after the call to listen, Benedict addresses his readers and himself, as follows:

> *It is high time for us to arise from sleep* (Rom. 13: 11). Let us open our eyes to the light that comes from God and our ears to the voice from heaven that every day calls out this charge: *If you hear his voice today, do not harden your hearts* (Ps. 94 [95]: 8). And again, *You that have ears to hear, listen to what the Spirit says . . .* (Rev. 2:7) . . . (Prologue to *RB*, 8–12; emphasis added).

All are exhorted to wake up, to open their eyes to see, their ears to hear, and their hearts to the One who shows the way to life. "Is there anyone here who yearns for life and longs to see good days? (see Psalm 33 [34]:13). If you hear this and your answer is 'I do,' God then directs these words to you . . . " (Prologue *RB*, 15, 16). God speaks to those who "have ears to hear." Given the sheer volume and variety of both exterior and interior noise with which most people contend today, the practice of attentive listening for God's voice can seem daunting. Benedict prescribes frequent prayer as a singularly effective means for developing a listening heart.

Common Prayer: Rooted in Scripture and the Liturgical Year

Frequent prayer, both in common and on one's own, is the integrating center of Benedictine spirituality; it is the necessary practice, the energizing force out of which, around which, and toward which every other activity flows. Prayer is the lodestone and magnet that draws us back to the center: God. A friend visiting our monastery remarked, "How do you ever get any work done when everybody stops to pray?" A wonderful question—an observation that goes to the heart of the matter. For Benedict, the primary "work" of the community is the daily common prayer or Liturgy of the Hours (Divine Office), which he refers to as "the work of God" and about which he says, "Indeed, nothing is to be preferred to the work of God" (*RB* 43, 3). Aware that human beings are prone to distraction, busyness, and lack of discipline, Benedict made ample room for prayer. In fact, the monks of his time gathered seven times daily for common prayer and spent two to three hours in meditative reading for the sake of prayer. Common prayer flowed in and out of a rhythm of listening and responding, silence, and speech.

Benedictine prayer is biblical and liturgical, that is, it is shaped by the Bible and the seasons of the liturgical year. The daily Liturgy of the Hours consists of hymns, psalms and canticles, readings from the Bible, from biblical commentaries and theologians both past and present. Most psalms are prayed antiphonally by all the participants, and the liturgy always includes song. The very manner and pacing of prayer promotes reflection and calm. Quiet times between the psalms and after the readings allow for attentive listening and responding to the Word of God addressed to those gathered for prayer. In a busy world of too many words, the daily discipline of common prayer punctuated with quiet spaces contributes to the formation of a *listening heart*.

Virtually all of the Bible is read over the course of a number of years, so that the entire story of salvation is proclaimed and remembered. The content of hymns, antiphons, and prayers reflects the liturgical year, which celebrates the mystery of salvation from creation through the history of Israel, through the life, death and resurrection of Christ, until the end of time. Year in and year out, from Genesis to Revelation, one hears and responds to the saving presence of God's Spirit active in the world. It is impossible to exaggerate the influence of the Bible in shaping the life, prayer, and imagination of Benedictines; they are literally "awash" in its language and images by virtue of daily exposure in communal prayer.

Contemporary Benedictines gather three times each day for common prayer: morning, noon, and evening. They also celebrate Eucharist, usually daily, with special attention given to the Sunday Eucharist. While more time is devoted to the Liturgy of the Hours, Eucharist brings the community together around the altar, uniting its members with the Paschal Mystery of

Christ and the worship of the larger Church. Liturgy of the Hours and Eucharist, the public prayer and worship of the whole Church, have been called the fountain and source of spirituality.

Perhaps the best way to decide whether the biblical/liturgical prayer described above nourishes your spirit is to visit a Benedictine monastery and participate in its common prayer and worship. At many Benedictine monasteries and colleges, lay faculty, staff, students, and friends join the monastic community for common prayer occasionally or regularly, as a way to begin or end the day's work. (Prayer in common is rarely longer than twenty-five or thirty minutes). A number of Benedictine communities have developed abbreviated versions of the Liturgy of the Hours, usually morning and evening prayer, complete with text and tapes for those not near a Benedictine monastery, or for those who prefer praying at home, by themselves, with a spouse or friend. Liturgy of Hours books, some with inclusive language, can be ordered through a college bookstore. Some faculty and staff members keep a book of hours or psalms in their offices for ready use during the day. With regard to Eucharist, the Catholic colleges with which I am familiar, welcome administrators, faculty, staff, students, and guests as active participants serving in various liturgical roles: planners, readers, musicians, cantors, choir members, Eucharistic ministers, and ministers of hospitality.

Prayer on One's Own: *Lectio Divina*, or Prayed Reading

> Sit every day for half an hour alone in the best room.

> The disappearance of the porch . . . is something to think about; . . . the porch represented a contemplative element in American life . . . a place to sit and think. . . . In the modern house there is no room that is built for meditation, prayer, or reflection.

> To pray is to pay attention to the deepest thing we know.[12]

All three quotations express human insight into the need for quiet reflective time, time that leads to awareness of God and to personal prayer. The Benedictine practice of *lectio divina*, variously translated as sacred reading, meditative reading, or prayerful reading, addresses that need. Benedict expected members of the community to spend two to three hours daily in reflective pondering of biblical texts. Texts were read slowly, over and over, often aloud, then committed to memory and repeated later during the day or night. The purpose of this form of reading was neither information nor the mastery of content, but an encounter with God who meets us in the Word:

> Daily individual reading, listening and responding to the Word of God, draws us more and more deeply into a personal relationship with the Word, Christ, so that finally his life becomes our life and our life becomes his.[13]

It was assumed that over time, a lifetime, the reader would be changed by exposure to God's Word. "God works in us while we rest in him" is the way Peter of Celles, a monk of the Middle Ages, phrased it.[14]

Other ways of describing the goal of *lectio divina* include finding our deepest identity in God; opening ourselves to Truth; listening for God's will in our lives; yearning for the simple presence of God; sharpening our capacity to hear God; losing ourselves in God's love, resting in God. Still others see its effects as awakening us "to the great gulf stream of love that will not let us go, awake to what each relationship in which we stand really means . . . cleansed, refreshed, and renewed in hope . . . "[15] *Lectio* can "rouse us . . . from sleepwalking . . . through our lives, never really there to our families, our children, our friends, our colleagues, our neighbors in need. . . . "[16]

While some or all of the above may result from the practice of *lectio divina*, its effects will probably be quite subtle and undramatic. We may notice that we are less anxious and harried, hopeful rather than cynical, more sensitively aware of the needs of others. If we approach *lectio* in faith, as a way of encountering God by means of a sacred text, when the time in *lectio* feels unproductive, as it often will when God is silent, we will be able to accept that experience with equanimity, content with simply being there, open and receptive.

Lectio is not complicated; however, faithfulness to the practice requires discipline and patience. Baron Friedrich von Hügel, the English philosopher of religion and spiritual mentor to Evelyn Underhill, Anglican scholar of mysticism, practiced *lectio divina* fifteen minutes each day for forty years. He said it sustained his life like food. "Such reading . . . is meant . . . to feed the heart, to fortify the will . . . to put these (heart and will) into contact with God—thus, by the book, to get away from the book, to the realities it suggests . . . "[17] The last point merits underscoring. While *lectio* begins with a biblical text, it moves beyond the text to the One the text suggests and evokes—God.

Although the Bible remains the reading of choice for the practice of *lectio*, there is no reason one cannot use poetry, literature, art, journaling, even film as a *lectio* text. All of these, if pondered and prayed, can reveal and lead to God. Because *lectio divina* is a central practice of Benedictine spirituality, a time-tested means of seeking God, easy to understand and make one's own, I have included a brief description of *lectio* hoping someone will try it. "Dare we not only listen to lectures on prayer, but be prepared to go into the laboratory as well?"[18] (Helpful resources for those desiring more information are listed at the end of the chapter.)

The Practice of *Lectio Divina*

Preparation for Lectio Divina
- Decide what your *lectio* text will be before you begin. One of the daily Scripture readings assigned for Eucharist, or the continuous reading of a book of the Bible might be choices.
- Find a quiet place where you can sit in an erect, attentive, yet relaxed

way. Place yourself gently in God's presence letting go of all thoughts and attend to the Presence. Begin by inviting God into your awareness with a simple spontaneous prayer.

Reading (Lectio)

* Read the chosen text reflectively and slowly, entering into it as deeply as you can. Read the text, or parts of the text, several times, either aloud or quietly. When the text or any part of it strikes or touches you, stop reading.

Pondering (Meditatio)

* Stay with whatever touches you, whether a word, phrase, image, or insight.
* Ponder and savor it, letting it penetrate your awareness, mind, and heart.

Praying (Oratio)

* If reflective pondering moves you to pray, whether to prayer of repentance, gratitude, hope, praise, need, love, desire, etc., give yourself to however your prayer chooses to express itself.

Resting in God (Contemplatio)

* At times, your prayer response may become wordless, imageless, a quiet resting in God. When this happens, let it happen, yielding yourself to God in trust and love.
* As the sense of resting in God ceases, return to reading the text and let the rhythm of reading, pondering, praying and resting in God play itself out naturally and fluidly.

End the time of *lectio* with a brief prayer.[19]

Work

Ora et labora (prayer and work) is a motto of Benedictines. In the *Rule*, the balance is weighted toward prayer, *lectio divina*, and study with less time devoted to work. "Four hours of each day were devoted to liturgical prayer, four to spiritual reading, and six to manual labor."[20] This way of dividing the day's activities reflects the primary goal of monastic life that is not any particular work, but seeking God.

If the data are accurate, Americans are working longer hours rather than fewer, struggling to balance work with personal and family life as well as countless other activities and obligations. Those of us engaged in higher education as administrators, teachers, student development staff, whether we work in admissions, alumni relations, food service, or a physical plant, are hard pressed, given present work demands and expectations. Like most people, Benedictines today spend more time working than praying. "The image of the cowled and hooded monk gazing placidly across a lake, with nothing to do all day but contemplate eternal verities, is pure myth."[21] At the same time, whether monastic or lay, because we need to work to support ourselves and others, because we value work and invest so much of ourselves in it, and because we spend most of our lifetime working, work is and has to be a significant part of our relationship with God and others.

The *Rule of Benedict* contains neither a developed theology nor an extensive discussion of work. One has to draw inferences about a "spirituality of work" from the monastery's daily schedule and from various comments found throughout the *Rule*. We know that Benedict understands work as necessary for self-support, as a form of discipline, and as service of others. Consonant with his sacramental perspective, we can assume that Benedict believed God could be found in work. Monks are to turn their thoughts frequently to God while working and to do their work willingly, calmly and without undue stress (*RB* 31, 17; 48, 24). Benedict would, I believe, have been comfortable with viewing work as stewarding creation, and as cooperating with God in bringing the kingdom to completion.

Work Is Good

There is much in the *Rule* that could shape both our attitude toward work and the way we go about it. All work is valued; no work demeans, since it is necessary for the sake of the community and as a way of serving others. Every able-bodied community member shares in the work of running a household, rotating the various tasks so no one is left with the most burdensome. The cellarer "should be given helpers, that with their assistance he may calmly perform the duties of his office" (*RB* 32, 17). "Additional help should be available when needed, so that they can perform this service (kitchen duty) without grumbling" (*RB* 53, 18). "This consideration . . . applies to all duties in the monastery; the brothers are to be given help when it is needed and, whenever they are free, they work wherever they are assigned" (*RB* 53, 20). Mutual assistance and working together helps build community and lightens work load.

In a highly competitive society, one that rates/ranks work according to categories of esteem and pay, Benedict's perspective challenges. It means seeing our work as part of a larger enterprise, and appreciating the contribution of all, whatever their work. It promotes working cooperatively rather than competitively. It suggests developing and using one's talents fully, but never arrogantly. Benedict's admonition to the monastery artisans is telling in this regard. They are not to become "puffed up" with undue pride in their work, forgetting that their talent is a gift from God (*RB* 57, 2). Rather, everything is to be done "for the glory of God."

Work Is Done Well and with Reverence

Before anyone used the language of quality control, accountability, or assessment, Benedict insisted that work be done well. Because what we do matters for something or someone, there is to be nothing mediocre, shoddy, or halfhearted about our work. Instead, respect and reverence for the actual task, for co-workers, and for the beneficiary of our labors should characterize our work. "He (the cellarer) is to regard all the utensils and goods of the monastery as sacred vessels of the altar" (*RB* 31, 10). "They should each try to be the first to show respect to the other" (*RB* 72, 4). Where to draw the line between perfectionism and minimal standards in work performance may be difficult to discern. Even so, the principle Benedict espouses is that both work and persons are to be treated deferentially.

Work Is Service

The first Benedictines were engaged mostly in manual labor and service of others: farming, carpentry, masonry, maintaining the monastery, meal preparation, laundry, caring for the sick and guests. Fairly early in their long history they became involved in education. The study of biblical texts and commentaries expanded to include the natural sciences, humanities, the arts, and the practical sciences. While we often imagine Benedictines as writers, copiers of manuscripts, musicians, and liturgists, today we know them as college presidents, teachers of every discipline, physical plant managers, nurses, psychologists, computer technicians, chaplains, artists, and environmentalists.

Whatever one's work, Benedict's description of work as service, and as a way of loving others still inspires. The sick, the old, and the young are to be served with the most sensitive attention out of consideration for their particular needs. Because Christ is encountered in every guest, especially in the poor and pilgrims, all are to be welcomed with gracious hospitality and served with utmost solicitude (*RB* 53).[22] The same respect and love is extended to community members for in everyone we encounter Christ. ". . . service fosters love. . . . Let all serve one another in love" (*RB* 35, 2, 6).

Anyone engaged in administration or teaching could find in Benedict's description of the kind of person the abbot ought to be, qualities we are called to bring to our work and an understanding of work as loving service. Wherever you read, "the abbot" or "he," substitute "the administrator," "the teacher," or yourself in your current role at a college or university:

> . . . the abbot is to show equal love to all (*RB* 2, 22).

> He must . . . accommodate himself to each one's character and intelligence (*RB* 2, 32).

> He ought to be learned . . . so that he has a treasury of knowledge from which he can bring out what is new and what is old (*RB* 64, 9).

> He should always let mercy triumph over judgment (*RB* 64, 10).

Let him strive to be loved rather than feared (*RB* 64, 15).

. . . He should be discerning and moderate . . . he must so arrange everything that the strong have something to yearn for and the weak nothing to run from (*RB* 64, 19).

Work Is Done in Moderation

Particularly wise and challenging is Benedict's mandate that everything, including work, be done in moderation. "Let everything be done in moderation" (*RB* 48, 9). For this reason, the monastery schedule makes room for prayer, work, study, time alone and with others, rest. A daily rhythm of alternating activities carried out in an atmosphere of peace and calm fosters a balanced and integrated life. Everything has its proper time and place.

Obviously, our lives are markedly different. Most of us are not monastics. And, even if we desire a more balanced life, actually achieving it can seem an insurmountable task. The demands of work together with personal and family obligations are not easily subject to our control. Acknowledging all this, but before dismissing *out of hand* Benedict's ideal of a balanced integrated life, each of us might consider the following:

• What are my regular habits of being and doing—how do I spend the hours of my day?
• In what ways is my life unintegrated and out of balance?
• Am I neglecting something that needs my serious attention?
• What could I change, even if slightly, to achieve more balance/ integration?
• If little can be changed, what can I do to make the inside and outside of my life more consonant?
• When can I make time for prayer and quiet reflection?
• Is my working style mostly competitive or cooperative?
• How could viewing my work as a way of loving and serving others shape what I do?
• How can my work be an expression of hospitality to others?

What seems most important is remembering Benedict's exhortation to be open, always, to the God who works in and through us whatever we do. Katherine Howard says it well:

Work comes into harmony when it flows from the inner source of divine energy. When done mindfully, animated by desire for good and an awareness of God working in us, work tends to take its proper proportion in our life, and we are able to work with more peace, perseverance, and joy. A life of prayer nurtures every good work whether spiritual or material.[23]

Community: Life with Others

If the primary reason for Benedictine life is seeking God, there is no finding God without loving others. Love is the goal; love is the way to God. Even the earliest desert hermits understood their solitary lives of prayer and asceticism as joined to the larger community of the Body of Christ. T. S. Eliot voices that awareness in "Choruses From 'The Rock'":

> What life have you if you have not *life together*?
> *There is no life that is not in community,*
> And no community not lived in praise of God.
> Even the anchorite who meditates alone,
> For whom the days and nights repeat the praise of God,
> Prays for the Church, the Body of Christ incarnate[24] (emphasis added).

For Benedictines, the common life is the arena in which one learns to love others not in theory but in practice. By the vow of stability they "cast their lot" with a particular group of people for life similar to the traditional marriage vow, "Until death do us part." Like marriage, family, and friendship, love in community is not general or generic, but terribly particular. We love real persons as they actually are—humanly flawed—"flawedly" human.

Benedict recognizes the challenge such loving entails given the *variety of characters* (his phrase) that comprise any community. And so, he exhorts everyone, beginning with the abbot, to *accommodate* and accept others no matter what their defects and limitations. Aware that community always involves the clash of egos and wills, Benedict wisely asks for honest self-examination, mutual obedience, balancing individual needs with the common good, humble acceptance of correction, and readiness to give and receive forgiveness.

Chapter four of the *Rule*, "The Tools of Good Works," is filled with specific instructions about relating to others respectfully, honestly, and affectionately. One finds there numerous directives describing desired behaviors, everything from the Commandments and Golden Rule, to the corporal and spiritual works of mercy, to pithy maxims like the following:

> You are not to act in anger or nurse a grudge (*RB* 4, 20).

> Never give a hollow greeting of peace or turn away when someone needs your love (*RB* 4, 25–26).

> Do not injure anyone, but bear injuries patiently (*RB* 4, 30).

> Do not speak ill of others (*RB* 4, 40).

> Respect the elders and love the young (*RB* 4, 70–71).

> Make peace before the sun goes down (*RB* 4, 73).

Lest anyone forget that it is the love of Christ that informs our relationships with others, Benedict inserts, in the middle of these prescriptives: "Your way of acting should be different from the world's way; the love of Christ must come before all else" (*RB* 4, 10, 20–21). Love of God, Christ, and others are intertwined—inseparable. That Christ-like love, deeper than differences, divisions, even animosity, is possible only because of Christ's presence mediated through the relationships that make up our lives. This is most obvious in chapter seventy-two, "On the Good Zeal of Monks," a chapter that has been referred to as the Magna Carta of community life. No paraphrase adequately captures its spirit:

> This, then, is the good zeal which monks must foster with fervent love: *They should each try to be the first to show respect to the other* (Rom. 12:10), supporting with the greatest patience one another's weaknesses of body or behavior. . . . No one is to pursue what he judges better for himself, but instead, what he judges better for someone else. To their fellow monks they show the pure love of brothers; to God, loving fear; to their abbot, unfeigned and humble love. Let them prefer nothing whatever to Christ, and may he bring us all together to everlasting life (emphasis added).

Zeal for the good of others reaches beyond the confines of the monastery to embrace the stranger and guest, especially the poor and needy. In fact, the *Rule* singles out the poor as deserving special solicitude. "Great care and concern are to be shown in receiving *poor people* and pilgrims, because in them more particularly Christ is received . . ." (*RB* 53, 15). Throughout their long history, Benedictines have cared for the sick, for orphans and the elderly. More recently, many Benedictines have focused on advocacy for the poor and oppressed, as well as on local and global issues of social justice and peace. Life in the monastery, and for that matter, in a Catholic university, is incompatible with indifference to the plight and pain of the whole world. Catholic universities, according to Jon Sobrino, a Latin American theologian, must be places where persons combine the pursuit of knowledge for its own sake with active concern for the poor: " . . . knowledge must be put at the service of the poor. Only in this way is the Catholic university's true catholicity affirmed—that is, its openness to the worth of all people and not just the economic elite."[25]

Our lives are webs of intersecting relationships, for we belong to many communities. It is in living and working with others that our struggle to love becomes most apparent. On any given day we can look at our lives and find evidence of failure to love and moments of genuine love. At times, we are self-centered, petty, irritable, and uncaring, but we are also kind, empathetic, supportive, and generous. Loving others over the long haul requires sustained effort, grace, a kind of "stretching" of the heart. Bernard Loomer calls it *SIZE*:

> By size I mean the stature of a person's soul, the range and
> depth of [one's] love, [one's] capacity for relationships. I mean
> the volume of life you can take into your being and still main-
> tain your integrity and individuality, the intensity and variety
> of outlook you can entertain in the unity of your being without
> feeling defensive or insecure. I mean the strength of your spirit
> to encourage others to become freer in the development of
> their diversity and uniqueness. . . . I mean the magnanimity of
> concern to provide the conditions that enable others to increase
> in stature.[26]

Loomer further asserts that persons of stature can only emerge out of communal relationships, out of authentic communities. "I believe . . . that the
individual is an emergent from [his/her] communal relationships. . . . For this
reason, we need great communities in order to have great individuals. . . . We
need . . . great academic communities in order to produce . . . fulfilled students and faculty" [students and faculty of stature].[27]

While he does not use Loomer's language, Benedict's vision of community intends a comparable expansion of the human spirit, a magnanimous
heart, a growing up into "the *full stature* of Christ" (Ephesians 4:13). The
Rule's language is biblical and lyrical: "As we progress in this way of life and
in faith, we shall run on the path of God's commandments, our hearts overflowing with the inexpressible delight of love" (Prologue to *RB*, 49). A sixth-
century monk and a twentieth-century process philosopher both understood
the critical need for communities of *love and learning*. How this hope can be
realized in our communities and colleges seems a *matter of consequence* for
us to ponder at length and work toward achieving. Stephen Pope sees the task
as follows: "Institutions of higher education that are at once true universities
and genuinely Catholic must be characterized in terms of both an 'enlargement of heart' and an 'enlargement of mind.'"[28]

Conclusion

These reflections began with the words of Hazel McComas who spent her
life seeking "the God we have known who has always known us." Her desire
for God reflects the contemporary hunger for a lived spirituality—concrete
ways of deepening a relationship with God. For Benedictines, these ways
include finding God in the ordinary, in work, in relationships and community,
in a balanced and integrated life, in biblical liturgical prayer, especially
Liturgy of Hours and *lectio divina*, and in the poor. Recent books on Benedictine spirituality, many written by non-Benedictines, describe this ancient
spirituality as "fresh," "free," "broad," "sane," "practical," "whole," "a seamless garment," "timeless."[29] Through their voices as well as through his own,
Benedict's invitation to the God-seekers of his day is being extended down
through the ages to anyone with *ears to hear*, anyone *who desires life*:

Listen carefully, my son [my daughter],
Let us open our eyes to the light that comes from God,
and our ears to the voice from heaven that every day calls
out. . . .
The Lord calls out to [you]: *Is there anyone here who yearns
for life and longs to see good days?* (Prologue to *RB* 1, 9,
14–15; emphasis added).

It is simply a matter of beginning—for God, for others, for
the world.

Notes

1. Robert Benson, *Between the Dreaming and the Coming True* (San Francisco: Harper, 1996), 4.
2. Benson, 4–5.
3. More will be said about Benedict and the *Rule of Benedict* later on in this chapter. The *Rule of Benedict* will be cited frequently as follows (*RB* 58, 7), that is, Rule of Benedict, chapter fifty-eight, verse seven. The edition used is that of Timothy Fry, et. al., *RB 1980: The Rule of St. Benedict in Latin and English with Notes* (Collegeville, MN: The Liturgical Press, 1981). Because the *Rule* was written for men, words like *monk, brother, abbot,* in an inclusive text, are often translated as *monastic, nun, sister, abbess or prioress.* The reader is invited to substitute feminine nouns and pronouns wherever appropriate. (There are actually twice as many Benedictine women as Benedictine men).
4. *Theological Investigations,* volume 13, trans., Cornelius Ernst (Baltimore: Helicon, 1961).
5. *The Sacred and the Profane* (San Francisco: Harper and Row, 1978).
6. Quoted in Diarmuid O'Murchu, *Reclaiming Spirituality: A New Spiritual Framework for Today's World* (New York: Crossroad, 1998), 21.
7. Quoted in a flyer distributed by *Daily Enterprises* (Waite Park, MN, December 18, 1998).
8. *Catalogus Monasteriorum OSB,* ed. Office of the Abbot Primate (Rome: Confederation of St. Benedict, 1995).
9. "The *Rule of Benedict* does not try to outline a theory of spirituality, but rather a practice of it." Remark made by Abbot Marcel Rooney, OSB, in an address to a gathering of Benedictines. *AIM Monastic Bulletin #64* (1998), 8.
10. *I Asked for Wonder: A Spiritual Anthology of Abraham J. Heschel,* ed. Samuel H. Dresner (New York: Crossroad, 1983), vii.
11. Abraham J. Heschel, *Man's Quest for Meaning: Studies in Prayer and Symbolism* (New York: Scribner's, 1954), 87.
12. See Douglas V. Steere, *Together in Solitude* (New York: Crossroads, 1982): first quotation, p. 21; second quotation, p. 112; third quotation, p. 25.
13. Katherine Howard, OSB, *Praying with Benedict* (Winona, MN: Saint Mary's Press), 49.

14. Thomas Merton, *The Climate of Monastic Prayer* (Washington D.C.: Consortium Press, 1973), 82.
15. Steere, 25.
16. Steere, 25.
17. Steere, 64.
18. Steere, 30.
19. There are many persons whose spiritual practice is centering prayer, the last movement of *lectio divina*. Several books on centering prayer are listed at the end of the chapter.
20. Esther de Waal, *Seeking God: The Way of Benedict* (Collegeville, MN: The Liturgical Press, 1984), 86.
21. Charles Cummings, *Monastic Practices* (Kalamazoo, MI: Cistercian Publications, 1986), 61.
22. Hospitality is an essential element of Benedictine spirituality and deserves much more discussion than is possible given the confines of this chapter. Stated succinctly: Christ is encountered in one's colleagues, in students, in guests—in everyone. For this reason, everyone, without exception, is graciously welcomed as Christ.
23. Howard, 58.
24. *The Complete Poems and Plays 1909–1950* (New York: Harcourt, 1958), 101.
25. Stephen J. Pope, commenting on Jon Sobrino's assertion that Catholic universities and graduates of Catholic universities must use their knowledge in service of the poor. This quotation appears in "A Vocation for Catholic Higher Education," *Commonweal* 28 (March 1997), 12.
26. Bernard Loomer, "Size Is the Measure," in *Religious Experience and Process Theology*, eds. Harry J. Cargas and Bernard Lee (New York: Paulist Press, 1976), 70.
27. Loomer, 73–74.
28. Pope, 13.
29. These adjectives were gleaned from some of the sources listed in the suggested bibliography and from my own memory of things read in the past.

Contemporary Books on Benedictine Spirituality, the *Rule of Benedict*, and *Lectio Divina*

(There are many more resources; the following are readable and easily accessible)

Casey, Michael, *Sacred Reading: The Ancient Art of Lectio Divina* (Liguori, Missouri: Triumph Books, 1995).

_____, *Toward God: The Ancient Wisdom of Western Prayer* (Liguori, Missouri: Triumph Books, 1996).

Chittister, Joan D., *Wisdom Distilled from the Daily: Living the Rule of St. Benedict Today* (San Francisco: Harper, 1991).

de Vogue, Adalbert, *Reading Saint Benedict: Reflections on the Rule,* tr. Colette Friedlander (Kalamazoo, Michigan: Cistercian Publications, 1994).

De Waal, Esther, *Seeking God: The Way of St. Benedict* (Collegeville, Minnesota: The Liturgical Press, 1984).

_____, *A Life-Giving Way: A Commentary on the Rule of St. Benedict* (Collegeville, Minnesota: The Liturgical Press, 1981).

Hall, Thelma, *Too Deep for Words: Rediscovering Lectio Divina* (Mahwah, New Jersey.: Paulist Press, 1988).

Howard, Katherine, *Praying with Benedict: Companions for the Journey* (Winona, Minnesota: Saint Mary's Press, 1996).

Keating, Thomas, *Open Mind, Open Heart* (New York: Amity House, 1986). [centering prayer].

_____, *Intimacy with God* (New York: Crossroads, 1994).

Leclercq, Jean, *The Love of Learning and the Desire for God: A Study of Monastic Culture*, Catherine Misrahi, third edition, (New York: Fordham University Press, 1982).

Margrassi, Mariano, *Praying the Bible: An Introduction to Lectio Divina.* tr. Edward Hagman (Collegeville, Minnesota: The Liturgical Press, 1998).

Merton, Thomas, *Contemplative Prayer* (New York: Doubleday Image Books, 1990).

Pennington, Basil, *Centering Prayer: Reclaiming an Ancient Prayer Form* (New York: Doubleday: 1980).

Stewart, Columba, *Prayer and Community: The Benedictine Tradition* (Maryknoll, New York: Orbis Books, 1998).

Taylor, Brian C., *Spirituality for Everyday Living* (Collegeville, Minnesota: The Liturgical Press, 1989).

Vest, Norvene, *Friend of the Soul: A Benedictine Spirituality of Work* (Boston: Cowley Publications, 1997).

_____, *Gathered in the Word* (Nashville, Tennessee: Upper Room Books, 1996). [helpful resource for group *lectio divina*].

20

Augustinian Spirituality for the Intellectual Life

Joseph T. Kelley

The life and work of St. Augustine of Hippo offer a heritage of distinction to enliven and enrich the vocations of contemporary scholars and teachers. Augustine's known writings include over five hundred sermons, one hundred thirteen books, and two hundred seventy letters. His early search for truth and happiness, his conversion to Christianity at the age of thirty-two, and his thirty-five years as Bishop of Hippo in North Africa still yield both insight and inspiration sixteen centuries later. Catholics and Protestants, theologians and philosophers, believers and agnostics, continue to find in Augustine a challenging companion, or a worthy adversary, for matters of the mind and habits of the heart.

There are recurring themes in his works that provide touchstones for a contemporary Augustinian spirituality. They include: the primacy of love; the mystery of Christ; the efficacy of grace; the importance of Scripture; and, a critique of human power and institutions. Each of these themes distinguishes the Augustinian philosophy and praxis of education.[1]

In addition to Augustine's own contributions, the religious men and women who have lived according to the monastic rule he wrote have enlarged and strengthened the Augustinian heritage. The medieval Augustinian school of thought, which originated in the early European universities, further broadened and deepened Augustine's insights and influence in Western thought. The following pages present Augustine's life and work, the Order of St. Augustine, and the medieval Augustinian school of thought. A review of these sources will be useful for considering how Augustine's heritage provides a dynamic and transforming vision for the interior life of educators and intellectuals today.

Saint Augustine of Hippo (354–430)[2]

Aurelius Augustinus was born on November 13, 354, in the North African town of Thagaste, the present Souk Ahras in Algeria, about forty-five miles south of the Mediterranean coast. His magnanimous and hot-tempered father, Patricius, was one of the thousands of proud but impoverished gentry of Rome's African Province of Numidia. His mother's name, Monica, suggests that she was a native Numidian, a descendent of the indigenous peoples closely related to the modern-day Berbers. Augustine had perhaps two sisters and at least one brother, Navigius.

When North Africa was the prosperous, pleasant, and secure home of Augustine's youth, it had already been a province of the Roman Empire for almost five hundred years. Africa provided wheat, corn, and oil for the Roman world. Its citizens were proud of their important role in the economy and culture of Rome, even if their more urbane cousins across the sea in Italia might have considered these southern colonials curious in their accent and extreme in their civic and religious passions.

Augustine's Youth

We know much about Augustine's youth, of course, from the early chapters of his *Confessions*. Doted on by his mother at home, he was bright and arrogant in school. He hated the quick hand and sharp cane of his teachers. The adventures and stories of Roman heroes like Aeneas excited his imagination and his feelings. Homer's tales were less accessible because Augustine had such distaste for Greek grammar. Augustine strove hard to be accepted by his peers as he grew into his second decade, engaging in juvenile pranks that provided him much thought for reflection and regret in his adult years.

After finishing his primary education in the local school of Thagaste, Augustine, at the age of sixteen, went to the town of Madaurus, fifteen miles to the south, for an additional year of studies. His parents could not afford more than that, however, and he had to endure a stormy year at home until Patricius secured a patron, an influential family friend named Romanianus. In 371 Augustine left for the port city of Carthage, about one hundred fifty miles east on the Gulf of Tunis. He admits that his motives for going on to "higher education" were mixed at best. "So I arrived at Carthage, where the din of scandalous love-affairs raged cauldron-like around me. I was not yet in love, but I was enamoured with the idea of love . . ." (*Confessions III,*1). The classical education waiting for him there, however, was one of the few tickets out of the poor, backcountry life in Thagaste.

During his student years in Carthage (371–374), Augustine began living with a girlfriend who was to be his companion of eleven years. He also became a "hearer" or novice in the Manichean cult, and suffered the death of his father, Patricius—a tumultuous and difficult "college" career in any century. Augustine reports, however, that during his second year at Carthage, he fell in love with learning. He was inspired to pursue wisdom upon reading *Hortensius*, a now lost work of the Roman orator and philosopher Cicero. From the vantage point of his later years, Augustine understood this to be the beginning of his search for truth, a search that led ultimately to his conversion to Christ.

The cult that Augustine joined, the Manichean sect, was a combination of Christian teaching and Persian dualism, founded by the second-century Persian teacher Mani. Manicheans preached two ultimate principles of good and evil: the spiritual world was good, and the material world, evil. These two forces were in constant conflict, even and especially in human beings:

our soul being good, but our body and its needs being evil. Augustine seemed to have found in this dualistic mysticism a compelling approach to the problem of evil—but for only a few brief years. Although he maintained social contact with the Manichean teachers up to and during his year in Rome, Augustine admits that after meeting the Manichean teacher Faustus, when the latter came to Carthage in 382 or 383, he found the sect's intellectual base weak and flimsy. Later, as bishop, Augustine spent significant time and energy in refuting the Manicheans whose influence in Europe lasted for several more centuries.

Professional Years in Italy

In 383, after teaching rhetoric in Carthage for seven years, Augustine left for Rome, where he heard that the students were better and less disruptive. In Rome, however, students had the habit of not paying their bills. Augustine, who was struggling financially, was frustrated by the situation. His unhappy year in Rome was made more miserable by a serious illness. His talent for rhetoric and teaching, however, had been noticed by Symmachus, the pagan Prefect of Rome. Through contacts and connections of Symmachus, Augustine was offered the desirable, prestigious, and lucrative position of Rhetor in Milan and speechwriter for the emperor. This meant a move to the imperial capital of the western empire, which by the fourth century was in Milan. Augustine moved there in 384 and was soon joined by his woman companion, son, mother Monica, brother Navigius, and assorted cousins and friends.

Several important currents in Augustine's life converged in Milan. In this cosmopolitan city he was introduced to the thought of the neo-Platonists. Augustine found this philosophical school very compelling. Plotinus (d. 270) had retrieved, revived, and reframed Plato's philosophy. It appealed to Augustine's growing metaphysical hunger and it challenged his intellect.

The second current of his Milan experience was the Catholic bishop of the city: Ambrose. This distinguished gentleman of noble background was a powerful rhetorician as well as a student of neo-Platonism. Even the critical and discerning Augustine could admire and strive to emulate Ambrose. Augustine would go to the cathedral church where Ambrose preached in order to listen to and learn from his rhetorical style. Since Ambrose was speaking about the Christian faith, however, Augustine began to hear the bishop's content even as he studied his style.

The third current of Augustine's life in Milan was a crisis of meaning and an enervating episode of life weariness. He had been responsible for supporting a family and the friends who would visit and stay. His intellectual search, always infused with passion and restlessness, was beginning to wear on him. Monica, never happy with his woman companion, finally prevailed upon Augustine to send her back to Africa. She then arranged a proper marriage for him, a marriage delayed, however, by the young age of the girl—which sent Augustine off on another romantic cul-de-sac. Finally, the competitive, corrupt, and deceptive world of fourth-century Roman politics, especially fierce in the imperial court, drained his energies.

Conversion and Return to Africa

Augustine recounts that, amidst all this inner turmoil and outer stress, he experienced a call to "Pick up and read" (*Tolle lege! Tolle lege!*) the New Testament. There, in his garden in Milan, he picked up Paul's Letter to the Romans and read the end of chapter thirteen. "Let us live honorably as in the day, not in reveling and drunkenness, not in debauchery and licentiousness, nor in quarreling and jealousy. Instead, put on the Lord Jesus Christ, and make no provision for the flesh to gratify its desires" (cf. Romans 13:13–14). This conversion experience was the beginning of his life in Christ. The next month, in September 386, an exhausted but newly confident Augustine left his position in Milan and retired to a villa in the foothills of the Alps, in the village of Cassisiacum. There, with son, mother, and friends, he hoped to regain his mental and physical health. The following spring, of 387, he was baptized by Bishop Ambrose during the Easter Vigil on April 24–25.

Augustine soon made plans to return to Africa. His party, traveling by ship back to Africa, was delayed in the Roman port city of Ostia because the harbor was closed by a military blockade. During that summer in Ostia, Monica died and was buried. Back in Africa Augustine set up a religious commune on the family land he inherited in Thagaste, intending to live a simple life of prayer and study with like-minded intellectual Christians. During the first or second year of this community living, however, his son Adeodatus died, marking the third great personal loss in a few short years for the thirty-five-year-old Augustine.

Bishop of Hippo

In the spring of 391 Augustine visited the port city of Hippo, about fifty miles northwest of Thagaste, where he interviewed a potential member for his community back home. The Christians of the city knew he was in town and, during a service in the cathedral, presented him to their bishop, Valerius, himself of Greek background, who had been seeking a Latin-speaking presbyter.

The recent convert was reluctant to leave his quiet community life of prayer and study. Augustine, however, moved to Hippo and was ordained to the presbyterate in 391. He gathered a community around him in Hippo, as he had in Thagaste, and thus was born one of the first Christian urban monasteries. In 395 Augustine became Bishop of Hippo, a ministry he continued for the next thirty-five years.

Bishop Augustine cared passionately for his people. He now employed his famous rhetorical skills and literary gifts for the preaching of the gospel. In his many letters, sermons, and books, he addressed difficult questions of Christian doctrine and discipline. He confronted the issues raised by the Manicheans (his former associates), by the schismatic Christian sect of the Donatists (the radical Christian purists of North Africa), and by the British monk Pelagius (whose teachings on the relationship between divine grace and human effort were not up to Augustine's standards). In addition to his writings, done mostly at night, and his daily pastoral duties, Augustine regularly heard civil cases brought to him by Christians and others for his discerning judgment.

Augustine's three greatest works, *Confessions* (397–399), *On the Trinity* (419), and *City of God* (413–427), are undisputed classics in Christian and world literature. Augustine's teaching again and again raises the centrality of God's freely given love and forgiveness, the universal presence and power of Christ, the importance of the Scriptures in Christian life and learning, and reliance on God and God's grace as opposed to civilization and human institutions.

Augustine died on August 28, 430, in his beloved Hippo, which was under siege by the Vandal tribes that were sweeping across North Africa, after crossing over from the Iberian Peninsula. To the good fortune of posterity, Augustine's library was saved by his friend, Possidius, who was also his first biographer. Catholic Christianity died in North Africa shortly after Augustine, since the invading Vandals were Arians. Two centuries later Islam swept across the northern coast of the continent, pushing back the Arian tide, and claiming the land for Allah. Christianity returned to this part of Mediterranean Africa only with nineteenth-century French colonists.

The Order of St. Augustine (1244/1256)

In 397 Augustine wrote a rule of common life for lay Christians. Upon his return to Africa, he lived in his community of lay Christians who sought to support one another in prayer and study. When he first moved to Hippo, he founded a new community of laymen there with whom he shared life and prayer. Then, as bishop, he invited his presbyters to live a common life with him. The rule that he wrote, if not specifically for one or other of his own communities, certainly expresses his ideas about living in such an intentional religious community.[3]

The Rule of St. Augustine is one of the oldest extant monastic rules. It is short on regulations and ascetic admonitions. Rather, Augustine puts forth a set of inspiring principles that serve as the foundation for a common life based on love and harmony with Christ as the center of the community. He grounds his rule in the Acts of the Apostles 4:32: "The whole group of believers was of one mind and one heart. No one claimed any of his possessions as his own, but everything was held in common." Christians come together to establish and enjoy a real and loving common life, centered upon God, striving for God. Material and spiritual goods are to be shared in humility, which is a necessary condition for love. Augustine is less interested in external observances than in inner transformation: seven times the rule invites the hearer to move from external action to interior conversion. The essence of the rule is to value community life as a victory over self-seeking, and as a practical model for the transformation of wider society.

This rule seems to have spread quickly as a guide for communities of Christians wishing to live out the gospel together in mutual support. The rule was known to be used across Europe from the fifth century on by small groups of hermit monks and nuns, as well as by diocesan clergy living, like

Augustine's presbyters, in cathedral communities of prayer and study with their bishop. It was the practical Christian life companion piece to Augustine's intellectual and doctrinal influence.

The Mendicant Movement of the Thirteenth Century

In the thirteenth century, Europe was in the midst of great social change. The new class of merchants was becoming an influential economic and political power, as their expanding wealth enabled them to rival the nobility. Urban centers were growing up around these mercantile endeavors, and new centers of learning or "universities" were organizing in these growing cities.

The Church's response to these social changes included new forms of religious communities. Monks had lived mostly hidden within the cloister; active clerics had clustered in the enclave of the court or environs of the cathedral. During the early thirteenth century, however, a new breed of religious community was emerging in Europe. These religious witnessed to their faith in the growing urban centers, among the merchants and their stalls, attending to the poor and to those dispossessed by the changes in European society. They did not retreat to grand monasteries, nor attach themselves to a bishop's cathedral. Rather, they preached the gospel wherever they discerned the need, and they lived off the generosity of God's people. Because of this dependency on alms, they became known as *mendicants*, or beggars.

There were four major mendicant orders, all founded in the first half of the thirteenth century: the Dominicans in 1216 in Spain; the Franciscans in 1223 in Umbria, Italy; the Augustinians in 1244 in Tuscany, Italy. The Carmelites, who originated in the Holy Land and spread throughout Europe in the latter part of the twelve hundreds. Dominic Guzman and Francis of Assisi are the well-known founders of their respective orders. The Augustinians, however, were founded by Pope Innocent IV. Because the pope wished to affirm and further the good works and preaching of the growing mendicant movement, he gathered groups of hermits living in various communities throughout Tuscany, gave them the Rule of St. Augustine, and coaxed them from their eremitic life to the active service of God's people. Alexander IV gathered more such communities into the new Order of St. Augustine to expand and strengthen it in 1256.[4]

Many members of the new mendicant orders quickly became leading scholars at the growing universities. The Augustinians, after the example of their spiritual father, Augustine, dedicated themselves to study and writing as part of their service of the Church. As early as 1245 there was an Augustinian house of study in Paris affiliated with the university. By 1248 the new order had established a community in the town of Clare in Suffolk, England, where they became known as the Austin Friars. (*Canterbury Tales* mentions their mendicant status in a somewhat condescending remark about "Austin-friar" by Chaucer's less observant monk.)

From Clare Priory they founded houses of study at the newly organizing centers of learning at Oxford (1266, now Wadham College) and Cambridge (1289, now Corpus Christi College). As the fourteenth century dawned, the

Augustinians had also established houses of study at Bologna, Padua, Rome, Florence, Prague, Strasbourg, Cologne, Vienna, Erfurt, and Magdeberg among other places. These houses of study, which granted degrees of bachelor, licentiate, and doctor, were an important part of the university movement, and Augustinian friars were among the renowned scholars and teachers of scholasticism in the high Middle Ages.

Reform, Upheaval, and a Friar Named Martin Luther

The theology of the German Augustinians was distinguished by a deep spirituality and interest in mysticism, as well as concern for reform in the Church. Perhaps the most famous German friar, a member of the Augustinian community in Erfurt, was one Martin Luther (1483–1546). Luther's theological training involved various, and undoubtedly misleading, understandings of St. Thomas's theology. His resulting discomfort with Thomistic scholasticism, as well as his reliance on Scripture and on Augustine (both very characteristic of the Augustinian school) formed the intellectual foundation for the German Reformation. Despite his original intentions, Luther's teaching at the University of Wittenberg led to difficulties with Rome. His calls for reform eventually split not only the Church, but the Augustinian order as well. The German provinces and congregations all but disappeared under the establishment of the Lutheran Church in the mid sixteenth century.

The Spanish Augustinians, however, led a revival in the late sixteenth and seventeenth centuries, and the order expanded in Latin America and, in the nineteenth century, in the United States and Australia. There are currently 3000 Augustinian friars worldwide, and scores of other religious communities that follow Augustine's rule of common life.

Distinctive Characteristics of the Augustinian Heritage

The life and work of St. Augustine, the charism and ministry of the Order of St. Augustine, and the writings of the medieval Augustinian school comprise a notable and distinctive tradition in Western Christianity. As mentioned above, the main characteristics of this intellectual, spiritual, and pastoral tradition include: the primacy of love; the mystery of Christ; the efficacy of grace; the importance of Scripture; and a critique of human power and institutions.

These characteristics are certainly not unique to the Augustinian tradition. Augustine's understanding of love and grace, his witness to Christ, his reading of Scripture, and his critique of social structures have all entered the mainstream of Western Christianity as foundations of its theology and spirituality. Recast in their original settings, however, and woven together in the fabric of Augustinian history, the subtle and varied hues of Augustine's thought present rich material for a cohesive and compelling contemporary spirituality. This Augustinian spirituality offers much to deepen and broaden the vocation of the Christian intellectual and the profession of persons of many and varied persuasions who study and teach at Catholic colleges and universities. These five characteristics, then, are reviewed for an appreciation of their Augustinian origins and for the possibilities they hold for the contemporary scholar.

1. The Primacy of Love

When reading Augustine's *Confessions*, his letters, or his sermons, one sooner or later notices that Augustine is almost never solitary, rarely removed from human companionship. His recollections of childhood and adolescence concern school, peer pressure, and friendships—are all very social experiences. The death of a friend, suffered when he was in his early twenties, devastated him, as he recounts at length in Book IV of the *Confessions*. Augustine's remembrance of that severe loss is immediately followed in the *Confessions* by his beautiful hymn to friendship. As a young adult he seems to require the steady and supportive companionship of a woman. When he arrives in Milan, a retinue of family and friends soon joins him, and he seems to think this very normal.

Even Augustine's deeply religious moments are shared. He immediately reported his conversion experience in the garden at Milan to his friend Alypius; his mystical experience in Ostia was shared with his mother; his ideal of Christian living was a community of friends; and he spent considerable energy on setting up and living in such communities. Friendships, relationships, community living, all held the highest value for Augustine.

Augustine's conversion to Christianity prompted him to reflect deeply on the nature of friendship and gave him new insights about love. In his works on the Gospel and Letters of St. John, Augustine delights in John's affirmation that "God is love" and that when we live in love we live in the divine reality. Inspired by faith and by his reading of Scripture, Augustine begins to write about the importance of loving properly, that is, in ways and means appropriate to the object of one's love. This "ordering of love" in the light of faith enabled Augustine, always the passionate lover and intense friend, to temper and tutor his desires so that all his loving led ultimately to the One Who Is Love. Aided by God's grace we can learn to love all persons, indeed all creatures, in the proper measure and always within the ultimate context of the Divine Lover. The gift of the Holy Spirit in turn inflames and directs our loving.

It is no surprise, then, that in his scholastic theology, Giles of Rome insists on the Augustinian principle that will is superior to intellect. The way in which we are most like God is not in our knowledge alone, but in our creative capacity to choose to love. The final purpose of theology, according to Giles and the Augustinian scholastics, is to deepen our desire for God and our love for God's creation. Knowledge and understanding are always in the service of love.

Augustinian spirituality, then, rests not on asceticism or methods of religious observance, not on meditation or ritual practice, not on the rarified knowledge of religious ideas or secrets, but simply on love. The spiritual life is itself made possible by the gift of God's love in the Holy Spirit—a gift that guides us in the ways of love. Any efforts on our part are both inspired and aided by divine love, and are all directed to the perfecting of our capacity to love God and each other.

The ideal of the Christian life for Augustine, then, is to live together in humble and sincere love, as a community of friends, centered in Christ who is the revelation of God's love. His rule begins, "Before all else, dearly beloved, love God and then your neighbor, because these are the chief commandments given to us. . . . The main purpose for your having come together is to live harmoniously in your house, intent upon God in oneness of mind and heart." The rule provides the guidelines for a practical experience in Christian community based on love. Where one might expect to find a reference to a spiritual director or religious mentor, Augustinian spirituality directs one's attention to divine love directing and forming us in and through the Christ-centered community. When one seeks personal transformation in holiness, Augustine recommends daily common prayer. To the earnest scholar seeking truth, Augustine extends the invitation to sustained and engaging conversation among those many and diverse members "who have come together" in intentional community.

Love and the Intellectual Life: It may be countercultural in contemporary American intellectual circles to suggest, as Giles did seven hundred years ago at the University of Paris, that learning should be ordered to love. An Augustinian vision of the academy, however, is founded on the primacy of love. It understands the academic community to be, above all else, a scholarly fellowship of friends.[5] Those friends, from very different backgrounds, disciplines, persuasions, and beliefs, can nonetheless be united by *caritas. Caritas,* or charity as Augustine understood it, involves a profound respect for and acceptance of one's fellow searchers for truth. It exercises the necessary, and sometimes difficult self-discipline to realize that respect and to sustain that acceptance. *Caritas* is willing to practice humility, that is, a realistic assessment of one's own strengths and limits in light of the common search for truth. All members of the academic community should be afforded this respect and acceptance as they engage one another in the important and sometimes difficult search for truth.

From an Augustinian perspective, the scholarly fellowship of friends is called to grow together through knowledge to wisdom. Learning is valued because it opens opportunities for personal and societal transformation. Passionate learning, supported by a compassionate community of students and scholars, can be the beginning of lifelong transformation of self and, through one's service to others, of society. This is wisdom in the Augustinian tradition: knowledge put to work in the building of a new society, a society whose outlines and blueprints can already be found in the respect and acceptance, in the *caritas* of the collegiate community itself.

This Augustinian theology of love can also have an influence on the curriculum or course of studies in higher education. In an age of specializations, of isolated and esoteric academic disciplines, people are calling for ways to help students make connections. The emphasis of the Augustinian school on the primacy of love provides a principle of integration and of connection across the curriculum. The respect and acceptance of one's academic colleagues includes, in an Augustinian approach, a respect for and acceptance of their particular disciplines, different from one's own. Augustinian education calls for the exploration of ways to invite and engage students and faculty from different disciplines and majors into sustained and meaningful conversations on civilization and its many and diverse aspects.

The medieval Augustinian school asserted that theology has as its final purpose not only love of neighbor, or *caritas*, but also love of God, or *affectio*. All members of the typical contemporary college or university may not believe in God or in the reality of a transcendent being. An Augustinian spirituality, however, considers and sustains the possibility that human learning, in its many and diverse particulars, is ultimately a participation in the divine. Teaching, research, writing, and study are sacred activities, containing within themselves the seeds of transcendence. The life of the student and the scholar are filled with a thirst for knowledge which knowledge alone cannot quench. As theology is ultimately directed to the experience of God's love, all learning in its proper way is directed to awakening within the student and the teacher an experience of self-transcendence that leaves one open to the possibility of the eternal. Indeed, for Augustine, all ventures searching for the "true" and the "good" are on the way to a discovery of God.

2. The Mystery of Christ

Augustinian spirituality is deeply Christ-centered. Augustine understood Jesus to be the very mystery of the Divine One breaking personally and powerfully into human history and experience. To enter into relationship with Christ through baptism, and to celebrate and sustain that relationship in the Eucharist, is to live in intimate and enduring love of the Holy One.

Augustine's sermons elaborate in many, powerful ways this aspect of Christian doctrine. He puts flesh on the Christological controversies of the third and fourth centuries, as he constantly invites his people into ever deeper relationship with God through Christ. He tells his congregations what it means in everyday life that Jesus is truly God and truly human. It means that they, and he, are invited by Christ into the mystery of the Eternal One.

Augustine's conversion involved not only the discovery of Christianity as a convincing system of belief, thought, and ethic. After his baptism, Augustine, ever the restless searcher for truth, found within himself a new source of confidence and curiosity, a new font of love and learning that intensified his intellectual journey and deepened his spiritual search. He explores the soul, studies the Scriptures, and critiques religion, philosophy, and society with this new inner confidence, a confidence built upon Christ his "Inner Teacher." Certainly Augustine's early life had been an odyssey of intellectual and existential searching. On his own, he would examine and explore various schools of thought such as Manicheism, Aristotle's categories, academic skepticism, astrology, and neo-Platonism. At the same time he would long for a teacher or mentor who might show him the way. Christ becomes for Augustine, after his conversion, that teacher and mentor, an inner compass, a Virgilian companion who guides him as he ventures forth into new territories of the soul and new vistas of Christian faith and philosophy.

Faith in Christ and the Search for Truth: It is clear that conversion to Christ did not mean the end of intellectual activity for Augustine. Christian faith for him rather inspired a return to a life dedicated wholly to study and reflection, as well as to prayer. Faith and reason were not only compatible; both were necessary and reliable guides in Augustine's search for truth. Christianity, in its best understanding, can never be used to foreclose any avenue of truth. The Catholic intellectual must cherish and nurture freedom and openness in intellectual, scientific, or professional research, writing, or teaching.

This continuing search for truth, however, presents an ambiguity for the Christian intellectual, an ambiguity canonized in the opening paragraphs of John Paul II's *Ex corde ecclesiae* where he appeals directly to the thought of St. Augustine: "A Catholic University's privileged task is 'to unite existentially by intellectual effort two orders of reality that frequently tend to be placed in opposition as though they were antithetical: the search for truth, and the certainty of already knowing the font of truth'" (n.1). How does one continue the search for truth after conversion to Christ, whom believers hold to be the Truth? This is a particularly acute question in the modern Catholic college or university, with its great diversity of opinions, religious traditions, and philosophical schools.

The question is less problematic perhaps when one is speaking of search for discernable facts in science, or in the interpretative and imaginative pursuits of literary exegesis. It is, however, in the areas of theology, philosophy, and ethics where difficulties about truth and search for truth arise. Are students and faculty who believe in Christ less engaged, by virtue of their faith, in a true, open, and continuing quest for truth? Are scholars and teachers who do not believe in Christ, or in God, by virtue of their positions or opinions, on an endless and fruitless search until and unless they eventually discover God in Christ? How can members of the scholarly fellowship of friends continue together on the search for truth within an academic community that includes everything from conviction to agnosticism to atheism about Ultimate Truth?

It is clear how Augustine continued that search after his conversion. Christ became his Inner Guide, his Inner Light, in the post-conversion intensification of his intellectual life. He explored the meanings and implications of Christian doctrines; he elaborated them and broke new ground in the theologies of grace, sin, ministry, and Church. He invited others, even those with whom he had basic disagreements, into continuing dialogue about religious and philosophical issues. He even had various friendly dialogues with contemporary pagan intellectuals of his day.

The contemporary Catholic college or university should be a place where Christians can explore faith and philosophy, science and business, in the context of a community of faith. Such a college, however, should also be a place where persons of other philosophical persuasions or religious commitments can, as full members of the scholarly fellowship of friends, follow their search for truth in ways that remain faithful to their best selves. Augustine would probably find the great diversity of faiths and philosophies in the contemporary Catholic college or university interesting and, indeed, invigorating. While he knew significant philosophical and religious pluralism in his time and place, the contemporary convergence of world religions would no doubt challenge his religious imagination in new ways. In the end though, were he to be consistent with the value he put on intellectual freedom and respect for all sincere adherents to truth, Augustine would enter the debates, conversations, and disagreements with his characteristic enthusiasm and passion. That passionate engagement should be a hallmark of the Catholic intellectual life, wherein the scholarly fellowship of friends entertain and enjoy and engage all seekers of truth.

The "Total Christ": A further aspect of Augustine's Christology is his use and development of Paul's image of the Church as the Body of Christ. This image appears again and again in Augustine's preaching and writing. To be baptized is to become part of, a member of, the infinite mystery of the total Christ, the *Totus Christus.* In inviting the assembly to share communion at the eucharistic table in Hippo, he proclaims: "See what you believe! Become what you receive!" To be a Christian then is to become one with the mystery of Christ in the world, loving the world, working to transform the world.

This theme of the Church as the Body of Christ is the foundation for Augustine's option for the poor. In writing and preaching about the Last Judgment scene in Matthew 25, Augustine calls his people to remember that Christ is truly present in the human community, and especially in those who suffer in any way. The Christian has a baptismal responsibility to respond to, care for, and relate to persons in distress, poverty, and persecution.

Recently discovered letters of Augustine show him involved in issues of his day which concerned justice for the poor and dispossessed.[6] He asked the emperor to promulgate new laws against slave trade, he worried about the sale of children by very poor families, and he administered his Church's aid and support of the poor of Hippo. It matters not who we are—prostitute, fighter in the arena, known sinner; in Augustine's way of thinking, we all stand in need of God's grace and forgiveness. Christians must never discriminate against anyone. Humility calls us to recognize that we are all in need of God's love and forgiveness, healed and made whole not by our own ministrations but by being made members of the Body of Christ. Ultimately, it is Augustine's Christology that informs his political and social themes in *The City of God.*

For Augustine, then, Christ is the foundation of his life; Christ is his Inner Guide and Teacher on the journey of life back to God. The mystery of Christ embraces all of humanity and calls Augustine and those who share his vision of the spiritual life to serve the needs of all.

3. The Efficacy of Divine Grace

The Christ-centeredness of Augustine's own spiritual life is the foundation for his understanding of divine grace. Grace is a continuing theme in Augustine's *Confessions.* As he looks back over his life, he sees God working in, through, around, and under all his experiences to draw him into loving union. This pervasive, persistent, yet gentle and loving divine work is grace. Grace is the ongoing divine creation wherein the Holy One continues to mold and shape all created reality into the divine image. The power of God, which made all that exists, is the very same power that guided Augustine to his conversion and life in Christ, God's "new creation." It is no accident that the *Confessions* end with reflections on the Book of Genesis.

For Augustine there is no compromising the importance of grace. As with St. Paul, who also had a powerful conversion experience, so for Augustine: all is grace, all is God's pervasive power and presence constantly calling and nudging us into ever closer union through Christ. While respecting our free will, since love must be free, God's purpose is to complete creation by reuniting all things in Christ.

A contemporary of Augustine, the British monk Pelagius, taught that we are called to grow in perfection and that God's grace can help us. That grace, however, as Pelagius understood it, is more an external aid provided us by God as we strive mightily toward holiness. Augustine responded to Pelagius's teaching, which had spread throughout the Mediterranean church, with his full rhetorical vim and vigor. In Augustine's experience, divine grace was not a spiritual add-on that assisted our efforts in becoming like Christ. Rather, grace illuminates our minds, strengthens our faltering wills, guides our insufficient efforts, shows us the way, and assists us with every step. Even our responses to God's continuing initiatives toward us are themselves also made possible by grace.

Augustine argued that human experience is much more complex and dynamic than Pelagius imagined. We cannot simply identify a goal, religious or otherwise, and naively begin the ascent to achieve it. Our wills are weak; we are compromised by conflicting desires; we lack insight and perspective; we hurt and betray one another. So we stand absolutely in need of divine grace, of God's ongoing creative, redemptive activity on our behalf. Our redemption is not the result of our efforts, but of our surrender to God's transforming love. This primacy of grace is reflected in the Augustinian School from Giles of Rome up to and including the Reformation and the theology of Luther.

Grace and the Complexity of Human Experience: Augustine's theology of grace contains an affirmation of God's freedom and creativity. Divine grace is not a commodity of the Church nor a monopoly of believers. Rather, grace moves where it will within society and the individual, creating ever new opportunities for the discovery of divine love. The "Inner Teacher" teaches each in quite different ways sometimes.

Augustine's radical affirmation of grace, therefore, calls Catholics and other Christians in the scholarly fellowship of friends to respect the consciences of those whose intellectual and religious journeys differ from their own. Augustine discerned a complexity in the many intertwining levels of intellect, will, and affect in human experience. The scholarly fellowship of friends in an Augustinian model acknowledges that complexity and its ensuing ambiguity by a profound respect for each other's thoughtful opinions, careful convictions and earnest doubts. A kind of intellectual humility is essential for the Augustinian scholarly fellowship of friends. This complexity of mind, heart, and will undergirds the basic paradox inherent in Augustine's intellectual Christianity, the paradox of continuing the search even as one believes that the Truth has been revealed in Christ. Appreciating such complexity and sustaining that paradox inspire a radical Augustinian tolerance of others and a profound Augustinian respect for differences. Complexity and paradox hold search and discovery in a creative tension. Complexity and paradox invite searchers and believers to recognize and respect that, in each and every person at diverse times and on different levels, there is believer, searcher, agnostic, atheist. Augustine's theology of grace affirms and is affirmed by recognition of the complexity in all persons. In parallel fashion, his theology of sin allows for the paradox of faith and failure simultaneously—*simul justus et peccator*, as Luther put it. An Augustinian spirituality affirms both complexity and paradox; it encompasses both the possession of truth and the continuing desire for truth; and it embraces all the many and varied expressions of both.

Augustinian complexity and paradox, founded on Augustine's theology of grace, not only call for intellectual inclusion. They also comprise an invitation to transcendence. Augustinian spirituality inspires a continuing and creative invitation to all members of the fellowship of friends to ask their questions, debate their positions, and construct their theories provisionally. It also encourages all members of the fellowship to consider how the possibility of transcendence might reframe their work, illumine heretofore ignored implications of their thought, and open new considerations of their basic presuppositions.

Augustine reinvigorated many aspects of Platonism and neo-Platonism when, after his conversion, he reconsidered them in light of his faith. Thomas and Giles expanded the uses of Aristotelian categories in light of faith in the Eternal and Holy. In the same way, Christian and other religious scholars both learn from and give to their agnostic or atheistic colleagues when conversation includes the possibility of the transcendent, even if only as a tempting proposition or friendly amendment. Complexity, paradox, and the possibility of transcendence do not lead to a unified school of thought. These do, however, provide enough common ground—indeed, a worthy and expansive *campus*—for serious, exciting, enriching, and ennobling work in the scholarly fellowship of friends.

To all this Augustine would add, relying on his understanding of the *Totus Christus*, an invitation to the fellowship of friends to travel beyond the campus, to embrace the less advantaged in society and in the world. An Augustinian spirituality, to be faithful to its heritage, must constantly ask questions about the relationships between the scholarship and the learning it encourages and allows, and the needs, problems, hopes, and crises of wider social, political, and economic communities. It is not enough to accept and explore differences among those in the fellowship of friends. That fellowship must extend itself, transcend the limitations often self-imposed by an academic community and, with the help of divine grace, engage the wider and diverse world by dialogue and service.

4. The Importance of Scripture

In his early years in Carthage, Augustine read some of the New Testament and found its literary quality so inferior that he dismissed both the text and its message. He was, indeed, reading Latin translations that had not yet had the advantage of Jerome's landmark literary translation, the Vulgate, which began to be available toward the end of the fourth century. Scripture, however, played a key role in Augustine's conversion, in his study and reflection as a new Christian, and in his pastoral role as bishop. His preaching, in fact, was filled with quotes from Scripture; his homilies were invitations to ever deeper understandings of the texts that had just been read during the liturgy. A close analysis of his sermons suggests that he would start a passage from the Psalms or the Gospel, and his congregation would often finish it, somewhat in the responsive style of African American churches today.

Augustine's exegetical works on Genesis, the Old and New Testaments, and his homilies on the Johannine books of the New Testament and on the Psalms comprise a large proportion of his entire corpus. These biblical commentaries by Augustine inspired the medieval Augustinian school's extensive use of Scripture, and its importance in the religious life of Augustinian religious.

The Role of Sacred Text in the Intellectual Life: The Hebrew Bible and the New Testament can have a significant place in the discourse and prayer life of the contemporary intellectual and of the academic community. Augustine's reliance on the Scriptures and the attention given to Scripture in the medieval Augustinian school challenge the scholarly fellowship of friends at a contemporary Catholic college or university to honor and cherish the sacred texts. Teachers and students at these schools can experience how Scripture enriches faith and prayer as they study the origins, genres, uses, and meanings of scriptural texts.

It is also of great value for teachers and students to learn and study the sacred texts of other religious traditions. Such consideration could make members of those traditions feel affirmed and valued in their faith, and accepted as full and equal members of the scholarly fellowship of friends.

Finally, because Scripture, by its very nature and purpose, led Augustine to prayer and praise, an Augustinian approach values opportunities for individual prayer and common worship in the academic or intellectual community. Habits of contemplation and considered reflection on experience can greatly benefit all contemporary scholars who so often are overburdened by committees and projects, and who can be distracted or enervated by the stresses of our extroverted, market-driven society. Sacred Scripture can provide categories and texts for such contemplation, as can the sacred texts of other traditions. Liturgical celebrations for the Catholic and Christian members of the community and worship services for other religious traditions can also affirm God's grace, power, and presence in ways that benefit the entire fellowship.

5. Critique of Human Power and Institutions

Augustine's knowledge of himself, his struggles with social institutions first as a teacher and then in the imperial court, and the social and religious conflicts that preoccupied so much of his ministry kept him from ever being Pollyannaish. His critique of power, and of its potential for corrupting individuals, institutions, and society, serves as a powerful preventive against naiveté in Augustinian spirituality.

From his early student days, Augustine struggled with the notion of evil. His detour into the dualistic world of the Manicheans was his first serious attempt to wrestle with the nature and existence of personal and social evil. The idealism he later found in neo-Platonist mysticism was soon balanced by his Christian understanding of sin and our need for redemption. Augustine's reflections on and convictions about evil coalesce in his teaching on original sin.

In elaborating the sin of the primal parents, Augustine challenged his readers to consider sinfulness at the "origins" of humanity as a compelling and convincing theological explanation for the pervasiveness of sin and suffering. In his understanding we enter, at our very conception, a world compromised by sin. Humans are not necessarily bad, in Augustine's understanding; rather, we are disabled by our immersion into this world of sin and we need the constant help of grace to do the right thing. We cannot escape sin on our own, whether by citizenship in some utopian society, by withdrawal from the world altogether, or by a program of self-improvement.

One need not accept every detail in Augustine's theory of original sin to appreciate his willingness to take evil seriously, to struggle to account for the very real pain, ambiguity, and suffering which he witnessed and participated in as a pastor. He understood that we all have mixed motivations; we are all sinners. A selfish love of self and a selfless openness to God and others coexist, even within the same person. As Augustine writes in *The City of God*, goodness and evil exist side by side in the same society or community. We cannot in this world ever escape the consequences of sin. It is only in Christ's redeeming love and by the power of grace that the way out of sin and evil becomes a possibility. Thus it is good to sustain a healthy critique of power, to develop a holy hermeneutic of suspicion toward our motivations, our society, our institutions, and—even, Augustine would agree—toward our Church.

The Transformation of Society: Augustine's trust in human power and institutions continued to diminish over the years. In many ways Augustine came to see civilization as a thin veneer over human greed and power. He did not, however, disengage from efforts to improve the lot of society and, especially, of the people in his city. His vision of human development and social improvement, however, drew more and more from his faith, from Scripture, and from his conviction that true and lasting change must be built on the personal, inner conversion of heart and mind made possible by divine grace. He learned to rely on God and God's grace alone when hoping and working for improvements in society. This is the major theme of *The City of God*.

Augustinian spirituality counsels scholars to engage in the issues of wider society beyond the academy and to strive to become critical catalysts in social development and human welfare. By an informed, inspired, and critical understanding of political and social theory and praxis, one can become part of the divine work of continuing creation, a "subcontractor" in the work of building the City of God. Augustinian spirituality invites the intellectual to leave the ivory tower of academe and venture into the streets of Babylon, just as Augustine himself was called by the Church of Hippo to forsake his idyllic retreat in Thagaste and to continue his journey of faith in the midst of the diverse and struggling populace of urban Africa.

Augustinian spirituality also counsels continuing self-critique, a constant and vigilant *semper reformanda*. The medieval Augustinian school was noted for its capacity to maintain a critical stance toward its own tradition and to revise, reframe, and recast even basic elements of that intellectual tradition. Augustine would agree. No institution, no person, no matter their history or accomplishments, should ever rest content with their laurels. The reality of sin is too pervasive for such inattentiveness; restless search and striving are essential to and salvific for our human nature. The vocation to the intellectual life, in an Augustinian perspective, involves the willingness and the humility to remain as open as possible to the gentle, persistent promptings of grace that call us to continual growth and redemptive change.

THESE FIVE CHARACTERISTICS of Augustinian thought have distinguished and enriched higher study and Christian education for centuries. The Augustinian intellectual and spiritual tradition has brought learning and love, grace and sacred text, social critique and service, to sustained inquiry and engaging search. Each of these characteristics offers much to deepen and broaden the contemporary scholar's understanding of her or his vocation to the intellectual life.

Notes

1. Father Tarcisius van Bavel, O.S.A., suggests these five themes as cardinal points in Augustinian spiritual inheritance. See his text *Augustine* (Editions du Signe, 1996), p. 20.
2. The two classic biographies of Augustine are Gerald Bonner, *St. Augustine: Life and Controversies* (London: Norwich, 1963, 1986) and Peter Brown, *Augustine of Hippo* (Berkeley: University of California Press, 1967).
3. For studies of the Rule of Augustine, its origins and history, see George Lawless, *Augustine of Hippo and His Monastic Rule* (Oxford: Clarendon Press, 1987); Adolar Zumkeller, O.S.A., *Augustine's Ideal of the Religious Life* (New York: Fordham University Press, 1986); and, Tarcisius van Bavel, *La Règle de Saint Augustin* (Paris: Études Augustiniennes, 1967).
4. See John Rotelle, O.S.A., ed., *Augustinian Spirituality and the Charism of the Augustinians* (Villanova, PA: Augustinian Press 1995).

5. I am indebted to Fr. Donald X. Burt, O.S.A., for the terminology of the "scholarly fellowship of friends" and its elaboration in an unpublished paper delivered at Merrimack College, Fall 1998.
6. Tarcisius van Bavel, O.S.A., "Augustine's Option for the Poor: Preaching and Praxis" (Roma: Publicazioni Agostiniane, 1992).

For more information and readings see <u>www.augustinian.org</u>, or contact the Augustinian Press, PO Box 476, Villanova, PA 19085; 610-527-3330 x248, or 800-871-9404.

21

Franciscan Spirituality: The Footprints of Jesus in the Classroom and the Marketplace

Ingrid Peterson, O.S.F.

Franciscan spirituality is a way to the God exemplified by Jesus, the visible sign of the invisible God. Franciscan spirituality centers around individual persons with their historical and human limitations, modeled on the human Jesus who was the Christ Incarnate. It is sacramental in that all created things are also seen as signs pointing to God as creator. In Franciscan spirituality, the path to God is learned by reading the Gospels to discover what Jesus did and said, for Francis said the gospel was his rule of life. Franciscan spirituality does not aim for divine perfection, but rather for the fullness of human experience as demonstrated in the life of the human Jesus. Franciscan spirituality leads persons to try to live, no matter where they are or what they do, by following in the footprints of Jesus.

Franciscan spirituality is drawn from the lives of St. Francis (1181–1226) and St. Clare of Assisi (1193–1253). The example of their lives and their writings provided material for later followers, such as theologians St. Bonaventure (1217–1274) and Duns Scotus (1266–1308) to systematize their thought into a theological system. These writers provide primary sources to consider Franciscan spirituality and its attraction for our time. Some actions that moderns might seize as their own involve: 1) grasping how all things in the world are revelations of God; 2) praying by paying attention to the mysteries of creation that surround us daily; 3) understanding Christ's primary role as the revelation of God's goodness; 4) sensing the sacredness of the particular and unique; 5) valuing presence more than productivity; and 6) cherishing the diversity of a global community. The universal attraction of Francis and Clare throughout the centuries stems, in part, from some of these tenets in Franciscan spirituality. A discussion of the value of Franciscan spirituality today must begin with a review of the lives of its co-founders, Francis and Clare of Assisi.

Walking in the Footprints of Jesus: Francis and Clare of Assisi

The beginning point in the adult life of Francis of Assisi was his experience of God through his encounter with a leper. From this event, he came to understand that knowing God is a personal experience, that God comes to us with human limitations, and that Jesus is the visible sign of the invisible God. From the example of Jesus' life, Francis came to know about God: that God is good and compassionate. This certainty of belief made demands on Francis. To be like God, Francis, too, must be compassionate, generous, and loving.

In many ways Francis's journey to a mature spirituality speaks again to our age and maps a way for the choices young people must make in the twenty-first century. It is a journey both birthed and validated by personal experience. It is a search for and discovery of God by walking a human journey in relation with others, not through metaphysical systems, philosophy, or theology. God is experienced here and now, not in the future or someplace other than where we are. For Francis, to be like God was to walk in the footprints of Jesus, not to try to reach beyond earth to find the presence of God. Consequently, the central metaphor of Franciscan spirituality is the footprint.

Many of the same concepts of spirituality are found in the adult life of Clare of Assisi. Clare's journey from childhood is also grounded in her experience with her family, her society, and her Church. Each institution made claims on her and attempted to define what she should do as a woman coming into her own at the cusp of the thirteenth century. Clare did none of it. Following the urging of her heart and intellect, Clare made her own path. She rejected her family's expectation to marry a rich noble and acquire land to augment the splendor of the Offreduccio household. In doing so she turned against the cultural norms for women of her time. She also found a new way to dedicate herself to a life of virginity and poverty that was outside the established monastic structure.

In listening to the voice within, Clare came to know the same God that Francis had met outside the walls of Assisi. God's love seemed to have no boundaries. Clare met the crucified Jesus of the cross and chose to imitate him in the poorness of his birth, in the humility and suffering of his life, and in his final generous act of love in laying down his life. She did not wish the Poor Ladies of San Damiano to be huge landowners or to come to the monastery with magnificent dowries to support themselves in style, as did many women religious during the Middle Ages. Because Clare could not confine herself to the religious or social structures of her time, she created a new way of life for enclosed religious women. To insist upon living without property and still remain faithful to the Church that continued to nurture her spiritual life demanded of Clare some fancy footwork with papal authorities. Clare's power of persuasion and the credibility of her life seem to have won over five popes, one after another.[1] She became the first woman to write and receive ecclesial approval for her *Form of Life*—her ideal of union with God lived in community. Clare had been relentless in her determination. Her indomitable spirit is one key to her spirituality and a model for contemporaries who face new times and the need for new ways. Clare looked to the past, acknowledged the parts that remained of value, and attempted to reform what needed repair. The spirit of Francis and Clare came from within, not from outside of themselves.

Franciscan spirituality comes from the experience and events in the lives of Francis and Clare, and other Franciscans, such as Bonaventure and Duns Scotus, who formed theological principles and systems to aid others to know and love God. While their writing never reached the popularity in academic circles of Thomas Aquinas's scholastic work, many of their teachings continue to speak to contemporary issues. Franciscan spirituality continues to thrive in persons who attempt to bring the values of the gospel to the challenges of their times.

Putting a Face on God: All Creatures as Sacraments

Francis was no theologian making investigations into the First Cause or the transcendent nature of God.[2] Quite the contrary. His experience of God was personal and immediate. In the confusion and darkness of his youth, God broke into his life as a personal and concerned participant.[3] Francis's writings demonstrate this intimate relationship with God. The earliest prayer of Francis was composed between 1205–1206, when he knelt before the crucifix in the small neglected Church of Saint Damien requesting God to untangle the struggles of his heart:

> Most High,
> glorious God,
> enlighten the darkness of my heart
> and give me
> true faith,
> certain hope,
> and perfect charity,
> sense and knowledge,
> Lord,
> that I may carry out
> Your holy and true command.[4]

This simple prayer expresses Francis's personal yearning for God's will. It was a good beginning to establish a more authentic relationship with God and a mature spirituality.

Because of Francis and Clare's attention to Christ, Franciscan spirituality is often described as christocentric, that is, a spirituality primarily based on the person and example of Jesus Christ. Ordinary Christian seekers easily grasp the spirituality of Francis and Clare because it is grounded on central mysteries of the Catholic faith: the Incarnation, the Redemption, and the Eucharist. Each of the key moments celebrated in these mysteries illustrates how God reaches out through Jesus to be in relationship to all human beings. What seemed to overwhelm Francis and Clare is that in the mysteries of the crib, the cross, and the chalice, God descends to earth. By pondering the meaning of Jesus' birth, his passion and death, and his continued sacramental presence in the Eucharist, Francis and Clare understood God's involvement in human life.

By their own experience and through the Scriptures, Francis and Clare knew that God is not removed from our earthly concerns. In 1225, to help the people in the little village of Greccio in the Rieti Valley comprehend that God came down to live among us, Francis reconstructed the manger scene at the birth of Jesus. Thomas of Celano, Francis's first biographer, tells how Francis ordered the celebration of Christmas: "For I wish to enact the memory of that babe who was born in Bethlehem: to see as much as is possible with my bodily eyes the discomfort of his infant needs, how he lay in a manger, and how, with an ox and an ass standing by, he rested on hay."[5] Francis understood and wanted all people to understand that, through Christ, God had come down to earth and was set before our bodily eyes. The immediacy and urgency of the Christmas event for Francis is evident from his words. For Francis, the Incarnate Christ is God's human face.

In the fall of 1224, when Francis was making a forty-day retreat, he experienced a vision of God in the descent of a man, like a seraph, fixed to a cross. Thomas of Celano provides the details of this miraculous event:

> While he was living in that hermitage called La Verna, after the place where it is located, two years prior to the time that he returned his soul back to heaven, he saw in the vision of God a man, having six wings like a seraph, standing over him, arms extended and feet joined, affixed to a cross. Two of his wings were raised up, two were stretched out over his head as if for flight, and two covered his whole body.[6]

The crucified man looked at Francis tenderly, which filled him with happiness—but it also filled him with fear, because of the suffering Francis could see. Celano describes how Francis attempted to find meaning in this experience: "While he was unable to perceive anything clearly understandable from the vision, its newness very much perplexed his heart. Signs of the nails began to appear on his hands and feet, just as he had seen them a little while earlier on the crucified man hovering over him."

In the Christian mystical tradition, the mystical experience of God is often communicated as an experience of fire or light. Saint Paul tells of being taken up into the seventh heaven; the movement is one of ascent from earth to God in heaven. For this reason the ladder of ascent, as expressed in works such as St. John Climacus's *The Ladder of Divine Ascent,* becomes a primary metaphor.[7] Francis reverses this, for he experienced God descending to him. Francis began to comprehend that Jesus as the human face of God was an exemplar for each human person.

The daily descent of God in the Eucharist became another example for Francis of God's immanence and continual revelation. In one of Francis's admonitions, or spiritual sayings, he describes the humility of God in the sacrament of the Eucharist. He explains that as Christ came on earth in his humanity in historical time, in the same way he comes in the sacrament:

> Behold, each day He humbles Himself as when He came from the royal throne into the Virgin's womb; each day He Himself comes to us, appearing humbly; each day He comes down from the bosom of the Father upon the altar in the hands of a priest. . . . And in this way the Lord is always with His faithful, as He Himself says: Behold I am with you until the end of the age.[8]

What is striking in Francis's conclusion is the way he understands the revelation of God to be ongoing. The following table summarizes the development of Francis's thought:

Mystery of Christ	**Place in Francis's life**	**Event**
Incarnation	Greccio	Birth
Redemption	LaVerna	Suffering
Eucharist	Admonitions to followers	Presence

The table illustrates how the experience of Jesus celebrated in the mysteries of the Church predicates Francis's experience and informs his spirituality. Francis realized that the revelation of God begun through the historical Christ continued in his life and in each human life.

Making a Home for God: Prayer Rooted in Human Experience

The writings of Clare also emphasize the Incarnate Christ. Clare instructs the Poor Ladies to make their souls a dwelling place for God. She reflects on how Mary carried Jesus "in the little enclosure of her holy womb and held Him on her virginal lap."[9] Since the human Mary was so dignified to be chosen to carry Jesus bodily, then Clare concludes that every human soul is also chosen to carry the life of Jesus spiritually: "Indeed it is now clear that the soul of the faithful person, the most worthy of all creatures because of the grace of God, is greater than heaven itself, since the heavens and the rest of creation cannot contain their creator and only the faithful soul is His dwelling place and throne." Then Clare quotes from the Gospel of St. John and his teaching on the soul as the dwelling place of God.

Clare makes an extraordinary plea for the sanctity of human life. She asks, "Who would not dread the treacheries of the enemy who, through the arrogance of momentary and deceptive glories, attempts to reduce to nothing that which is greater than heaven itself?" In a similar voice, Pope John Paul II has repeatedly pleaded with North American society to halt its violence and "culture of death." Contemporary Franciscans are united in an effort to protest the "hatred of the Incarnation" that characterizes contemporary culture.[10]

One challenge of Franciscan spirituality is to be a bearer of Christ, like the pregnant Mary, and to symbolically bring forth Christ in imitation of Mary's maternity. Bonaventure, the first great theologian of the Franciscan tradition, describes how God is born spiritually in the soul "when the soul begins to do that which it long had in mind."[11] Bonaventure's affectivity and personal experience of the tenderness of God is evident in his writing: "And in truth we find how good he is when we nourish him with our prayers, bathe him in the waters of our warm and loving tears, wrap him in the spotless swaddling cloths of our desires, carry him in an embrace of holy love, kiss him over and over again with heartfelt longings and cherish him in the bosom of our inmost heart." Bonaventure's personal encounter with the Incarnate God is tenderly expressed in his text.

Bonaventure's language characterizes the Franciscan way of prayer that flows from the senses.[12] This prayer involves stories, symbols, and concepts following the way God is revealed to humans through the sensory tools of vision, hearing, and feeling. Our contemporary barrage of television images, advertising sound bites, and the noise of contemporary culture produces a pragmatic, sensory-based society at home with the senses as the source of knowing. Franciscan prayer is not a trip on a "spiritual elevator" to an abstract ecstasy. That was neither Francis's nor Clare's experience. Rather, it is an encounter with the divine that begins with human rituals, such as bread and wine. In Franciscan spirituality, material things are perceived as vestiges of the divine, footprints of the creator. God is at home on our earth, present at our kitchen tables as well as in our churches and chapels.

Clare's letters of instruction to Agnes of Prague describe the activity by which contemplative prayer is internalized. Clare instructs her sisters to move from the outer world to the inner world; that is, in popular contemporary language, from the workplace to the spiritual world. She instructs the praying person moved by something seen to observe it closely, "to gaze" intensely upon it to develop an inner involvement. Such loving looking fosters contemplation, which, in turn, effects a reverse movement from the inside to the outside. Meeting God in prayer as the generous fountain of giving, the soul seeks to imitate God's generosity by giving service to others. Clare, who prayed for more than forty years before the figure of Jesus on the San Damiano cross, came to resemble him in her poverty, humility, and charity. In this way, looking creates resemblance.

Clare describes the activity of prayer as a formula: gaze, consider, contemplate. This is how resemblance to God in human virtue happens. She introduces the image of the mirror to help Agnes and her sisters understand how they reflect God and how they can sharpen God's image by imitating the virtues of Jesus: poverty, humility, and charity. Since Jesus is the visible sign of the invisible God, his birth, life, death, and resurrection become models for every human life. The spiritual journey of Clare does not detail the ascetic practices of the saints of the first millennium; rather, the center of her journey is Jesus. This is why she exhorts Agnes to follow in the footprints of the poor Jesus and his poor mother—to follow them in the self-giving and generosity of their lives.

Clare encourages active prayer in the effort to move deeper into God. The idea is to remove the things that keep us from entering fully into God's life. For many persons, the things of the world are distractions from the things of God. In the schema of Clare and Francis, created things are analogical reminders of the Creator. For spiritual progress, what needs to be weeded out is not necessarily material things, but whatever keeps persons from centering their lives on God.

The Franciscan way to pray begins with things. The prayer places of those who follow the spirit of Francis and Clare are filled with candles, incense, music, icons, books, holy cards, rosaries, stones, flowers, photos, or whatever it is that leads them to recognize the presence of God in the world, to see the vestiges of a loving God. Following Francis and Clare, Franciscan prayer begins with sense knowledge in a movement from the visible to the invisible world, and it is immediate and intimate. God is imminent in Franciscan prayer, not distant or unknowing. Francis and Clare believed that there was a connection between the material stuff of the earth and the God who created that matter. They believed that in prayer humans, as part of the created world, renew their awareness of their relationship to the Creator and to one another.

Seeing Christ as Center: From the Visible to the Invisible

Franciscan spirituality and theology is preoccupied with the place of Christ in human life and with God's activity in all parts of creation. Francis declared that because Jesus was born of Mary, he took on "the flesh of our humanity and our frailty"[13] The historical Jesus experienced the fullness of humanity with all the limitations of the human condition. He was born in a particular place—Bethlehem—and in a particular historical period—according to the Gospel of St. Luke, during the reign of Caesar Augustus.

The foundation of St. Bonaventure's theology is the conviction that Christ is the center of all reality and that he is the visible Incarnation of the invisible God.[14] These are the poles of Franciscan prayer, the movement from what is seen and heard to that which is not seen but can only be loved. Bonaventure taught that Christ is an example in the flesh of who God is and what God is like. Christ is an image or mirror of God. Moreover, according to Bonaventure, Christ is the model or blueprint for all of creation. Bonaventure's theology finds a scriptural base in St. Paul's Letter to the Colossians 1:15–20:

> Christ is an image
> of the God we cannot see.
> Christ is firstborn in all creation,
>
> Through Christ the universe was made,
> things seen and unseen,
> thrones, authorities, forces, powers.
> Everything was created through Christ and for Christ.

> And before anything came to be, Christ was,
> and the universe is held together by Christ.
> Christ is also head of the body, the church,
> its beginning, as firstborn from the dead
> to become in all things first.

According to Bonaventure's understanding of the Trinitarian life of God, the First Person, the Father, is a fountain overflowing with goodness and love, the *fontalis plenitudo*. The Second Person, Christ, is the outward expression of God's overflowing love. The Spirit, the Third Person, is an inward expression of God's goodness—God's Love aware of itself. Bonaventure uses the homely example of a shoemaker to illustrate how Christ is the exemplar for all creation. He explains that God is like a shoemaker who makes a perfect model of a shoe and places it on his workbench. All the other shoes made by the shoemaker are shaped according to that model, the blueprint. Christ is that blueprint for the human person and for all of creation. In becoming more and more like Christ, humans enter into a clearer likeness and an intimate relationship with God. This is why Christ is the primary example of what it means to become holy.

Bonaventure drew his theology from Francis, who described our human creation as modeled on Christ who is both human and divine. According to Francis, the human body is made in the image of Christ and the human soul is made according to the likeness of Christ.

> Consider in what sublime condition God has placed you and
> that you have been created in the Divine image of the Son of
> God according to the flesh and in his likeness according to the
> spirit.[15]

Therefore, Christ is the model of humanity in both our bodily and spiritual dimensions.[16] Up until the time of Francis, the soul was described as made in God's image, but the body was too infrequently thought of in the same terms.

A section of chapter twenty-three in Francis's *Earlier Rule* of 1221 demonstrates how Francis saw the greatness of humanity in its relationship to the Trinitarian God:

> All-powerful, most holy,
> Almighty and supreme God,
> Holy and just Father
> Lord King of heaven and earth
> we thank You for Yourself
> for through your holy will
> and through Your only Son
> with the Holy Spirit
> You have created everything spiritual and corporal
> and, after making us in Your own image and likeness,
> You placed us in paradise.

Through our own fault we have fallen.
We thank you
for as through Your Son you created us
so through Your holy love
with which You have loved us
You brought about His birth
as true God and true man
by the glorious, ever-virgin, most blessed, holy Mary
and You willed to redeem us captives
through His cross and blood and death.[17]

Francis reiterates that the only motive to account for the creation of persons is God's love, the fullness of love that compelled God to send Jesus as redeemer and savior.[18]

Bringing God's Presence: The Primacy of the Particular

Gerard Manley Hopkins was fascinated with creation's specificity, its "Pied Beauty." Hopkins' poetry flows from his understanding of the Franciscan, Duns Scotus, whom Hopkins read as a young Jesuit seminarian at Oxford. Rather than viewing each material thing as manifesting some attribute of God, such as the lion's strength, the honey's sweetness, or the sun's brightness, Scotus saw material things, each in its own way, as a total image of the Creator.[19] Created things do not reveal aspects about God, but God's beauty as a whole or, for Francis, God's goodness. In the common Thomistic view, things have matter and form. Scotus adds a third component: "thisness." It is a corollary to the Incarnation, for he considers Christ to be the "thisness" of God.[20] Because Christ is a particular example of God, Scotus placed knowledge of the particular as superior to knowledge of universals or abstractions.

Duns Scotus dwelt on the particularity of creatures in his doctrine of "thisness" (in Latin, *haecceitas*). He taught that each person and each material thing is sacred because in being what it is, it manifests God in a unique way. Simply because we are particular creatures, this and not that, we are loved by God. Thus, Scotus understood that things are God-like in their specificity.

The implications of the doctrine of particularity are important in realizing the importance of our individual prayer before God, and how, poor though we may judge it to be, each prayer proclaims the whole of God's glory and goodness. Realizing the sacredness of particularity calls us to know that the smallest act of kindness we perform for our peers, a single word of encouragement to a student, or even a seemingly incomplete job carries with it an entire statement about God and ourselves. Consequently, Franciscan spirituality is marked by diversity more than order, for "God's Grandeur" is evident in the beauty of each individual person and everything that is unique. The spirituality of Francis easily accommodates the fringe characters of life.

In Franciscan spirituality, Christ is seen as the model for all of creation; he is the first absolute in God's plan and greater than any human imperfection or sin. According to another teaching of Duns Scotus, the world is Christ-centered rather than sin-centered. In his doctrine of the absolute primacy of Christ, Scotus argues that even if Adam had not sinned, Christ would have come into the world. Christ's primary mission, then, is to reveal the goodness of God, rather than to redeem us from our sins.

Such an understanding has important implications for the followers of Christ who seek to imitate him. The primary mission of individuals on earth then is not to do a specific work, but to do what Jesus did, which is to reveal the goodness of God. What persons, in fact, bring to the world is not salvation, but the presence of God. Scotus taught that God's primary purpose in becoming human is to be with us, not to save us from our sins. To bring the presence of God must be the primary purpose of all human relations and of the Church in its missionary efforts.[21]

The doctrine of the primacy of Christ as the model for all creation, human and material, lays the foundation for what contemporary writers call the "cosmic Christ." The concept accounts for the universal relationship that Christ has with all of creation, one that inspires confidence that Christ rules over the universe and there is no need to fear the forces of evil. Theologians as early as Irenaeus of Lyons and as recently as Teilhard de Chardin visualize humanity and creation moving toward a point of perfection that finds its fulfillment in Jesus Christ.[22] An understanding of three aspects of Christ is necessary to grasp this concept of the cosmic Christ. Margaret Pirkl, OSF devised this table:

The transcendent Christ	Heart of the Trinity	divine
The historical Jesus	Heart of History	human
The cosmic Christ	Heart of the Universe	cosmic

The transcendent Christ is the eternal word, the logos, the hidden center of the divine. The historical Jesus, the word made flesh, lies at the heart of human history. The cosmic Christ pervades the entire universe "in all its parts" to use St. Paul's words to the Ephesians. Implied in understanding the cosmic Christ is the conviction that material things are christological and illustrate what the Body of Christ is like. Everything in creation adds to a picture of who Christ is in the Incarnation.

Scotus rejected hierarchy in nature for he saw all creatures pointing to nature as the body of Jesus, and the humanity of Jesus as the central point of all the created universe. For Scotus, what created things do that is of value is to be themselves. The activity of created objects cannot be separated from their being what they are. William Short calls this melding of doing and being, a Frank Sinatra kind of theology, do-be do-be do-be do.[23] Scotus follows the theory of association called the univocity of being in which being and doing are related. What the doctrine of univocity of being means in our vocational choices and intellectual work is that who we are as persons speaks with the same authority as what we do.

Cherishing Diversity: The Challenge of a Global Community

The recent realization of humankind as a global community demands that educators have new understandings to teach about the world of today. The so-called globalization of society and rapid advancement of technology create a new insistence on the primacy of persons over structures. The intercultura-tion of modern life places new demands on the meaning of the common good. In our complex society, students must be prepared to respond as whole persons, not as functionaries of an isolated task. Riding on the coattails of scientific advancement are a myriad of life issues regarding the quality of life for the poor, affordable housing, agriculture and the production of food, the distribution of goods, an adequate living wage, a just balance between the local and global economy, genetic manipulation, and the political responsi-bility of each individual for the whole. The present efforts of peacemakers touch these issues: to promote nonviolence, to reduce the effects of racism, to resolve civic and international conflicts, to protect human rights in all corners of the globe.

In 1986 the National Conference of Catholic Bishops raised ethical issues revolving around the globalization of our economy based upon the principle that society as a whole, acting through public and private institu-tions, has the moral responsibility to embrace human dignity and protect human rights.[24] Ewert H. Cousins illustrates how Franciscan spirituality can make a difference for the future life of the planet and its people.[25] Specifi-cally, he examines two areas to which he has recently devoted attention: the global network and interreligious dialogue.

Cousins argues that the Meadows report, *The Limits to Growth* (1972), has brought an increased awareness to the general public of the magnitude of the ecological crisis.[26] Many persons have become aware that this is more than a pragmatic problem to be solved: it is, first of all, an attitudinal prob-lem and, ultimately, a spiritual problem. Francis and Bonaventure provide rich resources for such a spirituality, for each of them sees the relationship between God, the human person, and physical nature.[27] Cousins turns to Bonaventure's "The Life of Saint Francis" to illustrate how Christ is the medium who links the divinity of God to creation:

> [Francis] rejoiced in all the works of the Lord's hands
> and from these joy-producing manifestations
> he rose to their life-giving
> principle and cause.
> In beautiful things
> he saw Beauty itself
> and through his vestiges imprinted on creation
> he followed his Beloved everywhere,
> making from all things a ladder
> by which he could climb up
> and embrace him who is utterly desirable.

> With a feeling of unprecedented devotion
> he savored
> in each and every creature—
> as is so many rivulets—
> that Goodness
> which is the fountain-source.
> And he perceived a heavenly harmony
> in the consonance
> of powers and activities
> God has given them,
> and like the prophet David
> sweetly exhorted them to praise the Lord.[28]

The passage illustrates Bonaventure's concept of exemplarism, by which all creatures are expressions of the Word in the Trinity. Bonaventure sees the reflection of God in the material world and the goodness of God penetrating to the depth of matter and drawing all things back to their source.[29] Consequently, the material world must be respected in its own right as a sacred manifestation of the divine. Such a holistic model can lay the foundation for a spirituality of the environment.

Bonaventure's system also serves as a resource for interreligious dialogue. Cousins names the tension between God who is a transcendent Other and the intimate God of the Trinity. Thus, in Franciscan spirituality all comes together: heaven and earth, humanity and divinity, contemplation and action, one nation and many. The nature of Bonaventure's coincidence of opposites provides a tool to see the disparate positions in Christianity and in various religions related to each other in paradoxical ways.[30]

Educating for Tomorrow in a Franciscan Key

The modern world finds the message of Francis and Clare an attractive one. Franciscan themes of forgiveness, peacemaking, care for the earth, and concern for the poor abound in our Church and society. Francis is the patron saint of ecology; Clare is the patron of television. Yards and patios are dotted with images of St. Francis illustrating his affinity with the birds and the earth. The so-called peace prayer of St. Francis is said and sung across the planet. The world gasped in horror at the destruction of Assisi's sacred shrines in the 1997 earthquake. Assisi is one of the busiest pilgrimage sites to celebrate the new millennium. There is abundant evidence of universal goodwill toward Francis and his simple message to follow in the footprints of Jesus.

Since the time that Anthony of Padua asked Francis how his brothers were to be involved in the intellectual life, Franciscans have struggled with this question. Francis's qualified his endorsement of advanced learning for his brothers, so that "they do not extinguish the Spirit of holy prayer and devotion to which all temporal things must contribute."[31] A later controversy brought a tirade against learning, caught in Jacopone da Todi's *Lauda* 31: "In sorrow and grief I see Paris demolish Assisi, stone by stone. / With all their theology they've led the Order down a crooked path."[32]

More recently, Zachary Hayes outlined positive principles for today's educators that can be garnered from Bonaventure's writings, given that we are "bent over" by the reality of sin.[33] Hayes considers what it means in modern culture to "stand straight" as we were originally created. He describes our modern tendency to limit our vision of reality to dimensions drawn from the positive-physical sciences and to see the world in terms of unlimited aggression and domination. In contrast to this view, to look at the world with the eyes of Francis or Bonaventure is not to see objects defined chemically or controlled for utilitarian purposes. To view the things of the world only as they help to satisfy our physical needs and nourishment is to overlook what is most important about created objects. In the Franciscan spirit, the value of an object is never more important than the fact that it is a "vestige" of the divine, an object that enriches us spiritually by providing us with a contact with the presence of God.

Bonaventure joins knowledge with charity in order that we may be both knowledgeable and loving. "For as humans, we are made not only to know, but also to find joy, peace, and fulfillment in loving transforming union with God."[34] For Bonaventure the goal of education is not only knowledge or power but also the ordering all aspects of life to foster the life of God within ourselves and within others. Education, then, is not a process of dispensing useful packages of knowledge, but rather a process that brings all information—from the arts and sciences and from philosophy and theology—into the service of persons as we struggle with the most basic questions of our existence. Bonaventure promotes what today we call an integrated education in which mind and heart, intellect and will, are bound together as our spiritual core.

Many writers continue to reiterate some of Bonaventure's principles about the vocational call in today's language. Frederick Buechner, one of today's popular spiritual voices, writes, "The place God calls you to be is the place where your deep gladness and the world's deep hunger meet."[35] The spirit of Francis is in this contemporary rhetoric. In the allegory, *The Sacred Exchange*, Lady Poverty asks Francis to show her his cloister. Francis replied, "The world is my cloister," clearly disavowing a separation of sacred and secular. Clare spoke of herself as a co-worker of God, understanding that while God's work of creation was finished, she was an important player to continue the sacred work of creation. At the end of his life Francis said, "I have done what is mine to do, may God teach you what is yours." Their lives are over, but their message is clear: read the signs of the times.

Educators, like all humans, find themselves full of frailty and with limited time and ability. So did Francis. Knowing that he was modeled on the humanity of Christ, Francis spoke often of his *fragilitas*. The human Jesus also possessed finite knowledge and was subject to every human imperfection. However flawed and inadequate our human progress, it is holy precisely because it is human activity. Perhaps acknowledging and grappling with the limitations of the contemporary world is the most important work of the twenty-first century. Embracing Franciscan spirituality means to view persons as good, the gifts of a loving, generous Creator. Believing that God is good and that the world is good gives hope for the next millennium. To follow in the footprints of Jesus in Franciscan spirituality is not a call to perfection, but to know and to love life in its fullness.

Notes

1. In her lifetime, Clare dealt with Popes Innocent III (1198–1216), Honorius III (1216–1227), Gregory IX (1227–1241), Innocent IV (1243–1254), and Alexander IV (1254–1261) as Cardinal Raynaldus.
2. See Regis J. Armstrong, OFM Cap., "Francis of Assisi and the Prisms of Theologizing," *Greyfriars Review* 10.2 (1996), 179–206 for a treatment of how Francis's experience and writing provide a foundation for theological conclusions.
3. Michael Higgins, TOR, "Franciscan Spirituality and Christology," *Resource Manual for the Study of Franciscan Christology,*" ed., Kathleen Moffatt, OSF (Washington, DC: Franciscan Federation, 1998), 229.
4. "The Prayer Before the Crucifix," in *Francis of Assisi: Early Documents. The Saint,* volume 1. ed., Regis J. Armstrong, OFM Cap., Wayne Hellman, OFM Conv., and William Short, OFM (New York: New City Press, 1999), 40. Francis's writings and primary texts will be taken from volume 1 of the translations based on Kajetan Esser's critical edition of the Latin texts and noted here as *FA:ED.*
5. "The Life of Saint Francis by Thomas of Celano," 84 (1228–1229), in *FA:ED,* 255.
6. "The Life of Saint Francis by Thomas of Celano," 94, in *FA:ED,* 263.
7. *The Ladder of Divine Ascent by St. John Climacus,* trans. Colm Luibheis and Norman V. Russell (Mahwah, NJ: Paulist Press, 1982).
8. "The Admonitions," 1, 16–18, 22, in *FA:ED* 129.
9. "The Third Letter to Agnes of Assisi," in *Clare of Assisi: Early Documents* (Saint Bonaventure, NY: Franciscan Institute Publications, 1993), 47.
10. At a national gathering of the Franciscan Federation, a network of groups of Third Order women and men, Joseph P. Chinnici, OFM named respect for life as critical to the Franciscan heritage and inspired a concerted effort to reclaim and proclaim reverence for the Word of God who became flesh and lives among us. His keynote address is published as "The Prophetic Heart: The Evangelical Form of Religious Life in the Contemporary United States," *The Cord* 44.11 (1994), 292–306.
11. *Bringing Forth Christ: Five Feasts of the Child Jesus, St. Bonaventure,* trans. Eric Doyle, OFM (Fairacres, Oxford: SLG [Sisters of the Love of God] Press, 1994).
12. Prayer of the senses is called cataphatic prayer. Apophatic theology, on the other hand, stems from the belief that no human concept is adequate to contain God. Such a theology holds that, except for revelation, God is unknowable, as declared in the title of the fourteenth-century English mystical tract,

The Cloud of Unknowing. Apophatic prayer searches for an unknowable God.

13. "Later Admonition and Exhortation to the Brothers and Sisters of Penance (Second Letter to the Faithful)" 4, in *FA:ED*, 46.

14. See *Bonaventure, The Soul's Journey into God, The Tree of Life, The Life of St. Francis,* ed. and trans. Ewert H. Cousins (New York: Paulist Press, 1978).

15. "The Admonitions," 5.1, in *FA:ED,* 131.

16. Francis's faith in God as the Creator of all things material and spiritual stands in opposition to the heretical beliefs of the Cathari and Gnostics of the early thirteenth century who held that a good god created the spiritual realm and an evil god created physical things.

17. "The Earlier Rule," 23:1–3, in *FA:ED*, 81–82.

18. Saint Paul's Letter to the Ephesians 1:13–14 lays out the human role in the great plan of God that will unite the entire universe in Christ.

19. J. Hillis Miller, "The Univocal Chiming," *Hopkins: A Collection of Critical Essays,* Geoffrey Hartman, ed., (Englewood Cliffs, NJ: Prentice-Hall, 1966), 113.

20. Seamus Mulholland, OFM, "Christ the *Haecceitas* of God, the Spirituality of John Duns Scotus' Doctrine of *Haecceitas* and Primacy of Christ," *The Cord* 40.6 (1990), 165–171.

21. See Margaret Eletta Guider, OSF, "Foundations for a Theology of Presence: A Consideration of the Scotist Understanding of the Primary Purpose of the Incarnation and its Relevance for Ministry in the Underworld of the World Church," in *Resource Manual for the Study of Franciscan Christology* (Washington, D.C.: Franciscan Federation TOR, 1988), 195–203.

22. Dermot A. Lane, *The Reality of Jesus* (New York: Paulist Press, 1975), 134, in Higgins, 214. See Pierre Teilhard de Chardin, *The Divine Milieu; An Essay on the Interior Life* (New York: Harper and Brothers, 1960).

23. William Short, OFM, "Pied Beauty: Gerard Manley Hopkins and the Scotistic View of Nature," *The Cord* 45.3 (1995), 30.

24. *Economic Justice for All; Pastoral Letter on Catholic Social Teaching and the U.S. Economy* (Washington, D.C.: National Conference of Catholic Bishops, 1996). See the commentary by Kevin M. Queally, TOR, "A Franciscan Reflection on 'Economic Justice for All,' the Pastoral Letter on Catholic Social Teaching and the U.S. Economy," *Franciscan Global Perspectives* 2.2 (1982). Also see David Flood, OFM, *Francis of Assisi and the Franciscan Movement* (Quezon City: Franciscan Institute of Asia: Contact Publications, 1989) and Davis Flood, OFM, *Work for Everyone: Francis of Assisi and the Ethic of Service* (Quezon City: CCFMC Office for Asia/Oceania, 1997) for two works that relate the Franciscan tradition to the contemporary social issues in Church and society.

25. Ewert H. Cousins, *Christ of the 21st Century* (Rockport, MN: Element Books, 1992).

26. Cousins, 292, n. 11, Donella H. Meadows, et al., *The Limits to Growth: A Report for the Club of Rome's Project on the Predicament of Mankind* (New York: Universe Books, 1972).

27. Cousins, 293.
28. "The Life of Saint Francis," *Bonaventure: The Soul's Journey into God, The Tree of Life, The Life of St. Francis,* ed. and trans., Ewert H. Cousins (New York: Paulist Press, 1978), 262–263.
29. Cousins, 294, n. 16 points to Francis's Canticle as another example of exemplarism, and he calls attention to Ilia Delio's "The Canticle of Brother Sun: A Song of Christ Mysticism," *Franciscan Studies* 52 (1992), 1–22.
30. Ewert H. Cousins, *Bonaventure and the Coincidence of Opposites: the Theology of Bonaventure* (Chicago: Franciscan Herald Press, 1978).
31. "The Later Rule," 5.2, in *FA:ED*, 102.
32. *Jacopone da Todi; The Lauds.,* trans., Serge and Elizabeth Hughes (New York: Paulist Press, 1982), 123. Jacopone, a thirteenth-century poet, was highly educated before entering the brotherhood of friars. "The Franciscan Charism in Higher Education" is a recent attempt by contemporary educators in Franciscan institutions to articulate how the Franciscan heritage attempts to understand the world through learning; that is, to bridge the gap between Paris and Assisi. "The Franciscan Charism in Higher Education," ed. Roberta McKelvie OSF, *Spirit and Life: A Journal of Contemporary Franciscanism* (Saint Bonaventure, NY: The Franciscan Institute, 1992).
33. Hayes in McKelvie, ed., 18–38. Hayes's essay, "Toward a Philosophy of Education in the Spirit of Saint Bonaventure," was originally published in the *Proceedings of the Seventh Centenary Celebration of the Death of St. Bonaventure* (Saint Bonaventure, NY: The Franciscan Institute, 1975).
34. Hayes, 35.
35. The preface of Jeffrey K. Salkin's, *Being God's Partner: How to Find the Hidden Link Between Spirituality and Your Work* (Woodstock, VT: Jewish Lights Publishing, 1997), eighteen quotes from Frederick Buechner's *Wishful Thinking: A Theological ABC.*

22

Carmel: "Way of the Spirit, the Contemplative Way"

Keith J. Egan

John of the Cross (d. 1591), Carmelite poet and mystic, composed his poetry and the commentaries on his poetry for those called to the "way of the spirit, the contemplative way."[1] In so doing he was harkening back to the origins of the Carmelite Order and was anticipating our need at the beginning of the new millennium for a more contemplative Church and for an academic life that fosters a contemplative disposition in its professors and students. For centuries the monastic life was referred to as the contemplative life, that is a vowed life centered on God. Ancient philosophers had seen contemplation as a higher intellectual function of the human person and, in Christianity, contemplation became a description of a deep and transforming experience of the presence of God. The Carmelite charism, that is, the order's unique gift to the Church, is its insistence on the primacy of the contemplative life, a charism that it offers to the world at large as the global village seeks a more humane, less violent, more centered existence. The goal of the Carmelite tradition is contemplation as the experience of God's transforming love, not in some abstract way but in the practical, everyday reordering of women and men into communities of love. Teresa of Avila's goal for the small Carmelite communities of women that she founded was precisely this transformation: "All must be friends, all must be loved, all must be held dear, all must be helped."[2]

The contemplative life, whether intellectual or religious, is not an esoteric way of life but a way of fully embracing one's humanity, a humanity that finds its completion in a higher wisdom, a higher love. A contemporary Carmelite, Fr. William McNamara, has described this contemplative approach as "taking a long loving look at the real," a description that involves the development of a contemplative disposition that can be a preparation for gifted encounters with God.

There have been centuries of debate over which is better, action or contemplation. This is mostly a false dichotomy. Action or contemplation may be primary, but each must include the other. The Jesuit William Johnston has put it this way: "The authentic mystic can never flee from the world. He or she must resonate with the suffering and the agony that is the common legacy of humankind."[3] The activist without a contemplative grounding is relegated to superficial do-goodism. On the other hand, we must admit that the contemplative way makes demands on the human person. As T. S. Eliot has said: "Humankind cannot bear very much reality." A certain sluggishness keeps the human person from generously opening up to transcendence, to the otherness of mystery and the largeness of the divine. The Carmelite tradition has experience and teachings that offer wisdom to the would-be contemplative, that is, to the person who wishes to develop an ordinary openness to the real wherein is found goodness, truth, and beauty, and who is open to whatever gifted perceptions of the divine one may receive.

There are many obstacles to leading a more contemplative life in the ordinary sense of that word—obstacles that lurk in the very fiber of modern culture. Who isn't confronted from time to time, if not daily, by cluttered schedules, over-busyness, the temptations to self-absorption and ambition (perhaps even to greed), the all-present individualism that so isolates moderns, and the absence of a lively faith that seeks God as the source and center of human existence? The Carmelite tradition seeks to liberate one from the chains or threads that hold one bound to an all-too-small reality. A contemplative disposition means that one seeks to become focused, attentive, mindful, other-centered, and passionate—qualities of life that come to play in study as well as in prayer.[4] A well-developed contemplative disposition makes one open to reality wherever it may be found and disposes one to be available for whatever gifts God may grant. In Carmel, the challenge and opportunity of living the contemplative life have been worked out in the context of a loving community whose aspirations and adaptations in various eras are worth examining.

Carmelite Origins

The Carmelite Order with its contemplative tradition stands as a witness to the primacy of the contemplative way—a means of being more fully human, of accepting one's humanity with its completion in the divine. The Carmelite Order originated on Mount Carmel about A.D.1200, when a group of lay hermits settled at the *Wadi ain es-Siah*, a wadi two and a half miles south of Haifa in what today is Israel. This wadi is situated in a valley looking out into the beautiful blue Mediterranean waters.

The "formula of life" of these first Carmelites describes a group of hermits living in separate cells around an oratory, later identified as dedicated to the Blessed Virgin. Life was utterly simple, with each hermit called upon to "remain in his cell or near it, meditating day and night on the law of the Lord and keeping vigil in prayer." Silence was prized. Eucharist was to be celebrated each day when that was possible, and the hermits were to live committed to a following of Jesus. One can easily see in this formula of life a creative tension between the primacy of solitude and of a supportive and challenging community. The staying power of the Carmelite tradition may well have to do with its ongoing struggle to be faithful to the creative tension which is, in fact, a challenge for every human person: the tension between being person (solitude) and being in relationship (community). The creative response to this tension makes for a lively academic life as well as for a committed life of faith. We, like these medieval Carmelites, if we wish a quality life, must find ways to be more mindful of the potential of the deeper human capacities of intellect and spirit.

Some of the early Carmelites had to leave their cherished home on Mount Carmel as early as 1238, when they emigrated to Cyprus, Sicily, England, and France. In Europe the Carmelite hermits encountered an extraordinary phenomenon: the Dominicans and Franciscans were taking Europe by storm. The followers of Dominic and Francis were ministering to the growing populations of the towns of Europe. These two founders of the mendicant way of life had a new vision of the monastic or contemplative life. As the Dominicans put it: they were intent on sharing the fruits of contemplation with their neighbors. However, the Carmelite hermits seemed, like St. Paul, to be born out of due time (see 1 Corinthians15:8).

By 1247 the Carmelites joined the ranks of the mendicant friars. Like other mendicants, the Carmelites preached, taught, and offered spiritual counsel to their neighbors. In order to participate in this evangelization of the new townsfolk of Europe, the friar orders became student orders, sending their brightest young members (friars like Thomas Aquinas and Bonaventure) to the medieval universities. The subsequent entry of the Carmelites into this evangelization and into university life saw the Carmelite charism develop into one in which solitude now stood in creative tension with ministerial community. No longer hermits, but still with a call to contemplation, the Carmelite friars joined in the great mendicant evangelization of the Western Church. As preachers and teachers, these Carmelites were expected to bring a contemplative spirit to the classroom as well as to the pulpit.

During the Middle Ages the Carmelites discovered the mystical orientation of their calling. The first person to articulate this mystical orientation explicitly was Felip Ribot, a Carmelite provincial from Catalonia, who died in 1391. Ribot spoke of this mystical calling in these words:

> The goal of this life is two fold. One part we acquire, with the help of divine grace, through our efforts and virtuous works. This is to offer God a holy heart, free from all stain of actual sin. The other part of the goal of this life is granted as the free gift of God: namely to taste somewhat in the heart and to experience in the soul, not only after death but even in this mortal life, the intensity of the divine presence and the sweetness of the glory of heaven.[5]

Ribot's work circulated widely, and in the sixteenth century, Teresa of Avila and John of the Cross had ready access to this part of the text, which emphasized the mystical character of the Carmelite vocation. The writings of Teresa and John resonate profoundly with Ribot's mystical orientation. The two Spanish Carmelites—especially Teresa—not only determined the understanding of Christian mysticism for centuries, but they firmly set the contours of subsequent Carmelite mystical horizons.

In the early Church the word *mystic*al referred to the hidden encounter with Christ in the Scriptures and the encounter with Christ in the sacraments of baptism and Eucharist. About the beginning of the sixth century, mystical took on the meaning that a Syrian monk gave it: the personal and extraordinary encounter with the divine. More and more, as time went on, mystical referred to this extraordinary personal phenomenon. However, in our day there has been an effort to return to the sacramental roots of mysticism. In other words, there is a contemporary concern to see the mystical in continuity with the presence of Christ in the sacraments. Ribot, Teresa of Avila, and John of the Cross stress that we can dispose ourselves to God's presence but that the special mystical experience is the complete gift of God's special grace. In our day, the mystical, at least in its foundations, seems more accessible to more people than was thought to be so in pre-Vatican II days.

The Carmelite tradition offers its charism—the development of a contemplative disposition and an openness to God's gift of contemplation—to all who seek to live beyond a superficial awareness of reality, and the Carmelite challenge is to pursue the good the true and the beautiful as they are found ultimately and fully in the divine. Access to this Carmelite tradition comes most readily through the writings of those who have penned the Carmelite classics. Readers will find that these Carmelite classics are for our time what they were for past readers—a vicarious experiences of the journey to a deeper life and an appreciation of the divine presence which writers like Teresa of Avila and John of the Cross describe. Sample yourself and share with your students Teresa's *Interior Castle* or John of the Cross's lush and beautiful poetry. By so doing you will expand the horizons of your students and your own as well.

Carmelite Figures and Their Classics

This brief essay can hardly convey even a partial picture of Carmelite spirituality and what it may offer to those involved in higher education. I shall confine myself to a consultation of some major Carmelite figures who offer guidance into living more effectively the creative tension between solitude and community.

In the following pages, I briefly profile the three Carmelite saints who have been named Doctors of the Church: Teresa of Avila, John of the Cross, and Thérèse of Lisieux. A Doctor of the Church is a saint whose teaching has been designated by the Church as having special significance for the whole Church and for all who seek the divine reality.[6] In addition, I propose to examine briefly the lives and teachings of Edith Stein, the first woman academic named a saint, and her fellow victim of Nazi brutality, Titus Brandsma. We shall seek from these Carmelite wisdom figures some guidance about the Carmelite tradition of solitude and the contemplative way to God.

Let me say at the start that external Christian solitude is always for the sake of a spiritual solitude, an inner awareness of God. Christians like Anthony of the Desert were called to long periods of physical solitude but always so that they may stand in the presence of God. Readers of Thomas

Merton, another contemplative, will note that he, more than anyone in modern times, reminded the modern world of the blessings of solitude. We academics know how crucial some kind of solitude is to effective study. The journey to God is also grounded in solitude. Study and the faith journey have more convergences than our culture supposes.

Teresa of Jesus and John of the Cross

I mention Teresa and John together because they were collaborators in the sixteenth-century reform of the Carmelite Order. This reform retrieved the value of solitude and contemplation for the Carmelite tradition. Moreover, these two Spanish contemplatives have continued to be associated with each other in Christianity's mystical imagination. One needs to interpret Teresa in the light of John and vice versa. Teresa was the primary reformer who invited John, her junior by twenty-seven years, to work with her to reform the Carmelite tradition. Whatever other choices Teresa made, she merits A+ for her choice of John of the Cross as her partner in renewing the contemplative life of the Carmelites. In reforming Carmel, Teresa and John have also made all Christians more aware of their contemplative calling as followers of Jesus. Recall how often the Gospels speak of Jesus going off alone to pray.[7]

Key to Teresa's reform was her conviction that the monastery where she had been living, the Incarnation at Avila, was much too large for the solitude needed for contemplative prayer. When Teresa began to found monasteries for women, she meant them to house no more than thirteen nuns. Eventually that number rose to twenty when it became clear that a larger number was needed so that the nuns could support themselves. The solitude that Teresa sought was inspired by her view of who the first Carmelites on Mount Carmel were.

> So I say now that all of us who wear this holy habit of Carmel
> are called to prayer and contemplation. This call explains our
> origin; we are descendants of men who felt this call, of those
> holy fathers on Mount Carmel who in such great solitude and
> contempt for the world sought this treasure, this precious pearl
> of contemplation that we are speaking about.[8]

Teresa wanted the nuns in her reform to practice what she called the prayer of (active) recollection, to know themselves well, and to be detached from whatever kept them from the love of God. She thought that such a life made them available for God's gift of contemplation. This prayer of active recollection, something like modern centering prayer, was an exercise in focusing often during the day on an event from the life of Christ,[9] a form of prayer congenial even to our overly busy culture. Nor did Teresa see contemplation as some private gift, but as a gift which prepared one to serve for the sake of the Kingdom of God. Toward the end of *The Interior Castle*, Teresa wrote: "This is what I want us to strive for, my Sisters; and let us desire and be occupied in prayer not for the sake of our enjoyment but so as to have this strength to serve."[10] For Teresa prayer and service were inseparable partners.

Teresa of Avila, who called herself Teresa of Jesus once she initiated her reform, realized what many late medieval reformers did not—that reform, new life, renewal, come not through invoking some new organizational structure but through allowing God to take over in one's prayer and life. Teresa knew that holiness is not a human achievement but a gift from God. The contemplative way is precisely that—to invite God to be the center of one's heart knowing then that one is led by God's Spirit. Teresa's initiatives on behalf of solitude and contemplation renewed the contemplative tradition in the sixteenth century. Today Teresa can serve that same function. She is a great storyteller and those who read her stories of God's work within her find in them what the contemplative way can mean for moderns faced with the demands of new and changing cultures. These stories about wisdom of the contemplative way may be found in her autobiography, called the *Book of Her Life*, in the book known as *The Way of Perfection* (which she wrote for young women who wanted her to describe for them how to live the contemplative life), in the *Book of Her Foundations* (which shows her at her storytelling best) and, of course, in her masterpiece, *The Interior Castle*, which is a thinly disguised autobiography of her prayer life. For a look at Teresa's very human and far-reaching interests, don't miss her letters.

Like all good storytellers, Teresa has wisdom about a God-centered life that transcends her own time, broadens our vision, and gives us direction even in this postmodern world where meaning and commitment seem so elusive at times. For Jesus, the great and first commandment was love of God and love of neighbor. Teresa knew that lesson well. In her always practical approach, the contemplative life was measured by one's growth in love of neighbor.

> Here in our religious life the Lord asks of us only two things: love of His Majesty and love of our neighbor. . . . The most certain sign, in my opinion, as to whether or not we are observing these two laws is whether we observe well the love of neighbor. And be certain that the more advanced you see you are in love for your neighbor the more advanced you will be in the love of God. . . . [11]

For Teresa solitude, the mother of contemplation, was the foundation for the growth of love in the human heart. In her guidebook for young nuns, *The Way of Perfection* (40, 4), Teresa wrote that "with contemplatives there is much love, or they wouldn't be contemplatives." Teresa's monasteries were to be communities of friends. What she taught her young sisters, we can learn from her insistence on friendship. From ancient Greece and Rome and St. Augustine, academics should know that we learn better when we are among friends. Teresa thought that we pray better when surrounded by true friends.

The poetry and commentaries of John of the Cross, Teresa's protégé, have given Christianity new understandings of the journey to union with God in love, the contemplative way to God. John did so with uncommonly beautiful poetry of the soul. On three of these poems, he wrote commentaries for those for whom he provided spiritual guidance: "Dark Night," "The Spiritual Canticle," and "The Living Flame of Love."

Like Teresa, John prized solitude. When Teresa met John for the first time, soon after his ordination to the priesthood, he was considering a transfer to the Carthusians. Of these Carthusian monks, Dom David Knowles has written that their "silence and solitude . . . were profound."[12] Obviously John wanted greater solitude than was then available to him as a Carmelite. He let Teresa know that she must not delay in making solitude possible in her reform of Carmel; otherwise she could not count on his collaboration.

John's premise is that not only do we find God in creation, but God is within the human person to be found there through contemplative prayer. In *The Spiritual Canticle* (1, 6), John wrote: "God then, is hidden in the soul, and there the good contemplative must seek him with love." For John, meditation and asceticism are mere preparations for the gift of God's loving presence in contemplation.

In this essay we are exploring John's search for God in solitude and the consequent gift of contemplation as a means of reminding us that the way of listening and waiting, of mindfulness and reflection, so crucial to the work of the academic, has a counterpart in the contemplative journey described by mystics like Teresa and John. The academic search for goodness, truth, and beauty is ever so congenial to the religious and to contemplative search for God. For those seeking God, John has this consoling conviction: ". . . if anyone is seeking God, the Beloved is seeking that person much more,"[13] a precursor to Francis Thompson and his "Hound of Heaven."

If one is intrigued by John of the Cross's sharing of his experience of God, one can turn to John's small corpus of lyrical poetry, some of which is considered among the world's great poetry and, without question, among Spain's finest poetry, especially poems like "Dark Night" and "The Spiritual Canticle" and "The Living Flame of Love." John's surviving letters show him to have been a compassionate spiritual guide. His commentaries on the three poems just mentioned offer one a taste of the demands and the joys that await one who is gifted with a loving union with God. One may object that John's mysticism is not one's cup of tea; yet, a reading of John's texts will greatly enrich one by what T. S. Eliot would call "hints and guesses" of the truth, the goodness and the beauty of God. John is especially lyrical about divine beauty that is shared with the contemplative who has been blessed by union with God. John shares with his readers the following bold conversation with God:

> That I be so transformed in your beauty that we may be alike
> in beauty, and both behold ourselves in your beauty, possess-
> ing then your very beauty; this, in such a way that each look-
> ing at the other may see in the other their own beauty, since
> both are your beauty alone, I being absorbed in your beauty;
> hence I shall see you in your beauty, and you will see me in
> your beauty.[14]

John of the Cross is the poet and the spiritual guide of the journey from solitude to a heart filled with love of God and consequently of love of creation and neighbor. The poem, "The Living Flame of Love," which describes John's deepest experience of God, concludes with these lines addressed to the Holy Spirit:

> . . . and in your sweet breathing,
> filled with good and glory,
> how tenderly you swell my heart with love.

As with Teresa's writings, those of John of the Cross are a gift for anyone who wishes to have a greater sense of the gracious goodness of the divine. Reading the texts of John of the Cross is a cure for the experience of the one-dimensional character of contemporary culture.

Thérèse of Lisieux

On October 19, 1997, during the year of the hundredth anniversary of her death, Pope John Paul II declared Thérèse Martin a Doctor of the Church, the youngest person ever so named. For many observers, Thérèse seems, at first glance, a most unlikely candidate to be ranked among the likes of Augustine, Gregory the Great, Bernard of Clairvaux, Thomas Aquinas, and Bonaventure. For years the popular perception of this young woman whose only schooling consisted of a few years of elementary education was as a pretty, sugar-sweet, and God-spoiled child. A restoration of original documents and careful scholarship, however, have revealed that Thérèse Martin was no Barbie Doll saint with a watered down reading of the Gospels. Thérèse, in only nine years of life in Carmel, became a wisdom figure in the Christian tradition whose life of early losses in the end were transformed into a rare maturity with deep faith and a vocation to love. "Yes, I have found my place in the Church and it is you, O my God, who have given me this place; in the heart of the Church, my mother, I shall be *Love*. Thus I shall be everything, and thus my dream will be realized."[15] Known popularly as the Little Flower, Thérèse, on the other hand, knew herself to be a "winter flower" who grew in unseasonable circumstances to be a wise woman. It was possible for her to hear in a direct and straightforward way gospel wisdom that had been obscured by pieties less inclined to sink deep roots into the ground of human experience and divine revelation.

From early childhood Thérèse knew that she wanted to join her two elder sisters in the Carmelite monastery at Lisieux. Boldly she made her case known to all who would listen, including Pope Leo XIII. She wanted permission to enter Carmel at an age thought unwise even at the time. She won her case and became a Carmelite nun at fifteen. In her short nine years in Carmel, Thérèse came to a profound yet uncomplicated understanding of the challenge of Jesus to love God and neighbor. She also presented Carmel's contemplative tradition, especially the teachings of John of the Cross, in ways that transposed those teachings into language intelligible to the modern mind.

In April 1897 Thérèse wrote to the young priest Maurice Bellière about the inspiration that Joan of Arc had been to her. She added: ". . . but instead of voices from heaven inviting me to combat, I heard in the depths of my soul a gentler and stronger voice, that of the Spouse of Virgins, who was calling me to other exploits, to more glorious conquests, and into Carmel's solitude."[16] The Carmelite contemplative tradition was a call to this young woman to spend her brief life living as fully as she could in the presence of a loving God whose painful absence she experienced in the last eighteen months of her "night of nothingness." During that time she also endured the excruciating pain of a tuberculosis unrelieved by what today would be considered ordinary treatments for this disease and its terrible pain, a disease that brought her young life to a premature end.

This young Carmelite nun left behind some notebooks that were soon gathered together as the *Story of a Soul.* There Thérèse tells of the presence and activity of God in her life. Her correspondence shows her as a wise guide even for others older than herself. And before legislation would allow, Thérèse served as guide for the novices in her community. Her poetry and plays[17] that she wrote for her community of nuns reveal her creativity. Thérèse's community preserved conversations that she had with them in the months before she died.[18] Much can be learned from these writings about a simple, direct journey to a loving God as experienced by Thérèse. Now that scholarship has alerted us that Thérèse Martin was no mere holy card saint but a young woman with a distinctive voice that offers insights into living more contemplatively, her writings have become a legacy that the Church has designated as possessing significant wisdom for modern God seekers. College-age students have much to identify with and much to inspire them in the writings of this youngest of the Doctors of the Church. I have found students avid readers of an autobiography that shares with them traumatic events in her life like the early death of her mother from breast cancer.

Edith Stein and Titus Brandsma

Two more recent Carmelites can serve as models for many of us. They were deeply involved in the academic life of the twentieth century, and their lives were snuffed out by the Nazi extermination of undesirables and those who opposed Nazi ideology. Both of these Carmelites reveal a contemplative approach to their academic life as well as to their search for God.

Edith Stein

Edith Stein was a Jewess, nonbeliever, philosopher, assistant to the phenomenologist Edmund Husserl, Catholic convert, educator, feminist, Carmelite nun, martyr, canonized saint and, as of October 2, 1999, a newly named co-patroness of Europe. All of these facets of the life and heritage of Edith Stein, known in Carmel as Sr. Teresa Benedicta of the Cross, make for a very rich *curriculum vitae.*

Edith Stein was executed at Auschwitz in 1942. The beatification and the canonization of this Jewess murdered during the Holocaust have evoked consternation on the part of some Jews. But no one can contest the intellectual acumen and commitment to the search for truth by this gifted German Carmelite who, as a woman, was excluded from consideration for a university position and later from teaching altogether because she was Jewish.

After her entrance into Carmel, Edith Stein's community at Cologne encouraged her to continue her research and writing. Edith had written her "dissertation" under Husserl on the problem of empathy.[19] Her publications cover a wide gamut—philosophy, pedagogy, women's issues, and spirituality, and Carmelite themes such as her incisive study of the teachings of John of the Cross.[20] When the whole corpus of Stein's writings are available in English, English-speaking academics and religious seekers will have at hand the writings of one of the twentieth century's major intellectuals who integrated so ably the life of the mind and the life of the spirit. Moreover, Stein's interest in and pioneering writings about the education of women are not known well enough outside of Germany.

Edith Stein, who died as a Jew and as a follower of Christ, is a model for intellectuals in a new millennium when there is a need to integrate academic pursuits with one's faith. Edith Stein combined fruitfully many aspects of her life, none more significantly than her academic search for truth and her religious search for God. One night in August 1921, when she was a guest of friends, she read through Teresa of Avila's *Book of Her Life*: "As I closed the book, I told myself: This is the truth." Later she reported: "From that moment on, Carmel was my goal."

As a Carmelite nun, Edith Stein became an exponent of the Carmelite charism. For a Sunday supplement of a 1935 Augsburg newspaper, taking the Carmelite patron Elijah as her model, she wrote: "To stand before the face of the living God—that is our vocation." In this article Stein claimed that the entire meaning of the Carmelite way of life is contained in the challenge of the Rule that "all are to remain in their own cells . . . , meditating on the Law of the Lord day and night and watching in prayer, unless otherwise justly employed."[21]

Edith Stein's solitude and contemplative life in Carmel culminated in the love that made it possible for her to accept a martyr's death. Her life[22] and her writings are a resource for anyone who seeks that all-important integration of faith and learning.

Titus Brandsma

Titus Brandsma was a Dutch Catholic, Carmelite friar, philosopher, exponent of Carmelite mysticism, ecumenist, faculty member and Rector Magnificus (1932–1933) of the Catholic University at Nijmegen, journalist and adviser to Dutch Catholic journalists, emissary of the Dutch Catholic bishops, martyr at Dachau (1942); he was beatified in 1985. This list samples only some of the more outstanding activities in the life of a friar whose actions on behalf of the Dutch Catholic bishops led to his martyrdom. The Nazis found Brandsma's defense of the Jews intolerable.

This contemplative Carmelite, frail and small in stature, with a scholarly bent and a poetic soul, confronted the Nazi oppressors with reasons for opposition to National Socialism. Moreover, he died after ministering to his fellow captives. At the Scheveningen prison where he was first held, Titus composed a poem that showed that the tradition of a separate cell for each Carmelite had so shaped his outlook that even prison cell 577 could not prevent him from living in the presence of Jesus. His poem, "My Cell," concludes with these words: "Stay with me, Jesus, only stay; / I shall not fear / If, reaching out my hand, / I feel Thee near."

Former prior general of the Carmelites Father Falco Thuis has said that the lines from this "simple but moving poem—composed in his cell—embody the nucleus of Carmelite spirituality: the experience of God's presence and of the soul's invitation to union with him"[23] Prisoner Brandsma composed a letter while at Scheveningen which shows him following in his cell a monastic schedule that included a solitude that made it possible for him to live in prayerful communion with God.[24]

During the 1930's Titus Brandsma conducted a lecture tour in North America. These lectures were published as *Carmelite Mysticism: Historical Sketches*, which is a pioneering work that offered English speakers for the first time historical glimpses of the evolution of Carmelite spirituality.[25] Titus Brandsma's appreciation of the Carmelite charism of solitude in community appears throughout these lectures which have inspired others to explore Carmel's charism as a gift for the Church and for all who seek God with that call for purity of heart that Carmel inherited from ancient desert spirituality.

On the feast day of Blessed Titus Brandsma, July 27, the Carmelite liturgy prays in honor of this scholar/teacher:

> Lord our God, source and giver of life, you gave to Blessed Titus the Spirit of courage to proclaim human dignity and the freedom of the Church even in the throes of degrading persecution and death. Grant us that same Spirit so that in the coming of your kingdom of justice and peace we might never be ashamed of the Gospel but be enabled to recognize your loving-kindness in all events of our lives.

Although Titus Brandsma was a busy friar and a very involved academic, his commitment to solitude bore fruit not only in love of God and neighbor but in extensive scholarship and teaching as well. Moreover, his contemplative approach to life prepared him to have the courage to die for his commitments. Prayer and study brought this priest/scholar to convictions that made him an enemy to a regime that scorned those convictions. As a young man, Cardinal Willebrands heard Brandsma lecture and, at his beatification, Willebrands said that Fr. Titus "had a passion for study and learning, inspired by his love for God, because he saw God as the origin and final explanation of all things." The homilist added: "He was a mystic in the true sense of the word: to be absorbed in God, to become one with God, but not to shut oneself up in God and seclude oneself from man and his world."[26] Like Edith Stein, Titus Brandsma's Carmelite charism enabled him to integrate the intellectual and the spiritual. Titus's writings can inspire the academic to strive to do the same.

Sharing in the Carmelite Charism

There are numerous other Carmelite saints, blessed, and just plain holy women and men whose lives have been shaped by the Carmelite tradition. And there is much more to Carmelite spirituality than what has been suggested here. I have long felt that the various spiritual traditions like the Benedictine, Dominican, Franciscan, Jesuit, etc., are not only perspectives on how to live the Gospels more fully. Rather, each tradition has been an exploration of a lived spirituality that consequently has become a theory of spirituality. The women and men of these traditions offer the rest of us tried ways to God, experiences of being Christian disciples. Moreover, their traditions have become what have been known as schools of spirituality. The Carmelite charism is one path to God that involves a call to solitude and to an openness to contemplation, whether that contemplation be a habit of reflection or ordinary sacramental mysticism or the gifted mysticism described by Teresa of Avila in the fourth to the seventh dwelling places of her *Interior Castle*.

The Carmelite charism offers scholars and teachers a spiritual tradition that enlarges and deepens the scholar's commitment to the search for goodness, truth, and beauty. How may one participate in this charism? Some share Carmel's commitment to contemplative ways of prayer through the practice of centering prayer and Christian meditation, the latter as taught by the Benedictine John Main. Carmel has not canonized a method of prayer but rather is eclectic in fostering whatever contemporary forms of prayer tend toward contemplative openness to God. Some scholars participate in the Carmelite tradition through lay affiliation with the order. Many contemporaries, no matter their religious tradition, have participated in the Carmelite charism through the prayerful reading of the texts of the three Carmelite Doctors of the Church and other Carmelite sources. As David Tracy has shown, classics have an excess of meaning to be mined anew by each generation. At the beginning of a new millennium that has inherited a very cluttered culture, the Carmelite charism can be shared by others as an opportunity to live, study, and teach more contemplatively. Study this tradition and you will soon find yourself searching for ways to find daily moments of solitude and moments for contact with the presence of God.

A charism is not for the individual but for the community, to be shared by all who find spiritual nourishment in a particular charism. The Carmelite tradition invites one, anyone, to lay claim to one's capacity for a deeper inner life, a life rooted in various experiences of solitude, so that one may live more fully in the divine presence. There is, of course, the solitude of the desert hermit, but there is also the solitude of a retreat, of meditation, of time alone by the lakeside, or the solitude of listening attentively to Mozart. There is also that inner solitude for which all other solitudes exist, where one can be alone before God so that one may find an imperative for greater attention to one's responsibilities, like teaching and service of neighbor. The solitude of living in the presence of the divine has a practical instructor in the Carmelite Lawrence of the Resurrection, who has reminded his readers to turn regularly to the graciousness of the divine presence.[27] The contemplative, secular or religious, lives with frequent reminders that there are deeper realities than lie on the surface of our consciousness. With T. S. Eliot, greater mindfulness of the ordinary beauty around us can lead to an awareness of the great mystery of the Incarnation.

> The wild thyme unseen or the winter lightning
> Or the waterfall, or music heard so deeply
> That it is not heard at all, but you are the music
> While the music lasts.
> These are only hints and guesses,
> Hints followed by guesses; and the rest
> Is prayer, observance, discipline, thought and action.
> The hint half guessed, the gift half understood,
>   is Incarnation.
> Here the impossible union.[28]

As with other spiritual traditions, the Carmelite charism is a way of being a more authentic human person, a more committed disciple of Jesus, of sharing in a church tradition where all humans must be seen as sisters and brothers. As she lay dying, Teresa of Avila said over and over again, "Finally, Lord, I am a daughter of the Church." Teresa challenged her order and her Church to be more contemplative. Today she challenges all humans to be more human through living and praying more contemplatively, that is, with a listening heart (a *leb somea* in Hebrew). The First Book of Kings (3:9) attributes Solomon's wisdom to his request for a listening heart. No greater gift can the academic wish for than that wisdom which is a combination of love and knowledge that comes from living, praying, studying, and teaching more contemplatively.

Notes

1. *The Ascent of Mount Carmel*, 2.14.1. *The Collected Works of St. John of the Cross:* revised edition, trans., Kieran Kavanaugh and Otilio Rodriquez (Washington, DC: Institute of Carmelite Studies, 1991).
2. *The Way of Perfection* 4,7 in *The Collected Works of St. Teresa of Avila*, volume 2; trans., Kieran Kavanaugh and Otilio Rodriquez (Washington, DC: Institute of Carmelite Studies, 1980), 55.
3. William Johnston, *Mystical Theology: The Science of Love* (London: HarperCollins, 1995), 364.
4. See Walter Burghardt, "Contemplation: A Long Loving Look at the Real," *Church* (Winter 1989), 14–18.

5. A critical edition of Ribot's *Institutio Primorum Monachorum* is being prepared by the Australian Carmelite Paul Chandler.
6. Bernard McGinn, *The Doctors of the Church* (New York: Crossroad, 1999).
7. See Lk 5:16; 6:12; 9:18,28; 11:1; Mk 1:35.
8. *The Interior Castle,* V.1.2.
9. Teresa describes active recollection in *The Way of Perfection,* 28–29.
10. *The Interior Castle,* VII.4.12.
11. Ibid. ,V.3.7–8.
12. David Knowles, *The Monastic Order,* second edition (Cambridge: University Press, 1963), 378.
13. *The Living Flame of Love,* 3, 28.
14. *The Spiritual Canticle,* 36.5.
15. *Story of a Soul; The Autobiography of Saint Thérèse of Lisieux,* third edition; ed. and trans., John Clarke (Washington, DC: Institute of Carmelite Studies, 1996), 194.
16. Thérèse of Lisieux, *General Correspondence,* volume 2; trans., John Clarke (Washington, DC: Institute of Carmelite Studies, 1988), Letter 224, 1085.
17. *The Poetry of Saint Thérèse of Lisieux*; trans., Donald Kinney (Washington, DC: Institute of Carmelite Studies, 1996). The plays are being translated for publication by the Institute of Carmelite Studies.
18. Thérèse of Lisieux, *Her Last Conversations*; trans., John Clarke (Washington, DC: Institute of Carmelite Studies, 1977).
19. Edith Stein, *On the Problem of Empathy,* third edition; ed. and trans., Waltraut Stein (Washington, DC: Institute of Carmelite Studies, 1989).
20. Edith Stein, *The Science of the Cross*; trans., Hilda Graef (Chicago: Henry Regnery, 1960).
21. Edith Stein, "On the History of the Spirit of Carmel, A *The Hidden Life;* trans., Waltraut Stein (Washington, DC: Institute of Carmelite Studies, 1992), 1–6.
22. Edith Stein, *Life in a Jewish Family: Her Unfinished Autobiographical Account;* eds., L. Gelber and R. Leuven (Washington, DC: Institute of Carmelite Studies, 1986).
23. R. Valabek, ed., *Essays on Titus Brandsma, Carmelite, Educator, Journalist, Martyr* (Rome: Carmel in the World, 1985), 8.
24. Ibid., 304–305.
25. Titus Brandsma, *Carmelite Mysticism: Historical Sketches* (Darien, IL: Carmelite Press, 1986, reprint). Another printing has the title *Beauty of Carmel.*
26. R. Valabek, ed., *The Beatification of Father Titus Brandsma, Carmelite (1881–1942), Martyr in Dachau* (Rome: Institutum Carmelitanum, 1986), 74–75.
27. Lawrence of the Resurrection, *Writings and Conversations on the Presence of God;* ed., Conrad de Meester, trans., Salvatore Sciurba (Washington, DC: Institute of Carmelite Studies, 1994).
28. T. S. Eliot, "The Dry Salvages," *Four Quartets.* See *The Complete Poems and Plays, 1909–1950* (New York: Harcourt, Brace & World, 1952), 136.

23

Ignatian Spirituality

Howard J. Gray, S.J.

Ignatius Loyola,[1] founder of the Society of Jesus,[2] described his spirituality as a journey towards God.[3] He envisioned most everything in life as part of that journey—as created realities that facilitated the journey or impeded its progress. Therefore, Ignatius also promoted the need for men and women—pilgrims all—to become people of discernment.[4] Moreover, in that discerning journey, Ignatius believed that there were three guides: Jesus Christ, the mission he gave to his Church, and human experience. Ignatian spirituality is at heart a discerning *pilgrimage* to God[5] guided by three important elements: the reality of *Christ*, the *mission entrusted to his Church,* and *human experience.*

The Pilgrimage

Ignatius did not intend to become a saint. He focused his sixteenth-century ambitions on the life of a courtier. However, battle wounds necessitated his convalescence at his family castle of Loyola. During his recuperation, Inigo, as he was then called, asked for copies of popular romances to lighten his boredom. None was to be found in Castle Loyola so, reluctantly, Inigo read what was available: a life of Christ and a collection of the lives of the saints.[6] This reading ignited in Inigo a desire to serve God alone, a desire that would have been unthinkable to him and all who knew him a few months earlier. Gradually, he determined to turn away from court ambition, to embark on a pilgrimage that was to last years and took him, finally, to studies for the priesthood at the University of Paris, where he gathered a group of disciples who, in turn, presented themselves to the pope as a new religious order.

What was pivotal in this process was Ignatius's—as he now called himself—self-designation as "the pilgrim."[7] He meant the title literally because after Loyola he traveled from Montserrat to Manresa to Barcelona to Rome to Venice to Jerusalem to a series of Spanish university towns, and then to Paris. From city to city, from university to university, Ignatius learned how to discern the movements within his own soul. Out of this inner and outer pilgrimage, Ignatius was also refining the notes of his *Spiritual Exercises,*[8] a guidebook to help other men and women move into Christian discipleship. He himself described this process in these poignant words:

God treated him at this time just as a schoolmaster treats a child whom he is teaching. Whether this was because of his lack of education and of brains, or because he had no one to teach him, or because of the strong desire God himself had given him to serve him, he believed without a doubt and has always believed that God treated him in this way. Indeed if he were to doubt this, he would think he offended his Divine Majesty.[9]

The *Exercises* represent a kind of spiritual journey, as they invite the one who makes them to consider the foundational truths of Christian life: creation as an act of love, human stewardship of creation, sin and forgiveness, the life and work of Jesus as a paradigm of discipleship, Christ's suffering, death, and resurrection and, finally, the surrender of all human life into the hands of a loving God. The Ignatian take on the Christian journey is to insist that it is a movement, an active progress towards a radical decision to live one's life in harmony with Christ's vision and values. The movement towards Christ is both inward and outward, horizontal and vertical, contemplative and active.

The *Exercises* present an intense interiority, a call to spend time noting what in a person's life has been leading to life or to death, to love or to enmity. In that sense, then, the *Exercises* represent the introspective dimension of Ignatian spirituality. The prayer form that captures best this self-awareness before God is the examen of consciousness.[10] In the examen of consciousness the aim is not recrimination but rather a developing alertness to what really motivates a person, to a person's pattern of choices that gradually reveal the character and personality of a woman or man before God. For example, if one notes that all his or her choices are made primarily out of a desire to succeed, then questions confront that man or woman: What do I think a successful life really is? How do I imagine happiness, contentment, fulfillment? This introspective inventory of the soul's desire, especially when conducted in the companionship of an experienced guide, reveals much about the values, ambitions, dreams, and desires of a person.

But the *Exercises* are not only oriented towards self-scrutiny; they also orient the one who makes them towards self-donation. A rhythm of prayerful reflection on the direction of one's life in comparison to the direction of Christ's life constitutes another dynamic within the experience of the *Exercises*.[11] The life of Christ moves from one act of self-donation to another until the climactic self-offering of his death on the cross. The Risen Christ does not exist in some eternal sabbatical, but continues to work through his Spirit—inspiring, challenging, healing, leading. The Ignatian pilgrimage leads towards the mission of this Risen Christ, inviting men and women involved in the Exercises to look outward, beyond themselves, to the mission of the kingdom.

The kingdom for Ignatius is a gift "from above,"[12] from the eternal design of the fatherhood of God who calls all people to be saved. This vertical movement—the descent of God into human minds and hearts and into human structures in order to make all creation a reflection of peace, justice, and love—constitutes another type of prayer in the *Exercises*. Contemplation of the life of Christ as portrayed in the four Gospels leads to discipleship, to a commitment to the Kingdom of God. God reveals in the incidents of Jesus' life the way God wishes to be known, to be loved, to be served.

The service of God, exemplified in Jesus, is also a horizontal movement. This movement reaches out to all other men and women, to all creation, to cultures and nations, to Christians and to people of other faiths. Service to God meant for Ignatius a service that "helps other people." As Ignatius moved through the early stages of his own pilgrimage, he found himself withdrawing from a lifestyle that had been dominated by isolation, penance, and asceticism to a growing solidarity with other people. He could understand this movement towards others only as a desire "to help people." "To help people" became a mantra for Ignatius, and later, for all the other early Jesuits. It was a phrase that epitomized all that gave them energy for their ministries and direction within their works.[13]

This desire to help people guides the discernment of the *Exercises*. The so-called "election"[14]of the *Exercises* is the peaceful resolution of a complex set of movements. Where, finally, does God call you to serve him through helping other people? Ignatian prayer leads to a practical choice about how to live in the world, how to make the gospel credible and vital, how to incarnate within oneself the values of the kingdom. Significantly, the climactic prayer of the *Exercises*, the Suscipe, incorporates these movements into a summary of a contemplative who acts within the world:

> Take, Lord, and receive all my liberty, my memory, my understanding, and all my will—all that I have and possess. You, Lord, have given all to me. I now give it back to you, O Lord. All of it is yours. Dispose of it according to your will. Give me love of yourself along with your grace, for that is enough for me."[15]

In his reflection on the life of Ignatius, the novelist Ron Hansen says, "I have simply been trying to figure out how to live my life magnificently, as Ignatius did, who sought in all his works and activities the greater glory of God."[16] The spirituality Ignatius presented does lay claim to magnificent ambitions and ideals. But the initial process that led to his greatness of vision and spiritual ambition was that of the pilgrimage of God. It was a sustaining metaphor that implied traveling light with the essential baggage being those values preached by Christ. The pilgrimage metaphor also meant a patient willingness to find God through the journeying. It also meant a willingness to risk a process of trial and error, of successes and failures, of some triumphs but also many humiliating defeats. The pilgrimage, finally, meant taking the journey to God by working for the kingdom in the midst of the world, not secluded from it.

Because every pilgrimage involves the willingness to be transformed along the way, Ignatius demands two conditions for every traveler through the *Exercises*. First, the one who makes them must be free enough to discern how God calls him or her, to give time and space for the endeavor.[17] Second, the one who makes them must be generous enough to embrace what God extends to him or her.[18] Thus, contemplative reflection and the generous implementation of what prayer reveals characterize Ignatian spirituality. It is an invitation to become a contemplative who acts.

Centrality of Jesus Christ

The *Exercises* present two dimensions of Christ. First, Christ is the gospel figure whose words and actions symbolize how God would live human life. Therefore, Christ is to be imitated—not in the physical details of his life but in the values, ideals, priorities, lifestyle he reveals.[19] To know Christ, Ignatius insists, is to love him and to love him is to want to serve him. And the service Jesus models is to preach, to teach, to labor, to make God's kingdom available to all people.

Second, Christ is the Crucified and Risen Lord who lives in the glory of the Father but who, through his Spirit, lives in his followers and in the world he loved and saved. This Risen Christ summons every man and woman to read the gospel narratives as invitations to a fuller life and a more liberating love. The gospel narrative does not simply inspire but it has an animating, spiritual power that reaches into the history, psychology, and ambitions of men and women who make the *Exercises*.[20] This communication of the Risen Christ through his gospel stories contributes the principal prayer of the *Exercises*: Ignatian gospel contemplation.[21]

How does Ignatius present this gospel communication, this transforming, religious narrative? There are two features of Ignatian gospel contemplation. The first involves the way one learns how to integrate the gospel story into his or her consciousness. The second involves how one comes to focus on the unique way Christ calls him or her through the narrative.

To understand the method of prayerful integration that Ignatius teaches, we have to look at another source of Ignatian spirituality, the Jesuit *Constitutions*.[22] The *Constitutions* represent the major work of Ignatius's generalship of the Society of Jesus. The *Constitutions* are themselves a kind of pilgrimage that lays out the developmental stages of Jesuit formation, incorporation, mission, and life. In an especially rich section of ascetical and mystical advice, Ignatius proposes the way a young Jesuit can become contemplatively engaged with his world, finding in the world God's activity, design, and direction. What Ignatius proposes we may term *attention, reverence*, and *devotion*.[23] While the immediate context for this Ignatian wisdom is Jesuit formation, the process that he proposes constitutes what he also means by gospel contemplation within the context of the *Exercises*.

By *attention*[24] Ignatius means allowing the reality of the other to be present to you in all its integrity. To be attentive is to be focused, i.e., gently alert to what has been revealed. In our context, it is the gospel narrative in whole or in part. To sustain such a focus demands time, energy, and generosity. Consequently, Ignatius demands these as pre-conditions for making the *Exercises*. It is difficult, if not impossible, for one to make the *Exercises* without taking time to listen, to see, to be present to what God may reveal.

Let us use an example of gospel attentiveness. In Luke 15, Jesus offers the lovely but challenging parable of a prodigal son.[25] A superficial reading tempts someone to go immediately to the core moment, the elaborate welcome and restoration of the younger son extended to him by his ever-patient father. The point of the narrative is that God forgives us. But attention slows this process down. The narrative is a chapter in Luke's Gospel. It is the third in a series of parables in Luke 15. The context is an exchange between Jesus and the religious leaders of his time. The issue is Jesus' intimacy with public outcasts—sinners and tax collectors. These are the people religious authority has judged unclean, to be shunned, but Jesus treats them as his friends, his table companions. Therefore, in the eyes of the righteous, either Jesus is himself sinner or ignorant or defiant of the prevalent ethico-religious social code. In any case, Jesus has pitted himself against the system. The parable is Jesus' answer to such accusations. His accusers have chosen to stand not with the father who forgives but the self-righteous older brother who condemns. Attention takes the time and energy needed to let the density of the episode become my story too. It is the difference between being merely a spectator or an active participant.

Once engaged by the reality of the gospel narrative, Ignatius then asks that the attentive viewer or hearer treat all that he or she has discovered with *reverence*. Reverence for Ignatius is not an artificial piety or a superstitious solicitude. *Reverence* means what one has been attentive to must now be accepted as it is, in its own terms.[26] Reverence is the exclusion of exclusion; e.g., my biases and prejudices, my fears and hesitancies. If attention symbolizes "letting in," then reverence is "embracing what I have let in." For example, I reverence the narrative of Luke 15 when I accept the universality of God's forgiveness as revealed in Christ: "I tell you, there will be rejoicing among the angels of the Lord over one sinner who repents" (cf. Luke 15:10), Or I reverence Luke 15 when I accept the extravagant generosity of the father in the parable as a hint of the free vulnerability of God before a sinner who returns to God. Or I reverence Luke 15 when I accept the profound significance of the words, "to them he addressed this parable" (cf. Luke 15:3). For this means that I accept the self-disclosure of Jesus himself, that this is the kind of God he represents and that these publicans, tax collectors, and sinners, are, indeed, the people he chooses to serve. Reverence helps the one involved in Ignatian gospel contemplation to see sacredness in all aspects of Jesus' teaching.

Out of attention and reverence the one making the *Exercises* progresses to *devotion*, a term rich in significance for Ignatius:

> [F]or Ignatius, devotion was the actualization of the virtue of religion by means of an affection for God which is prompt, compliant, warmly loving, and impelled by charity. Its goal is the worship of God which is accomplished in all things and actions of oneself and one's fellow men [and women], since it gives worship to God by finding and serving God in all things. In the Ignatian vocabulary 'devotion' is intimately linked to

> other key phrases . . . such as union with God, consolation,
> familiarity with God, charity, discreet charity, . . . love, fervor,
> finding God in all things, and the like.[27]

Within the context of the *Exercises*, devotion connotes those specific parts of a gospel episode that speak most tellingly, most personally to an individual. Such moments can be characterized as peace or as a strengthened sense of being called or of a renewed insight into the personality of Jesus. For example, as someone engages more and more with the parable of the prodigal son, he or she may be drawn to the seemingly limitless mercy of the father of the parable. And in this process of attraction, the one making the *Exercises* understands personally, in ways never experienced before, how profoundly Jesus is the Son of just this kind of Father. Devotion represents a privileged moment of personal revelation. It is also a moment when the heart is touched, drawing the person to greater love or deeper faith or surer trust or to a more courageous willingness to follow Jesus. Such moments and such movements are called consolations, movements towards God.[28]

Sometimes the experience of devotion may not be as gentle. There may be reverent attention that draws a person towards a harsh honesty where one experiences the discrepancy between his or her operational values and God's revelation. For example, I may find myself far more at home with the self-righteousness of the elder brother of the parable. I may recognize painfully that I do not want to live with the kind of generosity and forgiveness that the father of the parable dramatizes. I realize that in the deepest part of my heart I am not where God is. Such realizations can shock a person; and its significance can even sadden him or her. But these movements of honest confrontation are also consolations, if they lead to a deeper yearning to be converted into the likeness of Jesus or into a deeper harmony with his discipleship or into a freer acceptance that God's extravagant mercy extends to everyone.

However, if such insights tempt me to discouragement, to cynicism, or to trivialize the entire gospel event so that I move away from its truth or reject it as too idealistic, then I would be moving towards desolation, away from God.[29]

Gospel contemplation centers on persons, especially on the person of Jesus. The aim of such contemplation is to integrate the mind and heart of the person making the *Exercises* with the values and affections portrayed by Jesus. Gospel contemplation works towards union. As a prayer of union, gospel contemplation is both human disponability and divine grace. I bring a focused attention and reverence to the gospel narrative. God draws me through moments of devotion to dwell on a particular facet of the gospel event. This process gradually reveals how I am being drawn to follow Jesus. The question that emerges is: How does someone engaged in the contemplative prayer of the *Exercises* know how God calls him or her here and now, in this concrete situation? The response to this question involves the second feature of gospel contemplation.

The discipline of Ignatian gospel contemplation originates from the structure of the day spent in the *Exercises*.[30] Each day of the full Ignatian retreat has five distinct prayer periods. Each day centers on two gospel narratives, e.g., the Incarnation and the Nativity—the announcement of the birth of Jesus to Mary (Luke 1:26–38) and the birth of Jesus (Luke 2:1–26). These two periods of prayer are followed by two other prayer periods called "repetitions" and a fifth called "the application of senses." This daily structure and rhythm represents important characteristics and principles of Ignatian spirituality. It is crucial to unpack their significance.

First, repetition is not remedial prayer work nor is it a kind of stress-instruction. That is, the idea behind the Ignatian repetitions is not that of doing a prayer until you get is right. Neither is it a crude effort to dictate how a person should find grace or God's leadership. Rather, the repetitions are efforts to engage mystery, to center on the depth of riches within revelation and to discover how God specifically invites this particular man or woman to find the meaning of a gospel event for him or her. In other words, the aim of Ignatian repetition is to personalize prayer. For example, a person hears Mary's *yes* in Luke 1:38. In the initial encounter with this scene, the *yes* of Mary may have been admirable, challenging, and vaguely inviting. In the course of the prayers of repetition the man or woman making the *Exercises* may begin to feel drawn to pronounce his or her own *yes*, to recognize a developing attraction to stand with Mary in personal solidarity with her kind of discipleship. Such a movement will lead in time to a willingness to stand with Mary beneath the cross of her son.

Third, the process of increasingly intense personal engagement with the meaning of the gospel is a gift, a grace. Ignatian prayer is never a performance; it is an encounter. Ignatius insists that this encounter involves two freedoms, human and divine. So delicate is the moment of revelatory encounter that Ignatius insists one of the principal tasks of the guide of the *Exercises* (Ignatius himself avoided the term *director*) is to guarantee that there be no engineering of this encounter. In fact, in a document that guides the interview with candidates to the Society of Jesus, Ignatius instructs the interviewer to halt the process if the candidate indicates anyone had influenced his decision to apply for the Jesuits. The candidate is to be advised to rethink the attraction, to take time to make sure that he is totally free in his decision.[31] From his own experience Ignatius learned the essential importance of spiritual freedom. One can claim grace as genuinely and uniquely *his* or *hers* only if the conditions for a free encounter be sustained. Perhaps an even more crucial reason lies within the Ignatian understanding of discernment and its relationship to Christ. For Ignatius Christ symbolized the privileged moment of human and divine encounter both within Jesus' own consciousness and in his relationship to Abba, the beloved Father.[32]

Discernment is not so much technique as it is an awareness of how God moves within one's life and within the events that surround a person. Discernment for Jesus was whatever in him and in his mission—his work—led to life and to love not to death and enmity. Consequently, Jesus' choices, even his willingness to die faithful to his mission to reveal a loving Father, were expressions based on the affirmation of life and love over death and enmity. For this reason, in the act of discerning love, Ignatius saw the epitome of the Christian imitation of Christ.

The Jesuit poet, Gerard Manley Hopkins, has significantly caught the Ignatian purchase on Christ's significance in these words:

Mark Christ our King. He knows war, served this soldiering through;
He of all can reave a rope best. There he bides in bliss.
Now, and seeing somewhere some man do all must man can do,
For love he leans forth, needs his neck must fall on, Kiss,
and cry "O Christ—done deed!" So God made flesh does too:
Were I come o'er again cries Christ "it would be this."[33]

For Ignatius, then, Christ was the exemplar both of God's self-donation to the human and of the human person's self-donation to God. The *magis*—the greater good—was embedded within a harmony of two seemingly contradictory virtues, humility and magnanimity.[34] The following of Christ meant for Ignatius the freedom of humility and the willingness to risk all for the kingdom of magnanimity. Only in humility and magnanimity can one truly love God and the neighbor and journey confidently as a pilgrim in the spiritual life.

Of course, the question that demands some adequate response concerns this centrality of Jesus Christ in the *Exercises* and in Ignatian spirituality. Does this insistence on the centrality of Jesus effectively restrict this spirituality to believing Christians? One of the great early Jesuit confidants of Ignatius, Jerome Nadal, asserted that the *Exercises* were for anyone who sought peace with God and help in discovering his or her own path to God.[35] The reason Nadal could say this, I believe, was the Ignatian teaching on pastoral adaptation within the *Exercises*. An introductory directive to the one giving the *Exercises* advised the guide to fit them to the faith, education, and experiences of the one who made them. If the experience of the entire *Exercises* was not fruitful for a person, then give only part of them. If a person were capable of making the *Exercises* in their entirety but simply did not have time for thirty-day solitude and prayer away from family or work, then give them over a period of time and in a modified prayer form, e.g., one hour a day.[36] What was indispensable for the *Exercises* were the willingness to commit to them, a singleness of heart before God, a generosity of spirit, and the desire to deepen one's relationship to God in prayer and in everyday life. These dispositions know no creedal restrictions and are open to all men and women of goodwill. Moreover, the values that Christ lived, preached, and taught are founded on Jewish religious experience and have much in common with other religious traditions. In an age of inter-religious dialogue and increasing cooperation among people of goodwill, in professional environments that presume a diversity of beliefs and convictions, we have to live in mutual openness and honest dialogue. Much of the *Exercises* can help anyone. Christ's example can be adapted. What challenges Ignatian spirituality in an ecumenical and pluralistic culture is developing the imagination to make them available to others who are not Christian but who are genuinely seekers of deeper relationships with God.

The Mission of the Church

We have to be up front that as a man necessarily culturally conditioned, Ignatius could not be anything other than a Catholic Christian.[37] Catholicism was a birthright, a hermeneutic for interpreting the meaning of life, and the matrix for his religious and ethical world. What his conversion at Loyola had done was to transform him from a cultural Catholic to a dedicated man of gospel discipleship. We cannot discuss here the complex features of Ignatius's understanding of the Church. Despite what some commentators facilely assert, neither the *Exercises* nor the Society of Jesus were intended to be instruments of the Catholic response to the Protestant Reformation.[38] Rather Ignatius and his spirituality stand within the tradition of *Christianitas*, an effort to make Christian faith alive within a culture and to liberate whatever inhibited the gospel of Christ from informing society, especially in the case of the poor and socially and economically marginated.[39] *Christianitas* was an impulse towards helping people in every way, in soul, certainly, but also in mind, heart, and body. Ignatian spirituality was an effort to animate this mission of the Church. Consequently, Ignatius made an effort to tie the Society of Jesus to the saving mission of the Church and to avoid its politics and its controversies.[40] This particular purchase on church service, to animate its mission, does not neglect the development of Christian values within the believing community: prayer, sacramental life, union among the members, especially the hierarchy and the body of the community of the Church. But Ignatian spirituality is biased towards a Church that is a continuation of the itinerant ministry of Christ, particularly the mission of preaching, teaching, and incorporating the word of God into the lives of people. The model of such mission for Ignatius was Christ as the itinerant preacher, his disciples on their journeys, and Paul in his missionary work. Ignatius Loyola is more a saint of the book than of the altar, although his personal eucharistic devotion was intense and mystical. Ignatius forged a spirituality for the frontiers of faith, that land where belief and unbelief, where the churched and unchurched, where indifference to the lot of the poor and uneducated and profound human pain and need met.[41] Moreover, especially with the founding of the schools,[42] Ignatian spirituality engaged the cultures of the world, its learning, arts, and professions. In this engagement with the secular culture of its time, Ignatian spirituality found an even more profound application of its conviction that contemplation and action can fuse into a harmonious act of virtual prayer. The schools deepened what it meant to be a contemplative in action.

The fourth vow of the Jesuits is pronounced at the time of final profession and made in addition to the three traditional vows which designate a man or woman as a member of a recognized religious-life community in the Church.[43] The three traditional vows are chastity, poverty, and obedience. The fourth vow needs to be understood correctly:

As by now should be clear, no treatment of "mission and the early Jesuits" would be complete without some comment on the "Fourth Vow." The formula, as given in the *Constitutions*, runs as follows:

> I, [name], make profession, and I promise to Almighty God . . . poverty, chastity, and obedience; . . . I further promise a special obedience to the sovereign pontiff in regard to missions, according to the same apostolic letters and the Constitutions.

Seldom in the history of religious life has something as central to an order's identity been so badly misunderstood. The vow is often referred to as the Jesuits' "vow to the pope." This elliptical manner of speaking is misleading in the extreme for it seems to indicate that the vow is made not to God but to a human being. "Vow to obey the pope" is in that regard an improvement, but in every other way misses the point by misconstruing what the vow is all about. The vow does not concern the pope; it concerns "missions," as the formula clearly states. The pope of course figures in the vow, but, as these "missions" were interpreted in the Jesuit *Constitutions*, the superior general of the Society also had a similar authority "to send" members.[44]

What this fourth vow dramatizes is the way Ignatian spirituality describes its special relationship to the Church, i.e., as part of the pastoral mission of the Church. To be in the Church of Christ is to be with Christ on mission. While the historical Jesus no longer walks this earth, his Spirit continues to animate his followers to continue the entire gamut of his ministry: preaching, teaching, reconciling, healing. But it also means a willingness to do this everywhere and in all areas of human life. And it is this dimension of being sent to carry the Gospel message everywhere that especially drives the *action* within Ignatian spirituality. To be on apostolic pilgrimage, adapting the values of the gospel to business, politics, academic life, social action, art and theater, science and technology, is integral to the way Ignatian spirituality expresses itself.

But to be on the mission of Christ through the pastoral presence of his Church means even more. The early Jesuits spoke about their "way of proceeding,"[45] which indicated their particular style of life and service. One aspect of this "way of proceeding" is an overriding determination to work for reconciliation rather than confrontation. Reconciliation is not facile tolerance or a phoney ecumenism—a blurring of honest differences or a muting of essential belief or ethical commitments. For the early Jesuits, reconciliation meant the willingness to emphasize where God dwelt in seeming differences. The best Jesuit missionaries asked not "Can we bring God to you?" but rather, "Where in your culture, in your profession, in your occupation, in your religious experience, in your life does God already exist and act?" Reconciliation is an apriori desire to find how God dwells even in adversaries and to seek to make them friends or, at least, mutually respectful members of a dialogue.

Ignatian spirituality, then, risks leaving the security of domestic faith to find in apostolic pilgrimage new ways to explain the action of God and the significance of the gospel. The early Jesuits exhibited a trust in the generosity of God's presence so that between the culture of Europe and those ancient, but newly discovered, cultures of Asia, Africa and Latin America there could be communication and mutual benefit. This instinct for pastoral mediation was for them an expression of the deeper wisdom of the Church, a wisdom that understood God as at once embedded in a culture and yet greater and more generous than any one culture. Today we would say that from its beginnings Ignatian spirituality included a concern for inculturation as part of its mission in the service of the Church.[46]

As a consequence of this developing missiology, Ignatian spirituality also served the Church by confronting the narrow sectarianism that inhibited the Church from finding God in all things. Of course, some Jesuits failed in this ideal and proved to be as narrow and rigid as any other culturally myopic European. But when a Jesuit truly grasped his own spirituality and what service to the Church through the gospel really meant, he entered generously and, frequently imaginatively, into new pastoral and cultural situations.

Ignatian spirituality today retains its loyalty to the pastoral identity of the Church. It is only one movement among many others in the contemporary Church. But it remains a spirituality reconciling culture and faith, the world and the Spirit, learning and social concern, the human and the divine. Today Ignatian spirituality continues to work for "the greater glory of God" by proclaiming a Church that is a religious event, an epiphany of God's truth and goodness unafraid to reach out to today's world.[47]

As a consequence, Ignatian spirituality sees a Church in the world, and discerning, challenging, confronting, yes, but also in dialogue and, therefore, also learning, growing in self-knowledge through interaction with the world. Is such a spirituality within the Church a risk? Of course, but two realities make this a "holy risk."[48]

First, this is the process whereby the Church came into its consciousness as a world church, moving beyond the world of Jerusalem.[49] Second, it is a way that demands discernment, gospel judgments about how to be the Church here and now. The risk of being genuinely a Church on mission leads us to the third, and final, guide to the Ignatian journey to God: human experience.

Human Experience

Both Christ and the Church invite response. Out of the gospel narratives Christ continues to challenge and to confront, to call people to wisdom and to compassion, to define what God's kingdom is. The Church in all its historical reality and existential presence today continues to engage either the loyalty or the hostility of contemporary men and women. Both Christ and Church are relational realities. By this I mean both have the power to engage the human mind and heart. Engagement assumes relationship of some sort. For example, we say that we believe in Christ or that we belong to the Church. Or we say that we do not believe in Christ or that we do not belong to the Church. For Ignatius there were two aspects of relationships: Do these relationships belong to you? *or* Do you belong to these relationships? To say that something belonged to you meant that you freely chose to let someone else or something else become a part of your life but not to own your life. You remain free, capable of choosing your career, lifestyle, or human partner in the journey of life. True, once you let another reality into your life, you care for that reality, respond to it, and, somehow or other, put this reality into your set of personal priorities. Ignatius called this kind of response "ordered,"[50] meaning such relationships lead—again those words—to life and to love. For example, every human person needs food, drink, affection, knowledge, if she or he is to develop into an integrated human being. But all these realities, and the people who make them possible for us, are meant to help a man and woman to express themselves, to become bearers of ethico-religious realities that most characterize their moral and spiritual selfhood. In other words, I become my choices.

Consequently, if someone were to be so captivated by food, drink, affection, or knowledge that any one of these realities claimed ownership over that man or woman, Ignatius would see this as a kind of slavery, what he would term "disorder."[51] Thus, for Ignatius the foundational human experience was freedom: freedom from all created reality and freedom for God's ownership over a person's life. This kind of spiritual balance—i.e., freedom from and freedom for—he called "indifference."[52] Ignatian indifference does not mean an absence of feeling, affection, pleasure, or care. It does mean that nothing ultimately owns me except God. Therefore, those moments in which I find God, the private solitude of soul that mark my spirituality, lead to God's possession of me. This is not a possession of domination but of love, a blessed companionship, an experience of discipleship intimacy.

Such freedom from and freedom for—this Ignatian indifference—founds the ability to pray peacefully, to discern honestly, and to choose wisely. This is the reason that indifference is an essential element in Ignatian spirituality.

In this environment of freedom, Ignatius believed that one could find both union with God and with all other creation. Ignatius saw human experience not as a bundle of sensations or passing affections but as "memory, understanding, and will."[53] By *memory* Ignatius meant more than simple recall. For him memory was that personal history which constitutes identity, reveals a person's talents, strengths, and weaknesses, and, ultimately, orients a person's deep affections and desires.

By *understanding* Ignatius meant the ability to integrate one's past with his or her present: to see how my childhood was the seed for my adulthood, how every love bestowed prepared one to love, how every moment of grief or joy molded my heart into its humanity.

By *will* Ignatius meant the power to make my ambitions, my desires, my values, my personal priorities come into life so that these personal, treasured realities become the basis for companionship, competency, and service.

This understanding of human experience as freedom expressed in self-possession and in self-donation constituted the only way for Ignatius in which a man or woman could be fully human. Prayer would be both those formal moments in which one encountered God but also those informal, daily moments when a person encountered life and discovered God in the midst of action. The spiritual life became the animating force for both private development and public service.

For Ignatius the greatest human gesture was in those moments when human experience became free self-donation to the God of self-donation. Ignatius called this exchange *liberality*, "the embodiment of that interchange which concretizes and constitutes mutual love."[54]

> The structure of personal love involves two critical and developing insights in the *Spiritual Exercises*, insights that Ignatius frames as a preface the "Contemplation for Attaining Love," but that govern the understanding of love throughout the entire work. First, there is of necessity an integrity between love and life, an integrity in which love manifests itself through its objectification in deeds or in historical events much more than in words or declaration. Secondly, though the closeness of this sequence is not often recognized, the deeds in which love is manifested are mutual liberality. This is a giving and sharing that is termed "*communicacion de las dos partes*," a mutual communion: "Love consists in a mutual communion on both sides, i.e., the lover gives and shares with the beloved that which one has or can attain and also the beloved with the lover." Liberality in Ignatius is neither (as is sometimes preached) a *noblesse oblige* nor simply the love of gratitude; it is the donation and sharing of one's freedom with God as "He himself has given himself to me to the very limits of his power according to his divine ordinances." The liberality of the person is then the response to the divine liberality, because this interchange consists of love. Liberality is the conjunction of grace and human freedom, and it is the direction given to the manifold possibilities that a person is.[55]

Liberality celebrates the great virtue of Ignatian spirituality—magnanimous love.

Conclusion

Ignatian spirituality draws heavily on the personal religious experiences of Ignatius Loyola and the first Jesuits as well as on his *Spiritual Exercises*, the *Constitutions of the Society of Jesus*, his letters, and his dictated memoir of his conversion which is sometimes simply called *The Autobiography*[56] or *A Pilgrim's Testimony*,[57] or *A Pilgrim's Journey*.[58] But it is also a spirituality that has been illumined by centuries of study, research, and pastoral practice.[59] Sometimes a distinction has been made between Ignatian spirituality and Jesuit spirituality with the former representing the experiences of the early Jesuits and the latter expressing developments and interpretations after the death of Ignatius in 1556. In this reflection I have emphasized the Ignatian experience but highlighted the interpretations that have characterized modern readings of Ignatian spirituality.

What I hope has emerged from this reflection is a spirituality highly dependent on experience, tested in the crucible of pastoral ministry, developed through a variety of apostolic demands, notably those of the schools, and practical in nature. Ignatian spirituality is theologically rich but focused primarily on helping people to pray and to discern.

Another dimension I hope comes through these reflections is the flexibility and accommodating character of this spirituality. Of course, the vocabulary and the symbols of Ignatius, particularly in the *Exercises*, reflect his sixteenth-century culture. He saw Christ as the ideal King.[60] He read the Gospels as history.[61] His psychological insights were limited.[62] But when you dig beneath the vocabulary and live closely with his symbols, the wisdom of Ignatius comes through. He understood the human heart, grasped the dynamics of the gospel challenge, saw the mission of the Church afresh, and welcomed the continuous need to adapt principles of Christian spirituality to the concrete reality of persons and cultures.

In short, Ignatian spirituality is a spirituality of pedagogy, teaching ways to make the gospel tradition, Church tradition, and humanist tradition available to people. It is no wonder, then, that the Jesuits found their development of a school system totally compatible with their "way of proceeding." For them education was a spirituality, a way to teach future generations how to find God in all things.

I hope that two other Ignatian realities have emerged in these reflections. First, Ignatius came to trust his own experiences, believing that God dealt directly with him. Second, Ignatius also saw in that process how much God trusted him and all human reality. God revealed God's very self to people. God placed his message of salvation and holiness within the fragile reality of human minds, hearts, and imagination. And if God trusts what was human to bear the divine, so would Ignatius. Trust is the glue that holds Ignatian spirituality together—trust of God, trust of the process of the *Exercises*, trust in fellow Jesuits, trust in people's own experience of God, trust in God's presence in cultures, in learning, in art, in music, in technology. The litany of the objects of Ignatius's trust goes on and on. Ultimately, Ignatian spirituality trusts the world as a place where God dwells and labors and gathers all to himself in an act of forgiveness where that is needed and in an act of blessing where that is prayed for.

Such a spirituality breathes a plurality that is not a ploy but simply a result of its own integrity. It is a spirituality that rejoices in the multiplicity of Christ's presence in the world of his Father's making:

> . . . For Christ plays in ten thousand places,
> Lovely in limbs, and lovely in eyes not his
> to the father through the features of men's faces.[63]

Ignatian spirituality is, then, the Christian experience, faithful to its foundation in the gospel, eager for the translation of that gospel in and through the times we live.

Notes

1. Two helpful and available introductory volumes on Ignatius and his major works are: *Ignatius of Loyola, Spiritual Exercises and Selected Works*, ed. George E. Ganss, S.J. (New York: Paulist Press, 1991) and *Saint Ignatius of Loyola, Personal Writings*, trans. Joseph A. Munitz and Philip Endean (London: Penguin Books, 1996). A solid, readable biography is that of Jose Ignacio Tellechea Idigoras, *Ignatius of Loyola, The Pilgrim Saint*, trans. Cornenilus Michael Buckley, S.J. (Chicago: Loyola University Press, 1994).

2. The best English introduction to the Society of Jesus and its foundations is John W. O'Malley, S.J., *The First Jesuits* (Cambridge, MA: Harvard University Press, 1993).

3. The phrase is also translated "a pathway to God." It is found in *The Formula of the Institute* which incorporates the document the first companions and Ignatius presented to Pope Paul III in 1539, describing their proposal for a new religious order, cf. *The Constitutions of the Society of Jesus*, trans. George E. Ganss, S.J. (St. Louis: Institute of Jesuit Sources, 1970) [3], p. 67.

4. The literature on Ignatian discernment is extensive. The most thorough treatments in English are Jules Toner, S.J., *A Commentary on St. Ignatius' Rules for the Discernment of Spirits* (St. Louis: Institute of Jesuit Sources, 1982) and *Discerning God's Will: Ignatius Loyola's Teaching on Christian Decision Making* (St. Louis, 1990). A briefer popular summary is his "Discernment in the Spiritual Exercises," in *A New Introduction to the Spiritual Exercises of St. Ignatius,* ed. John E. Dister, S.J. (Collegeville: The Liturgical Press, 1993), pp.63–72.

5. John C. Olin, "The Idea of Pilgrimage in the Experience of Ignatius Loyola,"*Church History* 48 (1979), pp. 387–397; Howard J. Gray, S.J., "What Kind of Document," *The Way Supplement* 61 (Spring 1988), pp. 24–25.

6. Cf. Tellehea Idigoras, *Ignatius*, pp. 119–121.

7. *A Pilgrim's Journey, The Autobiography of Ignatius of Loyola*, trans. Joseph N. Tylenda, S.J. (Wilmington: Glazier, 1985), n.15, p. 23, Cf, Tolenda's note on 15–16, p. 22.

8. A succinct but authoritative narrative of the composition of the *Exercises* can be found in *The Spiritual Exercises of Saint Ignatius*, trans. George E. Ganss, S.J. (St. Louis: Institute of Jesuit Sources, 1992), the Introduction, pp. 2–4. It is this translation of the *Exercises* that I shall use in this essay.

9. This translation is from *A Pilgrim's Testament, The Memoirs of Saint Ignatius of Loyola*, trans. Parmananda R. Divarkar (St. Louis: Institute of Jesuit Sources, 1995), n. 27, p. 39.

10. For a thorough and helpful exposition of this prayer, cf. George A. Aschenbrenner, S.J., "Consciousness Examen," in *Notes on The Spiritual Exercises of St. Ignatius Loyola*, ed. David L. Fleming, S.J. (St. Louis: Review for Religious, 1981), pp. 175–185.

11. An excellent analysis of this kind of prayer, Ignatian gospel contemplation, is that of Brendan Byrne, S.J., "'To See with the Eyes of the Imagination . . .' Scripture in the Exercises and Recent Interpretation," in *The Way Supplement* 72 (Autumn 1991), pp. 3–19.

12. I.e., *de arriba*, cf. the comments in Ganss, *Ignatius of Loyola Spiritual Exercises and Selected Works*, p. 474. The classic exposition of the term and its significance is in Hugo Rahner, *Ignatius the Theologian* (New York: Herder and Herder, 1968), pp. 1–31.

13. O'Malley, *First Jesuits*, pp. 18–19.

14. *Exercises*, cf nos.135–189, pp. 64–80. An extended treatment on the meaning of the Ignatian election can be found in Michael Ivens, S.J., *Understanding the Spiritual Exercises* (Trowbridge: Cromwell Press, 1998), pp. 128–145.

15. *Exercises*, n. 234.

16. Ron Hansen, "The Pilgrim," in *A Tremor of Bliss, Contemporary Writers on the Saints*, ed. Paul Elie (New York: Riverhead Books/Berkeley, 1995), p. 112.

17. *Exercises*, nos. 5, 16, 18–20.

18. Ibid. nos. 15, 16, 19–20.

19. Ivens puts this well in his *Understanding the Spiritual Exercises*: "The 'imitation of Christ' is a total quality of life, a quality consisting not in external mimicry, but in a transformation of one's inner experience by the assimilation of Christ's own experience. Here one seeks to be taken into this experience in prayer, and hence to promote the further development of it in one's life. Such a prayer consists in contemplating the Christ of the Gospels as in the *Exercises* themselves, seeking the grace 'to feel with the Incarnate Word, as he reveals himself, looking and hearing, touching and tasting, in the gospel word'" (p. 185).

20. It is the same process outlined by Luke Timothy Johnson in "The Process of Learning Jesus," in *Living Jesus, Learning the Heart of the Gospel* (San Francisco: Harper, 1999), pp. 57–75.

21. Cf. note 11 above.

22. Cf. note 3 above.

23. *Constitutions*, n. 250.

24. An important discussion of *attention* can be found in Pierre Hadot, *Philosophy as a Way of Life*, trans. Michael Chase (Oxford: Blackwell, 1995), pp. 126-144.

25. My reading and application of the parable relies on: John R. Donahue, S.J., *The Gospel Parable, Metaphor, Narrative, and the Theology of the Synpotic Gospels* (Philadelphia: Fortress Press, 1988), pp. 151–162; *The Gospel According to Luke*, Introduction, Translation, and Notes by Joseph A. Fitzmyer, S.J. (Garden City: Doubleday, 1985) Vol. II, pp. 1082-1094; *The*

Gospel of Luke, Commentary by Luke Timothy Johnson (Collegeville: Liturgical Press, 1991), pp. 234–242.

26. Charles O'Neill, S.J., *Acatamiento: Ignatian Reverence* in *Studies in the Spirituality of Jesuits* 8/1 (January 1976).

27. *Constitutions*, Ganss note 5, pp. 155–156.

28. Michael Ivens comments in *Understanding the Spiritual Exercises* are a helpful addendum to my remarks: "It must be noted, first, that both consolation and desolation are defined as *spiritual*, the relation to the spiritual being positive in the case of consolation, negative in the case of the 'anti-spiritual' movement of desolation. To recognize these spiritual movements, one needs to be generally sensitive to the whole fluid and elusive realm of one's feelings and reactions: but not every kind of positive or negative mood or stirring recognizable by a self-aware person is to be equated with 'consolation' and 'desolation' as understood in the *Exercises*. In the last analysis, consolation 'consoles' because whatever its form, whether unambiguous or implicit and discreet, it is a felt experience of God's love building up the Christ-life in us. And what characterizes every form of spiritual desolation is a felt sense of dissonance which is the echo in consciousness of an influence tending of its nature to undermine the Christ-life, and hence in the case of a person who remains fundamentally Christ-oriented to contradict their most deep-seated inclinations"(p. 206).

29. Ibid. Also Michael J. Buckley, S.J., "The Structure of the Rules for Discernment of Spirits," *The Way Supplement* 20 (Autumn 1973), pp. 19–37.

30. *Exercises*, nos. 45–72 gives the paradigm of a day of the retreat.

31. *The General Examen*, c.3, n. 51 in the Ganss edition of the *Constitutions*:

> "Does he have a deliberate determination to live or die in the Lord with and in this Society of Jesus our Creator and Lord? And since when? Where and through whom was he first moved to this?
>
> "If he says that he was not moved by any member of the Society, the examiner should proceed. If the candidate says that he was so moved (and it is granted that one could licitly and meritoriously move him thus), it would seem to be more conducive to his spiritual progress to give him a period of some time, in order that, by reflecting on this matter, he may commend himself completely to his Creator and Lord as if no member of the Society had moved him so that he may be able to proceed with greater spiritual energies toward greater service and glory of the Divine Majesty."

32. Harvey, D. Egan, S.J. "A Christ Centered Mysticism," in *Ignatius Loyola the Mystic* (Wilmington: Glazier, 1987), pp. 86–118.

33. Gerard Manley Hopkins, *A Critical Edition of the Major Works*, ed. Catherine Phillips (Oxford: Oxford University Press, 1986), p. 168.

34. Ivens, *Understanding the Spiritual Exercises*, p. 75.

35. O'Malley, *The First Jesuits*, pp. 38–39.

36. *Exercises*, nos. 18 and 19.

37. The historical reality of Ignatius is increasingly emphasized by scholars, e.g., Ganss' general introduction in *Ignatius Loyola, Spiritual Exercises and Selected Works*, pp. 10–26.

38. John W. O'Malley, S.J., "The Historiography of the Society of Jesus: Where Does It Stand Today?' in *The Jesuits, Cultures, Sciences and the Arts, 1540–1773*, ed., John W. O'Malley, S.J., Gauvin Alexander Bailey, Steven J. Harris, and T. Frank Kennedy, S.J. (Toronto: University of Toronto Press, 1999), pp. 3–37.

39. O'Malley, *The First Jesuits*, pp. 87–88; p. 327.

40. Ibid., C8, "The Jesuits and the Church at Large," pp. 284–328.

41. John W. O'Malley, S.J., "Mission and the Early Jesuits," in *The Way Supplement* 79 (Spring 1994), pp. 3–10.

42. Ibid., pp. 6–7; O'Malley, *The First Jesuits*, pp. 239–242. Indeed, the entire volume, *The Jesuits, Cultures, Sciences, and the Arts* illustrates this.

43. John W. O'Malley, S.J., "The Fourth Vow in Its Historical Context: A Historical Study," *Studies in the Spirituality of Jesuits,* 15 (January 1983).

44. O'Malley, "Mission," p. 7.

45. This phrase is rich in connotation. In many ways O'Malley's *The First Jesuits* is all about their "ways of proceeding," cf. pp. 370–375. In the recently published volume, cited above in nos. 38 and 42, its contributors emphasize the same pervasiveness.

46. Again a recurring theme in *The Jesuits, Cultures*; see pp. 342–349 on Ricci and Valignano.

47. I am thinking of General Congregation 34 of the Jesuits, held in Rome from January 5 to March 22, 1995. Its pivotal decrees on mission, justice, culture, and inter-religious dialogue illustrate the commitment; *Documents of the Thirty-Fourth General Congregation of the Society of Jesus*, ed. John L. McCarthy (St. Louis: Institute of Jesuit Sources, 1995).

48. Cf. Decree, "On Having a Proper Attitude of Service in the Church," from General Congregation 34.

49. *The Acts of the Apostles*, ed. Luke Timothy Johnson (Collegeville: Liturgical Press, 1992), "Universality," pp. 16–18.

50. *Exercises*, nos. 2, 21, 97.

51. Ibid.

52. Ibid., n. 23.

53. Ibid., n. 50.

54. Michael J. Buckley, S.J., "Freedom, Election, and Self-Transcendence: Some Reflections upon the Ignatian Development of a Life of Ministry," in *Ignatian Spirituality in a Secular Age*, ed. George P. Schner, S.J. (Waterloo: Wilfrid Laurier University Press, 1984), p. 72.

55. Ibid.

56. Ganss, *Ignatius Loyola*, pp. 66–67.

57. Divarkar, *A Pilgrim's Testament*, p. vii.

58. Tylenda, *A Pilgrim's Journey*, p. ix.

59. Cf. O'Malley, "Historiography," footnote 38 above.

60. E.g., Hans Wolter, "Elements of Crusade Spirituality in St. Ignatius," in *Ignatius Loyola, His Personality and Spiritual Heritage, 1556–1956*, ed.

Friedrich Wulf, S.J. (St. Louis: Institute of Jesuit Sources, 1977), pp. 97–134.

61. Ganss, *Exercises*, n. 63 on p. 163.
62. W. W. Meissner, S.J., M.D., *Ignatius of Loyola: The Psychology of a Saint* (New Haven and London: Yale University Press, 1992).
63. Hopkins, "As kingfishers catch fire," in *Gerard Manley Hopkins, Critical Edition*, U. 12b–14, p. 129.

24

The Vincentian Tradition

Evangelizare Pauperibus Misit Mei

Dennis Holtschneider, C.M.

Introduction

Vincentian spirituality begins and ends with the evangelization and service of the poor. Ours is a mission-based spirituality, rooted in action, undertaken in partnership with a God who has a particular concern and love for those on the margins of human society. This love of God moves those who call themselves "Vincentians" to action on the poor's behalf.

Higher education, in this tradition, does not grow out of a particular intellectual framework or heritage. Certainly, there have been notable scholars among the Vincentian membership throughout the centuries, but the present work of higher education emerges from a social and ministerial mission. Higher education is seen as a powerful method of breaking the social evils of poverty and advancing the progress of poor people economically, socially, and spiritually.

Because this spirituality is so mission-based, it is best learned in the lives and activities of Vincent DePaul, his contemporaries, and present-day followers.

Vincent DePaul

Not unlike many others of his era, Vincent DePaul pursued and accepted ordination as a step out of the humble means into which he had been born. His farming family had been able to educate him at a local college of Dax for his preparatory studies and also for the first two years of his bachelors studies at the University of Toulouse, but difficult times at home soon forced him to seek employment privately tutoring and running a boarding house in order to meet his own expenses. After seven years formal study, Vincent was ordained to the priesthood in 1600 at nineteen years of age, six years under the minimum prescribed age. The French Church did not always enforce the minimum age but, to be safe, Vincent sought out an ordaining bishop who was both elderly and blind for the ceremony.

Vincent's earliest years of priesthood are somewhat unclear, although two stories remain of his attempts to reclaim a stolen inheritance and a controverted benefice he believed to be rightfully his. During these years,

Vincent studied in Rome and eventually sat for and passed his bachelors exam in theology from the University of Toulouse. He eventually relinquished his claim to the benefice and returned to Paris in 1609. Here he secured the position of "official almoner" to Queen Marguerite, the first wife of Henry IV. The position made him one of several cleric almoners and placed him in rank below other clerics who would have served as confessor and spiritual director to the queen. Such a position provided him the time to study and successfully sit for his licentiate degree in canon law from the University of Paris (the Sorbonne). Ironically, this position of privilege also introduced him to the bleak lives of the urban poor at the *Hôpital de la Charité*, one of the queen's favorite charities.

Vincent resigned the position of almoner in 1612 at the encouragement of his spiritual director, Cardinal de Berulle—founder of a priestly reform movement known as the Oratorians—and tried for a time to pastor the villagers of Cliche, France. In later years, Vincent would look fondly on those days in Cliche, but twelve months after his arrival, he returned to the halls of privilege to serve as family chaplain and tutor to the children of Monsieur de Gondi, Lieutenant General of the King's Galleys and brother of the bishop of Paris. As before, his position ironically immersed him in the life of the poor.

Madame de Gondi owned extensive property in Picardy, Burgundy, and Champagne, and frequently asked her young chaplain to accompany her on her trips to inspect her lands. Here, Vincent quickly became familiar with the lives of the rural poor who worked Madame's lands. He began to visit these workers regularly and to say Mass and hear confessions for them. These simple and regular interactions with their poor began to challenge Vincent's career path of chaplaining wealthy benefactors. One story in particular served to summarize the changes in Vincent's priorities. One day Vincent was called to hear the confession of an elderly, dying man on the de Gondi estates. Vincent heard the confession and was shocked to realize how close this man had come to dying with serious sin on his soul. For the simple lack of a priest, the man might have lost his soul. Within this theology that framed his concern, Vincent's heart was deeply moved. The incident illustrated to him, and to those who began to join him for periodic missions on the estates, how completely the poor had been abandoned by France's clergy at that time, and at what terrible cost to their salvation.

Nearly forty years of age, Vincent began to notice a progressively wider circle of people whose religious needs were unattended. He began organizing missions to the many laborers on Madame de Gondi's widespread lands. He soon extended those missions to the convicts sentenced to row the French fleet's ships, over whom Philip de Gondi was general. The desperate situation of these men and their families led Vincent to organize relief efforts on their behalf.

Desiring to apply himself full-time to the needs of the rural poor, Vincent accepted the pastorship of Châtillon-les-Dombes, in southeast France. Here he discovered a sick family at home who were starving simply because they were too sick to manage their lands, and Vincent preached on the situation

one Sunday. Chaos ensued for, by that afternoon, there was a line of parishioners all bringing food to the one house Vincent had mentioned. The food
would have gone bad had it all been left at the one house, and Vincent knew
well that there were other families in as much need as this one. In later years,
Vincent would tell the story of this chaotic moment and his realization that
the parish charity had to be better organized. He designed simple procedures
that following week so that poor people within the locale received dependable assistance from their neighbors. This simple, parish-based "Confrater-
nity of Charity," as he named it, soon spread to other parishes throughout
France.

According to Vincent, much of what followed in his life sprung from
these formative experiences. The combined entreaties of the bishop of Paris,
Vincent's spiritual director, and Madame and General de Gondi convinced
Vincent to return to Paris after only five months with the parishioners of
Châtillon-les-Dombes. There he was promoted to chaplain of the de Gondi
Estates and Chaplain-General of the Royal Galleys. The position offered him
regular contact with the powerful of France, making it easier to fund and pro-
mote his charitable works and organizations.

Tapping this network, he organized the Ladies of Charity, a circle of
France's wealthiest women, to fund and organize many charitable works
throughout Paris. In 1625, he organized a band of priests and brothers—the
Congregation of the Mission—to evangelize the poor and to see to their more
temporal needs. He offered priestly training for seminarians and weekly conferences for diocesan priests so that they might learn priestly practice and
spirituality, believing that the poor deserved good priests. At the request of
the queen, he sat on the Council of Conscience and led the effort to reform
the appointment process for bishops and abbots, ending the tradition of
appointing children and unqualified individuals. With Louise de Marrillac, he
founded the Daughters of Charity, a community of women who gave full-
time, direct service to the poor. Louise also assumed the day-to-day organization of the many Confraternities of Charity spreading throughout France.
Together with these many groups and individuals, Vincent and Louise provided religious education and spiritual guidance, created soup kitchens and
job training programs, taught young women to read, trained priests and seminarians, organized hospitals for the sick poor, ministered to prisoners and
galley slaves, nursed plague victims, raised abandoned infants and children,
and found food and shelter for the vast influx of rural poor into Paris during
the Thirty Years' War and Fronde.

Vincent lived long enough to see the work of his priests and sisters
spread beyond France, to Italy, Poland, Ireland, Scotland, and Madagascar.
He had organized charitable action on behalf of the poor throughout all of
France, and then on an international scale. Through his work on the Council
of Conscience, his training of priests and seminarians, the advice given to
royalty and episcopacy, and the work of his priests, sisters, and other collaborators, he had helped transform the French Church. Popularly called the
Father of the Poor and the Light of the Clergy, Vincent was given the hon-
orific, Patron Saint of Charity at his canonization in 1737.

A Vincentian Spirituality

In the midst of an extremely active life, Vincent DePaul created no formal school of spirituality, *per se*. He did, however, have strong, experience-based beliefs about the way in which his similarly active collaborators should advance in holiness and integrity of life. To his mind, activity and prayer reinforced each other. People best fed their spirits when they gave their energies and talents to the service of the poor. People best directed and sustained their activities when they took time to nourish their spirits. High-minded ideas or spiritualities that failed to lead to useful action were suspect to Vincent:

> Let us love God, my brothers and sisters, let us love God, but let it be with the strength of our arms and the sweat of our brow. For it often happens that the various affective acts of the love of God and the interior motions of a humble heart—even if they are good and desirable—are nonetheless suspect if they do not result in effective love. Our Lord himself says: "In this is my Father glorified: that you bring forth very much fruit."

Vincentian spirituality believes deeply that God works amidst the poor, and that time spent among the poor offers enormous opportunities for spiritual growth. One learns generosity, patience, deep respect, humility, and unconditional love. One grows in self-knowledge. The social values of fame, beauty, and wealth slowly lose their power, allowing the inherent beauty of all people, including the marginalized, to come forward. One also gains a fresh perspective on Jesus Christ, who was born poor and spent his own life among the poor.

Vincent considered all work for the poor to be a continuation of Jesus' labors. He summarized this frequently with the maxim, "Jesus Christ is the Rule of the Mission," by which he meant not Jesus' teachings, but Jesus' person. For that reason, Vincent encouraged his followers to examine deeply the life, motivations, and purposes of Jesus, with an eye toward incorporating those same virtues and goals.

> If the Congregation, with the help of God's grace, is to achieve what it sees as its purpose, a genuine effort to put on the spirit of Christ will be needed. How to do this is learned mainly from what is taught in the gospels: Christ's poverty, his chastity and obedience, his love for the sick, his decorum, the sort of lifestyle and behavior which he inspired in his disciples; his way of getting along with people; his daily spiritual exercises; preaching missions; and other ministries which he undertook on behalf of the people. [Common Rules, 3]

The goal of such meditation was never simply for one's own growth or salvation, but also to extend Jesus' historical ministry to the poor into the present. The present Constitutions of the Congregation of the Mission states it this way: "The love of Christ, who had pity on the crowd (Mark 8:2), is the source of all our apostolic activity, and urges us, in the words of St. Vincent, 'to make the gospel really effective'" (SV, XII, 84 [Constitutions, 11]).

Vincent knew well and spoke often of the difficulties of working with the poor: their unreasonable demands, lack of gratitude, offensive odor or demeanor; of the overwhelming river of human need. To sustain oneself for a lifetime of service, Vincent insisted that his followers care for their spirits. This was critical to Vincent. "It is necessary to tend to our interior life; if we fail to do that, we miss everything" (Dodin, Andre, *Vincent dePaul and Charity*, 54). Toward this end, he recommended regular participation in the Eucharist and a daily period of meditation. The meditation, he encouraged, could be quite simple. Often beginning with Scripture or some other inspirational text, Vincent taught his collaborators to linger on the topic being presented (nature), consider how and why this idea might be helpful (motive), and finally create some simple way in which the idea could be put into practice that day (means). Finally, Vincent also recommended that, sometime each year, his followers undertake a retreat experience for more extended prayer and reflection, allowing God to refresh and reorient one's spirit.

Although Vincent encouraged time apart from the work in order to nourish one's spirit, he did not necessarily separate the spiritual and earthly realms. Vincent's spirituality was strongly incarnational, believing that God was best encountered in the persons of the poor. Vincent firmly believed that God's voice could be found and heard in the midst of service and activity. "We have to sanctify our occupations by seeking God in them and by doing them to find God in them rather than to get them done" (Dodin, *Vincent dePaul and Charity*, 55). One heard the voice of God best when one "listened" within the gambit of a day's work—whether from a co-worker, a lesson learned in the doing, or from the mouths of the poor themselves. Vincent took quite literally the passage from Matthew 25, that whatsoever is done to the least of these, is done to Jesus. This engendered enormous respect for those being served: "I must not consider a poor peasant or a poor woman according to their outer appearance, nor in what I see of the capacity of their mind. But see the other side of the picture and you will see with the light of faith that the Son of God, who became poor, is personified for us in the poor" (*Like a Great Fire*, 23).

The social and spiritual initiatives that Vincent came to understand and accept as "God's will" were enormous in scope. In response, his spirituality grew both collegial and institutional. He drew into the work all who could be helpful, and insisted that one's spiritual progress could be forged alongside others. Whether Queen Anne of Austria, the highly educated doctors of the Sorbonne, the youngest, illiterate volunteer for his "Daughters of Charity," or the poor themselves, Vincent would welcome the generosity of whoever put their skills at the service of the poor. He believed in the power of large-scale organizations to accomplish God's will, provided that these institutions constantly adapted and changed according to the changing needs of the poor. God's will always needed to be sought out, not only because human beings are slow to understand God's plan but also because the world is dynamic, and

God may at any moment send us new needs to which to minister. Organized together—religious and lay, poor and wealthy, women and men, educated and illiterate—Vincent sought to create a worldwide force that simultaneously assisted the poor and enabled its workers to grow in holiness.

Foundation and Evolution of Vincentian Colleges in the U.S.

Vincent DePaul never envisioned his followers entering into the work of higher education outside of seminary formation (Poole, 1973, vii; Poole, 1988, 291). The early Vincentian missionaries to the North American territories, however, found higher education a useful means to accomplish their seminary goals. A small band of Vincentian priests and brothers came to the United States in 1816, accepting Bishop DuBourg's invitation to evangelize the settlers in the upper Louisiana Territories and to found a seminary there. They found in America, at the time, a tradition of opening college preparatory programs that served both local lay students and clerical prospects. This model suited the Vincentians' traditional works, for colleges could serve as a base for rural missionary outreach and the lay students' tuition supported the cost of seminary education (Power, 36; Gleason 4).

The dual-mission was not to last long, however. In the late nineteenth and early twentieth centuries, a trend toward free-standing seminaries progressively took hold. This trend contributed to the closure of several Vincentian colleges. Those that remained relinquished their programs or plans for clerical education, and adopted a new mission. Local bishops were concerned that the large waves of Catholic immigrants were not welcome or could not be accommodated in other U.S. colleges, thereby limiting Catholics' movement into the U.S. mainstream. The bishops hoped that new Catholic colleges would facilitate this movement, as well as reinforce the Catholic values of these young men as they graduated and entered more fully into the U.S. culture. The Vincentian priests and brothers accepted this mission. Soon, the Daughters of Charity and Sisters of Charity opened their own colleges to accomplish the same goals, focusing particularly upon the needs of young women.

By the 1980s, the Vincentian colleges and universities had grown substantially and had adopted Vincent DePaul's outreach to the poor as a primary source of institutional direction. Serving the children of the immigrant classes, the universities began to speak of the power of a college education to break the cycle of poverty, both for individuals and for the larger society. Financial aid was increasingly focused toward their needs. Statistics began to be kept on how many students from families below the federal poverty line were accepted into the universities. Opportunity programs to assist students from underprivileged backgrounds proliferated. Research centers were begun to investigate poverty. New employee orientation programs focused upon Vincent's life. Community outreach projects to poorer sections of the city were sponsored. Service-learning was required of students in the classroom, putting them in direct contact with economically poor people. Systematic efforts were begun to introduce all members of the university to the life and teachings of Vincent DePaul, with the hope that all members of the university community would take inspiration and guidance from his example. Individuals were hired and charged to advance the university's "mission" and "identity." Institutions that had been formed to continue Vincent's mission of educating the clergy had now reinvented themselves as bearers of his legacy to serve the poor.

Putting the Mission into Practice

One need not work at a Vincentian university, nor necessarily belong to one of the groups Vincent founded, in order to take on this legacy and mission. One must, however, place the poor at the center of one's concern; work on their behalf and do so in partnership with the God that cares deeply for the least of his people. Most post-secondary institutions do some outreach to needy students. Some serve large populations of such students.

There are many direct ways to put higher education at the service of the poor. Faculty are permitted what is perhaps the most central role in this process. Through their instruction, faculty—whether teaching Thomas Aquinas, Virginia Wolfe, or John Maynard Keynes—educate the poor and their children and thereby break the vicious cycle of poverty within family units. Their education of first-generation college-goers enables new immigrant groups to the United States to enter the social mainstream. The stronger the education, the higher the standards and the better a student's future prospects and personal development. Stubbornly believing in students' potential, at times when they themselves do not appreciate it, is perhaps the greatest gift faculty offer.

All college students experience times when they need the assistance of support personnel in order to stay in college. This is particularly true of students from impoverished backgrounds. Without the intervention and interest of financial aid counselors, mentors, academic enrichment, and support services, student life professionals, coaches, dorm supervisors, activity coordinators, health professionals, secretaries, and many, many others, students from poor backgrounds often leave college prematurely. By offering such support services to needy students, these individuals make key and critical contributions to the success of these young men and women, and thereby further the Vincentian mission.

There are also less direct, but equally powerful ways of furthering the Vincentian mission within the world of higher education. Research agenda turned toward the poverty in society can help identify and moderate the underlying causes of this social evil.[1] Universities' considerable institutional resources (e.g., knowledgeable experts, volunteers, meeting space, contacts) can be offered to other agencies and community groups with complementary goals and, thereby, join in a larger effort to combat poverty in a given community. Perhaps most importantly, a university can instill within all its citizens—rich and poor alike—a love for the poor and a desire to improve the lot of the poor. By so doing, a university develops another generation of "Vincentians" to carry Vincent's vision forward.

Regardless of the particular work one might undertake on behalf of the poor, no one can reasonably call themselves "Vincentian," unless they pray. A Vincentian spirituality asks us to integrate our work lives and spiritual lives. These cannot be mutually exclusive in a Vincentian spirituality. One must bring the work to prayer, and bring the fruits of one's prayer to the work. The prayer helps enormously to keep focus, perspective, and motivation. So long as one is always aware that the care of the poor is God's work, and that we only play a part, one can avoid the disillusionment and burnout that is so common to those who labor among the poor. It also helps one remember the love God has for these people, and their inherent dignity. More importantly, as we slowly come to realize our own inner poverty, and the love God has for us, we are freed to serve generously with full hearts. We incrementally come to see the poor as brothers and sisters, rather than the objects of our charity.

No amount of prayer or hard work, however, can substitute for coming to know the poor personally. To be a "Vincentian," one must go a step further than working and praying for the poor. One must meet a poor person and come to know her or him. Vincent believed, with all his heart, that God most works upon our souls through the poor themselves. Their lives, their stories, their worldviews: all transform our own perspective. We grow because of our relationships with them. The prospect of meeting or conversing with the poor can cause no small amount of fear. Those who do not come from poverty must overcome their fear of rejection by the poor, the fear of danger, or the simple fears of the immense difference between the lives of the poor and their own more privileged backgrounds. Any Vincentian can easily recall the days of their initial fears, their awkward moments of first conversing with poor people, and the relationships that soon blossomed. While the initial fears are real, the courage to meet the poor leads to wonderful relationships, the learning that the lives of the poor are not as different from ours as we first thought, and an immense freedom that one's world has gone beyond the boundaries of race or economic status. To be a Vincentian, one must come to know the poor. Academe's "ivory tower" cannot—by definition—be true of Vincentian education.

To be a Vincentian, one must also seek out a community of support. Vincent never permitted his missionaries or Daughters or Ladies of Charity to work alone. Instead, he required that they always have at least one other person alongside them for support. Work for and with the poor can be tiring and frustrating, and one needs the company and wisdom of others who are similarly committed. This community can be as simple as a friend with whom one labors; as wide-ranging as a group that meets by website; or as formalized as a group that meets regularly for prayer, reflection, and group service. Any work for the poor is commendable, but without some sense of community support, it is not Vincentian.

Finally, for work to be considered "Vincentian," one must have a larger view of a poor person's "need." It is not enough merely to work for the students' financial and social advancement, one must also work for their spiritual well-being. In the end, Vincent was most concerned for the salvation of the poor. While his theology may be somewhat different from our own, his central concern remains critical. The capitalistic and individualistic ethos of U.S. society is as easily assumed by the poor as by those with great means. Giving the poor money, resources, education, political power, and entrée into the mainstream of society does not guarantee that they will be any better off as human beings. Happiness and wholeness is not based upon one's resources, and Vincentians must always be careful to foster and support the values that lead to ultimate happiness. At Catholic universities, students can be taught the Roman Catholic tradition as an interpretive framework and spiritual support for their professional lives.

Presenting such students a religious tradition as an interpretive framework and spiritual support gives them a strong moral base for their professional lives and a protection against the real danger of confusing and reducing their economic advancement to mere financial enrichment.

Strategic Decisions of Who Will Be Served

Individuals and institutions that wish to implement Vincent's vision sometimes stumble on the question of who is to be served: Who are "the poor"? How exactly are "the poor" to be defined? The question is important, for definitions of who will be served are also definitions of who will be excluded. If one adopts a strict definition, such as limiting one's charity to those below the federal poverty index, the "working poor" would be excluded—a group that clearly struggles financially. Too strict a definition might also limit the number of wealthier students whose tuition dollars could offset the financial aid burden that the presence of needy students places upon a university. If one adopts a broad definition (e.g., all those without education are poor), the mission would apply to any student at all, and the ivy-league colleges could, in that one sense, call themselves "Vincentian institutions." The Congregation of the Mission itself wrestled with these questions through the 1970s and 1980s. In 1992, its Eastern province chose to define the poor using a U.S. government economic measure that included both those below the federal poverty line and those considered the working poor. Tacitly, the assembly also recognized the universities' financial need to enroll "full-pay" students as well, but encouraged the universities to expand the number of poor students who were served.

Strategically, the Vincentian universities in the United States have never aspired to become "Catholic community colleges," even if that would mean that larger numbers of poor people could be offered a college education. Nor have they sought to become highly selective, research institutions, since the attendant costs would prevent poor students from attending. Instead, they have sought to walk a delicate balance between selectivity and accessibility, between offering an excellent liberal arts education and keeping the costs low enough for poor people to attend. This strategic choice brings with it daily tensions and balances, but the Vincentian universities have chosen to live with those tensions in the name of providing an excellent education that is available to the poor.

Vincent himself did not have a narrow definition of the poor. When selecting those who would receive his charitable attention, he focused more upon the marginalized, unassisted, and needy, than upon a particular economic measurement of poverty. Generally, he responded to individuals and groups whose needs became known to him over time, rather than seeking out and restricting his charity to those fitting a predetermined economic profile (Carvin). At the same time, Vincent clearly believed that those with economic means had more access to resources than the poor, and preferred to give his energies to those without the financial resources to successfully manage their lives in society. This flexible but focused definition of "poverty" is important for those who would follow in Vincent's footsteps, for not all charitable work is necessarily "Vincentian." For example, offering tutoring to students whose grades are substandard is unquestionably an act of charity, yet Vincent himself left the tutoring of wealthy children to others, and focused his own energies upon those without economic means. Vincent's heart was always with the poor. Within this subset of human need, however, there is extraordinary variety and opportunity for charitable work.

Educational Institutions and Vincentian Spirituality

Vincentian spirituality is not a "top-down" spirituality, but the stuff of grassroots. People embrace this spirituality when they come to know and care about the needs of poor people. The power and advantage of institutions is that they bring together similarly committed people to support one another and to accomplish large works together. In the end, the Vincentian spirituality is a practical tradition meant to support those who accept and undertake this partnership with a God who actively cares for the poor.

Universities do not fully realize the Vincentian mission. Few of the world's peoples have or require a college education. Even in the United States, little more than half of the population attains a postsecondary degree. Worldwide, there are nearly two million individuals who claim Vincent DePaul as the tradition and inspiration behind their work for the poor. Educational apostolates are but a fraction of their work to feed, clothe, house, train, employ, heal, organize, enfranchise, and evangelize the world's marginalized.

Nor does the Vincentian mission fully encompass the mission of a university. Both are so much more than the other. As a *university*, a Vincentian university pursues all of the traditional purposes and activities of a university, particularly teaching, scholarship, and service—with rigor and generosity of spirit, for the poor deserve nothing less than a fine education. As a *Catholic* university, the university offers students the wealth of the Catholic intellectual heritage for their reflection and integration. It offers the Church a place where theological and philosophical scholarship is encouraged and nurtured.

The Vincentian character of the institution, however, adds additional focus and purpose. Those who work within the institution are part of a larger effort to educate the poor, to ameliorate the suffering of the poor, to instill a love for the poor. Education within the Vincentian tradition is a means to a larger social and religious goal: the evangelization and social advancement of the economically poor.

Notes

1. "Fathers and Brothers of the Mission, search out more than ever, with boldness, humility and skill the causes of poverty and encourage short and long term solutions; acceptable and effective concrete solutions. By doing so, you will work for the credibility of the gospel and of the Church" (Address of John Paul II to the delegates of the General Assembly of 1986. Osservatore Romano, English Edition, August 2, 1986, p.12).

Sources

Carvin, John. (1979). *Vincentiana*. "The Poor: An Attempt to Fathom the Mind of St. Vincent." Rome: Congregatio Missionis Curia Generalitia.

Gleason, Philip. (1995). *Contending With Modernity: Catholic Higher Education in the Twentieth Century*. New York: Oxford University Press.

Poole, Stafford. (1973). *A History of the Congregation of the Mission, 1625–1843*. Privately printed.

Poole, Stafford. (1988). The Educational Apostolate: Colleges, Universities, and Secondary Schools. *The American Vincentians: A Popular History of the Congregation of the Mission in the United States, 1815–1987*. Ed. John E. Rybolt. Brooklyn: New City Press.

Power, Edward J. (1958). *A History of Catholic Higher Education in the United States*. Milwaukee: The Bruce Publishing Company.

Part IV

Discipleship and the Practices That Sustain Us

25

Accidental Discoveries

Elizabeth Johns

"You shall love the Lord, your God, with all your heart, with all your soul, and with all your mind" (Matthew 22:37).

This has been my quest.

Yet, throughout my youth and early womanhood, to integrate the intellect, the emotions, and the spirit in a lived life seemed impossible. How strongly did the mystical poet Rilke's indictment of intellect ring true: "The mind is but a visitor: it thinks us out of our world" (Rilke, *Book of Hours: Love Poems to God*). I knew myself to be intelligent, I loved learning anything new, and I found my great solace in reading, but until my early thirties I could never have conceived of myself as having an intellectual autobiography—then or ever. My world was that of many women my age (I was born in 1937), subtly but clearly subordinate to that of men. It was practical, domestic and, on the emotional level, frequently miserable. I still regret this but, on the other hand, if I'd not had to recognize it and make the wrenching changes to leave it behind, I would not know much of what I think I know today.

This start from behind does not describe my spiritual life, however, and for this I'm grateful. Always I believed God was near, even through the years of college doubt that most of us embraced. Having been raised as a Protestant, I was a faithful Lutheran throughout young and early middle adulthood, even as individualist and matter-of-fact Reformation Christianity took a heavy toll on my spirit. During these long years I felt bogged down in words, and alone rather than part of a community. The spiritual world I lived in was certain but cold.

Then, in my early fifties, just after I'd moved to my present position in Philadelphia, a new acquaintance recommended that I try an eight-day retreat at the Jesuit Center for Spiritual Growth in Wernersville, Pennsylvania. Because I was quite tired and relished a "vacation" that would take place in the countryside an hour and a half's drive from Philadelphia, I signed up. That retreat, in the summer of 1990, was like an earthquake. Until then, I'd never even heard of spiritual direction. I'd never prayed with Scripture. Those eight days were the beginning of astonishing newness, a growth I look back on as breathtaking, but also as prepared for me by God from the very beginning of my life. From then on, with increasing sureness and depth, I lived into my awakened sense of the sacramentality of everyday life and the breadth of Christian community all around me. I became a Roman Catholic in 1992 and made the Spiritual Exercises of St. Ignatius on a thirty-day retreat the next summer. As I devoted myself to understanding and then practicing the Ignatian ideal of contemplation in action, I began to see in a new light what I had already done with my life and how I could hone and develop it. By that time, I'd been teaching on the college and university level for twenty-five years.

Just how has Ignatian spirituality informed this daily life?

In the first place, I have always found vitality in the imagination. Ignatius's instruction to imagine the scriptural passages in all their concreteness as we pray was a capability I'd long relished, in fact, absolutely depended on, in my reading. Even as a child I could not live more than twenty-four hours out of reach of a book without hazarding a dreadful emotional low. Typically I read novels. Over the years, after I finished college with an English major, I had long lists of major novels to "get through," lists I dreaded completing. I loved the establishment of place, the development of character, the language—the very sentence structure—with which authors accomplished their magic, and I found it easy to immerse myself in the imagined scenes. Eliot, Hemingway, Tolstoy, Defoe, O'Hara—I was almost indiscriminate. They all held me in thrall. But they didn't inform what I did with the rest of my time; they simply made the rest of my time manageable. In my mid-twenties, I got an M.A. in literature, luxuriating in the necessity that I spend hours every day with my nose in a book.

Not until I entered a doctoral program did I begin to sense that I had in fact an intellectual life. I realized that the work of the imagination is fundamental to *thinking*, and that, moreover, it did not have to separate me from who I was the rest of my day. I'd begun graduate study for practical reasons: at thirty-three, with two small children and three years of teaching literature, I knew I'd need a Ph.D. as a "ticket" to any future long-term job. During my first semester of course work in the interdisciplinary program in which I'd enrolled, I signed up for an art history course. It was my introduction to the field, and the topic was American art of the nineteenth century.

Within a month I was hooked on the discipline, and my fascination with the temporal character of reading began to yield to enthrallment by the spatial presence of images. Behind each static picture, I realized, were the worlds of temporality that I'd cherished in reading: the houses in which people loved and hated, the conversations in which they revealed themselves, the storms and snowdrifts that signaled their inner lives. Images were like a book pleading to be opened: a wondrous intersection of individual uniqueness, artistic tradition, and cultural history. They offered intimacy outside of my own life—closeness to the artist who made them and an irrefusable invitation to decipher the world at the moment of their making.

As a beginning scholar attempting to piece together these moments of creation, I found that I positively thrived in archives. They were the rich remains of the human past, of God's children living their lives. To read letters (especially in manuscript form but even on microfilm), to scan old newspapers (looking for something in particular but living thoroughly and with great expenditure of time in the details about everything else), to look through pamphlets and broadsides—I lost myself in sheer joy. I was mesmerized by the quotidian: lurid details in newspapers about murders, people who could write holding pens in their toes, and menageries with animals straight from "the dark continents"; holes cut out of letters by descendants anxious to preserve reputations, peculiar collections of prints and broadsides, books with uncut pages. The very smell of a library enchanted me, and much to my great fortune, in my first appointment as an art history professor (after several years of teaching literature and interdisciplinary humanities), I was able to roam the shelves of the Library of Congress to research first one project and then another. Without that privilege, I doubt I'd have found what I did in the way of evidence, nor ever conceived of even looking for such material in the future. From the beginning I had loved, it seems, the small and the large of human life. Novels had fed my imagination; now I used that well-exercised faculty to probe the endless implications of pictures, the possible meanings of historical moments. In flashes of insight about what I was doing, I saw myself as relishing the sacramentality of details out of love for God, for God's world and God's creatures—the human community.

This brings me to the second aspect of Christian spirituality that informed my intellectual life: one doesn't simply revel privately in richness of understanding; one acts on it, or acts out of the richness. I perceived that I was bringing my self with all my capabilities and failures and unperceived desires to probe the mystery of people who had lived before me.

The first artist I wrote on was Washington Allston (1779–1843), a South Carolinian who worked in Cambridge and spent much of his early career in England and Rome. He was a close friend of Samuel Taylor Coleridge, whose work I'd known since my days as a student of literature. Although I wrote a creditable thesis on Allston's theory of the imagination (1974), its relationship to that of Coleridge, and its embodiment in Allston's paintings, I didn't come into my own with the material until several years after I finished the dissertation and published from it. I wrote an essay on the relationship between Coleridge and Allston, calling their friendship "remarkable." That was twenty years ago, and I still think the essay itself was remarkable. From my vantage point I see that even then I did my best work in writing about individuals, in working from the inside out and the outside in to probe causes and effects, patterns, darknesses, foibles, blind spots, brilliance, and the strange and inexplicable character of what one creates from the uniqueness of personality.

After several short-term projects I jumped next into what became a complex study of Thomas Eakins (1844–1916), the Philadelphia painter known primarily for his portraits of rowers and surgeons. He was also famous, posthumously, for the many years in which he had been misunderstood and rejected. Planning a long article on one major picture, I undertook to "explain" the group portrait that first mesmerized me—*The Gross Clinic* (1875)—but in rummaging through archives I got caught up in the wealth of material from nineteenth-century Philadelphia that threw light on everything else Eakins painted. As if obeying a command from outside myself, I went on to write a fairly long book to cover the "everything else," as well. Sleuthing through archives, libraries, and historical societies up and down the East Coast, I worked for five years on the project, during which even my daily conversation became more and more preoccupied with Eakins. I felt my juices flow when I read a magazine article from 1870, or correspondence from and to people I did not know; I let out a whoop in more than one rare book room when I found things that had not yet appeared in the scholarship. I once even dated a check for 1880 rather than 1980. I was determined to create an Eakins that no scholar before me had found—and I did, for as I later saw, I'd not written a book on him before and so, of course, the book was unique, uniquely me. For this is another quality of "contemplation in action," or praying the lived life: even our most common acts are shaped by our uniqueness.

My book on Eakins was published in 1983, when I was in my early forties. Like Eakins and his sitters, I was ambitious, competitive, and convinced that I would achieve my success by dint of hard self-discipline and resistance to the opinions of others. Afterwards, I was exhausted. For at least a year I was in withdrawal, as I later explained it, from so intimate an involvement with another person and another time.

Recovered, I saw that discretion more than valor was called for in my choice of the next few projects. I was also "overdosed" on the late nineteenth century, had thought quite enough about portraiture, and was eager to learn about a different period. I retreated from engagement with one person, and one era, and took up involvement with an entire social world. I looked to several artists who, in the years before the Civil War, painted "genre pictures," or scenes of what misleadingly has been called "everyday life." For this project, I tried to understand the group mentality of the ambitious citizens who saw themselves as leaders of the American citizenry from what was the "center" of American culture: New York City. I studied the politics and economics of the period until my friends ran when they saw me coming; I looked at caricatures; I read stories, newspapers, and broadsides. I recognized stereotypes everywhere, and I bristled. The social thrust of my own politics came to the fore. I found the individual artists absolutely boring—it was the cultural collusion that had me in its grip: citizens at the "center" putting down Yankees, Westerners, blacks, women, and immigrants.

Publishing that book in 1991, and moving on to several small projects that made further use of some of the material, I next accepted an invitation to look at landscapes, a refreshing change from people to nature. This project was a comparative exhibition and book which three of us undertook as co-curators, to look at the ways that artists had presented the landscape in Australia and the United States in the nineteenth century. All my experience living in distinct regions of America came into play here. As I spent time in Australia, I noted how I was comparing the dirt, the vegetation, the light, the very smell of the air, with those phenomena I'd experienced across the U.S. As I'd known not one single Australian picture before this project, and had written hardly a word on American landscape, I brought almost no brief to the work. Throughout my years as an adult, however, I'd always pondered, What is "nature"? How do we make it our home? How do we want to see it? The book and the exhibition (1998) were at the same time the most expansive project I'd worked on and the closest to my spiritual awareness of my own physical rootedness in the earth.

I've about finished what I think will be my last big study, a book on Winslow Homer (1836–1910). Bold enough at last to return to individual biography and the late nineteenth century, I conceived the project in 1995, when I was in a hospital with serious pneumonia. Lying in bed with an I.V. in my arm, I kept thinking about what my career as an art historian had meant. How could writing about artists come most closely to God's perception of us as creatures? Four years later, I continue to see the manuscript on Homer as drawing on every capacity that is "me." Interpreting correspondence, an intricate network of family relationships, the minutest parts of pictures and, through it all, the spiritual life of a man who was intensely private, this book comes from the insights of my late fifties and early sixties into what I've learned over a lifetime. I'm using Erik Erikson's theories on identity and the life cycle to interpret Homer's decisions; they interpret mine as well.

The long and the short of my intellectual life as a scholar is that I have loved what I brought into being—what I researched and wrote and arranged exhibitions about—and I have needed heart, soul, and mind to do it. Putting words together that are truest to what I found in libraries and in pictures has been to bring new truths into being. If I couldn't see a truth coming, the projects never got off the ground: they didn't stimulate something in my history or my imagined future. I've hated the mechanical preparation of manuscripts and the endless correspondence for photographs and permissions to publish, but throughout this intellectual work I have been joyous to find that the "me," the "I," whom I'd earlier seen as beside someone else's main point, was very much a main point.

Yet, I might never have probed this capability to live a life of the mind, to say nothing of integrating it with a public life as a scholar, if I had not started teaching. In this matter, I'd come upon a situation that brought even more of my early fragmentation into clarity. I'd gotten my first position (in 1968) through something of a fluke. With a master's degree I arrived in a small town in the South just as the local college had an unexpected vacancy. It was August—and within two weeks I was in the classroom, teaching composition and literature and a team-taught interdisciplinary humanities course funded by the National Endowment for the Humanities. I was thrilled to have an "identity" that was clearly not subordinate to someone else's "real" work, not domestic, and not without utility. Yet, I hadn't the faintest idea of what to do.

And *doing* was essential. Christ enjoins us with "Whatever you do to the least of these, you do to me" (Cf. Matthew 25:40). Rilke has a particular resonance for me in his insistence that our dailiness is *to* the point rather than *beside* the point. He begins his poem about the intellect with, "Only in our doing can we grasp you. Only with our hands can we illumine you." When I had the opportunity to begin teaching, I was still wondering what literature could have in common with doing for most people, what the work of the mind had to do with the work of the hands. It wasn't only that culturally I was still very much a pre-feminist female. As early as middle school I'd felt the popular attitude that the intellectual life is remote from the practical world, for what we were learning, even though I found it fascinating, didn't have an obvious utility. And I had absorbed willy nilly the much-touted individualism that Americans bask in at all ages, a "self-sufficiency" that relegates intellectual matters to the sidelines. For me, Rilke's indictment was true: our entire culture thinks ourselves out of our world, out of our daily lives.

But I knew that, in my own undergraduate career, this wasn't quite so. I remembered that when I had begun to acquire some understanding of philosophy, history, music theory, and biology (my freshman curriculum), I had been thrilled to find that my everyday life—my world—had begun to take on new meanings. I didn't precisely argue with others about Platonic idealism and Aristotelian materialism, but the ideas made a difference in the way I saw myself and others. The Middle Ages came to be populated with individuals I wondered about as I walked across campus. As I found myself musing about whether my current mood was tonic or dominant, I took hope in the inevitable return of tonal compositions (and thus my temporary distress) to the "home" key, and the smell of formaldehyde on my hands from the biology lab called me back to the fact that my own body would decay. These moments of unity had been precious, but they did not inform my daily activities, especially after I graduated. My integration of learning and selfhood was tenuous, always ready to slip out of my grasp. In my frustration during that first teaching appointment, I looked back on the way I was taught and I realized that something had been out of kilter with that education (and not only with the "me" that I had brought to it).

What I had to ask, at first almost blindly, was: How does knowledge call on the whole person? What should be happening in the minds of the students sitting in the classroom? And more importantly: What was the relevance of students' time in class to their lives outside of class?

I was still close enough to my own studenthood to identify what many students brought to the first day of class—what I had tended to bring. Struggling to integrate my own passion for the material with the "me" that existed outside the classroom, I sat down and listed my students' suspicions and their consequences:

1. The content of a course is a definable body of material that can be attacked and mastered. An understanding of it does not lead to questions; rather, questions reveal that the process of assimilation is not complete.

2. Knowledge that is worth struggling to absorb is typically instrumental. Everything else may be interesting but its usefulness is uncertain. Courses in the core curriculum require students to learn information they will never use.

3. Most bodies of knowledge exist in a realm distinct from everyday life. The daily lives of Americans—a flow of tasks and details relieved by entertainment— are beside the point in relation to the bodies of knowledge students must ingest.

4. Learning or understanding is progressive and we, in our time, have the only valid set of understandings. The past is generally irrelevant.

These ideas, whether mere suspicions or hardened attitudes, spell emotional and mental death. I knew what that meant.

As I immersed myself in what came to be a professorial career, clarity about how I could help students integrate mind and world came slowly. I started with panic-driven adrenalin, as I consulted teaching guides and paid attention to my intuition. I experimented. Over the many subsequent years, in community college, historically black four-year colleges, universities with graduate programs (the types of institutions at which I've taught), and in literature, American studies, and art history (my specific disciplines), I attacked the separation of the work of the mind from self, from daily life, and from the connectedness of humanity.

The process came into maturity when I began teaching art history, in 1975. Now this discipline surely provides a test case of the relation of the work of the mind to "real" life. For most of the general public, art history is impractical, feminine, beside the point—in short, an indulgence. For uninitiated students, it is a graspable body of knowledge about as esoteric as imaginable: it is applicable to hardly anything in the way of making money; it has no conceivable relationship to everyday life unless one is an artist; and because most of it happened in the past it has little pertinence to today's larger world. Most of the undergraduates I've taught decided to take the course only because it was in the core curriculum and they'd heard it could be "interesting." They left thinking something quite different.

Here is what—I think—helped change their minds. Every feature is part of the larger enterprise of prayerful living.

Point one: The discipline requires careful looking. Students realize rather quickly that this is more complicated, more time-consuming, than they'd expected. Color, shape, dimensions, light, material: to notice everything in a painting or a sculpture or a print or a building requires several sessions. As I frequently point out, even experienced scholars are taken aback to realize, after months of acquaintance with an image, that they had never noticed a particular detail. Students learn that their expectations influence what they see and what they don't, expectations that are shaped by their past, their preoccupations, and the mystery of their own temperament. Other disciplines also require attentiveness—the laboratory sciences come immediately to mind—but the need to pay close attention to something stationary is not obvious. If the viewer—the thinking observer—is not careful and moves too quickly into analysis, the results are doomed. This is a humbling lesson. And so in life, and so in prayer: one cannot live or pray with integrity without attentiveness—to self, to others, to objects, to sequences of events, to institutional structures.

Point two: What students study in art history are pictures—paintings, sculptures, photographs, prints—that have everything to do with life outside the classroom. Knowledge of any kind always involves the macrocosm. For pictures are about the agonies and pleasures and mysteries of self, connectedness with others, and moment-to-moment daily life. Sexual desire, the physical body, nature as forest or field or mountain or sea, historical events, and God, Christ, the saints, Buddha: these are the top themes. Students ponder the nude as inspiring desire both male and female (and, in recent times, debasing desire); the body as the expression of shame or power or repentance or fragility; landscape as raising the question of our place in nature and the sacredness of the earth; historical or literary scenes as pointing to human actions that are noble or dishonest or laughable; religious images as didactic, inspiring devotion, or urging community. Students learn that pictures over the centuries (and television and films today) present a procession of "natural" human understandings: class and racial hierarchies, the relation between men and women, the place of children, the uses of nature. To attend to so frequently reproduced an image as Leonardo's *Last Supper*, for instance, is not only to review with students the Passion of Christ (a story with great power for even unbelievers), the principle of single-point perspective, and the processes of conservation. It also leads to questions about the distinct ways that even these specially chosen individuals react to the same announcement; a Providence in which even those who betray are granted a place at the earth's banquet; the relationship of our own worldviews to Leonardo's confidence that humanity was the center of an ordered universe. Perhaps most memorably, to study the *Last Supper* is to stand amazed that one individual could make an image so powerful that five hundred years later millions of dollars would be spent to preserve it. Across the history of art touchstones of the human story abound: the brute power in Assyrian reliefs, the journey of the soul in Asian landscape, the assumption of another self in African masks, the unconditional love in Rembrandt's *Prodigal Son*.

Point three: Art historians move from the details of an image to their meanings by studying context, whether that of the artist or the broader period in which the artist was working. In like manner, the person intent on living Christ's love surveys the entire context of perception and action. Amazed to learn that artists don't swirl paint onto the canvas or hammer at marble blocks in a simple ecstasy of inspiration, students in art history look at earlier images that the artists knew, diaries and journals and correspondence, statements of patrons and reviewers. They learn what can be proposed about the relation between the economy and the art, the social setting and the art, the religious beliefs and the art. They see themselves, just as artists, in historical continuity, and learn to question the heritage of assumptions and biases and purposes into which we all are born. To hypothesize about a particular work of art in the wake of generations of hypotheses by viewers and scholars, they find, is to move with an awareness of our own time. It is to respect the mystery that prevents positive answers; to assume the humility that makes living ever fresh. It is to begin to question critical judgments in all arenas of life.

Point four: The teacher is a model of integration. This capacity, especially, is not limited to art history. In lectures, the professor passionate about her material radiates a oneness of person and mind. Her well-ordered course with clear syllabus, lectures in which she frequently reminds students of the relation of where they are in the material to where they've been and to where they're going, and occasional references to other bodies of knowledge as integral to the present topic, reveal a life lived within guideposts that are at once clear and yet can be moved or adjusted in ongoing attention to the wider world. The professor who presents knowledge as always in progress in the very phrasing of his lectures—occasionally speculating, for instance, about how someone fifty years from now might approach the material—helps students situate themselves in the ongoing flow of human endeavor. The teacher who reveals her interest in contemporary popular culture brings the pertinence of intellectual work to the implications of mass movements.

The teacher connects mind and doing—knowledge and living—not only in lecturing, but in leading discussion. Discussion is a laboratory in which students learn to do the connecting. The very fact that their contributions are *part of the class process* is important in itself, for discussion is the class activity in which individual uniqueness is most impressively revealed. A class discussion can reveal the wealth of experience and individuality that participants bring to an art historical problem. Group analysis of images startles students who've not seen what others pick out. Similarly, when the class moves from description to interpretation, the leaps from evidence to conclusion also illuminate personal differences. Students begin to see that authority can rest in careful intellectual work—in *process*—rather than in a body of previous knowledge brought to a question. They identify the biographical and cultural situatedness not only of fellow participants in class but also of the authors of books that propose distinctly flavored—or even startlingly different—aspects of the same picture or artist. They sense themselves as capable of moving toward such authority in this and in many other dimensions of their lives.

And professors model respect for individual uniqueness in their grading—and grading is no simple matter. The task of responding to students' written work requires tact, directness, respect, encouragement and, at times, a dead-level skepticism. At least once in the semester, I state to the entire class that grades are only one measurement of what they have absorbed. Because people have distinct talents, regardless of how hard some of them work, they are not all A students. This does not mean that they are not valuable persons. The professor's respect for just how valuable they are is best revealed in responses to essays. In choice of vocabulary, specificity of reference, length of sentence, and emotional tone, each writer is a very specific person—and deserves to have this pointed out. I require reflection papers, so that I might respond to students' ideas with comments in the margins rather than specific grades, comments that give the papers the character of dialogue rather than evaluation. For one question on my final exams, I have often asked students to relate some aspect of the course content to questions they have been wrestling with over the last year.

WHEN STUDENTS LEAVE art history, I hope they will have begun to believe the following. I state this "creed" in secular terms, but it is a foundation for life in God:

We live in a universe that functions in dependable ways. Over the course of time we as human beings have been able to describe and analyze this world with certain fundamental questions driving our explanations. The knowledge most worth having, which *underlies* what is merely instrumental, is best understood as a large range of questions that we ask. These questions have materialized into specific poems, works of art, and social theories that provide us the working vocabulary with which to live our lives. Our answers are historically specific but, at the same time, they share with the conclusions of past generations our human passion for understanding. Knowledge always leads to new perspectives, to new relationships with other knowledge, and to newness in the people who absorb it.

As I look back over my years in the classroom, I still muse over a few disappointments. These, too, I state in secular terms, but every one of them diminishes the spiritual potential of the academic life. I'd like to have done more team teaching and to have taught more small classes, but the economic necessity for maximum student load per professor has prevented it. I regret that I was not able to stimulate much peer exchange on teaching techniques. The present student emphasis on preprofessional training at the cost of study in the liberal arts, and the consequent preoccupation with grades that will place them in top professional schools, has distressed me no end, for knowledge that is utilitarian doesn't offer much deep work in living. I have also seen, to my regret, that the teaching of disciplines with theory foremost, especially literatures, has meant that students come to art history (and presumably to later life) trained not to be attentive to specific details, but to see everything through minds that have already reached conclusions. And as I see myself further each year from the worldview of my students, and watch the average professorial age at my institution advance while well-trained young Ph.D.s cannot find jobs, I regret that so many of my older colleagues elect to continue teaching beyond a normal retirement age.

I wonder if we might define an ideal life course for the academic career that would replace the hectic race to tenure and promotion followed by either stardom or withdrawal with a thoughtful assessment of what activities might best be emphasized in turn. I suggest that scholarship, teaching, mentoring, administrative responsibilities, and time to read be given due—and separate—attention.

In the larger scheme of things, a relative few have read my books and essays. However, I have taught thousands of students. I hope they are still asking questions.

* * *

26

Intersections

Cynthia Russett

Half Irish, half German, all Catholic. Such was my birthright. Both my grandfathers immigrated to this country before the turn of the century: James Patrick O'Brien from Ireland, Jacob Eagle from Bavaria. Their wives, my grandmothers, were born here: Mary Fisher (or Fischer) married James O'Brien; Mary McDonald married Jacob Eagle. When my parents, Julia Grace O'Brien and Jacob Eugene Eagle, met at college, they were solidly churchgoing children of solidly churchgoing parents.

That tradition was maintained in our house throughout the years of my childhood. I don't, of course, remember my baptism, but I do have a photograph of myself as a sober seven-year-old with pigtails, dressed in the white dress and veil of a first communicant. Of that occasion, my only recollection is of feeling important. An aunt, appraising me in my veil, said she thought I would make an attractive bride, but that was hardly anything I gave any thought to.

More vivid is the memory of my first confession. It took place in the traditional confessional with its thick drapes and sliding panel that connected the penitent with the priest. We had rehearsed this moment in our religious instruction classes, and I was prepared, or so I thought. But I was not prepared for the silence that greeted me when the panel slid open to reveal the profile of the priest. In our class, the priest (was it a priest or one of the nuns taking the priestly role?) had spoken the first words in the ritual, a few gently encouraging comments meant to put us at our ease. But the priest before me said not a word; he had not been party to our rehearsal. So the panel slid back again, as I remained kneeling there; then, after a few minutes, it slid open again. Still he said nothing, and I said nothing. After a few fruitless rounds, I left the confessional distraught and discouraged, and whispered to my mother that the priest would not speak to me. She explained that I should take the initiative, using the formula ("Bless me, Father, for I have sinned") that we had been taught. Thus fortified, I returned to the confessional and successfully completed my first confession.

At that time, our family was living in a suburb of Washington, D.C. Our country had entered World War II, and my father, who was too old to join the military, wanted to do something for the war effort, so he took a job with the War Production Board. It was the task of the WPB to establish priorities for the allocation of critical materials like steel. Thus, for example, at its first meeting it forbade the continued manufacture of cars for the civilian market, so that automobile makers could concentrate on military production. My father's section of the WPB was non-ferrous (i.e., not steel) minerals. My mother stayed at home with her three children. (Years later, when I was teaching my course in American women's history, I asked my mother if she had ever considered joining the wartime workforce herself, as the government had exhorted women to do. She said, quite emphatically, "No." So much for any chance that I could claim a Rosie the Riveter for my mother.)

My brother and I attended the local public elementary school; my sister was already in high school. I don't know whether parochial school was ever discussed, but it would have required driving us to school and back, at a time when gasoline was strictly rationed. So, instead, we attended religious instruction on Sundays, provided by the Sisters of Notre Dame de Namur from the community at Trinity College. We would all go to Sunday Mass together, and then Jimmy and I would have religious instruction while my mother, father, and sister had coffee and pastry at a nearby coffee shop. The nuns were smart and kindly, and I liked them very much. I did not know at the time, of course, that I would one day return to Trinity College as a college student, in part because of this early exposure to their tutelage.

When I was ten years old, our family moved not far away to a suburb of Baltimore, where my father took a job with a company that manufactured colors for chinaware. Here the Catholic church and school were within walking distance, and it was almost a foregone conclusion that we would attend St. Rita's School. It was not a difficult decision because of its convenience, and also because the public schools of the town were not highly thought of. It was commonly believed that unruly behavior was much more prevalent in the public elementary school, that discipline was poor and learning haphazard. For most of our neighbors, St. Rita's was the school of choice.

Our town was named Dundalk. It had its origin in a foundry established by Henry McShane in the late nineteenth century. McShane called the depot Dundalk after the town in Ireland in which he had been born. Around 1916, the Bethlehem Steel Company decided to lay out a town for workers for its nearby Sparrows Point Shipyard—and the growth of Dundalk began. In keeping with its Irish roots, many Dundalk streets had Irish or pseudo-Irish names, a great many beginning with the prefix "Dun." There were Dunran, Dunlear, Dunhill, Dunmanway, and others. We lived on McShane Way, named for the old man himself.

Dundalk was a workingman's bedroom community for the great Sparrows Point works. The Bethlehem Steel shipyards at Sparrows Point had reached their apex during the war, when warships were sent down the ways into the Chesapeake Bay. But even after the war, Bethlehem Steel remained the largest employer in our area. As children, my brother and I learned that our friends' playtimes might not coincide with our own, since they had to conform to their fathers' shift schedules at "the Point." They were often called in to dinner at five o'clock, long before our family sat down to dinner. But most of them, like us, went to St. Rita's Church on Sunday and St. Rita's School during the week, since German, Irish, or central European, they were mostly Catholic too.

Saint Rita's School was for me a positive experience on the whole. We had our share of warrior nuns, so storied in the reminiscences of Catholic novelists and playwrights. There was Sr. Eustace, for example, whose bulk made us cower at our desks as she plowed down the aisle toward some hapless miscreant in the back of the room. Then there was Sr. Wilmette who, subject of much interested speculation about her close friendship with one of the parish priests, did not much like me. Once in fifth grade, when I was leaving the afterschool clean-up squad to go home to a piano lesson, she made it a point to tell me what a selfish little girl I was to leave when others were still working. But most of the nuns were agreeable, and we got a good education in the basics. I loved to diagram sentences with blue ink, drawing ruler-straight lines in red pencil. It gave us a feel for sentence construction that stood us in good stead thereafter.

Long ago Garry Wills described what it was like to grow up Catholic in the 1940s and 1950s:

> Catholicism was first experienced by us as a vast set of inter-meshed childhood habits—prayers offered, heads ducked in unison, crossings, chants, christenings, grace at meals; beads, altar, incense, candles; nuns in the classroom alternately too sweet and too severe, priests garbed black on the street and brilliant at the altar, churches lit and darkened; clothed and stripped, to the rhythm of liturgical recurrences; the crib in winter, purple Februaries, and lilies in the spring; confession as intimidation and comfort (comfort, if nothing else, that the intimidation was survived), communion as reverie and dis-comfort; faith as a creed, and the creed as catechism; Latin responses, salvation by rote, all things going to a rhythm, memorized, old things always returning, eternal in that sense, no matter how transitory.

Wills has much more to say, all of it achingly familiar. His *Memories of a Catholic Boyhood* I could with equal propriety adopt and entitle *Memories of My Catholic Girlhood*. Catholicism, American suburban parish style, approached something like national uniformity in its rituals. Wills concludes, "It was a ghetto, undeniably. But not a bad ghetto to grow up in." To which I say, "Amen."

Saint Rita's parish had erected a new church building shortly before we arrived in Dundalk. Neither modern nor nostalgically traditional, it was bland but not unattractive. During the first ten or so years we were there, the pastor was a curmudgeon named Father (later Monsignor) Wiedenhan. It was his practice, when saying the prayers at the foot of the altar after Sunday Mass, to whirl suddenly around and shout "Come back here!" to anyone foolish enough to attempt to leave the church early. The other priests were not made of such stern stuff, however. Some of them were quite nice looking as well as pleasant; these tended to be the ones who made up the sad litany my mother used to recite to me in afteryears of priests who had left St. Rita's and, indeed, had left the priesthood altogether. For she, like many women of the parish, set great store by the priests, and had a kind of maternal feeling for the young ones. It was well-known that St. Rita's was hard on its priests, perhaps because it was a big, sprawling parish and their numbers were stretched too thin, perhaps because all those steelworkers were tough customers. Some priests became alcoholics or left because of "mental exhaustion." It perhaps goes without saying that they were not intellectuals and that their sermons usually failed to inspire, but most of the parishioners did not ask for so much. On the whole, these were good men who served with devotion to the best of their abilities.

Our family was active in the parish. My father belonged to the Holy Name Society, my mother to Our Lady's Sodality. My brother was an altar boy. I knew all the Latin responses as well as he did (*Introibo ad altare Dei, Ad Deum qui laetificat juventutem meam*) because he practiced them at home. But, of course, as a girl I had no place before the altar of God. At the time, I did not think this odd or exclusionary—that was just the way it was. And I had my own bailiwick: the girls' choir, which, with little to recommend it, was the only choir the church had. Its limited excellence was particularly on display at funerals, when our chanting of the lugubrious *Dies irae, dies illa* must have made the deceased glad to have left this world behind. For social events we had the CYO (Catholic Youth Organization), which provided a safe venue for sports (I loved basketball, even though my lack of stature made greatness an impossibility) and for properly chaperoned dances.

At home, we were devotional, though not to the extent of some of the families you could read about in Catholic periodicals. My mother was punctilious about seeing that we attended Sunday Mass, and often daily Mass during Lent, and that we went regularly to confession. There were, as a matter of course, crucifixes over all the beds, and each of us was expected to kneel and pray by the bedside before going to sleep. I don't know whether my father did this, but I know my mother did. Too, those were the glory days of the Rosary, and each of us had our own. I had every Mystery of the Rosary down cold, and was sometimes called upon to lead the praying of the Rosary when my class was in church. For a while our family gathered to say the Rosary collectively in the evening, although this did not last long. And it now seems strange to me that we did not, like so many families whether Catholic or Protestant, say grace before meals. Still, the rhythms of the church year permeated our household, and there was never any doubt that we belonged to the great church family.

I was quite a pious child, through some combination of family tradition, school enforcement, and my own inclination. I remember how hard I tried to observe the three hours of Good Friday, from noon to three o'clock, sitting quietly in the church pew. This could only be done with the aid of a great deal of reading material, although I knew that saints tossed off three-hour meditations routinely without any assistance at all. When I was twelve or thirteen, I needed to have several teeth extracted prior to orthodonture. I was anesthetized with gas and dreamed that someone was insisting that I give up my faith. As I awoke, the nurse asked me why, when she told me to wake up, I had kept repeating, "I won't. I won't." I do not recall being troubled by doctrinal doubts even as late as high school, since I was swimming in the sea of faith and it was belief, rather than unbelief, that was for us in Dundalk the normal state.

The day came to bid farewell to St. Rita's School, sing its anthem for the last time ("Alma Mater, hear our song of joyous days of childhood"), and move on to the next pedagogical level. I would no longer be in classes with boys for coeducation ended with eighth grade; Baltimore Catholic high schools were all single sex. My brother, a year ahead of me, was at the Jesuit school, Loyola. I chose Trinity Preparatory School, which, although it was on the opposite side of the city and required two public buses and a school bus to reach, had an excellent reputation. A friend of mine was already there, and enthusiastic. And Trinity was run by the same order of nuns I had liked so much in Washington: the Sisters of Notre Dame de Namur.

Trinity, a former Episcopalian boys' boarding school, had a beautiful campus far out in the country. There were acres of woodland and a small farm, as well as a convent and a grammar school for both sexes (known as the "lower school"), in addition to the secondary school for girls only. Trinity Prep was devoted to the formation of Christian womanhood: we wore uniforms (skirts and blazers of gray wool not well suited to Maryland's spring temperatures) and maroon beanies. Our gym outfits had skirts also and, for the first few years, we had to cover our legs with hideous maroon cotton gym stockings. Classes were small; ours was the largest at twenty-seven. Our freshman year instructor was Sister Marie Julie, a nun from the Boston area who insisted on calling the closet a "press," and loved history. She was especially fond of having our class write historical lyrics to well-known tunes. One of our efforts began, rather improbably, "Disraeli, Queen Victoria come on and do your stuff," set to the tune of the Battle Hymn of the Republic. (In later years, when my knowledge of Queen Victoria was deepened by historical study and my image of her by film, I used to try to imagine what she might have made of an injunction to "do your stuff.") We celebrated National Book Week to the tune of "Tramp, Tramp, Tramp, The Boys Are Marching":

> "Make friends with books," the slogan's saying.
> You can pick and choose at will.
> If you like biography, you will certainly agree
> That the nearest books your hopes will all fulfill.

The Trinity chapel, inherited like everything else from the Episcopalians, was a little jewel of a place, all dark wood and somewhat in the English style. It was on the second floor and, on the landing, as you ascended the stairs, stood a little statue of the child Jesus as a kind of infant emperor. He was always exquisitely dressed in satin and silk robes with many hand-decorated details. Sometimes the robes were bejeweled. It must have been the nuns who sewed the wardrobe, probably delighting in each tiny stitch done for the glory of God. The robes changed with regularity. It was always fun to see what the infant Jesus would be wearing, and to choose favorite apparel, although this may or may not have conduced to greater piety on our part.

The beauty of the chapel and its small and intimate size made reflection seem natural. Like many, perhaps most, adolescent Catholic females, I began to mull over the possibility that I might "have a vocation." I had a friend one year older at Trinity, who planned to enter the Sisters of the Immaculate Heart of Mary, the order that had taught us at St. Rita's. She used to tell me that she expected one day to see me in the blue robes of the order. The thought did not please me, which I hoped was a sign that the vowed life was not for me, but I was not to be let off the hook so easily. Nuns and retreat masters liked to remind us that when God called, it did not matter whether you were attracted or repelled—it was God's call, and had to be accepted. In the end, with a somewhat uneasy conscience, I decided that, in any event, I would go on to college, as all my family had done. Meanwhile, religion was a part of all our days at Trinity, from the timely message on the bulletin board in February ("Now is the holy time of Lent, let every day with Christ be spent") to the glorious freedom of wandering the grassy hillside in silent meditation during springtime retreats, whether to reflect on one's shortcomings and the goodness of God or to revel in the Maryland countryside, who could tell?

There was only one college for me: Trinity College in Washington, D.C., the big sister of Trinity Preparatory. My mother, father, and sister had all gone to Alfred University in New York (my brother went on from Loyola High School to Loyola College), but I had no desire to do so. I had been won over by my experience at Trinity Prep, and by the persuasive powers of a Trinity Prep graduate who returned to sing the praises of the college. I would return to Washington, and to the nuns I had admired ten years before.

I loved my four years at Trinity. The college prided itself on being one of the premier Catholic women's colleges in the country, one of the most selective and intellectually challenging. Many, probably most, of the faculty had doctorates. The great majority were Sisters of Notre Dame, but we had Dominican priests as well as one Paulist priest for theology, and occasional other visiting lecturers. (One of these was a Croatian priest whose accent created amusing effects in our European history class. He spoke, for example of "Willem da tird Orange" of the Netherlands, and we drew three circles in our notebooks and labeled the third one William.) The students were largely from the East Coast, with large concentrations from New England and the New York-New Jersey area. Classes were small; our entering class numbered some 125. Almost all were Catholic, although at least one of the commuting students was not. So I continued, as I had since entering fifth grade, to experience my education, as well as the rest of my life, permeated by the signs and symbols of Catholic spirituality.

We took four years of theology with, since our instructors were Dominican, a great deal of emphasis on St. Thomas Aquinas. We were given to understand that the Dominicans taught the true theology, as compared to the temporizing of the more worldly Jesuits. Of those years of theological study I remember little, although the Dominican priests themselves are vivid in memory. One rather saintly Dominican, who later went on to become a missionary in Africa, loved to quote the phrase, "Taste and see that the Lord is sweet." He was a shining example of dedication. We adored him and felt ourselves to be better people because of his gentleness and evident love of God.

The Trinity chapel was magnificent, a Byzantine-style edifice of white marble with an interior decorated with marvelously brilliant mosaics. It seemed grander than our under-endowed college had any right to be, and must have been the gift of generous donors. It was a fine place to have ceremonial rituals. On special occasions, it would resound to the college hymn, work of alumnae of a previous generation:

> Be ever blessed, and thanked, and praised
> Through all eternity in endless unity
> Bowed down in rapture we adore
> O, holy Trinity, your daughters call to Thee,
> Veiled in thy majesty,
> We thee adore.

On class days, of which each class had one a year, "your daughters" could be replaced by the year of the celebrating class. Thus we sang "'58 calls to Thee" on our class day each March.

Thoughts of the sisterhood having by this time faded, I had, as I approached my senior year, no particular other occupational goals. Looking back from so many years later, I find this astounding; it is clear that I had not yet attained, at the age of twenty-one, any sense of myself as an adult with a calling. Despite the fact that I had attended a Catholic college, I did not yet understand the meaning of "vocation." But in the late 1950s, it was not expected that a young woman, even a well-educated one, would plan for a serious career, and I suppose, in the back of my mind, was the expectation that, like so many of my classmates, I would marry and raise a family. I was fortunate, however, to have as my primary history advisor a nun who believed that intellectually able Trinity students should go on to graduate school. She insisted that I should do just that, and she helped me plan which universities I should apply to. She also told me about the Woodrow Wilson Fellowships available to aspirant graduate students who wanted to teach at the college level. My interest and aspirations thus kindled, I arrived in New Haven, Connecticut, in the fall of 1958, to study American history at Yale.

It was really the first time I had ever been truly on my own, out from under the parental wing, the parish wing, the college wing. I was going to live much farther away from home than the forty-five or fifty miles that separated Trinity College from Dundalk. And for the first time I would be living in a truly secular environment, where religious faith would be a willed and intentional choice. Instead of being the very air one breathed, faith would be almost a countercultural option.

Yale had been founded in an aura of Protestant piety but it had long since shed most of the vestiges of that past. There was excitement in facing this wider world, but also apprehension, and I remember listening to the evening bells chime out from Harkness Tower on one of my first evenings and wondering whether I would thrive. As it turned out, I did, although some of my fellow first-year students did not. My next-door neighbor in the women's residence hall spent most of her first year asleep, in the kind of somnolence I later learned was characteristic of those in deep clinical depression. In addition to the general anxiety about succeeding at Yale, she was coping with the disappointment of a failed love affair, her boyfriend having announced that he was gay, and it was too much for her. She did not return the second year. Another resident tried to jump out of a third-story window but was prevented.

Fresh from my Catholic environment, I was somewhat shocked at these examples of desperation, and I wondered whether an absence of religion had made these students more vulnerable to life's vicissitudes. Certainly I had not found the same level of unhappiness in my friends and classmates at Trinity. This was probably a facile judgment. Desperation was not encouraged among good Catholics who should take their burden of woe to the feet of Christ or Mary or the saints in prayer. It may be that my fellow Trinity students were equally unhappy but careful not to seem so. Still, I did believe at the time, and still do, that religious conviction could fortify one for the battles of life.

Yale still had an official chaplain and a college chapel. Catholics accordingly worshiped at St. Thomas More Chapel, usually referred to as More House, an entirely independent entity not financially supported by the university. More House was the creation of an extraordinary Yale graduate named T. Lawrason Riggs, scion of a wealthy Episcopalian family, who became a Catholic priest determined to set up a Catholic center for the benefit of future Yale students. At the time of my arrival at Yale, More House was presided over by the kindly but uninspiring Fr. O'Brien. Although he welcomed all students, he understood his ministry as directed to undergraduates, so there were no programs for graduate students and no outreach specifically to them (or for that matter to medical and law and other professional students). Catholic graduate students did, however, manage to create a kind of community that sustained us.

That first year in New Haven I met and began to date Bruce Russett, a graduate student in political science, one year ahead of me. Bruce was from western Massachusetts and had graduated from Williams College. By the end of my first year, Bruce had proposed and we had an understanding that we would marry at the end of the following academic year. Bruce, however, was not a Catholic. Although his father had been born into a Catholic family, the experience with Catholicism had not been happy, and he had abandoned it long before he married the woman, a Methodist, who was to be Bruce's mother. Bruce was reared a Methodist but did not really consider himself a member of any church and had only vague religious convictions. Yet, he was not hostile to religion, and certainly respected my own faith. He agreed to the religious instruction that the Church required for non-Catholics who married Catholics. It was not possible in those days for a Catholic marrying a non-Catholic to have a nuptial Mass, but at least one no longer had to be married in the rectory as had formerly been the case.

In the months of our engagement, I thought long and hard about the issue of religious difference and eventually turned for advice to my older sister, who had also married a man who was not a Catholic. They had been happily married for four years and had one son, whom my sister was raising as a Catholic. She wrote me a long, eloquent letter that gave me much comfort. She, too, had been concerned about the matter of religion and had hoped that Walt would eventually convert to Catholicism. But this was not happening, and my sister no longer thought it would. However, Walt had never issued the slightest objection to her raising Kurt in the Catholic faith and, although she wished that they could all attend church together as a family, she had made peace with the fact that this was not to be. Walt was a loving husband and father, and she was grateful for her life with him.

My story did not end like my sister's. In the year after the birth of our eldest child, Bruce, who had gone from a tolerance of Catholicism to an increasing interest in it, was baptized into the Church. Through reading and reflection he had come to a conviction that the historical claims of the Church were indeed valid. Our marriage could have that unity of belief that my sister had yearned for.

After a year in Boston, where Bruce taught at M.I.T while I worked on my dissertation, our family returned to New Haven and to Yale. Bruce would teach full-time with tenure; I would teach part-time (and after many years full-time) while raising our four children. We continued as members of the More House community, as we do to this day, and it has remained the center of our spiritual life. Successive chaplains have broadened the vision of the chapel to include a stronger emphasis on intellectual as well as pastoral sustenance. Today, St. Thomas More Chapel and Catholic Center is a vibrant, liturgically rich, and intellectually alive community.

Early on, Bruce and I participated with a close-knit group of parents in organizing a religious education program for our children. There had not previously been a need for such a program as the presence of Catholic faculty at Yale was new, and the chaplains at More House had focused their efforts on undergraduates. Gradually, however, our group came to feel the need for further religious education for ourselves as well as our children, and so evolved the adult discussion group that continues to be active to the present day. It is a freewheeling group that meets once a month to discuss previously assigned readings on topics of spirituality, theology, church governance, social ethics and morality, and whatever else strikes us as interesting—providing, of course, that it has some relationship to Catholic belief and practice.

Over the years, this discussion group has been one regular impetus to reflecting on my faith. We have examined the Gnostic gospels, liberation and feminist theology, and the structure of authority in the Church. Recently, we explored the Gospel of Mark in conjunction with an essay on Mark written by a young British punk rocker. I remember reading with a real sense of shock Hans Küng's suggestion that the Resurrection did not necessarily mean that Christ's physical body had risen from the grave. The Jesus Seminar, were one to accept the results of its deliberations, takes us much further along the path of uncertainty. Some of its members go so far as to doubt the divinity of Christ.

Since college, if not before, we have been reminded that those of us who are born into the Church must exchange our child's faith for one that is adult.

But making that exchange is not easy. While we would love to hold on to the beautiful stories in the Bible, it is relatively simple to acknowledge their mythic elements—the manger, the Magi, and the star, for example—and yet to claim their symbolic truth. But how far can the deconstruction of the biblical texts go before faith itself crumbles? Between the poles of credulity and nihilism, the footing is unsure and the path constantly shifting. Meanwhile, in parishes across the land, priests preach and people listen to a message that maintains the old untroubled certitudes, and we who struggle with a more complex understanding wonder sometimes if this is truly the "one Church, indivisible" of the creed.

At the same time, we ourselves can seem unthinkably credulous to our colleagues in the university. Although Yale was founded as a Christian institution, and its presidents were all clerics until the twentieth century, it was not noted for its religiosity by the 1950s. It was, in fact, its hostility to religion, as he perceived it, which caused William F. Buckley to write his famous diatribe, *God and Man at Yale* (1951). Although exaggerated, the book was not all wrong: at that time one could, in fact, find examples of anti-Catholicism in Yale's classrooms. That is no longer the case and, over the intervening years, Yale has become quite a different place from Buckley's Yale, with a department of religious studies, a faith and science seminar, a campus Christian Fellowship, and an endowed professorship of Catholic thought. In my own department of history, there are two historians of American religion, one of the Reformation, an eminent historian of Christianity, and an intellectual writing on Cardinal Newman.

But intellectual inquiry is one thing, personal piety quite another. Although a faith conviction is no longer thought to be intellectually disabling by most people, it is still far from the norm. There is general tolerance of religious belief at Yale, but some religions are seen as more intellectually respectable than others. It is an odd fact that Judaism was respected intellectually at a time when Jews were still socially unacceptable, whereas Catholics, whose Catholicism was of dubious intellectual standing, were more socially acceptable than Jews. There are doubtless many reasons for the low esteem in which Catholicism has been held among American intellectuals, especially, I would suppose, the historical fact that the Catholics who immigrated into this country were, for the most part, peasants and workers, while immigrant Jews brought with them a tradition of scholarship and study of the Torah. The noted church historian Msgr. John Tracy Ellis castigated American Catholicism in an address in 1955 for "the impoverishment of Catholic scholarship in this country, as well as the low state of Catholic leadership in most walks of national life . . . the absence of a love of scholarship for its own sake among American Catholics . . . the absence of a sense of dedication to an intellectual apostolate." His lament helps to explain why, in a familiar witticism, anti-Catholicism has been called the anti-Semitism of the intellectuals.

Yet, although Ellis's indictment has lost much of its force over the years, the challenge it presents to Catholic intellectuals is as relevant as ever. What exactly is an intellectual apostolate and how might we live it out? It seems to me that we will each answer this question a bit differently, but that for me, at least, it involves some combination of work and witness. When Catholic students arrive at Yale, they are likely to face new challenges to the practice of their faith. We faculty members who are known to be Catholic can offer, by our very presence in the worshiping community, welcome reassurance that such challenges can be met, and that faith can remain the center of a life devoted to scholarship.

In our professional work, most of us as humanists or scientists or engineers will probably not be doing research that bears directly on religious issues. Unexpected opportunities may nonetheless arise, however, as when my husband agreed to serve as the academic expert on the committee writing the bishops' pastoral letter on war and peace, or when I took on the editing of a book of essays on American colleges founded by women's religious orders. As for our teaching, faculty at Catholic universities and colleges can more easily bring their faith into the classroom. To those of us in secular institutions, this is not permitted, but I consider it vitally important in my courses to convey the simple truth that religion has played a crucial role in the course of the nation's history. In my intellectual history class, for example, I introduce students to the work of Reinhold Niebuhr not just because he is one of the preeminent American intellectuals of this century, but because he offers a deeply informed religious perspective on society and politics. In my course on the history of American women, I make sure to include the relationship—sometimes positive, sometimes troubled—between women and religion. I do this for eminently academic reasons—my courses would be intellectually poorer without this attention to religion—but I do it in addition because of my own faith commitment.

Another dimension of my life as a Yale faculty member is individual conversation and counseling of students. Here certainly the ethical principles of the faith come into play. It is true that the obligation of all faculty is to honor the integrity of students and to help them both academically and, when necessary, emotionally to grow toward effective maturity. But always we who are believers are reminded of Jesus who grew "in wisdom, and age, and grace." For our students we wish wisdom as well as learning, and grace as well as maturity. In ways not easily measured, our beliefs will make a difference in our relationship with them.

That relationship, of course, is not a one-way street. We teach our students; we also learn from them. I think of two young women, Kalyanee and Teresa. Kalyanee was born in Cambodia of Cambodian parents, although raised in this country. She took a seminar with me, and I was the reader for her senior essay. Kalyanee's moral compass is set very high, the result of a loving upbringing by her devoutly Buddhist mother and father and her own innate decency. She spent last summer interviewing Cambodians to learn how they had survived under the Khmer Rouge regime, and will return to Cambodia this year to help document human rights atrocities in preparation for a war crimes tribunal. Ultimately she hopes to study international human rights in law school. Kalyanee is wise beyond her years; she has seen violence and trauma and become stronger in her resolve to be of service to the Cambodian people.

Teresa is a flame-haired, bubbling contrast to the dark-haired gentleness of Kalyanee. Last year she spent coordinating the social justice activities of Yale students. Perhaps her greatest challenge and achievement was to organize a group of students to demonstrate at the School of the Americas in Georgia, a place that has trained many of the repressive military leaders of Central and South America. Next year she will attend business school at the University of Chicago, and with MBA in hand, she will head for the Episcopal Divinity School. She will someday be an administratively skilled, female, red-haired Episcopalian priest, a category with, I suspect, few if any other members.

These two young women are living examples of goodness. If I have touched their lives, they have equally made a difference in mine—they have shown me something of the working of grace in the human spirit.

The relationship between the spiritual and the intellectual in my life is not always smooth. This is especially the case in my courses on the history of American women, which activate the tension always latent between my dual commitments to faith and feminism. It is a tension that is in part founded in the very philosophies of the two belief systems: religion encourages concern for others even to the point of self-sacrifice, altruism, and asceticism. American feminism, by contrast, arose in reaction to the forced self-sacrifice of women and, accordingly, emphasizes self-fulfillment, achievement, and self-assertion.

In addition to the generally dismal record of all the Western churches in their treatment of women, there are the painful places at which Catholicism in particular seems to come into direct conflict with feminism, above all at emotional flashpoints like the issue of abortion. And Catholicism has been slow to come to terms with its historic marginalization of women. Although today it affirms women as human persons with equal dignity to men, it has not practiced this message in the past, nor does it fully now.

If one finds little support for religious belief among one's university colleagues, it is sadly true that the Church itself, as a hierarchical organization, sometimes seems harsh and rigid. In exchanging the faith of a child for that of an adult, I have had to make the distinction between faith and Church, between religious conviction and the organization within which I choose to live out that conviction. There are times when I find myself at odds with the Church, unable to accept all its precepts. I cannot find validity in the arguments against contraception, and I am troubled by their policy implications. How can the Church plausibly engage with the poorer countries of the globe when its condemnation of abortion is accompanied by a ban on the very methods that would make abortion less prevalent? I am dismayed by the prohibition against even discussing the ordination of women and this, in turn, is only a small part of the much larger issue of the historic treatment of women by the official Church. Individual priests and local bishops may be warm and humane, but the Church in Rome speaks too often in a voice that is oppressively censorious.

It was certainly in part that voice that drove one of our children, no longer able to endure the heavy hand of patriarchy, away from the Church. I am saddened by our inability to pass on the legacy of faith to our four children. Several attend church only when they are visiting us; at least one does not attend church at all. But it would not be true to say that they have abandoned their legacy. All are principled young adults and, as our oldest child once put it, "If you grow up Catholic, you never leave it completely behind." The child who rebelled against the patriarchal Church is now living and volunteering in a Catholic Worker house in New York City, serving the hungry and homeless and reading Dorothy Day.

Will we as intellectuals ever arrive at a perfect integration of spirit and intellect? It is something to be hoped for, but in the New Jerusalem, not in the here and now. I count myself fortunate to have had the opportunity to reflect on this issue in the company of colleagues young and old at the summer institute called Collegium. It was moving to hear others express the same longings and to discuss them with the help of an intellectually accomplished corps of experts. Yet for all that, I doubt that we were meant to attain complete resolution. Although certainly not a postmodernist, I do feel that there is much truth in the postmodern description of the self as fragmented. The times we feel that we are in balance—physically, spiritually, and intellectually—are wonderful, but there are also times when we experience inner friction and disharmony. That may be just as well, since tension can be creative as well as debilitating. Insofar as we must constantly ask ourselves what we truly believe and renegotiate again and again the intersection, or perhaps better, interpenetration of knowledge and faith, both our scholarship and our belief are revivified.

In the end, and not withstanding reservations, I cannot imagine myself as other than Roman Catholic. The difficulties of holding to the faith are real. There will always be the times of doubt—the existence of God, after all, is not provable, and Jesus, although his earthly existence is provable, remains mysterious even to those who love him. Evil will always be a stumbling block. Still, on the good days—the days when the liturgy unfolds with mystery and majesty and the homily captures the urgent power of the word of God—I know that I am in the right place. I am at home.

27

Science, Faith, and World Politics

Bruce Russett

This is an autobiographical statement by someone who is both a Catholic and a political scientist, talking about the juncture between those two identities. Since I became a political scientist somewhat before becoming a Catholic, I'll start with the former, although the two are deeply entangled, as you will quickly see. The pieces, however, do fit together.

Origins

Despite growing up in a small, insular, New England industrial city (North Adams, Massachusetts), my earliest political memories are about matters of war and peace. The first (at age five) is of President Roosevelt's campaign for a third term, during which he appeared in public in an open car. My mother remarked that he shouldn't do that; someone might try to shoot him. "Who, a Republican?" was my response. She then explained to me about Nazis. My second "political" memory is of my father, with my toy ships arrayed on a large map of the North Atlantic, showing me how the British sank the battleship *Bismarck*. The third such memory is of Pearl Harbor Day.

I was not a refugee, my home was not bombed or occupied, no relatives went to the gas chambers, and I was too young for the army. Nonetheless, World War II was an intense experience. I was small for my age and not very strong; war games were an appropriate outlet for aggression. Another early memory is of air-raid drills and blackouts. Although I didn't know it, of course, it was pretty unlikely that the Germans would bomb North Adams. Much later I understood that the government was manipulating us to encourage patriotic self-sacrifice; that realization contributes to the strain of populism and distrust of authority that runs through my work. I also remember vividly the day the United States dropped an atomic bomb on Hiroshima. My mother, a woman usually with remarkable empathy for others, in this instance was overwhelmed by what I suppose were her maternal instincts, saying, "Now they'll do it to us." The Japanese couldn't, and later the Russians didn't. But this was my entry into what would be the world of the Cold War and nuclear deterrence.

My family was working class and ethnically mixed. Ethnicity mattered in Massachusetts. Mother was descended from a Mayflower family; my father was French-Canadian. His parents were nominally Catholic, but hardly devout. When he was fourteen years old, he suffered a ruptured appendix, and abscesses raged throughout his body. My grandmother's piety was such that she prayed—for his death. But despite that, he survived. An example of my grandmother's Christian charity is her behavior one day when my dad's sister, my aunt, brought a "beau" home to dinner. He was Protestant, and that did not sit well with my grandmother. He also had a large and misshapen nose. While the rest sat at dinner, grandmother went to the kitchen and returned holding a potato that had a twisted protuberance, remarkably like the beau's nose. My grandmother crept behind the poor unsuspecting gentleman and held the potato over his head for the entertainment of the other diners.

With this kind of example before him, it's not surprising that my father quickly fell away from the "faith" in which he was raised, and became agnostic. Years later he met my mother, a Methodist, and became a Methodist himself when he married her. His family was offended, but that hardly bothered him. He and his family cut many of their remaining ties.

Living in an area where ethnic and religious tensions were still palpable, my father made a thorough switch of identity. (For instance, he always insisted to us that he knew no French—although we knew that his parents had spoken French around the house when he was young.) He was content in his new life, deeply attached to my mother and her family, and correct if not devout in his religious practices.

I was raised as a Protestant, but my identity is split. Sometimes I can become sort of blueblood; at others I am an unmeltable ethnic. Although my examples were a good deal more inspiring than those my father had, I too fell away from religious belief and practice after adolescence. I was not hostile to religion, but very skeptical. Besides, life was too full of interesting things.

I was the first in my line to go to college, although cousins and uncles had done so. College (Williams) was six miles from home. When the Korean War came I tried to enlist in the navy—not with enthusiasm for service, but it looked a lot better than waiting to be drafted into the army. The examining physician rejected me as having a heart murmur. Although he was mistaken, I certainly had no desire to argue.

I never even traveled west of Rochester until I was nineteen. But the wider world held great fascination. Although I wanted to do good in the world, I turned away from the "do good" occupations, such as medicine and the clergy, that a working-class boy might aspire to. (About the latter, I now sometimes crack that I was repelled by the prospects of poverty, chastity, and obedience, in equal portion. But, of course, none of that would have been required of a minister.) So as my horizons broadened, I settled on college teaching in politics. And I cared about peace and war. So it had to be international relations, and first I had to see the world.

Williams came to the rescue by giving me a scholarship for a year of study abroad. Not much of a linguist, I prudently chose to do my study in England. At Williams I majored in political economy, a hybrid of the economics and political science majors. I was interested primarily in politics, but political science at the time seemed inadequate for reasons I did not at the time fully understand. Frederick Schuman's enthusiasm for the political implications of anthropology, psychology, and sociology helped broaden my horizons. I liked the rigor of economic theory. My roommate told me that if I wanted to be a political scientist I should take mathematics. I told him he was crazy. It was 1955, and he was crazy. But he was also right. I went to King's College, Cambridge, and did economics in the shadow of John Maynard Keynes, with some political philosophy thrown in. I also bounced around Europe pretty extensively.

The next step was Yale for a Ph.D. By then I knew I wanted political *science* in some sense, but didn't know how to get it. Fortunately, I was at exactly the right place and time. Three Yale giants, Robert Dahl, Karl Deutsch, and Harold Lasswell, were making the study of politics self-consciously scientific, and I became an enthusiastic spear-carrier. Deutsch was the man in international relations, and at his peak. Despite my absent mathematical training, my education in economics gave me a pivotal comparative advantage.

Going to Yale proved a great decision, with blessed cascading consequences. There I met Cynthia, who was to become my wife. She was a deeply committed Catholic, and I had to face a whole set of issues I had banished from my attention. Out of respect for her (and as was required in those days), I took instruction in the Catholic faith, at least so as to understand her beliefs. In fact, I was ready for this, and found myself increasingly convinced of Catholicism's truth. I was not to be hurried, however, and we wed with the ceremony then appropriate to a mixed marriage (no Mass). But I continued to think, read, and pray, and almost a year after our marriage, I was baptized and confirmed. It was a mature, considered, and joyous act of faith. I have now been with Cynthia for more than forty years, and a member of St. Thomas More Chapel at Yale nearly as long. Thanks to her personal and spiritual example, and to the intellectual and nurturing community at the chapel, I have had a privileged experience of the best of the Church. Without them I might not have stayed.

Soon I was doing a little free-lance writing on current affairs for Catholic periodicals, including *America* and *Commonweal*. Two of my earliest articles concerned the need to take the population problem seriously, and not to pretend, as many Catholic authorities tried to do, that the economic development of poor countries could be achieved without some easing of their population pressures. I was not advocating artificial contraception—that was beyond my own thinking, let alone anything acceptable to such magazines. But even insisting that there was a real problem to be addressed was against the grain.

After my degree and a year of teaching at M.I.T., a position at Yale opened up, carrying what was, for the time, an exceptional package of resources for pursuing my research. Most of my work in those first years was in the vein of statistical analysis of the characteristics and behavior of large-scale political systems. This work meant a struggle—not just one in the normal sense of trying to get tenure at an elite institution, but in the sense that the social scientific revolution in international relations was still being made.

We "scientists" were still relative outsiders in the profession. So although getting tenure meant "making it," it also left me, reinforced by my working-class background, feeling "in" but not really "of" the establishment. I found myself adopting the position of establishment critic; that is, using my newly privileged status as an opportunity to take positions critical of established political or scholarly wisdom. (I still think that's what tenure is for at a place like Yale.) I was no radical—a populist, but never marxoid—but felt somewhere on the left. Yale's political science department expected us to be social scientists, not ideologues, and that was fine. Yale also produces men of affairs like Dean Acheson and George Bush. Yale more broadly expected us to speak to our country's "leaders," present and future, about how the world was and could be.

As a child of the Cold War, I believed in containment, although I was no hawk. For a while I approved of the Vietnam War, not turning fully against it until 1967. I then did some of the activist things, like campaign for Eugene McCarthy, but saw my true niche as being a scholar. By then I had discovered Christian just-war theory and decided that the war was neither in the national interest nor just. Yet it still went on. So I spent the next ten years trying to understand what was driving some of the key propositions of the left about economic interest and ideology. I took those propositions more seriously than did many of my colleagues, but as hypotheses to be tested rather than as self-evident laws. Not surprisingly, the empirical results were mixed, and I called the shots as I saw them. With the war over, I could return to an earlier interest in international justice, equality, and human rights. For a while that meant taking Third World *dependencia* theories seriously, but again as scientific hypotheses.

One of the major empirical conclusions from my Vietnam-era work was that ideological motivations were more important than economic ones, at least as the latter were commonly understood. Ideology in this context included a "realist" view of the world as an anarchic struggle for power, epitomized by Thomas Hobbes's view of anarchy where life is brutal, nasty, and short. Within that view, World War II, my formative experience, was necessary and successful. Yet it also seemed to me that just such a verdict on World War II had formed much of the impetus for subsequent American military interventions around the world, and a key base of support for the Vietnam War effort. To delegitimate Vietnam required delegitimating at least some of the "lessons" derived from World War II. So I wrote a short book raising questions concerning the established wisdom about the necessity and success of World War II. The book remains in print with modest sales even now. I am not always comfortable with some of its fans; it was a youthful expression of some things that could have been said more circumspectly. But in its social context, and for its attempt to challenge a myth that was being put to a less-than-benign purpose, I still defend it and believe it has some useful lessons.

Catholics and Nuclear War

Realists are not supposed to be bemused by such matters as just-war theories. I was, and remain, in some respects a realist, recognizing the exigencies of the international struggle for power and security. Nuclear deterrence is a quintessentially realist doctrine. It was assumed by all but a handful of professionals, inside the government and out, that nuclear deterrence meant presenting the adversary with the threat of "assured destruction," and that, in Defense Secretary Robert McNamara's public formulations, meant, at a minimum, the destruction of some large percentage of the Soviet Union's people and industry. That formulation, and the possibility that it might be executed, I could not square with the just-war principles of proportionality and discrimination.

I was (and am) not a pacifist, but as a Catholic (although a leftish one skeptical of authority), I had to take the just-war tradition seriously at the same time that nuclear deterrence seemed so existentially inescapable. Also, my realist sympathies are seriously diluted not only with a sense that there is more to international relations than the struggle for power, but also with the liberal or idealist conviction that there *must* be more than the struggle for power. The risks of unlimited nuclear confrontation are not tolerable. So I tried to reconcile just-war principles with some form of nuclear deterrence in what I called a "countercombatant" strategy intended to concentrate on permissible military targets while largely sparing civilians. The formula, however, was imperfect on its own terms. Many civilians would not be spared, escalation from any use of nuclear weapons would be terribly likely and, by some arguments, a countercombatant strategy could even make war more likely. I acknowledged all those problems at the time and continued to try to ease them by narrowing the circumstances of, and emphasizing the need for, restraints on, any possible use. Imperfections nonetheless remain, in limited possibilities for actual command and control, and in the politics of public understanding. Nevertheless, it was the best I could do in the context of the Cold War.

Like my book on World War II, this work alienated me from some friends on the left—I was challenging their accepted wisdom too, and its meaning has sometimes been twisted by those on the right to purposes of which I heartily disapprove; e.g., a first-strike strategy. There never has been a straight-A paper resolving the normative and practical contradictions of nuclear deterrence. Limited nuclear war is an oxymoron truly believed in only by morons. Yet, in my life situation, I could not escape from the inquiry.

I couldn't escape, because I was drafted. After reading some of my work in 1981, Fr. J. Bryan Hehir, then Chief of International Affairs at the U.S. Catholic Conference, asked me to serve as principal consultant to the bishops' committee that was preparing to write a pastoral letter on war and peace. Maybe I could have pled conscientious objection, but it was conscience that had involved me in the first place. This was a serious opportunity. Major institutional statements of Catholic teaching on the moral dimensions of political and social issues take one of three forms. Two are papal encyclicals and documents from councils, notably Vatican II. The third are pastoral letters of national conferences of bishops. These have sometimes developed into big statements, drawing attention beyond the Catholic community and sometimes beyond national borders. The pastoral letter is an art form perhaps developed most highly in the United States. It also is now a phenomenon, and a process, currently under heavy stress with a clouded future.

So I signed on, and after several committee meetings was asked to prepare a first draft for discussion. I did, and since word processing on PCs was still in its infancy, put the draft into the word-processing system on the Yale mainframe computer. I almost expected our secular computer to crash from this content. But it did not and, over the next year and a half, the committee (chaired by Archbishop Joseph Bernardin, with four other bishops, a representative each of the female and male religious orders, Hehir, a lay member of the U.S.C.C. staff, and me) produced subsequent drafts in what proved to be a superheated political environment. The drafts proceeded dialectically, each correcting certain emphases in the previous one in response to our own learning, testimony to the committee, and intense public commentary.

The final version of *The Challenge of Peace: God's Promise and Our Response* was much longer and better than the first, but not too far from it in its essential position. In all I spent two years helping to produce a statement that was by my standards professionally defensible, politically and theologically acceptable to a wide spectrum of clergy and laypeople (not just Catholics; the ecumenical aspects of this effort mattered a great deal to me), and something I could live with in conscience. People disagree vigorously about whether we succeeded on the first two criteria, and only I can speak to the last. I think we did well enough to get an A minus.

Both the substance of the document and the process that produced it are worth recalling. It was both *universal* and *American* in substance. It was reflective of the universal Church, in that it built on two millennia of Christian and especially Catholic tradition: Scripture, church scholars like Augustine and Aquinas, papal and conciliar documents, recent writings by many analysts, and the contemporary statements of John XXIII and John Paul II and from the Second Vatican Council. It drew especially on the just-war tradition that strictly limits the legitimate reasons for going to war and the kinds of actions that can licitly be taken during war. But it paid much respect to the principles of nonviolence that would lead to acts of conscientious objection; it repeated Vatican II's affirmation, in *The Church in the Modern World,* of conscientious objection as a legitimate option for individuals. This, incidentally, is a very American option, although not exclusively so. Many governments do not permit it.

The letter proceeded by applying general principles from the tradition to the particular local conditions of the United States during the Cold War. Applying general principles to reasoning about local conditions is precisely what national bishops' conferences are supposed to do. Here it was applied to American political and strategic realities, and to the configuration of moral discourse in the United States in the 1980s. It made a careful distinction between general nondisputable principles (like the need to distinguish between civilians—who can never be targeted deliberately—and possibly legitimate military targets, and the need to keep any damage to military personnel and civilians proportionate to the good supposed to be achieved) and conditioned judgments about how those principles would seem to apply to specific choices about strategy or weapons.

The just-war tradition is not meant to forbid any use of military force whatsoever. But it is meant to apply tough constraints on the use of force. It requires careful judgment and weighing of options; different individuals, with different values and understandings, use it to arrive at very different moral conclusions. The letter was in this spirit. It was also very American in encouraging study, prayer, and dialogue rather than laying down binding statements such as "You cannot licitly work in a nuclear weapons factory." Although it applied very tight conditions to the possession and possible use of nuclear weapons, it did not absolutely forbid either. This derived in part from a practical judgment about the character of national as well as international politics. But it also reflected a particularly American commitment to freedom of conscience; the principle that moral teaching must be persuasive, not coercive. Indeed, one bishop member said at a meeting of the drafting committee: "*Humanae vitae*, issued by the pope after rejecting the recommendations of his own commission, destroyed all teaching authority on the topic. We mustn't let that happen here."

It was also a very American document in its process, which began with requests for such a letter from a wide spectrum of bishops, and a resolution of the conference to move forward. The letter was produced after uniquely wide consultation covering the full political spectrum: government officials and private experts on military-political matters, ethicists, theologians, and citizens. This consultation was also very ecumenical, ranging far beyond just Catholics. The committee was actively and publicly lobbied from all sides. In addition to incorporating statements from Catholic tradition and authorities, it cited Gandhi, Martin Luther King, Jr., Dorothy Day, and many other individuals. The drafting committee followed a very collegial process; clerics and nonclerics on the staff (including a sister) were treated as intellectual and moral equals by the bishops. But the bishop members would be the ones who signed it, so in that sense we quite properly could not be fully equal. All took their responsibility incredibly seriously. Those who had little expertise on the issues rapidly acquired it.

So too, in time, did most of the bishops in the country. They had to do so because the process was so public, and the document itself so controversial. It went through three drafts, plus what became a televised extravaganza of the 1983 annual bishops meeting in Chicago, to produce the final version. The drafts responded carefully to the various comments, moving repeatedly—but within sharp limits—between conservative and dovish positions. People made sure they understood what they were doing. (Perhaps with some help; at one crucial point in the great meeting at the Chicago Hilton I thought I felt the Holy Spirit move across that ballroom.) And in the end it was approved by a vote of 238 to 9. It was, I believe, a testament to pluralism and to the understanding of democracy embodied in John Courtney Murray's contributions to *The Church in the Modern World.* The process by which we operated became the standard against which later all subsequent bishops' statements would be judged. Even at the time, I thought this might prove even more important than the document itself.

There was one less-than-pluralistic glitch, however. Suddenly, in January 1983, then Cardinal Bernardin and Archbishop Roach (the elected head of the conference) were summoned to Rome for consultations. Rome had waited a long time to come into a process that had proceeded well without it. The Americans met with the Holy Father and other Vatican officials. They heard a variety of questions and reservations, but nothing that the Americans felt was fundamental. On returning, Bernardin and Roach wrote a report for the committee saying what points in the document needed clarification or modification, but we all thought the integrity of the document, and the process, could be preserved. Bernardin said verbally that the Vatican feared that conscientious objection, and hence nonviolence, would be treated as an option for the state (not just for individuals), but that the committee did not intend that and could make it clear. We all sensed also an undertone of displeasure with the American bishops for taking on a teaching function that Vatican officials would have preferred to keep in Rome.

Then, in March, came an imperious memorandum from the Vatican detailing a long list of reservations allegedly discussed at the Rome meeting. The substance of the memo was not so bad, expressing many opinions but not as a magisterial statement. But, said Bernardin, "its tone is more negative than I experienced," and if it should become public, "sentences could be taken out of context and used mischievously." That would destroy all our efforts to write a document that would both include specifics and achieve a consensus—end of project. And the memo indicated that in due time it would be sent to every American bishop—meaning, of course, that it would become public.

The committee members were dismayed—and furious. Blessed Joseph Bernardin (I use the qualifier deliberately; I believe he was, and is, blessed) said, "In terms of myself, I'd be happy to say 'Go to hell.' But we can't. We have to preserve the document." And it was Bernardin's brilliant stroke that saved it. He proceeded to distribute the memo to all the bishops, along with the Bernardin and Roach report to us on the meeting, and a committee commentary on the memo showing that we were in fundamental agreement with its principles. The storm blew away. But it came close to a total wipeout of the process and of the document.

I believe the substance of the document continues to be relevant for international relations, even after the Cold War. Here are a few highlights. It did not call for unilateral disarmament, nor did it explicitly prohibit any use of nuclear weapons for deterrence. But it drew on *The Church in the Modern World* statement, "Any act of war aimed indiscriminately at the destruction of entire cities or of extensive areas along with their population is a crime against God and man itself. It merits unequivocal and unhesitating condemnation" (see *The Challenge of Peace*, n. 147, cf. *Gaudium et spes*, n. 80). Regarding the probable escalation of any use of nuclear weapons to undiscriminating and utterly disproportionate consequences, the U.S. bishops declared, "We do not perceive any situation in which the deliberate initiation of nuclear warfare, on however restricted a scale, can be morally justified. Non-nuclear attacks by another state must be resisted by other than nuclear means" (n. 150). They also leaned heavily on a very careful statement by John Paul II in 1982: "*In current conditions,* 'deterrence' [actually, in the French original, "*une dissuasion,*" not any and all deterrence] *based on balance,* certainly *not as an end in itself* but as a *step on the way toward a progressive disarmament, may still* be judged morally acceptable" (see *The Challenge of Peace,* n. 173, drawing from John Paul II, "Message to U.N. Special Session," 1982, p. 3). Note all the qualifiers, which I emphasize with italics.

The just-war emphases on avoiding deliberate targeting of civilians, and on keeping the unintended damage to civilians in some way proportionate to the gains to be achieved by the war, have sharply constrained all subsequent American policy makers. One may well contend that the applications of military force by the United States against Iraq, or against Serbia, pushed beyond the proper just-war limits. But, whether they like it or not, policy makers have felt obliged, in terms of what is morally acceptable to their electorate, to observe much tighter limits than were applied in World War II, or in cold war strategy, when the indiscriminate bombing of civilians was presented as necessary and desirable. In light of the reception of the letter, I doubt that such indiscriminate acts will ever again be acceptable in Western democracies.

In a subsequent pastoral letter in 1993, *The Harvest of Justice Is Sown in Peace,* the U.S. bishops declared, "The eventual elimination of nuclear weapons is more than a moral ideal; it should be a policy goal" (see paragraph E16). Now, well into the post-Cold War era, when the threat of an attack on the West by the Soviet Union is lifted but weaker states are imitating the nuclear powers by developing nuclear weapons of their own, is it time to think again about demanding the negotiated elimination of all such weapons? Perhaps that is still utopian. But by the bishops' own reasoning, they should as a body explore it—and they haven't.

Is there likely ever again to be anything like the U.S. bishops' big letter? It would take a lot of bishops ready to address the question and to exercise some real independence in doing so. Yet the temperamental and theological makeup of the hierarchy in the United States has changed greatly. In 1985 (note, only two years after *The Challenge of Peace*), the Extraordinary Assembly of the Synod of Bishops asked for a study of the theological and juridical status of national episcopal conferences. That study worked its way through the Vatican and emerged as the July 1998 apostolic letter from Rome on "The Theological and Juridical Nature of Episcopal Conferences." That document declares that national conferences are not to take over the authority of the individual bishop in his diocese since his authority is by "divine institution." Yet in general, individual bishops are becoming increasingly reluctant to exercise much independence from anyone; perhaps some are even selected with the expectation they will not; and they risk penalties when they do. Furthermore, doctrinal declarations of a national conference not unanimously agreed to may henceforth be issued only if the Vatican gives its approval. One dissenting bishop is enough to stop it. This is, of course, a much higher standard than was applied to documents from the Second Vatican Council. (And remember that *The Challenge of Peace* garnered "only" ninety-six percent of the votes.) No national conference pastoral letter that really says anything can expect to achieve unanimity. If both individual bishops and national conferences are tranquilized, who then is left?

Reprise

So what was a self-proclaimed social scientist (with more than a hint of positivism in his philosophy of science) doing in such an enterprise? First, by now we all understand that our choice of research programs and our interpretations of our evidence are governed in part by our value systems. Mine drove me to look at policy questions like deterrence. Second, the enterprise of constructing theory about "oughts" is not alien to a social scientist. It means conducting rigorous logical analysis within a deductive system, with words if not with mathematical symbols. Third, it repeatedly requires empirical evidence about the world. A logically consistent argument about the morality of deterrence is worthless if some of its empirical or implicit premises (whether deterrence is really needed; the conditions under which it is likely to work) are grossly in error. To make normative arguments relevant and helpful, there is an essential role for systematic empirical social science, and I did a lot of that.

Before, during, and after the pastoral letter, I regularly taught an undergraduate class on Ethics of Nuclear Strategy. We used many of the materials that had shaped my thinking and, once it existed, the letter itself. I was somewhat apprehensive about the conflict of interest and how the students at this great secular institution might react to it and to me. I made my conflict of interest fully apparent, and tried to teach it as *an* approach, certainly imperfect but one that, as the most prominent statement on the topic, they needed to consider. Fortunately the response to the document was generally favorable, and to my role tolerant. (I did proclaim that my role of advisor to pastoral letters was limited to this topic, and that I had nothing to do with, for example, the letter on women.) It was probably my most successful lecture course.

My research of the past decade or so has returned intensively to a perspective from which I worked much earlier. It starts with a project on the epidemiology of war and peace, rather like what medical researchers do to understand the causes of heart disease or cancer by analyzing large databases on the heredity, behavior, and life experience of hundreds of thousands of individuals. Colleagues and I have put together that kind of big database, but on the characteristics and behavior of all countries in the international system over the past century and more. From it we are teasing out the patterns of who fights whom, under what circumstances—and finding some remarkable regularities.

World politics is conducted in a condition of anarchy. Anarchy is meant in its derivation from Greek: not chaos, but "without a ruler," with no overarching authority to enforce order. In a world far from ready for a global government, the characterization of anarchy is accurate. Realist theorists of international relations say that in such a condition every country is potentially an enemy of every other—intentionally or not, a threat to their security and very existence. This tradition, with a long and honorable history from Thucydides, Machiavelli, and Hobbes, shaped the perspective of theologians like Reinhold Niebuhr. Deterrence forms the heart of survival. Deterrence is also a miserable way of avoiding war, however, and a miserable way to live. To treat all international politics as unending struggle is, moreover, a self-fulfilling prophecy. As a self-fulfilling prophecy, it is a poor guide to practical action, and (therefore?) immoral.

Some of the regularities we are discovering in our work are exactly what the realist theorists predict; for example, alliances may restrain conflict between allies, and disproportionate power often deters weak states from challenging or resisting strong ones. But we are also finding things that realist theory does not predict; for example, that democracies rarely fight one another, that economically interdependent countries rarely fight one another, and that a dense network of international organizations often can prevent violence from breaking out. Some countries—although not all—learn to live peaceably with each other despite a centuries-long history of desperate, violent competition. The European Union testifies to this possibility. None of this constitutes a deterministic law of behavior, but represents the same kind of probability statement that a medical researcher can make about the risk that a smoker runs of developing lung cancer, relative to that of a nonsmoker. And like the medical research, it suggests points of intervention, like giving up smoking. Countries can support the emergence of democratic government in other countries, build economic ties with them, and construct crossnational organizational links.

Increasingly we are finding evidence that cooperative international relations, overcoming the probability of war, are possible—and are far more common than many people recognize. There is stability within the chaos, probability within the randomness, order within the anarchy. Furthermore, it is an order of cooperation and reciprocality consistent with basic precepts of moral behavior. This alternative conception of international relations derives from a tradition of Grotius, Locke, and Kant, owing much to Christianity. It speaks to me of a created order—a sinful order to be sure—that leaves us an opening for behavior that can be other-regarding while still self-regarding, imperfect but not condemning us to a choice between self-victimization and endless cycles of violence. Social science can help us to discern the music of the social spheres, and to comprehend some part of the social creation.

I certainly have not worked out the philosophical and theological implications of all this, and lack the capacity to do so. But I do have the capacity, however flawed and incomplete, to discover these patterns and begin to understand them. I think I see the hand of a demanding but benevolent Creator. In this sense, even when seeing a world of conflict, I can be an optimist and possibly a better Christian. I hope to conform with this instruction from *The Church in the Modern World,* paragraph 62: "May the faithful . . . blend modern science and its theories and the understanding of the most recent discoveries with Christian morality and doctrine. Thus their religious practice and morality can keep pace with their scientific knowledge"

To conclude, I return to some details of my personal life. When I became a Catholic, my parents took this well, certainly not as any kind of betrayal. It helped that they were very fond of Cynthia, and that they respected my conscience. But my decision opened up a crisis of conscience for my mother. She had long felt guilty about my father's conversion. Certainly she knew that he was a thoroughly lapsed Catholic when she met him, and that she had actually brought him back to some religious affiliation. But somehow she felt, at heart, that she had persuaded him to abandon something, and feared that his act—more than one of cultural rejection and affirmation than of faith—had not been in good conscience. She felt, therefore, that he had sinned, and that she had been the occasion of his sin. While maintaining a hopeful kind of piety, her own religious beliefs had never been very strong, and she had always suffered from a terrible lack of intellectual and social self-confidence. Faced with my example, she decided that she, too, should become Catholic. Her new conviction was impelled all the more by her own sense of guilt for my father's abandonment of Catholicism. Yet her conviction was not one she could bring herself to act upon. She was committed to my father. Given his attitudes, and experience of familial rejection as he married her, for her to become a Catholic would be an act of betrayal. So, as she confided to me, she knew she should become a Catholic, but could not.

It was a clear case of conflicting allegiance, posing a threat to her soul. I also sensed a difficulty for my father. He remained a somewhat indifferent Protestant, hostile to Catholicism although not to Catholics, uncomfortable with any discussion of religion and, in some degree, troubled. Did he now question his own departure from the Church? If so, he could not admit it. Even if he did, it was unthinkable that in that small town he could bear the social pressures involved in recrossing the line he had crossed thirty years before. I did not have to believe in outmoded doctrines of "no salvation outside the Church" to see the risks to both of them.

I could see no way out of this condition that I had unintentionally catalyzed. I did the only thing I could—ardently, I took it to the Lord in prayer. A year or so later, my prayers were answered. My father underwent what should have been minor surgery. Because of the anesthesiologist's blunder, he had a cardiac arrest on the operating table, and died three hours later without regaining consciousness. I was called at Yale immediately after the heart attack and, in turn, telephoned the local parish priest and asked him to go to my father. He did, and gave him the last rites. I knew that administration of the sacrament was no act of magic or mechanistic salvation. Unless my father was properly disposed, it would do him no good. But, in the theology of the time, if he was sorry for leaving the Church, or otherwise for the sins of his life, the sacrament would save him. Had he been conscious, his old antipathies likely would have hardened, leading him to reject the priest's ministrations. But since he remained comatose, his last—and perhaps uncomplicated—dispositions would have been operative. At the same time, his death removed my mother's double bind. She could convert to Catholicism without hurting him, and did so. By a mysterious and frightening route, here was an answer to my father's doubts, my mother's anguish, and my own prayers.

I never told my mother about my fears and prayers. She was prone enough to guilt without any hint that her husband had unwittingly died to save her. Maybe this sequence of events was just a coincidence, but it has made me ponder the ways in which prayers may be answered. On the one hand, this experience is reminiscent of many cautionary fables: one should be careful what one wishes or prays for. On the other, as one who believes that this life is a passage to the greater one, I had to be content. The outcome may have been, for my father, "a good death." And if I needed evidence for my own newfound faith, this could be it. This brings me to a story from the Hasidic Jews of Eastern Europe:

> When the Baal Shem had a difficult task before him, he would go to a certain place in the woods, light a fire and meditate in prayer—and what he had set out to perform was done. When a generation later the "Maggid" of Meseritz was faced with the same task he would go to the same place in the woods and say: We can no longer light the fire, but we can still speak the prayers—and what he wanted done became reality. Again a generation later Rabbi Mose Leib of Sassov had to perform this task. And he too, went into the woods and said: We can no longer light a fire, nor do we know the secret meditations that belong to the prayer, but we do know the place in the woods to which it all belongs—and that must be sufficient; and sufficient it was. And when another generation had passed and Rabbi Israel of Rishin was called upon to perform the task, he sat down on his golden chair in the castle and said: We cannot light the fire, we cannot speak the prayers, and we do not know the place, but we can tell the story of how it was done.[1]

Now there are nights when my own faith cools. I see members of the institutional Church trying to assert authority in a way I consider excessive, and I feel alienated. Often, in pursuit of my secular goals, I compromise my principles. My rationalist, scientific side can overshadow faith. I forget the words, I know not the place, and I cannot light the fire. But in the story of my father's death nearly forty years ago, I still can hear God's voice: "I AM." May it be sufficient.

Notes

1. Gershom G. Scholem, *Major Trends in Jewish Mysticism* (New York, 1946), quoted in Joseph R. Levenson, *Confucian China and Its Modern Fate: A*

Trilogy, combined edition (Berkeley and Los Angeles: University of California Press, 1969), volume 3, pp. 124–125.

Sources

Citations from the Second Vatican Council: *The Documents of Vatican II*, W. Abbott, S.J. ed.

28

"Where are you?"
A Journey Home

John Thompson

"Adam, where are you?" God asks in the opening of Denise Levertov's (1997, p. 17) poem, "On a Theme by Thomas Merton." God's initial query and consequent suffering over Adam's absence voiced in the poet's concluding reply refract my own story: ". . . Fragmented, he is not present to himself. God suffers the void that is his absence."

We live life forward. We tell it backwards framed by the present. The story I tell is a retrospective reply to the question, "John, where are you?" Past pieces patched together highlight themes of absence in darkness, a journey into uncertainty, a search for my father and a changed relationship with God, the Church, and the world. Mine is a tangled account of culture and faith, just trying to make sense of things.

To begin, I offer Buechner's description of vocation as "that place 'where the heart's deep gladness meets the world's deep hunger'" (Parks 1990, p. 360). Although such a meeting probably happens to only the great and the lucky, its possibility attracts me. Sometimes, even if by accident, what gives one joy might also encourage others.

At sixty-one years of age, I recount my story from later adulthood, glancing at encroaching old age. In the tension of Erikson's life-cycle stages, I struggle to care for those who come after while trying to resist the cocoon of stagnant self-importance. Warily I eye old age, hoping for some feeling of integrity to offset the threat of debilitating doubt that my life has been a waste. In tension. Incomplete.

This story needs a warning. The comment on a card which once hung on the college chaplain's door seems apropos. "It just may be that my sole purpose in life is to serve as a warning for others." I got most of it wrong. Only now am I where I probably should have started years ago. I take some solace, however, in Picasso's retort after age eighty: "It takes a long time to become young."

Beginnings

My life mirrors the American Catholic Church's contestation with modernity. Along with many Americans, the Depression pushed my parents' families from the Midwest to the West Coast in search of work. Jim Thompson found a part-time job at Goodyear Tire, while trying to get on with the fire department. Alice Hopkins had a stenographer's job with an insurance company. They met at a Catholic youth dance and three years later married. Several years later I arrived to live on Imperial Highway in Downey, a town of ten thousand, about thirteen miles from Los Angeles. The New Deal provided PWA work projects for two uncles and a social security pension for my grandparents who lived next door. FDR was a family icon. We were Democrats.

World War II images are my earliest memories: talk of Pearl Harbor, convoys of camouflaged army trucks rolling down Imperial Highway, the long barrel of a howitzer sticking out of a tent-covered bunker a block away. V-E Day, May 1945, is the first public celebration I remember. In August, Hiroshima, Nagasaki, and A-bomb entered our talk as Japan surrendered. American and Catholic were my family's identities and loyalties, and the parish church and hall and Catholic school were the focus of our community. Priests, sisters, and parishioners constituted the relationships that counted. Sunday Mass, evening devotions and saying the rosary, not eating meat on Friday, and voting Democrat were regular rituals that distinguished us. Catholic institutions marked our boundaries as daily conversations buttressed our certitudes. Although my family ancestry was mostly German, our world was Irish Catholic. My father liked pointing out the Polish names of Fighting Irish football players, yet he didn't miss a game on the radio. Fierce loyalty to Notre Dame symbolized the odd mixture of our American Catholic pride and feisty inferiority. Although my father had not completed high school, Carl Sandburg's *Abraham Lincoln* graced our bookshelves and his two sons were going to Notre Dame. My mother and father gave us children a dime for each A on report cards and a nickel for each B. Doing well in school was important, the way to a better job and life.

Several years after the war ended, my father was promoted to captain on the fire department. My mother was at home raising my brother, my adopted sister, and me. My father's political bent and union allegiances found causes in civil service negotiations for the firefighters' association, in the Knights of Columbus, and in supporting local candidates for office. As the youngest son, he possessed an atypical sense of equality that overrode his German, Irish, Catholic, and Caucasian tribal ties. He encouraged African Americans, then called Negroes, to take the civil service exam for the fire department, and more than once he walked out of the room when his brothers told anti-Jewish jokes. My father gently invited anyone with an air of superiority or complaints about hard work to "join the human race." In the post-war mood of optimism, affluence, and influx of veterans with families, orange groves were uprooted for housing subdivisions as Downey became a suburb.

Plans Change

The fabric of our family future unraveled early one foggy morning in late 1949 when I awoke to the terror in my mother's words, "I've called Father Doyle. Dad won't wake up." At forty-three, my father had died of a heart attack during the night. My mother was thirty-eight; I was twelve. In my dazed reaction, I remember a favorite uncle on my mother's side of the family holding me tightly around the waist as we walked up the aisle in church, the sight and smell of so many flowers, a funeral procession two miles long going to Calvary Cemetery, off-duty firemen everywhere. I heard my paternal grandmother say, "Parents should die before their children." Within several years, she and my grandfather died. Somehow I felt responsible.

My mother began working outside the home. I worked weekends and summers at a dairy. Trying to grow up, I buried my father's death. Adrift in adolescent confusions, I desperately clung to the stability and certainty my Catholic beliefs and practices held out. I submerged my grief, meeting my need for approval and achievement with high grades and getting into Loyola High School. Thoughts of becoming a Jesuit held out the allure of a future securely embedded in the certain Catholic world—beyond death. These years saw the Cold War spread and a war in Korea break out in mid-1950. Our neighbors' grandsons, Gene and Ronnie, joined the navy and served on aircraft carriers in the Pacific.

The fall of 1950, I started high school, leaving home early each morning to make the hour-and-a-half streetcar ride to Loyola in smoggy LA. By working morning recess and part of lunch hour in the cafeteria, I paid tuition. Loyola meant college prep classes, lots of homework, and classmates from wealthy families. I met Jesuits, some of whom I admired. I began to see myself associated with them. I did well academically, motivated by high grades and a delight in learning. Math and physics fascinated me. In late 1952 America tested an H-bomb in the South Pacific, "five hundred times more powerful" than an A-bomb—and we called it "atoms for peace." As the Korean War stalemated the next summer, the Soviet Union tested its own H-bomb—and we called it a nuclear threat. Gene and Ronnie returned home safely, very good ping-pong players. As the Cold War became an arms race, a few people built bomb shelters in their backyards. "Godless communism" became the new enemy. Jesuit missionaries expelled from Communist China visited Loyola High vividly to affirm this enemy of the Catholic Church. Fear of communist sympathizers spread alongside signs of affluence. TVs with rabbit ear antennas appeared in store windows and some living rooms. We bought our first new car, a 1953 Chevrolet with powerglide. Downey was the site of McDonald's first golden arches drive-through. Drive-in theatres redefined dating. A senior retreat confirmed my plans to enter the Jesuits. Holiness meant becoming a priest.

Joining the Jesuits

On August 14, 1955, I took the train to San Jose with two others to enter the Jesuit novitiate at Los Gatos. The enclosed world of the novitiate quickly seized my thoughts and demeanor, demarcating a sharp break with "the world." Two weeks after arriving, still struggling to learn Latin words and phrases for everything from dishwasher to excuse me, we postulants received our cassocks and entered a world of silence and certitudes, monastic routines and ideals, affirmed by the novice master in his talks on the rule, obedience, and "God's will." In pursuit of holiness, "perfection," I strove to fit in. Sports and outdoor work brought relief from the isolated hours of silence and scrupulosity. In late fall, a thirty-day retreat was a time of "consolation," as St. Ignatius called it in the rules for discernment. The assurance of a vocation filled me with the comfort and joy of certitude in doing "God's will." Within several months, however, I was assailed by doubts about everything. Darkness descended everywhere—including prayer. In fledging efforts to use St. Ignatius's rules for discernment, I concluded I should leave. The novice master's assurances about a vocation did not diminish my "desolation." I envied the apparent ease and joy of other novices. I was told to take vows, a day I remember as filled with intense isolation, anguish, and abandonment by God.

The next two years meant Greek and Latin studies, Shakespeare and English literature, history and speech. Reading *Orthodoxy* started a binge on Chesterton's writing, which ended suddenly a few pages into *The Man Who Was Thursday*, when paradoxes turned sour. Although studies gave spotty relief to darkness and depression, spiritual practices proved painful, as did the continuing advice to go on. In fall 1957, Sputnik, a basketball-sized Soviet satellite, spooked the West over Communism's threat to "bury the West." Pope Pius XII died in 1958. The new pope, an old man, called himself John XXIII. I remember nothing about this "caretaker" pope calling a council.

In fall 1959 I began a B.A. in scholastic philosophy along with courses in mathematics and physics at the Jesuit House of Studies at Spring Hill College, Mobile, Alabama. Getting off the train in Mobile, I saw the first of many signs of segregation, bathrooms for "colored." Although I remember some initial excitement at the prospect of grappling with "truths of reason," I found most philosophy courses remote to my concerns, although philosophy of science did interest me. While darkness continued to dog me, spiritual advisors still told me I had a vocation. Although I spent Sunday afternoons visiting in a black community near the residence, the emerging racial turmoil and protest were kept from our view. Despite Spring Hill College's courage in integrating in 1954, we were exposed to little on the social encyclicals or the race question. Holiness meant separation from the world, yet the House of Studies erupted in support at John Kennedy's election as president. In August 1961 the Berlin Wall went up. The following May, I graduated with a B.A. in philosophy, against the backdrop of old oaks, azaleas, and William F. Buckley, Jr.'s commencement words.

Teaching

After summer short courses on teaching, I was assigned to Loyola High School in Los Angeles. At 8:25 on an early September Monday morning in 1962, I stepped into 3C to teach twenty juniors, armed with an Algebra II book and a black cassock—and filled with trepidation. But within ten minutes, I knew I wanted to teach for the rest of my life.

With access to newspapers, magazines, and television, I followed public affairs. The opening of Vatican II that fall fascinated me. Although exhausted from teaching, I stayed up nights reading whatever I could find about the council. In late October, the Cuban missile crisis turned the Cold War into an imminent nuclear threat. Late some nights, I found odd comfort walking in the shadows behind the floodlights illuminating the school building, trying to extinguish darkness searing my soul. Finally, I struck a deal with God. More than thirty-five years later, it still sounds blasphemous. "I will no longer ask what you want. And you won't again tell me." The search for God's will was officially off. Darkness deepened. Was God keeping his end of the bargain, or . . . was there only darkness? Fall 1963 was punctured by John Kennedy's assassination.

Three years at Loyola High confirmed and deepened my desire to teach. Teaching evoked my energy, gladness, and care for students. In teaching, I felt at home where I had least expected it. Teaching did not, however, dislodge darkness and depression. Despite another prayerful effort to leave the Jesuits, a different spiritual director again discerned a vocation. I went to theology, deeply uneasy.

Theological Studies

Theological studies brought two significant encounters: introduction to the Scriptures as historical and literary documents and introduction to the background, documents, and implications of Vatican II, under the guidance of Fr. Dan O'Hanlon S.J., an expert on ecumenism at the council.

Paragraph 1 of "The Church in the World Today" (*Gaudium et spes*) still startles me in its expression of solidarity with humanity, our collective affirmation as Catholics to "join the human race." A profound return to and retrieval of what *catholic* meant.

> 1.(The close link between the church and the whole human family)
> The joys and the hopes and the sorrows and anxieties of people today, especially of those who are poor and afflicted, are also the joys and hopes, the sorrows and anxieties of the disciples of Christ, and there is nothing truly human which does not also affect them. Their community is composed of people united in Christ who are directed by the holy Spirit in their pilgrimage towards the Father's kingdom and who have received the message of salvation to be communicated to everyone. For this reason it feels itself closely linked to the human race and its history (Tanner 1990, p. 1069).

The next summer, I took two sociology courses at UCLA. This new perspective immediately attracted me, representing an affinity with my changing, expanding sensibilities, bringing me into intellectual and emotional engagement with social and cultural change in American life, civil rights, black power, and feminism. I saw the American Catholic Church and Vatican II reforms through a new lens. What C. Wright Mills called "the Sociological

Imagination" brought different questions, refocused my intellectual interest and drove my curiosity. I began to realize my story as imbedded in a larger historical story. Sociology offered me a new window on American society, the Church, and myself. That summer closed with violent riots in Watts, only a few miles south of Loyola High, expressing graphically much of what I had begun to probe in sociology courses.

In theology, I was attracted by organizational, thematic, and comparative approaches to the Gospels generally and to the parables specifically as part of the "new quest" for the consciousness of the historical Jesus. "Abba" and "suffering servant" were among the clues. I studied the suffering servant songs of Second Isaiah in Hebrew and their presence as themes and echoes in the New Testament, particularly the Lord's Supper. Was it possible that darkness, unanswered questions, were also Jesus' experience, despite what I had grown up believing about Jesus' foreknowledge? Had Jesus drawn on the suffering servant songs to make sense of himself, of his relationship to his Abba, and of the emerging conflicts in which he found himself? e. e. cummings (1954, p. 455) voiced my identification with Jesus beset by darkness and loneliness, a stranger:

no time ago	jesus)my heart	close as i'm to you
or else a life	flopped over	yet closer
walking in the dark	and lay still	made of nothing
i met christ	while he passed(as	except loneliness

During this time, I read Thomas O'Dea's *The Sociology of Religion* (1966). I began reading American novels. Studying sociology and religion seemed a way critically to encounter and appropriate American society and culture, the Catholic Church and my own identity in response to *Gaudium et spes*. Ironically, as a kind of stranger, I was trying to enter into American society and culture at a time of its deepening crisis.

Being Found

On another front, I found myself a stranger. Here was this Jesus with whose humanity I had increasingly identified. His paradoxical life of care and detachment, articulated in the beatitudes and parables, attracted me. His identification with the marginalized felt God-like. Yet, darkness, persistent and relentless, had eroded my faith. I felt like a stranger to the now opaque religious symbols I inherited. I was about to walk away from the deadened religious practices—in my utter absence from God. Late one night in December 1967, after studying, I turned off the light to sit quietly before going to bed. Leaning back in the swivel chair, I kept my fingers lightly on the edge of the desk to keep from tipping backwards. My mind, usually racing with thoughts, started to shut down. Its deepening silence left me feeling as though I were about to fall, evoking a terrifying claustrophobic childhood memory of a little girl who had fallen down a well shaft. Wedged one hundred and two feet below the surface, she died before workers who had tunneled down alongside the well shaft could rescue her. My fingers now clutched at the desk's edge to keep from falling. Something drew me to let go. As I did, I felt myself falling down a well shaft. Suddenly, I was floating, as though in outer space. No down or up. Floating, outside of time. A bright white-light presence flooded me in my darkness. Held me. I felt God's presence as a father. Although not in words, I heard, "I love you without conditions." Joy. How long the experience lasted or what time I went to bed, I don't know. I awoke fully dressed in the morning to the intense feelings of God's care still there. Over the next several days, love of neighbor tied to God's love grew clear. Somehow I was my neighbor. Despite repeated efforts to debunk the whole experience, I could not do it.

A sense of presence remained. So did darkness. Several months later I entered the worst depression I had yet endured. In suffocating fright, daily I felt myself plunging down a well shaft. Although wanting to hang on, I struggled to be silent, to let myself fall into emptiness. That summer, I went to San Diego to take sociology courses in religion and collective behavior. I lived in a black parish. The reductionist assumptions of sociology of religion confronted my faith convictions protected until now by compatible philosophical contexts. In facing the critiques of Marx, Durkheim, and Weber, which exposed the underpinnings of modernity, I felt their relativizing undertow on my faith. Herberg's *Protestant, Catholic, Jew* (1960) presented the revival of religious belonging and practices as simply allegiance to the American way of life in denominational disguise—secularization. *Humanae vitae* was released on July 25, 1968. The confluence of the jolt from sociology of religion, rancor of racial tensions on the streets of southeast San Diego and in the parish, and debilitating depression brought terrible headaches and the conclusion I would end up on skid row. A failure. The odd amalgam I had hammered out of American dream and sainthood disintegrated.

One August morning the sky was blue. "One day at a time" lengthened into two; eventually a week. At the ocean I listened to the rhythmic rumble of breaking waves as they rolled thousands of small stones toward the beach, paused in silence, and receded back in a rush to the sea. Then a month. The fragrance of flowers surprised me. Nearly nineteen years after his death, my dad touched me through surfacing memories and emotions—a man motivated by justice, hard work, and care, who had a playful sense of humor and sometimes swore while asking his children to remind him not to swear. He had been waiting for me. The next visit home was filled with questions about Dad. Was it surprising that eight months earlier I had experienced God as a caring father? Finding my dad alive in memories I had submerged in suppressed grief and hidden in depression, I found myself. Like my dad, I sometimes swore.

By Christmas, I completed an M.A. in theology. I found odd comfort in the harsh and pounding sounds of Bob Dylan's 1965 "Highway 61 Revisited." In January 1969, I returned to San Diego State to continue sociology courses. Sociological theory attracted and challenged me. Like many on campuses, I questioned U.S. involvement in Vietnam. Despite continued bouts of depression, out of a sense of obligation and suspicion that I had been avoiding commitment, I accepted ordination to the priesthood that June.

Graduate Studies in Sociology

As I continued with sociology courses and took the GRE, I applied for admission to Ph.D. programs. In November, I met Professor Thomas O'Dea at his Santa Barbara home. In his backyard, we talked of Bernard Lonergan's *Insight* (1957), secularization, and the renewal of Vatican II. That afternoon was my introduction to Tom O'Dea, the storyteller-teacher, sociologist, Catholic intellectual, who agreed to accept me as one of his graduate students.

The next fall I started a Ph.D. program in sociology at UC Santa Barbara amid continuing campus protest over Vietnam and Cambodia. Professor Walter Capps's course, Methods in the Study of Religion, marked an interior transition. After my presentation of Heinz Schlette's *Towards a Theology of Religions* (1966), Walter Capps asked me: "Do you ask yourself the truth question about your faith?" Without hesitation, but with some surprise, I replied, "No. But until you just asked me, I didn't know I'd stopped." I heard in my words what I had not yet realized. We talked about this shift as he asked: "Is your Catholic faith true for you?" "Yes, it's how I must live my life." "Is it necessary that it be true for others?" "No, but it's still true for me." "Are other faiths a threat?" "No. Actually, I am curious about them." In reference to Newman (1947), he spoke of the need for a "grammar" of this complex transition to personal conviction, intensified curiosity about and dialogue with "the other," and a tolerance that was not indifference. My obsessive quest for certitude, pursued in an apologetics of difference, had ceased. Already another quest had begun for elements of congruence in others' views and lives different from mine, for assumptions informing my own views and life, for tolerance toward ambiguity. I had begun to hear and ask questions in a dialogue with modernity.

That fall I read O'Dea's *The Catholic Crisis* (1968) where I found a description of these shifts and a framework for making sense of them in his analysis of the historical context of Vatican II and four conciliar documents. Through O'Dea's insights into the dilemmas of institutionalization and the strains of "overinstitutionalization" in the Catholic Church's defensive response to modernity, a shift from a classical and invariant form of theological formulation to a consciously historical and experiential approach to theological reflection, I recognized the minute and intimate ties between the personal features of my identity and the defining institutional structures of the Church. Despite my earlier lack of interest in philosophy, I now had an intense interest in epistemology, phenomenology, qualitative research, and methodological assumptions. Courses and many conversations with Tom O'Dea allowed me to explore these issues in the study of sociology and religion. Heller's *Catch 22* (1961), however, revealed our generational differences. His service in the army during World War II made *Catch 22* unpalatable, even repulsive, while I found laughter at its satiric mocking of modern warfare and society redemptive.

With these shifts in thinking crystallizing and my continued uneasiness about ordination, I decided to leave the Jesuits and seek laicization. Although much more is left out than said here, the painful oscillation over whether I had a vocation or not had the practical ending of the Jesuit provincial accepting my decision. The sky was blue that day too. After receiving laicization papers a year later, I married the woman with whom I had developed a close friendship through correspondence. She had previously left religious life.

My dissertation research involved extensive fieldwork on Charismatic Renewal among Catholics in Southern California, through which I examined the dynamics and forms of this movement in relationship to institutional church structures. Participant observation allowed me to study a self-avowed movement of renewal from a sociological vantage point. It marked an enduring intellectual and existential concern about renewal of Roman Catholic institutions within the contexts and changes of Vatican II and modernity.

The years with Tom O'Dea were the gift of a mentor passionately engaged as an intellectual in identifying and analyzing relationships between religion and culture, with particular attention to the American Catholic experience. His extensive readings in philosophy, literature, theology, and history informed his sociological analysis of religious institutions and religious responses to the contemporary world. He took the sacred and the religious quest seriously. Despite his many contributions to understanding American Catholic life, he felt the charge of disloyalty leveled from within against the religious intellectual.

Following a year-long struggle with Hodgkin's disease, Tom O'Dea died on November 14, 1974. A week before we had prayed the Lord's Prayer together and said goodbye. I grieved for this man who had become a second father to me and to whom, during four short years, I had been an admiring and caring son, blessed as a student in his presence, genius, and stories. After the funeral Mass at Mission Santa Barbara, Fr. Vincent Martin, OSB, a fellow graduate student with Tom O'Dea at Harvard after World War II, spoke at the graveside about the gratitude and joy that we who had known Tom O'Dea experienced in his touching our lives. The simple concrete gravestone reads, "Thomas F. O'Dea. 1915–1974. U.S. Army."

St. Thomas More College in the Canadian Prairies

In Summer 1975 my wife and I moved to Saskatoon where I had been offered a position in sociology at St. Thomas More College (STM) at the University of Saskatchewan. STM met my hopes to teach in a Catholic liberal arts college, while offering the unexpected but welcome context of its federation with a provincial university of more than 900 faculty, 12,000 students, a sociology department of sixteen colleagues, and a graduate program. Named after the great Catholic humanist scholar and statesperson Thomas More, and offering humanities and social science courses in university degree programs, STM struck me as conducive to and representative of Vatican II's response to the contemporary world: service and search for truth in dialogue and cooperation. My wife and I joined the STM worshiping community.

On Easter Tuesday, 1976, our first child, Andrew, was born. I was overwhelmed by feelings of fatherly care that this infant evoked in me, no doubt much like what my dad must have felt toward me. Our son was an overwhelming gift to my wife and me. We felt blessed and fascinated in his presence and development.

Learning to Teach

The next fifteen years involved sustained engagement in scholarly activity into which I threw myself with delight and long hours. These years represented developments that seemed to emerge from some inner logic in the desire to teach. My desire to teach can be heard in a 1972 application for a Kent Fellowship:

> I intend to become a teacher. I see a teaching career in sociology with an emphasis in religion as enabling me to help students formulate approaches to knowledge in the context of questioning and intellectual disciplines. By "approaches to knowledge" I mean getting some perspective on the influences in one's own life, becoming aware of the limitations and advantages of theoretical knowledge, relating knowledge to personal questions of social and moral importance. It involves learning how to think and formulate implications, in the context of sensitivity to and concern for others, without overestimating one's impact and without surrendering control of one's life to outside influences.
>
> I view my intended teaching career as a way of usefully serving others, and as a way in which I can contribute to man's [sic] struggle for self-transcendence and a sense of brotherhood [sic].

"Demythologizing modernity," the title of my first graduate student's thesis on Peter Berger's sociology of religion, expresses the concern which has informed and unified my teaching sociology: identifying the character and dynamic of modernity, locating it historically, and making explicit its practices, values, and truth claims as a culture. Rather than have students reject modernity or reject their experience, unmasking modernity tries to show modernity as a culture, socially constructed and ordinary in character, and thereby to make students aware of its pervasive, although hidden, claim on their consciousness. Jim Kelly (1982, p. 128) succinctly states modernity's claim as it proclaims itself in positivistic sociology. "The myth of social science is that it has no myth." Teaching with this humanistic concern represents a hope of bringing students to informed choices and commitments (Westhues 1982).

I have taught sociology as a story that took shape as varied responses to the Enlightenment and the rise of science, the Industrial Revolution, the French Revolution, and the emergence of the modern state. I present the critiques of Marx, Durkheim, Weber, and their followers within the contexts of their lives and times, and as lenses focusing economic, moral, and cultural forces at work. Rather than have students choose among these theorists and theories, I attempt to have students enter into these thinkers' insights, often incompatible in their underlying assumptions about society, culture, key processes, and the human person, as vantage points that reveal modernity's strikingly contradictory faces. Following Nisbet's *Sociology as an Art Form* (1976), I treat these thinkers as sensitive artists sketching with broad strokes the landscapes and portraits of modern society. Alienation, anomie, and "demagicification of the world" are offered as metaphors to illuminate the mysteries and maladies of modernity and to reduce its totalizing claim. Charles Taylor's *The Ethics of Authenticity* (1992) allows students to identify sources shaping our modern sense of self. Taylor's retrieval of authenticity, care, and personal responsibility as an ethical core in a culture of modernity offers a methodology as well as a sense of personal agency for students to connect their stories with their times.

Learning about Canada and Saskatchewan informed my efforts to encourage students' critical appropriation of their identity as Canadians. My becoming a citizen in 1980 proved a source of not only personal meaning but also of outsider insights to explore and question students' taken-for-granted attitudes toward Canadian society. Newcomer status has allowed me to encourage students to see the distinctiveness and contributions of as well as the challenges facing Canadian society and culture.

Teaching and Writing to Learn

My beliefs and practices about the importance of writing and its relationship to learning and thinking, probably an obsession by now, informed and shaped my own developments as a teacher and my changing approach to students' learning. In a phrase now current, "write to learn" (Murray 1984), emerged early on as a central concern of and vehicle for my teaching. In the fright and risk of writing an impromptu essay in front of students, I became a student with those in my classes. More than thirty-five impromptu essays later, my in-class essays are still first drafts, no better than the initial essay twenty years before. I am now, however, more at ease in showing students a live sociologist at work exploring a topic of their choice through writing.

When I realized that the search for meaning through writing required serious and sustained revision, I moved beyond one-shot or first-draft-last draft assignments. I began using topic selection papers, first drafts with my typed comments as conversation for revision, and second drafts. Free writing and one-minute memos at the end of each class became a regular part of my teaching. Writing had given me a window on students' thinking, their efforts to connect their lives to societal structures and issues, and their risk-filled struggles to form identities, to address ethical issues, and to make occupational choices in the pluralism of modernity. My teaching now focused less on me as the teacher and more on students and their learning. This meant long hours of student conferences and early mornings and weekends of marking and preparing classes. In 1988, STM students gave me the college's first teaching award. Although deeply honored, I felt embarrassed, since only then was I starting to get the hang of how students learned and hence how I should be teaching.

Students now felt like my grandchildren, evoking care I hadn't noticed before. Concerns about epistemological, intellectual, ethical, and faith issues grew out of my interactions with them and my questions about how sociology as a perspective influences their development toward adulthood. From the early 1980s into the 1990s the writings of Kenneth Westhues (1982), Donald Murray (1984), Parker Palmer (1983, 1987), William Perry (1970), Carol Gilligan (1982), Donald Schön (1983), Mary Belenky et al. (1986), Ann Berthoff (1988), and Sharon Parks (1986, 1990) gave voice and form to many of my inchoate concerns about student learning and development that had arisen out of "writing to learn." These authors allowed me to notice and make sense of changes in students' interrelated ways of knowing, and to appreciate the centrality of a community supportive of students moving toward and making adult commitments in the face of uncertainty.

I have had the privilege of accompanying many graduate students, listening as they courageously unravel the meaning and effects of modernity. Their questions have probed marginality and anomie, secularity and powerlessness, professions and control, change and identity in topics that range from the influence of patriarchy and technology on the lives of Hutterite women and the social construction of nursing as a profession to the inner-worldly mystical orientation of Aurovilians (Tamil Nadu, India) and the social consequences of near-death experiences on those who report them. These students' sensitivity to the stranger motif mirrors contemporary sensibilities (Bauman 1997). Their intellectual efforts reflect heroic attempts to make meaning in a culture in which, in Marx's words, ". . . all that is solid melts into air" (Berman 1982).

My own research has focused on religion and renewal: Catholic participants in an anti-cult conference; religion as a major factor in the quality of marriage and family life; the influence of reading the Catholic and secular press on the beliefs, attitudes, practices, and parish participation of prairie Catholics; the influence of Vatican II on the beliefs, attitudes, and practices of active Catholics in the context of a diocesan synod.

Our second son, Mark, was born in 1983, during the four-year research project on the quality of marriage and family life. My wife did ask about the quality of our family's life during my extended absences doing research. To our joy of a second child was the added joy of Andrew's delight in a baby brother.

Shifting Frames in Higher Education and a Different Darkness

By the mid-1980s, an anti-religious and positivistic bias in the university subculture began to show signs of crumbling. New voices began to be heard: women, visible minorities, Aboriginal people, persons with gay and lesbian orientation. Questions related to spirituality and ethics—even though sometimes uncritical and first thoughts—began to be heard. The first hints of what has come to be called "post-modernity" appeared in campus criticism of quantitative methodology, interest in neglected and new questions related to meaning, culture, marginality, and injustice, and desire for interdisciplinarity (Westhues 1987). At the same time other voices, louder, could be heard advocating education in marketing metaphors—clientele, commodities. information transfer, economic impact. The liberal arts core of the university and students' personal appropriation of informed, critical, and compassionate judgment were devalued to bottom-line measures of career and business success in the marketplace. For me it was a time of growing critique and discontent.

In the thirteen years at STM, I had unwittingly taken on the life and mission of the college. I had just wanted to work with students and do research, not take responsibility for the place and its direction. I was emerging now as a critic. Our failure to face and work through divisions over Vatican II that had bedeviled the college from the early 1970s had now hardened into a conspiracy of silence with a veneer of public politeness. One day at noon, going through the nearly empty cafeteria, I felt as though I had walked in on the college's funeral in progress. I sensed the college as an academic and faith community had gone dead without notice. As my alienation grew and my wife and I considered leaving the college, I was seconded to a university project on renewal of teaching and learning. An invigorating year with thoughtful colleagues allowed me to work through my disappointment and grief. In the fall of that year, I was unexpectedly asked to be a candidate for the STM presidency. Since my being chosen seemed out of the question, I agreed to speak and did so candidly about the college's loss of direction, reduced conversation with the university, failure to promote the ideals and practices of a liberal arts education beyond isolated classrooms, deadlock over Vatican II, isolation from the Catholic community, and need for renewal of our Basilian ideals of education. My critique didn't save me from being chosen for a job I didn't want. Friendly handshakes and congratulatory notes did not hide the prospect of a different darkness in my advocacy of college renewal.

I felt affinity to *Ex corde ecclesiae*, the Apostolic Constitution on Catholic Universities promulgated in fall 1990. Despite the conflict its implementation through ordinances later set off in the U.S., I found its ideal of inculturation of faith and learning close to what the Basilian Fathers had accomplished at STM as a federated college years before the council. Citing Newman four times and Vatican II documents more than twenty times, including *Gaudium et spes* eleven times, *Ex corde ecclesiae* represented a positive vision of intellectual inquiry in a dialogue between faith and contemporary culture and learning. Members of Catholic universities were called to engage in critical inquiry that included epistemological and ethical reflection as part of transforming culture in light of the gospel. The dual vocation of the Catholic university—to community and to scholarship in a context of faith—recognized the significance of a faith both personal and immersed in a living culture. Dennis Murphy (1992, p. 82) observes:

> The best of both our biblical tradition and our Catholic theological tradition holds for this intimate relationship between knowing and loving and between the learner and the world.

> Our Catholic tradition does not admit finally of a detached kind of knowing. . . . [T]here is more in learning than a subject who comes to know objects that lie outside oneself.

Within a year the college was embroiled in open conflict. My actions provoked anger, accusations of destroying the college, and attempted retaliation. Morale plummeted. I tried to absorb the hostility, without returning it, calling on the sociologist in me to frame conflict in institutional rather than personal terms. While renewal lacks orderly stages and clear outcomes, it does exact the price of division, even vilification. Gerald Arbuckle (1988) aptly frames this ordeal in creation imagery: "out of chaos." Could the college survive? Darkness was now joined to powerlessness, with no assurance of success. Peck (1993, p. 90) characterizes such experience as "the emptiness of not knowing . . . terrifying emptiness." Although he endows it with religious meaning and sees it as the price of civility, it felt only like dark isolation, without much civility. What I did know and feel was an obligation to care for the college in the throes of change, even when others would not or could not care. I could not walk away from renewal despite the personal cost.

I met daily reminders of Dietrich Reinhart's (1992, p. 55) understated observation: "All of you know what a challenge it is to ensure vitality in a mission grown old, what a challenge it is to keep such a mission in focus while nostalgia and bereavement for what once was keep distorting the lens." Three years later, in the face of continuing turmoil and against strong objections by some faculty, the review committee ignored my request not to be given a second term. Reappointment for a second five-year term felt like an extended sentence. Within two years, faculty initiatives appeared, with open and frank discussions starting to take place. Morale improved. Contacts with the Catholic community have become more frequent. Discussions about the direction of STM as a liberal arts college with a renewed commitment to the Basilian tradition of higher education were in evidence. My discontent had quieted. Others are appropriate judges for whether the college has become engaged in a renewal which translates Vatican II and *Ex corde ecclesiae* into actuality for students and the college's constituencies.

What Was the Question?

As I end this account, spring returns to the Canadian prairies. The news reports thousands of Albanians killed in Kosovo Province with many more thousands displaced from their homes and towns. Further north, NATO bombs rupture the nights and lives of Serbian people. The Dow Jones Index surpasses 11,000. *Catch 22* revisited. Violence and the problem of evil have filled our century and our souls. A prolonged and confusing recovery from pancreatic surgery has left me feeling life's fragility, the suffering of so many, the absurdity of war (Mowat 1979). My privileged position in the affluent world and academic life continues to trouble me in light of Jesus' life, his words in Matthew 25, my late night encounter with God's presence, and recognizing my neighbor as myself. So often I have "passed by on the other side of the road," as my neighbor lies beaten up and robbed in the ditch of the contemporary world.

For years, darkness' ugly presence reduced me to feeling God's absence and my own. Although I prayed, pious practices felt fraudulent. Darkness stubbornly stayed. I found Jesus walking there, too. Eventually, I was less afraid of it. Sometimes we furtively talked. A decade into darkness—now over thirty years ago—God found me, breaking through grief I suppressed at my father's death when I was twelve. I felt God's caring presence. As sociology interrogated the darkness, the Gospels, and me, I began to hear replies in a new voice, shaping my sensibilities to our times—fragmented, ambivalent, questioning, longing. Only recently I remembered words opening Simon and Garfunkel's *Sounds of Silence*: "Hello, darkness, my old friend. I've come to talk with you again . . ." The silence of modernity's multiplicity has not been mute. God has been in the darkness. God is even the darkness, suffering.

Out of the text and context of Vatican II, my identity as a Catholic and an academic has been reconstructed: a bricolage of a desire to teach, the vantage point of sociology, the call to be a Christian. *Gaudium et spes* remains "joy and hope" for me, affirming a changed and changing relationship with God, the Church, and the world, in solidarity with humanity.

"If you expect to see the final results of your works," an Arab proverb teaches, "you have simply not asked a big enough question" (Chittister 1992, p. 12). Like other Catholics whose lives Vatican II interrupted "in the middle of things," I have moved from assured certainty with clear answers insulated against questioning to intrusive, even uninvited, questions complex in their context and ambiguous in their consequences. The locus of faith has moved from the mind in the head to the hearts in the minds of persons in community. Incarnation and Eucharist mean taking Jesus' humanity seriously and ours too—in history, in culture and community, in experience (Cooke 1992, 1997). God is present in our times too, calling us to compassion, to presence to each other, Christian and non-Christian (Hellwig 1983). Ours is a pilgrim people journeying home, as my dad used to say, to "join the human race," and as our older son now says, "to join the planet." Within darkness I have heard a suffering presence ask, "John, where are you?"

> By night, by night, we journey—simply to find the source.
> Only our thirst lights the way, only our thirst lights the way . . .
> (Taizé)

Acknowledgments

The books and articles listed below are the works of some authors who have both challenged and accompanied me on the path of the Catholic faith tradition, in the reflective practices of teaching and doing sociology, and in telling my story.

Arbuckle, Gerald A. *Out of Chaos: Refounding Religious Congregations*. New York: Paulist Press. 1988.

Bauman, Zygmunt. *Postmodernity and Its Discontents*. Washington Square, NY: New York University Press. 1997.

Belenky, Mary F., Blythe M. Clinchy, Nancy R. Goldberger, Jill M. Tarule. *Women's Ways of Knowing*. New York: Basic Books. 1986.

Berman, Marshall. *All That Is Solid Melts Into Air*. New York: Simon and Schuster. 1982.

Berthoff, Ann E. *Forming/Thinking/Writing*. Second edition. Portsmouth, NH: Boynton/Cook. 1988.

Chesterton, G. K. *The Man Who Was Thursday*. New York: Sheed and Ward. 1975. (1908).

_____. *Orthodoxy*. London: J. Lane. 1908.

Chittister, Joan. "Spirituality for the Long Haul." *Compass* May/June 1992. pp. 12–13.

Cooke, Bernard. *God's Beloved*. Trinity Press International. 1992.

_____. *The Future of the Eucharist*. New York: Paulist Press. 1997.

cummings, e. e. *Poems 1923–1954*. New York: Harcourt, Brace and World. 1954.

Gilligan, Carol. *In a Different Voice*. Cambridge, MA: Harvard University Press. 1982.

Heller, Joseph. *Catch-22: A Novel*. New York : Simon and Schuster. 1961.

Hellwig, Monika H. *Jesus: The Compassion of God*. Collegeville, MN: The Liturgical Press. 1983.

Herberg, Will. *Protestant, Catholic, Jew*. Garden City, NY: Anchor Books. 1960.

John Paul II. *Ex corde ecclesiae*. Origins Vol. 20, No. 17. 1990. pp. 266–276.

Kelly, James R. "Fact and Value in Contemporary Sociology." *Thought* Vol. 57, No. 224.1982. pp. 128–147.

Levertov, Denise. "On a Theme by Thomas Merton." *The Stream and the Sapphire: Selected Poems on Religious Themes*. New York: New Direction Books. 1997. p. 17.

Lonergan, Bernard. *Insight: A Study of Human Understanding*. New York: Philosophical Library. 1957.

Mowat, Farley. *And No Birds Sang*. Toronto: McClelland and Stewart. 1979.

Murphy, Dennis J. "Catholic Education: Towards the Third Millennium." *Grail* Vol. 2. No. 2. 1992. pp. 69–91.

Murray, Donald. M. *Write to Learn*. New York: Holt, Rinehart and Winston. 1984.

Newman, John Henry. *An Essay in Aid of a Grammar of Assent*. New York: Longman, Green. 1947.

Nisbet, Robert. *Sociology as an Art Form*. New York: Oxford University Press. 1976.

O'Dea, Thomas F. *The Sociology of Religion*. Englewood Cliffs, NJ: Prentice-Hall. 1966.

_____. *The Catholic Crisis*. Boston: Beacon Press. 1968..

Palmer, Parker J. "Community, Conflict and Ways of Knowing." *Change* Vol. 19, No. 5. 1987. pp. 20–25.

_____. *To Know As We Are Known*. San Francisco: Harper and Row. 1983 (republished in 1993).

Parks, Sharon. *The Critical Years*. San Francisco: Harper and Row. 1986 (republished in 1991).

———. "Social Vision and Moral Courage: Mentoring a New Generation." *Cross Currents* Fall 1990: pp. 350–367.

Paul VI. *Humanae Vitae*. Encyclical on the Regulation of Birth. 25 July 1968.

Peck, Scott M. *A World Waiting To Be Born: Civility Rediscovered*. New York: Bantam Books. 1993.

Perry, William G. Jr. *Intellectual and Ethical Forms of Development in the Student Years: A Scheme*. New York: Holt, Reinhart and Winston. 1970 (republished in 1997 by Jossey-Bass).

Reinhart, Dietrich OSB. "A Good Stewardship of Paradox: The Identity of a Catholic College." *Current Issues* Vol.12, No. 2. Winter 1992. pp. 55–58.

Schlette, Heinz. tr. W. J. O'Hara. *Towards a Theology of Religions*. New York: Herder and Herder. 1966 (original in German, published in 1963).

Schön, Donald A. *The Reflective Practitioner*. New York: Basic Books. 1983.

Tanner, Norman P., editor. *The Decrees of the Ecumenical Councils*. London: Sheed and Ward and Washington, D.C.: Georgetown University Press. 1990. *Gaudium et Spes*, the Pastoral Constitution on the Church in the World Today, promulgated by His Holiness Pope Paul VI, December 7, 1965, is found in Vol. 2, pp. 1069–1135.

Taylor, Charles. *The Ethics of Authenticity*. Cambridge: Harvard University Press. 1992.

Westhues, Kenneth. *First Sociology*. New York: McGraw-Hill. 1982.

———. editor. *Basic Principles for a Social Science in Our Time*. Waterloo, Ont: University of St. Jerome's College Press. 1987.

29

Leading a Life of Faith in the Secular Academy

Peter Dodson

I am, in no particular order, a geologist, a dinosaur paleontologist, an evolutionary biologist, a veterinary anatomist, a lecturer, a traveler, a sometime fossil collector, a student, a reader, an author, a grant-writer, a mentor, a neighbor, a citizen, a husband, a father and, above all, a deeply committed Christian. I am surpassingly lucky to have prospered in many if not all of these activities. Any one of these could potentially consume a disproportionate amount of my time. Part of the art of being a successful academic *and* a successful person is to do well all of these sometimes contradictory things, in their turn; it is surely impossible to do them all simultaneously.

I am in general reluctant to speak or write of myself, but I am acutely aware of the value of role models. Clearly, there are ever so many articulate models for the scientist as atheist today. If my experience as a scientist who practices his Christian faith openly in a highly secular academic environment can have some value, then I am pleased to proceed with this essay. I draw on my experience of twenty-five years at the University of Pennsylvania, where I am a professor of animal gross anatomy in the School of Veterinary Medicine, and also a professor of earth and environmental sciences (formerly geology) in the School of Arts and Sciences. This is perhaps an eyebrow-raising combination, but I have three degrees in geology to prepare me for a career in dinosaur paleontology. The accident of taking human gross anatomy at Yale Medical School in the final year of my graduate program opened the door to my present position. I always tell my students that an anatomist switching between a human and a dog is like a mechanic switching between a Chevrolet and a Toyota.

In my opening comments, I misstated that all of my attributes are in no particular order. It is categorically true that my Christian faith overarches and colors all of my activities, indeed every breath I take. This fact makes me the husband and father that I am, the scholar and teacher and mentor that I am, the friend and neighbor and citizen that I am. It is an inseparable part of the unity that is Peter Dodson.

We all accept that faith is a gift of the Holy Spirit. I received the gift of the Catholic Christian faith from my parents, both converts. I was baptized and raised in the faith, and it has been my joy to practice the faith throughout my life. I am a simple person; I never had need to pass through a stage of adolescent rebellion. I grew up in a kinder, gentler era before drugs and sex were invented, or at least before they had become the pervasive social problem they are today. My life borders on the boringly upright—no one will ever make a movie of my life! The faith always made sense to me and appealed to me.

With only a couple of years' hiatus, I spent most of my education in Catholic schools, with little regret. A few minor details: I was born in California in 1946, while my dad was competing his Ph.D. in biology from the University of California at Berkeley. I lived in South Bend, Indiana, where Dad taught biology at Notre Dame until I was eleven. The family then moved to Canada, where I grew up in suburban Aylmer, Quebec, and Dad taught biology at the University of Ottawa until his retirement in 1981. As a result, I had the advantage of learning reasonably fluent French and studying Latin in high school for four years. I studied geology at the University of Ottawa, and later pursued paleontology, anatomy, and evolution, first at the University of Alberta (M. Sc. 1970) then at Yale University (Ph.D. 1974).

Upon graduation from Ottawa in 1968, I married Dawn Swank, my sweetheart from freshman-year science. Dawn has been my best friend and companion, and the mother of my two splendid children, Christopher (born 1973) and Jessica (born 1976). We spent the first two and a half months of married life in a tent in southern Alberta, where I did field studies for my master's degree. Life has been a bed of roses (comparatively!) ever since: every subsequent address we have lived at has had hot and cold running water, electricity, and indoor plumbing!

My first and only position since leaving graduate school has been at the University of Pennsylvania. In retrospect, the early days of my career in Philadelphia were somewhat difficult. There was much joy in raising a young family, and our urban parish of St. Francis de Sales in West Philadelphia proved to be a delightful, warm, and welcoming Christian community; it continues to be our spiritual home twenty-four years later. Yet the demands of the job were considerable: learning to teach gross anatomy, learning to meet the requirements of collegiality, establishing a funded research program, and publishing the papers to secure the reputation that would be required for tenure in a few short years. Added to these stresses were the demands of a young family. Fortunately, my particular branch of science is not a demanding laboratory discipline, and I was able to maintain a reasonable 9-to-5 schedule for the most part, or an 8-to-5:30 or 7-to-6 schedule. I have always been jealous about reserving weekends for my family (the exception being when I travel and the airfare requires Sunday travel). My laboratory was the great outdoors, typically in summers. For a number of years, I packed up my family and headed for Alberta or Montana, where we camped for the summer in the course of my professional research.

I achieved tenure in 1981. It was neither an easy process nor a foregone conclusion—perhaps understandable inasmuch as a geologist in a School of Veterinary Medicine is a legitimate oddity. (I received my first student-teaching award in 1988, and a number of others since then—so I don't believe tenure was a mistake!)

As for the practice of faith, it was not an issue in any explicit way in the academic setting. I think students who were perceptive knew about my faith. Occasionally a student would come to discuss some personal issue because he or she recognized something in me; this has always flattered me.

I regard teaching as a ministry. It is a charism I have been given. It is what I do. It allows me to touch peoples' lives. It is one of the first ways that I served my parish in Philadelphia. When the influx of Vietnamese began in 1976, another parishioner and I began teaching English to the new immigrant families. We continued for nine months, until more professional support services were in place. I believe my effectiveness as a teacher stems from my Christian faith: it involves contact with the whole person, the individual. In my professional teaching, I often find that I have greater contact with the struggling student than with the top-drawer student who needs nothing from me. It is always a source of great personal satisfaction when my extra efforts have made the difference between success or failure for a student.

I note two other forms of evangelism: the silent witness of ashes on the forehead every Lent, and the very satisfying ministry of choral music. Our church has a splendid choir; indeed our parish has a rich tradition of music. Saint Francis de Sales is an old stone church with a beautiful Byzantine dome and a truly magnificent French organ. I praised the choir a little too enthusiastically one day twenty years ago and found myself in the tenor section the following Sunday—and have been there ever since.

The choir is one of the major contributing factors to my mental well-being and habitually happy outlook on life. We sing a rich repertoire of sacred music that ranges from the earliest fifteenth-century polyphony through Bach and Handel to nineteenth-century Romantics such as Brahms, Gounod, and Bruckner (our favorite) to twentieth-century artists. We sing together, we pray together, we laugh together, and we cry together.

Our choir is a community within a community, and has always been welcoming to families and children. If I discover that a vet student or a grad student is a singer, I instinctively recruit. In that way I enjoy a deeper and continuing relationship with that person than is typically possible. In any case, although I rarely made an explicit thing of it, my faith and its importance to me gradually became known to my colleagues, never to my detriment.

My family at work is close knit, as we have been colleagues and friends for years. I arrived there nearly twenty-five years ago, and I am still one of the new kids on the block. We know one another very well. Like any family, of course, we have our ups and downs but on the whole we get along well. One of my colleagues is as Catholic as I am, educated by priests and nuns from kindergarten through college. Our secretary also is Catholic. One technician is a delightful Seventh Day Adventist, devout, intelligent, and committed. Another technician, however, has shunned his mother's faith for many years, but is now asking the profound questions of life and browsing Scripture. A senior colleague is agnostic, but a respectful and sincere seeker, interested in religion although he cannot yet leap off the precipice of rationalism. All in all, the environment of the department, where neuroscience and evolution flourish, is remarkably open to good, honest religious discussions, which can break out without warning at any time. I must also mention a close friend who is a devout and highly intelligent atheist. He is the most literate, witty, opinionated, and articulate person I have ever known, and he has done wonders for my knowledge of letters. I was not liberally educated; in Canada, at least in the 1960s, a science education was just that. My friend, a biologist and linguist from Brown, has repaired some of the deficiencies in my education, for which I am deeply grateful. He is a valued confidante, a reader and editor of all my writings, and he bears the brunt of all my religious sentiments. I witness to him constantly as that strange animal, the scientist as believer. His worldview remains intact, even as I invite him, in the words of John Polkinghorne, to take a broader view of reality.

Thus I lived my life with a fine family and a rich set of friends and colleagues. My complacency changed, however, on December 15, 1988, when I attended a scientific seminar at the Academy of Natural Sciences in Philadelphia that literally changed my life, although I didn't know it at the time. The seminar was entitled "The Evolution of Human Morality," by William Provine, a distinguished historian of science from Cornell University. Because the title was intriguing enough, I naively failed to anticipate that this was to be an atheist manifesto by an evangelical atheist, a born-again scientific naturalist. The speaker was a consummate rhetorician—one might almost say preacher, and he played his crowd masterfully. At one point he had his audience joining him in peals of laughter as he read from Pope John Paul II's 1982 statement to the Pontifical Academy of Science about the harmony of science and religion. His major point was that evolutionary biology shows us that there is no God, there is no soul, there is no life after death, indeed there is no such thing as free will (every one of the hundreds of decisions we make every day being the result of either our genes or our environment). Moreover, a scientist who professes to believe in God is a hypocrite.

I was stunned by all of this—by the comments themselves and the apparent approval of the audience. During the discussion period afterward, I was too overwhelmed even to raise an objection; I did not know where to begin. At first I was depressed; after all, this was not the message I wanted to hear as I prepared to celebrate the birth of Christ.

Then my depression turned to resolve and, on December 23, I wrote Provine a four-page letter, professing my faith in Christ and passionately outlining my thoughts about the reasonableness of religious faith. In particular, I objected to being labeled a hypocrite (whatever else I am, I don't think I am a hypocrite). Provine generously responded in five pages, allowing that I might not be a hypocrite but "merely blinded by powerful cultural traditions!" (Aha! Peter Dodson is blind and Will Provine sees clearly—now I understand!) He ended his letter by inviting me to Cornell to debate him in public. Knowing his superior rhetorical skills and home-field advantage, I declined his invitation, doing so in six pages. That ended our correspondence, but the fifteen pages of letters exchanged were of incalculable value to me in ways I am still learning.

My first reaction to the encounter was the thought that I was alone, that I was the only scientist in the United States who was also a religious believer.

Of course, nothing could be further from the truth: a survey taken several years ago revealed that forty percent of American scientists believe in God, a number essentially unchanged since early in the century. But because there are ever so many models for the scientist as atheist, one has to look much harder for the model of scientist as believer. Thus, I set out on a project of discovery. Who were believers among scientists? Provine, ever the evangelical, actually went so far as to state that there was only a mere handful of believers among evolutionary biologists—even though he had not asked me, my father, my friends, or anyone to my knowledge; evidently this wildly imaginative statement was to be taken on faith!

The first scientist I encountered on my project of discovery was Owen Gingerich, a distinguished astronomer and historian of science from Harvard University. Gingerich happened to give a seminar on our campus sponsored by the Intervarsity Christian Fellowship. His seminar, entitled "Modern Cosmology and Genesis," was dazzling, a deft exposition of science, philosophy of science, and personal witness. I was deeply moved and inspired, and I knew that my journey had indeed begun.

Through my father, I encountered another man whose writings have loomed large in my worldview: John Polkinghorne, a distinguished Cambridge University particle physicist who left the physics laboratory at age forty-three to take Anglican holy orders. Since then he has written a steady stream of substantial but highly readable books explicating and exploring the relationship between the science he loves and understands deeply and the Christian faith he has embraced and practiced throughout his life. Two of his recent books are my favorites: *Faith of a Physicist* (Princeton University Press, 1994); and *Belief in God in an Age of Science* (Yale University Press, 1998). Another important American author is Ian Barbour, who has a Ph.D. in physics from Chicago and a master's in divinity from Yale. I was in awe of this combination: Why hadn't I thought of that? Barbour taught me that a sense of wonder and awe—the moment of aha!—is itself a prayer! This point was driven home to me when I read the account of a paleontologist handling skulls of human ancestors in an African museum. He described his sense of reverence and awe at holding these treasures in his hands and then, almost in embarrassment, added that to keep the record clear, these of course were not religious feelings! Too late—the cat was out of the bag!

By this time, I was pretty certain that I was not alone as a religious scientist. Several other truly wonderful things happened in my professional life. One was that an engineer and a musicologist put out the call for Christian faculty and grad students to meet at the Newman Center to explore the faith and in particular to consider the role of religious belief in a hostile academic environment. (I can only conclude that the Holy Spirit is alive and well on our campus.) We called our group Coffee, Croissant, and Christianity, or CCC. (Croissants are such a rarity that we sometimes call the group "donuts and dogma," although we are far from dogmatic!) Unfortunately, the date of founding is not recorded, but it must have been 1990 or 1991. In any case, we have met continuously since then, every Tuesday morning following the 7:30 Mass, until we depart to our various home bases around campus. Our numbers have varied, rarely more than twelve, sometimes as few as six; only two of the charter members remain. The grad students and postdocs have turned over, but the mix has always been delightful and eclectic, a nice balance of humanities and the sciences, sometimes emphasizing one, sometimes the other. Currently we include a physicist, a protein chemist, a European historian, a medieval musicologist, a Renaissance art historian, an Ethiopian orthodox priest, a pair of law librarians, and a Romance languages grad student. We also have various interesting drop-ins. In the past we have had nursing students, a med student, a psychologist, a Quaker philosopher, a Presbyterian administrator, a priest-Sumerologist, a truck-driver-classics student, a young laboratory worker who left us to join a convent, a merchant marine, and an Intervarsity Christian Fellowship leader.

Our discussions have been wide-ranging, at times terribly apt, at times barely intersecting with any reality I know, but collectively marvelous—both the liberal education I never had and an examination from every conceivable angle of the faith we all cherish. We normally focus on a reading—a chapter from a book, a sermon of John Henry Newman, a papal encyclical (currently *Fides et ratio*), a topic from the news, sometimes Scripture, a segment of the *Catechism of the Catholic Church*, regularly a paraliturgy, a video of a play (*St. John in Exile*) or of a significant program ("The Life of Edith Stein"). It is a special treat when a member shares his or her special scholarly expertise, as with the analysis of Sir Edward Elgar's *Dream of Gerontius* by our musicologist, or of a painting of Raphael by our art historian. CCC is one of the most cherished activities of my academic life. I really try to plan my life in such a way that I do not miss it.

Another of my life supports grew out of CCC in a way that some would describe as coincidence, but of which we Christians know better. A nursing student in the group, knowing of my interest in faith and science, suggested I contact Fr. Tom King, S.J., at Georgetown University. I did, and Fr. Tom invited me to participate in the Cosmos and Creation meeting at Loyola College in Baltimore. The Cosmos and Creation seminar is usually held over Memorial Day weekend, and is sponsored by the Jesuits in science—the most canny minds in Roman collars! The gathering includes Jesuits who teach and/or research at various colleges, universities, and institutes, and lay persons, like myself, who are scientists vitally interested in the dialog with religion. I attended my first meeting in May 1990, and have not missed one since. The speaker on that occasion was the distinguished German Teilhard scholar, Karl Schmitz-Moorman. The group was so welcoming, Karl so stimulating, and the size of the gathering and the format so conducive to discussion and fellowship that I returned home bubbling with joy and a profound sense of re-creation. It was so clear that my personal quest stimulated by my encounter with Provine was no fool's errand but a realistic goal and a reasonable scholarly endeavor. I was so gushing in my enthusiasm that the next year my father and mother joined me! And in later years, both of my brothers and my son have attended—so it has become an occasion for a family reunion each year, making it all the more joyful. Over the years we have been joined by one after another of the giants in the field of science and religion:

Ian Barbour, Arthur Peacocke, Thomas Torrance, Jack Haught, even John Polkinghorne himself. I count myself extremely lucky indeed to have made all of these acquaintances. My knowledge has expanded enormously on account of these conferences.

So far, I have said little of my father, Edward O. Dodson. He is a giant in my life, a role model for the integration of science and faith. He is also a legitimate scholar in the field, the author of a study on Teilhard de Chardin, *The Phenomenon of Man Revisited* (Columbia University Press, 1984), as well as *Evolution or Creation? Correspondence Between and Evolutionist and a Creationist* (University of Ottawa Press, 1991). Because it was important for me to find my own way, both in science and in faith, I think perhaps early on I did not give him sufficient credit for his insights and scholarship. During my undergraduate and graduate education, I was striving to gain the foundation I needed in my chosen field of science. It was not until I received the stimulus from my greatly appreciated "enemy," Will Provine, that I was moved to begin to grow in knowledge about the relationship between faith and science. I think it was through Cosmos and Creation that I matured enough to understand and appreciate Dad's depth.

In 1994, I had the wonderful blessing of attending a conference at Queens College, Cambridge University, with my parents. The conference, held for two weeks in July, was entitled "Cosmos and Creation," sponsored by the C. S. Lewis Society and hosted by Rev. John Polkinghorne, Ph.D., F.R.S., S.O.Sc. (Society of Ordained Scientists). Here again were my heroes, including Polkinghorne, Gingerich, and Barbour, as well as many others, including authors Peter Kreeft and Thomas Howard, Cornell President and paleontologist F. H. T. Rhodes, and earnest young comers such as John Medina and Keith Miller. It was a marvelous time for worship, fellowship, family time, and growth in knowledge and faith. This was my first real visit to England, and I enjoyed Cambridge immensely, including such highlights as punting on the Cam, visiting Isaac Newton's Trinity College, and Charles Darwin's Christ College, dining in the Great Hall of St. John's College and, above all, attending evensong in King's College Chapel. For years I have enjoyed Christmas Eve lessons from King's College Chapel broadcast on PBS. As recreated year after year on television, the glorious sound fills the Gothic, fan-vaulted space to create an other-worldly experience. As a choral singer myself, I had longed to experience the thrill of hearing the famed and inspiring King's College singers in their own space. Moreover, it was none other than Stephen Jay Gould, in a famous paper with Richard Lewontin, *The Spandrels of San Marcos* (Philosophical Transactions of the Royal Society of London 1979), who sang the praises of this, one of the most splendid ceilings in the history of architecture! God sometimes sees fit to gift us with our heart's desire. Not only did I attend evensong four times, but the choral work on my first visit was the choral setting (*Agnus Dei*) of Samuel Barber's sublime Adagio for Strings. I just about had an out-of-body experience. As tears stained my cheeks, I was literally speechless. All-in-all, the two weeks I spent in Cambridge were two of the happiest weeks of my life, and I think, two of the most productive in my growth in the study of science and religion.

Up until now I have emphasized the process of my formation, a process that, to this point in my narrative, had consumed forty-eight years of my life. Of course, the process continues. Has it borne any fruit? I hope so. Part of the explicit goal of our CCC group is to determine ways for Christian faculty to be a presence, a witness, on campus. This is also the goal of Christian Leadership Ministries, a Protestant group whose weekly meetings I sometimes attend. The obvious place to begin to witness is in one's own classroom. There I sometimes begin an introductory lecture by saying something like, "I am a dinosaur paleontologist, an evolutionary biologist, and a deeply committed Christian. Go figure!"; or "I profess geology, paleontology, anatomy, and Christianity." The object is not to make a big deal about it, but to make a simple statement that students can do with as they wish, including to ignore it. But it is there. This step takes small courage.

A somewhat larger step is to witness outside the classroom or even off campus in a decidedly secular/hostile environment. The Spirit suddenly moved me to do so in the fall of 1994, at the annual meeting of my professional organization, the Society of Vertebrate Paleontology. At the business meeting, a somewhat surprising resolution was presented, I suppose in response to some perceived threat by local Creationists. The resolution expressed the official position of the SVP that evolution by natural selection is *the* method by which the diversity of the biological world has been achieved. I, normally a silent observer, was moved to stand and offer what I described as a friendly amendment, to wit: "Acceptance of evolution in no way precludes belief in God. And the religious beliefs of scientists mirror those of the population at large."

Unfortunately, I was too clever by half. If I had confined my statement to the first half, the tenor of the discussion suggests that it may have passed. I had badly misspoken, however, on the second statement. What I had meant to say was that the *range* of religious beliefs of scientists reflected those of the population at large. I knew this to be true, as I knew that among the paleontologists present in the room, there were those like myself who attended church every Sunday, and there were those who have never set foot inside a church. The discussion on the second sentence turned hostile very quickly. My attempts to undo the damage were in vain, and the amendment was voted into oblivion. I was not disappointed inasmuch as I had not offered the amendment because I thought it would carry but because I felt it was the correct time to stand and witness; I felt called to do so. I cannot say that it failed because I do not know what lives this action may have touched.

Further opportunities have arisen for more explicit witness. In 1996, for example, I had the pleasure of publishing a book, *The Horned Dinosaurs*, with Princeton University Press. On the dedication page I placed the slogan *Ad Majorem Dei Gloriam,* presumably cryptic enough for those who are ignorant of the Christian faith or of Latin, but an unequivocal advertisement for those who are aware. Throughout the text, I sprinkle the "G" word in several places. The message should be there for those who are perceptive. Rather more explicit, I devoted an entire essay for the column I write in *American Paleontologist*, a quarterly newsletter published by the Paleontological

Research Institute in Ithaca, New York. My essay in the May 1997 issue is entitled "God and the Dinosaurs." In it, I literally come out of the closet and confess my faith in Christ. I state:

> I am inspired by the example of a number of other evolution-ary scientists and philosophers who have come out of the closet. I am comforted by the company of Stephen Jay Gould, E. O. Wilson, the late Carl Sagan, William Provine, Daniel Dennett and Richard Dawkins, to name but a few. These courageous individuals have shared with us their religious views, which as a group range from respectful agnosticism to evangelical atheism. I can no longer hide the fact that I am a deeply committed Christian. All of my life I have practiced the faith of my fathers; this gives meaning and joy to my life, informs each breath that I take and everything that I do.

In the essay, I appreciate Stanley Jaki's position that modern science grew out of the Judaeo-Christian understanding of the relationship between God and nature, and I develope the four-fold typology of John Haught, about the different postures between science and religion: conflict, contrast, contact (dialogue), and confirmation. I concluded: "Dinosaurs were the jewels of God's creation. They graced the planet for 160 million years. Like all of His creation, they gave Him praise. God loved them."

American Paleontologist has a modest circulation, but I got more response from that essay than any other I have published there. The responses were basically ones of gratitude. One southern geologist thought that I had put in to words what perhaps half of the geologists he knew felt but had never been able to express. Another letter was from an Episcopal priest, ordained after a career in science, who was excited to read some attempt to put together the two activities that mean so much to him. I got two negative letters, or at least letters of challenge. One was from a biologist at a creationist college who felt I had been unjust to that camp. Our exchange of letters was subsequently published, giving me further chance to witness:

> I have a serious problem with young-Earth creationism because it implies a deceitful God, one who "antiqued" the Earth, giving it only an impression of great antiquity. This is not the God I worship as Sovereign Lord. It also implies that the senses God gave us are inadequate for comprehending creation—that is, that science as a method is fatally flawed and cannot stand by itself without the aid of the Bible.

The other challenging letter I received was a very thoughtful three-page letter from a geologist who had abandoned the faith of his youth forty-five years ago. He asked me a series of very specific questions about just how my faith impacted my life as a scientist. As for what I believe about the course of evolution, I wrote:

> It makes no difference to me whether God breathed upon the
> face of the waters or a lightning bolt discharged into the pri-
> mordial soup three and a half billion years ago. My faith is in
> Jesus and the Resurrection—and He came to save you and me,
> not bacteria, trilobites or dinosaurs. If you look to the Bible for
> a scientific account of nature, then of course it has a bad
> record. If you look to it for a hard-eyed and realistic descrip-
> tion of human nature, as a source for values and moral guid-
> ance, as a prescription for leading a good life, and for a just
> society, it is unsurpassed. Shall we look to Darwin for these?
> Surely not!

I conceded to him that it might not make a difference in the way I swing my
hammer to break open a rock or in the way I use my calipers to measure a
specimen. However, I pointed out that as a full professor in an Ivy League
university, I occupy a position of power. Every day I review manuscripts for
publication and grants for funding, write letters for students seeking positions, and review dossiers for promotion. Each one of these activities provides an opportunity for abuse. "I do not cease to be a person when I act as
a scientist. Inasmuch as science is a social enterprise, my actions are always
informed by my faith. This is expressed by the way I treat students, colleagues, collaborators, and competitors." I poured my heart and soul into
those five pages. I hope they may have done some good, but I never got a
reply. But I feel enriched by having collected and written my thoughts.

Writing an essay is a somewhat anonymous activity; I have little indica-
tion that my professional colleagues that I care the most about will ever see
this publication. When it came time for me to decide what papers to distribute in a general biannual mailing of my reprints, I had to decide whether I
had the courage to send "God and the Dinosaurs." It was really a no-brainer.
After all, chance to evangelize is not to be missed! Again, several warm
responses were generated, including one colleague who came up to me at our
national meeting and hugged me! Wow!

Once I came out of the closet, opportunities began to materialize. I was
invited to lecture at a Catholic college in Philadelphia, at a Christian college
in Iowa, at a Templeton workshop in Texas. In the fall of 1999, I lectured at
the national meeting of the Geological Society; my topic: "The Faith of a
Paleontologist!" One of the most exciting challenges now is the development
of the Philadelphia Center for Science and Religion, which became public in
February 1999. In this center, we host monthly lectures to foster the dialogue
between religion and science. My fellows in this enterprise span a wide range
of beliefs; I was deliberately asked to be president because of my firm faith.
In 1996, while I was on sabbatical, I had the privilege of sitting in on a wonderful undergraduate course on science and religion called Science and the
Sacred. It was tremendously stimulating, and I encountered a wide range of
literature and religious thought. The instructor, Dr. William Grassie, has
become a valued friend. It was Billy Grassie who founded (and is the executive director) of the Philadelphia Center for Religion and Science. Now my

turn has come to teach Science and the Sacred. I have just been awarded a Templeton course award for religion and science. In the fall of 1999, I had the chance to share my thoughts with twenty of the best and brightest undergraduates. For a lifelong science geek like me, this was a slightly frightening but very exciting challenge. For someone who deals with animal guts and dinosaur bones every day, the challenge of teaching a genuine humanities course was very real. I hope it was rewarding for all involved.

In summary, my twenty-five years as an academic has been extraordinarily rewarding in every way. My experiences have been varied and ever interesting. I have touched many lives, I have done interesting research, I have traveled to many parts of the globe. Early in my career it was incumbent on me to establish a scholarly reputation both nationally and internationally. Attending meetings in Europe early on was probably one of the most valuable career moves I made, because the contacts I made became the international referees I needed for my promotion dossier. Later on, especially in the last ten years, I have branched out of the confines of my narrow academic field. Now, developing in knowledge of my faith and sharing my joy in Christ rank among the activities that I treasure the most. At times there is a temptation to make a career of them. But I value my teaching and my professional research too highly to abandon either.

To everything there is a season. Now is the season of my life when I can afford to divide my activities. To have done so twenty years earlier would have been disastrous. I am profoundly grateful for the privileges of the academic life.

30

A Continuing Search

William G. Gray

When I was department chair, the same scenario was repeated a couple of times each academic year. The parents of a prospective undergraduate student would call the office and schedule a meeting with me, ostensibly to discuss the educational opportunities for their son or daughter offered at Notre Dame in the Department of Civil Engineering. At the appointed hour, the parents and student would arrive and nervously arrange themselves to absorb the wisdom they expected I would be dispensing. After some informal social introductions, we would get down to the agenda. The prospect would ask about the courses required for a major in civil engineering, about the laboratories, and about the flexibility in the schedule. Then the parents would ask the questions that would climax the visit, questions that I expected but disliked. "What is the job market in civil engineering? What are the starting salaries for individuals graduating with a degree in civil engineering?" No matter how the conversation had gone prior to this point, I knew that these questions would arise, that these questions were viewed as of the utmost importance in the minds of the visitors.

From my perspective, these questions have almost nothing to do with reasons for selecting a college or major. My strategy at this point was to reply by talking around the questions without actually providing any specific answers. Concerning the job market, I would disclaim, "The job market in engineering tends to fluctuate with the economy. Thus the current job market is no indicator of what the market might be like in four years and certainly is not an indicator of the job market throughout the career of a new engineer. Also, many individuals who major in engineering decide to pursue other fields, such as medicine, business, or law, as their professions." The question of starting salaries is a bit trickier. My answer tried to provide a broader perspective. I would note, "The starting salaries in civil engineering tend to be lower than those in other engineering disciplines. However, civil engineering provides more opportunities for entrepreneurial activities than other engineering disciplines. Thus, although salaries are low on average, the motivated individual who wishes to go into consulting or start his or her own business has opportunities to earn a well-above-average salary." These answers seemed to satisfy my visitors. In hindsight they seem to be alternative ways of saying simply, "I don't know," and "It doesn't really matter."

I do not know when the process of selecting a college and major became infected by overriding concern for future financial success. In my own selection process, a close family friend, a gregarious priest with connections at the University of Notre Dame, spent several years trying to convince me and my parents that Notre Dame was emerging as an outstanding educational institution and was certainly a school I should consider. I was also being recruited by the lawyer for one of the leading California wineries to major in oenology at the University of California at Davis. He promised me a terrific job at graduation, not knowing that I really didn't much care for wine. I decided against Notre Dame, in large part because of fear that a kid from San Francisco would freeze to death in the harsh Midwestern weather. It seemed that I would have an easier time learning to love wine than winter.

The flawed reasoning used to decide which school to attend nevertheless led to a wonderful choice. I enrolled at UC Davis. A couple of summers working in the vineyard and the winery, however, along with a dose of common sense, finally prevailed in leading me away from oenology and toward a major in the sciences. I was becoming a chemistry major when I was exposed to a bit of engineering just before my junior year and switched into chemical engineering so that I could use more math in the analysis of chemical processes. I was naive about job prospects in any of these fields, but being in school in the late '60s assured staying out of the military and Vietnam, making all majors somewhat attractive. I was both apolitical and an eager student. Although I didn't know where it would lead me, I was happy with my major and enjoyed learning to analyze and solve problems of fluid mechanics and chemical reactions. I recall being amazed that physics was well enough understood that one could model systems such as those involving flow through tubes or the spreading of chemicals with equations that actually describe the operative processes.

My curiosity about being able to model fluid movements led me to pursue graduate studies. At this point, I decided it was time to get away from California to see if the rest of the country was as lacking in quality of life as Californians said it was. Then, on completion of graduate school, I could return to the West armed with experience confirming this common wisdom. From what I had heard, the East was not as unlivable as the center of the country, so my developing decision-making skills led me to pursue a doctorate at Princeton University.

My years as a graduate student were both important and difficult. While studying for exams, I became even more fascinated with the order that exists in physical processes. I loved to draw connections between apparently disparate phenomena. Taken to its logical conclusion, my goal was to know only one fundamental principle, and to be able to derive all the information that I needed from that principle. The analogy with knowledge of God was not lost on me, and I often found that when I was able to make new derivations, I was not only gaining a clearer understanding of physics, but I was also learning how God had ordered the universe. I had moments of joy when, while studying alone in my office or a corner of the library, I would gain a new insight that provided closer unity with the fundamental principle. It became clear that the discovery of new descriptions of physical processes, and even coming to an understanding of known descriptions, was what I was drawn to as the great prize for intense study. I wanted discovery to be the focal point of my disciplinary studies.

Graduate school was also a personal challenge. I was not a particularly brilliant student. I struggled with courses and examinations. It seemed to me that my difficulties lay not with the work being too complex, but more that I did not look at the problems from the right perspective. In any event, the result was that I did not distinguish myself; fortunately, I survived the hazing process, whose hurdles included courses and qualifying examinations. My research was on a topic that interested neither me nor my advisor. This strained our relationship and forced me to turn my preparation of a dissertation into a rite of passage to be endured rather than the authoring of some new understanding of cutting-edge problems.

I was very fortunate during the last year of my studies, when interest in my research was at a mutual minimum, to meet a faculty member from a different department: civil engineering. He and I would stand around the computer card reader—a great socialization spot long since outmoded by personal computers and terminals—loading our boxes of computer code and discussing what we were each doing. I was modeling flow and heat transfer in chemical reactors; he was modeling flow and chemical reactions in subsurface geologic regions. The similarities in the equations that described these systems were obvious, and I began to wonder if I could adapt some of his solution techniques to my problem as a way of getting some advanced analysis into my studies. When I suggested this to my advisor, he responded definitively that the finite element method I wanted to examine was an outdated technique that people formerly used when computers had vacuum tubes.[1] He told me not to deviate from the path of inquiry that had been outlined. I was frustrated because I knew the assessment was not correct and because I was in need of someone to be supportive of my research efforts. I therefore decided to work with my computer room colleague on a problem of interest at night while I worked on my dissertation during the day, making sure my advisor did not know that I was finding intellectual stimulation elsewhere. Although this strategy consumed much energy, the excitement of discovery of new things while working with someone who shared in that excitement more than compensated for the inconvenience.

In the meantime, I began my search for a job. Because my record was not strong, I decided that I would look for positions in industry. There was no regret in this decision, only realistic assessment that concluded I could not compete for an academic job. My search went badly, and I accumulated a pile of rejection letters. Some of these I earned on my own demerits; others, I found, were inspired by my advisor's unwillingness to be supportive. Finally, when my options seemed to be disappearing, I contacted a large oil company; and I asked my clandestine research colleague to serve as a recommender. He agreed to do so and told me that in his letter he had written that the company should discount anything my advisor had to say concerning my qualifications. To my great pleasure and relief, I was contacted by this company for a recruiting visit.

In the interim, my night work had begun to bear fruit, and I was interested in pursuing this direction of research. My friend had managed to obtain funding for a post-doctoral position for me that was very attractive and which provided the advantage of allowing me to distance myself, professionally, from my mediocre graduate student career. Also, it allowed me to pursue some of the unified aspects of flow analysis that intrigued me so much by modeling tidal estuaries analogously to my models of chemical reactors while investigating the numerical techniques I had not been allowed to employ in my dissertation. I took the position in the Department of Civil Engineering, and also had the liberty, after accumulating all those rejection letters, of finally being the one to reject a potential industrial employer.

About a month after I finished my degree, I was approached by one of the senior members of the chemical engineering faculty. He said he knew that I had had an unreasonably difficult time as a student, and he wished to apologize. He said he felt the unpleasantness was largely his fault because he was responsible for bringing my advisor to Princeton. At present, I prefer to avoid apportioning blame for difficulties in my graduate school experience, but I do know that this comment was a great kindness. It essentially freed me from my past and allowed me to begin my career as a Ph.D. holder unencumbered by self-doubt, able to try to build a career on the aspects of engineering and science that held my interest.

My year as a post-doc was a wonderful beginning to the academic life. I was able to publish, attend meetings, learn, and think about challenging and relevant problems. I had a great colleague to work with. Whereas my graduate student years seemed to stifle all initiatives, I was now free to go outside bounds and pursue problems simply because they were interesting to me. This was a most refreshing activity and gave me a new perspective on life in a university. As the year was finishing up, I was getting ready to move on when a member of the faculty resigned his position. I was asked to fill in for the following year as a lecturer while the department did a search for a tenure track replacement. Because this seemed like a good opportunity, affording me an additional chance to build my resume before entering the job market, I agreed to postpone beginning my "actual" career for another year.

The first course I was asked to teach was a graduate course in hydrology, the study of water and its interaction with the earth. This was quite a challenge as I had never taken any courses in hydrology. I realized that some aspects of the subject could be taught based on the conservation principles that are universal, but I still had to adapt to the specific contexts of rainfall, river flow, and groundwater movement. My lectures took a long time to prepare and represented my full understanding of the topic. My fear was that if I ever ran out of notes before the end of class, I would have had nothing to add as I knew no more than what was in those notes. Nevertheless, the class was great fun and proved to be a fantastic learning experience. I had to have the material well sorted out and organized since the incredibly sharp graduate students seemed poised to pounce on any inconsistencies or nonsequiturs. Their expectations forced me to learn the subject and to prepare well for class. I wouldn't have wanted it any other way.

A little more than half way through the academic year, the department chair approached me and said that the department had done its search for a new faculty member and had decided that I was the top choice. I was surprised. I had not applied and had not even considered the possibility of staying on. Because I was enjoying my research and teaching, as well as the interactions with the other faculty, I accepted a tenure track position as an Assistant Professor of Civil Engineering at Princeton.

In considering this turn of events from a distance of twenty-five years, I find it truly quite improbable. I had an undistinguished record as a graduate student in chemical engineering and had been rejected from virtually every position I applied for. However, within two years of finishing my degree, I had a tenure track position at one of the best universities in the world. I had been offered this position despite the fact that the discipline I was hired into was one in which I had no formal education. Additionally, I had not applied for the position, was not interviewed for it, did not give a seminar, was not introduced to the college administration. While working hard in a general field of study that I enjoyed, an opportunity came along that I was able to accept, an opportunity that I had not envisioned.

I am certain that this development in my career was driven, unwittingly, by vocation, by my intellectual passions leading me along a career path. In hindsight, my graduate school experience destroyed notions I had about selecting a job based on the quality of my education, geography, salary, or opportunity to advance. Instead, circumstances led me to search for an atmosphere free from discouragement in areas of study that I enjoyed. Through no considered decision of my own, I was freed to pursue research and teaching with confidence that by doing good work in these important areas, job prospects would develop. However, I was unaware of the wisdom of this strategy; it was not my strategy but rather the consequence of being called to a vocation.

My years as an Assistant Professor were possibly the most enjoyable I have had in academia. Perhaps because of my accidental path to a faculty position, I was oblivious to demands to publish. I simply enjoyed working with colleagues and students. The publications came naturally. Teaching was a chance to learn something new. Our department had been charged to improve, so we were in a building situation. Such a situation is ideal because there is so much work to be done that political intrigue is minimized. We put our energies into developing good undergraduate and graduate programs, attracting quality graduate students, and doing productive work as educators. Quantification of improvement was left to others to recognize. After two years, the chair appointed me to be the Director of Graduate Studies for the department. He told me I was selected, in part, because of my unhappy experience as a student. He felt that I would be sensitive to situations that led to difficulties and would be able to help our faculty and students avoid them. Several years later, promoted and tenured, I began to think that I was in charge of my career and started to make plans for how I wanted that career and my life to develop in New Jersey.

I find it interesting that my spirituality did not develop through contacts at Princeton University. In fact, my faith life grew in intensity, but it was definitely distinct from my activities at the university. One person that I knew said that no one in her discipline believed in God, almost as if that were the litmus test for membership in that intellectual community. Memories of discussions with my peers about religion are few, with the strongest relating to the annual college Christmas party. Since the faculty was spread among several buildings, this gathering provided a chance to meet some colleagues who were otherwise invisible. I recall that each year I would be cornered at the punch bowl by one individual who worked in an area related to mine. In the course of small talk, he would ask how many children I had. To my response of "five," he would step back and say, "Oh, you must be Catholic," and then withdraw to chat with someone else, only to return the next year with the same question. My faith and my career were in different compartments.

After I had been on the Princeton faculty for about nine years, a subtle sense of restlessness began to set it. I was happy in my job; but because my academic career, including graduate school, had been experienced only through Princeton, I began to wonder about the situation at other institutions. I had no intention of leaving, but as the activities involved in building a program began to transform into activities needed to maintain that program, I missed some of the excitement and enthusiasm of the earlier years.

At about this time, I was contacted by the University of Notre Dame and asked if I would be interested in considering their open position as department chair in civil engineering. My immediate response was that I was not interested, but eventually I agreed to take a look with the understanding that I planned to remain at Princeton. To my surprise, the position held many attractions. There was a desire to build the department, especially at the graduate level; the university had resources such that it could grow wherever it decided to; the expressed interest of the university in providing moral and religious dimensions to its education was attractive; even the size of my family would become a non-issue. Father Theodore M. Hesburgh, C.S.C. was the President who provided energetic, unambiguous, and forceful leadership. His vision, that one does not honor God with mediocrity, provided a direction and rationale for improvement of the university that resonated with a need on my part to better integrate spirituality into my life. Over the course of several visits to Notre Dame, spanning a number of months, my wife and I came to the conclusion that while many advantages of Princeton would be missed, Notre Dame offered some possibilities for me, for us, and for our family. Because none of my children had yet started high school, the timing seemed right for moving. So, to my surprise, I decided to risk the security of my situation at Princeton for the unknowns awaiting at Notre Dame.

During the period of transition to my new job, I had a number of conversations with people in Princeton about the changes that lay ahead. Three conversations, in particular, are especially memorable. There was a person on staff whom I had known since my graduate student days. She had been encouraging during the hard times and the good times. When I told her I was leaving for Notre Dame, however, her only response was, "Isn't that in one of those boring Midwest states that begins with a vowel?" I was disappointed that she did not wish me well, but I suppressed the urge to respond that for someone who grew up in San Francisco, neither New Jersey nor Indiana had made the list of desirable places to live. This brief meeting reminded me that the opportunities provided by the job, and not its location, were what had driven my decision.

One day when I was sitting in my office, one of my colleagues on the faculty stuck his head in the door and said, "My wife is glad to hear that you are leaving Princeton." I was a bit startled by this remark as I barely knew this person and could not recall having ever met his wife. My colleague grinned and then explained that when his wife heard I was leaving, she was surprised because, "No one ever leaves Princeton." Then she had told him that my departure gave her hope that they might leave some day, too. I realized that it is easy to become so numbed by the *status quo*—either geographic, professional, or by affiliation—that it is hard to recognize other possibilities, other chances for growth, additional nuances in God's call. I, too, was pleased to be leaving.

The third memorable conversation occurred during the course of my decision-making process and was with a colleague whom I admire for his insights and his ability to identify critical issues. One day he said to me, "You should realize that right now you are one of the best people in your research area in the world. If you stay at Princeton, you will have a chance to become the top person. You won't necessarily make it, but you will have a chance. If you go to Notre Dame, you will not become the best. What's more, you will never know if you could have made it." For success in academia, research must be reviewed and recognized. Indeed, the positive evaluation of that research by others in the community is an essential component of promotions and advancement; but these evaluations cannot be orchestrated. Faculty can only choose their areas of investigation, the problems they wish to address and solve, their approach to interacting with students. These provide the real satisfactions of academic life. Following one's passions must take a higher priority than seeking recognition. Vocation is a call to a productive activity, not a call to recognition; following that call into uncertainty is an expression of faith. I did know that being at Princeton gave me an advantage in gaining recognition, but I had reached a place of security in what I had accomplished that I was more concerned with my own assessment of my performance than with others' views. I considered my career to be an ongoing search for satisfaction and for consistency with the will of God. It was personal and not subject to peer review. I had confidence in myself, perhaps too much, but also confidence that I was acting in concert with God's will for me.

I found the move to Notre Dame to be refreshing, an exciting new experience. There was much to be done, but the key ingredients of faculty and administrative support made even the tough decisions possible. During my first three-year appointment as chair, the department was in need of focusing its programs, recruiting faculty to support those foci, attracting quality graduate students, and building the size of its undergraduate programs to justify the faculty positions. The faculty made extraordinary, creative efforts in these areas. I enjoyed the students in my classes, and I was fortunate to have an exceptional post-doc to work with to keep some of my research on track. The sense of community at Notre Dame, of being a part of building a special

educational institution, was invigorating. I loved my job and the sense of satisfaction it provided. I believe this was another case of so much work needing to be done that people were too busy building to let petty jealousies cause
problems.

When I was asked to consider accepting a second three-year term as
chair, I agreed to undergo the required review. I believed that the department
had made much progress but that some of the new programs and procedures
needed to mature a bit to become part of the normal operation. The review
was reported to me as positive, so I agreed to continue on. Although I had
maintained a hectic pace through my first term, I think this began to wear on
me in my fourth year. Some of my engineering momentum was beginning to
ebb because of the demands of administration, and I felt I was too young to
have my career as a regular faculty member active in teaching and research
derailed by administrative duties. As a result, I interviewed for and was
offered a faculty position at another university, but in the end decided that my
commitment to serve as chair and the real potential for uniquely effective
educational programs in my department argued in favor of staying at Notre
Dame. I was still convinced that, given its resources, Notre Dame could
achieve at whatever level it wished; and my department had much room for
improvement before it would be in a position to test that hypothesis. The
development of the climate of learning in my department was exciting. I
believed in the ideals that Notre Dame professed and in an institutional will
to achieve, although I was concerned about the loss of Fr. Hesburgh to
retirement. Within a year, I was given an endowed chair, which I took to be
the administration's expression of confidence in me. I was happy and looking forward to the continuing unfolding of what had been a rewarding academic life in the "boring" Midwest.

While in the sixth, and possibly last, year of my service as department
chair, I was approached by the top layers of administration with an idea. They
had decided to investigate merging the Department of Earth Sciences in the
College of Science with my department. Earth Sciences had no graduate program and was graduating about four students per year. Its chief mission
seemed to be the offering of large service courses for nonscience majors.
This mode of operation was not consistent with the vision Notre Dame had
for itself, and so the merger was being discussed. I was told that before the
merger talks reached full flower, the administration wanted to know if I
would remain as chair of the new department. If I was not willing to continue
as a chair, the merger would not go forward. I agreed that some reorganiza-
tion of Earth Sciences was warranted for the good of the university. A case
could be made that some synergy could be found by combining the study of
geosciences with environmental engineering, water resources, and the reduction of natural hazards. Although this merger would increase the size of the
department by fifty percent, add an additional set of educational programs,
and create some tensions between science and engineering faculty members,
I believed that it would also provide better educational opportunities for our
students. I made a decision then that I now question: I agreed to continue as
a department chair.

Many bad decisions are recognized only in hindsight. In this instance, the decision was bad for me, at least in part, because I needed a break from administration. The need for this break coincided with the very real challenge of trying to pull together a department consisting of engineers who had a sense of direction and understanding of what they were accomplishing, and scientists who had been dragged into a different college and told their ways would have to change. Quite understandably, there was a deep suspicion on the part of the geoscientists that their programs and positions were to be phased out in favor of more engineering positions. In the face of such uneasiness, it is essential for the leadership to be unambiguous in its expectations so that a spirit of mutual respect and constructive interaction can be fostered. However, once the merger had been accomplished on paper, the administration retreated from its supportive stance. Commitments of resources at the time of the merger that had induced faculty approval were not honored. Subsequently, particular interest groups on campus asserted their historic ties with the old Earth Sciences Department, ties unlikely to withstand a genuine merger but ties they wished to preserve. These maneuvers only served to interfere with departmental efforts to achieve a genuine integration.

Despite the management challenges, the new department grew in many ways during its first three years. It was clear that large strides were made in faculty and student quality and in the effectiveness of our educational programs. Although I had some very satisfying classroom experiences and advised a couple of terrific graduate students, I was edgy and began to feel that I was drifting, being dragged away from what I needed to be doing professionally, personally, and spiritually. I was further frustrated by a growing climate of thought control in the college in which ideas were not discussed and communication with some individuals in the university community was discouraged or forbidden. I think it is fair to say that I had lost sight of my activities in the context of vocation.

While completing my third term as a department chair, I was asked to stay on for yet another additional term so that the merger could be cemented. I was disinclined to continue but felt some responsibility to shepherd the merger since I had agreed to take it on. I made it absolutely clear that this would be my last term as chair and hoped that I could begin the process of disengaging myself from administrative duties. I was eager to become a regular faculty member.

The following two years were devastating. Shortly after I was reappointed, the Dean of Engineering was reviewed by the faculty of the college and somehow came to the erroneous conclusion that I and the faculty of my department had undermined him and bore responsibility for his weak assessment. I have not been provided with the rationale, if any, for what followed and have been rebuffed in all attempts to gain understanding. In any event, a campaign of unfettered, vicious personal and professional attacks was launched against me, some faculty in the department, and the programs we had established. The upper administration chose not to intervene or to promote an atmosphere where discussion could take place. This was a brutal period for me where my disbelief at what was happening was exceeded only by the realization that the attacks were being allowed to continue at a place which so boldly proclaims its Catholic character. I resigned as chair when the bullying and harassment grew, unabated, far beyond what I could tolerate. This did not end the spreading of malicious and slanderous lies within the university community; nor did it end overt action by some who wished to damage the department and then point to the damage inflicted as corroborating prior allegations.

At the present time, four years after I resigned my administrative duties, I cannot honestly say that I have come to grips with the bizarre turn in fortune I experienced. I have moved beyond immobilizing depression to a place where some hope for the future has sprouted. Unfortunately, I retain measures of wariness, anger, mistrust, disillusionment, discouragement, and disappointment. So much of what I poured myself into has been dismantled. My department's life, which had become so intertwined with my own life, is no longer a part of me—and I need to start over. I am like the young student beginning to embark on a new phase of life wondering how to decide what to do.

Although I am not far enough separated from my experiences to be dispassionate, I have identified several issues on which I reflect and pray, issues that must be resolved for me to be at peace. A call to a vocation is not a call to a charmed life of controlling one's own experiences such that nothing goes wrong. Therefore, a vocation is different from simply using one's talents. People in academia are intelligent people who have all achieved at a consistently high level. It is a jolting experience when the academic environment that has offered success, rewards, and a sense of accomplishment for many years turns harsh. Yet following a vocation viewed as a call to live consistently with God's will does not imply an easy path, does not assure freedom from discouragement. If being faithful to a vocation is a high value, then this value remains regardless of the human obstacles constructed. Many heroic and saintly people have faced enormous obstacles in living their vocations. Their saintliness and heroism comes precisely from the fact that they persisted and overcame. In comparison, my obstacles are rather trivial. However, they are my obstacles, the obstacles I know, the obstacles I have experienced during sleepless nights and painful days, the obstacles that challenge me. I have no doubt that my own vocation lies in education and research. At times I have felt abandoned, but the overwhelming support from colleagues, students, and my profession—especially at points in my odyssey when most needed—confirms my vocation and strengthens my resolve to pursue it. Still, the evil grinds away and gnaws at me.

Above all is the fact that my vocation to married life and as a father outweighs my other callings. Marriage in particular has been a great source of spiritual strength, of perspective, of encouragement at the low points and celebration at the high points. By sharing my life, my wife has enriched it and filled it far beyond what misguided politics can take away. The constant demands of being a husband and father are blessings because sharing life with other people is so much more uplifting than focusing on self. I also am a Permanent Deacon which has put some discipline in my spiritual life. In particular, at times when I would have preferred to turn away and focus on myself, I had the responsibility to read, pray about, and reflect on the Scripture readings of the week to prepare a homily. I was often struck by how the readings related to my situation and how embarrassingly short of the call to discipleship I fell in comparison to what I was proclaiming. Because of my commitment to minister, I had no option but to face Scripture and allow it to work at transforming me. That task is ongoing.

I have spent two of the four years since completion of my term as chair on sabbatical leaves that I negotiated with the university at the time of my hiring. I have also spent one other year on academic leave, working to satisfy the requirements of a research grant. This period has provided me with some opportunity to heal. Although I have been able to strengthen my ties with research colleagues during this time, I have missed the interaction with students. I had a meeting with the new Dean of Engineering who categorized the treatment I had received in the preceding years as "inhuman." Although this assessment bears some similarity to the apology I received on completion of my graduate studies, it has not produced a comparable sense of freedom. I am preparing to return to full-time presence on campus uncertain that the atmosphere has changed but determined to concentrate on the teaching and research activities that form the heart of my academic vocation.

When I look back on the years since I embarked on my career in academia, I can see clear patterns, instances when, despite my clumsy wanderings in some other direction, my vocation held me on course. Life in an academic setting is both privileged and fraught with frustration and disillusionment. Perhaps the unpleasant aspects enter in when one becomes too enamored with the possibilities for making a difference and loses sight of merely trying to live out a call in academia, while leaving the results to others to evaluate. It is a spiritual challenge. Academia is a place of rankings and stature, of prestige and influence, so much so that these qualities are viewed as goals in themselves rather than natural consequences of meeting more concrete goals—such as doing quality research or educating and motivating students. Thriving in such an environment requires that one not be distracted into following paths likely to earn the most academic currency. Rather, primary consideration must be given to a sense of fulfillment in the work accomplished, the intrinsic satisfaction of being an educator, researcher, or mentor. The search for vocation is not unlike that of a prospective student, although recognizing the signposts of someone else's search is much easier than living one's own.

In assessing the past fifteen years, I am struck by the contrast between arriving at Notre Dame supposedly unconcerned that this might diminish my standing in the research community while now being distressed that my contributions as a department chair have been savaged. It seems that my need for approval must be greater than I had thought. This strikes at the very heart of vocation as a call from God. I am convinced that I did the right things as chair, but I should have better braced myself against the irrationalities of this world. Perhaps I should have discontinued my service as chair earlier without being seduced by the notion that my continued leadership was important. Perhaps I needed to stay on to recognize how insignificant and fleeting human accolades are in the scheme of trying to live in relationship with God. For sure, my experiences led me to assess whether I am responding to God's call in my career or am simply getting caught up in the culture of academic life. I am most fortunate that, as I undertake the difficult task of freeing myself from the wounds of my experiences, I have my family, the opportunity to interact with good students, and the undiminished support of loyal and gifted colleagues. I do not know where my career is headed, yet history shows me that when I have been able to place my future in God's hands rather than try to dictate it, I have found the greatest happiness, fulfillment, and reward. I look forward to renewal of my continuing search for my vocation.

Acknowledgments

I am grateful to Gail Gray, Genny Gray, Guerin Gray, Maria Kolar, Randy Kolar, Tom Landy, Julia Muccino, and Ralph Stansley for many kindnesses and particularly acknowledge here their perceptive comments in response to various versions of this essay. I am also grateful for the enrichment that Collegium has brought to my life.

Notes

1. This technique has continued to grow in applicability for the last thirty years and remains one of the most useful and researched numerical methods for the solution of differential equations.

31

On Becoming a Disciple: Finding God and a Vocation in the Academic Life

Ed Block, Jr.

As I conclude my twenty-third year of teaching in the Department of English at Marquette University, I realize that I am still a learner, the literal meaning of the word "disciple." And I sometimes wonder what formed and nurtured that discipleship. What has continued to sustain my intellectual, emotional, and spiritual commitment to the academic life and—surrounding that—my life as a committed Catholic? It's easy and fairly predictable to point to the importance and mutually supportive effect of relationships, meaningful work, and the acknowledgment of achievement. Reflecting on those years, however, I find that the answer is a providential combination of events, experiences, and people. They have called me out of myself and made me aware of a profound mystery not only at the heart of creation but within myself.

It is the effort to keep alive that awareness of mystery and a consequent gratitude for it that have enabled me to take each successive step toward being a better disciple—seeking and, sometimes in surprising ways, finding God in the academic life. But I also have to point to some uniquely formative features of the Jesuit tradition: its respect for experience, its emphasis on reflection, and its reverence for passionate involvement with all of creation. So the story of what sustains me in my discipleship and my academic vocation is just that, a story of memorable events and experiences. It is because I have been so powerfully affected by what it means—experientially—to seek God in all things that I have felt called to live out this vocation. I shall try to frame this reflection in terms that, I hope, will raise questions, derived from readers' own experiences and the stories that are their lives.

But first a bit of background. I am a "cradle Catholic." I attended Catholic grade and high school, and St. Thomas College in St. Paul, Minnesota. I was an English major at St. Thomas and can still recall the thrill of reading the poetry of John Donne and Gerard Manley Hopkins for the first time. I also remember several individual faculty members whose example I later imitated, both deliberately and unconsciously. I left St. Thomas with a Woodrow Wilson Fellowship to Stanford University in fall 1967.

Stanford in 1967 was an inhospitable place for believing Christians, let alone Catholics. I recall being shocked at the anti-Christian comments of my professor of Old English, as he led us through the construing of the Blickling Homilies. I also recall the materialistic bent that the faculty's scholarly interests took. I kept my faith alive by attending Mass at the off-campus Newman Center and participating in its retreats, hikes, and other events.

In retrospect I realize how much Stanford's secular ethos affected my early professional development. Working toward a Ph.D. in English and comparative literature, I increasingly conceived of myself as a scholar, but a secular scholar. It was not until the final year or two writing my dissertation—and continuing to participate, with my wife, in Newman Center activities—that I began to realize how little my professional development integrated intellectual with spiritual concerns.

When, in December 1976, I interviewed for a tenure-track position in Victorian literature and literary criticism at Marquette University, I was brought up short before the question that my interviewer posed: "How do you feel about working at a Jesuit, Catholic university?" I recall trying to make the most of my Catholic high school and college background, and even threw in a caustic remark about Stanford. It was to become my standard putdown: on the walls of Stanford's Memorial Church one saw many edifying moral statements, but most reflected the philosophy and morality of the school's robber-baron founder more than anything in the Christian tradition.

For the first few years at Marquette, my experiences of faith and intellectual life were dissociated. My wife and I participated fully in university life, but our faith life was largely a family and parish affair. Although we also took part in major liturgical events of the university—like the all-university Mass of the Holy Spirit at the beginning of the fall semester—we found our weekly home at a local parish. Frankly, despite a few individuals who felt strongly about Marquette's Jesuit Catholic character, the English department as a whole was intent on its "professional" status. It wanted to compete with departments at larger, and often more intently secular universities. For those reasons the department was not a place to talk about—let alone live—an integration of faith and intellect.

A bright spot in the first years—from a professional perspective—was a reading group that gathered to discuss Hans-Georg Gadamer's *Truth and Method*. An interdisciplinary group of faculty and graduate students from English, philosophy, theology, and communications, we met weekly for almost four years. With these colleagues and friends I absorbed and began to apply Gadamer's ideas about the dialogical nature of understanding and the hermeneutics of hope. Without my knowing it, Gadamer's ideas also began to form the basis for a renewed understanding of the Christian tradition, and a scholar's potential place in it. In time I would publish a number of articles on Gadamer's work and its application to literature. If I took the time to look back on it, I think I might be able to trace the outlines of Gadamer's work in most of the scholarly research I did at that time.

It goes without saying: most of the pre-tenure period was a time of intense professional activity and stressful personal, familial relations. A rancorous environment in the department made life doubly difficult. Denied tenure on a first try, I seriously looked for positions outside of the academic world, in heuristic computer programming, personal banking, and human resources management. As difficult as that period was, however, the need to consider other career options energized me to think and imagine new possibilities, to "reach beyond my comfort zone." I developed a network of contacts. One later became the source of some part-time public relations consulting. Having to think of a new career made me more of a risk-taking extrovert than I had been before. I also became more sensitive to the anxieties and struggles that others have experienced in looking for a job. These changes in attitude would not have likely happened without the threat of termination. It may seem easy to say we are "strengthened by adversity." The experience itself, however, is seldom an enjoyable one and never without stress and anxiety.

During this time it was our growing family and our parish activities that sustained my wife and me. We participated actively in the first archdiocese-wide RENEW program that took place in the early '80s. As its name suggests, RENEW was an opportunity for parishes, through a series of sustained, small Scripture, prayer, and discussion groups, to enable individuals and couples to renew their faith life. It was, in fact, the dialogue sustained in our small group that provided us with friends and support that lasted for over a decade after the last meeting of RENEW. With these friends, my wife and I suffered, prayed through, and survived to a second, successful bid for tenure.

Looking back, I see the immediate post-tenure year or two as a period of letdown and lack of direction. I had built my immediate pre-tenure research on Victorian science, literature, and values. But, ironically, the values I was studying had little directly to do with my own religious values and spiritual background. Largely because of this lack of direction and integration, my first sabbatical semester yielded less in the way of professional, personal, and spiritual satisfaction than I had expected. Besides realizing the limitations of my long-term research plans, I realized that you have to learn how to do a sabbatical, just as you have to learn anything else.

Back from sabbatical, I discovered that one result of the Gadamer group's discussion of dialogue was to provide a foundation for an interdisciplinary colloquium and lecture series on John Henry Newman that I organized in 1989. The success of a lecture series, both at Marquette and within the wider Milwaukee community, awakened me to the possibility of a wider dialogue on issues that Newman's thought had raised, and which related back to what we in the Gadamer group had been reflecting on for years.

The focus on Newman, it turned out, also gave renewed focus to my research interests. A colleague in the department, Dr. Joseph M. Schwartz, was editor of *Renascence: Essays on Values in Literature*, a journal that had been part of Marquette since just after World War II. Doctor Schwartz invited me to edit a special Newman issue, based on the talks given during the colloquium. So, gathering a selection of those talks, and inviting additional contributions, I edited the special issue. With the addition of other contributions, I subsequently published an entire collection: *Critical Essays on John Henry Newman*.

The whole Marquette campus was further stimulated by the first discussion of *Ex corde ecclesiae*. That occurred in February 1990, when the late Fr. James Sauvé S.J., one of the document's authors, responded to questions about *Ex corde* at a joint meeting of the university's faculty governance bodies. It was the first time in a long time—it seemed to me—that the issues of Marquette's Jesuit Catholic mission and identity were being taken seriously on our campus again.

An event that followed the opening of such dialogue and gave me, at least, further inspiration, was Marquette's celebration of the 500th anniversary of Ignatius's birth and the 450th anniversary of the founding of the Society of Jesus. This occurred in the summer of 1991. The "birthday party" brought Jesuits and former Jesuits of the Wisconsin province together for a week of social, intellectual, and spiritual events. We "collaborators" (the first time I'd heard that expression) were also invited. Witnessing, enjoying, and participating in the moments of reconciliation and healing among Jesuits and former Jesuits; listening to the stories of former Jesuits and their families: all these were eye and spirit-opening experiences.

At about this same time my colleague and mentor invited me to investigate the work of Hans Urs von Balthasar. I began my study of the late Swiss theologian and humanist's work with *Theo-Drama*, the second part of his theological trilogy. I came as a literary scholar seeking literary critical insight; I continued to read because, as Balthasar commentator Medard Kehl observes, in Balthasar "forgotten or hidden things are made to speak in an original and often surprisingly up-to-date way."[1] I found that Balthasar's "theological aesthetics" starts from a distinctly dialogical foundation similar to Gadamer's, but adds to that the perception of beauty and drama, along with a deep sense of gratitude and wonder at existence (which he rightly calls the foundation of both philosophical and religious speculation).

Balthasar's life and thought have remained an important theme of my research, my thinking, and my spirituality. His work was the subject of my second, much more successful sabbatical, and I now read or reread favorite works regularly. In time I began publishing literary essays employing Balthasar's ideas, as well as giving lectures and including his work in courses and discussion groups. It was, in part, the continuing desire for the deeper dialogue which the Gadamer group had inspired, and which the reading of Balthasar renewed, that made me take the next step toward a fuller realization of my vocation.

In early 1992 I began to plan a faculty seminar on Jesuit Values in Undergraduate Education. Inaugurated with a lecture by David Tracy on Gadamer, the seminar began in January 1993 and involved some twenty-seven arts and sciences faculty in a series of presentations and discussions. Urged on by another lecture delivered by Joseph Appleyard, S.J., at the mid-semester, the seminar lasted into early May. It culminated in a conference, "Ideas for the University," which took place just before commencement that spring. The conference brought to campus a number of nationally known figures who spoke on the challenges and opportunities facing higher education, particularly colleges and universities committed to sustaining their religious affiliations in the face of increasing secularization.[2]

Although neither seminar nor conference developed a clear definition of qualities, let alone values, that characterized a Jesuit undergraduate education, participants agreed that the conversations were fruitful and should be continued—with the audience expanded to include all interested faculty, administrators, and staff. In fall 1993, therefore, I sent out invitations to all full-time employees—and received twice as many positive responses as I could accept. Renamed the Marquette Mission Seminar, the meetings began in October. For each of the next three semesters a group of twenty-seven to thirty voluntary participants gathered four to five times per semester to discuss important texts relating to Jesuit higher education, Jesuit spirituality, or the challenges to Catholic higher education. Response from the broad university community was overwhelmingly positive. Each semester the seminar had to put between ten and twenty would-be participants on a waiting list.

A significant change in my spiritual and intellectual life occurred in the fall of 1994. Preparing for my second sabbatical, I did a 19th Annotation retreat in daily life through Marquette's Center for Ignatian Spirituality. My retreat director was the center's director, Sr. Carol Ann Smith, S.H.C.J. That retreat set burning in me the fire for greater understanding of the Ignatian spirit and tradition. I read Candido de Dalmases' biography of Ignatius[3] and began reading John O'Malley's *The First Jesuits*.[4] I found myself discovering Ignatian qualities at Marquette that I hadn't seen before.

The fire of that retreat was somewhat dampened just after New Year's 1995, when I learned that a colleague I had asked to moderate the Mission Seminar during my sabbatical had been passed over for an important appointment and had left the university. I found the university's decision difficult to understand. The colleague, an administrator genuinely devoted to Marquette's mission, had been a seminar participant and had even published a fine essay in *Conversations on Jesuit Higher Education*. Because of his leaving, however, I was forced to let the Mission Seminar go into hiatus during my sabbatical, and I concentrated on my Balthasar research.

That spring I was invited to be a mentor for the third annual *Collegium Colloquy on Faith and Intellectual Life*, to be held in June at Loyola Marymount University, in Los Angeles. Those nine days became another turning point in my spiritual and intellectual life. As a mentor I was supposed to help a small group of the participants—graduate students, young faculty, and a few academic burnouts seemingly sent by their deans. With me as discussion facilitator, they were to reflect on their own lives and to see the opportunities available for integrating faith and intellectual life within the academic environment. But I found that I received more than I was able to give, and the entire week was like an intense seminar and retreat rolled into one. The openness of the non-Catholic participants was particularly inspiring. Their desire to understand Catholicism and Catholic higher education gave new meaning to what the Mission Seminar had begun to realize in its discussions: to be a genuine university, a Jesuit institution had to be generously open to the diversity of faiths and vocations that it gathered to itself. That openness had to begin in conversation, but it also had to manifest itself in the celebrations, rituals, and other sharings—the very fiber of the university's activities.

Having nearly decided at the end of the spring sabbatical that I would let the Mission Seminar die peacefully before the next fall, I returned to Marquette inspired by the *Collegium* experience. Realizing that the seminar was something that others at *Collegium* wished they could have on their campuses, I determined to reinaugurate the seminar at Marquette. With the help of a young Marquette alumna working in the university's annual fund office, the seminar sent out personal invitations to all the vice presidents, deans, and chairs, asking them to encourage Seminar participation among their faculty and staff. The response was again overwhelmingly positive, and the Seminar's "second life" began.

I also returned from *Collegium* determined to make the Ignatian tradition a more explicit part of my pedagogy. Among the things I began doing differently in my undergraduate courses were the practice of beginning class with a prayer from the Marquette prayer book, *Finding God in All Things*, and the explicit relating of classroom activities (particularly oral presentations, dramatic performances, recitations, and the like) to the Jesuit educational ideal of eloquence. The more I read about Ignatius and the Jesuits, the more I could see at Marquette the sometimes dim realization—or clear potential—for realizing more of the Ignatian tradition. My reading of Ignatius's life and the early history of the Society had made me want to share that with undergraduate students; so I began offering one "Ignatian Fact" per class, right after the opening prayer. In time I made a short narrative of Ignatius's life an extra-credit option in every undergraduate class I taught. On teaching evaluations, students often made a point of saying how much they appreciated the "Ignatian Facts."

In fall 1995, I also became editor of *Renascence*. The job of reading and making the final decision on what essays to publish in the quarterly journal has further transformed my sense of vocation. For decades I had considered myself a Victorianist with an interest in comparative literature and theory. Now I had to be a generalist, evaluating scholarly essays on Christian values and belief in literature. Submissions ranged across many different national traditions and periods from Anglo-Saxon to the present. At the scholarly conferences I attended I was now as interested in the papers other people were presenting as I was in my own. I was always on the lookout for potential submissions to *Renascence*.

It was genuinely providential when, in spring 1996, I attended a conference on Christianity and Literature at Santa Clara University. There I heard two fine papers on religious aspects of the poetry of Denise Levertov, and I invited one of the presenters to submit his essay to *Renascence*. I also became so fascinated with Levertov's work that I decided to develop a special issue of *Renascence* devoted to "Spirit in the Work of Denise Levertov." Over the next year and a half the issue grew to a double issue, and my own research interest in Levertov's poetry expanded. I invited Ms. Levertov to read at Marquette, and while she was in Milwaukee for the reading, I arranged to interview her for the special issue. It made for a bittersweet culmination of the work that our special Levertov issue came out scarcely two months after Denise's death in December 1997.

The effect of this—and other—special issues of the journal has been to make me re-examine not only many of my research interests but also the purpose of my professional vocation. While I continue to read, write, and publish on a variety of authors and topics, I now see part of my vocation as fostering and encouraging the work of younger scholars, particularly those working in the area of literature, belief, and spirituality. Editing *Renascence* has transformed my vocation and made me even more aware and grateful for what I can do to nurture the integration of faith and literary study in the work of others.

In 1997 I got a practical sense of how an often overused Jesuit word, *magis*—meaning "more"—expresses a genuine sense of how vocation and discipleship can grow. While I continued to teach classes, do research, edit *Renascence*, and moderate the Mission Seminar, I applied for and received funding for a second honors colloquium and speakers' series: this time on the life and work of Hans Urs von Balthasar. What I now refer to as "the Balthasar semester" became another aspect of my growing sense of vocation and discipleship. The four lectures on Balthasar[5] brought out a truly interdisciplinary response from colleagues around the university, and the community at large.[6] It also fostered a number of smaller reading and discussion groups besides the honors seminar I taught to undergraduates. In time, the Balthasar semester made me acquainted with a number of others, graduate students and faculty, who were interested in fostering Marquette's Jesuit Catholic character.

I would also claim at least some credit for inspiring efforts to bring Chicago's Francis Cardinal George to campus in the spring of 1998. For it was a group of graduate students and faculty who began a *Communio* reading group after the Balthasar semester that made that visit possible. It was they who found funding, made overtures, and carried to completion an important and exciting event on Marquette's campus. Although its long-term impact is hard to judge, that visit further sustained the dialogue on mission and identity which it has been a major part of my vocation to foster over the last seven years.

I now look forward to my third sabbatical. After finding a successor to moderate the Mission Seminar during the coming year, I hope to devote my time to completing a book on the literary critical implications of Balthasar's *Theo-Drama*. In preparation for the sabbatical, I did another 19th Annotation retreat in the spring: as a way of helping to discern the direction that the sabbatical will take my life, my vocation, and my further professional development. Despite numerous commitments which at times weigh upon me, I continue to find myself sustained by the efforts of colleagues and friends whom I have made during the past seven years. It is particularly with these colleagues that I can now share the triumphs and the challenges that we and the university continue to face. It is, as I said at the start, because I have been so powerfully affected by what it means to seek God in all things that I have felt "missioned" (a very Balthasarian term), as part of my professorial vocation, to seek greater integration of my faith and intellectual life.

What the Mission Seminar Has Meant

Of all the events I speak about in my essay, it should be clear that a central event has been the experience of the Mission Seminar. As a kind of "appendix," therefore—and as an incentive for others—I offer the following look at the way the seminar operates.

The Mission Seminar has been a regular source of renewal and reassurance. Even at the end of the busiest of days, I find it deeply encouraging to enter the Henke Lounge of our Alumni Memorial Union to find seminar members gathering around the modest rolling table where catering has laid out refreshments. On the clothed and skirted table—usually decorated with seasonal flowers or centerpiece—are cookies, a big wooden bowl of "Marquette Mix," a glass bowl of lemonade, canisters with coffee and hot water for tea, cups and glasses. Seminar participants are getting reacquainted, comparing notes from the day, and otherwise catching up on campus news.

About ten after the hour we're all seated around the clothed and skirted conference table with large stand-up name placards in front of us.[7] Because of the print size, the placards include only first and last names and the participant's unit. My one acknowledgment of status is for the Jesuits and the occasional religious who are part of the seminar. Otherwise we come together as persons, equal around the table.

The conversation begins. Sometimes the opening questions or observations do not elicit immediate response, but I have learned to trust the "creative silence." It usually takes less than twenty seconds for someone to address the opening question or to offer an entirely new perspective on the day's reading. As the meeting proceeds, the depth of insight and the measure of trust expands. Each semester finds about half of the group new to the seminar experience. Nevertheless, it seldom takes more than a meeting before all are sharing at a deep personal level their sense of vocation as well as the triumphs and frustrations that attend their efforts.

For me the seminar is a source of renewal; for other participants I hope it is many things. It is a place for social and institutional contacts, what we have come to call horizontal networking—as opposed to the vertical (hierarchical) lines of communication that we are used to in our departments and units. The seminar is also a resource for information about the Jesuit and Ignatian tradition of education, as well as for an informal "passing along" of the names and issues in the history of Jesuit higher education, in the U.S., and the world. I do not want to discount the importance of the seminar for making professional—or institutional—contacts. Colleagues have nurtured closer disciplinary relations with each other through their being on the seminar in a given semester. Young faculty also meet the people who go with the names they have heard about around campus.

Though the seminar began as a more or less "academic" group, our subsequent conversations have been by no means narrowly "professional." They range across and so unite the academic with the administrative and the student affairs sides of the university. The seminar is also one form that an ongoing orientation to the university can take. Around 1995 Marquette instituted a formal, one-day orientation program for new faculty and administrators, an orientation which has increasingly emphasized institutional mission and identity. Since 1996 the orientation package includes copies of the seminar's "history" and an invitation to each new hire. Over the last three years we have had new hires in the seminar almost every semester.

Lately the seminar has also become another place where administrators can communicate information of importance to the university. Since 1997 we have invited the President, the Executive Vice President, and the Academic Vice President to address a few words to the seminar, particularly at the start of a semester's meetings. The President surprised us, a couple years ago, by remaining after his comments and responses to questions, in order to participate in over half of our discussion.

An immediate implication, and one that has been borne out in each of the last fourteen semesters of the seminar's existence, is the fact that seeing God in all things means seeing God in the diverse community that makes up Marquette. To be "open" to the way that God through the Spirit works among my colleagues, my students, and other members of the Marquette community means realizing that—in a turn of St. Paul's statement—we are neither Catholic nor Protestant, believer nor secularist. In the seminar, even those who might not consider themselves religious recognize something about the "ethos" of Marquette. It is something that we recognize; it is also something that we recognize the absence of.

This ethos is not something that just happens. Neither is it something that can be mandated, like indoctrination to a corporation's "core value." While corporations do seek to get their employees to "own" the core value, such enforced adoption of the "corporate model" in order to "manufacture" a sense of the university's mission would be the surest way to condemn it to becoming a cliché at best, an empty and hypocritical phrase at worst.

A continuing frustration that I experience is the realization that the Mission Seminar is not reaching some of the people who need our conversations most—and whom we need just as much: the members of the Marquette community who know little and may care even less about mission and "mission talk." We need them to join the conversation because they are part of the Marquette community, and it will only be by hearing all parts of the conversation that we will be able to respond better to the needs of all. In some units—especially where a "corporate model" pertains—morale can be low and concern with mission negligible. It is people from these units that we need in the seminar.

Another source of frustration is the realization that many tenured faculty were hired when a different ideal of Catholic higher education drove not only Marquette but many of our sister schools around the nation. In that period (post "Land 'o' Lakes," i.e., late 1960s and early 1970s)[8] mission was less important than Marquette's becoming "mainstream" in American higher education. Many faculty hired at that time may think that the new emphasis on mission excludes them. Others represent the almost unavoidable cases of "burnout" and professional frustration or disgruntlement that occurs in any human institution.

What will make a place like Marquette different will be the way that embodied mission responds to these inevitable, human problems. A practical application of the Jesuit understanding of Incarnation can help. Ignatius speaks about (spiritual) desolation, and I can attest that much of what he says applies to the normal, run of the mill "desolation" that occurs in everyone's life, and which—at times—can deepen to take the form of job dissatisfaction, declining productivity, depression, and a whole clinical manual of unhealthy conditions. Not only as members of the Mission Seminar, but as fellow employees, we need to take some responsibility for helping those who feel hurt, isolated, alienated, dissatisfied, frustrated. One way is to talk about, then try to achieve the very Ignatian ideal of being people for others.

Questions

I will conclude by posing and seeking to answer some questions that have come up in the course of seminar discussions.

Where does the seminar go from here?
The seminar has spun off a number of other, largely *ad hoc* groups and activities. The first was what we called "The Next Level." In fall 1996, shortly after the arrival of Fr. Robert A. Wild, S.J., as the new President of Marquette, a number of members of the seminar suggested that we organize a forum for all seminar alumni and invite Fr. Wild to come. He accepted the invitation and participated in a panel discussion on Marquette's Mission and Identity. Over sixty—out of one hundred—alumni of the seminar attended.

What about seminar members who desire to move from discussion to action?
A second group spun off from the seminar was the Action Committee. Two longtime participants suggested that we invite a group of dedicated Mission Seminar members to meet and talk about possible actions which would concretize some of our discussions. The action committee began meeting in early 1997 and in time identified a number of priority actions that would further foster a sense of mission and identity. Uppermost on the list was reinstitution of the Religious Commitment Fund, a source of money for initiatives aimed at heightening awareness of Marquette's Jesuit Catholic identity. By the end of academic year 1999 the committee was surprised to realize that this—as well as some other lesser—goals had been achieved.

What is a critical mass?
The Mission Seminar has varied from twenty-seven to over thirty participants. Early on it became clear that, despite strong encouragement that participants attend all meetings during a given semester, unforeseen circumstances would prevent a certain percentage from doing so. To insure that the total number attending never fell below twenty, the number of acceptances has risen from twenty-seven to thirty-five. That generally insures that a critical mass of from twenty-five to thirty attends each meeting.

How important is the quality and the choice of readings?
Although the notes of past meetings show that the readings are often an important springboard for discussion, one cannot predict how much or how often discussion will focus on the readings. What is clear to me, however, is that phrases, ideas, and ways of thinking about certain issues are absorbed over time, and thus a kind of Ignatian way of approaching an issue develops.

How might one assess the effectiveness of the Mission Seminar?
Because we began the seminar with the conscious idea that it would be an open-ended conversation, without a particular agenda or concrete goal, it remains in many ways difficult to assess. Participants regularly attest to the seminar's importance for their growing awareness of Ignatian ideas and Marquette's mission but, beyond a palpable sense of the trust and willingness to confide and share one's deeper joys and frustrations with personal mission and vocation, we have not sought to assess the seminar's effect in any conscious or deliberate way.

Why has it been so hard to find ongoing funds for the seminar?
After its first two or three semesters the seminar literally "went begging" in order to proceed. Different units contributed paper, reproduction services, and the time and labor necessary to put out invitations. At each meeting I pleaded for individuals who had unrestricted access to operating budget accounts to "sponsor" the refreshments for one meeting. Both University Ministry and the Center for Ignatian Spirituality were for a long time the biggest supporters in terms of time, talent, and financial resources.

Clearly, the Mission Seminar does not rank with other claims for funding. Depending upon how one classifies our endeavor (faculty discussion group, support group, or ongoing orientation), it will usually take a backseat to more pressing categories of need. That is a reality of modern university life. Until faculty and staff development are seen as important, if not essential long-term goals, efforts like the Mission Seminar will continue to exist at the margin, at least as far as university administration is concerned.

Notes

1. *The Balthasar Reader* (New York: Crossroad, 1982).
2. *Ideas for the University* is available from Marquette University Press.
3. *Ignatius of Loyola: Founder of the Jesuits: His Life and Work*, translated by Jerome Aixalá (St. Louis, MO: Institute of Jesuit Sources, 1985).
4. Cambridge: Harvard University Press, 1993.
5. By David Schindler, Edward Oakes S.J., Virgil Nemoianu, and Aidan Nichols O.P.
6. Publicity for the lectures went out to almost two hundred parishes in the Milwaukee area and all the religiously affiliated colleges, universities, and seminaries.

7. I produce the stand-ups from my seminar roster database, making for a relatively easy job. At the first meeting of every semester I also provide stick-on name tags for people to wear when they come in, and before they take their places at the table. Such extra efforts to encourage hospitality and a sense of belonging goes a long way toward helping people from across campus, and across disciplinary and other boundaries, to get better acquainted.

8. A conference, named for Land o' Lakes, Wisconsin, where it took place, is generally agreed to have set the stage for Catholic colleges and universities to enter the mainstream of American higher education. See a historical overview by J. A. Appleyard, S.J., and Howard Gray S.J., in *Conversations* 18 (fall 2000).

32

Arriving at Valhalla

Sidney Callahan ·

Looking back on a journey can be perilous. Can I be reduced to a pillar of salt dissolved in regret? Or tempted to explain chance events as astute life choices? No, not if I can help it. Like St. Augustine, I know one thing for certain: I don't want to be deceived. Despite the new psychological findings about the possibility of false memories, reconstructions of the past can succeed.

In any event, I can be sure that at the present time I am embarked on a quest. My vocation is threefold. I am called to be a Christian who is a wife, mother of six adults, grandmother, friend, parishioner, neighbor, and citizen. At the same time, I am a seeker of truth for its own sake and a public Catholic intellectual trying to resolve civil and church questions. I work within an interdisciplinary framework of psychology and moral theology.

Unfortunately, the threefold demands of my vocation conflict with one another. Writing and thinking require solitude; being a good family member is relentlessly social; while public speaking and advocacy require travel. There is never enough time, energy, or resources to get all the different tasks done. In collisions of conflicting obligations, I have always put family ahead of work, but never without lament and complaint. It is no accident that the first book I ever wrote was devoted to the conflicts besetting educated women. Working out these problems, I went on to publish books on the working mother, sexual ethics, and the challenges of parenthood.

After I completed graduate training in psychology, I wrote a book on psychology and religion and one on conscience. I plan to write more books on psychology's challenge to faith and am almost finished with a book on suffering. Along the way, I have published hundreds of popular and scholarly articles. One form I've used often has been the column of opinion—for the *National Catholic Reporter,* for *Health Progress,* the official Catholic health-care magazine, for Religious News Service, and now for *Commonweal* eight times a year. A brief opinionated essay gives me a chance to voice ideas that I will never have the time or the energy to develop into an article or book. When columns are reprinted, I am doubly satisfied. It's a fine thing to get more work in print without more labor.

I've also spent two decades as a college psychology professor. But at this point, I've set aside my tenured position in order to concentrate on writing, lecturing, giving workshops, and taking part in conferences. Classroom teaching was not an intellectually stimulating experience for me but rather a process of nurturing students. Perhaps this is because I've mostly taught first-generation nonresidential working undergraduates, many of them immigrants. There was a real sense of mission in my teaching, but little of the traditional collegial life of academia. At Mercy College, in order to accommodate our students, we had several different campuses with many three-hour classes, often held in the evenings. While I lived next door to the Dobbs Ferry campus, I spent much of the academic year driving to and from our campuses in the Bronx, Yorktown, or White Plains. Teaching in bread-and-butter non-elite academic settings can be exhilarating but with a full-time load of four courses every semester, it is an exhausting schedule.

A recent family emergency occasioned my exit from the classroom. The sudden death of my son's wife in childbirth catapulted my husband and me into a new phase of family life: the three-generation household. We brought my son and his infant daughter, Perry, home to live with us in our apartment. After many decades of the freedom of an empty nest, we have started over again with an enchanting child. For three and a half years, I have been intensely rewarded and very tired. My role of actively nurturing grandmother squeezed out the role of nurturing professor, and I quit. Fortunately, we have enough money to hire a 9-to-4 nanny during the week, and I have not had to give up writing.

Every morning, even if I've been up in the night with Perry, I struggle to the computer and try to keep working as long as I can stand it. Deadlines loom and are finally met. Delays occur when our nanny, who is an aspiring actress, gets a part, or my son the scriptwriter gets a chance to direct a movie made from his script. Admittedly, much of the pressure I feel over thwarted work schedules is self-generated. I accept paper assignments and forget how much more time everything takes than I estimate. But who can resist the excitement of writing a paper that will be challenging, or one that means going to a conference and arguing with smart people?

At last I have arrived at the intellectual's Valhalla: think, write, read, lecture, and argue. The only thing I lack is a local circle of like-minded people to work with. But then I've rarely found more than a few persons anywhere who share my particular passions. Those who love psychology don't love theology—or the other way round. Isolation is a common penalty paid by those engaged in interdisciplinary work. If specialization continues to increase in academia, all intellectuals and scholars will find themselves longing for more discussions, unless they can travel freely. At least as a Catholic intellectual, I get to go to many conferences where all the participants share a commitment to the Church. The Church has given me an intellectual community as well as all its other graces and benefits. God is a God of surprises and I confess that I have done more in life than I could ever have hoped or imagined.

How Did I Get Here?

My beginnings would not predict the end of this journey. In my childhood world, there were no Catholics, no intellectuals, and scarcely a middle-class working woman. Men had careers but women stayed home and managed the household: the family's meals, help, clothes, parties, trips, holidays, school-ing, and cultural forays. Religion was not important, although as Scotch-Irish, French Huguenots in ancestry, we were decidedly Protestant. I say I was raised lapsed Calvinist since my parents had left their strict Baptist, Pres-byterian, and Methodist religious roots behind in the South. We were a trans-planted Alabama family living in Washington, D.C. As a youngster, my father enlisted in the navy, came north, and eventually got an education and became a dentist. When the Second World War began, my loyal father rejoined the navy and retired as a captain. Because his brothers had gone to West Point and Annapolis, most of our friends were army and navy families (mostly southerners) who formed an extended clan, meeting each other at various tours of duty.

In this highly social world, you won praise for being courteous, attrac-tive, having a good reputation, displaying backbone, working hard, playing hard, and having wit and charm. It was important to be smart but not so smart that you became odd. You should be good but not pious. My father had an antagonism against religion which he judged to be superstitious, hypocritical, and against science's march to a better future. Despite the allegiance to progress, my family brought their backward southern prejudices with them when they came north. My father was anti-Catholic, anti-Semitic, a kindly racist, and a male chauvinist military man who looked down on Yankees. Northerners were considered rude, pushy, ambitious, and dull. They were judged to be ill bred and tone deaf to the requirements for acting like a true gentleman or a real lady.

Naturally I, too, should grow up to be a southern lady, but with a certain hardy twist. Ladies should have all the feminine refinements but also be indomitable; they should be able to cope with any crisis. Tales of the heroic struggles of the Civil War were told: Robert E. Lee was glorified as the supreme gentleman, and spunky female forbears who had routed marauding Yankees were admired. The modern women most respected in my family were charming, capable navy wives who could move house, paint rooms, entertain, raise good children, and keep the household going while their hus-bands were at sea.

I received a double dose of the family's ideals because I was expected to display all the female virtues along with the male ones. I had the same name as my father and was the firstborn of two girls. Because I was thought to have inherited my father's strong character, expectations were high. I received the message that I must be responsible for my little sister and be brave, wise, honorable, and true. We even raised our hand and took oaths on our family honor swearing that what we said was true. "You can be anything you want," my father would tell me. "If anyone else can do it, it should be duck soup for you." He joked that our husbands would have to take our family name—although we should not marry young, have too many children, or work after marriage. Women were supposed to get educated and work successfully but, upon marrying, they were to drop any thoughts of a career.

My trajectory into female adulthood went smoothly but did not fully conform to the family program. If it had, when I graduated from Holton

Arms, our good private girls' school, I would have gone on to Sweetbriar, and married a naval officer. Externally, I looked, dressed, and flirted like a southern belle, but all the while other currents were flowing under the surface. I was religious and seriously committed to the intellectual life. Always we had plenty of books in the house—children's books, old college texts of my parents, and Book of the Month Club selections that my stepmother had collected. But I can't remember anyone else but me reading books, especially not my father. Every evening when he came home, he put his feet up and my stepmother, sister, and I were required to sit around, eat, play games, and have fun. We had a constant stream of company, and my hospitable father was always inviting people to come and live with us when they needed a place to stay. In a way, he recreated the jolly open house of his southern boyhood—with the addition of the drinking, smoking, card playing, and dancing forbidden to Baptists.

I loved all the company and parties but, early on, found reading to be a competing passion. I read constantly, often covertly. Hiding my reading habit was necessary since my parents thought it vaguely unhealthy. Undeterred, I read everything in the house, everything in the local library. Reading helped me to do well in school so I loved school, too, always trying to be first in the class. Coming from my family, I also wanted to be the most popular girl, to be elected president, to be the best athlete, the best actress in the school play, and so on. Yet, the love of learning for its own sake was real. I used to get up at dawn and eagerly wait to go to school. My parents thought my academic success was nice, but they were definitely not invested in my school achievement. We were taken to museums and battlefields and expected to know about geography and current events but not to be deeply learned. Learning was my own private thing and I cherished it.

My thirst to know was fused with spiritual searching. I have early memories of feeling wonder and awe at nature's beauty and the excitement of being alive. I identified these experiences of heightened consciousness with God, because a residue of religion remained in the household and the culture. Someone had taught us "Jesus Loves Me, This I Know," and my sister and I said grace at meals. In the Virginia public schools at the time, the Lord's Prayer and Bible reading began the day, along with the Pledge of Allegiance and the singing of "My Country 'Tis of Thee." But at home we were not instructed in religion or taken to Sunday school.

Private meditative moments continued as I observed the world and tried to understand things. I can remember lying in bed and trying to imagine the end of space. I was also worried about death and dying. My sister and I had been told that our real mother had died and that was why Daddy had brought us up alone until he married our stepmother. (The real story was more complex, but family secrets are often a part of southern histories.) Death became an immediate threat when the Japanese bombed Pearl Harbor and many army and navy friends were caught in the fighting. One reaction I had to my fear of dying reflected my father's attitude toward progress. When the thought of dying came up, I said to myself, "Oh well, when I grow up, science will have solved all that and I won't have to." This defense didn't last long in the face of the war news.

During these anxious years (would the Nazis and Japanese win?), a magnetic religion teacher started visiting our two-room school. Hume School was built in 1824 on Arlington Ridge Road with a great view of Washington, D.C. We had two maiden-lady teachers who each taught three grades in one room. Visiting teachers of music, art, and religion supplemented the program. Mrs. Davis, our religion teacher, told us Bible stories and about God and Jesus. Most importantly for me, she said that dying would be just like a caterpillar turning into a butterfly. I believed this good news. Mrs. Davis also had each student construct a personal chart upon which we could paste a gold star when we attended the Sunday school of our choice. This presented a problem for me as a decidedly Protestant but unchurched child.

I solved the problem by walking with a friend to the Methodist Sunday school, a mile and a half down the hill from my house. The Baptist Sunday school was closer but stricter; there you had to attend church service every week and be immersed to join up. In the more lax and disorganized classes of the friendly Methodists, I soaked up what knowledge I could. My father allowed me to go to Sunday school with the instruction that, while he did not believe in this stuff, if I started to go I should be prepared to finish. Steadfastness and staying the course was an important value for him. So for several years, I got up by myself, tiptoed my way through the remains of my parents' Saturday night party, and plodded down to Sunday school and back. Often I sensed God's presence and love on these solitary walks. At twelve I wanted to join the church and did so after the elders visited my parents and arranged it.

I found out then that my mother had insisted that my sister and I be baptized as Episcopalians. Getting sprinkled again as Methodists was our second baptism. When in college, I became a Catholic and was baptized for a third time. Back in those unecumenical days, converts were rebaptized and required to take an oath affirming as true everything that any Protestants had ever questioned. But I am getting ahead of my story.

In my early adolescence we moved from Arlington into Washington D.C. and, with no church home, my faith began to fade. Sleeping in on Sundays seemed more attractive than church.

Then at this crucial juncture came a chance event that changed my life. Daddy went to sea and my stepmother, who remained quiescently religious, would go to church. One day she went to a tiny experimental church that had just started around the corner from our house near Dupont Circle.

This church in a townhouse, calling itself the ecumenical Church of the Savior, eventually become renowned for its creative witness and mission. Members were required to embrace the discipline of tithing, study, and work. It was led by a charismatic thirty-five-year-old ex-Baptist Virginia minister, Gordon Cosby, and his wife, Mary. They were witty and attractive southerners who made religion immensely appealing. Gordon had been a chaplain in World War II and decided that Christianity needed a renewed kind of church: communities that could reach out to the world by displaying the power of Christianity. In this new and exciting company of believers, I studied the Bible, learned to pray, and read the spiritual classics; Gordon gave me C. S. Lewis to read and he became a decisive intellectual influence on my thinking. At the age of fifteen, I joined the church. My sister and I became its youngest members. For me it was a decisive adult conversion to Christianity.

My membership in the Church of the Savior changed my life. Commitment to Christianity helped me fend off the worldliness of my private girls' school, where becoming a debutante and coming out conferred status. I still loved going to parties, especially at Annapolis, but loved church and learning more. My father was not thrilled with either my intellectual or my spiritual aspirations. Only reluctantly did he let me go off north to Bryn Mawr College, where I had won a scholarship. He had sent me to Holton Arms to be certified as a lady, not to become a bluestocking. But as I insisted, I won my point and went off to college—where I was duly shocked by the secular atheism of my teachers and the general intellectual rejection of religion. I was also out of step with the sophisticated, cool culture of the East Coast establishment. Yet, I bloomed in an academic enclave where I was encouraged to be as intellectual and scholarly as I could be. I can still remember the intellectual ecstasy of studying at night in the Gothic library huddled within the pool of the green reading light in each cubicle.

Challenged by this new kind of secular milieu, my faith also flourished. Those of us who were Christian believers found one another and had cell meetings for prayer and Bible study. The College Chapel services were mostly an excuse for the choir to perform, but we made efforts to revitalize the chapel committee and create some interesting programs. During the academic year I searched for a worshiping community and began to attend Haverford's Quaker meeting. The Quakers cultivated the inner Light and prayed to the Spirit in their silent worship services. They were committed social activists and pacifists. Sitting silently for an hour in Sunday meeting nearly killed me at first. Later, however, I could not stand it when people (usually the same people every week) were inspired by the Spirit to speak and disturb the peace. Gradually I recognized that I desired more order, form, art, ritual, and silence in worship.

As I progressed in my studies of English literature, history, and philosophy, I also began to seek a more theologically developed religious life. Even my beloved but far away Church of the Savior was not intensely intellectual or formal in its life. After taking a course in the Enlightenment, I found out where all my ingrained American Protestant prejudices and unexamined assumptions came from, and I became more open to an institutional sacramental Christianity. I began to go to the Episcopal church, first a low church and then a high Anglican church. I might be there still if, at this point, I had not met Daniel Callahan, or someone like him.

Dan, my husband-to-be, was a junior at Yale and a devout, intellectual Roman Catholic who was taking philosophy courses from John Courtney Murray. He became a major intellectual influence upon my life and thought—and has remained so during our forty-five-year marriage, even though we often disagree. Dan introduced me to many new ideas, new authors, and new theological worlds. I resisted romance, so we pursued a stimulating intellectual friendship that included a lot of fun. Eventually, friendship led to love and we married at the end of my junior year, while Dan was a sergeant in the army's Counter-Intelligence Corps.

Through Dan, I was introduced to Roman Catholic thought, worship, and intellectual journals such as *Cross Currents* and *Commonweal*. Like so many secular intellectual converts of the fifties, I was enthralled to discover the richness of the Catholic Church. Compared to my provincial WASP world, Catholicism was universal, sacramental, dense, intellectual, and practiced a formal fulsome ritual in its sacramental life. It was also able to retain the loyalty of all classes and ethnic groups, and had a growing commitment to a theology of social justice. Gradually, I overcame my anti-Catholic heritage, became convinced of Catholicism's truth, and joyfully entered the Church—where I gratefully remain.

My parents and friends deeply disapproved of this move to Rome, of course, but explained it away as the result of marrying an Irish Catholic philosopher. When my husband left the Church in the late sixties and I remained an enthusiastic member, it become clear that, while marriage may have been the occasion of finding the Church, it had not motivated my conversion. Indeed, becoming a Catholic confirmed me in an intellectual vocation. With no formal theological education, I immersed myself in reading and study. As a young couple, Dan and I enthusiastically entered into all the intellectual, spiritual, and apostolic movements that existed before the Second Vatican Council. The council came as one of God's happy surprises but it articulated and confirmed many of the springs of renewal bubbling up in the Church. Of all these movements, I found the Catholic Worker most inspiring.

Dorothy Day was an impressive and inspiring figure whose influence continues in my life. A dedication to peace and social justice, first stimulated by the Quakers, was enlarged by the witness of the Catholic Worker Movement. Today I am a member of Pax Christi and remain committed to the other movements for justice in and out of the Church. I work for reform in our Church governance and in the prolife causes in the civil society. These causes have stimulated me to write on topics concerning rights, authority, and the need to include everyone in a just society: women, the unborn, prisoners, the poor, the ill, and the dying.

I became personally acquainted with poverty during our time as a young graduate-school family in Cambridge, Massachusetts. After the army, my husband was struggling to obtain his Ph.D. in the anti-Catholic Harvard philosophy department. Inspired by Dorothy Day and the Catholic Worker, we thought having many children and living well below the poverty line in near slum conditions was a valiant way to give glory to God. Catholics in those unassimilated days were a minority at Harvard who were subject to mild persecution and scorn for their "regressive" beliefs. Anti-Catholicism was the anti-Semitism of the intellectual elite. Secular disdain made the Harvard Catholic community mutually supportive and devotedly loyal to the Church. Dan and I started a Catholic graduate school group and had lots of parties that got people to meet one another. We were too poor to afford alcohol or food, but we had wit and energy—energy that was important because Dan had to work all the time to support us and to pass his comprehensives. I needed

energy, too, to throw myself into childbearing and childrearing (seven children in ten years) under difficult conditions, i.e., no money and no help.

Nevertheless, my morale was high because I was fulfilling my plan to
have six children by the time I was thirty, a Ph.D. by thirty-five, and to begin
college teaching at forty. My husband had thought that having twelve children would be great, but I assured him I could only manage six, because I
wanted to have a career. Obviously, we were both spoiled middle-class children who, as the eldest in two-child families, had never done any childcare
or housework. For us, the brave struggle of youthful poverty was an adventure—and spiritually bracing. But I am also glad that our poverty came to an
end when Dan got a job with a salary—and we finally had to pay taxes.

I survived all of the stressful years because prayer and study had inspired
me to want to love and serve, especially through the manual labor prized by
the Catholic Worker and the Benedictine ideal. Then, too, my family, and
especially my father, had imbued me with confidence and a "can do" American spirit that valued hard work. Occasionally, after some domestic disaster,
I would give way to a fit of anxiety but, for the most part, I felt exhilarated
and challenged by the fight to survive and protect my home. At the same
time, I spent every spare minute reading and studying in order to remain true
to my intellectual calling. It pained me to be denied the chance for graduate
study, and I often envied Dan's opportunities. Still, I believed in my call to
valiant motherhood and enjoyed our friends and intellectual community in
Cambridge.

Things changed for the worse when our fortunes improved. Dan became
an editor of *Commonweal,* and we moved to suburban Hastings-on-Hudson
to be within commuting distance of the office in New York City. I found the
move traumatic. I was now isolated—living in a house with no friends or
intellectual community around. The local parish was not a lively one. My
depressed state after the move was probably due to just having lost our fourth
son in a sudden infant death. This traumatic loss of a child produced dreadful grief, guilt, and anxiety, but did not make me doubt God's love. In retrospect, I can see how psychologically naive we were not to get help for our
children and ourselves in order to cope with this tragedy. But I had been
brought up to scorn psychotherapy as weakness, and so adopted the stance of
the stoic: endure and get on with your work. I ardently desired to triumph
over death by having more children, but I did not recognize that the family
healing process could take a long time.

During this low period, I began to be intensely bored with the domestic
routine. I was rescued from these doldrums when I took up the suggestion
made by an editor we knew at Sheed & Ward, that I should write a book on
the topic of women's changing roles, a topic I had been avidly studying. Dan
and some of our Harvard friends had written books, so naturally I was confident that I could do it, too—even though the only thing I had ever written had
been a brief book review. What's more, I had never had any ambitions to be
a writer and the thought of publishing a book had never crossed my mind.
Yet, I was desperate and felt thwarted by the inability to get to graduate
school. In those benighted days, women could not attend graduate school

part-time, and those who were married with children had a tough time getting jobs. So I sat down at my desk like many another housebound woman and turned to writing for escape.

I knew Virginia Woolf had written all her works in two hours a day, and Sertillanges, the Dominican author of my cherished *The Intellectual Life*, had claimed two hours of study was enough if you were disciplined. With my three-hundred-dollar publisher's advance from Sheed & Ward, I was able to get a babysitter for several hours a day—and I typed and typed, throwing out the first one hundred pages.

Despite having two more babies, I persevered and, in 1965, published *The Illusion of Eve: Modern Woman's Search for Identity*. This effort to synthesize Christian faith and feminist insights was the right book at the right time. It was the beginning of the women's movement so my book received a lot of notice, was reprinted in foreign languages, and led to lecture invitations, writing assignments, and more book contracts. The month I delivered my manuscript I got pregnant with my last child. But I had become disciplined; I had developed an ability to focus on my work for a few hours in my study and then open the door, come out, and throw myself into domestic life. Eventually, I was able to hire enough help to go back to graduate school part-time in a program that Sarah Lawrence set up for women returning to school. An M.A. in psychology led to a brief stint working part-time doing psychotherapy in a clinic. This job may have been decisive in my finally getting accepted in a full-time Ph.D. graduate school program at C.U.N.Y. In 1980, twenty-five years after receiving my B.A. at Bryn Mawr, magna cum laude and magna cum baby, I received a Ph.D. in Social and Personality Psychology.

My ambition to be a psychotherapist, however, faded after three years practice in the clinic. Psychotherapy is incredibly draining. I realized that I was an academic intellectual at heart who would rather write and teach. While finishing my degree, I had worked full-time, teaching in a small graduate program at Fairfield University in Connecticut. With the Ph.D. in hand, I could get a job at nearby Mercy College.

The seventies had been an exhausting decade for me. For three years I commuted an hour each way to Fairfield to teach evening classes. I cared for six teenagers, gave wifely support to Dan in the founding of a bioethics think-tank, continued fulfilling many writing and lecture assignments, conducted my research, and wrote my dissertation. Later decades have not been equally frantic, although the pattern continues of teaching, writing, lecturing, and coping with family life. Our big family presented many crises during the troubled, turbulent, and rebellious years of protests, assassinations, drugs, and the sexual revolution.

During this period, I was often heartsick over family troubles but was always sustained by prayer, worship, and intellectual work. In my worst moments, I found comfort working in the quiet library and praying quietly at Mass. Through the years, I have received the energy to live one day at a time following St. Thérèse's little way of love. Families bring demands for sacrifice, as well as joy. Today, my grown children are all a source of happiness and support. But I have been fortunate to have professional fulfillments and rewards outside of the family. My career has been unconventional but privileged. As Dan founded and ran the Hastings Center, I got to take part in an intellectual adventure and sit in on the birth of the new field of bioethics. By virtue of attending hundreds of ethical meetings and working on some of Hastings's projects, I have been able to meet many of the leading academic figures of the day. My own work on religious questions has given me the chance to meet most of the prominent Catholic thinkers in America today. On my own and with Dan, I have traveled to many conferences abroad.

What Now?

Today, I confront new challenges for the future. Intellectually I want to focus more narrowly and undertake more scholarly work. Over the years, I have grown intellectually as I tried to overcome the gaps in my education. Now I feel ready to dig deeper and attempt more significant work. I am not seeking money or academic positions, but I am still ambitious to do good work and have it recognized as such. I want to pursue internally generated projects that I believe need to be done, rather than reacting to invitations from others. Involvements in public causes remain important, but I now want to focus more exclusively on writing. Many intellectuals start out specializing in their field and, once established, engage in larger public arenas. I want to follow the opposite path and go from the more general to the specific.

My main worry is that I will not have enough energy and good health to continue working toward my goals. Other family emergencies could also arise. I pray that God will sustain and inspire me, and help me rise up with eagle's wings. My aspirations toward more focused intellectual work are matched by a desire for a deeper spiritual life. I have rarely doubted or been tempted to commit serious sins, but I am prone to laziness. I'm afraid I have never made the spiritual progress that I could have because of inertia and self-indulgence. In fits and starts, I have managed to go to daily Mass and pray at regular times of the day. Then some demand arises and I fall back to weekly Mass and only sporadic prayer. A disciplined regulated spiritual devotion has been beyond me.

Can I finally break through the barrier and enjoy a spiritual growth spurt? I want to overcome my limitations and finish the race with steadfast esprit. I desire to desire God more ardently and to love others more fully. My simple spiritual life seems so mediocre considering the graces and opportunities I've been given. My intellectual appreciation of the faith outstrips my practice. And all the while, I am mindful that the endgame approaches. I've been grateful for good health and good fortune, but these cannot last forever. Science has not done away with death yet. The challenge of old age and dying awaits. As Montaigne said of the dying process, "Now we will see what's at the bottom of the pot." Every day I thank God for my wonderful life and try to be worthy of the promises of Christ. If it weren't for the care and comfort of the Holy Spirit, I could have been derailed and brought low a thousand times. When at church we sing "Amazing Grace," a hymn which my faithful Alabama forbears sang, my favorite verse is this one:

Thru many dangers, toils and snares
I have already come;
'Tis grace has brought me safe thus far,
And grace will lead me home.

Contributors

Ed Block, Jr., is Professor and former Chair of English at Marquette University, where he also chairs the Marquette Mission Seminar. Author of a number of books, he recently became editor of *Conversations*, the magazine of the National Seminar on Jesuit Higher Education. He has a special interest in the work of John Henry Newman and Hans Urs von Balthasar.

Russell Butkus is Associate Professor and Chair of the Department of Theology at the University of Portland.

Sidney Callahan recently retired as Professor of Psychology at Mercy College, is author of eight books on psychology, spirituality, and parenting, and is a columnist for *Commonweal*. She has lectured at more than two hundred colleges, universities, and medical institutions, been consultant to the U.S. Catholic bishops, and received numerous honorary degrees.

Peter Dodson is Professor of Veterinary Anatomy at the University of Pennsylvania, where he also teaches Vertebrate Paleontology. He has conducted dinosaur research in Western Canada, Montana, India, China, and Madagascar. In addition to books like *The Horned Dinosaurs* (Princeton, 1996), he has coauthored several children's books on dinosaurs.

Dennis Doyle is Professor of Theology at the University of Dayton. His published work is primarily in ecclesiology.

Keith J. Egan holds the Joyce Hank Aquinas Chair in Catholic Theology at Saint Mary's College where he directs the Center for Spirituality. He is also Adjunct Full Professor of Theology at the University of Notre Dame, and is well known as an expert on Carmelite spirituality.

David Gitomer is Associate Professor and Director of the Masters of Arts in Liberal Studies Program at DePaul University. His specialty is the religions and literatures of premodern India. Among other projects, he recently translated the *Bhagavad Gita* and is doing the same for portions of the *Mahabharata*.

Howard Gray, S.J., is a director for Ignatian Spirituality for the Jesuit Institute at Boston College, and an internationally regarded lecturer on Ignatian spirituality. He is trained in English literature and has taught at Boston College, Fordham and John Carroll Universities, and Loyola University of New Orleans. He served as rector of the Weston School of Theology, and provincial of the Detroit Province of the Society of Jesus.

William Guerin Gray is Massman Professor of Civil Engineering at Notre Dame. He is author of numerous books and articles on porous media physics, computational methods for environmental simulation, and multiphase flow. He is also a Catholic deacon.

Diana Hayes is Associate Professor of Theology at Georgetown University. Author and editor of several books, her particular interests include Black Catholic theology, liberation theology, and African American and women's studies.

Michael Himes, Associate Professor of Theology at Boston College, taught Theology at the University of Notre Dame and served as a seminary dean. Author and editor of a number of books, he is best known for his *Fullness of Faith* (Paulist, 1993), which he coauthored with his brother, Kenneth Himes.

David Hollenbach, S.J., is Flatley Professor of Theology at Boston College. A well-known social ethicist, he is author of a number of books and was a principal contributor to the U.S. Catholic bishops' pastoral letter on the economy in 1987. His current project is a book on the common good.

Dennis Holtschneider, C.M., is Executive Vice President and Chief Operating Officer of Niagara University, New York. He is coauthor, with Melanie M. Morey, Ed.D., of "Relationship Revisted: Catholic Institutions and Their Founding Congregations" (Association of Governing Boards of Universities and Colleges, Washington DC, 2000).

Eva Hooker, C.S.C., is Professor of English at Saint John's University, Collegeville, Minnesota, where she also served as Academic Vice-president. A member of the Congregation of the Holy Cross, she teaches poetry and Shakespeare, and has recently published a new collection of poems, *The Winter Keeper* (Chapiteau Press, 2000). She is a longtime Collegium mentor and board member.

Elizabeth Johns, a Fellow at the Center for Religion, Ethics and Culture at the College of the Holy Cross, has held faculty positions in English, humanities, American studies and fine Arts, most recently as Silfen Term Professor of Art History at the University of Pennsylvania. She specializes in American painting, sculpture, photography and prints, has written several major books on American art history, and curated several major exhibitions. She spent the last year studying spiritual direction.

Joseph Kelley is Vice President for College Mission and Adjunct Professor in Religious Studies at Merrimack College. His research has been in the areas of pastoral psychology, psychoanalysis, and ritual. He is a clinical psychologist, editor of *Augustinian Heritage* journal, and consulting editor for Augustiniana in *The New Catholic Encyclopedia*. In 1999 he led a group of faculty and staff on a "pilgrimage" to a number of sites important to Augustinian heritage.

Katherine Kraft, O.S.B., is a Professor of Theology at the College of Saint Benedict, and a spiritual director. Her particular interests are foundational theology, Christology, and monastic spirituality.

Thomas M. Landy is founder and Director of Collegium, a consortium of sixty Catholic colleges and universities led by Fairfield University, which sponsors annual colloquies on Faith and Intellectual Life. He also serves as Associate Director of the new Center for Religion, Ethics and Culture at the College of the Holy Cross, where he teaches sociology.

Richard Liddy, a priest of the Archdiocese of Newark, is University Professor of Catholic Thought and Culture and Director of the Center for Catholic Studies at Seton Hall University, and a Senior Fellow at the Woodstock Theological Center at Georgetown University. He has written about the thought of Bernard Lonergan, under whom he studied, and also has a special interest in interdisciplinary dialogue and in the life and works of John Henry Newman.

Brian Linnane, S.J., teaches Christian Ethics at the College of the Holy Cross. He has written on fundamental moral theology, health-care ethics, and the ethics of gender relations. His book, *Karl Rahner's Theocentric Ethic of Discipleship*, will be published in 2001 by Peter Lang Publishers.

M. Therese Lysaught is an Associate Professor at the University of Dayton, with an expertise in bioethics. Her most recent writings are on ethics of genetic and stem-cell research. She serves on several national editorial and advisory boards in these fields.

Alex Nava is Assistant Professor of Religious Studies at the University of Arizona in Tucson. He is the author of *The Mystical and Prophetic Thought of Simone Weil and Gustavo Gutierrez: Reflections on the Mystery and Hiddenness of God* (forthcoming, SUNY Press). His research interests include religion and culture, especially Hispanic traditions, philosophy of religion, liberation theology, and Christian mysticism.

John Neary, Associate Professor of English at Saint Norbert College, recently completed a term as Chair of the college's Humanities Division. He is author of two books, including one on the sacramental imagination in literature, *Like and Unlike God: Religious Imaginations in Modern and Contemporary Fiction* (AAR Press, 1999), which expands upon the themes of his chapter in this volume. John is a Collegium board member.

Dennis O'Brien taught philosophy at Princeton University and Middlebury College, where he also served as Dean. He subsequently served as President of Bucknell College and as President of the University of Rochester. Through his years in administration, he remained an active teacher and scholar. His most recent book is *All the Essential Half-Truths About Higher Education* (University of Chicago, 1997).

Michael Patella, O.S.B., is a theologian and monk of Saint John's University, Minnesota, with expertise in Biblical Studies. He recently published *The Death of Jesus: The Diabolical Force and the Ministering Angel, Luke 23: 44–49* (Paris: Gabalda, 1999). Having completed his studies at the École Biblique et Archéologique Française de Jérusalem, he now directs Saint John's Jerusalem Studies Program.

Ingrid Peterson, O.S.F., is a popular teacher, lecturer, and retreat director on Franciscan spirituality. She is author of *Clare of Assisi: A Biographical Study* (Franciscan, 1993) and coauthor of *Praying with Clare of Assisi* (St. Mary's, 1994). She is an Assistant Editor of *Greyfriars Review*, and a contributor and consultant for a forthcoming omnibus collection of sources, *Francis of Assisi: Early Documents* (New City Press).

Jill Raitt retired this year as Professor and Chair of Religious Studies at the University of Missouri, a department which she founded. A well-known scholar on spirituality, she is a past-President of the American Academy of Religion. She also enjoys teaching the history of Christianity and the theology of Augustine and Aquinas.

Bruce Russett is Dean Acheson Professor of International Relations and Political Science at Yale University, author of nearly two dozen books and two hundred scholarly articles, and the Editor of the *Journal of Conflict Resolution*. Bruce was a lead author of the United States Catholic bishops' pastoral letter on peace, served on the Collegium board for several years, and has been active in the Thomas More Center at Yale.

Cynthia Eagle Russett is Professor of History at Yale University, where she specializes in women's history, intellectual history, and American cultural history. She has written on the Victorian construction of womanhood, and is editor of a forthcoming volume on the history of colleges founded by Catholic women's religious communities.

Paula Powell Sapienza has taught Russian and East European Studies at the University of Michigan, Union College, and Fairfield University, where she served for two years as Associate Director of Collegium before heading west to Denver. Her research specialty if Russian literary theory and poetry.

John Thompson recently completed a ten-year term as President of Saint Thomas More College at the University of Saskatchewan, which has allowed him to return to teaching. His academic research has been in religion, marriage, and family.

Joanna Ziegler is Associate Professor of the History of Art and Architecture at College of the Holy Cross. She has written and lectured on medieval mysticism as art and is currently exploring the implications of "seeing" for fostering a more contemplative dimension to human existence. She lives with her husband and two cats in Douglas, Massachusetts.